9

CU00820366

The Political Diary
of Hugh Dalton

1918–40, 1945–60

The Political Diary of Hugh Dalton

1918–40, 1945–60

Edited by Ben Pimlott

JONATHAN CAPE
IN ASSOCIATION WITH THE LONDON SCHOOL OF
ECONOMICS AND POLITICAL SCIENCE

First published 1986
Diary copyright © The British Library of Political
and Economic Science 1986
Introduction and editorial matter copyright © Ben Pimlott 1986
Jonathan Cape Ltd, 32 Bedford Square, London WC1B 3EL

British Library Cataloguing in Publication Data

Dalton, Hugh
The political diary of Hugh Dalton 1918–40, 1945–60.
1. Dalton, Hugh – Correspondence, reminiscences, etc.
I. Title   II. Pimlott, Ben
941.083′092′4   DA581.D

ISBN 0–224–01912–0

Typeset by Ace Filmsetting Ltd, Frome, Somerset
Printed in Great Britain by
Ebenezer Baylis and Son Ltd
The Trinity Press, Worcester and London

Contents

Illustrations

Cartoons

Acknowledgments

This volume of Dalton's diary and its predecessor were made possible by a generous grant from the Leverhulme Trust Fund to the London School of Economics and Political Science. Both volumes were edited as part of the same project, and the personal and professional debts mentioned in the Acknowledgments to the *Second World War Diary* apply equally here. I wish to express my special gratitude to the two other members of the small editorial team: Dr Dorothy Tarry, my research assistant, who examined the text, investigated sources and drafted notes; and Greta Edwards, who deciphered Dalton's handwriting in order to type from the manuscript, and later typed both volumes of the edition. I would also again particularly like to thank Jane Hill, my editor at Jonathan Cape.

For permission to reproduce illustrations I am grateful to: the B.B.C. Hulton Picture Library, for plate nos 1, 4, 6, 7, 8, 11, 12, 14, 15, 17, 18, 19, 20, 22, 23, 24, 25, 27, 28, 29 and 30; the Press Association, for nos 5 and 16; Syndication International/the *Daily Herald*, for no. 13; Douglas Jay, for no. 31; London Express News and Feature Services, for cartoons by Low on pp. 46, 57, 159, 179, 189, 203, 391, 482, 538, 562 and 633, and by Vicky on pp. 375, 394, 408, 416, 463 and 572; and the Labour Party Library.

Gower Street
London WC1
September 1986   B.J.P.

Introduction

This book is about an unusual, even implausible, adventure: the trials and exploits of a royal chaplain's son who joined the Labour Party, confounded the companions of his youth, and became a socialist Chancellor of the Exchequer. The hero is the narrator; the villains are the fools and charlatans who attempt to frustrate him. It is not always an edifying tale.

There are two sections. The first covers the author's long apprenticeship before he held major ministerial office; the second his period as a senior statesman, initially active, then elder. A selection from his diary for the years of Churchill's wartime Coalition has recently been published in a separate volume.[1]

Hugh Dalton aroused strong feelings. Opponents detested him, while many on his own side were confused or disturbed by an element of self-parody in his performance. There was a story about him entering the Cabinet Room, 'his eyes blazing with insincerity'. He seemed to revel in the image of the cold-hearted manipulator, the master of manoeuvre and deceit. 'Dr Dalton is one of the relatively few contemporary politicians ... with a well-defined personality', Malcolm Muggeridge once observed. 'He is a card.'[2] His humour had a puckish quality which drove sober, respectable persons to bitterly enraged contempt.

Yet there was a gap between manner and substance. Dalton was not an entirely successful political leader, but for a time he was a highly effective and creative one, guided by clear principles. In the 1930s the Labour Party's move towards a foreign policy based on collective security owed much to his finesse. Many of Labour's post-war

1 B. Pimlott (ed.), *The Second World War Diary of Hugh Dalton 1940–45*, Jonathan Cape (in association with the L.S.E.), London, 1986.
2 *News Chronicle*, 8th April 1957.

measures were of his inspiration, and it is no coincidence that the most radical years of the Attlee administration were those of his Chancellorship. Politically, he was driven by two desires: to prevent war, and to increase equality. These were supported or impeded by a number of vigorous prejudices. He was an ardent friend of miners, refugees from Nazi Germany, Slavs, the French, Zionists, Australians, hikers, ex-students of the London School of Economics, young and clever Labour politicians or economists. He was an intolerant hater of the rich, the pompous, political rivals, Germans, most Bloomsbury intellectuals, many civil servants, almost all Tories. He was also a man in whom private and public emotions were tightly enmeshed.

The peculiarities of Dalton's character owed much to his unusual background. Born in 1887, he was the son of a former tutor to the young sons of the Prince of Wales, one of whom reigned, during the middle years of Hugh's life, as George V. Hugh grew up in the Trollopean world of St George's Chapel, Windsor, overshadowed by the royal castle. He was educated at St George's Choir School, Summer Fields (an Oxford prep school), Eton and King's College, Cambridge, where he read mathematics and then economics, taught by Pigou and Keynes. While at Cambridge he formed a close friendship with Rupert Brooke, a King's contemporary, and the two together adopted the currently fashionable Fabian socialism of Beatrice and Sidney Webb and H. G. Wells.

Rupert soon abandoned politics; Hugh, on the other hand, had found his vocation. Beatrice Webb, encountering Dalton at the age of twenty-one, wrote that he was 'by nature an ecclesiastic – a sort of lay Jesuit – preparing for political life'.[1] What kind of political life he imagined for himself before the emergence of the Labour Party as a national body is not clear, but his choice of training related directly to his beliefs. Influenced by the Webbs, he studied at the L.S.E. for a doctorate (later published as a book)[2] on the inequality of incomes. Shortly before the outbreak of war he married a fellow student, Ruth Hamilton Fox, who shared his Fabian commitment.

In 1915 he enlisted, obtained a commission and joined the Army Service Corps. Early the following year he was posted to France. He started to write a journal, in a small lined notebook, on the eve of embarkation. At first the diary consisted of brief, stiff accounts of routine activities. Gradually it became more vivid and reflective, filled with descriptions of French peasant life, the irritating habits of fellow

1 N. MacKenzie (ed.), *The Letters of Sidney and Beatrice Webb*, vol. II, *Partnership 1892–1912*, Cambridge University Press, Cambridge, 1978, p. 316.
2 H. Dalton, *Some Aspects of the Inequality of Incomes in Modern Communities*, Routledge, London, 1920.

officers, the incompetence of army bureaucracy, and the terrible evidence of death and mutilation brought back from the Front. There are also records of some of the incidental horrors of war, like the savagery of British military justice:

> Two cases of recent shooting in our division, one for 'desertion' and one for 'Cowardice in face of the enemy' ... The first was in the Royal Scots, and the execution nearly caused a mutiny. A young boy, aged 17, but 'official age' 21, as given in a patriotic lie on enlistment, had a wire that his father was dead. He couldn't get leave. A week after he heard that his mother was dead. He couldn't get leave. He went broody and went up the transport lines instead of into the trenches the following night. He was there found, half in a dream. Sentenced to death for desertion. He sat calmly in a chair and smoked a cigarette, up to the moment when they carried out the sentence.
>
> Case of machine gunner. For a quarter of an hour he got in a funk and left his gun. Then realising what he had done, and, in order to atone, he took his machine gun out into No Man's Land and stayed out there two days and night. But it did not atone in the eyes of the Court Martial for initial 'Cowardice in face of the enemy'. Having miraculously escaped death at the hands of Germans, he found it at the hands of his own people. These two cases illustrate the spirit and the necessities of militarism.[1]

Dalton knew about the fighting in the trenches only at second-hand. But he could both see and hear the artillery fire which preceded infantry attacks. His diary reveals a growing fascination with what Wyndham Lewis called the 'fearful flashing of a monstrous cannonade',[2] just beyond the horizon:

> We can hear the steady boom of big guns away southward, and also a bit up north. We have a good view in the twilight from the top of a green hillock, half a mile away. Star shells in the distance, the constant whistle of trains, the hum of our returning aeroplanes, the woods lying quiet and still, the millions of lives of unseen fighters hanging in the balance. It is hard to realise the immensity of all these things on this hot evening, after the warm summer rain.[3]

It was the start of the Allied bombardment that preceded the battle

1 Diary, 16th June 1916.
2 W. Lewis, *Blasting and Bombardiering*, Eyre & Spottiswoode, London, 1937, p. 121.
3 Diary, 24th June 1916.

xiii

of the Somme.

In 1917 Dalton was transferred at his own request to the Royal Artillery and was sent to Palmanova in the Italian Alps. The landscape, and the hope of seeing action, raised his spirits. 'After the Somme and Arras', he wrote later, 'I fell in love with the Italian Front at first sight.'[1] On the day of his arrival he recorded a new resolve:

I shall write a book, if I survive, and call it 'With British Guns in Italy'. It will be a War Book, and sell well ... It will contain some purple passages and some home truths about War, and some indelicate descriptions of sights, sounds and smells.[2]

Subject matter was soon provided. In October the Italian Front suddenly collapsed. Dalton heard that British battalions were to be moved north, where the battle was most intense. 'Anything that I may have written that is publishable, in my wife's judgement, I would like published', he wrote in his diary, as a kind of testament.

The expected move never happened. Instead, the Italian Third Army was forced into a general retreat from Caporetto westward to the River Tagliamento. Dalton found himself in command of thirty bombardiers, and responsible for the last British artillery pieces on the road. 'Villages everywhere have been set alight ...' he wrote as the withdrawal began. 'The whole country is blazing and exploding.'[3] Hampered by traffic jams caused by the huge movement of soldiers and equipment, he led his men slowly away from the advancing enemy column. There was an imminent risk of being cut off. After dragging the guns through rain and mud for three days, the small British force at last reached the bridge over the Tagliamento, just before the arrival of the victorious Austrians.

Dalton was much affected by this episode. The experience of physical danger, the test of courage and endurance, stirred him. There were two direct results. One was the best account of the famous retreat in any language, the 'War Book' Dalton had pledged himself to write.[4] The other was a rekindling of his desire for a public career. The observation of military chaos gave his opinions a sharply practical edge. 'It was the belief that politics, rightly handled, can put an end to war, which, more than anything else, drew me into the life of active

1 H. Dalton, *Call Back Yesterday: Memoirs 1887–1931*, Muller, London, 1953 (henceforth CBY), p. 88.
2 Diary, 18th June 1917.
3 Diary, 27th October 1917.
4 H. Dalton, *With British Guns in Italy*, Methuen, London, 1919, p. 120.

politics when the war was over', he wrote later.[1] Within weeks of the Armistice he was back in England, throwing himself into the civilian conflict of a general election, with Labour fighting as an independent party for the first time. It is here that the selection from the diary included in this volume begins.

'My own New Year's Resolution', Dalton wrote at the beginning of 1932: '(1) Never give the appearance of being cynical (2) tell no one that I keep a diary.'[2] He held firm on (2). 'I didn't know the bugger kept a diary like that', was Herbert Morrison's reaction to the first volume of Dalton's memoirs.[3] Only a handful of people were aware of the diary's existence until the last decade of its author's life.

Why did Dalton write it? A diary kept over many years is a habit, and habits cannot be explained in rational or practical terms. But we may guess at how the habit came to be established, and why he found it congenial.

Dalton's background contained a number of diarists. His clergyman grandfather had kept a diary.[4] Perhaps inspired by this example, or by that of Queen Victoria herself, Hugh's father had kept a weekly log of his royal pupils' progress and had taught the young Prince George to write a journal during an extended round-the-world trip.[5] George continued the practice until his death. Another possible model for Hugh was the writer A. C. Benson, a family friend, who published extracts from his diary in 1906.[6] But the most interesting and possibly the most potent influence was that of Dalton's Fabian mentor, Beatrice Webb.

Dalton knew about Beatrice's diary-writing in 1911. '... I want to tell you about the Webb Diaries', he wrote to Rupert Brooke. 'We all come into them. They will be published twenty-five years after she dies.'[7] Here we may speculate: did Dalton also have future publication in mind? We have seen how he had decided in 1917 to write a war book, and used the diary kept in Italy as the basis for it. The possibility of building on this early success may have occurred to him quite early on.

1 H. Dalton, *Towards the Peace of Nations: A Study in International Politics*, Routledge, London, 1928, p. ix.
2 Diary, 1st January 1932, p. 165, below.
3 Diary, 30th April 1953, p. 612, below.
4 Joyce Parker Papers.
5 A heavily edited version of this document was later published. (Prince Albert Victor and Prince George, with additions by J. N. Dalton, *The Cruise of Her Majesty's Ship 'Bacchante' 1879–1882*, London, 1886.)
6 A. C. Benson, *The House of Quiet: An Autobiography*, John Murray, London, 1906.
7 Cited in CBY, p. 75.

Such an idea first appeared in the diary during the Second World War, when, in a dark moment, Dalton began to consider writing 'scabrous memoirs' after his retirement.[1] He started to put the idea into operation in 1950, while still a Cabinet Minister. Thereafter the writing of autobiography increasingly replaced diary-keeping. Three volumes were published: *Call Back Yesterday* (1953), *The Fateful Years* (1957) and *High Tide and After* (1962),[2] the last appearing a few days before his death. Each caused a tremor in Westminster and Whitehall, helping to undermine prevailing standards of decorum and reticence in published reminiscences. The political scientist Robert McKenzie described the final volume as 'the most important contribution to an understanding of the post-war political scene so far made by any of those who played a part in it'.[3]

Yet the diary never reads as though it were intended for public consumption. There is certainly no coyness or false modesty, and Dalton is engagingly (or distressingly, according to taste) open about his wiles and stratagems. Much of the early diary in any case was non-political: Dalton was far more faithful to it before he entered Parliament, often writing about academic matters or foreign holidays, than in the first five years of his career as a politician. For a time, politics threatened to kill the habit altogether. 'How do M.P.s keep diaries?' he wrote when he took it up again after a long break.[4] Only when he became a minister in the 1929 Labour Government did he resume diary-writing on a regular basis, looking at the details of politics and policy much as, in 1916–18, he had examined the incidental details of war.

Was he a 'literary' diarist? Recently it has become common to ascribe to quite down-to-earth diarists high artistic aspirations, even to see in their work a master plan. Beatrice Webb has been subjected to this approach. Both the editor of her diary, Professor Norman MacKenzie, and a literature scholar, Deborah Epstein Nord, claim to see in the Webb diary the hand, not just of a good writer, but of an imaginative one as well. MacKenzie likens Beatrice's diary to a novel or a play. Nord, even more boldly, presents her diary-based *My Apprenticeship* as a reworking of the life of St Theresa, with a theme familiar to students of Victorian hagiography: a morbid childhood followed by a guilt-ridden adolescence, then Temptation (in the form

---

1 Diary 13th–14th March 1943 (see *Second World War Diary*, p. 567). The thought occurs again in April of the following year (ibid., p. 734).
2 All published by Muller, London.
3 *Observer*, 4th February 1962.
4 Diary, 1926.

of Joseph Chamberlain), conversion (socialism) and ultimate, though dubious, fulfilment (Sidney Webb).[1]

Perhaps we should learn to play such critical games with all diarists; possibly with none of them. Whatever may be said of Beatrice Webb, it would be an imaginative reader who could find in Dalton's diary the outline of a 'novel' – a form which must surely require, of its creator, a final control over the plot. Yet there is enough art and style in Dalton's writing to make it more than a mere chronicle or random collection of thoughts and impressions.

It is a narrative diary, with a series of overlapping stories that weave in and out of the text. The author is not a camera: he has feelings, often fierce ones, towards those he observes. At the centre of a cast of thousands are a handful of individuals towards whom he relates strongly and recurrently. These usually include a hated figure upon whom the diarist unloads the full weight of his anxiety and fear. The hated figure is balanced by a loved friend, always a younger aide or protégé, who offers sympathy, common sense and companionship and becomes a trusted confidant. The interplay between enemy and friend gives the diary its rhythm.

There are other symmetries. Dalton kept his diary with increasing frequency in the late 1930s, reaching a peak of productivity in 1942, outside the period covered by this volume. After the war the length and regularity of entries declined. In consequence the post-war diary broadly mirrors the pre-war diary in shape; but there is something more. If there could be no awareness of the end at the beginning, there is a powerful recollection of the beginning at the end. Dalton's eager, altruistic pursuit of seats for young friends (especially Anthony Crosland) in the 1950s seems to reflect a similar quest on his own behalf in the 1920s. Even more strikingly, Dalton's vivid account of Bevan's resignation from the Government in 1951 contains echoes of his own diary description (which he had recently been reading) of the resignation of Sir Oswald Mosley more than twenty years before. 'I whisper to Morrison beside me: "This is Mosley speaking!",' wrote Dalton, after Bevan addressed the P.L.P. '... [Bevan] was sweating and screeching and seemed on the edge of a nervous breakdown.'[2] The words bear a strong resemblance to his account of an equivalent meeting in 1930.[3]

Unlike Beatrice Webb (whose diary Professor MacKenzie characterises as a 'lifelong attempt to explore the complex interaction between

1 D. E. Nord, *The Apprenticeship of Beatrice Webb*, Macmillan, London, 1985.
2 Diary, 24th April 1951, p. 539, below.
3 See the entry for 20th November 1930, p. 130, below.

her *doppelgänger* and herself')[1] Dalton was not an introspective diarist. There are painful moments of self-revelation or despair, as in the moving entries which recount, with simple economy, the illness and death of his little daughter Helen in 1922. He clearly turned to his diary as a psychological release: it is noticeable that entries become longer at times of strain. Keeping a diary (especially, perhaps, dictating a diary to an attentive secretary) must have been a balm in a hectic life. But he seldom used the diary to brood on personal matters. Where Beatrice often focuses on the turmoils of her inner world, Dalton projects outwards, expressing his moods in public terms. Some subjects are almost never touched. Feelings about the loss of the child ('... of Her, for fear of tears, I never speak'),[2] about tensions in his marriage, or about his ignominious fall from the Chancellorship in 1947, may only be guessed by reading between the lines.

A diary is often supposed to show 'the truth' about its author. Yet the truth of a diary is always partial, and in spite of the diarist. Whether or not a diary is intended for public scrutiny, its author selects and fashions with great care. A diary may be a depository for disagreeable attributes – a confessional, as in the case of Beatrice Webb, or a kind of emotional latrine, as with the startling, explosive diary of Lord Reith.[3] On the other hand, it may be an expression of conceit, or a vehicle for self-justification. A diary may only be written up at moments of unhappiness, or only at times of light-hearted relaxation. A cheerful person can write a gloomy diary, or an arrogant person a humble one.

Dalton's diary certainly does not give us a proper picture of Dalton. He was both more formidable, and less cocksure, than the hero of his narration. What the diary does show is how he liked to regard himself. This volume opens with its author emerging from a world of military assumptions, and setting his sights on a political career. Creating a suitable persona required a script. The diary provides it: I am this kind of politician, he seems often to be saying, with these kinds of views and this kind of skill. Instead of a psychiatrist's couch, the diary is the means to establish an identity. Later, more positively, it becomes a sounding-board for new ideas, a private seminar where facts and thoughts are pondered before an opinion is established and made active.

How much of what Dalton wrote about events or people should be taken at face value? Where does satire or caricature end and fabrica-

1 *Index to the Diary of Beatrice Webb 1873–1943*, Chadwyck-Healey, Cambridge, 1978, p. 14.
2 Diary, 26th July 1929, p. 61, below.
3 C. Stewart (ed.), *The Reith Diaries*, Collins, London, 1975.

tion begin? One answer is that diaries are both the best historical sources available, and the worst: the best because close to the action and uncensored, the worst because uninhibited in their special pleading. Of Dalton it may be said that his biases are so blatant that they are unlikely to mislead.

It is the wealth of detail in Dalton's record and his rare understanding of policy, combined with his extreme political nosiness, which have helped to make the diary a classic. There is also another, more fortuitous, aspect: during the period Dalton's diary covers, most political diarists were Tories. At least until the late 1940s, Dalton was the only prominent Labour politician keeping a diary. Anybody who has worked among the political papers of an age before investigative reporting, intrusive television or *Private Eye*, will be powerfully aware of this uniqueness, and of the beacon Dalton is able to shine on areas of history for which the only other unpublished sources are government papers or party minutes.[1]

The hitherto unpublished Dalton diary has exerted as great an influence on historical writing as the published memoirs, partly because it has been available to scholars for almost as long.[2] Lady Dalton deposited the Dalton Papers in the British Library of Political and Economic Science shortly after her husband's death in 1962, and gave the copyright to the L.S.E. Since then, many episodes known only or mainly from Dalton's diary (or a combination of the diary and the memoirs), have passed into the folklore of contemporary history, having left little trace in the press or the official records.

Thus, the attempts by Cripps and others to depose Attlee in 1947 would have disappeared from history with the deaths of the conspira-

---

1 Before releasing his papers Dalton's literary executors, Anthony Crosland and Sir Robert Fraser, removed Cabinet Office and related documents and material which they considered defamatory or too personal. The censorship does not appear to have been rigorous. Evidence that some material has been lost (perhaps as a result of the Daltons' own prunings) is, however, provided in the autobiography, which contains quotations from diary passages no longer to be found in the manuscript. There are also a few other unaccountable gaps in the surviving document, where sheets appear to be missing. A check of the Dalton Papers in 1975 showed that a number of items had been removed after their arrival in the B.L.P.E.S., presumably as a result of theft.

2 The earliest reference to unpublished material from the Dalton Papers is in an article by D. C. Watt (of the L.S.E.) in the *American Review* for April 1963 ('American Aid to Britain and the Problem of Socialism 1945–51'). Dalton's diary first affected the writing of history a quarter of a century earlier, however. In her excellent biography, *Arthur Henderson* (Heinemann, London, 1938), the writer and former M.P. Mary Agnes Hamilton based the account of Henderson's tenure of the Foreign Office in 1929–31 on diary entries lent by her friend Hugh Dalton. This was a rare departure from the principle of keeping the habit secret.

tors without Dalton's record, and the post-war Labour administration would appear a much more harmonious team than we now know it to have been. The best accounts that have been written of the 1931 political crisis, the fall of Chamberlain in 1940, crises over convertibility in 1947 and devaluation in 1949, and the Cabinet resignations of 1951, are all heavily dependent on the Dalton *oeuvre*.[1]

The whole diary is contained in fifty-six notebooks and folders. It is more than one and a half million words long, of which almost half was written during the Churchill Coalition (the period of the *Second World War Diary*). From 1916 until 1937, and from the autumn of 1947 until the end, it was handwritten – at first carefully and clearly on lined pages, then in red ink on loose sheets of austerity paper which often smudged and blurred illegibly. Between 1937 and 1947 it was dictated to a secretary (from 1937 to 1944 Mrs Dean, thereafter Miss Wagstaff), who visited Dalton in his Victoria flat or at his ministry, usually once a week. Because the diary was frequently written or dictated in bunches of several entries at a time, a period of days often elapsed between the events described and the recording of them. The pace and regularity of entries varied: dictation and the attendance of a secretary encouraged Dalton to write more often, in greater detail and at greater length. After the 1924 election, Dalton gave up the diary because he won. After the 1931 election he wrote it less frequently because he lost. For much of 1934 and 1935 he did not keep a diary at all. He resumed the diary when he returned to Parliament at the 1935 election, and maintained it thereafter, with few major lapses, until the mid-1950s. From 1955 the spaces became longer and the entries shorter as he disengaged from politics and his mind concentrated more on the past than on the present.

This volume contains a selection from the diary for the years not covered by the *Second World War Diary*, apart from the 1916–18 period.[2] I have used very little of Dalton's travel and holiday diaries. Sometimes (as, for example, during his tour of the Soviet Union in 1932 or his visit to Australia and New Zealand in 1938) there are fascinating glimpses of the countries visited, and their politics. This material, however, is generally tangential to the main story. On the other hand, part of Dalton's account of his visit to Italy in 1933 has

1 The biographers of Herbert Morrison refer to Dalton's memoirs or diary more than a hundred times for the period of the Attlee Government alone. (B. Donoughue and G. W. Jones, *Herbert Morrison: Portrait of a Politician*, Weidenfeld & Nicolson, London, 1973.)
2 Much of his diary for the First World War appears in *With British Guns in Italy*.

been included because of the special interest of his meeting with Mussolini.

Choosing material for inclusion was not easy. No simple criterion could be applied, neither could passages be judged in isolation on some abstract scale of merit. Often a line in an otherwise colourless paragraph provided a vital link, or a sequence of individually unremarkable entries developed an idea or built up an atmosphere. In deciding what to put in and what to leave out, I have sought not to anthologise but to treat the selection as a unified work.

A particular difficulty with this volume has been the use Dalton made of the diary in writing his autobiography. On the whole, I have not included passages which Dalton himself quoted or closely paraphrased. Applying this principle, however, has involved some tricky editorial manoeuvres. It also inevitably gives a distorted impression of the diary. Thus, there is relatively little material in this selection about Dalton's Chancellorship between 1945 and 1947, not because he neglected his diary during this period, but because he used a large portion of what he wrote in *High Tide and After*. Similarly, I have included little from Dalton's account of his early election campaigns (he fought four contests unsuccessfully in the 1920s before winning at Peckham) because these are extensively covered in *Call Back Yesterday*. However, there are a few episodes where Dalton's contemporary record is so interesting that I have abandoned my rule. Dalton's accounts of the August 1931 crisis and of the period preceding Chamberlain's resignation in May 1940 have been included, even though the versions in the published memoirs are quite full.

Dalton was not always a scrupulous interpreter of his own text. Often he quoted or paraphrased his diary accurately, but there are many other places where he toned up or down in order to give a different meaning. Occasionally I have included passages where, it seemed to me, Dalton's autobiography bowdlerised himself. Frequently I have re-used sentences or paragraphs which appear in the memoirs in order to place new material in context.

As a result this volume and the memoirs complement each other, with emphases in different places. The memoirs contain more about Dalton's politics before he became an M.P., and more about his financial policy as Chancellor. This selection contains much more about the second Labour Government, foreign policy in the late 1930s, the 1949 devaluation crisis, the 1951 Cabinet resignations, and divisions in the P.L.P. in the early 1950s.

Each of the ten chapters is preceded by a survey intended to fill gaps and to provide necessary historical and biographical background.

Otherwise, the editorial conventions followed in this volume are the same as in the *Second World War Diary*.[1] Contractions have been expanded and surnames substituted for initials, sometimes with the first Christian name as well. Where organisations or official bodies are referred to by initials, these have been expanded if they are brief, and retained where they are long or familiar. Dates have been standardised, with the day of the week added. Breaks involving the exclusion of material *in the middle* of entries are indicated by three dots (...). No indication is given if an entry is left out altogether, or if material has been excluded at the beginning or end of an entry, unless the break occurs in the middle of a sentence. Where Dalton himself used multiple dots, these have been distinguished from those indicating missing material by the use of six dots, rather than three. Spelling and other obvious textual errors have been corrected.

The aim of biographical footnotes has been to provide basic information which may be of use in reading the diary. I have given title or form of address at the time of the diary entry, followed by the last known title, and any earlier name if different from the current one. Each note starts with the position or occupation of the character mentioned at the time of the entry, followed by other facts of contemporary relevance. Earlier or later career details may then be given. Senior ministerial posts are automatically listed, junior ones only if held at the time of the entry. Otherwise, except for Treasury and Foreign Office posts, junior offices are included under the general rubric of 'junior minister'. With officials, apart from the post or department at the time of the entry (where this information is available), usually only the most senior posts are mentioned. In a few cases the reader is referred to a biographical appendix at the back of the book.

1 See *Second World War Diary*, pp. xxxix–xl, for a fuller account of them.

Abbreviations

A.A.	Anti-Aircraft
A.V.	Alternative Vote
B.A.	Bishop Auckland
B.E.F.	British Expeditionary Force
B.I.S.	Bank for International Settlements
B.L.P.E.S.	British Library of Political and Economic Science
B.M.A.	British Medical Association
C.A.S.	Chief of Air Staff
C.C.F.	Co-operative Commonwealth Fellowship
C.I.D.	Committee of Imperial Defence
C.I.G.S.	Chief of Imperial General Staff
C.L.P.	Constituency Labour Party
C.O.S.	Chiefs of Staff
C.W.S.	Co-operative Wholesale Society
D.L.P.	Divisional Labour Party
E.A.C.	Economic Advisory Council
E.C.	Executive Committee
E.D.C.	European Defence Community
E.P.C.	Economic Policy Committee
F.S.T.	Financial Secretary to the Treasury
G.M.C.	General Management Committee
G.U.S.	Great Universal Stores
H.C. Debs	House of Commons Debates (Hansard)
H.M.G.	His/Her Majesty's Government
I.F.T.U.	International Federation of Trade Unions
I.L.P.	Independent Labour Party
I.M.F.	International Monetary Fund
L.C.C.	London County Council
L.E.A.	Local Education Authority

L.N.U.	League of Nations Union
L.S.E.	London School of Economics and Political Science
L.S.I.	Labour and Socialist International
M.A.P.	Ministry of Aircraft Production
M.E.W.	Ministry of Economic Warfare
M.R.P.	Mouvement Républicain Populaire (French Christian Democrats)
N.A.T.O.	North Atlantic Treaty Organisation
N.C.B.	National Coal Board
N.C.L.	National Council of Labour
N.E.	National Executive
N.E.C.	National Executive Committee
N.F.R.B.	New Fabian Research Bureau
N.S.	National Service
N.U.R.	National Union of Railwaymen
O.E.E.C.	Organisation for European Economic Co-operation
O.G.P.U.	Obyedinyonnoe Gosudarstrevennoe Politicheskoe Upravelenie (Soviet Political Police)
P.A.	Personal Assistant
P.E.P.	Political and Economic Planning
P.L.P.	Parliamentary Labour Party
P.O.U.M.	Partido Obrero de Unificación Marxista (Spanish Revolutionary Communists)
P.P.S.	Parliamentary Private Secretary
P.Q.	Parliamentary Question
P.R.	Proportional Representation
P.S.	Private Secretary
P.U.S.	Permanent Under-Secretary
R.P.M.	Retail Price Maintenance
S.E.A.T.O.	South-East Asia Treaty Organisation
S.F.I.O.	Section Française de l'Internationale Ouvrière (French Socialists)
S.O.E.	Special Operations Executive
S.S.I.P.	Society for Socialist Inquiry and Propaganda
T.U.C.	Trades Union Congress
T.V.A.	Tennessee Valley Authority
U.L.F.	University Labour Federation
U.N.E.S.C.O.	United Nations Educational, Scientific and Cultural Organisation
U.N.O.	United Nations Organisation
U.N.R.R.A.	United Nations Relief and Rehabilitation Administration
W.E.A.	Workers' Educational Association

W.T.A.   Workers' Travel Association

In footnotes, PRO refers to documents in the Public Record Office, Kew. Dalton's three volumes of memoirs have been abbreviated as follows: CBY, *Call Back Yesterday: Memoirs 1887–1931* (1953); FY, *The Fateful Years: Memoirs 1931–1945* (1957); HTA, *High Tide and After: Memoirs 1945–1960* (1962).

I

Long Weekend

1

The Three Party System 1918–29

Dalton's war ended in northern Italy, with a triumphant advance against the Austrian army and a delirious welcome from liberated villagers 'crowding around our car, weeping and cheering, pouring out their stories, touching and holding and kissing us'.[1] He returned to England on 4th December, and at once began campaigning for Labour in the general election.

In the months that followed, we find Dalton – one of many former soldiers facing an uncertain future – looking hopefully for a job at the bottom of the academic ladder, and pursuing political openings at the same time. His immediate step was to gain an early release from the army, by securing a secondment to the Ministry of Labour. Once established here, he set himself two goals: a permanent appointment at the London School of Economics, and a parliamentary seat. The first was soon attained, and Dalton consolidated his position at the School by publishing books and articles on economic theory and public finance. Within six years he had also achieved the second, though with more difficulty and mishap than he had bargained for.

Gaining from the extension of the franchise and from the disarray of the Liberals, Labour's success in winning constituencies was outpacing its ability to find suitable people to fill them. Dalton's search for a seat coincided with the period of Labour's breakthrough from minor to major party status. In 1918 the Labour Party obtained 2.2 million votes. By 1922, the Labour vote had risen to 4.2 million, and with 142 seats the Parliamentary Labour Party became the official Opposition.

Spurred by these successes Dalton worked to exploit every opportunity, securing the support of organisation staff in Eccleston Square for his quest. But the newly-formed constituency parties (still loose federations mainly in

1 *With British Guns in Italy: a tribute to Italian achievement*, Methuen, London, 1919, p. 257.

3

the hands of trade union branches) maintained an obstinate independence, and it was harder for the Party leadership or for national officers to arrange selections than it later became. An additional hazard was the difficulty of assessing constituency chances. In the electoral anarchy of the 1920s, apparently promising seats returned Conservative or Liberal M.P.s, while others that had been written off as hopeless produced surprise victories. Dalton was particularly unlucky in his choices. In all, he fought four unsuccessful contests – at Cambridge, Maidstone, Cardiff East and Holland-with-Boston – before winning the fifth, at Peckham, in December 1924.

Once in the House of Commons, Dalton rose fast, quickly establishing himself as a leading authority on financial and international affairs. It was an indication of his abilities (and also of the paucity of professional talent among Labour colleagues) that he was elected to the Labour Parliamentary Executive at the end of his first session in 1925, and became a member of the Labour Party National Executive a year later.

Dalton's skills as a parliamentarian contrasted sharply, however, with his maladroit handling of local party matters. A simmering row between the Peckham M.P. and his agent became so bad that the N.E.C. was called in to investigate, failing to resolve the dispute. Faced with an implacably divided party, Dalton decided not to stand again for the same constituency. It was a dangerous but – as it turned out – fortunate decision. Aided by Arthur Henderson, the Labour Party Secretary, Dalton was selected for the County Durham seat of Bishop Auckland, which he was to hold, with one break, until his retirement.

The 1920s were a time of rapid progress, but they also contained a personal tragedy. While Hugh was in Italy in 1917, his wife Ruth had given birth to a daughter, Helen. In June 1922, Helen died of a kidney disease that had initially been mis-diagnosed. Hugh reacted with bitter grief, and both he and Ruth continued to feel the loss deeply, apparently blaming themselves. Yet this bereavement barely slowed the pace of Hugh's career.

Wednesday 11th to Saturday 14th December
Speaking for Mallon[1] in Saffron Walden Division. I enjoy myself and am a great success, especially at Saffron Walden itself which is very Tory and loves a soldier. A great meeting, with tumultuous opposition, at Saffron Walden Corn Exchange on eve of poll. I shout them down with vulgar repartee.

1 J. J. Mallon (1875–1961). Warden of Toynbee Hall 1919–54. Social reformer.

Saturday 21st December
Lecture on 'eighteen months with Italian Army' at King's College (London) for W.E.A. [Workers' Educational Association] Funds. An audience of eighty, very stodgy, largely my relations. I keep them listening to me for an hour and forty minutes.

The general election held between 2nd and 19th December 1918 produced a large majority for the Lloyd George Coalition, based on a greatly-strengthened Conservative Party. Asquith's group of independent Liberals was reduced to 34 seats. Labour representation increased from 42 seats in 1910 to 61; but with candidates standing for the first time without benefit of the pre-war Lib–Lab pact, the real improvement was much greater.

Sunday 29th December
Election results worse than I had expected. Not much hope of another election for at least four years. I don't see much hope of resurrection for the Squithian body. On the other hand, if the Coalition Liberals, or a large proportion of them, cross over and join up again with the Squithian residue a Liberal buffer party might again come into being between Conservatism and Labour. But I don't think it would have a long life.

Though the Labour Party has made smaller gains than I had hoped, it *has* made gains. I hope it will take over official Opposition. It has suffered, for the moment, for keeping most of its brain in its left big toe. It polled surprisingly well in many unexpected plots of virgin soil. I was specially struck with the beginning of an awakening among agricultural labourers in Essex. Also the soldiers at the front either couldn't vote, or voted in a hopeless atmosphere.

Four years hence Labour ought to poll a tremendous vote, and meanwhile win a lot of by-elections. What is chiefly needed is (1) improved organisation in the constituencies, (2) an influx of brains and middle-class non-crank membership. It is very weak now in knowledge on foreign and imperial policy, and army and navy. Also it will want some good lawyers (but not too many). I wish Simon,[1]

1 Sir John Simon, later 1st Viscount (1873–1954). Liberal M.P. 1906–18, 1922–31; Liberal National 1931–40. Solicitor-General 1910–13; Attorney-General 1913–15; Home Secretary 1915–16. Joined the National Government in 1931, and became Leader of the Liberal National Party. Foreign Secretary 1931–5; Home Secretary 1935–7; Chancellor of the Exchequer 1937–40; Lord Chancellor 1940–45.

for instance, would come in. But no 'agreements' with the Liberals as a separate party are entertainable.

Thursday 2nd January 1919
Mallon to dinner. He talked incessantly, always interesting and, whenever possible, amusing. The Labour Party are B.F.s not to give him a good seat. He would be invaluable to them in the House with his knowledge, personality and quick wit. He pointed out the difficulty of good bourgeois being adopted for good seats under the present constitution.

Friday 17th January
Visit London School of Economics to see Cannan,[1] Miss MacTaggart,[2] Director,[3] Lees-Smith,[4] Withers.[5] I am received effusively by the second. It seems clear I can get in there in the autumn, as Cannan's assistant. He says it oughtn't to be difficult to make a reputation there, once I get my foot in, as Lees-Smith and co. have got very slack and there are no new people coming on. A large number of young economists have been killed in the war.

Sunday 26th January
Tea with Cole.[6] He looked ill and unhappy. His chief interests I think are narrow, though his knowledge pretty wide. We talk of Italian Labour movement, publishers, etc., etc. His wife[7] I didn't much like.

1 Edwin Cannan (1861–1935). Professor of Political Economy at the London School of Economics 1907–26. Cannan had supervised Dalton's research before the war.
2 Miss C. S. MacTaggart. Secretary and Registrar of the L.S.E. 1917–20; Dean 1920–21. The power behind the ailing and increasingly inadequate Director.
3 William Pember Reeves (1857–1932). Director of the L.S.E. 1908–19. Former New Zealand politician. Fabian.
4 H. B. Lees-Smith (1878–1941). Lecturer in Economics and Public Administration at the L.S.E. Liberal M.P. 1910–18. He joined the I.L.P. in 1919, having previously been a member of the Union for Democratic Control. Labour M.P. 1922–3, 1924–31, 1935–41. Postmaster-General 1929–31. President of the Board of Education 1931. Acting Chairman of the P.L.P. 1940–41.
5 Hartley Withers (1867–1950). Editor of *The Economist* 1916–21.
6 G. D. H. Cole (1889–1959). Philosopher, historian, polemicist and socialist campaigner. Secretary of the Labour Research Department and leading figure in the Guild Socialist movement. Fellow of Magdalen College, Oxford 1912–19. Fellow of University College, Oxford and University Reader in Economics 1925–44. Chichele Professor of Social and Political Theory, Oxford 1944–57.
7 Margaret Cole, later Dame (1893–1980). Writer and socialist campaigner. Assistant Secretary of the Labour Research Department 1917–25. Secretary of the New Fabian Research Bureau 1935–9; Chairman of the Fabian Society 1939–53. In an interview shortly before her death, she recalled having first met Dalton during the war through the Labour Research Department. The dislike was mutual.

A fine lot of black hair, however. Passes rather for a very William Morris type. Yellow blouse. A pipe smoker. The pair of them a little difficult. He a better talker than listener. But his books are damned good.

Thursday 30th to Friday 31st January
Fix up with Miss MacTaggart and Cannan my entry on L.S.E. staff ... She fixed with me to give Cannan's Public Finance Lectures next term and in the autumn. Next term forty guineas for a course of nine, repeated in the evening. Not bad pay to begin with. I have a free hand, taking general principles one term, and concrete facts the next. Arrange with Cannan that he will set such Public Finance exam questions as I suggest. When I have a book out on something economic, they think I shall be acquired without difficulty as a Lecturer in London University. Cannan gives me his lecture notes, but I shan't do more than use them in conjunction with others.

Tuesday 4th to Thursday 6th February
At Cambridge after an absence of about six years. Rather heart-rending at first, but after two days all the places have grown so familiar that they no longer hurt, another phase of Nature's queer self-protectiveness. She is very cunning, as Dickinson[1] says. If we weren't blunted by repetition of even the worst experiences we should, perhaps, stop breeding, which wouldn't suit Nature's book at all. Khaki is beginning to disappear from the streets, and a number of quite normal looking undergraduates are walking about the streets. A number of young Naval officers in Cambridge. Thought that this may be permanent, which would be very good for the Navy.

Union Debate on Tuesday rather a dead dull thing. Not dramatic enough to be painful. A list of the dead read aloud. I quote Rupert's war sonnets[2] and Pericles. They all sit and stare in front of them. I doubt how far Englishmen, or any one, realise our war losses at all.

---

1 Goldsworthy ('Goldie') Lowes Dickinson (1862–1932). Fellow of King's College, Cambridge and part-time lecturer at the L.S.E. Political theorist and writer on international questions. 'The Don who had most influence on me was Lowes Dickinson', Dalton wrote (CBY, p. 56). 'He lectured on political ideas, was a man of the Left and an anti-clerical.' In the 1920s, Dickinson served on the Labour Party's Advisory Committee on International Questions.
2 Rupert Brooke (1887–1915). Poet and classical scholar. Dalton and Brooke had been exact contemporaries and close friends as undergraduates at King's.

Wednesday talk to Fay,[1] who suggests my coming up to Cambridge for a night or two a week in term time to coach and lecture. I doubt if this is very feasible. I see Pigou,[2] who has been humanised a bit by the war. Still hates stupidity more than anything, especially Hughes[3] over indemnities, etc. We talk also of aeroplanes, Italy, etc. Dine with Dickinson and stay with him till late. The most beloved personality of them all. I must go again to Cambridge when it has grown still more normal, perhaps by October. Snow still on the ground. Damp and rather cold. Dickinson wants me to become secretary to Educational Committee of League of Nations Union to infuse internationalism into our education. I doubt if it will be feasible. I am rather overflowed at present with offers of employment which are not quite good enough.

Dickinson on War Cabinet, not five lively specialists on conduct of war, but a confused body of about twenty, including officials and private secretaries. No one knowing what has been decided, agenda and minutes very scrappy. Scene. Enter Carson[4] in midst of discussion on what you will. 'By the way, Prime Minister, I've just come back from Ireland. I noticed a lot of books on the bookstalls. I think it's a great waste of transport having books carried about from one place to another. I think we ought to stop it.' Smuts.[5] 'I don't agree with you, Carson. This is a war of ideas. The more thinking everyone does the better.' Carson. 'I don't agree with you, Smuts. Only an ignorant people can be great in war. Thinking should only be done by the men at the head of affairs. Titus Oates, for instance – ' Lloyd George[6] looking up, suddenly interested. 'Speaking of oats reminds me of my young days at Llanystymdwy. We used to have some fine crops of oats there. And, by the way, that reminds me. I hear there are 40,000 mules down at Aldershot, eating their heads off and doing

---

1 C. R. Fay. Economic historian. Fellow of Christ's College, Cambridge.
2 A. C. Pigou (1877–1959). Economist. Fellow of King's College, Cambridge; Professor of Political Economy 1908–43.
3 W. M. Hughes (1864–1952). Prime Minister of Australia 1915–23, and delegate to the Paris Peace Conference.
4 Sir Edward Carson, later 1st Baron (1854–1935). Unionist M.P. for Duncairn Division of Belfast 1918–21. Solicitor-General 1900–6. Attorney-General 1915. First Lord of the Admiralty 1916–17, Minister without Portfolio 1917–18.
5 Jan Christian Smuts (1870–1950). Prime Minister of South Africa 1919–24, 1939–48. Minister without Portfolio and member of the War Cabinet 1917–19.
6 David Lloyd George, later 1st Earl (1863–1945). Prime Minister 1916–22. Liberal M.P. for Caernarvon District 1890–1945. President of the Board of Trade 1905–8; Chancellor of the Exchequer 1908–15; Minister of Munitions 1915–16; Secretary of State for War 1916.

nothing.' (Sudden excited intervention of military personage. Whispering.) 'Well, not perhaps 40,000 but 4 or 5,000. We must do something about it.' ...... Dickinson, when talking to Smuts, found he had a quite un-English mind, a speculative, free moving mind, more like a Frenchman's.

Friday 7th February
Am demobilised, without regret.

Monday 10th February
Start work at Ministry of Labour.

Sunday 16th February
To Miss N. Young's[1] flat with Ruth.[2] Present Mallon, the Coles and Keeling, a photographer painter just back from Russia.[3]

Cole very narrow and impractical outside his own shop, and without humour. Ruth expecting an Etonian Bolshevik, as Dent[4] calls them, disappointed. Cole thinks Wilson[5] 'rather a nasty fellow, one of those old fashioned Liberals, rather like Asquith.' Proposed League of Nations worse than useless. Asked if alternative isn't old Balance of Power, replied no, World Revolution. Then forced to admit that no Revolution to be looked for at present in England, France or America. Cole has no regard for truth in general, but only for vicious propaganda. Doesn't want a Committee of Enquiry to go to Russia, because it would probably, finding out the truth, report adversely on the Bolsheviks. Doesn't want anything authoritative said against Bolsheviks.

This sad looking, delicate, argumentative, truculent, conceited young man has a fine intellect of a very narrow kind, and great power of constructive thought, again on very narrow lines. His wife is very

1 Not identified.
2 Ruth Dalton, née Hamilton Fox, later Lady Dalton (1890–1966). She and Hugh married in 1914. See Appendix.
3 H. V. Keeling went to Russia in 1914 to instruct Russian workmen in photo-litho processes. After working for the Bolshevik Government's Education Department, he left the Soviet Union in January 1919 (shortly before this entry) and published a book (*Bolshevism: Mr Keeling's five years in Russia*, ed. E. H. Hayward, Hodder & Stoughton, London) criticising the regime.
4 E. J. Dent (1876–1957). Musicologist. Fellow of King's College, Cambridge 1902–8, 1926–57. Professor of Music 1926–57. The Daltons rented Dent's house in Cambridge for two years, while Hugh was Labour candidate for the city.
5 Woodrow Wilson (1856–1924). President of the United States 1912–21.

intense, and ought to have had her teeth knocked in when she was little. But more practical than her husband.

Wednesday 26th February
Lecture at Battersea Polytechnic on 'Making of Italy, Mazzini, Garibaldi and Cavour'. A bad and dull lecture, very properly criticised by Ruth who says that neither facts nor history are my strong point, and that I had better stick to political campaigning or general economic principles. I said that Cavour promised to marry Princess Clothilde to Napoleon III himself, when apparently it was some relative of the latter. Ruth said, quite rightly, that I didn't know that Bomba's family came from Spain. However I carefully refrained from coughing and made a less bad impression upon the audience than upon my better informed and more critical spouse.

Sunday 23rd March
Ruth and I are summoned to lunch with the Webbs.[1] No one else there. I am put through my paces, and questioned as to my present opinions, occupation and intentions. We learn that the Labour leaders 'won't come and consult us', and 'are not good teamsters' being very suspicious of one another. They invited all the newly elected Labour Members to dinner. Thirty accepted, but only seventeen came, one on the wrong night. One said he 'wanted to take up finance'. None knew anything of foreign affairs. Next time every seat except the City of London and Westminster should be winnable.

An election we learn will probably come in two years, and an election next autumn is 'not outside the bounds of possibility'. 'We think' that Lloyd George will probably go into Opposition, propose much more daring things than the Labour Party have ever done, arrive at an electoral understanding with the latter, win the election and offer Labour 2/3rds of the posts in the Ministry. How could they refuse?

Much mockery of Adamson[2] coming and announcing that, to become His Majesty's Opposition, all the Labour Party needed was

1 Sidney Webb, later 1st Baron Passfield (1859–1947) and Beatrice Webb, née Potter (1858–1943). Fabian reformers and writers on social questions. Sidney Webb became a Labour M.P. from 1922–9 and served as President of the Board of Trade in 1924 and (having accepted a peerage) as Colonial Secretary in 1929–31.
2 William Adamson (1863–1936). Leader of the Labour Party in the House of Commons 1918–21. Labour M.P. for West Fife 1910–31. Secretary of State for Scotland 1924, 1929–31. Ex-miner.

two additional clerks, a typist and a messenger. The Speaker refused to recognise the Labour Party as unqualified Opposition, because of Sinn Fein[1] and the possibility of this and Liberal sections reuniting.

In the evening we read Wells on Uncle Kidney and Aunt 'Altiora' in *The New Machiavelli*.[2]

Wednesday 16th April
With Ruth to Corfe Castle. I have been feeling only a quarter of a man, or less, for some time and intensely oppressed by the futility of the Ministry of Labour, or at any rate my work there. Once away I find myself rapidly cheering up, and begin to have a stream of ideas for *The Inequality of Incomes*[3] and several other books ...

A superb holiday, with unbroken good weather. We walk sixty-five miles, and cover most of the Isle of Purbeck. The first proper holiday we have either of us had since our honeymoon in May 1914.

Friday 25th April
W.E.A. tutors' conference. A lot of talk about salaries. In the evening with Ruth to a meeting of the Latchmere Ward Committee of the Battersea Labour Party.[4] Small attendance, but rather pets. Talk about organisation, etc. Must keep up contact with these people. It *might* be feasible to stand for this constituency, but the drawbacks are obvious, and Burns[5] a disconcerting factor.

Saturday 26th April
I shake the dust of the Ministry of Labour off my feet, and am full of inarticulate joy and relief.

On 29th April, Dalton began lecturing on public finance at the L.S.E. He continued to teach at the School (part-time between 1924 and 1929) until

---

1 Sinn Fein won 73 constituencies in the 1918 election; all the successful candidates declined to take their seats.
2 H. G. Wells (1866–1946) published *The New Machiavelli* in 1911, lampooning the Fabian morality of the Webbs, whose characters were thinly disguised. Dalton would have been amused by this book for another reason: its description of a group of progressive undergraduates which closely resembled his own Cambridge circle.
3 See entry for end of September, beginning of October 1920, p. 19, n. 6.
4 Hugh and Ruth were living in rented accommodation in Albert Bridge Road, Battersea. Apart from Dalton's involvement in the 1918 election campaign, this is the first reference to any direct participation in Labour Party activities.
5 John Burns (1858–1943). Independent Labour, then Liberal, M.P. for Battersea 1892–1918. President of the Local Government Board 1905–14. President of the Board of Trade 1914. Resigned on declaration of war.

1935, with a break in 1929–31, when he was a minister in the second Labour Government.

Saturday 3rd May

With Ruth to Albert Hall for Co-operative and Trade Union demonstration. Bernard Shaw[1] speaks very well, without squibs or verbosity, but with humour, power of phrase and distinction. Ruth admires the cut of his clothes. He has a better head for economics than Smillie.[2] The latter has a great reception. He is not a great orator, but a very effective speaker, especially in his frankness and emotional appeal. 'Kings and Queens are not generally shown the slums. Kings and Queens should have the intelligence to ask to see the slums.' His economics are vaguely Marxian.

The co-operative leaders strike one as rotten sticks. It's difficult to understand how they do as well as they do. But no doubt they have a certain shrewdness in business matters.

Monday 2nd June

Dine with Dickinson at the Athenaeum. He is very pessimistic, as usual, about the 'Peace'. He says Winston[3] has now got some big and vague ideas into his head about an inevitable conflict between east and west. 'East' apparently means Russia and China and Japan. Hardly a likely combination I should have thought, and 'West' includes Germany, and Winston is in favour of making concessions to Germany. What a dangerously vigorous and untrained intellect. He needs to go to a House of Rest.

In July, Dalton was adopted as prospective Labour candidate for the Abbey Division of Westminster, where it was thought a by-election might be held. In fact, there was no by-election, and Dalton was shortly afterwards adopted as candidate for Cambridge.

---

1 George Bernard Shaw (1856–1950). Playwright, social critic and Fabian pioneer.
2 Robert Smillie (1857–1940). President of the Miners' Federation of Great Britain 1912–21. Member of the Sankey Commission, which advocated the nationalisation of the mines. I.L.P. pioneer. Labour M.P. 1923–9.
3 W. S. Churchill, later Sir Winston (1874–1965). Secretary of State for War and Air 1919–21. See Appendix.

Friday 6th June

I meet the Propaganda Committee of the Westminster Labour Party. . . . Sanders,[1] Houlihan,[2] Marion Phillips[3] and a few others. Haden-Guest[4] and I are apparently the alternatives, and I think the Committee would prefer me. I'm not so sure about the Executive, on which the Webbs sit, and of which Henderson[5] is chairman. Burdett-Coutts,[6] the sitting Member, is expected to die at any moment. He has twice offered his resignation, but it has not been accepted. Christabel Pankhurst[7] is in the field as an independent candidate, but it is not thought that she will get the coupon. There will possibly be an official Unionist, and possibly a Liberal also.

It is agreed that, if I am adopted, I shall be bound to Westminster for a by-election only. At a general election the seat would probably not be fought by the Labour Party. Also that I should not be expected to break up my present summer plans, which include two to three months in the country, unless the seat actually becomes vacant. The crucial point is expenses. Sanders says he thinks a well run election shouldn't cost more than £500, including the Returning Officer's fee of £150. The Committee think they *could* raise the lot locally, but they want a guarantee of the Returning Officer's fee at least. I promise to let them know in a few days.

Sunday 8th June

I write to the secretary of the Westminster Labour Party undertaking, if adopted, to guarantee the Returning Officer's fee, on condition, if sufficient money is raised from other sources, I shall be reimbursed.

Friday 13th June

See Houlihan in the evening, and learn that I have been approved as

---

1 Captain W. S. Sanders (1871–1941). Secretary of the Fabian Society 1914–20. Labour M.P. 1929–31, 1935–40. Junior minister 1930–31.
2 J. T. Houlihan. A member of the Union of Post Office Workers and Labour Party activist who was backing Dalton for the nomination.
3 Dr Marion Phillips (1881–1932). Lecturer in Social Science at the L.S.E. Chief Woman Officer of the Labour Party. Labour M.P. 1929–31.
4 L. H. Haden-Guest, later 1st Baron (1877–1960). London County Councillor 1919–22. Labour M.P. 1923–7, 1937–50.
5 Arthur Henderson (1863–1935). General Secretary of the Labour Party. Labour M.P. for Widnes. See Appendix.
6 William Burdett-Coutts, originally W. L. Ashmead-Bartlett (1851–1921). Unionist M.P. for the Abbey Division of Westminster 1918–21; Westminster 1885–1918.
7 Christabel Pankhurst, later Dame (1880–1958). A leader of the Women's Social and Political Union, working for female suffrage. Eldest daughter of Mrs Emmeline Pankhurst.

candidate by the Westminster Labour Party Executive. Sidney Webb was in the chair and said he knew Mr Dalton and thought he would make a very good candidate.

Monday 16th June

To Caxton Hall with Ruth to hear Christabel Pankhurst. Such stuff! and delivered with such gestures! It would be immense fun to have a public debate with her. A crowd of middle-class women, a very few probably electors in Westminster, come to hear her.

Wednesday 18th June

Ruth and I dine with Lady Byles,[1] and drop hints that we don't want a Liberal to run in Westminster, if there's a by-election. I think she understands. She is very lovable and wonderfully conscious of the debt which the old owe to the young who have survived the war.

Thursday 19th June

Talk to Lees-Smith at the School of Economics. He is just joining the Labour Party, and I.L.P. [Independent Labour Party], after six months' intensive study of them. He says the Tories are very much afraid of Labour in the country districts.

Saturday 28th June

Go round with Ruth to see the Houlihans in the evening, and their three girls. The second is a beautiful child. The first has at least beautiful hair. The third is pale and frail looking. Houlihan has started a Labour Party in Chelsea (he has boundless energy!), and they will contest nine seats at the Borough Council in November. He gives some astonishing instances of meanness in the treatment by the Post Office of disabled soldiers in their employment.

The railway unions had been negotiating with the Government (which had taken control of the railways during the war) for a new agreement. In September the negotiations broke down, and on 27th September the unions called a national strike.

Thursday 2nd October

Railway strike. On first night of strike I hear Lloyd George had two

1 Sarah Anne, Lady Byles, née Unwin. Widow of Sir William Byles, a Radical M.P. and social reformer.

fire engines with steam up in Downing Street! But no one came near him ...

Chief features of strike, when in progress, (1) the extraordinary orderliness of the strikers and the admirable leadership of Thomas,[1] (2) the tone of the Government announcements, *Bad*. Lloyd George's 'anarchical conspiracy', etc. (3) the tone of most of the press, *Worse*. *Times* 'fight to a finish, as in the Greater War against Germany'. Lesser rags howling about bolshevism, blow at community, etc.

Many of the 'public' taken in by all this. 'Class feeling', I'm afraid, will be intensified. Attended a strike meeting outside Henry VIII Gateway one evening. Much impressed by orderliness and good sense. Next day people were going about saying they had heard that attacks had been made on the King! The success of Government's skeleton service of passenger trains and food distribution by lorry. This is the plan worked out during war for use in event of invasion. But of course the Government couldn't move goods to any extent and the economic effects of strike, though a little camouflaged, as a result of mechanical transport developments, are almost as profound as in 1911.

Sunday 5th October
Go to Albert Hall with Ruth. Mass meeting of N.U.R. [National Union of Railwaymen]. Hall packed to overflowing. A less anarchical or bolshevik audience would be difficult to imagine. Cramp[2] announces settlement. He, Thomas (evidently exhausted) and Bromley[3] all speak persuasively.

Settlement a very marked compromise. Better so. If Government had won outright, labour feeling would have been very bitter, and anti-labour extremists would have been emboldened to try to break Trade Unions. If N.U.R. had won outright, labour extremists would have been correspondingly encouraged, and there would have been more 'lightning strikes', and talk of direct action.

---

1 J. H. Thomas (1874–1949). General Secretary of the National Union of Railway-men 1911–31. Labour M.P. for Derby 1910–31; National Labour M.P. 1931–6. Colonial Secretary 1924. Lord Privy Seal and Minister for Employment 1929–30; Secretary of State for the Dominions 1930–5; Colonial Secretary 1935–6. Forced to resign from the Cabinet and the House in 1936 after leaking Budget secrets.
2 C. T. Cramp (1876–1933). General Secretary of the National Union of Railwaymen 1920–33. Member of the Labour Party N.E.C.
3 John Bromley (1876–1945). General Secretary of the Associated Society of Loco-motive Engineers and Firemen 1914–36. Labour M.P. 1922–3, 1924–31.

Monday 17th November
Much depressed by flow of essays at School of Economics, and inability to get on with *librone*.

Tuesday 18th November
See Susan Lawrence[1] about possibility of contesting Cambridge (Borough).

Saturday 6th to Monday 8th December
Spend weekend at Cambridge. Stay in Fay's rooms in Christ's ...

Sunday morning call on Mrs Rackham.[2] Question of my possible candidature at Cambridge discussed. She would like me to stand, but they have no organisation and practically no money. But many Liberals, she thinks, would vote for me against E. Geddes.[3] A Liberal candidate unlikely, if a Labour candidate is first in the field. She will bring the matter up at the next Party Meeting. I explain that I am in negotiation with another constituency and should have to choose, if I got a firm offer from Cambridge. She thinks I shouldn't be required to contribute anything. But this may be optimistic.

Lunch with Fay, Mrs Fay and the three little Fays, all male and rather ugly.

Tea with Dickinson in King's. Much talk of Keynes's[4] book on Economic Consequences of the Peace, coming out within a week. Fay calls him Jeremiah Malthus Keynes. Dickinson despairs of Fay's point of view.

Tuesday 24th February 1920
Giving lessons in economics to Grand Duke Dmitri Pavlovich, who

---

1 Susan Lawrence (1871–1947). Organiser of the National Federation of Women Workers 1912–21. Labour M.P. 1923, 1926–31. Later served on the Labour Party N.E.C. (Chairman 1929–30). Junior minister 1929–31.
2 Clara Rackham, née Tabor (1875–1966). Fabian and social reformer. Fellow of Newnham College, Cambridge. Married to Harris Rackham (1868–1944), Fellow of Christ's College.
3 Major-General Sir Eric Geddes (1875–1937). Industrialist and politician. Minister of Transport 1919–21. Conservative M.P. for Cambridge 1917–22. First Lord of the Admiralty 1916–18. Minister without Portfolio 1919. President of the Federation of British Industries 1923, 1924.
4 J. M. Keynes, later 1st Baron (1883–1946). Economist. Keynes represented the Treasury at the Paris Peace Conference, and disagreed strongly with the terms of the Versailles Treaty. His book, *The Economic Consequences of the Peace* (Macmillan, London, 1919) helped to convince liberal opinion that Germany had been unfairly and unwisely treated. Dalton remained sceptical of this attitude. See Appendix.

helped to kill Rasputin.[1] Aged twenty-eight. Handsome, elegant and distinguished. Intelligent and quick at the uptake. Felt war was coming in 1913 when he was in Paris. Chief reason – decline of morality, Russian ballet, Bakst[2] colour schemes, etc. Dmitri thinks Viennese waltzes were the passion of a more moral age.

After killing Rasputin (actually he was playing Yankee Doodle on the gramophone upstairs, while others were first trying to poison, and then shooting, the lousy and lascivious monk), he was exiled as a political prisoner to Teheran. Here he was guarded by soldiers who, when the First Revolution came, wore red cockades on their uniform and saluted less smartly, and when the Second Revolution came, threw down their arms and went off. Then being unguarded, he escaped and came to England.

Today we were talking of banking and credit, and he showed me his Passbook. He explained that he had got an advance of £1000 from the British Minister at Teheran on the latter's personal security. Barclays Bank were willing to make him a large advance six months ago, when it was thought that Kolchak[3] and Denikin[4] were winning in Russia. For, if they had, he would probably have been chosen Tsar 'on a plebiscite'. Barclays would have wanted no security then except a promise that he would remember them when he came to the throne. But the other day, when he mentioned the matter again, they said they would 'have to consider it'.

Dalton was selected as prospective Labour candidate for Cambridge on 28th February 1920. Until March 1922, when he contested the seat at a by-election, he divided his time between London and Cambridge, living for long periods in Cambridge and commuting to the L.S.E.

---

1 Grigory Rasputin was assassinated by a group of Russian aristocrats at the Yusupov Palace in December 1916. The conspirators, extreme conservatives aiming to save the Russian autocracy, included Grand Duke Dmitry Pavlovich, the Tsar's nephew, mentioned in this passage as Dalton's pupil. Rasputin was induced to consume poisoned tea-cakes and wine at the home of Prince Felix Yusupov. When he failed to die, Yusupov shot him. The unfortunate monk collapsed, but succeeded in running into the courtyard where he was shot again. Rasputin was then bound and thrown through a hole in the ice into the Neva River, where he died by drowning.
2 Leon Bakst (1868–1924). Artist and designer with the Diaghilev Ballet.
3 A. V. Kolchak (1873–1920). Russian admiral. Supreme Commander-in-Chief of the Russian anti-Bolshevik forces in 1918–19. Arrested in 1919 and executed by order of the Irkutsk Military Revolution in 1920.
4 A. I. Denikin (1872–1947). Russian military commander and leader of the White opposition during the civil war. Handed over command of the remnant of his troops to General Wrangel in 1920, and emigrated to U.S.A.

Saturday 28th February
To Cambridge with Ruth. I stay with Rackhams, she with Eileen Power[1] at Girton. Lunch in King's Hall, Keynes having mistaken the date of my coming, and expected me the previous week.

Monday 22nd March
Finish verifying references to *Inequality of Incomes*. Nothing remains but the proof reading. What a travail over! It flatters my sense of my own obstinacy and persistence.

Thursday 15th April
Dine at Drapers'[2] with Canon D.[3] and Clive Wigram,[4] Stamford-ham's[5] understudy, who asks me questions about the Labour movement, its chief personalities and its attitudes to the Crown. A reasonable sort of fellow, and fairly manageable, I should fancy.

Monday 3rd May
Women's meeting with Marion Phillips in the evening. She speaks well. Ruth says my speech wasn't very good. *I* thought it was. I made myself, and a number of my audience, cry over my peroration about women and battlefields.

Wednesday 19th May
Meeting in Guildhall, Cambridge. Good platform, 'hand and brain'.

1 Eileen Power (1889–1940). Medieval historian. Director of Studies in History at Girton College, Cambridge 1913–20. A student contemporary and friend of Hugh and Ruth Dalton at the L.S.E. before the war. Lecturer at the L.S.E. 1921–4; Reader in Economic History 1924–31.
2 Drapers' Hall. Daltons had been members of the Drapers' Company, a City Guild, since the early nineteenth century, when ancestors had been involved in the cloth trade, importing silks from the Far East. Like his father, Hugh Dalton valued this connection, and both served as Masters of the Company. The Drapers held ceremonial dinners and performed charitable works.
3 Canon John Neale Dalton (1839–1931). Father of Hugh Dalton. While a young curate at Whippingham in the Isle of Wight (where Queen Victoria was one of his parishioners), John Dalton had been asked to act as personal tutor to Prince Albert Victor (later Duke of Clarence) and Prince George (later George V). Dalton accepted, and served in this capacity from 1871 to 1884. He was rewarded with a Canonry and a knighthood, and spent the last half-century of his life in a house in the Cloisters of St George's Chapel, Windsor. Here the Canon brought up his two children, and attended to the politics of the Chapter House.
4 Clive Wigram, later 1st Baron (1873–1960). Assistant Private Secretary to the King 1910–31. Private Secretary 1935–6.
5 1st Baron Stamfordham, formerly Lt-Col. A. J. Bigge (1849–1931). Private Secretary to King George V 1910–31.

Arthur Greenwood[1] made a goodish speech in support of me, in the course of which he told them that I was 'as good as any member of the present Cabinet – and I would say better'. (Loud cheers.)

Tuesday 6th July
An American luncheon. Felix Frankfurter[2] and his wife, Miss Elizabeth Brandeis,[3] Laski[4] and Feis,[5] to meet Eileen Power. A great success. These American Jews of the New Republic are vivacious, cordial and not particularly Jewish. They have a large and decent view of the world. Laski, who is to be my colleague at the School of Economics in the autumn, falls on my neck and is very effusive. A brilliant talker, with a retentive memory, but not always a sure witness, and a little too apt to give the impression of knowing everyone.

End of September, beginning of October
Inequality of Incomes[6] out. A good format. My view of the merits of this book fluctuates. On the whole, I think it's pretty good!

Wednesday 20th October
Clynes[7] and I at the Cambridge Guildhall. A fine meeting. Some undergraduate interruption from the rear, and incipient attempts at

1 Arthur Greenwood (1880–1954). Secretary of the Joint Research Department of the T.U.C. and Labour Party. See Appendix.
2 Felix Frankfurter (1882–1965). Byrne Professor of Administrative Law at Harvard 1914–39. Associate Justice of the U.S. Supreme Court 1932–62. Friend and correspondent of Harold Laski.
3 Elizabeth Brandeis. Later married to Paul Rauschenbusch. Younger daughter of Louis Brandeis, Associate Justice of the U.S. Supreme Court 1916–39.
4 Harold Laski (1893–1950). Political theorist and socialist campaigner. Lecturer at the L.S.E. 1920–22; Professor of Political Science 1926–50. Member of the Labour Party N.E.C. 1936–49 (Chairman 1945–6). Shortly before this entry Laski had returned from Canada and the United States, where he had been lecturing at McGill, Harvard and Yale.
5 Herbert Feis (1893–1972). U.S. economist and historian.
6 *Some Aspects of the Inequality of Incomes in Modern Communities* (Routledge, London, 1920), based on Dalton's doctorate, surveyed theoretical literature on inequality since Adam Smith and J. S. Mill. It was also a political tract, attacking the principle of inherited wealth.
7 J. R. Clynes (1869–1949). Labour M.P. for Manchester North-East 1906–18; Manchester Platting 1918–31, 1935–45. President of the National Union of General and Municipal Workers 1912–37. Minister of Food Control 1918–19. Chairman of the Parliamentary Labour Party 1921–2. Lord Privy Seal and Deputy Leader of the House 1924. Home Secretary 1929–31.

a rag. But we reduce them to silence pretty quickly. Fay in the chair. Clynes very quiet and effective but rather old fashioned. 'Treat the workman as a man', etc.

Thursday 21st October

To London with Clynes by the 9.05 a.m. train. We get on well together ... He admires Synge's plays.[1] He thinks his consumers' council at the Food Ministry was a great invention, capable of being generalised, and well adapted to back up bureaucrats. He says Beveridge[2] was very able and resourceful, but not good at dealing with people and making out the best case for his own plans in debate. He says the Labour Party want more people like me in the House and that constituency organisation should more often seek the advice of the centre. I said that I thought it would all come in time and middle-class people couldn't expect to be taken at their own valuation, in view of their general attitude in the past.

Friday 31st December

Have got on a bit, but not much, with Public Finance.[3] Ruth in bed with tonsillitis and laryngitis, but over the worst stage. A pity to have made holes in a free week we would otherwise have had together. I'm a little brain stale and over economic, and, to a less extent, over politic. Also sententious and reflective at the turn of the year. Not a bad year for me really in which I've become Prospective Parliamentary Candidate in a possible constituency, made a lot of speeches, learned a good deal about practical politics and organisation, published a fat academic economic tome, written an *Economic Journal* article[4] that few can understand and none refute, become a University Reader,[5]

---

1 J. M. Synge (1871–1909). Irish dramatist.
2 William Beveridge, later 1st Baron (1879–1963). Writer on social questions. Director of the L.S.E. 1919–37, in succession to Pember Reeves. Second Secretary, then Permanent Secretary, at the Ministry of Food 1916–19. A member of many government committees and statutory bodies. Responsible for the 1942 Report on Social Insurance and Allied Services, the basis of the modern Welfare State. Liberal M.P. 1944–5.
3 *The Principles of Public Finance* (Routledge, London), Dalton's second book on economics, was published in December 1922.
4 Dalton's article 'The Measurement of the Inequality of Incomes' had been published in the September issue of the *Economic Journal*, of which Keynes was editor.
5 Dalton had been made Ernest Cassel Reader in Commerce in June (Diary, 4th June 1920), with an increase of salary from £400 to £750 per annum.

and Examiner, and Doctor of Science, with a perceptible rise in screw, and brought myself in a few miscellaneous ways into the public eye. But it seems a long way to go to anywhere real yet, and life is passing, and in some moods it all seems very empty and silly. Reading poems to Ruth in her bed tonight ...

Saturday 30th April 1921
To Cambridge to stay with Rackhams.

Sunday 1st May
Most successful May Day demonstrations. Procession to Great St Mary's Church in the morning, headed by Railway Silver Band and including a number of banners. Unending streams of Trade Unionists fill floor and gallery to evident consternation of Tory and Liberal Councillors. In the afternoon a procession from Parker's Piece for an hour's route march. Two bands, ten banners and according to *Cambridge Daily News* more than 2000 people in procession. Further huge crowds on Parker's Piece awaiting our return. Speeches from two platforms. An excellent show. Probably at least 100 votes gained on the day's proceedings!

Tuesday 21st to Friday 24th June
To Labour Party Conference at Brighton as delegate of Cambridge Trades Council and Labour Party. A quiet conference, industrial gloom and distant political hope. The platform, and especially Henderson and MacDonald,[1] dominate the Conference. A sense of general mediocrity, but in what conference would that not be felt?

Sunday 2nd October
Have M. H. Dobb[2] to supper, in order to propound to him the possibility of coming to the School next year. He has good brains, evidently developing now at a good pace. Probably ambitious. Reticent about himself. Said by some to be a timeserver. He seems to like the idea. He would be an acquisition to the social life of the School and would raise the average of presentability. Also he would help to block out

---

1 James Ramsay MacDonald (1866–1937). Labour pioneer and future Prime Minister (see Appendix). In 1921 MacDonald was out of Parliament, having lost his seat in 1918. He was re-elected a few months later, and was immediately chosen as Party Leader.
2 Maurice Dobb (1900–76). Economist. Later Fellow of Trinity College and Reader in Economics at Cambridge. Dobb helped Dalton in his 1922 Cambridge election contest, and afterwards became a research student at the L.S.E. Dalton was examiner for Part II of the Economics tripos in 1922, and awarded Dobb a First.

Beveridge's idea of a provincial dull dog in the Economic Theory Department.

Wednesday 19th October

Make the acquaintance of Professor Roberto Michels,[1] of Universities of Basle and Turin, an Italian subject and Reformist Socialist. He tells me that all the Italian economists are to be found in the summer in the Valle d'Aosta and offers to put me up there in his own villino. A large cheerful man with a pretty daughter, who acts as his secretary.

Monday 24th October

U.L.F. [Universities Labour Federation] meeting at Eccleston Square.[2] Little Arthur[3] tells me, very confidentially, that my name has been submitted by the Labour Party to the Cabinet as one of four nominees for the Advisory Committee on the Trade Facilities Bill. ... The other three are Webb, Chiozza Money[4] and Emile Davies.[5] Little Arthur tells me that Big Arthur[6] has a high opinion of me as an economist and that anyhow 'it is a big leg up for you to have your name put before the Cabinet.' And, indeed, it would appear that I am getting into the position of being one of the recognised authorities of the Party on financial questions.

Tuesday 25th October

Go to the House of Commons seeking Willie Graham,[7] to discuss

1 Roberto Michels (1876–1936). Political theorist. Professor of Political Science at the University of Perugia. German by birth and Italian by adoption.
2 The national headquarters of the Labour Party were at 33 Eccleston Square, Pimlico, S.W.1, near Victoria Station.
3 'Little Arthur', to distinguish him from his father, 'Big Arthur' or 'Uncle Arthur', q.v. Arthur Henderson, later Baron Rowley (1893–1968). Labour M.P. 1923–4, 1929–31, 1935–66. Junior minister 1942–7. Secretary of State for Air 1947–51.
4 Sir Leo Chiozza Money, originally Leo Chiozza (1870–1944). Author, journalist and politician. Liberal M.P. 1906–18. Junior minister 1916–18. Resigned, joined the Labour Party and fought unsuccessfully as a Labour candidate in 1918. As a young man, Dalton had admired Money for his book *Riches and Poverty* (Methuen, London, 1905) and offered to work for him in the January 1910 General Election.
5 Emil Davies (1875–1950). City Editor of the *New Statesman*. Fabian.
6 Arthur Henderson senior, q.v. Henderson's opinion of Dalton was even better than the younger man imagined. Four months after this entry, Henderson was privately suggesting Dalton's name as an alternative to Ramsay MacDonald for Foreign Secretary in a possible Labour government (Scott Papers: C. P. Scott's unpublished diary, 28th February 1922).
7 William Graham (1887–1932). Labour M.P. for Edinburgh Central 1918–31. Financial Secretary to the Treasury 1924. President of the Board of Trade 1929–31.

University Commission matters.[1] Graham is not forthcoming, but I am entertained by Big Arthur, who is very friendly and communicative. (Quite different from our last meeting when he was intolerably pompous. In the meantime someone has been singing my praises. I learn later that it is not only Little Arthur, but Greenwood.)

Thursday 27th October
Talk to Graham at the House ... A solemn little man of the W.E.A. student type, but with rather more go than is usual in this type.

Tuesday 17th January 1922
Talk to Willie Graham with Tawney[2] about the University Commission. Graham speaks very slowly, though he thinks a little quicker. We are to prepare reservations for him. He admits to knowing nothing about Oxford and Cambridge and places himself unreservedly in our hands.

Thursday 19th January
Go to the Charles Trevelyans'[3] At Home. A lugubrious atmosphere. Talk to Admiral Drury-Lowe[4] who is verging towards Labour from Christian premises. He belongs to the Cavendish Club, is appreciative of Clynes and Graham and Tawney, and interested in the W.E.A.

Wednesday 25th January
Lecture on inherited wealth at Ruskin College, Oxford. Walk out, in the rain, to tea with Cannan and wear a pair of his trousers while mine

1 The Cambridge University Statutory Commission, like its Oxford equivalent, had been set up to pass statutes in accordance with the proposals of the Royal Commission on the Universities of Oxford and Cambridge. Lord Ullswater was Chairman and Dalton, representing the Labour Party, was one of eight commissioners. Dalton successfully pressed for the adoption of a fixed retiring age for all Fellows and University teachers.
2 R. H. Tawney (1880–1962). Historian and social theorist. Fabian. Lecturer at the L.S.E.; Professor of Economic History 1931–49. Fellow of Balliol College, Oxford 1918–21. Member of the Consultative Committee of the Board of Education 1912–31. Adviser to the Labour Party, especially on educational questions.
3 C. P. Trevelyan, later Sir Charles, 3rd Bart (1870–1958). Liberal M.P. for Elland 1899–1918. Labour M.P. for Newcastle Central 1922–31. Junior minister 1908–14. Wartime recruit to the I.L.P., via the Union for Democratic Control. President of the Board of Education 1924, and 1929 to March 1931 when he resigned. Lord Lieutenant of Northumberland 1930–49. Friend and patron of Dalton since before the war.
4 Rear-Admiral S. R. Drury-Lowe, later Vice-Admiral (1871–1945). Served in the 1914–18 war. Retired 1921.

are drying.[1] Thus attired I am presented to a highly cultured Oxford lady with whom I discuss Italian life, literature and natural beauty.

Saturday 28th January

G. L. Dickinson and Rivers[2] to Lunch. A good mixture. Rivers thinks that this is the age of human science, following that of physical. Dickinson is not quite reassured. Walk with Dickinson, and talk about politics and Army brothels.

McNair[3] rings me up very solemnly, and announces that he has a confidential communication from Cope Morgan.[4] I go round in the evening. Morgan writes that, if I will retire from Cambridge, he has a pledge from Geoffrey Howard[5] that I shall have a choice of seats in the London area, in which there shall be no Liberal opposition. A Labour victory could only come in Cambridge by a miracle, but a Liberal victory in a straight fight with the Coalition would be quite on the cards.

Sunday 5th February

Meet Morgan at breakfast with McNair. Quite a nice fellow but with no real knowledge of politics or economics. Produces a list of London constituencies, marked by Isaac[6] of the London Liberal Federation, in which we are offered Woolwich, where there is no Liberal organisation and has never been a Labour candidate, plus a bunch of dud seats in return for keeping out of all the good seats. Geoffrey Howard undertakes that, if I will go to Woolwich or any of the dud seats, I shall not be opposed by a Liberal.

The Isaac list may have been seen by members of the Labour Party National Executive, who are in favour of the idea. Much else of a plausible, but rather unreal kind. I dwell on the obvious objections, in principle and detail. McNair is obviously rather keen on an agreement – his faith in the future of Liberalism has lately revived. But,

1 Cannan lived in Oxford, and commuted to the L.S.E.
2 W. H. R. Rivers (1864–1922). Fellow and Praelector in Natural Science, St John's College, Cambridge.
3 Arnold McNair, later 1st Baron (1885–1975). International jurist. Fellow of Gonville and Caius College, Cambridge. Whewell Professor of International Law 1935–7, President of the International Court of Justice 1952–5; President of the European Court of Human Rights 1959. Undergraduate contemporary and friend of Dalton.
4 Sydney Cope Morgan (1887–1967). Liberal candidate for Cambridge in 1922 and 1923. Barrister.
5 G. W. A. Howard (1877–1935). Liberal M.P. 1906–10, 1911–18, 1923–4. P.P.S. to Asquith (as Prime Minister) 1908–10.
6 Walter Isaac. Secretary of the London Liberal Federation 1919–26.

when I ask Morgan if he is prepared to consider the offer of an alternative seat elsewhere without a Labour opponent, he gives a flat refusal, owing to 'obligations to his local supporters'. Why should my obligations, I ask, be less strong? Because, perhaps, he suggests, I may be keener than he to be a member of the next Parliament. I reply that I feel like Eve in the presence of the serpent, and remind him that the serpent never got to Heaven.

In the end, I part from him with the warning that I see nothing in the proposal, but will ask Eccleston Square about the Isaac list.

Thursday 9th February
See Wake[1] at 33 Eccleston Square and tell him of the Morgan incident. He says that Ammon[2] has been trying for a straight fight in N. Camberwell and has been conducting, probably, clandestine negotiations with the neighbouring Liberals. Ammon put up Isaac's list to National Executive. He didn't advocate a deal. There was a look of disgust all round the table. It was unanimously decided to take no action. I am authorised to state this.

In March 1922, following the resignation of the sitting M.P. for Cambridge, Dalton contested the by-election and lost. He decided not to fight the seat again, and began to look elsewhere. In May, he was adopted as candidate for the Maidstone Division in Kent.

Friday 24th March
Lecture to the Fabian Society in consideration of their election grant, on the Capital Levy[3] at Essex Hall. Dialectics with Bernard Shaw, who tells me afterwards that he has no objection to a Debt-Redemp-

1 Egerton Wake (1871–1929). Labour Party National Agent.
2 Charles Ammon, later 1st Baron (1873–1960). Leader of the Labour Party on the London County Council 1922. Organising Secretary of the Union of Post Office Workers. Labour M.P. 1922–31, 1935–44. Junior minister 1924, 1929–31. Chief government whip in the House of Lords 1945–9.
3 Dalton published a short tract called *The Capital Levy Explained* (Labour Publishing Co., London) in March 1923, after lecturing and writing extensively on the subject over preceding months, especially during the 1922 election campaign. 'It was by the association of my name with the Capital Levy that I first became widely known in the Labour Movement', Dalton wrote later (CBY, p. 122). Dalton's policy (which the Labour Party adopted) called for a reduction in the War Debt by a once-and-for-all graduated tax on large fortunes. It was not implemented when Labour came to office.

tion Levy, which is what I had called it, though he is strongly opposed to a Capital Levy. I had disarmed part of his opposition by saying that, of course, the capital wasn't there!

Down to Oxted in the evening for a country holiday.

Saturday 25th March

Ruth joins me at Oxted in the morning. We visit Helen[1] at Blue Lane House, and have tea with the family. The atmosphere and arrangements of the place are very good for small children, but there is no education, except a rather mingy-looking governess, for the older ones. Helen had an attack of asthma, as it was thought, the other day, with great difficulty in breathing. She was taken to a London doctor, who recommended dieting experiments. This seems rather rot, but she has not had any more attacks.

Sunday 26th March

Ruth, Helen and I go for a walk and climb tree stumps and pick primroses. Helen is very perky.

Monday 27th March

Ruth goes to Forest Row and I to London to lunch with the Webbs and meet Arthur Henderson. This is rather a nuisance, as it breaks up our time in the country, but I go in the hope that something may come of it. Nothing does ... I aim to leave with him and talk walking to the House. But Beatrice (damn her!) engages me in pointless conversation and I miss the chance.

Tuesday 18th April

Tea with Gerald[2] and Fredegond Shove.[3] I dislike her more every time I see her – squirming, sentimental, self-consciously-diseased, clinging, feeble little creature! He seems fitter and cheerfuller than I should be. I should run away.

Saturday 13th May

Return to Cambridge, leaving Ruth in London. Disquieting news of

---

1 Helen Dalton (1917–22). The Daltons' only child, who had been sent to a residential nursery at Limpsfield in Surrey.
2 Gerald Shove (1887–1947). Economist. Fellow of King's College, Cambridge. A member of Dalton's undergraduate circle, and Secretary of the University Fabians in 1909.
3 Fredegond Shove, née Maitland (1889–1949). Wrote poetry and kept a large number of cats. Daughter of the historian F. W. Maitland and a cousin of Virginia Woolf, q.v.

Helen, kidney trouble and curious swellings on stomach and in the face.

In the evening a number of young men (University Labour Club) come in; they *are* a jolly crowd ... They matter tremendously to the world, the first of the new generation unscarred by the war. Politics, if it means dedicating oneself to their happiness and opportunities, is a trade well worth following.

Tuesday 16th May

Helen has kidney disease and is very swollen, but in good spirits. She will, probably, have to be in hospital for a month. Apparently there is not much danger of its getting really bad. But it is a nasty jar just at this time.

Wednesday 17th May

Ruth brings Helen up from Limpsfield to the Chelsea Children's Hospital. Very swollen and weighing four stone instead of three. But apparently without pain and quite unaware of what she looks like.

Saturday 20th May

Adoption meeting at Maidstone. A good spirit in the delegates' meeting. ... A few questions, one from a Communist (aged twenty-one) asking whether Labour leaders should be Privy Councillors. I said I thought the best thing would be, if the whole P.C. were Labour. Then the King would be sure of good advice. I added that, if I thought there was an incompatibility between the oath of a Privy Councillor and the duty of a Trade Union leader, I should take a different view, but I didn't consider there was. The young Communist rose and said that my answer was very satisfactory. Another man asked what were my views on workers' control. I said I was in favour of a large measure of it in all industries, whether ripe for nationalisation or not. This reply was received with applause, but kept out of the press by Hunt, our voluntary agent, who is indeed a 'realist'!

Evening meeting at Sutton Valence, a pretty little village over-looking the Weald of Kent. A. J. Ellis, of the Liberal Executive, in the chair. Hunt and I had tea with him before the meeting. Very friendly. At the meeting declared himself a Gladstonian Liberal, and said that it was the duty of all such to vote Labour, and that the next fight in the division was likely to be a straight fight of Labour v. Coalition. A useful man, who used to work for the Liberal Party as Honorary Agent. Has a jolly view from his garden over the Weald, and a fine collection of maples.

Monday 22nd May

Call, with Hunt, on Armstrong, draper and chairman of the Liberal Association, and Norman Carter, another leading light. On the whole friendly. Armstrong asks if I would accept nomination as an Independent Progressive. I said this was impossible, but that I thought there was great scope for friendly co-operation. Carter raised difficulties about nationalisation. I said I limited myself to coal, railways, land, liquor and armaments. Carter said he was willing to go this far, but wore a hostile look. Armstrong said there was no present intention of running a Liberal candidate. Good evening meeting at Yalding, one of our country strongholds, outside a pub, the proprietor of which is Labour.

Tuesday 23rd May

Back to London. Ruth in rooms at 4 Wellington Square. The landlady looks like a rather dirty prostitute, but the rooms tolerable and the maidservant, from S. Wales, a counterpoise to her mistress ... Helen better. Swelling down a bit, as a result of hot air baths. Hospital arrangements satisfactory.

Saturday 27th May

To Cambridge for weekend. Tea with Peases[1] at Girton. Wedgwood[2] and his deaf wife staying there. Wedgwood says it's very tiresome being the only gentleman in the P.L.P. ... He says that some of the newer members, Morgan Jones,[3] Ammon, etc. are a great improvement on the old gang. Henderson and Clynes, to say nothing of Thomas, are still very much subject to Lloyd George's influence. Special weekly meetings of I.L.P. Group, disapproved of by Henderson who calls them 'a section within a Party', very useful in providing ginger, etc.[4]

---

1 Michael Pease (1887–1966) and Helen Pease, née Wedgwood. Michael Pease was a scientist and an undergraduate friend and Fabian contemporary of Dalton at Cambridge; Helen was the daughter of Josiah Wedgwood, q.v.

2 Josiah Wedgwood, later 1st Baron (1872–1943). Labour M.P. for Newcastle-under-Lyme 1919–42; Liberal M.P. for same constituency 1906–19. Advocate of tax on land values. Chancellor of the Duchy of Lancaster 1924. Member of the Wedgwood china family. He married Florence, née Willett, in 1919.

3 Morgan Jones (1885–1939). Labour M.P. for Caerphilly 1921–39. Junior minister 1924, 1929–31.

4 The I.L.P. group within the Parliamentary Party became even more of a 'ginger' element after the 1922 election, with the influx of new members from Clydeside, led by James Maxton, q.v., and John Wheatley, q.v.

Monday 29th May
Back to Wellington Square. Helen slightly better or stationary all through this week. A slow business.

Tuesday 6th June
Chill on stomach, probably due to throwing off all bedclothes on a hot night.

Wednesday 7th June
Chill worse. Knock off lecturing at School. Cambridge Tripos papers to be corrected, not at all inclined for this. Next few days stay in bed. Chill diagnosed as colitis. A damnable complaint. Kept awake at night by the pain of it and dieted on slops. ... Helen is not making progress, and we are both rather anxious about her.

Wednesday 14th June
To Cambridge, with a struggle, for Tripos Examiners' meeting. ... On the whole the young Cambridge economists are not as good as they ought to be. The later stages of Pigou are, I think, rather beyond them, and they are encouraged to run before they can walk.

Thursday 15th June
Back to London. Helen has a cold. This is dangerous. Ruth and I now go to the hospital every day, and sometimes more than once. She lies flat on her back now.

Friday 16th June
Helen's complications, on top of nephritis, have become a new peril. Her cold is bronchitis.

Saturday 17th June
Helen tonight looked so bad, as she lay asleep, so unhealthily pale and swollen and breathing so hard, with her eyes not properly closed, even in sleep, that we felt the odds were very heavily against her. Her cough has been hurting her more than before that day.

Sunday 18th June
Helen seemed better in the morning, naturally perhaps, as it is normal to look worse at night. But there is a danger of further complications now – pneumonia, peritonitis, meningitis. In the afternoon and early evening she was less comfortable and, almost for the first time, looked frightened. She gave once a queer little sudden cry – that was meningitis striking at her brain – and then, as though to

find a reason, pulled out a piece of chocolate from under the bed-clothes and signed for it to be taken away. Several times she tried to speak, but we couldn't hear what she said. I read her a story, which she knew, about Peter Rabbit and showed her the pictures. Ruth began to sing her a lullaby, but couldn't go on. Just before we left, she held out her arms to Ruth and said, 'O Mother, I want to go away with you.' The fear of something unknown had come to her, and she associated it with the hospital ward. These were the last words we heard her speak. We came back in the evening. I signed an authorisation for the doctor to perform an operation to draw liquid from her spine to ease the pressure. She was sleeping or unconscious, and we did not see her then. We left about 11 p.m. and they were to send for us if a crisis came.

Monday 19th June
At 1 a.m. there was a knock on the door at Wellington Square. We went round to the hospital. They were giving her oxygen. She was unconscious and breathing with a terrible effort, a gasping, groaning sound.

At 2.55 she died, still unconscious. Her breathing had stopped suddenly. I waved the nurses away from the bed. Ruth and I kissed her hair and little lips and forehead, still warm, and held her little hands, already cold. Then we went.

At 10 we went back and saw her lying in the mortuary, with her hair bound up with a piece of white ribbon and holding some white flowers in her hand. Beside her, under a sheet, was another little girl who had died in the same ward this morning. On the wall above was written 'Of such are the Kingdom of Heaven'. Ruth had never seen a dead body before ...

Then a hocus pocus with death certificate and undertakers. We had just moved that morning from Wellington Square to 19 Margaretta Terrace.

Tuesday 20th June
We took Helen's body to Golders Green. It was cremated and her ashes were scattered on a bed of roses. Only Canon D. was there then. L'Ometto[1] and John[2] had come up with the body but had gone, at my request, at the end of the few prayers which Canon D. very

1 'L'Ometto': Thomas Hamilton Fox, Ruth's father. Retired businessman. Former Treasurer of Beatrice Webb's Society for Promoting the Break-Up of the Poor Law.
2 J. Forbes Watson, later Sir John (1879–1952). Director of the British Employers' Confederation 1921–52. Married to Hugh's sister, Alexandra Mary (Georgie), q.v., since 1918.

beautifully read. He came back to lunch at Margaretta Terrace. When he had gone, I went upstairs and wept alone for three hours.

......

As that little coffin slid out of sight, I wept and kissed my hand to her.

......

She is safe anyhow now. Safe from disappointment and disillusion, miseries and a broken heart and the next war and growing old. Safe too, from love and beauty and the sunshine.

Wednesday 21st June
With Ruth to Whitby, to escape from London and all who know us, and to be alone and face it out together.

Hugh stayed away from London and the L.S.E. for most of the next four months. He began serious campaigning for the election in August. The new Prime Minister, Bonar Law, dissolved Parliament in October, following the break-up of the Coalition. In his own fight Dalton concentrated on the Capital Levy issue. 'This suits me very well on the platform', he wrote. 'Two very good meetings at the Corn Exchange. Maidstone is not accustomed to good public meetings and is duly astonished.'[1] He came third, though only 924 votes behind the Conservative victor. Nationally, however, Labour made gains and became, for the first time, the official Opposition. Ramsay MacDonald was elected as Party Leader.

Friday 29th December
With Ruth to dine with Webbs. He thinks that if there is a Labour and Liberal majority, and if we are more numerous than the Liberals, we should form a government and offer them places on condition they accept a Labour policy, including Nationalisation of Mines and Railways and Capital Levy in first session. If they are more numerous than we, we should let them form a government and support them so long as they go right. Possibly the evolution will be slow and steady Labour advances, and Liberals shelling off to Tories and ourselves gradually. Asquith said to be in favour of Capital Levy as soon as bankers are willing, but not until. He thinks that Liberal reunion under Lloyd George would drive many Liberals and some of their press into our arms.

1 Diary, 31st October 1922.

31

Saturday 30th December

So ends a year, dark with Helen's death and in which Peter[1] also died and two elections passed by on the stream. The future will be quite other than we imagined a year ago. At first up at Clapham, we thought of a year of break-away in China and more seriously of the same project later. But after two elections within a year it seemed unfeasible from the point of view of the School. Now we are talking of the Austrian Tirol and Dalmatia in the summer and no more politics for a year at least. Yet what shadows we are and what shifting shadows we pursue!

Wednesday 24th January 1923

Laski tells me that Wallas[2] is retiring in May and that he is going to tell Beveridge that either he must succeed him or he will go into politics and give only half time to the School.

Sunday 11th February

I receive a letter from Marion Phillips, asking if I would be willing to stand for Swindon. I reply that at present I can't afford either time or money to be a candidate.

Last Thursday (8th February 1923) we went to an At Home at the Charles Trevelyans'. Ammon, who was there, very pleased with himself for being a Labour whip, told us of the annoyance of the Tories during the last short session at our people keeping them up all night. Major Barnston,[3] one of the Tory whips, heard having an altercation with an elderly hound who wanted to go home. Barnston said, 'Very well! I shall send in your name to the office.' Then he came across to Ammon and said, 'See that old bugger? I wish to Christ one of your chaps had beaten him.' We were also officially refusing pairs. One young Tory came up and asked for one in the small hours, but Ammon said that, now that all the trams and buses had stopped, our people might just as well wait till they began to run again. The young man said he had a car and would give any of our people a lift. Ammon said that probably they all lived in other parts of London. The young man said, 'I will take them home, *wherever they live*, if only you will get me a pair!'

1 Sir Arthur Peterson (1859–1922). High Court Judge. Known to Hugh and Ruth as 'Peter' or 'Pierrot'. Ruth's mother, Valentine Fox, had lived with him for many years. He died early in June 1922, a few days before Helen Dalton. Income from his estate provided Ruth, and hence Hugh, with comfortable private means.
2 Graham Wallas (1858–1932). Fabian pioneer and social theorist. Professor of Political Science at the L.S.E. 1914–23.
3 Major H. Barnston, later Sir Harry, 1st Bart (1870–1929). Junior government whip 1921–4, 1924–8. Conservative M.P. for Eddisbury 1910–29.

Monday 12th February
A brush with Beveridge, who says Stamp[1] has told him that my *Public Finance* will 'do harm to the School' and is unsuitable for use as a text book.[2] Beveridge asks what truth there is in these statements. I ask if he has read the book. He says no, but gives the impression of having read Stamp's anonymous review in *The Economist* (which makes reference to a red tie under a scarlet doctoral robe, and asks whether all my views form part of the 'officially accredited teaching' of the School or are my own personal adventures in political thought). On leaving Beveridge I feel very angry at his remarks. Going on to the Labour Party reception on the eve of the session, there is a dramatic change of atmosphere. Henderson, very friendly, asks me to keep myself free from constituencies at present as they want me for a bye when a suitable opportunity offers. MacDonald says, 'I wish you were with us' and adds that he tried to jockey me into Darlington (now vacant), but that the local people would stick to their candidate at the General Election, a Trade Unionist 'who will only get in, because other people will go down and get him in'. Many other people greet me with enquiries about my capital levy book. Raging to Ruth about Beveridge, as we go away, I feel that politics and not anaemic academicism is my spiritual homeland.

Thursday 15th February
Lunch with the Webbs and tell Uncle Sidney[3] about my row with Beveridge. He says that he has expected for some time that this sort of trouble would arrive, that if it does become acute he will be prepared to take action, that it will be easy to blow the City people out of the water if necessary, but that meanwhile we should act cautiously and make it as easy for Beveridge as possible. I say that Beveridge is inclined to be the prey of the last person who speaks to him. Webb says that he thinks we shall find that 'ultimately Beveridge is all right'. Dine with the Mairs.[4] I like this mythical husband of hers.

1 Sir Josiah Stamp, later 1st Baron (1880–1941). Economist and financial expert. Member of Senate of University of London 1924–6. Vice-Chairman of the Governors of L.S.E. 1930–34; Chairman 1935–41.
2 Though generally impartial, *The Principles of Public Finance* contained passages which were strongly political – in particular, on the capital levy.
3 Sidney Webb had been Chairman of the L.S.E. Governors before the war. He had also been responsible for the foundation of the School – 'Sidney's child' as Beatrice called it.
4 David Beveridge Mair (a cousin of William Beveridge) and Janet Mair, née Philip (1876–1959). Janet Mair was Secretary of the L.S.E. 1919–38. Her forceful behaviour in this post, combined with her hold over Beveridge, led to criticism and gossip. When David Mair died in 1942, Janet Mair and William Beveridge married.

Saturday 17th February
Dine with Malones.[1] Wedgwood and his deaf wife. Wedgwood has
personality, vitality and courage, but no judgment and no economics.
All against any agreement with Liberals ... Leah Malone[2] is busy
pushing her husband. A hard job after his record of bloomers. He
doesn't say much nowadays and is rather obviously out of things.

Saturday 10th March
Dine with Sydney Arnold[3] at Reform Club and talk about Capital
Levy. (My little work on this is going well.) He has a good deal of
useful knowledge on the other financial questions, and is helping
the Party at the House. He says that more of the younger Tories are
specialising in finance, and few of our people know anything about it.
Henderson said to him the other day that he wanted to get me in the
House.

Thursday 29th March to Tuesday 3rd April
At Red Lion, Avebury. Some good walks on the Wiltshire Downs.
See Keynes and Lopokova[4] lunching at Marlborough and again at
Savernake Station on the way home. Keynes says he has been 'riding'.

Saturday 7th to Friday 13th July
At Bangor Summer School. Lecturing on the Future of Trade
Unionism to a group mostly composed of Lancashire cotton opera-
tives. I lead them, in spite of themselves, up Carnedd Llewelyn. A
jolly crowd and good week's holiday, with a small profit. Whilst at
Bangor, I get a letter from Fenner Brockway[5] saying I.L.P. branch

---

1 Lt-Col. Cecil L'Estrange Malone (1890–1966). Coalition Liberal M.P. 1918–22.
   Following a trip to Russia at the time of the Revolution, Malone joined the British
   Socialist Party and then the Communist Party, yet remained a Member of Parliament until the general election. He returned to the Commons in 1928, this time under
   Labour auspices, losing his seat three years later after turning down the offer from
   Ramsay MacDonald of a post in the National Government.
2 Leah Malone, née Klingenstein (d. 1951).
3 Sydney Arnold, later 1st Baron (1878–1945). Stockbroker. Liberal M.P. 1912–18,
   1918–21. He joined the Labour Party in 1922, and resigned in 1938. Having taken
   a peerage, he served as a junior minister in the 1924 Labour Government and as
   Paymaster-General 1929–31. Like Dalton he was a keen advocate of the capital
   levy, and was regarded as one of the Party's financial experts.
4 Lydia Lopokova, later Lady Keynes (1892–1981). Russian ballet dancer. She married Keynes in 1925.
5 Fenner Brockway, later Baron (b. 1888). Organising Secretary of the I.L.P. General
   Secretary 1928, 1933–9; Chairman 1931–3. Journalist and writer. Pacifist. Labour
   M.P. 1929–31, 1950–64.

at Huddersfield want to nominate me, and asking if I am a member of the I.L.P. I thereupon join, or rather rejoin after a lapse of years, but suspend judgment on Huddersfield.

Friday 26th October
To Oxford to address the University Labour Club on Capital Levy. A good audience. Meet Malcolm MacDonald,[1] a sensible fellow but not very brainy.

In November 1923, Dalton accepted a last-minute invitation to stand as Labour candidate in Cardiff East.

Sunday 18th November
Good reception at Cardiff and at first things look well, but snags develop later. The next two and a half weeks spent in electioneering. I have amazing platform successes and next to Ramsay[2] in Aberavon I am more fully reported and more attacked by the South Wales press than any other candidate. Our meetings surpass all my previous experience for enthusiasm, but it gradually appears that there is no organisation ...

I find that scriptural quotations are popular, indeed almost essential, in Cardiff. I have to dig hard in the fields of memory. Mond,[3] who is fighting nearby in Swansea, is a ready butt. Whenever his name is mentioned at our meetings, there are cries of 'Who pinched the babies' milk?' At one meeting a Liberal asks me what I mean by accusing Mond of pinching the babies' milk. I reply by quoting his famous economy circular to local authorities. My questioner then asks what my policy is. I reply, 'To carry out the old injunction, "feed my lambs".' This is received with great applause, which encourages

1 Malcolm MacDonald (1901–81). Undergraduate at Queen's College, Oxford. Son of Ramsay MacDonald, q.v., Labour M.P. 1929–31; National Labour 1931–45. In 1931 he joined his father in the National Government. Junior minister 1931–5; Colonial Secretary 1935, 1938–40; Secretary of State for Dominion Affairs 1935–8, 1938–9. Minister of Health 1940–41. High Commissioner to Canada 1941–6. Thereafter he served as a roving ambassador in Africa and Asia.
2 Ramsay MacDonald was Labour M.P. for the Aberavon Division of Glamorganshire 1922–9.
3 Sir Alfred Mond, 1st Bart, later 1st Baron Melchett (1868–1930). Liberal M.P. for Swansea West 1918–December 1923. Liberal, later Coalition Liberal, M.P. for Chester 1906–January 1910; Swansea Town January 1910–18. Liberal M.P. for Carmarthen 1924–6. Conservative M.P. for Carmarthen 1926–8. First Commissioner of Works 1916–21. Minister of Health 1921–2.

me to add that Mond, of course, doesn't get beyond the Old Testament.

I consent to be known as 'Doctor Dalton', as I am told that the Welsh like academic distinctions. Two days after my arrival, the hotel porter asks if he may speak to me privately. 'Doctor,' he says, 'I'm suffering from piles. What would you recommend?' The obvious reply is 'Join the Labour Party and vote for the Capital Levy, our sovereign cure for excessive piles.'

In the election on 6th December, 191 Labour M.P.s were returned, against 258 Conservatives and 158 Liberals. New M.P.s included Margaret Bondfield, Herbert Morrison and Susan Lawrence – but not Dalton, who was again narrowly defeated.

Wednesday 12th December
Back to London. Squash at the Webbs'. Candidates victorious and vanquished. Congratulations and condolences. Short speeches by MacDonald, Webb, who tells us all to be discreet and not ask for jobs, Uncle[1] and Wake. Holford Knight,[2] who was beaten at Swindon and had told MacDonald that he lost on Capital Levy, tells me that all ex-Liberals were vindictively tracked down and kept out by Liberal machine. He says that this was specially unfair in his case, since he had been the means of withdrawing two Labour candidates and enabling two Liberals to win, including the Liberal who beat Sanders,[3] the Tory Minister for Agriculture in the Bridgwater Division! (I hear later that he went to the Liberal leader at Swindon and offered to drop Capital Levy if they would support him.) He then goes round telling several people, including deaf Mrs Wedgwood, that he hopes it will be realised that the Solicitor-General need not be in the House, and that the Law Officers should include a common and a criminal lawyer. (I hear later that he said at public meetings at Swindon that, if he were returned, he would be a Law Officer.) He and Bennett[4] are a fine pair of throw offs from the Liberals!

1 'Uncle' or 'Uncle Arthur': Arthur Henderson (senior), q.v. From this Dalton derived 'Aunt' for Henderson's wife.
2 G. W. Holford Knight (1877–1936). Barrister. Unsuccessful Liberal, and then Labour, candidate at 1910–24 general elections. National Labour M.P. 1931–5.
3 Sir Robert Sanders, 1st Bart, later 1st Baron Bayford (1867–1940). Minister of Agriculture and Fisheries 1922–4. Conservative M.P. for Bridgwater 1910–23, when he lost his seat, and 1924–9. Junior minister 1921–2.
4 E. N. Bennett, later Sir Ernest (1868–1947). Liberal M.P. 1906–10. Joined the I.L.P. 1916. Labour M.P. 1929–31. Like Holford Knight, he supported the National Government in 1931. National Labour M.P. 1931–45. Junior minister 1932–5.

Saturday 19th January 1924
Dine at Beveridge's. Ramsay Muir,[1] whom I meet for the first time, is a pompous creature. I hope we shall be able to avoid giving the Liberals either Proportional Representation or Alternative Vote in this Parliament. Then they mayn't live to ask for either in the next.

On 22nd January 1924 Ramsay MacDonald accepted office as first-ever Labour Prime Minister, at the head of a minority government. Among new ministers were several of Dalton's friends and patrons, including Arthur Henderson (Home Secretary), Sidney Webb (President of the Board of Trade), Josiah Wedgwood (Chancellor of the Duchy of Lancaster), and C. P. Trevelyan (President of the Board of Education).

Saturday 2nd February
To Ripley for Belper Selection Conference. My first experience of a 'singing competition'. Two other applicants ... We are limited to twenty minutes and five minutes' questions. I make a fair speech, and get one question. 'Are you in favour of old age pensions of £2 a week at sixty?' I say, 'Yes, but I'm afraid the financial position won't allow of it in this Parliament.' Back by night train.

Wednesday 6th February
At Ruth's suggestion I have told the I.L.P. that I will do a lot of propaganda speaking for them in the near future in good areas, where it would be well to be known.
   I won the Belper 'singing competition', but have declined the offer on the ground that the constituency is so scattered and would be so expensive to work. I hope for an early by-election.

Thursday 7th February
Charles Trevelyan At Home. Various members of the Cabinet, and Under-Secretaries, in a tight squash with their wives, daughters and the miscellaneous young women and old men whom one is always meeting on such occasions, but never remembering by name. Ammon bursting with pride.[2] Tells how they always open the door for him at

---

1 Ramsay Muir (1872–1941). Liberal M.P. for Rochdale 1923–4. Chairman and then President of the National Liberal Federation 1931–6. Professor of Modern History at Liverpool and Manchester Universities 1913–21.
2 Charles Ammon, q.v., had been appointed Parliamentary Secretary to the Admiralty.

37

the Admiralty and how the successive Sea Lords are announced and call him 'Sir'. How last of all they announced 'The Civil Lord' and 'in walked Frank 'Odges![1] Leach[2] rather puzzled about the Air Force. Henderson and Haldane[3] stand together on the hearth rug and declare loudly that Wheatley's[4] Poplar decision was taken without consulting the Cabinet, or even the P.M. Henderson annoys me by saying 'So I hear you're flitting again.' Eccleston Square are hopeless about finding seats. Henderson himself always gets fixed up in rotten places. I hope he gets Burnley all right and clears the way for successive by-elections.[5]

Thursday 21st February

Brailsford[6] and Barbara [Wootton][7] to supper. A good evening. Brailsford is very sensible and not soppy like so many of the Left. Our most distinguished journalist, I think. The *New Leader* is just paying. So is the *Herald*. What a change from a little while ago! Brailsford hates the subs more than is really reasonable. Probably they are unkind to animals.

　　Stories about our new ministers ... William Lunn[8] went to the

1　Frank Hodges (1887–1947). Civil Lord of the Admiralty in the 1924 Government. Labour M.P. for Lichfield 1923–4. Secretary of the Miners' Federation of Great Britain 1918–24.

2　William Leach (1870–1949). Under-Secretary of State for Air in the 1924 Government. Labour M.P. for Central Bradford 1922–4, 1929–31, 1935–45.

3　1st Viscount Haldane, formerly R. B. Haldane (1856–1928). Lord Chancellor 1912–15, 1924. Liberal M.P. 1885–1911. Secretary of State for War 1905–12.

4　John Wheatley (1869–1930). Minister of Health in the 1924 Government. Labour M.P. for Glasgow Shettleston 1922–30. A leader of the radical group of Clydesider M.P.s, Wheatley was regarded as the most left-wing member of the Cabinet. His first act as Minister had been to revoke regulations imposed by the outgoing Conservative Government on the Poplar Board of Guardians, who had gone to prison in 1921 for refusing to pay sums due to the London County Council. The Poplar councillors had agreed that the Borough could not afford both to meet the needs of its own poor, and pay charges which placed an unfair burden on the least prosperous areas. Liberals objected strongly to Wheatley's decision.

5　Arthur Henderson (who lost seats with embarrassing frequency) had just been defeated at Newcastle upon Tyne East. In February 1924 he returned to Parliament in a by-election at Burnley.

6　H. N. Brailsford (1873–1958). Socialist writer and journalist. Editor (1922–6) of the I.L.P. newspaper, the *New Leader*, whose regular luncheons Dalton attended.

7　Barbara Wootton, later Baroness (b. 1897). Research Officer in the T.U.C. and Labour Party Joint Research Department 1922–6. Economist and educational administrator. Served on many Royal Commissions and statutory bodies.

8　William Lunn (1872–1942). Parliamentary Secretary, Department of Overseas Trade in the 1924 Government. Labour M.P. for Rothwell (West Riding) 1918–42. Parliamentary Under-Secretary of State, Colonial Office 1929; Dominions Office 1929–31.

Department of Overseas Trade, where he is Parliamentary Secretary, and went to the door of his Chief Permanent Official – Sydney Waterlow![1] – and *knocked*! Entering timidly he asked whether Waterlow could recommend him a bed-sitting room in a quiet and respectable street near the office. Waterlow would be a better authority on bed-sitting rooms that weren't respectable!

This over, Waterlow discovered to his horror that Mr Lunn had never heard of the Trade Facilities Act, on which the work of the Department hinged. He applied to go back to the Foreign Office having been given a cab horse to train instead of the racer he had hoped for, to build his reputation on.

Walsh[2] at the War Office is generally accompanied by Mrs Walsh, who sits in his room. Cavan[3] came in with a very confidential document. He wanted Mrs Walsh to leave the room, but she showed no sign. At last he hinted broadly that this was for the Secretary of State alone. To which the latter replied, 'Oh never mind mother. She's always there.'

Saturday 19th to Tuesday 22nd April
To York for I.L.P. Conference. MacDonald's famous observation that Socialism is 'bookish'. Wonderful tameness of the I.L.P. beneath the scowl of the platform, except when H.Q. and District Finance is under discussion. Oswald Mosley[4] appears as a new convert and addresses the Conference from the platform. But well received. A young conference on the whole, and this is a hopeful sign.

In July 1924, Dalton fought a by-election at Holland-with-Boston – losing his fourth contest, again by a slender majority. 'I'm utterly sick of politics and feel a fool to have come on this adventure', he wrote after the count.[5] In October, MacDonald announced an immediate dissolution. 'I was stiff against standing again, except for an A1 seat', Dalton later recalled.[6] Never-

1 S. P. Waterlow, later Sir Sydney (1878–1944). Director, Foreign Division of the Department of Overseas Trade 1922–4.
2 Stephen Walsh (1859–1929). Secretary of State for War in the 1924 Government. Labour M.P. for the Ince Division of Lancashire 1906–29. Lancashire miner. Vice-President of the Miners' Federation of Great Britain 1922–4. Junior minister 1917–19.
3 F. R. Lambart, 10th Earl of Cavan, later Field-Marshal (1865–1946). Chief of Imperial General Staff 1922–6.
4 O. E. Mosley, later Sir Oswald, 6th Bart (1896–1980). Former Conservative, then Independent, M.P. who had recently joined the I.L.P. See Appendix.
5 Diary, 2nd August 1924.
6 CBY, p. 151.

theless, when he was offered the candidature at Peckham (which the Tories had held in 1923 with a majority of 176), he accepted. The tide was against Labour, which lost sixty-four seats across the country. But it also gained twenty-two – and Peckham was one of them. Dalton obtained 13,361 votes against 12,414 for his Conservative opponent. 'A strange sensation, that victory at last, while others are falling before the Zinovieff letter!' he wrote a few months later.[1]

Thursday 4th June 1925
Nearly ten months after! I have neglected my diarying! But it is the Whitsun Parliamentary recess, and I have a few rare, idle moments. I am quite used to being an M.P. by now, and so is Ruth to being a London County Councillor![2]

Late 1925
At the end of the session the Executive of the Parliamentary Party must be elected for next session. 'Left Wing' flutters cause heat and anger and, in the confusion, I am elected after tying with Ponsonby[3] and drawing lots for it, in the Whips' Room. This is an amazing result at the end of my first session and I must have been even more agreeable in personal relations and impressive in debate than I had realised!

A good Christmas present.

Friday 15th October 1926
Returning from Poland I go to Labour Party Conference at Margate and am elected, at first time of asking, to National Executive! Another record! One is touched and almost apprehensive at faith of rank and file. 'God make us worthy of the men we lead!' as Ellen Wilkinson[4] said during General Strike.

1 Diary, 4th June 1925.
2 Ruth had been elected a Councillor in Peckham earlier in the year.
3 Arthur Ponsonby, later 1st Baron (1871–1946). Labour M.P. for Sheffield Bright-side 1922–30; Liberal M.P. for Stirling Burghs 1908–18. Page of Honour to Queen Victoria 1882–7. Under-Secretary of State for Foreign Affairs 1924. Junior minister 1929–31. Chancellor of the Duchy of Lancaster March–August 1931. Leader of the Labour Party in the House of Lords 1931–5. Pacifist.
4 Ellen Wilkinson (1891–1947). Labour M.P. for Middlesbrough East 1924–31; Jarrow 1935–47. National Organiser of the National Union of Distributive and Allied Workers. Junior minister 1940–45. Minister of Education 1945–7.

December 1926
Shindig on National Executive over Mosley and Smethwick.[1] In the end the peace party wins by one vote, I voting in the minority.

A deplorable session ends with miners hopelessly beaten ...

Christmas Eve. Off to Windsor and then to Swallowcliffe till 10th January. Pretty tired. I have marched surprisingly fast this year. May I hold the ground worthily next year! Sincerity, courage and unity, three watchwords.

Dalton did not keep his diary regularly in 1927. He returned to it early in 1928.

Monday 6th February 1928
Meeting of Party Executive at 4 at Transport House[2] ...

Snowden[3] is sick, having strained himself at a recent meeting. MacDonald thinks – a little gleefully I thought – that it may be a rupture. Johnston[4] says MacDonald seems to have had 'a sniff of the bottle' today, and Uncle thinks him less 'alert' than usual ...

Eve of session Reception at Victoria Hall, Bloomsbury. I walk there with Uncle from National Labour Club. MacDonald and Mosley still hostile to one another. He [Henderson] thanks me for *Peace of Nations*, which, however, he hasn't yet read.[5] I say I want

1 Mosley had been selected to fight a by-election in Smethwick in December 1926 by the local Labour Party. The National Executive initially refused to endorse his candidature after accusations that he had 'bought' the nomination. After Mosley had won the seat, the N.E.C. discussed his statement 'to the effect that he had no confidence in the Head Office and had no intention of working or communicating with them ... ' Dalton was a member of a sub-committee set up to look into the matter (N.E.C. minute, 22nd December 1926).
2 In 1928 the Labour Party Head Office had acquired a new home as a tenant of the Transport and General Workers' Union at Transport House, Smith Square, S.W.1.
3 Philip Snowden, later 1st Viscount (1864–1937). Labour M.P. for Colne Valley 1922–31; Blackburn 1906–18. I.L.P. pioneer. Chancellor of the Exchequer 1924, 1929–31. Joined MacDonald in the National Government in 1931, but resigned the following year on the issue of Free Trade. As a result of a spinal injury in his youth, Snowden was in constant pain and walked with a stick.
4 Thomas Johnston (1882–1965). Labour M.P. for Dundee 1924–9; Stirlingshire West 1922–4, 1929–31, 1935–45. Founder of the Scottish I.L.P. paper, *Forward*, in 1906. Editor 1919–46. Junior minister 1929–31. Lord Privy Seal 1931. Secretary of State for Scotland 1941–5.
5 Dalton's book on foreign affairs, *Towards the Peace of Nations* (Routledge, London), published in January 1928.

41

him to go to the Foreign Office in the next Labour Government, and so do many others, including the Geneva Secretariat. He tells me again of his difficulties with MacDonald especially at the Burnley by-election in 1923,[1] when he advocated Revision of the Peace Treaties, especially as regards Reparations, and how MacDonald repudiated him in the House and sent a telephone message from a civil servant in Downing Street to a clerk in the Committee Room that 'The P.M. wishes Mr Henderson to "pull up" a bit in the speeches he is making at the by-election.' He agrees with me that MacDonald is like a star actress, jealous of every other leading performer in the cast. Unless one feeds him with adulation and admiration, one can't hope ever to get very near him.

Monday 19th March
Ruth off tomorrow to Aiguebelle. She saw Mrs Redgrave on Friday, who was full of Baldwyn's[2] disloyalty to me. Ruth very gloomy and thinks I may have to threaten resignation to get him out. He has collected a clique round him, whose minds he is steadily poisoning against me. The fellow has no sense of his own self-interest. I think he is a little off his chump. But it is a bloody nuisance to have all this fuss, when things might be going so well.

Thursday 26th April
Peckham Executive[3] from 8.15 p.m. till about 1 a.m.! For the first time in my life, almost, I don't sleep a wink! Adjourned till following evening.

Thursday 10th May
Second meeting of National Executive Committee of Enquiry with Peckham delegation. Baldwyn asked up early and seen by Uncle and Shepherd.[4] They suggest that he should resign, but he refuses. At the subsequent meeting Baldwyn continues his reply 'point by point' to my statement, dodging many of the most serious points and twisting on the others. He wearies the Committee and comes rather badly out of some of the questions put to him. His 'final suggestion'

---

1 The Burnley by-election took place in February 1924, not 1923.
2 E. Baldwyn. A local milkman in Peckham, and Dalton's agent. A row between M.P. and agent had been brewing for some time, and Dalton badly mishandled it. Faced with a serious split in his local party, he decided not to contest the seat again.
3 Peckham Divisional Labour Party Executive.
4 G. R. Shepherd, later 1st Baron (1881–1954). Labour Party National Agent 1929–46, in succession to Egerton Wake.

is that he and I should 'agree to work together'. Cramp[1] asks me what I think of this. I say that it is quite impossible, either he or I or both of us must leave Peckham.

Saturday 19th to Sunday 20th May
Weekend at Blanco-Whites.[2] Rather uncomfortable cottage, newly built on old model with lots of dogs and draughts. But company quite pleasant and good woods near. He rather solemn and earnest and less of an intellectual snob than he was. She still talking of 'H.G.' and her past conquests. Now an authority on currency and very busy coaching Pethick[3] on amendments to Government Bill.

Wednesday 23rd May
Uncle, Cramp and Morrison[4] trying to patch up Peckham. Afraid, after their meeting with Executive Committee last Monday, that there will be a serious split in the Party if either Baldwyn or I go. I told them my view, that it was impossible to make a disloyal man loyal by talking to him, and that I had taken my political life in my hand before and could do so again, preferring to fight with the enemy in the open rather than to be poisoned in a corner. They urge me to agree to their seeing Baldwyn and 'talking to him as he has never been talked to before'. I say I don't disagree, though I have no hope of their turning out to be miracle workers.

Ruth very anxious to have no compromise, but a clear decision quickly. She loathes the prospect of continuance of a hairshirt, and subjective costs have been, and will be, much heavier than can really be worth while.

1 C. T. Cramp, q.v., was a member of the Labour Party N.E.C. (Chairman 1924–5).
2 G. R. Blanco-White and Amber Blanco-White, nee Reeves (1887–1982). Amber Reeves had known Dalton at Cambridge, where she had been Treasurer of the University Fabians. She married Blanco-White (a barrister, and Recorder of Croydon 1940–56) in 1908, after a celebrated affair with H. G. Wells, by whom she had a child. She wrote a number of books, mainly on finance, literature and ethics, including one with Wells (*The Work, Wealth and Happiness of Mankind*) published in 1932. In 1928 she was lecturing in Moral Science at Morley College, where she continued to teach until 1965. She stood as a Labour candidate in the 1931 and 1935 elections.
3 F. W. Pethick-Lawrence, later 1st Baron (1871–1961). Labour M.P. for Leicester West 1923–31; Edinburgh East 1935–45. Financial Secretary to the Treasury 1929–31. Secretary of State for India and Burma 1945–7. Prominent supporter of women's rights.
4 Herbert Morrison, later Baron (1888–1965). Member of the Labour Party N.E.C.; Secretary of the London Labour Party; London County Councillor. See Appendix.

Thursday 24th May

Away to 'Trevelyan's Man Hunt'.[1] ... I tell Trevelyan about Peckham, and we discuss possible northern constituencies. I could have had Elland[2] a few weeks ago, if he had known! The transition will be difficult to explain, I fear, unless there can be talk behind the scenes. But Trevelyan will keep his ears open.

Saturday 26th to Monday 28th May

Hunting. Good fun and, except 27th, which is misty and rainy, good weather. Sing songs at night. Beer obtainable. This is new! The party, much of which only sees each other at Hunts, fits together surprisingly well.

I grow a blister on my left heel which quite disables me on the third day. I become a very lame hound indeed. But no matter!

Monday 4th June

Broadcast for the first time – fifteen minutes on 'Poland and its People' in between Polish music. An interesting experience, speaking to an invisible multitude of scattered listeners. I felt handicapped by having to read, word for word, from a prepared typescript. The unaccustomed procedure, as distinct from speaking from notes, increases my natural tendency to speak in a level, monotonous voice. But the subsequent comments from M.P.s and others seem very sincerely laudatory. They say that I was very clear and distinctly interesting. Price ten guineas.

Friday 20th July

To Liphook to spend the night with the Webbs and walk next morning.

This morning I send off my letter to Peckham, definitely resigning the candidature and recapitulating the case against Baldwyn. I also send a news paragraph to the *Herald* for Monday morning. The voting for next session's Executive will be finished by then. I don't want a sort of Red Letter sensation created in the minds of my colleagues.

The Webbs are getting old gently but surely. But she the faster of the two, and the more self-consciously. They think of leaving the

1 'Trevelyan's Man Hunt': a 'hare and hounds' walking party organised by the Trevelyan family from their country house, Wallington Hall, Northumberland, each Whitsun. Dalton had first taken part before the war.
2 Trevelyan had been M.P. for the Elland Division of the West Riding of Yorkshire from 1899 to 1918. C. R. Buxton won it for Labour in 1929.

house and garden at Passfield Corner to the School when they die. I think it might be very useful. We talk, rather flatly, about people and, rather old fashionedly, about unemployment and poor law and, rather inconclusively, about constituencies. She thinks Lord Oswald,[1] with his connections and wealth, had a sure and early future with the Tories and might have become their Leader, a prospect very remote, she thought, with us, though I pointed out that he was still very young. But we all agree that he is very uninstructed. Wheatley, Webb says, is a thorough Tammany type. His stock has never been lower than now ... The Webbs are not enthusiastic about Trevelyan. They once went round the world with him, and thought him very mean. Their servant often had to pay his cab fares. He was assertive and used to shout people down in argument. He once declared, at their house, that he considered himself Mr Gladstone's intellectual superior, because he did not believe in God. This, however, was only facing the logical conclusion of a heated argument. He was so unpopular with the Liberal heads in 1906 that, though Bannerman[2] circulated his name on a list of possible Under-Secretaries to members of the Cabinet, none of them would have him. It was not until his friend Runciman[3] became President of the Board of Education some years later that Trevelyan became an Under-Secretary. But, since his resignation on the outbreak of war, he had done well, Webb thought ...

Webb thinks that we can't get a majority at the next election, but shall poll more than the Tories, though we shall win fewer seats. He forecasts 100 gains for us and 20 losses, a net gain of 80 bringing us up to about 230, with 65 Liberals and a Tory majority of about 25 over all. In practice a little more, because some Liberals will always vote with them. He doesn't see the Liberals winning anything much, except in the West Country and the agricultural East.

Saturday 21st July
From Liphook to Windsor. The old man's health seems wonderful;[4] much better than a year ago. The heat, enabling us to be out of doors all the time, makes the weekend less hard work than usual.

---

1 'Lord Oswald': Dalton's name for Mosley.
2 Sir Henry Campbell-Bannerman (1836–1908). Prime Minister 1905–8. Liberal M.P. 1868–1908.
3 Walter Runciman, later 1st Viscount (1870–1949). Liberal M.P. for Swansea West 1924–9; Oldham 1899–1900; Dewsbury 1902–18; St Ives 1929–31. Liberal National M.P. for St Ives 1931–7. Junior minister 1905–7; Financial Secretary to the Treasury 1907–8; President of the Board of Education 1908–11; of Agriculture 1911–14; of the Board of Trade 1914–16, 1931–7. Lord President of the Council 1938–9.
4 'The old man': Dalton's father, Canon J. N. Dalton, q.v. He was eighty-eight.

In October, Dalton was re-elected to the Constituency Parties Section of the N.E.C. (until 1937 chosen by the whole Party Conference), having lost his place the previous year to Oswald Mosley. This time, both men were successful, Mosley in third and Dalton in fifth place. Others elected were George Lansbury, Herbert Morrison and Charles Trevelyan.

Monday 1st to Friday 5th October
Elected again, after a year's interval, to the National Executive ... All the winners, except Trevelyan, get the Miners' vote ... This is a good

1 'The Labour Star Turn', 6th October 1928

year to be on the N.E., with the final stages of the Programme, and the General Election, and after. I said to Mosley, 'How reassuring to find that this little world is large enough to hold us both!' He, rather taken aback, I think, said, 'Yes, rather a surprise, isn't it?' How the fellow stinks of money and insincerity! A row at the first meeting of the new Executive over J. B. Melville[1] and Gateshead. One Gillis,[2] a young barrister, has been to Gateshead, trying to get nominations reopened for Melville on ground that MacDonald and Uncle both want him in the House and that he is certain to be in the next Labour Government

1 J. B. Melville, later Sir James (1885–1931). Labour M.P. for Gateshead 1929–31. Solicitor-General 1929–30.
2 B. B. Gillis (b. 1905). Recorder of Bradford 1958–64. Circuit Judge and Additional Judge, Central Criminal Court, from 1964.

either as Solicitor-General or Home Secretary, and 'in any case with a seat in the Cabinet'. MacDonald hotly denies. W. A. Robinson,[1] who is also on the list for Gateshead, is very furious and persistent in his suspicions, not unnaturally.

Monday 8th October

School Michaelmas Term begins. I take charge of four bright young things, with three scholarships and a bursary. When other chores don't press too hard, I quite love the School!

Tuesday 16th October

Conversation with Lees-Smith. He says that Tory H.Q. estimate that, at worst, they will come back with a clear majority of 30 over all parties, and will probably do better than this. He thinks we should not take office as a minority government. We two and some others should take counsel together before long. There may be a heavy mortality among the older leaders soon, and an uncertain situation will then arise. The present Parliamentary Executive must be kept in being until a new one can be elected at the beginning of the new Parliament.

Monday 5th November

National Executive from 10.30. The case of Melville at Gateshead comes up. Robinson threatens, through N.U.D.A.W. [National Union of Distributive and Allied Workers], to circularise all Trade Unions on the incursion of middle-class candidates. Quite a sense of class-war in the air! We are rather intimidated by this, but shouldn't have endorsed Melville anyway. It is alleged that Melville offered Forster (the ex-Gateshead secretary, Robinson's chief backer) the refusal of the Agency at £350 a year with a five year contract. This greatly shocked Cramp and others. Agreed that we don't endorse, owing to irregularity, but that Uncle and Morrison see Melville and try to persuade him to withdraw altogether, and also that they go to Gateshead. A fine mess these lawyers make of their affairs!

More important. Discussion on policy for General Election. We have now 497 endorsed candidates. Last time we ran 514, of whom 27 lost their deposits. The question is, how many more to run? Going much further will mean risking the loss of a good few extra deposits. Shall Head Office encourage or discourage marginal candidatures? Uncle doesn't give a lead on this, but propounds a scheme

1 W. A. Robinson (1877–1949). Member of the Labour Party N.E.C. (Chairman 1934–5). General Secretary of the National Union of Distributive and Allied Workers. Labour M.P. 1935–45.

for deposit insurance, each endorsed candidate to pay over £10 out of his election expenses. If 500 candidates did this, it would give £5000, enough to pay 33 deposits.

On the main issue, Mosley proposes that we limit to 520. He advocates 'concentration' rather than 'diffusion' and uses military metaphors about generals attacking where enemy line is weakest and not along whole front. This proposal is made in the course of a rather confused discussion, on an amendment to a proposal by me that we should fight everywhere possible. I speak of importance of big aggregate vote, and of the need to begin the process of winning backward areas by fighting them continuously. I also point out, in reply to Mosley, that the military metaphor doesn't really apply. For you can't move local workers about like pawns. Mosley gets no seconder, and my proposal is then unanimously carried. MacDonald is on my side. He says, what I thought but didn't say, that a small Tory majority would be better for us than to have the Tories just in a minority, with the Liberals holding the balance. It wouldn't pay us, in short, to put 20 Liberals in by not running candidates, when we could have kept 20 Tories in by running ourselves. *Very sound sense!* This is a most important decision. Arthur Jenkins[1] and Mrs Adamson[2] both say to me afterwards that they are very glad I spoke as I did.

Committee appointed to draft election manifesto – MacDonald, Uncle, Morrison, Susan, myself, Cramp, Dennison,[3] Mosley. This will be a job!

Parliamentary Executive dine at Trevelyan's and hear King's Speech read. Much more social than dining at the Labour Club. But not *very* social really. They are an uncomfortable lot, these colleagues. No ease of manner. On to Albert Hall. MacDonald and Morrison announce that we shall run 600 candidates. But the huge place is only half full. It is too big and in the wrong part of London.

Early in October, Dalton was selected as candidate for the Durham mining seat of Bishop Auckland. 'Clouds pass away', Dalton wrote when he heard the news. 'My position with a safe seat and a place on both Executives in this critical year, is a very strong one, come what may.'[4]

---

1 Arthur Jenkins (1882–1946). Miners' representative on the Labour Party N.E.C. Labour M.P. 1935–46. Junior minister 1945. Father of Roy Jenkins, q.v.
2 Jennie Adamson, née Johnston (1882–1962). Member of the N.E.C. (Chairman 1935–6). Labour M.P. 1938–46. Junior minister 1945–6.
3 Robert Dennison (1879–1951). Member of the N.E.C. Labour M.P. for King's Norton 1924–9.
4 Diary, 7th October 1928.

Tuesday 6th November

Parliament meets. Everyone very congratulatory about Bishop Auckland. MacDonald in good form in his opening speech. 'He has still got plenty of fresh air inside him', says someone. Lunch with John Beckett[1] who is after Peckham. (Good luck to him!) Silkin,[2] Blake, W. A. Robinson and an unknown plasterer are also said to be after it! Dine with Arnold, fussing about Free Trade and Johnston's 'Protectionist tendencies' and 'lack of Parliamentary judgment'. I try to pacify him. Beckett says that MacDonald is now being motored about by Paddy Nasmith,[3] a film actress, said to be engaged to Derwent Hall Caine[4] – a little bit of fluff with an elegant car. I saw her hanging round at Birmingham. They motored to and from Wolverhampton. People are wondering where they really slept!

Saturday 1st December

Lunch with Robbins[5] in New College. He is making a reputation as a teacher and is, I think, rather happy at Oxford. Tea with Cannan, who is getting on with his book.

Wednesday 5th December

Trevelyan and others are thinking of the political repercussions of the King's death, if it comes. A loyal reaction, for what it's worth, will help the Tories. And there will be a difficult situation over the new Civil List with every possibility of internal squabbling in the Party and loss of heads and judgment both on Left and Right.

Sunday 9th December

Highly successful Young Labour squash at 5 Carlisle Mansions.[6]

1 John Beckett (1894–1964). Labour M.P. for Gateshead 1924–9; Peckham 1929–31. Beckett took Dalton's place at Peckham, and was elected Labour M.P. for the seat in 1929. In 1931, he stood as an I.L.P. candidate against an official Labour nominee and lost. Later he joined the British Union of Fascists, and was co-founder with the Duke of Bedford of the ultra-right British People's Party in 1938. He was imprisoned under the Defence of the Realm Act during the Second World War.
2 Lewis Silkin, later 1st Baron (1889–1972). Labour M.P. for Peckham 1936–50. Minister of Town and Country Planning 1945–50. Father of Sam and John Silkin.
3 Paddy Nasmith. Film starlet. Appeared in Victor Saville's *The Iron Duke* (1935).
4 Derwent Hall Caine, later 1st Bart (1891–1971). Publisher. Labour M.P. 1929–31.
5 Lionel Robbins, later Baron (1898–1984). Economist. Fellow of New College, Oxford 1927–9. Professor of Economics at the L.S.E. 1929–61. Director of the Economic Section of the War Offices of the Cabinet 1941–5. Robbins had been a student of Dalton, who helped his career in its early stages, engineering his return to the L.S.E. in 1929.
6 The Daltons' rented flat in Victoria. This remained their London home until 1941.

Ellen the central figure; also Arthur Shepherd,[1] Will Henderson[2] (very Head Office!), a bunch of candidates under forty, and a bunch of young Socialists from the School, headed by Fraser[3] and Bakstansky.[4] Will Arnold-Forster,[5] whom we have been looking after in the flat – rather a little piece of wreckage, going through the same treatment as Ruth for unhealthy gums – asks Fraser and others to spend Christmas at St Ives. I have my eye on Fraser, as a future politician of importance.

Tuesday 11th December
Find myself in MacDonald's room at the House after a division and talking about Spoor[6] and Bishop Auckland. He is very close and unexpansive, as usual, but not unfriendly. Very pleased with his trip to Paris and with the compliments which everyone, including Poincaré,[7] paid him. He was the only person who could make Poincaré smile; Poincaré was preparing himself to face a Labour government, etc. (Petica Robertson[8] said the other night that she had the most profound distrust of MacDonald; she always felt like that about people who might equally well be actors or clergymen.)

Thursday 13th December
Meeting of I.L.P. M.P.s at the House, arising out of Dr Salter's[9]

1 A. L. Shepherd (1884–1951). Labour M.P. for Darlington 1926–31.
2 W. W. Henderson, later 1st Baron (1891–1984). Transport House official. Labour M.P. 1923–4, 1929–31. Under-Secretary of State for Foreign Affairs 1948–51. Son of Arthur Henderson (senior), q.v.
3 R. B. Fraser, later Sir Robert (1904–84). A student of Dalton's at the L.S.E. and later a close friend. Australian by birth. Leader writer on the *Daily Herald* 1930–39. Director of the Publications Division at the Ministry of Information 1941–5. Director-General of the Central Office of Information 1946–54. Director-General of the Independent Television Authority 1954–70. Chairman of Independent Television News 1971–4. One of Dalton's two literary executors.
4 L. Bakstansky (1904–71). Student at L.S.E. 1926–32; President of the Students' Union 1929. Later General Secretary of the Zionist Federation of Great Britain and Ireland. Barrister.
5 William Arnold-Forster (1885–1951). Writer on peace issues. Member of the Labour Party Advisory Committee on International Affairs. Secretary to Lord Cecil, q.v. 1929–31. Later worked for the research staff at Transport House.
6 B. C. Spoor (1878–1928). Labour M.P. for Bishop Auckland 1918–28. Government Chief Whip 1924.
7 Raymond Poincaré (1860–1934). French Prime Minister 1911–13, 1922–4, 1926–9. President of the Republic 1913–20.
8 Petica Robertson (d. 1941). Married to Professor Donald Robertson, Emeritus Professor of Greek at Cambridge 1928–50.
9 Dr Alfred Salter (1873–1945). Labour M.P. for Bermondsey West 1922–3, 1924–45. Temperance reformer.

move against Maxton.[1] This is an adjournment from a previous meeting, at which Salter and others ('No Drink in our Time' Brigade, every one of them!) had attacked Maxton, and the *New Leader* ... Trevelyan and I and a few others were anxious for an adjournment *sine die* but hadn't prearranged anything, though we had canvassed for peace. The No Drinkers were terribly combative, and had prepared a resolution of censure, and were talking of 'thirty supporters' and wholesale resignation. They were, I think, in touch with Mac-Donald (silly ass!) behind the scenes. But most of them had exhausted their right to speak last time. Tonight, John Potts[2] moved, straight away, an adjournment *sine die*, and Trevelyan seconded. Maxton made a wandering, but not too provocative, defence from the chair, and among other speakers, Willy Lunn made a good appeal for unity, and Bob Smillie pronounced his customary blessing. Immediately on this, the closure was moved and carried by 29 to 11, and then Potts's motion was carried by 35 to 10. A very good ending. The enemy press got nothing to bite on, and were greatly disappointed. Maxton and Brockway will, I think, have learned a lesson. Salter and Co. were absolutely furious, and said this wouldn't be the end of it. But they were badly outnumbered and discountenanced. Their final 10 were Salter, Morgan Jones, Ammon, Graham, Hudson,[3] Viant,[4] Cecil Wilson[5] and 3 others. Rhys Davies[6] and Margaret Bondfield[7] regretted absence. But every miner, and all the Left and Left-Centre, were for Peace, and couldn't see 'the fundamental differences' which so agitated Salter and his friend. Another win for common sense! I laughed a lot afterwards over the discomfiture of this silly minority.

1 James Maxton (1885–1946). Labour, later I.L.P., M.P. for Glasgow Bridgeton 1922–46. Chairman of the I.L.P. 1926–31, 1934–9. Maxton led the I.L.P. out of the Labour Party in 1932.
2 J. S. Potts (1861–1938). Labour M.P. for Barnsley 1922–31, 1935–8. Ex-miners' agent. Methodist lay preacher.
3 J. H. Hudson (1881–1962). Labour M.P. for Huddersfield 1923–31; Ealing West 1945–50; Ealing North 1950–55. Secretary of the National Temperance Federation and Parliamentary Temperance Group.
4 S. P. Viant (1882–1964). Labour M.P. for Willesden West 1923–31, 1935–59. Junior minister 1929–31.
5 C. H. Wilson (1862–1945). Labour M.P. for Sheffield Attercliffe 1922–31, 1935–44.
6 R. J. Davies (1877–1954). Labour M.P. for Westhoughton 1921–51. Junior minister 1924.
7 Margaret Bondfield (1873–1953). Labour M.P. for Wallsend 1926–31; Northampton 1923–4. Chief Woman Officer, National Union of General and Municipal Workers 1921–38. Junior minister 1924. Minister of Labour 1929–31, and first-ever woman Cabinet Minister.

Wednesday 19th December

National Executive all day. Row with Lord Oswald all about nothing, arising out of my remark that it was abominable how some seats were simply auctioned to rich men. Beckett endorsed for Peckham! We couldn't, it was felt, be a court of morals, and nothing in this case was really public[1] ...

At a recent Parliamentary Executive MacDonald said that Dawson of Penn[2] had told him that he 'would like to give the King a good kick on the backside'. The reason why he was making such a slow recovery was because he seemed to have lost the will to get better. Clive Wigram had corroborated this, in other language over the telephone.

On 22nd December 1928 Ben Spoor, M.P. for Bishop Auckland, died suddenly. This created an awkward situation for Dalton, who was still M.P. for Peckham and could not, therefore, stand in the by-election that would inevitably follow. The problem was solved when Bishop Auckland Labour Party suggested that Ruth Dalton should stand and hold the seat for her husband, pending a general election. Ruth agreed, and was elected on 8th February 1929 with a majority of 7,072. For the next three months, therefore, Hugh and Ruth were both in the Commons together.

Wednesday 20th February 1929

Ruth asks her first Questions (very confidently). The question of a Private Secretary for MacDonald is still in many of our minds. Ponsonby is running King-Hall[3] very hard, and has taken him to see MacDonald who talked to him about constituencies etc. but ended by advising him not to leave the Admiralty till next August, when his present appointment is up. Ponsonby has also been telling Mosley about all this, and there is talk of amalgamating Research Departments – I.L.P. information, and Mosley's and Wedgwood Benn's[4]

1 In the summer Dalton had been told by Sidney Webb of a rumour that Beckett had been having an affair with the widow of a leading I.L.P. propagandist (Diary, 20th July 1928).

2 Bertrand Dawson, 1st Baron, later 1st Viscount Dawson of Penn (1867–1945). Physician-in-Ordinary to the King and Queen. President of the Royal College of Physicians 1931–8.

3 Commander Stephen King-Hall, later Baron (1893–1966). Writer and publicist, especially on defence and international affairs. Elected a National Labour M.P. in 1939, he resigned the whip in 1942 and was defeated in the 1945 election.

4 William Wedgwood Benn, later 1st Viscount Stansgate (1877–1960). Labour M.P. for Aberdeen North 1928–31. Liberal M.P. for Tower Hamlets St George's 1906–18;

private enterprise affairs – and giving King-Hall a salary on the strength of this. This does not sound at all pleasing, and I warn Ernest Hunter[1] ...

Sir Lonsdale Webster,[2] Chief Clerk of the House, owed £12,000 for gambling debts, and was on the edge of the bankruptcy court. A Conference of Party Leaders was held. Lloyd George paid for the bulk of these debts, and the Tories for a little. Garro-Jones[3] and I put this tale together from scraps of separate information.

Thursday 28th March
Easter break. Ruth to Cornwall to stay with Will and Ka.[4] I north by car with Bob Fraser. An experiment.

Friday 29th March to Saturday 6th April
My experiment is a very great success. Sleep at Appleby and then to Ousby, where we leave the car and walk Ousby–Crossfell–Ousby–Alston–Langdon Beck (2 nights) – Cauldron Snout. High Cup Nick–Dufton–Ousby. Glorious weather and very good companionship. He is quite α for politics, though only, I think, $\beta+$ for academics. Having enough money not to *have* to earn his living, and also a high moral tone in public things, he ought to go quite far. Only twenty-four, and only eighteen months in England. Spotted as an introvert by Ruth at her first sight of him. But self-possessed, easy and capable of falling quickly into a good relationship of casual, slangy equality.

Wednesday 10th April
At the School I work to secure the return of Lionel Robbins as Junior Professor of Economics and to keep the main chair open, with Beveridge as Head of the Department. Great jealousy of Lionel in the Ghetto, but I think I shall succeed in getting him back.[5]

1 Ernest Hunter. *Daily Herald* journalist.
2 Sir Lonsdale Webster (1868–1930). Chief Clerk of the House of Commons 1921–30.
3 G. M. Garro-Jones, later 1st Baron Trefgarne (1894–1960). Liberal M.P. for South Hackney 1924–9. Joined the Labour Party in 1929. Labour M.P. for Aberdeen North 1935–45. Junior minister 1942–5.
4 Ka Arnold-Forster, née Cox (1887–1938). Married to Will Arnold-Forster, q.v. Former girlfriend of Rupert Brooke.
5 The American economist Allyn Young, Cannan's replacement as Professor of Economics at the L.S.E., had died unexpectedly during the 1929 influenza epidemic. Dalton recommended that Robbins, still only thirty, should succeed him. His advocacy prevailed (see Lord Robbins, *Autobiography of an Economist*, Macmillan, London, 1971, p. 122).

Leith 1918–27. Labour M.P. for Manchester Gorton 1937–41. Secretary of State for India 1929–31; Air 1945–6. Father of Anthony Wedgwood Benn, q.v.

2

The Second Labour
Government 1929–31

The general election which took place on 30th May 1929 seemed to establish Labour once and for all as a party of government and power. For the first time it was the largest group in the House of Commons, with 288 seats – compared with 160 Conservatives, 59 Liberals and 8 others. Its leaders now had the experience of the 1924 administration behind them, and Whitehall was beginning to adjust to the prospect of periodic Labour governments as part of the new pattern of British politics. Though still dependent on Liberal support, the second Labour administration seemed capable of doing many of the things of which the pioneers had dreamed. Instead, it turned out to be the most ill-starred in the whole of the Party's chequered history.

MacDonald accepted office as Prime Minister at the beginning of June, and proceeded cautiously in choosing ministers. Most members of the 1929 Cabinet were taken from the 1924 team. Only Lord Sankey (Lord Chancellor), William Wedgwood Benn (India Office) and George Lansbury (Works) were new. For Dalton, this was a disappointment. Having gained election to both Parliamentary and National Executives, he was widely expected to obtain high office. But the Prime Minister disliked him, and so apparently did Philip Snowden and J. H. Thomas. For a time, Dalton feared that he might be left out altogether. Then, to his relief, Arthur Henderson, the new Foreign Secretary, asked for him as Parliamentary Under-Secretary.

This appointment had an important influence on Dalton's later career. Until 1929, his interests had been divided between finance and international affairs. Now they shifted decisively towards the international sphere. After 1931 Dalton's private ambition was always directed more towards the Foreign Office than the Treasury.

Although from 1929 Dalton represented a mining constituency that was particularly hard hit by the slump, he took little part in the growing controversy over unemployment policy. This was partly because his own attitude was ambivalent. He was contemptuous of the Chancellor, Philip Snowden, yet also retained a suspicion – part personal and political, part intellectual – of Snowden's academic critic, Maynard Keynes, and deeply distrusted the leading advocate of expansionist remedies within the Government, Sir Oswald Mosley. When it came to the final showdown in August 1931, Dalton sided unhesitatingly with the spenders – Arthur Henderson and the Cabinet minority – against the ministers who wanted to cut unemployment benefit. Up to this point, however, Dalton was far more concerned about Snowden's aggressive incursions into foreign policy than about his failings as a minister responsible for finance.

The main reason, indeed, for Dalton's lack of interest in financial and economic policy was a single-minded preoccupation with his own job. Dalton was closer to his chief than was usual for a junior minister, and had a greater influence on policy. Though a shrewd judge of men and situations, Henderson was weak in debate, and no master of detail. Hence he surrounded himself with politically-minded experts – Dalton, Philip Noel-Baker, Lord Robert Cecil and William Arnold-Forster. Dalton was leader of the team, with access to the Foreign Secretary at all times, helping to guide his decisions to an extent that upset permanent advisers – especially Sir Ronald Lindsay, the Permanent Under-Secretary, who regarded Dalton as a dangerously un-couth and unpredictable trouble-maker. Dalton, for his part, viewed the whole diplomatic caste with suspicion. He liked some officials individually: his own private secretary, Gladwyn Jebb, for example, and Lindsay's suc-cessor, Sir Robert Vansittart. But his distaste for the social rigidities that pervaded the service did not make for easy relationships.

Nevertheless, foreign policy was the one field in which the second Labour Government could claim some temporary success. Henderson and Dalton focused on three ideas: security, arbitration and disarmament. The Tories, they argued, had hampered disarmament and obstructed the League of Nations. Labour would pursue disarmament and support the League. The new Government emphasised this difference in September 1929 by sending a particularly strong delegation to the League Assembly in Geneva. Henderson also signed the so-called 'Optional Clause' which required governments to accept compulsory arbitration of international disputes, and he succeeded in persuading other countries to follow suit. In December, Britain exchanged ambassadors with the Soviet Union. Further steps aimed at reducing the danger of international friction followed. From the London Naval Con-ference early in 1930 there emerged the Three Power Treaty, which pledged the biggest Naval Powers (Britain, the United States and Japan) to end competitive building of warships for a period of five years. In 1931 an inter-national Disarmament Conference was arranged for the following year, and Henderson was invited by the League Council to act as President. Dalton was proud of these achievements, though not unduly optimistic about their long-term effectiveness.

In Parliament, Dalton was developing an effective, and highly personal, style. 'Nothing delights him more as an old Etonian than to face a group of his ex-school fellows on the warpath at question time', observed Ellen Wilkinson, 'as though he were the headmaster come down in wrath to deal with a Rag.'[1] Neither the battles within his own party – the rebellions of the Maxtonites, the defections of the Mosleyites, the constant quarrelling among the Big Five – nor the constant threat that the Liberals would bring down the Government, dampened his enthusiasm for the political game.

Saturday 1st June
The question now is will Baldwin[2] resign? A Labour government a practical certainty now. To wirepull or not to wirepull? I decide not to wirepull.

Dalton was appointed Parliamentary Under-Secretary of State for Foreign Affairs on 11th June.

Mid-June
On 17th June I accompanied Uncle when he received the ambassadors, and again on the 19th when he received ministers. No official was present. The Portuguese, the Albanian and one of the South Americans could only speak French and I translated.

I hear that my presence has caused comment in diplomatic circles. They think I am to be an influence in the office!

Monday 24th June
A series of good interviews.
Brailsford – a French Communist Lady – Wertheimer[3] – Mitrany[4] –

---

1 *Peeps at Politicians*, Philip Allen, London, 1930, p. 29.
2 Stanley Baldwin, later 1st Earl (1867–1947). Prime Minister 1923–4, 1924–9, 1935–7. Conservative M.P. for Bewdley 1908–37. Joint Financial Secretary to the Treasury 1917–21; President of the Board of Trade 1921–2; Chancellor of the Exchequer 1922–3. Lord President of the Council 1931–5.
3 Egon Wertheimer. German journalist. London correspondent of *Vorwärts* and the *Sozialdemokratischer Pressedienst*. Author of *A Portrait of the Labour Party* (1929).
4 David Mitrany (1888–1975). Economist and journalist.

Gillies[1] – Bartlett.[2] Lunch with Lansbury.[3] Dinner with … P.M., Ishbel,[4] non-Cabinet Ministers and their wives.

The French Communist Lady comes on behalf of Trotsky. Not skilful.[5] I say his case is before the Cabinet. I can make no statement, but will pass on her observations to the Secretary of State. I ask why Trotsky prefers England to France or Germany. She says that Germany has turned him down, on the representation of the Soviet in Berlin, and he has not applied to France, because he knows that the

LEFT TO RIGHT: SNOWDEN, JIM THOMAS, CLYNES, MOSLEY, NOEL BUXTON, TOM SHAW, WEDGY BENN, LORD THOMSON C. TREVELYAN, MAGGIE BONDFIELD, THE LOW PARTY, THE LIBERAL PARTY, WINSTON DISGUISED AS KEIR HARDIE, ETC

2 'Part of the Unemployment Problem Is Being Solved, Anyway', 6th June 1929

Soviet Ambassador in Paris has persuaded the French government to refuse. But here we have a Labour government, she says, and no relations with the Soviet!

1 William Gillies (1885–1958). Secretary of the Labour Party International Department 1920–44.
2 Vernon Bartlett (1894–1983). London Director of the League of Nations 1922–32. Journalist. Independent M.P. for Bridgwater 1938–50.
3 George Lansbury (1859–1940). First Commissioner of Works 1929–31. Labour M.P. for Bow and Bromley 1910–12, 1922–40. Leader of the Parliamentary Labour Party 1931–5; Leader of the Labour Party 1932–5. Christian socialist and pacifist.
4 Ishbel MacDonald, later Ridgley, later Peterkin (1903–82). London County Councillor 1928–34. Daughter of the Prime Minister, and his hostess at No. 10 Downing Street.
5 One of Henderson's first acts as Foreign Secretary was to refuse Leon Trotsky political asylum in Britain.

Mitrany wants the succession to Phil Noel-Baker[1] at the School. He says the Americans want Gilbert Murray.[2]

Wertheimer is very quick and intelligent. He says the diplomatic corps has been told that Uncle will always require a written statement to be brought and left behind, whenever an ambassador or minister comes to see him. This is interpreted to mean that he must submit everything to the P.M. I say that this interpretation is wrong. Uncle is cautious and knows his limitations. As Garvin[3] says in the *Observer* last Sunday 'he is not exactly a rusher, but he is a moving weight.' Wertheimer says that it is being put round that I am pro-French and 'even', ultimate horror, 'pro-Polish'! I say that this may come from reading between the lines of my book.[4] In truth, I am simply objective. I have no pet lambs. All foreigners are comrades. I seek sometimes to correct the lack of objectivity of my party, or sections of it. Even Poles have a case, of sorts, and should be given credit for it. Who, I say, says these things of me. The *Germans*, he replies.

I say that the worst enemy of Germany is Snowden, with his anti-French passions, which may delay evacuation.[5] Let some of Snowden's German friends advise him, for Germany's sake, not to attack France publicly and to accept the Young Plan.

Wertheimer agrees that one of Germany's worst friends was Morel.[6]

He asks my view about the Saar. I advise the Germans to content themselves, for the moment, with the Rhineland, and not to ask for a second helping with their mouths full.

1 P. J. Noel-Baker (1889–1982). P.P.S. to the Foreign Secretary 1929–31. Labour M.P. for Coventry. Professor of International Relations, University of London (L.S.E.) 1924–9. See Appendix.
2 Gilbert Murray (1866–1957). Regius Professor of Greek at Oxford 1908–36. Chairman of the League of Nations Union 1923–38.
3 J. L. Garvin (1868–1947). Editor of the *Observer* 1908–42.
4 *Towards The Peace of Nations: A Study in International Politics*, Routledge, London, 1928.
5 On Henderson's instructions, Dalton was trying to bring about the evacuation of occupying troops from the Rhineland. This was achieved at the Hague Conference in August, and a phased withdrawal began in September. Snowden was later applauded by the Right, and sharply criticised on the Left, for hard bargaining with the French over the Young Plan and a settlement on German reparations. It was felt by some that Snowden's financial 'jingoism' jeopardised agreement on the military issue.
6 E. D. Morel, formerly G. E. Morel-de-Ville (1873–1924). Writer on international questions. Founder of the Union of Democratic Control 1914. Labour M.P. 1922–4. Pacifist. Liberal opponent of 'secret diplomacy'. A major influence on inter-war internationalist thought.

Lansbury says Thomas having begun by pitching the note very high is now terrified of the difficulties everywhere. He is specially wobbly on pensions and the school leaving age. Lansbury and Lord Oswald have not been consulted till yesterday. They will have to fight. He is an old man, and careless of reputation, but Thomas and Lord Oswald will be broken by failure.[1]

The 'Optional Clause' of the statute of the Permanent Court of International Justice committed signatory nations to compulsory arbitration in legal disputes. The Conservatives, and many Foreign Office officials, were opposed to Britain signing it. Labour was strongly in favour of doing so. Henderson made Dalton responsible for pushing ahead negotiations in order to secure a British signature. This was achieved in September 1929, when Britain and several other nations signed the Clause in Geneva.

Saturday 29th June
Uncle and I walked out together at lunch time. He told me that he had 'had his first row with Lindsay',[2] who, in conversation with his chief, had remarked that he had suggested to the Prime Minister Sir P. Loraine[3] to succeed Lloyd[4] at Cairo, and had hinted at diffi-culties over the signing of the Optional Clause. Uncle had 'pulled him up' and said he didn't quite understand 'the inwardness of all this'. Lindsay had asked whether this meant that he was never to speak to the P.M. Uncle had refused to be caught in this trap and had repeated that he didn't understand the inwardness, etc. There had been an estrangement between them for two days. He had mentioned it to Selby[5] today who had said that he thought Lindsay would welcome a *rapprochement*.

1 J. H. Thomas, q.v. (Lord Privy Seal), given the job of co-ordinating unemployment policy, had been placed at the head of the Unemployment Committee, whose other members were Johnston, Lansbury and Mosley. The terms of reference of this committee were vague and there was soon friction among its members, leading eventually to Mosley's resignation from the Government in May 1930.
2 Sir Ronald Lindsay (1877–1945). Permanent Under-Secretary at the Foreign Office 1928–30. Ambassador to the United States 1930–39.
3 Sir Percy Loraine, 12th Bart (1880–1961). High Commissioner to Egypt and the Sudan 1929–33.
4 G. A. Lloyd, 1st Baron (1879–1941). High Commissioner to Egypt and the Sudan 1925–9. Conservative M.P. 1910–18, 1924–5. Governor of Bombay 1918–23. Colonial Secretary and Leader of the House of Lords 1940–41.
5 W. H. M. Selby, later Sir Walford (1881–1965). Principal Private Secretary to the Foreign Secretary 1924–32.

Monday 1st July
I send for Cadogan,[1] who, Phil Noel-Baker says, has been feeling rather out of it, and saying that he doesn't know whether he will be taken to Geneva any more.[2] He supposes we shall think he isn't internationally minded enough. I talk sympathetically to him about the understaffing of his department and its lack of status. Then of the reputation of the British delegation at Geneva as bad mixers. He admits the substance of this, and will try to get the Treasury to grant a larger sum for entertaining this year!

Friday 5th July
My maiden speech as a Minister (of the Crown)! ...
    My speech is short, only ¼ hour, picking up odds and ends, and showing fight at the Tories. Our people like its manner, though its matter was necessarily thin. 'There shall be no Chanaks in our time.'[3] But most people didn't understand the allusion. Ruth also thought, allowing for the thinness of matter, that it was all right, and she is bloody critical!

Saturday 6th to Monday 8th July
Weekend at Avebury with Beveridge, Mrs Mair, Elspeth Mair, Eileen Power. Ruth very critical here too! Beveridge and Mrs Mair chipping at each other a good deal. The little man can't rest and is always scratching the place where his *cazzo*[4] ought to be!

Arthur Henderson, backed by the Foreign Office, was planning to negotiate an Anglo-Italian Treaty to determine the future status of the Sudan. Those who opposed concessions to the Egyptians included the Conservatives, some Liberals, the King and the Prime Minister.

---

1 A. G. M. Cadogan, later Sir Alexander (1884–1968). Head of the League of Nations Section at the Foreign Office 1923–34. Permanent Under-Secretary at the Foreign Office 1938–46.
2 The Labour Government was planning to include the Prime Minister and Foreign Secretary as part of a strengthened delegation to the League of Nations Assembly in Geneva at the end of August, in order to demonstrate support for the League.
3 The Chanak crisis of 1922. Lloyd George, then Prime Minister, had tried to force the Turks to accept partition in Asia Minor, ignoring the rising tide of Turkish nationalism. The British were eventually compelled to give way. Dalton used this episode to stress the determination of his government to avoid the mistake of giving blind opposition to popular movements abroad.
4 '*cazzo*': prick.

Monday 8th July
MacDonald said to Phil Noel-Baker, 'We must be very careful about this Optional Clause. The Liberals are just waiting to pounce on us and turn us out. I have been lunching today with some of the Great Powers. I hear that the Liberals will turn us out if we make no reservation on Egypt. I think we might be able to find a form of words.' Phil very indifferent at this – suspects Hankey[1] at work. Doesn't believe the rumour. I ask Wilson Harris,[2] concealing all names. He thinks it a highly unlikely story, but will enquire. He doesn't know who speaks for the Libs on Foreign Affairs.

Thursday 18th July
School age to be raised on 1st April 1931. Trevelyan makes the announcement in the House this afternoon. This is a triumph for back-bench pressure. The date is rather late. On educational grounds it is better to delay, but we delay also the effect on unemployment. It may be useful, however, if we last three years or more, to have something in hand as a reducing factor. But, like other things, we have done it badly and undramatically and unwillingly, so far as the Cabinet is concerned.

Friday 26th July
Preside over an Inter-Departmental Committee on League Assembly work, and so, by an evening train, to Lockeridge,[3] following Ruth who went down earlier. It is a house, encircled for us with a crown of golden memories, tarnished by deep intervening sadnesses – Helen and the war – of Her, for fear of tears, I never speak.

Under pressure from the Foreign Office, Henderson had replaced Lord Lloyd with Sir Percy Loraine as High Commissioner to Egypt and the Sudan, as a first step towards securing an Egyptian Treaty. His objective was that Britain would give up control of Egypt's domestic affairs, and restrict her

1 Sir Maurice Hankey, later 1st Baron (1877–1963). Secretary to the Committee of Imperial Defence 1912–38; Secretary to the Cabinet 1916–38. Minister without Portfolio 1939–40; Chancellor of the Duchy of Lancaster 1940–41; Paymaster-General 1941–2.
2 Henry Wilson Harris (1883–1955). *Daily News* journalist. Editor of the *Spectator* 1932–53. Independent M.P. for Cambridge University 1945–50.
3 The Daltons had spent their honeymoon in 1914 in a house at Lockeridge (near Marlborough, Wiltshire), lent to them by the wife of A. N. Whitehead, the Cambridge mathematician and philosopher.

troops to the Suez Canal Zone. Henderson deflected criticism from Lloyd's Tory supporters by disclosing clashes between Lloyd and the former Foreign Secretary, Sir Austen Chamberlain. The King, however, was angered by the sacking of Lloyd and remained suspicious of the Egyptian negotiations. Meanwhile the Prime Minister (reflecting the attitude of the Palace) was taking an unwelcome interest in Anglo-Egyptian negotiations, especially those concerning the Sudan.

Tuesday 30th July

More stew over Egypt. Stamfordham[1] and MacDonald both in a terrible state over the Sudan. King George very indignant, says Stamfordham, because not kept informed of what was being done at the Foreign Office. Has written 'I protest' in the margin of one of the Egyptian documents. The Sudan is a place in which he has always taken a very keen interest; it always irks him that he can't sign the Commission of Officers in the Sudanese Defence Force; he has always insisted on a fair share of decorations going there; he always remembers the welcome the chiefs gave him at Port Sudan many years ago; he wants it to be a British Colony; we have kicked the Egyptians out and we mustn't let them come back; we have treated Lord Lloyd very badly. MacDonald also shying at the proposed Egyptian battalion in the Sudan. It was he who had turned the Egyptians out in 1924. 'The P.M. has a diehard streak, you know', said Selby to me, with special reference to this point. Uncle says to me, and the officials, that the Palace and the P.M. seem to be echoing one another, and that it's difficult to fight such a combination. He will try to convince the P.M. who said to him late last night, however, that he didn't want to discuss the question with Uncle, as he 'had seen Lindsay'. But Lindsay says his interview was very unsatisfactory. Uncle says to me (alone) that, if it was only the Palace, he would be prepared to tackle it in another way, 'especially with our own people'. After all, we are a constitutional monarchy. He knows he is unpopular at the Palace, but that doesn't worry him. But MacDonald, no doubt, is deceiving him behind his back.

Wedgwood writes very appealing letters both to Uncle and to me asking to be given the succession to Lloyd! What an idea!

Anglo-American negotiations going well – almost too well, Cecil thinks, and we may be getting such good cruiser terms out of the U.S.

1 Lord Stamfordham, q.v., the King's private secretary.

that Hoover[1] mightn't be able to get an agreement through the Senate. Treaty of Versailles over again?

It is clear, by the way, that not only Lloyd and Winston Churchill, but admirals and generals, are in the habit of running to the Palace behind the backs of ministers. This must be checked. The Service Departments evidently leak all over the floor when it suits them.

Saturday 3rd to Monday 5th August

At Lockeridge. Greenwoods down for weekend. Arthur Greenwood terribly tired, but revives. Will be a first class Minister of Health. Full of plans and ideas. If we have time to turn round, say three years, we shall, I think, do substantial things. And we shall hold the Liberals for a long while, I hope, on the string of electoral reform enquiry! Thomas and the Bondfield[2] are weak spots. I fancy that in the autumn there will have to be a better machine set up for dealing with unemployment.

Saturday 10th to Monday 19th August

Peace and some sun, but a Foreign Office pouch with my breakfast each morning to remind me that I'm not really on holiday. Mechanised evenings with wireless and gramophone.

Nightly news of Snowden. Cripple psychology. Waving his crutches round and round his head, and yelling insults at foreigners, amid rapturous applause from all the worst elements in England. ...

Petica [Robertson], the perfect guest, for two nights. Very interested and intelligent in all that concerns us. Lord Lloyd in Bombay,[3] Mrs Garrat[4] had told her, used to sit down when the National Anthem was being played and expect everyone to *back* out of his presence, and always come twenty minutes late to dinner parties, etc., everyone having to stand meanwhile and some ladies fainting in the hot night air.

Lionel Robbins comes over for a Sunday and we have a good jaw about the School. He says we are the most popular government since the war, chiefly due to the Prime Minister's flying about in service aeroplanes, and Snowden standing up to the foreigners.

1 Herbert Hoover (1874–1964). Republican President of the United States 1929–33.
2 Margaret Bondfield, q.v., Minister of Labour.
3 Lord Lloyd, q.v., had been Governor of Bombay 1918–23.
4 Probably Dilys Garrett, née Silvanus, married to J. H. Garrett, later Sir Hugh, Indian Civil Service 1903–39.

Wednesday 21st to Thursday 22nd August
Dine tonight (22nd) with Lindsay, tête-à-tête, not dressed, at 52 Eaton Square. A maidservant; a simple meal; everybody diplomatically adjusted to suit an Etonian Labour Under-Secretary. Lindsay has an easy manner, which does not however conceal a certain quality of slyness without depth. We speak of foreign lands, and the army and the war, and personalities. The Hague fills us both with gloom.[1] Snowden he says has created a real war mentality in this country. I quote Greenwood's warning before the Conference began, that Snowden has had no experience of negotiation all through his life. Lindsay says this is shown by his failure to divide the French from the Italians.

Friday 23rd August
Optional Clause Committee of Cabinet. Sankey,[2] Passfield,[3] Parmoor,[4] Alexander,[5] Wedgwood Benn. I represent Foreign Office.
...

I am infuriated by poor old Passfield reading out as 'Foreign Office view' Lindsay's minute to P.M. pressing the view that unity of Empire is more important than signature of Optional Clause.[6] It is difficult, in absence of Uncle, to make a protest against Lindsay's relation to P.M. But it is a bad, disloyal business.

Monday 26th August
I am forty-two! Many happy returns as a Minister of the Crown! We've never said *that* before.[7]

1 At the Hague Conference the Foreign Office had been unable to restrain the Chancellor of the Exchequer (see entry for 24th June 1929, and p. 58, n. 5). Snowden had sent an ultimatum on 14th August to the Conference chairman, indicating that if serious proposals to meet British financial demands were not made by the 17th, he would go home. Eventually, Snowden yielded some ground, and a compromise was reached on 28th – largely at the expense of the Germans. (See D. Carlton, *MacDonald versus Henderson*, Macmillan, London, 1970, pp. 46–9.)
2 John Sankey, 1st Viscount (1886–1948). Lord Chancellor 1929–35.
3 Lord Passfield, formerly Sidney Webb, q.v., Colonial Secretary.
4 Sir Charles Alfred Cripps, 1st Baron Parmoor (1852–1941). Lord President of the Council 1924, 1929–31, having joined the Labour Party. Conservative M.P. 1895–1900, 1901–6, 1910–14. Brother-in-law of Beatrice Webb and father of Sir Stafford Cripps, q.v.
5 Albert Victor Alexander, later 1st Earl (1885–1965). First Lord of the Admiralty 1929–31. Labour M.P. for Sheffield Hillsborough. See Appendix. Dalton often referred to him as 'King Albert' or 'Albert Victorious'.
6 Some resistance to signature of the Optional Clause came from the Dominions.
7 In my biography (*Hugh Dalton*, Jonathan Cape, London, 1985, p. 3, and in a quoted passage on p. 4) Dalton's birthday is given incorrectly as 16th August.

On 27th August, agreement was reached at a meeting with Dominions' representatives that all should sign the Optional Clause in Geneva. The British delegation left for Switzerland next day.

Wednesday 28th August
Leave for Geneva with Ruth and Aunt[1] and Selby by the Golden Arrow. Seen off by Fullarton,[2] several Office Keepers and Ka Arnold-Forster. Good crossing. Met by functionaries at Dover and Calais and at Paris by two Embassy cars and Holman,[3] engaged to Tyrrell's[4] daughter. Snowden's face has been hissed at a Paris cinema last night. The Prefect of Police has forbidden its further exhibition ...

Dine out in Bois de Boulogne – at the Armenonville – with Ruth, Aunt, Selby and Holman. Selby says that Lloyd sent a message to the Sudan that, on his last visit, he had noticed that civilians did not spring to attention when he spoke to them. In future they must do so. Further, when he passed through villages in the train, all local officials, in full bib and tucker, must parade with their wives and do obeisance. What *folie de grandeur*!

Sunday 1st to Wednesday 25th September
What a pity Cadogan always looks such a sad stick. But Jebb was very ornamental and quick and useful, though never, one feels, quite fool-proof. Willert[5] was really excellent. The Press had never been done so well before. Strang[6] reasonably competent, but a bit squirmy, and said to have been seen laughing (with Clutterbuck,[7] God's own

---

1 'Aunt': Eleanor Henderson, née Watson, wife of Arthur Henderson, q.v. ('Uncle').
2 Rear-Admiral E. J. A. Fullarton, later Admiral Sir Eric (d. 1962). Naval Secretary to the First Lord of the Admiralty 1927–9.
3 A. Holman, later Sir Adrian (1895–1974). Paris Embassy 1926–31.
4 Sir William Tyrrell, later 1st Baron (1866–1947). Ambassador to France 1928–34. Permanent Under-Secretary at the Foreign Office 1925–8.
5 Sir Arthur Willert (1882–1973). Head of the News Department, and Press Officer, at the Foreign Office 1921–39.
6 William Strang, later 1st Baron (1893–1978). Acting Counsellor, then Counsellor, to the Soviet Union 1930–39. Assistant Under-Secretary at the Foreign Office 1939–43; Permanent Under-Secretary (German Section) 1947–9. Permanent Under-Secretary 1949–53.
7 P. A. Clutterbuck, later Sir Peter (1897–1975). Principal at the Dominions Office and Member of U.K. Delegations to the League of Nations Assembly 1929, 1930, 1931. Permanent Under-Secretary at the Commonwealth Relations Office 1959–61.

Englishman from the Dominions Office) quite openly at foreigners in one Commission. Fullarton has good manners and is restful to have with one, but a little soft and fat, and an R.C. convert. Kirkpatrick[1] is R.C. from birth, capable, brown eyes and a sense of humour. But the League isn't really what it ought to be in the Foreign Office organisation ...

My silly brush with Cecil[2] was over a meeting to be held to exchange ideas on the last day, after Uncle had gone. Phil suggested it to me by minute, and I told Cadogan to summon it *in my room*. Cecil cut up rough, and wrote that if I desired it, he would summon a delegation meeting, but it should be held downstairs. I also cut up rough. On the ceiling or in the cellar? What an issue to fight on!

I must remember in future that he has the sensitiveness of the aristocrat.

William Martin of the *Journal de Genève*, reputed to be anti-English, soon yields to information and courtesy. He has never had either from the English here before.

I addressed Zimmern's[3] students and some solemn grown-ups one evening. I spoke as I should have lectured at the School of Economics, with many jokes. I even laughed at Austen and his Garter,[4] by way of a reply to critics of our signing the Optional Clause. Well received by the great body of the audience, but some were incredibly shocked. One man wrote to *The Times*, hinting heavily at me, but not mentioning my name. Some Americans went away wondering whether I was

---

1 I. A. Kirkpatrick, later Sir Ivone (1897–1964). First Secretary at the Foreign Office 1928–30. Permanent Under-Secretary (German Section) 1949–50. Permanent Under-Secretary 1953–7.
2 E. A. R. Gasgoyne-Cecil, 1st Viscount Cecil (1864–1958). President of the League of Nations Union 1923–45. Son of the Marquess of Salisbury. Conservative M.P. 1906–10, 1911–23. Minister of Blockade 1916–18. Lord Privy Seal 1923–4; Chancellor of the Duchy of Lancaster 1924–7. Resigned from Baldwin's government in 1927 on the disarmament issue. In June 1929, Henderson had asked Lord Cecil to join the League of Nations delegation in Geneva, and to advise on League questions. Cecil took William Arnold-Forster, q.v., as his private secretary.
3 A. Zimmern, later Sir Alfred (1879–1957). Political scientist and foreign affairs specialist. Director of the Geneva School of International Studies 1925–39. Professor of International Relations at Oxford 1940–44.
4 Sir Austen Chamberlain, K.G. (1863–1937). Conservative M.P. for Birmingham West 1914–37; Worcestershire East 1892–1914. Son of Joseph Chamberlain, and half-brother of Neville, q.v. Junior minister 1895–1900; Financial Secretary to the Treasury 1900–2; Postmaster-General 1902–3; Chancellor of the Exchequer 1903–5, 1919–21. Secretary of State for India 1915–17; Minister without Portfolio 1918–19; Lord Privy Seal 1921–2. Foreign Secretary 1924–9. First Lord of the Admiralty 1931.

really a Minister or was I drunk? My God! One must never joke in public while in office. Wilson Harris,[1] too, was profoundly shocked. Next day, at the Cambridge lunch, three clergy sat in a row eyeing me or twittering among themselves, hoping I wasn't going to make another speech like last night.

Friday 27th September to Friday 4th October
At Brighton for Annual Conference. Incommoded by a cold. Outstanding event of the Conference is Uncle's speech on the Wednesday, 2nd October. A plain survey of all that has been done – Iraq, Palestine, Egypt, Evacuation of Rhineland, Geneva, Russia. (His meeting with Dovgalevski[2] at Lewes the day before fits in perfectly.) At the end an ovation such as I had never heard before at a Party Conference. Not carried away by rhetoric or sobstuff, but conscious of honest, big achievement all along the line. Applause, quick at first, but rising steadily to a crescendo till everyone was on their feet – the applause of appreciation of straightforward policy and straightforward character. He had been squittering for days, and had been dealing also with all the small change of the Conference, just as if he was still simply the secretary of the Party. Thomas the day before and Snowden the day after were miserably poor by comparison.

Friday 11th October
A rush to Bishop Auckland and back. Leave King's Cross 10; arrive B.A. 3.38; motor with Bull to Town Hall; receive deputation of unemployed 4; conference on relief scheme with Urban District Council 4.15; similar conference with Rural District Council 5.30; tea with Mrs Bull 6.45; motor to Town Hall; receive deputation from British Legion 7.30; lecture with C. Curry[3] in chair 7.45 to 9.15 on 'Impressions of an Eye Witness at Geneva', jointly for League of Nations Union, Wesley Guild and Dramatic Society; talk to constituents after meeting; supper with Mrs Brown 9.45 ... catch train from B.A. station 11.25. Arrive King's Cross 5.15 a.m. [on 12th October].

Monday 21st October
Lionel Robbins to dine. He has made a very good start this term, as I knew he would. Professor at thirty-one (Pigou I think was Professor

1 Wilson Harris, q.v. Diplomatic correspondent of the *Daily News*.
2 V. S. Dovgalevski (1885–1934). Soviet Ambassador in Paris 1928–34.
3 Probably A. C. Curry (1887–1957). Chartered accountant. National Liberal M.P. for Bishop Auckland 1931–5. Later Newcastle upon Tyne City Councillor, Alderman and Lord Mayor.

at twenty-six), he has a long run home. Success is the great stimulant.

Tuesday 22nd October

I meet King Albert [A. V. Alexander, q.v.], First Lord of the Admiralty, in Whitehall. The Admirals, I fear, have got a firm grip on him. They talk unemployment, whenever he talks of reduced estimates. He is paralysed by this prospect.

He has been to sea with the Battle Fleet, and believes that there is a new gun which will shoot down aeroplanes from the sky. 'I could fire it myself', he says, 'and write my name in the sky in letters of smoke. No aeroplane could live under such fire.' He denounces the Air Force. They are very dangerous. They have the ear of the Cabinet, of every Cabinet. They undertake to do all the work of the Navy and the Army, and do it on the cheap, but they can't deliver the goods. We, with all our commitments, can't afford to give a lead in disarmament, etc. Departmental loyalty is easily grown, I know that. But O my poor co-operator![1] I interview the new boys at the Foreign Office. This has never been done before. They seem a good bunch.

Wednesday 23rd October

National Executive all morning and half afternoon. Uncle is not looking very fit yet, and has heavy days ahead of him. I am not very happy about this. Phil Noel-Baker, on the other hand, seems very well rested. Nicolson[2] comes to see me. I like him, and think well of his brains. Full of constructive ideas. His mother-in-law[3] has behaved so badly that he is leaving the service and writing for Beaverbrook.

1 Alexander was a leading figure in the co-operative movement.
2 H. G. Nicolson, later Sir Harold (1886–1968). Diplomat, politician, author, journalist, diarist and gardener. In September 1929 Nicolson resigned from the Foreign Office in order to join the editorial staff of the *Evening Standard*. But (as this entry makes clear) he was already thinking of switching to politics, and over the next twenty years he engaged in a strange flirtation with the centre and the Left. In 1931 he helped to start the New Party, leaving it after Mosley took up fascism. From 1935 to 1945 Nicolson served as a National Labour M.P. and in 1940–41 as junior minister. After the war, he joined the Labour Party, fighting and losing a by-election in 1948.
3 Victoria, Lady Sackville, née Sackville-West (1862–1936). Mother of Harold Nicolson's wife Vita Sackville-West and widow of Lionel, 3rd Baron Sackville. After the death of her husband in 1928, Lady Sackville began to spread malicious gossip about her daughter and son-in-law (both of whom were, or had been, actively homosexual). This seems to have been one reason, though not the only one, for Nicolson's decision to give up his diplomatic career.

But we must use him, one way or another. He would like to come into politics on our side. I doubt whether this is the best use that can be made of him. But we shall see.

Friday 25th October
In the evening to Cambridge. Addressed large meeting of Cambridge University Labour Club. Slept in King's as Goldie's [Lowes Dickinson] guest. He very much rejuvenated, and very cheerful at our foreign doings.

Wednesday 30th October
Meet Alexander at lunch with Webbs at L.S.E. Cheerful, very pleased with himself and his job. He is not very clever at putting the Admiralty case. I speak to him about a recent intercept, which I have been sitting on for a day or two. The Japanese Naval Attaché reported to his Admiralty at Tokyo that he had a conversation with one of our Naval Officers (Head of Far Eastern Section of Intelligence), who said that 'a certain politician' had told him that the Liberals would support a vote of no confidence in H.M.G. owing to their having negotiated with Dovgalevski. The result would be the defeat of the Government and a dissolution. Whatever government was formed after the election, it was clear that 'there would be a certain change in the situation, as regards naval disarmament'. Intercepts throw light in unexpected places! This British Naval Officer was certainly very indiscreet, almost certainly ill informed, possibly somewhat disloyal to His Majesty's Government's policy and willing to encourage the Japs not to take it very seriously. I told King Albert I would send him a note about this. A word from him, I said, might prevent a repetition of such incidents. He said he would gladly look into it. I consequently sent him that evening a 'personal and secret' letter, giving the reference number, etc.

On the intercept itself I wrote a minute drawing attention to the indiscretion of this Naval Officer, and giving it as my opinion that in a few days it would be found that his estimate of the Parliamentary situation was utter moonshine. I added that the fact that such a conversation should have taken place at all was very unpleasing, that I had written privately to the First Lord suggesting an admonition, and that we should watch for similar incidents in the future. My letter to King Albert having been written, Jebb[1] appears to say, in effect,

---

1 Gladwyn Jebb, later 1st Baron Gladwyn (b. 1900). Private secretary to Dalton as Parliamentary Under-Secretary of State 1929–31. See Appendix.

that Bland[1] suggests that I should hold it up until Lindsay had had an opportunity of seeing me about it!! Lindsay, just back from leave, was at the House with Uncle. Bland had merely read my minute. I told Jebb to send the letter off at once. Later in the evening, to cover my tracks, I mentioned to Uncle that I had spoken to King Albert at lunch and written to him this evening.

Thursday 31st October

Party Meeting.[2] Margaret Bondfield on her defence. Left at noon, with discussion in full swing, because she 'had to see Parliamentary Draughtsman'. Discussion adjourned, amid general discontent and indignation. She is *very* inept! She could have the Parliamentary Draughtsman to come and see her at any hour that suited her. It's a good Party,[3] with a sense of drive. If it's well handled, it'll do great things. Snowden makes a 'powerful appeal' for loyalty and team work. If Government defeated by votes of its own supporters, it will resign. They must resist temptation to support specious 'widening' amendments by Liberals and Tories.

Ponsonby[4] wants to be Ambassador to Moscow. He springs this on me today. Bloody fool! He has left it much too late. It is practically decided now that it is to be a diplomatist. The thing is very uncomfortable. I said that I had thought of him long ago as an excellent candidate, but had supposed that his wife's health would be an insuperable bar. He said, 'No. She and I have had it all out together.' He hates his present job. He thinks he is specially qualified for Moscow, that the Foreign Office couldn't object to him and that both our own Party and the Bolshies would warmly approve his appointment. He would like me to speak to Uncle. He is going to blow his own trumpet now, he adds rather pathetically. He is tired of keeping quiet and being treated like dirt. He is going to speak to MacDonald and others.

Uncle, to whom I speak later, has no use for the idea at all. His mind is increasingly set on a diplomat and a Russian speaker ...

I have a word with Lindsay on the intercept. He is quite friendly, but says that 'nothing happens at the Foreign Office for the first time'. They have had similar incidents before. There is always an indignant

---

1 G. N. B. Bland, later Sir George (1886–1972). Private secretary to the Permanent Under-Secretary for Foreign Affairs (Sir Ronald Lindsay and then Sir Robert Vansittart) 1928–35.

2 'Party Meeting': a meeting of the Parliamentary Labour Party.

3 i.e. Parliamentary Labour Party.

4 Arthur Ponsonby, q.v., was Parliamentary Under-Secretary for the Dominions June–December 1929.

denial of authenticity, followed by an awkward period of paralysis, during which no one dares to say anything to anyone. 'The Marquis'[1] on several occasions took up such questions and began telegraphing protests all over the world. But nothing ever happened.

Friday 1st November

Poor Ponsonby sees Uncle, but gets nothing out of it, and is very unhappy at his stolid reception. Uncle tells me that he said he wanted a Russian-speaking diplomat, but that, if the Cabinet turns down this idea, he will submit Ponsonby's name along with the large number of others which have already been brought to his notice. He adds, to me, that MacDonald thought so poorly of Ponsonby that 'he nearly left him out altogether', when he was making up the Government. Later that afternoon the Cabinet, at MacDonald's strong suggestion, decided that this was a Foreign Office matter.

Monday 4th November

Events march. Uncle sees MacDonald. Result Ovey[2] to Moscow, Lindsay to Washington; Vansittart[3] to be head of the office. Probably also myself to League Council meeting in January, as Uncle will be at Five Power Conference. I don't know Vansittart; he mustn't start running to MacDonald behind Uncle's back, as Lindsay did over the Optional Clause and Loraine. ...

Thomas makes a bloody awful speech on unemployment. How much longer is he to go on uncontrolled?

Wednesday 6th November

I unearth a class of 'No distribution' telegrams, which have hitherto been withheld from me. This includes both trivial and rather important communications. I tell Jebb to arrange that all such telegrams come to me in future; if there is any obstruction he is to tell the officials concerned that I shall go straight to the Secretary of State and secure authority. This is agreed to, though it is explained that this was never done for my predecessor! King Albert tells me that he had looked into

1 G. N. Curzon, 1st Marquess Curzon, 5th Baron Scarsdale (1859–1925). Foreign Secretary 1919–24. Conservative M.P. 1886–98. Junior minister 1891–2, 1895–8. Viceroy of India 1898–1905. Lord Privy Seal 1915–16; President of the Air Board 1916; Lord President of the Council 1916–19, 1924–5.
2 Sir Esmond Ovey (1879–1963). Ambassador to the Soviet Union 1929–33.
3 Sir Robert Vansittart, later 1st Baron (1881–1957). Principal Private Secretary to the Prime Minister 1928–30. Permanent Under-Secretary at the Foreign Office 1930–38. See Appendix.

the question of the intercept. Domvile[1] assures him that there is no truth whatever in the alleged conversation of his intelligence officer with the Japanese Naval Attaché. They have found the latter romancing before. I thank King Albert for receiving my letter in such a friendly spirit, and add that it will no doubt be useful to the Admiralty to have this additional evidence of the unreliability of the J.N.A. [Japanese Naval Attaché]. It will also, I think, though I don't say so, be a warning to the Admiralty to bridle their tongues.

Friday 8th November

Ask Ovey to see me. I think he should do well in Moscow. He is keen and has a sense of humour. He does not take 'propaganda' seriously. He suggests that we might give special passports, marked 'propagandist', to as many Russians as care to come to England and promise them police protection and all facilities. He is anxious to get in touch with as many leading people in Moscow as he can, 'even if they don't care to put on evening dress' when they come to the Embassy. He doesn't want anyone on his staff who will abuse the Bolsheviks 'if he has had a couple of glasses of port after dinner'. He would like to do his share of negotiations on debts and claims at the Moscow end.

Vansittart also calls to make my acquaintance. Begins with Eton and Canon D. Then to business. My first impressions are favourable. Relations will undoubtedly be easier than with Lindsay. He is younger, has easier manners and is much more adaptable, and with fewer prejudices. His views on appointments are much more in line with mine. He is all for passing over duds, and wants to bring in commercial people occasionally, on their merits and in order to encourage consuls, etc. I tell him that I don't like the block of home stickers among the Under-Secretaries – Wellesley[2] has been twenty-three years continuously in office, Oliphant[3] eighteen and Mounsey[4] ten. This blocks e.g. Selby's promotion to Under-Secretary. I think one at least of the three should go to South America, where Rio and Buenos Aires are

---

1 Admiral B. Domvile, later Sir Barry (1878–1971). Director of Naval Intelligence at the Admiralty 1927–30. President of the Royal Naval College at Greenwich 1932–4. Retired list 1936. He founded the Link, an Anglo-German friendship association, in 1937, and became a Nazi apologist, with strong anti-Semitic leanings. He was interned in 1940 under Regulation 18B.

2 Sir Victor Wellesley (1876–1954). Deputy Under-Secretary at the Foreign Office 1925–36.

3 L. Oliphant, later Sir Lancelot (1881–1965). Assistant Under-Secretary at the Foreign Office 1927–36.

4 G. A. Mounsey, later Sir George (1879–1966). Assistant Under-Secretary at the Foreign Office 1929–31. Secretary at the Ministry of Economic Warfare 1939–40.

both vacant now. The fact that Vansittart has no wife[1] will be a great help to personal intercourse. Also the fact that he is on friendly terms with Phil [Noel-Baker].

In the afternoon an Appointments Committee. I ask them point blank whether one or other of the Under-Secretaries wouldn't like to go to Rio or Buenos Aires. They all make excuses, and say that they haven't the private means required for B.A. (This is absurd. We ought to adjust the *frais de représentation*.) Then Wellesley hurriedly proposes Waterlow[2] for Rio, and the others all eagerly support this idea. They know that I have backed Waterlow and think I can't resist this. It is agreed that Waterlow shall have the offer. I head off the proposal of Macleay[3] for B.A. Vansittart had told me this morning that he was against this, and thought little of Macleay, of whom at Prague, Rennie Smith[4] had reported rather unfavourably. Ovey's counsellor comes up. Osborne,[5] now at Lisbon, is suggested, but Selby hands over to me his telegram of acceptance, in which he says 'I detest Bolshevik principles and practice so much that the idea of going to Moscow is sometimes like a nightmare. None the less ... ' I say abruptly that in view of this, if the Committee were to recommend him to the Secretary of State, I should have to recommend the other way. We do not require that our people at Moscow should be pro-Bolshevik, but at least they should be objective. Lindsay says, rather feebly, that this telegram shows that Osborne is objective. But they don't press him.

Saturday 23rd to Sunday 24th November
With Ruth to Oxford to spend a weekend with the Furnisses.[6] He had been expecting a peerage in the summer. He had heard from Lees-Smith and Greenwood that it was imminent, and had hung about London waiting for a call. He had been told that he was fourth on a list of twenty-five possibles. Rather pathetic ... Call at Ruskin and

---

1 Vansittart's wife had died the previous year. He remarried in 1931.
2 Sydney Waterlow, q.v. Minister to Bulgaria 1929–33; Abyssinia 1928–9.
3 Sir James Macleay (1870–1943). Minister to Czechoslovakia 1927–9. Ambassador to the Argentine 1930–33.
4 Rennie Smith (1888–1962). P.P.S. to Dalton as Parliamentary Under-Secretary for Foreign Affairs 1929–31. Labour M.P. for Penistone 1924–31. Journalist.
5 F. D'A. G. Osborne, later 11th Duke of Leeds (1884–1964). Counsellor to Portugal 1929–31.
6 Henry Sanderson Furniss, later 1st Baron Sanderson (1868–1939). Principal of Ruskin 1916–25.

find young Maddison[1] very radiant and absorbing new ideas.

Monday 25th November

At 10.15 the seven Under-Secretaries of State visit No. 10! Mac-
Donald, confused, long winded and havering about the peerage,[2] and
the odd man out! A certain disinclination to oblige was evident in
some of his hearers. But Willy Lunn went outside for five minutes and
told the Prime Minister that if he were given a permanent job with a
decent salary elsewhere, he would resign his seat in the House and his
Under-Secretaryship. This, however, was not thought to afford a
solution. Finally Ponsonby, who is both unhappy and incompetent
in his present job, said he would be quite willing to go to Russell's[3]
place at the Ministry of Transport, thus dropping £300 a year which
was the curse for some, and allowing, e.g. Short[4] to take his place at
the Dominions and Russell to go to the Home Office. We left it all
in a very undecided state.

Tuesday 26th November

Tom Johnston to lunch at 5 Carlisle Mansions with Ruth and me.
Very interesting and very amusing. He hears all the Cabinet secrets
from Old Willie [Adamson]. He, George Lansbury and Mosley
presented their scheme for retiring pension at sixty to Thomas a week
ago, and had an interview and a row with him yesterday. 'Great

---

1 Jack Maddison. Young friend of Dalton from Bishop Auckland, studying at
   Ruskin. Later he and his wife Mary ran a centre for the unemployed at Spennymoor, Co. Durham.
2 On 19th November, MacDonald asked Dalton to go to the House of Lords while
   retaining his present office. This was in order to meet a constitutional requirement
   that no more than six Under-Secretaries should sit in the Commons. Dalton discussed the offer with Henderson and Ruth, and then refused. His diary (19th
   November 1929) shows that he was not quite so certain about this decision as he
   later claimed (CBY, p. 248). At the time he wrote: 'I should lose my Parliamentary
   salary when we go out of office, and it would be a trifle grotesque for a Peer to
   return to the teaching of economics ... Ruth is clearly for refusal, as indeed am I,
   though I try to make her weigh the arguments on the other side – freedom from
   constituency labours, more time for Foreign Office and Geneva work, more time
   together for the two of us.' The prevailing view was that peerages should go only
   to men who had the means to maintain an appropriate life-style. It was regarded
   as natural, therefore, that the Prime Minister should offer to ennoble Dalton or
   Ponsonby but not a working-class minister like William Lunn.
3 John Russell, 2nd Earl (1865–1931). Parliamentary Secretary at the Ministry of
   Transport 1929; Parliamentary Under-Secretary at the India Office 1929–31.
4 Alfred Short (1882–1938). Labour M.P. for Wednesbury 1918–31; Doncaster
   1935–8. Parliamentary Under-Secretary at the Home Office 1929–31.

political difficulties', said Thomas, 'what about the man of fifty-nine?' Mosley said, 'Everything we put up is turned down. Our reputations are at stake.' It was finally agreed that Thomas should put up the scheme to the Cabinet and suggest that three members of the Cabinet should discuss it further with its authors. It would, Johnston says this is now admitted, lift 280,000 off the total of the unemployed at a net cost, after allowing for saving in unemployment benefit and poor relief, of £13 million a year, initial cost and rapidly declining. As Ruth says truly, this might mean the difference between life and death for this Government.

Monday 2nd December
Arnold to dinner. He is to lead our team, not a very strong one, on Electoral Reform Commission. He says that plural voting, business and university, is outside the terms of reference. This infuriates both Ruth and me. To abolish plural voting is the most necessary of electoral reforms and the most helpful to our party, and is a Radical project of fifty years' standing. ... As to Furniss's peerage, Arnold says that it was Mrs Furniss who spoilt it by gassing in Oxford and London about it in the summer. This upset the Prime Minister.

Tuesday 3rd December
Will and Ka [Arnold-Forster] to dine with Ruth. (I dine at the French Embassy, braided and powdered flunkeys, Sir Austen [Chamberlain] and other adornments, male and female. What a world!)

Will on Cecil's havering. He is half inclined to join our Party, and half not. He is not sure whether the Prime Minister or Uncle really want him to. Will thinks that if he were offered a place in the Cabinet, without portfolio or salary, he would join. But it is all very doubtful. Ruth and I both rather impatient. Cecil's position is very ambiguous and unsatisfactory now. If he believes in our policy, he should join us and have done with it, without conditions. And office would soon follow, with Cabinet rank. He will put it off until we go out, I suppose, and then do it too late!

The question of naval disarmament had been revived by President Hoover. MacDonald responded quickly to the President's initiative, and after the Prime Minister's visit to the United States in October 1929, arrangements were made for a naval conference in London in January 1930, to be attended by representatives of Britain, the United States, Japan, France and Italy.

MacDonald presided. The five powers agreed, *inter alia*, to a five-year holiday in the construction of capital ships and the early scrapping of a few battle-ships. There was also agreement on the tonnage and armament of submarines and on aircraft carriers. But France and Italy failed to settle their differences, and both remained outside the main treaty.

Wednesday 4th December

Wedgwood Benn and Phil [Noel-Baker] to lunch to talk Five Power Conference, and battleships in particular. Wedgwood Benn is to be our fourth principal delegate with P.M., Uncle and King Albert. We are to provide him with a Foreign Office secretary, probably Makins.[1] Ruth has been pressing me to arrange this lunch for some time. I think Wedgwood Benn will be on the side of the Angels. He says truly that the leaders of our Party have talked so long, without having the power to act, that now they are excessively timid in action. Within their different sphere, the old whips were bolder, through habit. Phil and I press on him the need to cut down battleships, thus making a Peace gesture and saving money. We must never lay down a battleship again. We haven't done so since 1922 and it would be intolerable to start again in 1931, even the smaller, cheaper kind which our Admiralty propose. We must mobilise The Chin, Snowden, at the right moment.

At the office I exercise my veto for the first time on a proposed appointment on Ovey's staff for Moscow. This time on Waite, a Consul, who was there with Hodgson,[2] was attacked in the Bolshevik press when the mission left, and has a White Russian wife, even though consumptive ...

On the suggestion of Arnold and Vansittart, I write to the latter recommending Furniss for a peerage. His chances seem to have im-proved. The reshuffle of Under-Secretaries is now complete. Ponsonby to Transport dropping £300 a year and his title of Under-Secretary of State, Lunn to Dominions in place of Ponsonby, Shiels[3] to Colonies

---

1 R. M. Makins, later Sir Roger, later 1st Baron Sherfield (b. 1904). Entered Foreign Office 1928. British Ambassador to the United States 1953–6; Joint Permanent Secretary at the Treasury 1956–9. Chairman of the U.K. Atomic Energy Authority 1960–64.

2 R. M. Hodgson, later Sir Robert (1874–1956). Chargé d'Affaires in Moscow 1924–7. Minister to Albania 1928–36.

3 T. D. Shiels, later Sir Drummond (1881–1953). Parliamentary Under-Secretary at the Colonial Office 1st December 1929–August 1931; India Office June–December 1929. Labour M.P. for Edinburgh 1924–31.

in place of Lunn, Russell from Transport to India in place of Shiels. Several of these are distinct improvements. But Ponsonby tells me that the first Morrison, his new chief, knew of it was when he read it in Monday's *Times* (2nd December)! Really MacDonald might take a little more trouble.

As to Warsaw and the possibility of an anti-democratic move, I wrote privately to Savery,[1] two days ago, asking for a report and inviting him to let it be known that Poland would lose all her friends and they aren't many, among His Majesty's Government's supporters, if she goes Fascist. We have made her legation an Embassy, and supported her re-elections to the League Council, since we came in and it would be a poor political *quid pro quo* if she played to the unconstitutional Right ...

Tonight a dispatch, quite worthless, from Erskine,[2] our Ambassador at Warsaw. I minute that I have the sensation, as in 1926, that our Warsaw Mission is out of touch with political personalities, that I wonder whether even Daszynski,[3] a most agreeable and handsome old gentleman, has ever been invited to lunch or dine at the Embassy, that a hint might be dropped to Erskine to cultivate more personal contacts (as Phipps[4] had lately so well done in Vienna), and report again, that there is still, I think, a tendency for some of our representatives abroad to move in rather narrow social circles, and so to give partial and incomplete accounts of political situations. This, Ruth thinks, will make some of them furious.

Thursday 5th December
Phil says that the King wrote a personal letter to Tom Shaw[5] and King Albert when they took over office, saying that he hoped they would keep on Milne[6] as C.I.G.S. [Chief of Imperial General Staff] and Madden[7] as First Sea Lord beyond the impending dates of their retirement, so as to preserve continuity. And they both did. Madden especially is hopelessly reactionary and Milne during the past year or two has become more and more so.

1 Frank Savery (1883–1965). British Consul in Warsaw 1919–39.
2 Sir William Erskine (1871–1952). Ambassador to Poland 1929–34.
3 Ignacy Daszynski (1866–1936). Veteran socialist leader from Austrian Poland who helped to set up the Polish state in 1918.
4 Sir Eric Phipps (1875–1945). Minister to Austria 1928–33. Ambassador to Germany 1933–7; France 1937–9.
5 Thomas Shaw (1872–1938). Secretary of State for War 1929–31. Labour M.P. for Preston 1918–31. Minister of Labour 1924.
6 General Sir George Milne, later 1st Baron (1866–1948). Commander-in-Chief, General Staff 1926–33.
7 Sir Charles Madden, 1st Bart (d. 1935). First Sea Lord 1927–30.

Phil also gives me an account, rather more plausible than Will's, of Cecil's state of mind. 49 per cent for joining the Government, chiefly to impress foreigners, 49 per cent against, chiefly to impress L.N.U. [League of Nations Union], 2 per cent wavering. Doubts whether MacDonald really wants him to join. Can't contemplate joining the Party, and *later on* having office. Wants Cabinet rank, without portfolio or salary, on analogy of Lansdowne[1] in the war. I speak to Uncle about this, walking home at midnight. He is very unsympathetic. Cecil should have come over before like Wedgwood Benn if he could swallow his scruples about co-partnership, etc. It would be impossible for him to have Cabinet rank, without joining the Party first, and difficult even so. He has the reputation of not being good at team work and of resigning too easily. Uncle and the P.M. both think he made a mess of the trained reserves point at Geneva and needlessly antagonised the French. Uncle isn't inclined to try to proselytise him again.

Margaret Bondfield's Unemployment Insurance Bill, published on 15th November, had been sharply attacked by Labour back-benchers and by the trade unions. On 5th December, after a confused debate in the House, the Minister of Labour conceded the General Council's main demand: that the sole disqualification from unemployment benefit should be proof that a claimant was 'definitely offered suitable employment and had refused it', and was not merely 'not genuinely seeking work'.[2]

It has been a shocking day in the House. Jowitt[3] splendid, but Bondfield at her worst ... Metallic mind, says Uncle. You can make no impression on it by argument. Tonight the Government would have been defeated, in spite of all loyalties, by a solid lump of Trade Union votes, if Clause 2 hadn't been withdrawn. A wasted day and a wrecked time-table. They had Bondfield up in Cabinet, and again before a small Cabinet committee, and told her she must be prepared

1 H. C. K. Petty-Fitzmaurice, 5th Marquess of Lansdowne (1845–1927). Junior minister 1872–4, 1886. Governor-General of Canada 1883–8. Viceroy of India 1888–94. Secretary of State for War 1895–1900. Foreign Secretary 1900–5. Minister without Portfolio 1915–16.
2 See R. Skidelsky, *Politicians and the Slump*, Macmillan, London, 1967, pp. 114–29.
3 Sir William Jowitt, later 1st Earl (1885–1957). Attorney-General 1929–32. Labour, later National Labour, M.P. for Preston 1929–31. Liberal M.P. for The Hartlepools 1922–4; Preston 1929. Labour M.P. for Ashton-under-Lyne 1939–45, having rejoined the Labour Party 1936. Solicitor-General 1940–42; Paymaster-General, Minister without Portfolio 1942; Minister of Social Insurance, then of National Insurance 1944–5. Lord Chancellor 1945–51.

to meet objection and bring clause into line with party policy. Clynes took her over to the Trade Union group. But she is as stiff as a poker. Uncle thinks, if we had been in two years, MacDonald would have asked her to resign. She says administration would become impossible, if amendments accepted. Uncle said to her, 'Margaret, you have the reputation of all the women in England in future Cabinets in your keeping, and I am amazed at your attitude.' She is under the thumb of her officials. The staff of the Ministry of Labour is ruining this Government.

Friday 6th December
Party Meeting at 10. Opinion against Margaret Bondfield very strong, but still surprisingly kindly, until she speaks of possibility of having to withdraw the Bill. Then a general outbreak. After a speech by Mac-Donald on difficulties of time-table and impossibility of sitting over Christmas for ministers who are up to the neck in preparations for Naval Conference, etc., and by Snowden, who paints the financial situation very gloomily, dwells on his coming defeat, thinks it will take three budgets to put national finances into proper order, adds up the new commitments he has already undertaken, estimates the cost of the amendments on the paper to new Unemployment Insurance Bill, asserts that he cannot accept any which involve increased ex-penditure, explains that we cannot carry out the whole of *Labour and the Nation*[1] in one session, and offers to resign in favour of anyone who will take over his crushing burdens with a light heart – it is agreed that we must pass the Bill before Christmas, that we will take off the paper all further amendments costing money, and that we will sit late, if need be. ...

To Cambridge in the afternoon for King's Founders Feast, to which I am an invited guest. A very happy binge, in the course of which, especially in the Junior Combination and afterwards, I wholly put off the responsibility of office, and join in hunting Sheppard,[2] our Vice-Provost, all over the College without finding him and in the end to bed!! (Nightingale[3] next morning says, 'Not much changed sir.')

Saturday 7th December
I wake, rather amazingly, at 7.45 unaided, eat a very small breakfast, and walk in a wet wind along the Backs. Cambridge is the most beloved place in the world, and its youth the most attractive. As this gap of

1 Labour's election programme (adopted in 1928).
2 J. T. Sheppard, later Sir John (1881–1968). Vice-Provost of King's College, Cambridge; Provost 1933–54. Classicist.
3 King's College head porter.

years slowly widens between me and them, in their eternal replenishment, my heart softens to them more and more. It seems a long morning and I call on Goldie. He is impressed by the effect of the Ten Year Period of stunned consciousness after the war, and the signs of its passing, with the flood of war books and the spreading interest in international relations, and by the immense powers of wireless to reach those who read little. He recalls how his bedmaker, a kindly lady, said to him during the war, 'We always 'ave 'ated the Germans, 'aven't we sir? I remember my father always used to 'ate them.'

Tuesday 10th December
Fuss over Anglo-American visa which I'm trying to abolish. An Inter-Departmental Committee sitting on it. Treasury are obstructing. Mounsey, representing Foreign Office, spends more time arguing against abolition, which Home Office and Board of Trade both want, than for reduction. I have put a taut minute on the papers and spoke to Uncle last night about it ... This minute has upset Lindsay, with whom I have a mutually disagreeable conversation. He thinks my minute 'most unfair', I think the procedure with this business 'very slow'. ... I say that we have to answer a question in the House tomorrow and that from the Parliamentary point of view there are great annoyances in prolonged delay. We then pass to discuss the Secret Service. A lot of hush and humbug about this subject. Lindsay says that 'No Embassy or Legation of ours would do this work.' But they must have 'cover'. This is provided, it seems, by Passport Control Officers. With the general abolition of visas, this system it seems will collapse. But Lindsay is now prepared for this. I think again, after this rather snappy conversation on both sides, that it will be a good thing when Lindsay goes. But to each his due! Phil says, when I tell him of this incident, 'He'd be a good man to be with in a trench.' And this, I think, is true.

Wednesday 11th December
Anxious not to have hurt Mounsey's feelings, I ask him to come and see me, and lay myself out to be friendly. I gather that he was more vexed with Lindsay than with me. He felt he had been put in a very difficult position, but that Lindsay had let him down by suddenly withdrawing the Secret Service argument against abolition of visas. Mounsey can hardly bring himself to say 'Secret Service'. It is like an old lady trying not to say 'W.C.' He calls it, in a hushed voice, 'certain arrangements'. He had, he says, always been taught, while he was in the Treasury Department, to regard the maintenance of these

'arrangements' as his first duty, to which everything should be sub-ordinated.

I told Jebb, after this talk, that I didn't wish to turn him into a Secret Service agent but that I didn't wish, either, to cause needless offence to anyone in the office, and should be glad if he would report to me from time to time what he heard said, so that I shouldn't be treading on people's toes without knowing it. He told me that he had heard it said the other day that I was the first Parliamentary Under-Secretary since Curzon who had shown any capacity to get myself disliked in the office. But that several who had begun by disliking me had come to like me very much when they knew me better. Even if the last part is a polite Private Secretary the first, I suppose, is a compliment!

Cecil talked to Uncle yesterday about battleships, urging their abolition. Without this there will be nothing dramatic in the Five Power Conference and no large savings to the Exchequer. Uncle listened rather well. He didn't see either why we needed these huge and expensive ships. If all would agree to abolish them he would certainly be for it. He should think that Snowden would too. But it must be remembered that we were a minority government. We couldn't do all we wished.

This gives me a clue. We must try to get the Liberals shouting to sink battleships.

Friday 13th December
Late in the evening to Aldbourne.

Saturday 14th December
Ruth wants to buy a cottage or a farm in Wiltshire! She has been bottling this up for weeks! She wants Mere Farm. We go to see it. It has a lovely position and would just fit many of our conditions. But it has no communications and is too far from accessible stations. But we will go on with the search.

The Coal Mines Bill provided for a $7\frac{1}{2}$-hour working day, a National Wages Board and a system of levies designed to boost exports and help the least profitable districts to pay an increased minimum wage. The Bill was opposed by the Conservatives (for the coal owners) and strongly criticised by Liberals. Although the Second Reading was carried, the proposal for a central levy was defeated in committee. The Third Reading was carried after changes had been made, but the House of Lords emasculated the Bill, all the levy provisions were dropped, and the Wages Board never operated effectively.

Thursday 19th December

Today the Government all but fell. Majority down to eight – 281–273 – on second reading of Coal Mines Bill. If defeated, we should have resigned. Too early for a dissolution. Baldwin, one supposes, would have refused. Lloyd George could hardly have had a serious offer. So it would have come back to MacDonald, I think, and we should have gone on, without the Coal Bill. But it would have been a bad fall.

In tonight's division 44 Liberals voted with the Tories against second reading, 6 abstained though present, 2 voted with us (Edge[1] and Mander[2]). The Tories were much above their usual or expected strength. Lately their attendance has been very slack. But their whips put forth all their efforts today and they returned from the ends of the earth, by ambulance and aeroplane. Our Party polled within 10 of our full strength and each of those 10 were unavoidably away and paired. A fine achievement by the whips.

Lloyd George made a vicious speech today. A very clever attack on the Bill, but ending with jeers at Graham, Jowitt and Ben Turner.[3] His bitterness against us proves ever greater. He desired to bring us down, and his speech was designed to make all accommodation impossible. He had been in conclave with Winston and Austen for hours. They are still dreaming of another Coalition. Baldwin either deliberately deceived Graham, or didn't know what was going on. Almost certainly the latter. For he said early in the evening, 'I suppose you will take the Committee stage on the floor of the House. Of course you will win easily.' And so most of us thought. Uncle thought the majority would be about 50. He counted on fewer Tories brought up and more Liberal abstentions.

But, though Lloyd George desired to bring us down, Samuel[4] had

---

1 W. Edge, later Sir William, 1st Bart (1880–1948). Liberal Whip 1929–30. Liberal M.P. for Bosworth 1927–31; Bolton 1916–23. National Liberal M.P. for Bolton 1931–45.
2 G. Le M. Mander, later Sir Geoffrey (1882–1962). Liberal M.P. for Wolverhampton East 1929–45. Joined Labour Party 1948.
3 B. Turner, later Sir Ben (1863–1942). Labour M.P. for Batley and Morley 1922–4, 1929–31. President of the National Union of Textile Workers 1922–9. Chairman of Labour Party N.E.C. 1911; T.U.C. 1928.
4 Sir Herbert Samuel, later 1st Viscount (1870–1963). Liberal M.P. for Darwen 1929–35; Cleveland 1902–18. Junior minister 1905–9. Chancellor of the Duchy of Lancaster 1909–10; Postmaster-General 1910–14, 1915–16; President of the Local Government Board 1914–15; Home Secretary 1916, 1931–2. High Commissioner in Palestine 1920–25. Leader of the Parliamentary Liberal Party 1931–5.

been seeking for days to find a bridge, and I think we were at fault in not responding better before things grew finally critical. The root of the difference was as to compulsory amalgamations.[1] We were needlessly stiff on this. It was part of our 'immediate programme' for the Mines. But the trouble is that the Bill, largely as a result of Thomas's influence, is a deal with the coal owners, and they hate compulsory amalgamations. But it will pay us better to do the right thing in combination with the Liberals, than the wrong thing in combination with the owners. And a 'dear coal bill' will be a bad slogan against us.

Uncle and I walked back together after the Division, very slowly and very tired. To me the emotional strain was very exhausting. Suddenly all our work in foreign affairs, and all the personal interest, ever increasing, of my work at the Foreign Office, seemed to hang by a thread. It would be very bitter to see it all fall with a crash. The precariousness of the life of the Government, and of all politics, is very live tonight. Shall we go to the next League Assembly? Or will the foreigners say, 'We always knew they wouldn't last. They came here and made a few speeches and went away and were soon kicked out. Labour governments are not real things in England.' Shall we last out 1930? But on the other hand, we have beaten the Tories and Liberals combined. All the powers of Hell have not prevailed against us – though they came bloody near it. We have time to think and talk things over before Parliament meets again. Then the Bill will be in Committee, and nothing need be a question of confidence. And, with the Five Power Conference sitting, there will be a disinclination to turn us out.

Monday 23rd December
Debate in House of Commons on Egypt. Austen [Chamberlain], opening, very moderate. Uncle very solid and as effective as usual. Winston speaks early to catch the press, and rants wildly. P.M. decides, only this morning, that he won't speak, so I wind up, after a long series of back-bench speeches. I go for Winston, and score a debating point over him regarding the Egyptian battalion in the Sudan. He looks pretty drunk, but rising at the end, after the House has been adjourned, says to me 'Good speech'. To which I reply by saying 'Cheerio' with a wave of the hand. He was heard outside saying 'That

1 'compulsory amalgamations': the Liberals wanted the Bill to provide for compulsory amalgamations through a Coal Mines Reorganisation Commission. The Labour Government, anxious to carry the coal owners, refused to put this into the first draft of the Bill. Under pressure from the Liberals, the Government then relented, inserting such a provision after the Second Reading. However, the House of Lords effectively removed this provision before the Bill became law.

fellow Dalton made quite a good speech.' Uncle congratulated me quite excitedly. 'Very much better than your speech on Russia,' he said. 'You dealt with every point they raised. That expository style you adopted tonight went down much better than lecturing the House, or appealing to emotion.' He is off to Brighton, pretty tired.

Tuesday 24th December
First Christmas Eve sitting of the House for forty years! Tories rather indignant, but they asked for it ...

I write a minute on battleships, urging that we ought to have a Foreign Office policy, and not simply echo the Admiralty. Our policy should be the maximum disarmament consistent with the general condition of security. This should include the abolition of battleships, for without this no appreciable reduction of Naval estimates is possible. Hoover's remarks to the P.M. at Washington on this subject seemed very promising. But they are not being followed up on our side.

(I am discouraged at the slowness of our back-benchers to cotton on to battleship abolition, or anything else in the way of practical ginger. The formation of the Government has sucked in the talent, I fear, and the residue is very weak.)

In the evening to Windsor. Increasing evidence of the cumulative weight of age and weakening intelligence.[1]

Monday 30th December
At the office. Talk to Craigie[2] about battleships, arising out of my minute, and to Lindsay about Austria, arising out of another of my minutes. Craigie doesn't believe, in spite of Hoover's remarks, that the U.S. are willing to abolish battleships. He quotes the arguments of the present Board of Admiralty in favour of keeping them. These are very unconvincing. It is said that only a battleship can have a deck so thick as to resist a bomb dropped by aircraft, and battleships are more immune than smaller vessels from submarine attack. There is also a practical danger that, if H.M.G. proposes abolition, the Sea Lords would resign, and we should be defeated, with reactionary effects on the prospect of disarmament generally. My opinion of Craigie has fallen in recent months. An essentially over-cautious and conservative mind, though a very hard and conscientious worker.

1 A reference to his father or to both parents.
2 R. L. Craigie, later Sir Robert (1883–1959). Counsellor, Foreign Office 1928–34. Ambassador to Japan 1937–41.

Tuesday 31st December
We see the New Year in at the Beveridge-Mair bungalow.[1] Rather a dull show and the rum punch not up to much! And so back in Beveridge's car to Aldbourne rather late, missing good sleep.

End of 1929
1929 has been an historic year. Ruth's election to Parliament, the General Election and $6\frac{1}{2}$ months at the Foreign Office.

How long shall we last? After the shake up on the Coal Bill one feels pretty insecure, but, though we might go out at any time, it is possible that we might yet last two years. Stamfordham told Canon D. that the King wasn't going far from London in the New Year for fear of an early general election. What would happen at an election? Have we become markedly unpopular yet? I think not, but even a loss of 20 or 30 seats (net) would upset the Parliamentary position pretty fatally. Issues, however, rise and fall, and we may do well in the New Year. Unemployment will fall at least seasonally, for a month or two,[2] and some of our Bills should be popular – Housing and Slum Clearance, and the Budget, for instance – and should also afford a basis for Lab–Lib co-operation in the House.

The Labour Government as a whole is already pretty disappointing with bright patches. Uncle's star has been very much in the ascendant, both in the Party and in the House, and George Lansbury is trying to brighten people's lives and let in more sunlight, and Morrison is very competent, and Johnston very persistent and Greenwood is first rate. But Trevelyan is terribly disappointing. This is a bitter discovery after our good political comradeship. But he is almost incredibly stupid, and is said always to put his case badly in Cabinet and can't even see that he ought to carry his Higher School Leaving Age Bill this session, so as to get it safely passed, while there is yet time, and make the L.E.A.s [Local Education Authorities] realise the need to get schemes ready for 1931. The effects on unemployment which will, I believe, be very striking, can't in any case come till the autumn of 1931. And this may be too late for *us*. And pensioning off the old is hung up too. Damn!

Thomas and Maggie Bondfield are the two most obvious failures of the Government. Few have anything good to say of either of them. MacDonald has been messing about again with the idea of the Economic General Staff, and having economists to lunch. But nothing concrete comes of it. Alexander is weak and in the hands of the Ad-

1 At Lockeridge, Wiltshire.
2 In fact, unemployment rose from 1,251,000 (9.7 per cent) in 1929, to 1,991,000 (16.2 per cent) in 1930 and 2,700,000 (22 per cent) in 1931.

mirals. Buxton[1] is only half alive. And so on, through the list. And they will all be a year older next June than when they took office!

The back-benchers are weak, as I have just said, on practical ginger – except on unemployment insurance. But this may improve, as some of the new recruits grow more experienced.

As to Foreign Policy, I am not so unhappy though my hopes of any big achievement on naval disarmament are rather dim. But Uncle has asked for 27th January for the Optional Clause in the House, and we should make another good show at Geneva, if we live so long, next September. The Russians, however, will be very troublesome – the new Communist Party daily in London is quoting stuff from the Third International already![2] Also the Egyptians and the Chinese won't be very easy. But they aren't really urgent, especially the Chinese.

India – thank goodness! – isn't our pigeon. The recent proceedings of the National Congress, with their outcry for 'independence', are not exactly comfortable. But, if the Simon Commission[3] produces a good report, and we act on it quickly, things may brighten up. 'Storm over India' is a dramatic caption, and some say the Government will fall over India. But I doubt this.

Wednesday 8th January 1930
Parmoor told Cecil that Snowden had said to him that MacDonald wasn't doing so badly as P.M., but added, 'I should like to have a shot at that job before I finish.' Cecil was delighted, and amazed, at the frankness of both Snowden and Parmoor.

At the beginning of 1930, the Government sent the same delegation to the League of Nations Assembly as in 1929, with a couple of minor changes, in order to consolidate the work of the previous year.

---

1 N. E. Buxton, later 1st Baron Noel-Buxton (1869–1948). Minister of Agriculture and Fisheries 1924, 1929–30. Labour M.P. for North Norfolk 1922–30. Liberal M.P. for Whitby 1905–6; North Norfolk 1910–18.
2 The *Daily Worker* started publication in January 1930.
3 The Indian Statutory Commission, under the chairmanship of Sir John Simon, q.v., had been set up in 1927 to examine the problem of nationalisation in India. Late in December 1929 the Indian Congress Party published a 'declaration of independence', proclaiming a boycott of central and provincial governments, and launching a campaign of civil disobedience and non-payment of taxes. By the time the Simon Report appeared in June 1930 (recommending democratic reforms and an Anglo-Indian conference) widespread disorders had broken out, and the authorities had embarked on a policy of mass arrests.

Friday 10th January
Off to Geneva by 11 a.m. from Victoria. Uncle, Ruth, Jebb and I on
the Golden Arrow, with Cadogan and others on the next train.

Arrive at the Gare du Nord, met by Tyrrell, and go to British Embassy, where dine and sleep. A too vast building, which stops being
superb or even comfortable, on the second floor. Bedrooms uninteresting and lifts very primitive ...

Tyrrell spoke strongly to me after dinner in favour of abolishing
battleships. He could see no real argument against it. The Admiralty
always tried to have a foreign policy of their own. Madden after a
C.I.D. Committee[1] at which Ronald McNeill,[2] alone against the rest,
had advocated a policy of low belligerent rights, had said to Tyrrell,
'I hope you didn't agree with that man.' Tyrrell replied, 'I have been
urging this policy upon him for months.' Madden said, 'You are no
better than a pacifist.'

The proposal to abolish battleships, Tyrrell thought, would create
an excellent impression in Europe and might move the French from
their position on submarines. The idea that it might offend the U.S.
he thought should not influence us. My only criticism of Tyrrell's talk
would be that he is inclined to be anti-American. He had a Hindoo
grandmother and gesticulates and organises his talk like a Frenchman.

Saturday 11th January
Leave Paris in the morning and arrive at Geneva at 8.30. Uncle
preparing his Optional Clause speech in the train.

Sunday 12th January
Walk with Uncle in the morning ...

Frank talk about leaders. If anything happened to MacDonald
now, there would be a close division, we agree, between Uncle and
Philip Snowden. But Uncle, who had begun by saying, on my quoting
Snowden's recent remark to Parmoor, 'Well, my chance of that is
gone now,' went on to say that he wouldn't want it by a narrow majority. His chances, he thought, would have come if MacDonald hadn't
been elected Leader in 1922. Clynes couldn't have been P.M., especial-

---

1 'C.I.D.': Committee of Imperial Defence, made up of Cabinet Ministers, military
  leaders and senior civil servants. Its job was to advise the Prime Minister. It was
  set up in 1904 and finally ceased to exist in 1946. Dalton had sometimes acted as
  Henderson's substitute on the C.I.D. in 1929.
2 Ronald McNeill, 1st Baron Cushendun (1861–1934). Conservative M.P. 1911–27.
  Parliamentary Under-Secretary of State for Foreign Affairs 1922–4, 1924–5;
  Financial Secretary to the Treasury 1925–7; Chancellor of the Duchy of Lancaster
  1927–9; Acting Foreign Secretary August–December 1928.

ly with MacDonald always intriguing on his flank, and Uncle's chance would have arisen 'to come in between them'. But I doubt if he realises how quickly his prestige has risen lately above what it was in those days.

The Daltons returned to London on 19th January.

Monday 20th January

To the office. The battleship problem has passed through rapid changes in the past five days! On Wednesday [15th January] Mac-Donald made his statement to the journalists.[1] Something had made him move sharply to the left on battleships. What was it? Cumulative encouragement in the press. A minute by Cecil. Uncle's stand at the delegation meeting. A strong memorandum from Snowden. A petition signed by 77 Labour M.P.s. Pressure in the Cabinet even with Snowden at The Hague and Uncle at Geneva. What else?

Anyhow he threw over the Admiralty, and the Blue Print doctrines, without a word of warning or consultation. And he played before the assembled journalists of all the nations. Phil Noel-Baker gave me tonight, in a taxi between the Foreign Office and South Eaton Place, a sketch of events. Uncle on Wednesday saw MacDonald for a few minutes before the latter's meeting with the journalists. He said to Phil afterwards, 'Now we've got them on the run!'

The Admiralty were furious, not without reason. Here was a completely new policy, or clear reversal. They prepared a violently argumentative document. They had gone as low as they possibly [could]. Not another ton could be surrendered. If there was a war with Japan they would need all their capital ships to beat up the Jap fleet and leave one or two 'to control the situation in Europe', etc.

The Americans were, it seems, slightly peeved, again not without justification, in view of MacDonald's attitude at Washington three months ago. But Phil has come into his own. MacDonald has been ringing him up to produce counter arguments, and to demolish the

1 Hitherto, MacDonald had resisted President Hoover's proposal for a complete 'naval holiday' in the construction of capital ships, on the grounds that this would cause 'dislocation in the yards'. Early in January the Prime Minister had persuaded a Cabinet Committee to endorse the so-called 'Blue Print', an Admiralty-approved document which upheld this position. On 15th January, however, he suddenly altered his position, indicating at a press conference that he now supported the naval holiday. It is possible that Snowden and Cecil helped to change his mind. (See Carlton, *MacDonald versus Henderson*, pp. 121–3.)

Admiralty case. He has been round to No. 10 in conference with MacDonald and King Albert, who doesn't quite know where *he* stands(!), and Craigie. And tonight he is labouring late preparing an urgent memorandum for No. 10. And tomorrow the Conference opens. It is Phil's great hour and he is playing his part very well indeed, though he admits to being terribly tired. He has won his way to Mac-Donald's confidence, as well as Uncle's and will, Uncle says jestingly, win back Snowden's! But what a strange animal is this Prime Minister of ours. It was almost too late, but he has taken at the eleventh hour the simple course!

Tuesday 21st January
[Naval] Conference opens. Everyone in morning coats and top hats. I succumb to the former mode, but not the latter. Vast crowd in Royal Gallery. The King's speech very commonplace, without an arresting phrase or any warmth of greeting. Others fairly good. Difficult to believe the thing can really fail. But how much will it succeed? ...

Hubert Henderson[1] and Cole are to become the nucleus of an expert staff on unemployment. I am not sure that Hubert isn't too negative. But he is keen on national development.

I recall here a few incidents. It was on 9th January that Uncle made his stand for a bold policy in the Naval Conference Delegation. It was to Makins that I said, 'Never forget that we are a Foreign Office, and not a mere basement to the Admiralty.' Cecil's original minute to the Blue Print was the one word 'Alas!' But he altered and expanded it on Will [Arnold-Forster]'s suggestion. Cecil sat next to Wedgwood Benn the other day at lunch and tried to push him on battleships. But the latter said that he didn't feel that he could take a strong line about anything in the Conference. He was only Secretary of State for India. In other words, he wants to keep in with MacDonald and is quite willing to be a passenger. Phil, I fear, has been taken in by his bright manner! ...

'The surest way of ensuring security of sea passage is to remove that which threatens it' (Sir C. Madden in 'very secret' document prepared for the Conference) ... The 'very secret' document contemplates a simple contract between the British Empire and Japan on the most serious naval possibilities. How and why this should arise is not discussed. It is agreed that a proportionate reduction of capital ships would make it very difficult for us. Now we have, under Washington Treaty, 15 to Jap 9. In case of trouble we could send 11 East to defeat

1 H. D. Henderson, later Sir Hubert (1890–1952). Economist. Joint Secretary of the Economic Advisory Council 1930–34. Economic Adviser to the Treasury 1939–44. Professor of Political Economy at Oxford 1945–51.

Japan, and keep 4 in Europe. But if we reduced to 10 and Japs to 6, we should need 8 East to beat them up. This would only leave us two, of which one might be undergoing repairs. This would only leave us one, with which 'to control the European situation'.

Today I sat behind the Japs and the Italians at the Conference. The latter are very familiar *tipi*. I know where I am with them. But the others are strange, inscrutable beings, as from another universe. Kirkpatrick tells me that, at the Guildhall the other night, a Jap picked up a list of the guests, and pointing to the name of 'Mrs King', said to his neighbour the one word 'Queen'. This was his solitary utterance all night.

Cecil and Salter[1] at Geneva, and Tyrrell in Paris, have all said to me recently that until the Sea Lords are allowed to resign, we shall never see the politicians really on top of the Admiralty. They have always been allowed to bluff so far, and they have learned to calculate, to a nicety, just when and how to threaten resignation. They are gallant fellows, in the simplest sense, but they are for the most part weak in logic, when it threatens the foundation of their traditions, but less weak in certain kinds of political and press intrigue.

Wednesday 22nd January

Dine with Trevelyan to meet Admiral Sir Herbert Richmond.[2] Norman Angell[3] also present. It is significant of our 'almost too late' way of doing things and also of poor Trevelyan's lack of sense of urgency, that, although Richmond is his brother-in-law, and an important ally in the anti-battleship fight, he has done nothing hitherto to introduce him to our leaders, and now introduces him first to me, who was outside the Conference. (I am rather acutely conscious of this last fact and find it galling.)

Richmond is not a pacifist, nor an internationalist, but he is a high naval authority,with a first class intellect, and plenty of courage. He thinks that no warship need exceed 6,500 tons to perform all necessary tasks, provided there are none bigger. The monster battleship is a hopeless attempt to make an 'immense' ship. His letter to *The Times* called down upon his head a sharp reproof from the Admiralty. He is

1 Sir Arthur Salter, later 1st Baron (1881–1975). Director of the Economic and Finance Section of the League of Nations 1919, 1920, 1922–31. Independent M.P. 1939–50; Conservative M.P. 1951–3. Junior minister 1939–41. Chancellor of the Duchy of Lancaster 1945. Minister for Economic Affairs 1951–2; Minister of Materials 1952–3.
2 Admiral Sir Herbert Richmond (1871–1946). Admiralty 1929–31. Master of Downing College, Cambridge 1936–46.
3 N. Angell, later Sir Norman (1874–1967). Writer and journalist. Labour M.P. for North Bradford 1929–31. Editor of *Foreign Affairs*.

pretty annoyed with the ruling group there. He gave me a large lump of memoranda, etc., setting out his point of view and answer to criticism. He thinks we could reduce Naval estimates to between £20m and £30m, and still have the strongest in the world, provided others scrapped big ships too.

Monday 27th January
Optional Clause ratification approved by the House of Commons without a division, after defeat of a Tory amendment proposing to add a further reservation on belligerent rights. This is the crown of $7\frac{1}{2}$ months' labour and opposition from many quarters. My 7 months baby is thus delivered!

Tuesday 28th January
Arnold[1] wants to resign because, he says, we have agreed to accept a Lords' amendment to the Unemployment Insurance Bill on the time limit. I tell him that this is not a big enough issue. But he is in a terrible fluster.

Wednesday 29th January
Arnold rings up, while I am having breakfast, and says that things are not as bad as he thought, so he is not resigning! Lord Oswald, however, tells me in the course of the evening that *he* is seriously thinking of resigning, because such a mess is being made of unemployment. We are faced, he thinks, with three years of rising figures, and all his proposals for bringing them down have been rejected. I express sympathy with him in being confronted with such a combination of stupidity and cowardice. But I don't, in fact, believe that he will resign in a hurry! (Optional Clause Ratification has now gone to Sandringham. Officials suggested holding it up till all Dominions were ready! But I impatiently vetoed this.)

Wednesday 5th February
Trevelyan to dinner to meet Leah Manning[2] and Mrs Lowe. They two and Ruth and I all hammer him to get the School Leaving Age Bill through this session. He is awfully stupid and irritatingly complacent. Quite oblivious of problems of training teachers, etc.

1 Lord Arnold, q.v., was Paymaster-General 1929–31.
2 Leah Manning, later Dame, née Tappin (1886–1977). Elected Labour M.P. for Islington East at a by-election in February 1931. Labour M.P. for Epping 1945–50. National Union of Teachers Organiser. When Dalton was an undergraduate and she was at a teachers' training college, he had recruited her to the Cambridge University Fabian Society.

Go out to Admiralty House, where King Albert is giving a reception to the Naval Conference delegates and a host of conventional others. A sense of atmosphere, sailors with open faces, saluting and leaping to attention. As a Sunday paper says there is nothing much changed here. No sharp discontinuity. No collapse of society, or even of 'Society'! But terribly boring. I have seen most of these people before, and there is nothing new to say to them. Small talk and inanities, with the Japs particularly hard work. *The Times* has gathered again, from Riga, that 300 naval officers have been shot by the Bolshies. It is arranged that masses shall be held for their souls. It appears to be a fake. The Soviet contribution towards naval disarmament, I suggest.

On 23rd January 1930, Sir Oswald Mosley sent the Prime Minister a memorandum outlining proposals to deal with unemployment, including a programme of public works, import controls and reform of the machinery of government. On 7th February, details of the memorandum appeared in the press, and next day there were reports of an impending revolt by the three advisory ministers on the Unemployment Committee – Mosley, Johnston and Lansbury.[1]

Saturday 8th February
Today's papers and those of

Sunday 9th February
have varieties of the yarn about the three threatened resignations. I must find out tomorrow.

Monday 10th to Wednesday 12th February
Excitements in, and on the outskirts of, the Cabinet over the 'leakage' of Lord Oswald's and the rest's memorandum. Lord Oswald sent copies to eight selected Cabinet Ministers, before it became a Cabinet paper. The rest are furious. It is also alleged that Strachey[2] gave a

1 See Skidelsky, *Politicians and the Slump*, pp. 167–89.
2 John Strachey (1901–63). Labour M.P. for Birmingham Aston 1929–31; Dundee 1945–50; Dundee West 1950–63. Junior minister 1945–6; Minister of Food 1946–50; Secretary of State for War 1950–51. Strachey was closely associated with Mosley at this time, and helped to set up the New Party a few months later. When Mosley moved towards fascism, Strachey broke with his former mentor and became a communist, writing the most widely read British Marxist tracts of the decade. Later he returned to the Labour Party.

copy to Joad,[1] of all people. This is denied. Lord Oswald's Allan Young[2] was seen sitting with Master Wheatley's[3] Jim Scanlon[4] in the Strangers' Dining Room. I fear they are more concerned with tracing the leakage than finding some new ideas for dealing with unemployment. Ruth is very helpfully active over the School Leaving Age Bill. But Thomas was heard in a corner of the lobby telling Campbell Stephen[5] that 'in a working-class home' a mother would find that this maintenance allowance of 5/- a week 'wouldn't keep 'er boy in bread'.[6] Trevelyan is hopelessly stupid in all this.

Friday 14th to Saturday 15th February
Bishop Auckland. Some improvement in employment and trade. People wonderfully patient and easily satisfied. Only persistent demand is for better pensions for old people, especially in the mining industry. Stay Friday night with Hodgson.[7]

Meetings at Coundon, New Shildon and West Auckland on Friday, and Bishop Auckland on Saturday. All about half full. Not bad for this dreary interim. Hodgson says of MacDonald that 'he is a frightened man' and of Uncle that he 'has the iron moulder's stroke'. Both shrewd comments. He wants the vacant Deanery of Lincoln. He *should get* a slightly better living in a Durham colliery village.

1 Cyril Joad (1891–1953). Philosopher, author and broadcaster. Professor of Philosophy, Birkbeck College, London University 1930–53. A member of Mosley's New Party in its early days.
2 Allan Young. Birmingham I.L.P. organiser who (with Strachey) had helped Mosley to write *Revolution by Reason* (Borough Labour Party, Birmingham, 1925). Founder member of the New Party, which he soon left. Later secretary to Harold Macmillan, q.v.
3 John Wheatley, q.v.
4 Probably *John* Scanlon, a former miner and shipyard worker, and a prominent I.L.P. journalist. Author of *The Decline and Fall of the Labour Party* (Peter Davies, London, 1932). An associate of the Mosley group in 1930, Scanlon continued to follow Mosley in his fascist phase, writing for fascist publications in the late 1930s.
5 Rev. W. Campbell Stephen (1884–1947). Labour M.P. for Glasgow Camlachie 1922–31, 1935–47. I.L.P. Clydesider.
6 Trevelyan's abortive Bill (which aimed to raise the school-leaving age from fourteen to fifteen) proposed that a maintenance allowance should be paid to meet the cost of keeping a child in school for an extra year.
7 Rev. William Hodgson. Secretary of the Bishop Auckland Constituency Labour Party.

Monday 17th February

Johnston says he thinks they are making progress with pensions,[1] but Mosley says Cabinet committee hasn't met yet.

Unemployment is now 177,000 more than a year ago. It is rising week by week at a season when it ought to be falling. The situation is incapable of defence. The recent increase is in cotton and wool, but there is nothing big enough to offset this.

Tuesday 18th February

Addison[2] rages to me about the weakness of Buxton. MacDonald gave Addison an undertaking, when the Government was formed, that Buxton would soon be appointed to a Colonial Governorship, or Dominion Governor-Generalship, and Addison would take his place. But such promotion lingers. I like Addison more and more as a politician. He is one of the live wires.

Friday 21st February

I go to a boring official dinner and levée at the Speaker's. All my bloody colleagues in a crowd. Willy Lunn says to me of Lord Oswald, 'If I had legs like that, I wouldn't wear knee breeches.' A proportion wear plain evening dress.

Sunday 23rd February

Ruth persuades me that I give way much too easily to nervous irritation, and tire myself needlessly. At fifty-five, she says, I shall not, at this rate, be an efficient Cabinet Minister!

Thursday 27th February

Critical division on the Coal Bill Part I, quotas. Government wins by 280 to 271. Four Liberals vote with us, and 8 abstain. A great

1 Mosley and Johnston were both members of a Cabinet sub-committee set up to consider a scheme for retirement pensions for industrial workers. Mosley had estimated that a plan with an Exchequer cost of £2½ million would cut unemployment by 280,000. Thomas was unconvinced, and the Cabinet rejected proposals put forward by the committee in December 1929.

2 Dr Christopher Addison, later 1st Viscount (1869–1951). Parliamentary Secretary, Ministry of Agriculture and Fisheries (under Buxton as Minister) 1929–5th June 1930. Minister of Agriculture and Fisheries 1930–31. Labour M.P. for Swindon 1929–31, 1934–5. Liberal M.P. for Hoxton January 1910–22. Junior minister 1914–16. Minister of Munitions 1916–17; Reconstruction 1917–19. President of the Local Government Board 1919; Minister of Health 1919–21; Minister without Portfolio 1921. Secretary of State for Dominion Affairs 1945–7; Commonwealth Relations 1947. Lord Privy Seal 1947–51; Paymaster-General 1948–9. Lord President of the Council 1951.

victory. If we had been beaten, we should have dropped the Bill, but not either resigned or dissolved. Willie Graham made a very fine speech, and Aneurin Bevan[1] did well.

Monday 3rd to Sunday 9th March

... [T]here is general misery and stagnation this week. The Naval Conference in a bad rut. Uncle, however, is to take on more of the negotiations with the French ...

A certain drive in the political and press background for more decisive results. But only the Admirals are really hanging on. Everyone else is losing grip, or courage, or interest, or all three at once. There is a cut of nearly £5 million in the Naval estimates this year, and no new construction. But there's a threat of supplementaries if the Naval Conference doesn't turn out well.

The Russian negotiations are sticking. Sokolnikov[2] comes and talks for an hour and three-quarters, and then goes away to refer everything to Moscow. Literally no progress at all. Wise[3] talks about orders and credits, but nothing materialises there. The Export Credits Committee will give no credit beyond twelve months for Russian orders. And Gillett[4] won't seriously try to move them.

Domestic legislation is sticking. Coal drags wearily on. Another $4\frac{1}{2}$ days on the floor of the House. Graham broke down the other night, and is obviously under a heavy strain. Ben Turner is utterly useless, and can't even move the closure in the correct formula. In another month the Budget will be here. Housing and Slum Clearance Bill next. That will be a good Bill anyhow and a change from Coal.

School Attendance Bill. Pressure very persistent from a number of our M.P.s, from the press, Liberal as well as our own, from the

---

1 Aneurin Bevan (1897–1960). Labour M.P. for Ebbw Vale. Bevan was closely associated with Mosley at this time, and backed the Mosley memorandum. See Appendix.

2 Grigori Y. Sokolnikov (1888–1939). Soviet Ambassador to Britain 1929–33. Commissar for Foreign Affairs 1934–6. Arrested and convicted in 1937 for alleged Trotskyist activities. Died in prison.

3 E. F. Wise (1885–1933). Labour M.P. for Leicester East 1929–31. Former civil servant. Economic Adviser on Foreign Trade to the Russian Co-operative Movement 1923–9. Leader of the 'affiliationist' wing of the I.L.P., which stayed in the Labour Party in 1932 when the majority, led by Maxton, q.v., broke away. First Chairman (1932–3) of the Socialist League. In the last years of his life he had a love affair with Jennie Lee, q.v.

4 G. M. Gillett, later Sir George (1870–1939). Parliamentary Secretary for Overseas Trade 1929–31. Labour M.P. for Finsbury 1923–31; National Labour 1931–5. Served briefly as a junior minister in the first National Government in 1931. Commissioner for the Special Areas 1936–9.

teachers' organisation. But Trevelyan can't, or won't, put up a decent case in the Cabinet. Denman,[1] who is working very hard on this, saw the P.M. alone one night this week. The P.M. said he didn't think there was time for the Bill this session; that it wasn't really practicable to raise the age by April 1931, as the Bill proposed; that he had met a lady – some painted social woman I suppose, like Mrs George Keppel in the old Capital Levy story![2] – who was a member of the Kent Education Committee, and had told him so; that it wouldn't make more than about 20,000 difference to unemployment – (he'd forgotten a nought!) – that he had met a business man who had said that, if he couldn't get boys of fourteen to employ, he wouldn't employ anyone, and that anyhow the Bill's effect on unemployment would be limited to the first year.

Perfectly ghastly!!!

He also told Denman, who suggested sitting until August to pass it, that this was utterly impossible, and that if Parliament didn't rise at the end of July, he and others would resign. A tired frightened snob, our great Prime Minister.

One despairs of politics in such days as these. Cotton goes from bad to worse. In Mossley, Lancs, 80 per cent of Gibson's[3] constituents are out of work. The total figures mount week by week, just when the seasonal decline should be operating.

The Cabinet is full of overworked men, growing older, more tired and more timid with each passing week. Pressure from below and from without is utterly ineffectual. High hopes are falling like last autumn's leaves. There is a whisper of spring in the air, but none in the political air. One funks the public platform, and one wishes we had never come in. We have forgotten our Programme, or been bamboozled out of it by the officials. One almost longs for an early and crushing defeat.

1 R. D. Denman, later Sir Richard, 1st Bart (1876–1957). Labour M.P. for Central Leeds 1929–31; National Labour 1931–45. Liberal M.P. for Carlisle 1910–18.
2 Mrs George Keppel, née Alice Edmonstone (d. 1947). A Society hostess and friend of Royalty. Dalton told 'the old Capital Levy story' in his memoirs (CBY, pp. 143–4), based on his diary entry for 8th December 1923. After the 1923 election, MacDonald was travelling to London where he was shortly to become Labour's first-ever Prime Minister. Dalton happened to be in the same compartment, having failed to win Cardiff East. In the course of the journey, the Party Leader informed the young candidate that the Capital Levy had lost Labour fifty seats. His evidence was the remark of a certain lady, who had told him that she agreed with all Labour's policy except the Capital Levy. 'A pause … "You would be interested if I told you who that lady was", said MacDonald … A long silence … At last he says, "It was the Honourable Mrs George Keppel." '
3 H. M. Gibson (1896–1954). Labour M.P. for Mossley 1929–31.

Sunday 9th March

... I recall, as a tiny grain of comfort, that last August I enumerated all our efforts at the Foreign Office and nothing done, and was on the point of resigning – at least I thought I was – and then the ice broke and we *did* them all. So may it be again!

Ruth is forty years old today. There is, at any rate, a fine perfection in my *private* life! We may be able to retire to the Lodge soon! or go together to Marrakesh.

Lunch with John Strachey, who always just fails to be interesting, and a young woman, secretary to Lloyd George and living with Strachey, whose wife is in America ...

Bob Fraser acting as leader writer on the *Daily Herald* on proposal of Laski to Mellor.[1] A hopeful adventure for him. But Ruth finds him rather heavy and humourless this evening. He comes to discuss his plans with us.

Tuesday 11th March

Government defeated by 8 votes on amendment to Coal Bill to strike out levy for export. Great excitement. All Liberals present vote against us, even Mander. Three ministers unaccounted for – Greenwood who was attending an official dinner – Trevelyan who was dining at home and whose division bell failed to ring for the first time in twenty years, and Craigie Aitchison,[2] who, it is said, was lying drunk at his hotel, not an uncommon condition. Earlier we were in danger of defeat, on a vital amendment, but had a majority of 30. This defeat is not vital, but it is an awkward knock. It will, however, emphasise the fact that we're a minority government to our supporters. Liberals sat, looking glum, while first the Tories and then our crowd rose and cheered and waved order papers. Fists were shaken at the Liberals from our benches, and insults shouted. Some of them went to Mac-Donald afterwards and explained that they only did [it] because it wasn't an essential amendment and Isaac Foot[3] told Graham that night and Mander told me next day, that on any *vital* vote at least a dozen of them would always at least abstain and some perhaps vote with us.

1 William Mellor (1888–1942). Editor of the *Daily Herald* 1926–31. Later Chairman of the Socialist League, and first editor of *Tribune*.
2 Craigie Aitchison, later 1st Baron (1882–1941). Lord Advocate for Scotland 1929–33. Labour M.P. for Kilmarnock 1929–31; National Labour 1931–3.
3 Isaac Foot (1880–1960). Liberal M.P. for Bodmin 1922–4, 1929–35. Backed Mac-Donald in 1931, and served for a year as Parliamentary Secretary at the Mines Department. Father of Michael Foot, q.v., and Dingle Foot, q.v.

Wednesday 12th March
Thomas addresses a Party Meeting and says that he's only carrying out the policy of the Cabinet. The Party Meeting is an unorganised rabble and he gets away with it. Rumour in Fleet Street that Lord Oswald has resigned. But Lansbury says he had dissuaded him.

Thursday 13th March
Johnston to lunch. Always very refreshing. Thinks Lord Oswald is on the point of resignation. But Lansbury and Johnston are both doing good work, apart from Unemployment, while Lord Oswald has nothing else.

An all-party conference on electoral reform had been set up in December 1929, presided over by Lord Ullswater, a former Speaker. The Liberals wanted proportional representation, but neither the Conservatives nor Labour would accept this. Hence the conference ended in July 1930 without agreement.

Tuesday 18th March
Uncle sees Lloyd George twice. Our inner Cabinet meets. Liberals will abstain on Thursday on Coal – nominally because there is a Naval Conference on. Electoral Reform Pact in the air. Uncle leans towards Alternative Vote. This is very ticklish. I think we should only agree to this – and in no case, or in any degree, to Proportional Representation – if we abolish the business and university votes in the same Bill, and also limit the use of cars. A real Reform Bill that the Lords would throw out twice. The idea of another two years of this Parliament fills me with mixed feelings. I should like another two years at the Foreign Office. And no doubt a certain amount of solid stuff would be put through the legislative machine. But what will the state of the Party be at the end? And the state of public opinion?

Wednesday 19th March
Uncle speaks frankly about Buxton. He can't see a successor. I praise Addison. He disagrees and thinks he has no drive. He is averse to losing North Norfolk, even to get rid of Buxton. MacDonald asked Buxton whether he would go to Australia as Governor-General. Buxton thought it over very carefully and discussed it with his wife and finally said Yes. Now MacDonald has told Uncle, who asked whether he realised that this would mean the loss of a by-election, that he hadn't. And now poor Buxton doesn't know where he is!

Thursday 20th March
Colonel Mitford,[1] Ovey's Private Secretary and Honorary Attaché, blew in today. No night life in Moscow, he says. A great crush at all theatres, etc. The Mission is living under 'active service conditions' in a hotel, largely, I gather, on imports from Fortnum and Mason. He is informed of the Five Year Plan. The Russians will certainly make good. The stunt about religious persecution is all moonshine. The priests whom he sees all look fat. They have shut up a lot of churches, of course. But no one ever went to them, except a handful of old people. Weren't a lot of City churches shut up a few years ago? There are no brothels, nor venereal disease – fucking not being morally prohibited and marriage easily contracted and dissolved – and illiteracy is being rapidly wiped out. The Embassy are a united party, except for Patrick[2] who is a bit of a diehard. Mitford ought to run about the West End talking this stuff. It's grand!

Friday 21st March
Vansittart tells me that he wanted all along to make a political formula for the French and to tackle Baldwin, who he thinks would have agreed. A member of the Cabinet, either Wedgwood Benn (silly little chirpy cipher) or King Albert, I fancy – told him that the country wouldn't stand it. All rot. I suspect that Hankey has been active over all this, pulling towards militarist isolation.

Vansittart fears a period of Anglo-French recriminations and, incidentally, the League rendered unworkable. Of the Great Powers, only France, he says, besides ourselves, is really devoted to the status quo in Europe. All the rest have ambitions inconsistent with this, which may cause trouble. Vansittart is a sound fellow but not strong in action.

Monday 24th March
Jebb tells me that Hugessen,[3] who kissed hands on appointment to Riga, reported that the King had heard that Mitford had been telling everyone at St James's Club that the Bolsheviks were very good fellows. The King was displeased at this, and would have preferred more impartiality. I wonder whether he would have taken the same objection to a good word for the Germans or Danes. Good old Mitford!

1 Lt-Col. W. B. J. Osbaldeston-Mitford (1877–1955). Honorary Attaché, British Embassy in Moscow 1930–31.
2 C. M. Patrick (1893–1942). Diplomat. First Secretary in Moscow 1930. Conservative M.P. 1931–42.
3 H. M. Knatchbull-Hugessen, later Sir Hugh (1886–1971). Minister to the Baltic States 1930–34.

Megan Lloyd George[1] is a very simple little thing. She told Ellen [Wilkinson], after the last Liberal Party Meeting, that 'they were all perfectly horrid to Dadda. They said they wouldn't turn the Government out. And Dadda was frightfully upset about it.' So he discovered the Naval Conference!

The Naval Conference is showing more hopefulness. Foreign Office officials working hard at a formula which shall satisfy the French. Phil was suddenly rung up by the P.M. after a silence of four weeks at his house at 9 a.m. this morning. But he was away at Coventry, having hung about vainly for four weekends on the chance he might be wanted. The P.M., he says, always rings up himself, doesn't give his name, but only says, 'I want to speak to Mr Noel-Baker. It's very important.' All day since, the P.M. has said nothing, and has passed Phil uncomprehendingly in the Lobby. A queer man!

Uncle is now willing to try to satisfy the French, but the P.M. is still very nervous about it.

Sunday 30th March
Ruth in the North. Dine with Lionel and Iris [Robbins] and Colin Clark.[2] They think trade will begin to improve this summer.

Tuesday 8th April
Dine with Egyptian Delegation at Hyde Park Hotel. Ruth, in a new dress, looking very pet and talking confidently good French, Uncle and Aunt, Vansittart and Loraine ... Very cheerful evening and excellent dinner. Ruth says Loraine was rather pained at hearty loud laughter of Uncle and me.

On 22nd April 1930, the United States, Britain and Japan signed the Three Power Treaty, limiting naval strengths to an agreed ratio and accepting a 'battleship holiday'.

Sunday 13th April
The Naval Conference was, for all practical purposes, wound up this

1 Megan Lloyd George, later Lady Megan (1902–66). Liberal M.P. for Anglesey 1929–51; Labour M.P. for Carmarthen 1957–66. Daughter of David Lloyd George, q.v.
2 Colin Clark (b. 1905). Economist. Member of the staff of the Economic Advisory Council 1930–31.

week. The Three Power Pact is a reality; the surviving elements of the Five Power are mere window dressing. The search for a formula of security has been fruitless, and the isolationist anti-covenant crowd has made very ugly showing. We must let this wind die down, or it may blow us to shipwreck. The battleship holiday till 1935 is a good thing in a small way. I can't see this holiday ever being broken, unless there is a sharp turn for the worse in the international situation. But we should have got down to 10:10:6, instead of only to 15:15:9. We have, however, 'carried the Board of Admiralty with us', and that, some timid people think, is the greatest achievement of all.

In short, we have succeeded, in 1930, after tremendous labour, in doing what the Tories failed, with no preparation at all, to do in 1927. But, in spite of that tremendous labour, we have failed to do more. The Peace Pact avails little as yet, to diminish, or even to check, the growth of Navies. But to finish with this wearisome and often mishandled affair lifts a weight from my mind, and I feel unexpectedly lighthearted, though tired.

The Egyptian negotiations stuck badly this last week, especially on the Suez Canal (Art. 9) and the Sudan (Art. 13). But Uncle is a far better and subtler diplomat than the Foreign Office officials. Astonishing, but undoubted. They wanted him to bludgeon the Egyptians all the time, even on secondary points, but he was firmly, or even sometimes jovially, conciliatory all the way. He is making a big effort to settle before Easter. Yesterday he was to see Nahas[1] in the evening. Today he and the delegation have been down to Parmoor's house in the country. Tomorrow Makram[2] is lunching with me alone before the Budget. I think we shall pull this off.

I was outside the cage in the Naval Conference, but I am inside with Egypt, and this makes all the difference. I feel the truth of Mallet's[3] saying 'optimism was the prevailing attitude of everybody in the War who was doing something, and pessimism the prevailing attitude of everybody who watched what was being done'. And not in the war only.

My natural impatience is irked by delays.

---

1 Nahas Pasha (1876–1965). Prime Minister of Egypt 1928, 1930, 1936–7, 1942–4, 1950–52. Leading member of the Wafd Party.
2 Makram Ebeid. Egyptian Minister of Finance under Nahas Pasha in 1930, and again in 1946. Leading member of the Wafd Party.
3 Sir Charles Mallet (1862–1947). Barrister and historian. Liberal M.P. 1906–10. Junior minister 1910–11. The quotation is from *Mr Lloyd George: A Study*, Benn, London, 1930, p. 106. Mallet had been discussing the view that Lloyd George's attitude changed from 'pessimistic criticism' to the 'utmost optimism' as soon he became Prime Minister in 1917.

In August 1929 the Cabinet had accepted Henderson's proposals, based on negotiations with the Egyptian Prime Minister, Mahmud Pasha, for the withdrawal of British troops in Egypt to the immediate vicinity of the Suez Canal, while keeping the Sudan under Anglo–Egyptian (which meant, in reality, British) control. Sir John Maffey, Governor-General of the Sudan, had supported the possibility of an Egyptian battalion in the Sudan not on 'progressive' grounds but because, as he put it to the King's Secretary, 'Egypt's share in the condominium is, in actual fact, purely nominal, and its only outward and visible sign will be this one Battalion, which from a Military point of view will be quite innocuous.' In the elections of December 1929, however, Mahmud was swept from power and replaced as Prime Minister by Nahas Pasha, leader of the Wafd, who were dissatisfied with the Mahmud–Henderson proposals. Nahas and several colleagues therefore came to London, and new talks began on 31st March 1930. Despite strenuous efforts by Henderson to reach a compromise, the British were not prepared to make concessions on the issue of control over the Sudan, and so no agreement was reached. Nevertheless Anglo-Egyptian relations seem to have been improved by these meetings.[1]

Monday 14th April
We end in a late sitting with the Egyptians ...

Loraine and Vansittart both seemed terrified of success. Loraine wanted to raise a new point, who was to command the troops in the Canal Zone? Shouldn't it be made clear that they were to be under British command? The whole thing is a fetish. We don't defend the straits of Dover by posting infantry permanently along the Kent coast. And, if there was a serious war, probably all Australian ships would come to British ports through the Panama Canal, which is a shorter route. The real truth that we keep troops in Egypt and in future in the Canal Zone, as a source of supply for the whole of the Middle East, is never, of course, told to the Egyptians and Tom Shaw seems only half to realise it, though Thomson[2] and the generals do. But, even on this basis, Cyprus would be pleasanter and equally effective, and as Passfield in a famous despatch has refused to return this island to Greece it would be as well to make some use of it.

Uncle is conscious of the attitude of Loraine and Vansittart. 'They

---

1 See Carlton, *MacDonald versus Henderson*, pp. 170–73.
2 C. B. Thomson, 1st Baron (1875–1930). Secretary of State for Air 1924, 1929–30.

1 Cambridge by-election candidate, March 1922

2 Ruth at Frogmore, 1914

3 Helen, *c.* 1920

all want wakening up,' he says to me afterwards. 'They're all right so long as they're doing their routine. But they're lost when they get taken outside it.'

Once in the small hours of the 15th he shouts angrily at Loraine in front of all our own crowd. It is Art. 13 (the Sudan) and Loraine wants Maffey[1] to be consulted and his consent obtained to a certain formula, before the point is even mentioned to the Cabinet. Maffey, who began last summer by being very progressive and recommending us to promise to have an Egyptian battalion back in the Sudan after the ratification of the Treaty if this concession would purchase peace, had his tail severely trodden on by his Council in the Sudan. Now he is terrified of any suspicion of change or 'unsettlement', if the latter could be prevented. His Council is wildly diehard and remote. And Loraine talks of him as if he were a Mussolini, or a Jesus Christ, which is irritating at times. He is, after all, only a civil servant, not a civil master. Entitled to be heard, but not necessarily to be obeyed.

Wednesday 16th April
We all dine by long prearrangement at the Egyptian Legation. Ruth sits between Thomas and Hankey, who *tutoient* one another across her all through dinner. Hankey explains how all Prime Ministers and Cabinets are really very much the same, though they think they're so different. Also how at present we have absolute 'security' which would vanish with the Channel tunnel. Ruth says something about an air attack, but that is 'quite different from having your country occupied by troops'.

Thursday 1st May
Foreign Office dinner to Schober,[2] Austrian Chancellor, who makes a good impression. I have a talk in a corner with Sir Richard Hopkins,[3] once of the Inland Revenue and now at the Treasury, who says that today's reduction of Bank Rate to 3 per cent is possible, because

---

1 J. L. Maffey, later 1st Baron Rugby (1877–1969). Governor-General of the Sudan 1926–33. Permanent Under-Secretary of State for the Colonies 1933–7.
2 Johannes Schober (1874–1932). Chancellor of Austria 1921–2, 1929–September 1930. Leader of the *Nationalen Wirtschaftsblocks* in the *Nationalrat* 1930–32. Vice-Chancellor and Foreign Minister 1932.
3 Sir Richard Hopkins (1880–1955). Controller of Finance and Supply Services at the Treasury 1927–32. Chairman of the Inland Revenue 1922–7. Permanent Secretary at the Treasury 1942–5.

Norman[1] has squared the French and Americans at Basle where the Bank for International Settlements has just been born. Moreau,[2] the Frenchman, is the great obstacle to intelligent international co-operation in monetary policy. He is quite ignorant of modern ideas, full of national prejudice and personally difficult. If, however, we can keep the Bank Rate down to 3 per cent for the next twelve months, Hopkins thinks we shall see a big fall in unemployment. The slight reductions in the past three weeks may well make a real turn in the tide. Such an opinion from such a source is very interesting and encouraging.

After the dinner, go out to a party, with classical music, at the Austrian Legation. But it goes on too long and I'm not in bed till 2 a.m. on

Friday 2nd May
Thus do diplomats sit up doing nothing in particular. Schober comes to see Uncle at 11 a.m. Franckenstein[3] and I are also present. Uncle asks whether internal situation in Austria is steady, and mentions that he knows Austrian Socialist leaders very well and that Bauer[4] in particular is a very able man. Schober is optimistic. He will be able, he says, to prevent all serious trouble and to bring about disarmament. His visit to Rome was a great success, and has brought about distinct improvements in South Tyrol. He has warned the Heimwehr leaders[5] that he will not tolerate disorders. The Socialists, though they oppose him publicly, admit to him in private that in some things they have gone too far, and that though they must put up a show of public indignation, they realise that certain changes must be made.

Leave for Durham in the evening for May Day demonstrations. All Durham Labour M.P.s, except the P.M., on the train.

---

1 Montagu Norman, later 1st Baron (1871–1950). Governor of the Bank of England 1920–44.
2 E. Moreau (1868–1941). Governor of the Banque de France 1926–30.
3 G. Franckenstein, later Sir George (1878–1953). Austrian Envoy Extraordinary and Minister Plenipotentiary 1920–38. In 1938 he became a naturalised British subject.
4 Otto Bauer (1881–1938). Austrian Socialist leader. Served in the *Nationalrat* until 1933, when he was forced into exile, eventually living in Paris.
5 The Austrian Heimwehr was a right-wing movement led by Ernst Rüdinger, Prince von Starhemberg. It grew rapidly between 1927 and 1933, when the authoritarian regime of Dr Dollfuss was established with Heimwehr backing. On 18th May 1930, a couple of weeks after Dalton's meeting with Schober, the Heimwehr issued a programme that became known as 'the Korenburg Oath', a mixture of nationalist, pan-German and fascist ideas.

Wednesday 7th May

There have been strained nerves and tempers these last few days. Uncle has shouted at Van[1] and Loraine in front of our side of the circus and has said to me several times that 'these officials don't seem to want a settlement. They do nothing but raise difficulties. They have no elasticity of mind.' Loraine took me aside and said that no suggestion which he had made from start to finish had seemed to be welcome, and that he gathered that the Secretary of State did not value his advice nor desire his presence. I assured him, as best I could, that this wasn't so, and that we all had our heads bitten off at times, that Uncle had many fine qualities, but that superficial politeness was not one of them; that it was a great strain on him and on all of us, etc. I asked Uncle to try to be nice to Loraine. He tried, but not very successfully in these dim, long, small hours. He said, 'There's poor Van going about like a bear with a sore head, because I spoke rather sharply to him. He'd make a fine Tory politician, but he's an awfully nice chap.' ...

Later a heart to heart talk with Van. What a nice fellow! I spoke of the roughness of Uncle to Loraine and himself, and said I hoped he hadn't taken it too seriously. He said that many conferences he had attended had been much tougher on the British side. Lloyd George had once thrown some figures back at him and practically called him a liar. Then he *had* protested. And Curzon had always been awful. Nursing grievances for days and weeks. Loraine was too thin skinned. He had urged him several times to assert himself more. But it would all blow over. If he still had Uncle's confidence, all was well. It was his duty to indicate difficulties jealously, and stand the racket. I said, 'Yes, you have his confidence, though Lindsay hadn't.' Willert afterwards said that Van should have sat next to the Secretary of State and not far down the table. This would have saved half the personal trouble.

Monday 12th May

Taking P.Q.s. Fear of adjournment being moved on us over *Daily Worker* article of last Thursday, congratulating Indian Regiment on having mutinied and urging British Regiments to do the same. Fortunately India has been quiet over the weekend. If there had been news of blood and rape the whole House would have been in wild turmoil. We prepare a delaying answer 'not yet in a position to announce the decision of H.M.G. in regard thereto.' It goes off very quietly. In a

---

1 'Van': Sir Robert Vansittart, q.v.

supplementary to Smithers[1] I say, 'This is clearly a serious matter and I think it would be best to leave it there for the moment.' The House had been very 'uppety' earlier on about nothing at all, the number of copies of the League Committee Report on Pact and Covenant in the Library, etc. The critical question came later, and the Tories had exhausted their energies.

I talk to Jowitt about the possibility of a prosecution. And later Van and I have a further talk with him. The memory of the Campbell case[2] is vivid. I feel that there should be nothing that could be called 'consultations' with politicians by Law Officers, or we shall be in difficulties answering P.Q.s. Jowitt thinks we should be sure of a conviction on the article. The Home Office officials are inclined to favour a prosecution; so is Van; so, a little less strongly, am I, though both Van and I make it a condition that we should be reasonably certain of winning. The Home Office have suggested an immediate conference of Cabinet Ministers with the Attorney-General. Van and I have objected to this, since Uncle can't be there. Jowitt objects to it on principle, since it would compromise his position. It is finally agreed between the three of us that he shall speak to the P.M. tonight and if, as we anticipate, the P.M. tells him that it is his responsibility, that clears Uncle along with the rest.

Later Jowitt tells me that the P.M. was very much worried at the incident, didn't much like the idea of prosecuting, thought it was all terribly like history repeating itself. (Wraiths of Campbell in the night sky!) But finally told Jowitt to do what he thought best. He will sleep on it.

This same evening I have talked to Arnold about Electoral Reform. The Liberals, he says, now won't look at A.V. [Alternative Vote], but stick out for P.R. We agree that no agreement is possible if this mood persists. Arnold saw Lloyd George a few days ago.

Later I have a word with Mander. *He* is indignant with Lloyd George. He realises that P.R. is out of the question for us, though he

1 W. Smithers, later Sir Waldron (1880–1954). Conservative M.P. for Chislehurst 1924–45; Orpington 1945–54.
2 'The Campbell case': in August 1924, J. R. Campbell, acting editor of the Communist *Workers' Weekly*, was arrested and charged under the Incitement to Mutiny Act 1797 for writing an article which urged soldiers not to fire on their fellow-workers. The Attorney-General told the House that charges would be pressed; but after Parliament adjourned, the case was withdrawn. In September 1924, the Conservatives tabled a motion of censure, and the Liberals proposed an amendment calling for a Select Committee of Inquiry. MacDonald insisted on making the issue a matter of confidence, lost the crucial vote, and lost the election that followed. (See C. L. Mowat, *Britain Between the Wars*, Methuen, London, 1955, pp. 184–6.)

would like it on merits. He, and a number of other Liberals he says, would gladly agree on A.V., plus all other obvious democratic reforms, plus three years of solid work in legislation and administration before a general election. He says Lloyd George has no authority from the Party to take this line. There has been no discussion of this question at a Party Meeting. He can only suppose that Lloyd George has been listening to a three-hour lecture from Ramsay Muir.

Tuesday 13th May
Tom Johnston tells me a few things. The three authors of the memorandum (he, Lansbury and Mosley) saw tonight the P.M. and Thomas.[1] The P.M. said they had before them a proposal from Snowden's Cabinet Committee (which had sat on the memorandum and turned it down – Snowden, Shaw, Bondfield and Green), to refer the Retiring Pensions Scheme to the Cabinet Committee, which is 'surveying the whole field' of pensions (etc.), the 'survey committee' as it is called. Whereupon Johnston asked the P.M. whether he was unaware that this Committee hadn't met since 29th October 1929. Sensation! P.M. nearly in tears. Who *was* the chairman? Clynes. Who else was on it? Thomas, Bondfield. He will raise this at tomorrow's Cabinet. He has been let down. (And so he has and badly too.) Johnston also informs me that the Unemployment Committee, Thomas and the three authors, has only met once this year. When they sent in the memorandum, he, Johnston, sent a covering note to the P.M. proposing that this Unemployment Committee should now be dissolved on paper, as it had long been dissolved in fact. 'If the Party Meeting only got to know of a few things like this', he said to me, 'they [would] all be climbing up the walls! It wouldn't be just Buchanan[2] and Campbell Stephen, it would be the soberest trade unionists in the Party.' Meanwhile Thomas says that we can do nothing; we are in the hands of Providence; in America they have 5 million unemployed, while we have only 1¾ million!

---

1 In fact, the other two advisory ministers on unemployment, Lansbury and Johnston, were not co-authors of the memorandum, though they supported its conclusions. A Cabinet Committee headed by MacDonald, and including Morrison, Thomas, Greenwood and Margaret Bondfield, interviewed Mosley, Lansbury and Johnston on 19th May. Mosley demanded £200 million for a programme of public works to provide 300,000 jobs. Discouraged, and determined to put the issue to the Party, Mosley handed his resignation to the Prime Minister at lunchtime on 20th May. (See R. Skidelsky, *Oswald Mosley*, Macmillan, London, 1975, pp. 206–10, and below, entry for 20th May.)
2 George Buchanan (1890–1955). Labour M.P. for Glasgow Gorbals 1922–48. I.L.P. Clydesider. Junior minister 1945–7; Minister of Pensions 1947–8.

The death of Wheatley[1] will make some difference to the Left I think. They will be like sheep without a shepherd.

Wednesday 14th May

A late sitting on Mental Treatment Bill till 4.30 a.m. 22 Foreign Office questions to answer. The House is soon a bear garden. Tories yelling with passion and some response from our side. It is said by some that I am 'provocative', by others that I adopt a 'superior tone'. I insti-gated, in the small hours of this morning, some supplementaries. When young Gibson, of Mossley, rose to put one of these, immediately after Austen Chamberlain had put a supplementary, which I was about to answer, the Tories started to yell 'Answer, Answer!' I said, 'If honourable members opposite will show a little courtesy, I am quite prepared to answer the right honourable gentleman's question. But I am not prepared for my honourable friend behind me to be howled down.' Then the row started and grew and continued through-out my oration. And perhaps I *might* have gone out to meet trouble a little less than half way! Alexander, next to me, whispered to me afterwards that he thought I had trailed my coat a bit too much, that, of course, our own people liked it, but that it lowered one's personal status in the House. And some of our tamer back-benchers thought, I heard, that I had been ill-advised and had asked for trouble. The placards, as I left the House a little later, had 'Uproar in the Commons' but it was really Red Ellen [Wilkinson] who made me do it. For, precisely today, she had a Bo-peep sketch of me, uncannily full of insight, in the *Evening Standard* and I had to live up to it!

Thursday 15th May

Yesterday's strong breeze hasn't quite died down! Our Party, on the whole, very pleased with me. Tories very angry. I had a late Question to answer today, and on rising was greeted with a prolonged demon-stration from both sides of the House, 'ironical' from the other sides, approving from our own.

Friday 16th May

Electoral Reform. Susan Lawrence has heard that the Tories and Liberals are now tending towards an agreement in favour of Pro-portional Representation in the boroughs and compact counties, and Alternative Vote in the scattered counties, and that A.V. all over the country is dead. This means, if true, no electoral reform in this Parliament and an earlier general election. But it will force our hands.

1 John Wheatley, q.v., had died on 12th May.

My splash of publicity continues. The *Evening Standard* Londoner's Diary (Harold Nicolson) on the whole takes my side. But Jebb hears from Nicolson that it took my side even more decisively before the Editor cut it about.

Monday 19th May

Tory demonstration at Questions in favour of Uncle and against me is a bit of a fizzle. The thing has pretty well blown over as a Parliamentary incident, and in spite of my semi-misgivings of having gone too far, I find the most unexpected people in strong support. MacNeill Weir[1] has written, he says, in praise of me in *Forward*. The Tories, he says, are angry, because they're afraid of me and realise that my answers are not only sarcastic but also well informed. And was it by chance that the P.M. smiled at me twice and spoke to me once? (MacNeill Weir is his P.P.S.!) This has hardly ever happened before.

Tuesday 20th May

9.30 a.m. National Executive on Electoral Reform. Arnold and the rest of our Ullswater Committee team present. No support from anyone for P.R. either total or partial. Arnold inclined to favour the offer of A.V. on condition we can get all our other democratic reforms accepted, and a good list of these is put in: reduction of election expenses; prohibition of expenditure by political parties outside election expenses; publication of political parties' accounts, nationally and locally; prohibition of use of cars on polling day, except under regulations laid down by Returning Officer for infirm, sick and disabled; abolition of all plural voting and repeal of business premises and University qualification for franchise, etc.

In ensuing discussion the P.M., Morrison and I speak in favour of this course. Lansbury, Compton,[2] Mrs Gould[3] and Susan against. Uncle, very unfortunately, has to go out to Buckingham Palace while the critical stages of the discussion and vote are being taken. So he doesn't speak. Decided by 11 votes to 6 that our representatives should only put up the above mentioned list of electoral reforms, and nothing on A.V. Of the team, Marion Phillips is in favour of this and E.N. Bennett against – a talkative and unatmospheric fool – audibly and

1 L. MacNeill Weir (1877–1939). P.P.S. to MacDonald as Prime Minister 1924, 1929–31. Labour M.P. for Clackmannan and Stirlingshire East 1922–31, 1935–9. Journalist. Weir later wrote a vituperative biography of his former master (*The Tragedy of Ramsay MacDonald*, 1938).
2 Joseph Compton (1881–1937). Labour M.P. for Manchester Gorton 1923–31, 1935–7.
3 Barbara Ayrton Gould (d. 1950). Member of the Labour Party N.E.C. (Women's Section). Chairman 1939–40. Labour M.P. 1945–50.

visibly half a Liberal who, by his continual intervention, creates suspicion against himself.[1] Those who voted in the majority feared a depressing effect on the psychology of our supporters, both immediately under the belief that we had made a bargain with the Liberals (grist to the Left Wing mill!) and more permanently in inclining us so to speak and act as to appeal for Liberal Second Preferences. There is weight in these arguments. On the other side, a possibility presents itself of prolonging this Parliament for another $2\frac{1}{2}$ years, i.e. till 1933, of outstaying the trade depression, getting through a good block of social legislation, consolidating peace, effecting some real disarmament and getting through the real Electoral Reform, by either coming back with a clear majority of our own, or at least keeping out the Tories for a generation. This possibility attracted me strongly. And I don't think today's vote has settled the question.

Gillies tells me that Breitscheid[2] told him that Harold Nicolson told *him* in Berlin that he hoped to stand as a Labour candidate at the next election. And Breitscheid added that in the German Socialist Party they would never tolerate such a thing. They would require service in the Party for a period of years first. Gillies, rather sore and jealous, poor little object, and indignant because *he* has been barred from standing, is strongly in agreement with Breitscheid. I am more interested in the news item!

Tonight Lord Oswald has resigned from the Government. I understand that he goes alone. Lansbury tells Uncle that he disapproves of this action, and that the P.M. has done his best to settle the points in dispute between Thomas, and the three authors. Cynthia[3] told Rennie Smith last night that Lord Oswald was going, that for the fourth time running he had not been allowed to speak in an unemployment debate. (Thomas and Lansbury spoke last night.)

The sequel to this resignation will be very interesting. Will Lord Oswald show judgment? He has a very difficult game to play. Rumour is that he will try to form, and lead, an inside Left ginger group, appealing especially to some of the younger members who are not associated with the present Left Wing group. All the resources of

1 E. N. Bennett, q.v., backed MacDonald in the 1931 crisis, and was rewarded with the post of Assistant Postmaster-General 1932–5.

2 Rudolf Breitscheid (1874–1944). Leading German Social Democrat. Minister of Interior in the First Revolutionary Government in Prussia in 1918. He fled to France when Hitler came to power. He was handed over to the Gestapo by the Vichy regime, and died in Buchenwald concentration camp.

3 Lady Cynthia Mosley (1898–1933). Labour M.P. for Stoke 1929–31. Daughter of Lord Curzon, q.v., and married to Sir Oswald Mosley. She followed her husband into the New Party in 1931.

wealth, flattery, intrigue, proximity of his dwelling to the House, and his wife's beauty to be brought into play. Touch to be kept with Keynes and McKenna,[1] etc.

But it will be very difficult for him to steer quite clear of the Sore-headed Left, who are greatly hated by most of the rest of the Party. And many will say, 'Why couldn't he play in the team?'

And he has antagonised, one supposes, at least nearly all the leaders.

Wednesday 21st May
Lord Oswald reads his letter of resignation to the P.M. first to the Party Meeting at 1.30 and then to the House at 4. In the Party Meeting he said that it was his duty first to announce this to his Parliamentary colleagues; he ended by giving notice of his intention to move a motion in the Party Meeting expressing dissatisfaction with the work of Government on unemployment and calling for bolder action in accord with the pledges given at the General Election. He was moderately, but not at all warmly, received. The meeting then went on, after Uncle had proposed another meeting tomorrow night to discuss rules and discipline, and became a bloody bear garden.

In the House in the afternoon, Lord Oswald stalked in towards the end of Questions, and took his seat in the corner seat of the third bench below the gangway, just below The Mountain,[2] not a very happily chosen position, though the traditional place of the resigning minister. A very quiet reception, neither jeers from over the way, nor cheers from our side. He again read his letter to the P.M. Some applause on our side, when he said he would remain a loyal member of the Party. Not much at the end.

Lobbies buzzing for the rest of the day. Lord Oswald has played his cards badly. His motion for tomorrow is a vote of censure on the Government. The Loyal Lump will rally against him. A loyal amendment is, indeed, being drafted in the Map Room. The Clyde Group, as it is still called, is ruining him, as I expected, by canvassing for his motion. Lansbury and Johnston are furious with him. He resigned without consultation. They say that they were just beginning to win on essentials. The P.M. had played a good part in the three meetings which they had with them and Thomas. Meanwhile this, coming on

1 Reginald McKenna (1863–1943). Liberal M.P. 1895–1918. Financial Secretary at the Treasury 1905. President of the Board of Education 1907–8; First Lord of the Admiralty 1908–11; Home Secretary 1911–15; Chancellor of the Exchequer 1915–16.
2 'The Mountain': a reference to the Clyde Group of I.L.P. M.P.s. 'The Mountain' was the name given to the extreme revolutionary party in the legislatures of the French Revolution.

top of the abstention of the 15,[1] and in the middle of the Nottingham by-election, looks very sinister.

There is talk of the election next week, and of an ultimatum tonight from Lloyd George based on our Executive decision on Electoral Reform. Uncle tells me that this is untrue. They had a long talk with Lloyd George tonight, and he was very much upset about Electoral Reform. But the ghost wasn't yet given up. If the Liberals would frankly accept all our proposals, some deal might still be possible.

Thursday 22nd May
In anticipation of tonight's Party Meeting, the Lobbies and Smoke Rooms are agog. Strachey and Aneurin Bevan are visibly active on behalf of Lord Oswald. Strachey wandered into the Map Room last night for the first time in his life. The minority is estimated at 30. Paling[2] thinks it may be as high as 40. Two days ago it was probably as high as 70, but the tide has set the other way. At 6.30 the Trade Union Group meets. I hear, just before 8, that they have decided to 'support the Government'. Bevan was vocal on behalf of Lord Oswald but Ebby Edwards[3] went for him and threatened to have this reported to the M.F.G.B. [Miners' Federation of Great Britain]. Ritson,[4] at one time a little under Lord Oswald's influence, says 'we've muzzled Bevan'. The Loyal Lump in action!

Committee Room 14 packed out at 8 p.m. Lord Oswald gives a long harangue which rather impresses the meeting. A parade of loyalty and no personalities. 'Not a general vote of censure on Government, but only a vote of censure on its unemployment policy.' This doesn't help very much. A great parade of statistics. Long term reorganisation. Imports Board. Loans for work-retiring pensioners. Raising school leaving age. All these last three to cost the Budget only £10m a year, and retiring pensions of £1 a week, plus 10/- for wife at sixty to cost only £2m a year. (Fantastic jugglery!) ... Present inequity between depressed and prosperous areas. (This passage much applauded.) Ends with a typical Mosley peroration about saving Government, and Party, and millions whom we represent. Considerable applause at the end. At one point, not quite sure of himself, refers to himself as 'a

---

1 'abstention of the 15': Dalton wrote in his diary on 19th May (in a passage not included here): 'Only a majority of 15 tonight on proposal to reduce J.H.T.'s salary. Liberals abstain, and also 15 of our Left Wing.'
2 Wilfrid Paling (1883–1971). Labour M.P. for Doncaster 1922–31; Wentworth 1933–50; Dearne Valley 1950–59. Junior minister 1941–5. Minister of Pensions 1945–7; Postmaster-General 1947–50.
3 Ebby Edwards (1884–1961). Labour M.P. for Morpeth 1929–31. Miner.
4 Joshua Ritson (1874–1955). Labour M.P. for Durham 1922–31, 1935–45. Miner.

newcomer and an outsider'. Then MacDonald. Not at all convincing
or effective. Then Hayday,[1] critical of Lord Oswald. What would be
thought in the Trade Union world of an Executive member who resigns
and then tries to turn membership against Executive. Then he moves
an amendment, encouraging the Government's policy, its executive
and administrative record, reaffirming that unemployment is in-
separable from capitalism, recognising that the present depression is
partly due to world causes, but urging a more vigorous policy. Bromley supports Lord Oswald in a speech of garrulous egotism. Rhys
Davies throws doubt on efficiency of offer of retiring pension of £1
a week at sixty. Thomas, half hysterical, speaks of 'we who built up
the movement on the soap box ...... and took on a job that I knew
would shatter my reputation ...... I have always been loyal to my
colleagues ...... I have always played in the team ...... the greatest
moment of humiliation in my life.'

Uncle at 10.30 rises to wind up. A difficult atmosphere, not very
friendly to the Government ... Congratulates all on high level of
discussion. Critical moment in history of Party. Bouquets for Lord
Oswald. He also has had to face resignation. Not true that principle
of retiring pensions has been abandoned. It couldn't be. We fought last
election on it. If it were to be suggested that this Government would
never, at any time or in any form, bring in such a scheme, there would
be at least one more resignation. (Mild sensation.) A vote tonight
would be disastrous whatever its results. Appeal to Lord Oswald and
Thurtle[2] to withdraw both resolution and amendment. Then a further
discussion on unemployment can follow at another Party Meeting.
Situation has changed. P.M. has been released from heavy work of
Naval Conference. He is now taking charge of unemployment discussion. Let us not give any comfort to our enemies. Let us do the big
thing. He is the oldest Labour Member here. Twenty-seven years ago
he entered the House. He has never made an appeal in all this time
more earnestly, or more conscious that he is right, than tonight.

Lord Oswald rises. He wishes to make a few observations. He
noticed that Uncle said retiring pension scheme was not abandoned.
But Snowden in his Report of Cabinet Sub-Committee had said that
'the Government should repudiate this scheme, and grandiose loan
plans'. Snowden who had sat silent all the evening, snaps, 'That's not
true.' Lord Oswald says, 'Then will you tell us what you did say?'

1 Arthur Hayday (1869–1956). Labour M.P. for Nottingham West 1918–31, 1935–45.
  Official of the National Union of General and Municipal Workers.
2 Ernest Thurtle (1884–1954). Junior government whip 1930–31. Labour M.P. for
  Shoreditch 1923–31, 1935–50; Shoreditch and Finsbury 1950–54. Junior minister
  1941–5.

'No,' snaps Snowden. Lord Oswald, very ruffled, then says that he has been appealed to by senior member[s?] of the Party to withdraw. He thinks a decision now would be more courageous than postponement. But he is seeking an accommodation and he will be willing to postpone a decision till after further discussion, and to move that the discussion be adjourned. Uncle jumps up and says that this is not what he meant. We must decide tonight. Lord Oswald says, if this is so, he must ask for a decision on his resolution tonight. An amazing blunder! He had the ball at his feet. He might have left the meeting a hero, the darling of the back-benchers, a moral victor. But his last words provoke a growl of surprise and indignation. One can feel votes turning away from him. There are shouts for a straight vote. (Thurtle withdraws his amendment.) On a vote Mosley gets 29 votes against 210. It is a crushing defeat.

The Left has sat all night, drilled and silent. Lord Oswald has so safeguarded himself, after much preparation clearly, from their direct embrace. But not many young men in the vote – Chuter Ede,[1] Haycock,[2] Morgan,[3] Seymour Cocks[4] and a few more.

And so we go forth at 10.45 with a passage thronged with waiting pressmen. Lord Oswald is the worst tactician of the age! 'Whom the Gods wish to destroy ...... ' A head swollen to the size of an elephant. Phil Noel-Baker ran away and did not vote. He is still very thick with Lord Oswald and Cynthia [Mosley]. Uncle cursed him roundly. Rennie Smith tells me afterwards that, while Uncle was making his appeal, Strachey and Bevan were in consultation with Lord Oswald. Lord Oswald said, 'How many can we count on?' 'Fifty,' said one of the minions. 'Then we'll go ahead,' said Lord Oswald.

Early today the Ullswater Committee met. All the Tories have come round to Proportional Representation as the least of evils. Our people talked and delayed a vote, till next Thursday.

And next Wednesday there will be another debate on unemployment. That night we may fall!

Wednesday 28th May
We didn't, however, though it was a humiliating day. We had a majority of 29 at the end.

---

1 James Chuter Ede, later Baron Chuter-Ede (1882–1965). Labour M.P. for South Shields 1929–31, 1935–64; Mitcham 1923. Junior minister 1940–45. Home Secretary 1945–51.
2 A. W. Haycock (1882–1970). Labour M.P. for Salford West 1923–4, 1929–31.
3 Dr H. B. W. Morgan (1885–1956). Labour M.P. for Camberwell North-West 1929–31; Rochdale 1940–50; Warrington 1950–55.
4 F. S. Cocks (1882–1953). Labour M.P. for Broxtowe 1929–53.

And on 24th May Ruth decided that we should call it 'West Leaze'.[1] This is local, legitimate and apt for the westering sun and senile memories at the hour of sunset!

Sunday 1st June
Colin Clark to dine. The Economic Advisory Committee has not yet begun to work.[2] All its proposed enquiries have been turned down. It wanted, for instance, to enquire into Free Trade as an immediate policy in Great Britain, but Snowden wouldn't have this. Nor would he agree to an enquiry into monetary policy, since the Macmillan Committee was sitting. Nor into the function of the state in relation to unemployment policy, which Keynes wanted – the businessmen have backed up Snowden. Keynes hurts the P.M.'s feelings by describing himself at one meeting as 'the only socialist present'. So Henderson has written a memorandum for the Cabinet Ministers deprecating very solemnly the idea that unemployment can be cured only by public expenditure, but proposing a 10 per cent import duty on all manufactured goods, the proceeds of which shall go half to national development and half to the unemployment insurance fund. This piece of folly is neither Free Trade, nor Liberalism, nor Practical Politics. I always doubted Hubert's positive side.

Colin is for an export duty on gold – a much more practicable proposition.

Hankey sent for him the other day, and said he wanted some material for a paper on unemployment he was writing for the Cabinet. It seemed to him that the French had no unemployment, because they worked longer hours for lower wages, and had fewer amusements (charabancs, etc.) and didn't give all these expensive social services which no one seemed to appreciate in this country. O Hankey how is thy head swollen and thine office grown too big for thee!

Another pretty little incident. Uncle wants a paper from the Cabinet on the General Act.[3] Howard Smith[4] told to preface it. His draft

1 The Daltons' new house near Aldbourne, Marlborough, Wiltshire.
2 'Economic Advisory Committee': in January 1930, the Prime Minister had announced the setting up of an Economic Advisory Council, with himself as chairman. Its staff of five included three economists: Hubert Henderson, Colin Clark and H. V. Hodson. The Council itself consisted of ministers, businessmen, trade union leaders and socialist intellectuals. See below, p. 123 and n. 1.
3 'the General Act': the General Act for the Pacific Settlement of International Disputes, which laid down procedures for settling 'non-justiciable disputes'. It was intended to complete the work begun with the signing of the Optional Clause. The Government obtained the agreement of the House of Commons to British accession in March 1931.
4 C. H. Smith (1888–1942). Diplomat.

begins with a quotation from *Labour and the Nation*. Very good discpline this. But Uncle cuts this paragraph out. 'It puts Them off', he said, 'to be told that anything is in *Labour and the Nation!*'

Shades of Them! Amended, this memorandum is passed by the Cabinet!

Saturday 7th to Sunday 15th June
At Aldbourne. Measuring on the site with Little Macmanus[1] and sunbathing.

Run into Beveridge, Mrs Mair, Postmaster-General[2] and his wife at Polly's[3] on the 14th. Walk to Avebury with Ruth on the 15th. Lees-Smith has relaxed the moral code at the Post Office. Hitherto if two employees of the Post Office are caught fucking, they have been dismissed. Now they are merely separated and transferred to other localities. 'You have reversed our traditional doctrine,' says Murray,[4] 'hitherto a Post Office employee could sleep with anyone, provided she wasn't also a Post Office employee.'

Wednesday 9th July
We only escape by 3 votes on Liberal amendment to Finance Bill exempting sums put to reserve from income tax. Liberals mostly voted against us, and were terribly upset, most of them, at having come so near to defeating us. Lloyd George had been in an intrigue with the Tories to put us out, and had told his Liberals that there was no danger of our being defeated ......

Later Lloyd George told MacDonald that he hadn't spoken to Baldwin for six weeks. (Liar!) He also told Hore-Belisha,[5] who passed it on to some of our disgruntled people, that he, Lloyd George, threw up his hands in despair over the Government and Unemployment. Whenever he suggested anything 'up jumped some scrubby-faced civil servant and said it couldn't be done. And that was always fatal.'

Lady Astor[6] had been tittle-tattling all round the lobbies about

1 Frederick Macmanus (b. 1903). Architect. Assistant to Sir Thomas Tait, designer of West Leaze.
2 H. B. Lees-Smith, q.v.
3 Polly's Tea Room in the High Street, Marlborough.
4 Sir Evelyn Murray (1880–1947). Secretary to the Post Office 1914–34.
5 I. L. Hore-Belisha, later 1st Baron (1893–1957). Liberal, then Liberal National, M.P. for Plymouth Devonport 1923–45. Financial Secretary to the Treasury 1932–4; Minister of Transport 1934–7; Secretary of State for War 1937–40; Minister of National Insurance 1945.
6 Nancy, Viscountess Astor (1879–1964). Conservative M.P. for Plymouth Sutton 1919–45. Married to Waldorf Astor, 2nd Viscount.

MacDonald and Lady Londonderry.[1] And Virginia Woolf[2] – with whom Ruth and I dined on 11th July – supported this, describing a dinner party she had been at, when MacDonald and Lady L. had withdrawn after dinner into a half-darkened room and sat together – the common herd being herded into another, more brightly lit chamber.

What easy social prey some of our people are! And how they are laughed at behind their backs, and ignored when they are out of office! And what would the loyal comrades say if they knew!

Lord Oswald, incidentally, is putting about the story that when he took MacDonald to dine at the best restaurants in Berlin and elsewhere, MacDonald always asked for the most expensive wines. No abuse is too caddish now.

...

Virginia Woolf quoted Beatrice Webb as having said to her, 'Marriage is the waste-paper basket of the emotions'.

Tuesday 15th July

Mander to see me in my room at the House. There was a row at the Liberal Party Meeting. The number who are determined not to be led into voting against the Government, except on some really grave matter, is steadily rising. It has gone up from 12 to about 20, nearly half the Party. Lloyd George said, 'I hear that a dozen of you are planning to form a separate group to support the Government. I advise you to do nothing of the kind. And, even if you did, there aren't enough of you to keep the Government in.' Mander thinks he is simply out to smash, but he has practically no funds left ... and the Liberals would have very few candidates if a general election came now. In other moods Lloyd George simply wants a Coalition – with anyone who will join up with him. An old man in a hurry, with the dusk falling. He will try next to break in on India.

Thursday 17th July

The state of the Party and the Cabinet is pretty bad. Party Meetings every day, and Cabinets and Committees almost every hour. Thank

1 Edith, Marchioness of Londonderry, née Hon. Edith Chaplin. Married to the 7th Marquess, a former Conservative M.P. and minister. After the formation of the National Government, MacDonald invited Lord Londonderry to serve under him as Secretary of State for Air 1931–5.
2 Virginia Woolf, née Stephen (1882–1941). Writer. Married to Leonard Woolf, who was Secretary of the Labour Party Advisory Committee on International Affairs. Like Dalton, Virginia Woolf had been a close friend of Rupert Brooke. She and Dalton were distant cousins.

the Lord the session is nearly over. Everyone is tired and helpless and angry.

Hubert Henderson says unemployment should reach its peak, well above 2 million, about November and thereafter gradually decline. And there will be a realised deficit, owing to unemployment charges, in this year's Budget and a still larger prospective deficit next year! If we can ride out this economic storm, and stay in for two or three years, the situation, as to unemployment, might improve substantially. Otherwise we shall have a shattering defeat.

Following the report of the Simon Commission on India in June 1930, it was decided to hold a Round Table Conference in London in November, at which the British and the Indians should discuss the future of the subcontinent. Although Congress boycotted the Conference, the Indian princes attended and agreed on an all-Indian federation of states, which led the British government, in turn, to seek new consultations with the Indians in order to frame a constitution. A second Round Table Conference was arranged for the autumn of 1931.

Tuesday 29th July
Uncle went four days ago to Champneys, Tring, to do a three weeks' course of orange cure and irrigation. No solid food, only oranges. And 16 gallons of water a day. Some, I think, must be squirted up from behind.

Meanwhile, today is Foreign Office vote. Egypt and Russia. MacDonald takes Egypt, following one of Winston's reckless rants ... I wind up on Russia and oddments. It is thought by all, including the Tories and Foreign Office officials, that I did well. Courtesy, light handedness, etc. The sense of contrast! *But in the House one grows muddly-mouthed and muddly-minded.* As Belloc[1] said to me long ago, 'A man can no more make a good speech in such a place than sing a good song in it!' The session drags to a weary end. All are tired, ragged, disappointed ...

Right at the end of the session there was a scare of a government defeat on India – Lloyd George and the Tories combining to press Simon into the Round Table Conference. A general election in

1 Hilaire Belloc (1870–1953). Poet and author. Liberal M.P. for South Salford 1906–10. As an undergraduate, Dalton had been an admirer of Belloc, and helped to form a 'Belloc Society' shortly after leaving Cambridge.

August? A Tory government in time for the Imperial Conference? But it blew over. The Liberals decided unanimously at a Party Meeting to abstain; Simon said he didn't want to be a cause of contention ... So we disperse for three months, till 28th October.

Friday 1st August

And not a day too soon. The thing was becoming utterly unendurable! On the final day we debated the Amendments to the Covenant on the Adjournment. I spoke very wearily, but dropped no brick, I think. On this same day Snowden announced our agricultural policy – an agreed Cabinet statement – at great length. Addison has fought well and done wonders.[1] He has found his colleagues hopelessly slow or timid. Their unwillingness to take a decision is the terrible thing. (Henderson said just the same thing to me last month. They turn, after a long discussion, and say helplessly to civil servants, 'Well, what can you suggest?') Trevelyan, Addison says, has been very bad, in floundering opposition to everything constructive. But we have a very good little agricultural group in the House. They have plodded along loyally and have kept in touch with the Ministry, and been persistent behind the scenes, and here it is. Better than posing peacocks and professional soreheads. Next time we may lose in the industrial centres and win in the agricultural areas!

The Consultative Committee[2] elections were interesting. 230 odd members voted ...

Lord Oswald astonished me and himself too, I'm sure, by not getting on. It was being given out by his friends that he was unwilling to stand, and would only do so if overwhelmingly pressed to come forward. And he polled 54, and was 16 short of even the last place! Leaving out his own vote, and Lady Cynthia's and John Strachey's and Bevan's, he only polled 50, or less than 1 in 4 of voting. And each had 12 votes to give away ...

Philips Price,[3] in a lucid interval, composed a creed on Lord Oswald's resignation, copies of which were typed and circulated pretty widely. (I had six typed in the Foreign Office.) Price showed a copy to Lord Oswald, who seemed to think it rather a joke, and to

1 Christopher Addison, q.v., had succeeded Buxton as Minister of Agriculture on 5th June 1930.
2 The Consultative Committee was elected from among Labour M.P.s who were not members of the Government.
3 Morgan Philips Price (1885–1973). Labour M.P. for Whitehaven 1929–31; Forest of Dean 1935–50; Gloucestershire West 1950–59. Signatory of the Mosley Manifesto, published a few months later. Former communist (though never a Party member). Old Harrovian.

Lady Oswald, who, he said, seemed to think it less of a joke. Here it is.

On the resignation of Sir Oswald Mosley. May 1930.
New Left Wing Creed on Unemployment
(Appointed to be said at all meetings of the Left Wing
– open or secret)

I believe in one Lloyd George, the Father Almighty, the giver of political wisdom, and in all his promises, possible and impossible.

And in one Lord Oswald Mosley, the only Begotten Son of the Father, from whom all Yellow Books are made.

Who for us rank and filers and our Salvation, came down from the Birmingham School; and was incarnate of the ghost of Karl Marx and of the Virgin I.L.P.

He was made Chancellor of the Duchy and was crucified for us under Jimmy Thomas; He suffered and was buried on the back-benches.

And the third day he rose again from below the gangway, according unto Hansard.

He ascended into the Constitutional Left Wing and sitteth on the right hand of Lloyd George, from whence he shall come to judge our theories on unemployment, whose numbers shall have no end.

And I believe in one J. M. Keynes, the Lord and Giver of inflation, who with Lloyd George and Sir Oswald together is worshipped and glorified; who spake through the 'Nation'.

And I believe in one Catholic and Apostolic Labour Movement (without Thomas, Snowden and other deflationists).

I acknowledge one Mosley Memorandum for the gingering up of policies.

I look for the Supercession of the Front Bench

And the life of 'Socialism in Our Time'

(If Maxton does not queer the pitch meanwhile).

Beckett – Sandham[1] – Mosley. The Posing Peacocks and the Booby. But against the Tired Timidity of Leaders, not a quite unnatural foreground.

A rumour ran round the Lobbies and the Press in the first days of August that there was a move on, organised by Mosley, to substitute Uncle as P.M. and get rid of MacDonald and Snowden. In one version, which, however, did not get into press, Phil Noel-Baker and I were also mentioned. Lord Oswald to be Foreign Secretary, with Phil

1 Elijah Sandham (1876–1944). Labour M.P. for Kirkdale 1929–31. I.L.P.er.

as Under-Secretary and I to be Chancellor of the Exchequer! Childish
and silly boomerangery!

Friday 8th August
Ewer[1] visiting me at the Foreign Office on 5th August said that Cole
had told him of a talk he recently had with Mrs Snowden[2] at No. 11.
She asked him to help her to get rid of Sir J. Reith[3] from the B.B.C.
Who, he asked, would she suggest as a successor. 'I would gladly
take it on myself,' she said. Then, suddenly, she pulled him back into
the room. 'Come away from the windows,' she said, 'we are always
watched by spies from the windows of the Foreign Office.'

Tuesday 26th August
My birthday – forty-three is a great age! – and the beginning of summer coincide. Really hot. To Cherhill by bus and then walking by the
Lansdowne Monument (this monument is dangerous, already two
great lumps of stone falling from its base, though it only heralds the
Edwardian Age, commemorating Victoria's success in at last bearing
a son). And so over new downs, walking with my shirt in my hand,
and sunbathing for hours, down to a cowman's cottage on the Haigh-
Lockeridge road (New Town), where, very thirsty, we drink tea, and
go by foot to West Overton along the Ridge Way, and back to Marlborough by bus, looking out at a fine sunset.

Thursday 28th to Friday 29th August
I come back to the Foreign Office and Labour Party Executive Committee. Ruth comes back on the 29th. She has had a lot of trouble with
her teeth at Marlborough, which has spoiled her holiday. But she has
had four out now, and is past the immediate trouble, I hope. It has
been a damned nuisance for her. I look forward to her having a good
restful and interesting time at Aldbourne next month. The walls of
the house should be leaping up by then.

   Uncle seems very fit after three weeks at Tring and two at Llandrin-
dod Wells. He has lost a stone, his face looks thinner and he is very
much on the spot in handling business.

1 W. N. Ewer. Diplomatic correspondent of the *Daily Herald.*
2 Ethel Snowden, née Annakin, later Viscountess (1881–1951). Married to Philip
  Snowden. Beatrice Webb later wrote of her that she and Jimmy Thomas 'had
  caricatured social climbing' (diary, 19th March 1932). Member of the first Board
  of Governors of the B.B.C. 1927–33.
3 Sir John Reith, later 1st Baron (1889–1971). Director General of the B.B.C. 1927–
  38. Minister of Information 1940; Transport 1940–41; Works (later Works and
  Planning) 1941–2.

Friday 3rd October

To Llandudno for Labour Party Conference. What a jump! A good conference. Very loyal and sensible on the whole, but not contented with the Government's record on unemployment. Lord Oswald did a dramatic piece of tub-thumping late on Tuesday afternoon. Cheers were led by Strachey and Aneurin Bevan. On Wednesday the vote for the Executive was taken. I was re-elected pretty comfortably, though, if I had not got the miners for the fourth year in succession, I might have come off. Lord Oswald got on again, but below me, in spite of much canvassing.[1] I was very passive, having a cold in the head. Morgan Jones went off in our section. The sensation was the defeat of Thomas who was bottom of the poll in the Trade Union Section. MacDonald made a good conference speech, but really said nothing, and was quite bowled over by Thomson's death in the R101 two days before.[2] Susan Lawrence did extremely well in the chair.

Tuesday 14th to Friday 17th October

In the Constituency. I had some apprehensions, but these are soon dissipated. The spirit is surprisingly good, though pits have been closing again – some say in order to create an atmosphere for wage reduction when the shorter day comes into operation in December. But the quotas and control of production begin next month and much faith is pinned to these by those entitled to be heard.

Eight good public meetings and a frank and friendly talk with the Executive. A plain narrative of what was accomplished, in face of great difficulty, in our first session is very well received. 100 per cent grants to local authorities are much appreciated, and rates are down by 2/- in the £ in Bishop Auckland and lesser amounts elsewhere, chiefly as a result of the Unemployment Insurance Act which put men back from poor relief on to unemployment benefit.

Thursday 23rd October

Dine with Lionel Robbins at Reform Club. He has had a very stiff time on the Economists' Committee appointed by the E.A.C. [Econo-

---

1 In Section III (Constituency Parties) of the National Executive, Dalton came third (after Lansbury and Morrison) with 1,431,000 votes, and Mosley fourth with 1,362,000.
2 Lord Thomson, q.v., the Air Secretary, and forty-eight out of fifty-four passengers, died on 5th October when the airship R101 burst into flames near Beauvais in northern France while on a test flight. It was believed by some that references to the victims of this disaster in MacDonald's Conference speech were designed to divert attention from Mosley's political demands.

mic Advisory Council]. But he has done very well.[1] Keynes, Stamp and Hubert Henderson have all gone protectionist – 10 per cent General Tariff, plus special duties for iron and steel and pigs and poultry, plus a lot of foolish additions, export bounties, wage subsidies, etc.

Pigou has been against all the protectionist proposals, but won't join Lionel in writing a Minority Report. Indeed [Robbins] says that Third Degree Methods have been employed to prevent his writing such a Report. First they tried to make him believe that it would be ungentlemanly. 'One never does that,' said Pigou, 'one tries to reach the greatest possible measure of agreement and then, if necessary, adds a minute of dissent on particular points.' 'If you want to make a row outside,' said Pigou on another occasion, 'can't you find some other way of doing it.' Then Keynes said that he had consulted Hankey and that there was no precedent for a Minority Report by one member. Lionel asked, 'What about the Sankey Report?' Someone said, 'Sankey never signed a Minority Report for one.' Lionel asked for the files. They were brought and, of course, he was right. Then they said, 'Oh, a Minority Report by the Chairman is a different thing.' Then he was referred, on Hankey's authority, to the Channel Tunnel report, to which Lord Ebbisham[2] added only a short dissenting minute on his fears for the Kentish fruit growers. Lionel said this seemed more important than that. Then he said that the Lord Chancellor (Sankey) had expressed the view that a Minority Report was perfectly in order. Hemming,[3] Hankey's second in command, wrote on a piece of paper 'I know the Lord Chancellor and don't think much of him.' Hemming, looking a year or two older, had previously tried to bully Lionel in a corner. Lionel said he would be quite willing to refer the question to the P.M. and to the Cabinet. But they said there was no precedent for this.

In the end he said he would send in a short Minority Report and if they didn't print it he would send it direct to the Chancellor of the

1 This was the occasion of Robbins's famous rift with Keynes – the culmination of a series of clashes at the Economists' Committee of the Economic Advisory Council. Robbins had refused to entertain any form of expansionism, or to compromise on the issue of free trade. Keynes, in the chair, refused to let Robbins write a minority report dissenting from the view of the Committee as a whole, on the grounds that Robbins was in a minority of one. Much of the personal bitterness in the division between Cambridge and London economists in the 1930s derived from this row. It is interesting to note that at the time Dalton took the side of his pupil rather than of his tutor.
2 G. R. B. Ebbisham, 1st Baron (1868–1953). Conservative M.P. 1918–28.
3 A. F. Hemming (1893–1964). Civil servant. Secretary to the Economic Advisory Council 1930–39.

Exchequer. He then left the room. Pigou buried his face in his hands. The others said goodbye. His reports, both long and short, are excellent. The tariff stuff is pitiable. I was taught to despise Protectionists at Cambridge. I do so still.

Lord Oswald is much with Keynes at present. But, of course, he can only take in the cruder arguments.

Tuesday 28th October
Parliament reassembles.

In the evening Molly Hamilton[1] and I talk to the Royal Institute about the Assembly. Sit next to Mrs Snowden at dinner and praise, quite sincerely, Snowden's Free Trade Speech at Manchester. In face of the protectionist wave, and some of its adherents – economists, and politicians – I am quite a keen anti-Protectionist now. She says that she hears that Lord Oswald has been spending weekends with Beaverbrook.[2]

Mander tells me after the meeting that a small minority of the Liberal Parliamentary Party want to turn us out at once. But most of them would like an excuse to keep us in.

Wednesday 29th October
I see Snowden and tell him of Lionel Robbins's experience. A very friendly interview. He has just read the report. He speaks with withering scorn of Keynes and Stamp. The latter was very soapy just before he made his Manchester speech and said he was very glad that he was going to make a Free Trade speech; people were beginning to forget the force of the Free Trade case; his *only doubt was* whether, perhaps, a temporary tariff on iron and steel wouldn't be wise. Snowden said, 'But you know that no tariff ever is temporary.' Stamp said, 'Yes, that's the difficulty.' Snowden had liked Lionel's report. He thought it 'a most trenchant reply'.

(Lionel told me that I had a very bad press with the Stamps. Lady Stamp had heard that I had said once in a lecture at the School, 'Sir

---

1 Mary Agnes Hamilton (1882–1966). Labour M.P. for Blackburn 1929–31. Member of the British delegation to the League of Nations 1929, 1930. Writer, journalist and biographer of MacDonald and Henderson. She became a close friend of the Daltons, and especially of Hugh.
2 Sir Max Aitken, 1st Bart, 1st Baron Beaverbrook (1879–1964). Proprietor of Beaverbrook Newspapers. Conservative M.P. 1910–16. Chancellor of the Duchy of Lancaster and Minister of Information 1918. Minister of Aircraft Production 1940–41; Minister of State 1941; Minister of Supply 1941–2; Lord Privy Seal 1943–5.

Josiah Stamp is one of our greatest authorities on public finance. And
he knows it.')

Lord Oswald made a speech in the House today with large protectionist patches ('insulation from the shocks of price fluctuations in the
outer world'). Ernest Hunter tells me that there are many rumours of
comings and goings and a new group forming. Lord Oswald is said
to be in touch with Beaverbrook, who claims to have tried to dissuade
him from resigning when he did and urged him to 'raise hell inside'
instead, also with Young Tories – Boothby,[1] Oliver Stanley[2] and
Walter Elliot[3] – also with Lloyd George, Edge being a go-between for
this purpose, and also with Keynes. But in the Party he carries only
Lady Cynthia [Mosley], Bevan and Strachey and perhaps W. J.
Brown[4] and Oliver Baldwin.[5] He holds himself rather aloof from the
Maxtonites. But he has bought (one supposes) the Presidency of the
new Trade Union Club in Holborn.

Saturday 1st to Sunday 2nd November
Lunch at Upham. Currie[6] says that Addison is terrifying his permanent
officials by the roughness of his policy. Good! That is the sort of
Cabinet Minister I like!

Monday 3rd November
Arising out of this last remark, have I anywhere recorded the story
of Winston, who, as First Lord of the Admiralty, had trouble with

1 R. J. G. Boothby, later Sir Robert, later Baron (1900–86). Conservative M.P. for
  Aberdeenshire East 1924–58. Junior minister 1940–41. Tory reformer and Keyne-
  sian.
2 Oliver Stanley (1896–1950). Conservative M.P. for Westmorland 1924–45; Bristol
  West 1945–50. Junior minister 1931–3. Minister of Transport 1933–4; Labour
  1934–5. President of the Board of Education 1935–7; Board of Trade 1937–40.
  Secretary of State for War 1940; Colonial Affairs 1942–5. Tory reformer.
3 Walter Elliot (1888–1958). Conservative M.P. for Kelvingrove 1924–45, 1950–58;
  Lanark 1918–23; Scottish Universities 1946–50. Junior minister 1923–4, 1924–9.
  Financial Secretary at the Treasury 1931–2; Minister of Agriculture and Fisheries
  1932–6; Secretary of State for Scotland 1936–8; Minister of Health 1938–40.
4 W. J. Brown (1894–1960). Labour M.P. for Wolverhampton West 1929–31.
  Independent M.P. for Rugby 1942–50. General Secretary of the Civil Service
  Clerical Association 1914–42. Brown supported the Mosley Manifesto and re-
  signed from the Labour Party in March 1931. He did not, however, join the New
  Party.
5 Oliver Baldwin, later 2nd Earl (1899–1958). Labour M.P. for Dudley 1929–31;
  Paisley 1945–7. Son of Stanley Baldwin. Joined the New Party 1931.
6 J. Currie, later Sir James (1868–1937) and Hilda Currie, née Hanbury. The Curries
  were neighbours of the Daltons at Aldbourne. Principal of the Gordon College,
  Khartoum, and Director of Education in the Sudan 1900–14.

his Sea Lords? Something he wanted to do was said to be contrary to
all the traditions of the British Navy. The Sea Dogs sat solemnly and
obstinately in a row with protruding chins. Then Winston rose from
his chair and said, 'The traditions of the British Navy, Gentlemen,
what are those traditions? Rum, lice, sodomy and the lash!'

Tuesday 4th November

A bad Parliamentary day. Tory amendment to the Address on unemployment defeated. 5 Liberals voted with the Tories, 4 with us and
the rest abstained. The 5 included Simon, who tried hard to get others
to go with him. In spite of a party decision to abstain, and Hutchison,[1]
their chief whip. Our majority was 31. Mander, who abstained, told
me that a dozen or more of them were 'standing by' ready to come into
our Lobby if too many went the other way. But it was a bad day by
reason of MacDonald's inconceivably bad speech at the end – no
policy, no sense of the impetus of the problem, impotent and irritable.
We can't go on like this much longer.

Thursday 6th November

Uncle raised Palestine urgently. The Jews all over the world, and in
Whitechapel particularly, where a by-election is pending,[2] are off
their heads with indignation. Passfield, Uncle and King Albert are
appointed on a committee to go into the question and, if possible,
meet the Zionist leaders. The Cabinet also decided that, in future, all
Colonial Office pronouncements on Palestine are to be submitted to
the Foreign Office before publication. But this is shutting the stable
door after the horse.

Minister babble of 'abuses' in Unemployment Insurance. Uncle
'walks into them', in his own phrase, and reminded them that ever
since Keir Hardie,[3] we had stood for work or maintenance.

Will Henderson tells me that a certain Labour candidate, one of the
best, had been told by the P.M. that the gravity of this question of
unemployment is greatly exaggerated. On the other hand, 'these
Conferences' – Imperial and Indian Round Table – 'will live in history'.
The candidate was inclined to retire from the field!

1 Major-General Sir Robert Hutchison, later 1st Baron (1873–1950). Liberal Chief
  Whip 1926–30. Liberal, then Liberal National, M.P. for Montrose Burghs 1924–32.
  Liberal M.P. for Kirkcaldy Burghs 1922–3. Paymaster-General 1935–8.
2 Voting took place in the Labour-held seat of Whitechapel (following the death of
  the sitting Member) on 3rd December 1930. The Labour candidate, J. H. Hall, q.v.,
  was elected with a reduced majority.
3 James Keir Hardie (1856–1915). I.L.P. leader and founding father of the Labour
  Party. Independent Labour M.P. 1892–5. Labour M.P. 1900–15.

Friday 7th November
We have lost the Shipley by-election. Only our second in seventeen months, but everyone is in a temper or a panic. 'We can't last more than three months,' etc.

Saturday 8th November
In gloom owing to Shipley and a tale of an imminent split in the Cabinet told by the *News Chronicle* – afterwards officially denied. Political life hangs by a frayed thread.

Sunday 9th November
Walk twenty-three miles with Ruth and feel better!

Monday 10th November
Plotting proceeds apace. Brown writes to Uncle that he and Lord Oswald want to see the latter, privately and away from the House, to discuss the affairs of the Party.

Ernest Hunter tells me that the article in the *News Chronicle* on Saturday, and another in the *Daily Express* which I didn't see, were practically word for word the same. Both contained two references to Mosley, to his resignation and to his Memorandum. Evidently inspired by Mosley, today the *News Chronicle* says that 'dramatic developments' will take place this week.[1] It is being said, says Hunter, on the one hand that a group of 30 or 40 of our Party have signed an ultimatum to the P.M. demanding Snowden's resignation, failing which they will vote against the Government (I doubt this), and on the other, that talk of a 'National Party' is far from finished.

Scott Lindsay[2] says that he spoke candidly to MacDonald the other day, and told him he ought to prepare his speeches, if he was going to make any, and try to do something about unemployment. I said that I had told Uncle that the Government ought at least to try to *look* as though it was going to do something. Lindsay said, 'No good saying that to him. He is watching every mistake MacDonald makes with a sardonic smile. The worse things go the more likely he is to get the leadership.' I said, 'But not in this Parliament, and at the rate things are going, there will be no Labour representative from Lancashire in the next Parliament.' Lindsay said, 'I hadn't thought things were quite as bad as that.' But I fancy I had put a new idea into his head!

1 Later insertion: 'P.S. In the end they didn't.'
2 H. Scott Lindsay (1879–1959). Secretary of the P.L.P. 1918–44. Assistant to the Secretary of the P.L.P. 1906–18.

He went on to say that Hartshorn,[1] when asked to tell the Consultative Committee what he had been doing about unemployment, said, 'How can I tell them anything? All my proposals were put in last August and no decision has been taken on them yet!'

Walton Newbold[2] – dirty bore – said that he had had a conversation with Allan Young – Lord Oswald's hireling – and had asked whether Lord O. didn't think that Morrison and I were serious rivals for the future leadership, and that Young had replied that Morrison had been completely shown up by his failure at the Ministry of Transport, and that I was 'submerged at the Foreign Office and out of the picture'. I only said, 'Really. Did he say that?' Lord Oswald has no sense of the slow transitions of real life. Having joined the Party last week, he wants to lead it tomorrow afternoon.

Wednesday 12th November

10.30 I find Uncle closeted with Weizmann[3] and Namier.[4] He has taken charge of the Cabinet Committee on Palestine and is negotiating with the Jews, who won't meet Webb or Colonial Office officials.[5]

10.50 The Jews are in the Ambassador's waiting room examining a suggested formula. I am with Uncle. Ronald[6] comes in and says that Passfield wants to see Uncle urgently before the opening of the India Round Table Conference at 11.45. Uncle says, 'Tell him I will meet him in the Court outside at 11.20 and walk down to the House

1 Vernon Hartshorn (1872–1931). Lord Privy Seal 1930–31. Labour M.P. for Ogmore 1918–31. Postmaster-General 1924. President of the North Wales Miners' Federation.
2 J. T. Walton Newbold (1888–1943). Journalist and lecturer. Communist M.P. for Motherwell and Wishaw 1922–3; Labour candidate 1929. Joined the National Labour Party in 1931, and supported Churchill at Epping in the 1935 General Election.
3 Chaim Weizmann (1874–1952). Zionist leader. President of the World Zionist Organisation and of the Jewish Agency for Palestine 1921–31, 1935–46. First President of Israel 1948–52.
4 L. B. Namier, later Sir Lewis (1888–1960). Historian. Political Secretary of the Jewish Agency for Palestine 1929–31. Professor of Modern History at Manchester University 1931–53.
5 The Colonial Secretary, Lord Passfield, q.v., had published a White Paper in October 1930 which declared that until Palestine's productivity improved, there could be no Jewish settlement outside the reserve lands already in Jewish possession. This declaration was much criticised by Jews and their sympathisers, and Jewish immigration was not immediately curtailed. Passfield, however, was 'pilloried as the worst enemy of the Jewish people since Haman'. (A. J. P. Taylor, *English History 1914–1945*, Clarendon Press, Oxford, 1965, p. 276.)
6 N. B. Ronald, later Sir Nigel (1894–1973). Private Secretary to successive Foreign Secretaries 1929–34.

with him.' Obviously he mustn't come here and run into the Jews in the passage.

10.55 Ronald returns and announces that 'Lord Passfield is here.' Consternation! The Jews are still in the waiting room, but may emerge at any minute. Passfield is put in Selby's room down the side passage, to wait till they have gone. French farce scene! In the end no collision occurs.

Round Table Conference opens 'in a good spirit'. No formal meeting of British All Party delegation has been held. This is deliberate. 'We don't want to go in as a white bloc,' says Uncle. 'If all the Indians unite in asking for Dominion status, it can't be refused, so far as the Government are concerned. I'm not going into this Conference with an open mind. I have been saying for twenty years that India ought to have self-government and I'm not going to change now. Wedgwood Benn and I ought to be able to carry Sankey with us, and MacDonald ought to be able to carry Thomas. Even if he carries him the other way, we shall still be 3 to 2.'

Friday 14th November

At lunch Wedgwood Benn was in very high spirits about the India Conference. (A little while ago, even *he* was very depressed.) He hopes it may be over by Christmas, and that we may send them away with Provincial Autonomy and a comfortable preamble to other reforms, the details of which they will work out in India at their leisure. These are the tactics, but they seem optimistic. From another point of view, we want the Conference to last a long time, for we shan't, I think, have an election while it is still going on.

Colin Clark comes to see me in the afternoon, and gives me a Cabinet paper prepared by Attlee[1] last July. It is not a very distinguished production, but it recommended that a Ministry of Industry should be set up to rationalise on socially sound lines – armed with considerable powers. The only result has been that Horace Wilson[2] (of all people) has been set up as Industrial Adviser, to rationalise, with no powers!

Clark says that the Government seems to have made up its mind that nothing can be done, or should be attempted, to deal with unemployment through industrial action. At the Unemployment panel

---

1 C. R. Attlee, later 1st Earl (1883–1967). Chancellor of the Duchy of Lancaster 1930–31; Postmaster-General 1931. Labour M.P. for Limehouse. See Appendix.
2 Sir Horace Wilson (1882–1972). Chief Industrial Adviser to the Government 1930–39. Permanent Secretary at the Ministry of Labour 1921–30. Seconded to the Treasury for duties with the Prime Minister (Baldwin and Chamberlain) 1935–40. Permanent Secretary at the Treasury and Head of the Civil Service 1939–42.

ministers spend all their time talking of the 'abuses' of the Unemployment Insurance System, and asking the civil servants what to do next.

Thursday 20th November
Party Meeting. Case of W. J. Brown brought up. He had read out a private communication, which had gone out with the weekly whips, on pre-war pensioners, and told the House where it came from, and spoken disrespectfully and publicly of the Chief Whip! But it was almost settled at the Party Meeting and he had more or less apologised, when Kennedy[1] and Lord Oswald flared the whole thing up by two provocative speeches. The meeting was in an uproar. I have never seen it so agitated. Kennedy mechanically demanded that the case should go to the National Executive. Lord Oswald, apparently quite out of control, barged in and shouted that 'if there is no place in the Party for a good socialist like Brown there are many others of us who will have to reconsider our position.' Then a denunciation of the Government (quite out of order). Then, in response to rising shouts of opposition, a threat that, if there's to be a scrap, he'll be in it. 'But it will not be fought out in this Parliamentary Party, but on the floor of the Annual Conference.' When he sat down, it was carried by 116 to 38, that the case go to the National Executive (where we dismissed it a few days later).

Attlee's comment got into the press, deservedly. 'Why does Mosley always speak to us as though he were a feudal landlord abusing tenants who are in arrears with their rent?'

Friday 21st November
Colin Clark to lunch. Depressing account of unemployment discussions. Time wasting, wandering from the point, no grip, no courage, no policy. Whitehall littered with derelict organisations.

Saturday 22nd to Sunday 23rd November
Weekend with Critall.[2] ... Visit Silver End. Should be much better known. Critall is very wheezy and out of condition. And his business is, quite naturally, depressed. Gives a pessimistic account of British industrial methods, especially in iron and steel. He gives an amusing account of receiving his knighthood. A crowd of recipients, including

---

1 Thomas Kennedy (1876–1954). Labour Chief Whip 1927–31. Labour M.P. for Kirkcaldy Burghs 1921–2, 1923–31, 1935–44. General Secretary of the Social Democratic Federation.
2 Sir Valentine Critall, later 1st Baron Braintree (1884–1961). Knighted in 1930. Industrialist. Chairman of Critall Manufacturing Co. Ltd. Labour M.P. 1923–4. Director of the Bank of England 1948–55.

old George Edwards,[1] and several very oleaginous characters, who kept asking questions such as 'Am I to understand that I do not back out of the presence of His Majesty?' and getting snubbed. Jack Hayes[2] much the smartest and most impressive of the Court officials. Clynes, on the other hand, 'came in looking like the man who had come to see about the gas.' Critall congratulated George Edwards on his knighthood – very old and deaf – who shouted very loud, 'Oh, yes, I *could* have had the whole thing.' Critall. 'What whole thing?' Edwards. 'Yes, I could have had the whole thing. The Baronetcy. But my Union wouldn't put up the money.'

Monday 24th November
Aneurin Bevan tells me that *he* stopped Lord Oswald from forming a National Party. There would have been members of all three parties in it, it would have had two national newspapers behind it, and a fighting fund of £250,000 and could have put 400 candidates into the field at the next election. So this was the game! Lord Oswald has never understood *modern* political mechanics.

Tuesday 25th November
Party Meeting. MacDonald talks woolly nothings and gets a good reception from the majority. Trevelyan gets an overwhelming majority – only 10 dissentients – for his compromise with the Liberals over the Education Bill. Postponement till September 1932 and a local means test. Surely this is the easiest Party that leaders ever had to lead, if it is treated frankly! ...

National Executive in the afternoon. Lord Oswald has given notice of a motion drawing attention to the failure of the Government to deal adequately with the economic situation and urging that the N.E. should send a deputation to the Cabinet, but instead of a row, he withdrew it, after Uncle had stated that he had sent the P.M. a statement from various constituencies of the reasons for recent setbacks at municipal elections. Lord Oswald, however, is going to speak at East Renfrew in favour of the unendorsed candidate.[3]

1 Alderman Sir George Edwards (1850–1933). Knighted 1930. Founder of the National Union of Land Workers 1906. A Primitive Methodist lay preacher for sixty years. Labour M.P. 1920–22, 1923–4.
2 John Hayes (1889–1941). Vice-Chamberlain of H.M. Household 1929–31. Labour M.P. for Liverpool Edge Hill 1923–31.
3 'East Renfrew': an I.L.P. nominee, Bailie Thomas Irwin, had been selected to contest the East Renfrew by-election, caused by the death of the Unionist M.P. The Labour N.E.C. refused to endorse Irwin's candidature because he had declared his support for the rebellious I.L.P. Clyde Group. Many I.L.P. members gave

Wednesday 26th November

Spoke at two meetings in Whitechapel by-election. Disorder and chaos caused by Communists and Zionists. Hall[1] a poor candidate. Lord Oswald had addressed a meeting of members last night to explain his 'views' on employment. Some 60 were present, largely P.P.S.s (including my own Rennie Smith) who were listening in by instruction.

Wednesday 3rd December

Russia is a bloody hair shirt! As Uncle said, 'If only it wasn't for Russia, we should be having quite a good time at the Foreign Office!' As it is, following up a protest by Ovey at Moscow on Monday on allegation against *past and* present government in sabotage trial. (Hansard is worth reading these days!) We bring in another today, stimulated by a private notice question by O. Locker-Lampson,[2] on a propaganda wireless address in English from Moscow. All my time from 11 a.m. till 3.45 p.m. is taken up with this rot today. Post Office listened in last night at three stations and men came in taxis to Foreign Office this morning bearing separate sheets. The answer is rushed, and scribbled down in Uncle's room at the House. He and I 'have words' in front of Phil [Noel-Baker], Selby and Seymour.[3] I say, 'You are giving an answer that will please the Conservatives.' He says, 'Can't you look at this question from a wider point of view than party?' I say, 'Where are you letting these Tories lead you? They will lead you on from point to point with these protests, until you find you have nothing left to do but break.' He says, 'Can you deny that this is propaganda? I can't understand why you always want to shield these people.' I say, 'Not one listener in a million will have heard this. You want a set worth £100 to get Moscow.' He says, 'Oh, no, that is denied.' I say, 'Well, I believe it's true nevertheless. I think it is a great mistake to make such heavy weather over such trifles. You will get a private notice now every day after a Moscow wireless talk.' ...... The officials, I think, all agree with me in not wanting another protest. But Uncle

1 J. H. Hall (1877–1942). Alderman of Stepney Borough Council. Labour M.P. for Whitechapel and St George's 1930–31, 1935–42.
2 O. S. Locker-Lampson (1880–1954). Conservative M.P. for Birmingham Handsworth 1922–45; Huntingdonshire 1910, 1918–22.
3 H. J. Seymour, later Sir Horace (1885–1978). Counsellor at the Foreign Office. Ambassador to China 1942–6.

active backing to Irwin in his campaign, in defiance of N.E.C. rulings; Mosley and Strachey also gave their support. Though Irwin was decisively beaten in the by-election on 28th November, this dispute foreshadowed the voluntary disaffiliation of the I.L.P. from the Labour Party nineteen months later.

has got a Soviet complex at the moment. We shall see the result of giving way to it!

Thursday 4th December
Meet von Neurath,[1] the new German Ambassador, at lunch at Van's. Not an interesting nor an able man, I thought, and speaks poor English.

Friday 5th December
Evening papers contain a speech by Lloyd George to the Liberal candidates, practically saying that, if we give them Alternative Vote, they will keep us in long enough to pass it; abusing the Tories, and now, for form's sake, jeering at us. Very deservedly! 'Pot bound Ministers. Taken out in prams by their departmental nurses.' Very funny and very just.

But it puts the election well away, if he means business. Uncle, Snowden and Arnold were in the negotiation for us. Lloyd George, Samuel and I don't know the third – for them.

Rumours in the press that MacDonald is to be the next Viceroy of India. Uncle is inclined to think that it is a kite, put out by MacDonald himself, and with the expectation that Buckingham Palace take the hint and press him strongly to take it. Of course, he would fill the part splendidly, and be free of Party worries and 'go down in history' more than ever, and enjoy every moment, especially of the Pageants. His going, I think, would be grand. Uncle is fussed about it. Mac-Donald, he says, has never said a word to him about it, but has dropped hints once or twice. 'If I am here when this comes up', etc. Uncle says he wouldn't take the succession if it were offered him. There would be great rivalry between his supporters and Snowden's. And some would push for Clynes, who might come in as the compromise third. If the hour [?] had come to him ten years ago, it would have been different. Or even a year ago, before all the splits in the Party. But those who [were] shouting for MacDonald to go now, would be shouting for him to go a year hence.

I urge him not to refuse it, if it *should* come. He has the qualities, I tell him, to pull the Party together and to push policy through. I speak bitterly of MacDonald's vanity and his habit of hoarding personal grudges. Uncle agrees that these are two of his great defects.

The Mosley Manifesto is promised for this weekend. Five Dictators and a Tariff.

1 Baron Konstantin von Neurath (1873–1956). German Foreign Minister in von Papen, von Schleicher and Hitler Governments 1932–8. Ambassador to Britain 1930–32.

The so-called 'Mosley Manifesto', incorporating many of the ideas of the earlier 'Mosley Memorandum' on economic and unemployment policy, was published on 13th December over the signature of seventeen M.P.s and that of Arthur Cook, the Miners' Secretary. Those who signed included Oliver Baldwin, Aneurin Bevan, W. J. Brown, Morgan Philips Price and John Strachey. The Manifesto was presented as 'an immediate plan to meet an emergency situation'. It advocated a Cabinet of five Ministers without Portfolio, subject only to the general control of Parliament.

Sunday 7th December
The Mosley Manifesto is featured in the Sunday press. It differs from the earlier Mosley Memorandum in that social services and especially retiring pensions are out, and tariffs, under impossible administrative conditions, are in. It is a move towards Toryism.

And the Five Dictators are new too!

It was subsequently applauded by Amery,[1] Sir William Morris[2] and other Tories! But it fell flat on the whole. It was a forty-eight hours' wonder.[3]

Friday 12th December
Talk with Nevile Henderson, our Minister at Belgrade. Very pro-Yugoslav. Uncle thinks he has more vitality than most of our ministers abroad. I agree. I also think he has more intelligence.

Wednesday 17th December
National Executive approves by 16 votes to 3 (Compton, Jowett[4] and Barbara Gould) the inclusion of the Alternative Vote in our Electoral Reform Bill. Lord Oswald, challenged on his participation in the East Renfrew by-election on behalf of the I.L.P. candidate, whom the Executive refused to endorse, expresses his 'contempt' for the

1 L. S. Amery (1873–1955). Conservative M.P. for Birmingham Sparkbrook 1918–45; Birmingham South 1911–18. First Lord of the Admiralty 1922–4. Secretary of State for Dominions Affairs 1925–9; India 1940–45. Journalist and writer on constitutional questions. Father of Julian Amery.
2 Sir William Morris, 1st Bart, later 1st Viscount Nuffield (1877–1963). Motor manufacturer and philanthropist. Chairman of Morris Motors Ltd 1919–52.
3 This paragraph was inserted later.
4 F. W. Jowett (1864–1944). Labour M.P. for East Bradford 1922–4, 1929–31; West Bradford 1906–18. Bradford textile worker and socialist pioneer. Chairman of the I.L.P. 1901–10, 1914–17.

4 Labour weekend at Easton Lodge, home of the Countess of Warwick, 1923.
Standing, right: Emanuel Shinwell. *Seated from left:* Arthur Henderson,
Countess of Warwick, Ramsay MacDonald.

5 Dalton and Sir Charles
  Trevelyan, May 1929

6 MacDonald as Prime
  Minister, with Churchill,
  1929

Government and says that he considers that the Government does not get a bad deal, if he refrains from voting against them in the House, as he has hitherto done, while reserving the right to criticise their policy in his speeches. The matter was then allowed to drop.

Trevelyan was in a mess again with the Bill at today's Cabinet. He wanted authority to bring in another Bill on the religious question as soon as the House met again. He said he had now practically reached an agreement with the Catholics, but he was incapable of explaining clearly what it was. So the Cabinet asked for a further memorandum on the subject.

Monday 29th December

Ruth thinks, and I can't disagree, that for the last three months I have been ineffectual and not sufficiently pushing outside the narrow routines of the Foreign Office. The gloom and sense of futility and exasperation have been awful. The black cloud of the Unemployment Figures has overshadowed everything and robbed all the political field of every glimmer of light. Tired and timid ministers. Discouraged private members. Depressed rank and file in the country.

Coal troubles over the new condition of working last Session's Act.[1]

A gleam of hope in the rumour that MacDonald might go to India as Viceroy has been dashed by the appointment of Willingdon.[2] We shall never get rid of MacDonald now. Uncle will never be Premier, I fear.

The economists can't yet make a prophecy as to when the world forces will reverse.

I am going to Bishop Auckland in the first days of January and hate the prospect of meeting my constituents again. It is all tragically different, so far as economic questions go, from what one had hoped and dreamed a Labour government would be like. And, even in the international field, there is fear in Europe, and Old Adam stalketh in the noonday. We go on signing new bits of paper but who believes in the undertakings they enshrine?

The consolations are only in my private life. West Leaze is promised to be handed over by 22nd January, barring unforeseen delays. *There*

---

1 Although the Coal Mines Act of 1930 had set up a National Industrial Board to protect wages, this never operated effectively, and the Government had not been provided with powers to enforce reorganisation of the industry.

2 F. Freeman-Thomas, 1st Marquess of Willingdon (1866–1941). Governor-General of Canada 1926–31; Viceroy and Governor-General of India 1931–6. Liberal M.P. 1900–10. Governor of Bombay 1913–19; Madras 1919–24.

will be peace and beauty and wide skies, and all the sunshine that England knows.

Tuesday 30th December
Walk to Avebury, through Ogbourne and Rockley in 4½ hours. Raining nearly all the way. Beveridge and Mrs Mair, who have recently been to Churt, report that Lloyd George is in favour of keeping us in for 'quite a long time', but very vexed at our ineptitude on unemployment.

Tuesday 20 January 1931
Parliament reassembles. Clynes at lunch is pessimistic. Says the Liberals are being bribed by the Tories with promises of straight fights at the General Election if they will vote against the second reading of the Trade Disputes Bill and that 28 have taken the bribe. If so, we are probably out next week.

Wednesday 21st January
Beaten by the Catholics on their amendment to the Education Bill. 36 Labour members vote and tell against the Government and 10 or 12 abstain. A bad business! There is always trouble when Uncle's away. We could have done any of these alternatives – (1) postponed further consideration of the Bill till agreement had been reached, (2) planked for the majority view at the recent conference. This would have rallied the Church and the Catholics; the Tories couldn't have opposed; nor the Lords, I fancy. But we should have lost the Liberals, and that might have been awkward at this moment. (3) Deliberately lost the Catholics, while gaining the Church and the Nonconformists. This would have been a less sure majority than (2), since the Catholics can bring heavy pressure on Tories and on many of our people. But I think we would have got through.

But what we actually did was worst of all! Trevelyan has no brains and no negotiating skill.

There can be no more discipline in the Party after this. At any rate the I.L.P. and the Mosleyites have never defeated the Government!

Thursday 22nd January
The Party very demoralised after last night's division. A lot of talk about its being better to go to the country, than to continue to be humiliated. Silly nonsense really especially for those with rocky seats, some of whom, none the less, are 'something in the City'. But the immediate political future looks very unsafe today.

Saturday 24th January
Move up in the morning to West Leaze and sleep there for the first time that evening. Very exciting, but a sea of muddy chalk surrounding the house. No paving, no made drive yet. Will Arnold-Forster arrives in the evening, without having given proper notice. Rather a nuisance. But he works out some good ideas about trees and shrubs.

I go back to London tonight.

Tuesday 27th January
Lord Oswald beaten at Party Meeting by 97 to 13 on his proposal that a national conference should at once be summoned to discuss unemployment policy.

Wednesday 28th January
Lord Oswald beaten at National Executive by 19 to 2 (only Jowett supporting him) on same issue. The fellow always forces these points to a division. I suppose in order to exhibit himself afterwards to crowds as the only righteous man.

Tonight we win on the Second Reading of the Trades Disputes Bill by a majority of 27. Better than most of us hoped. All our men accounted for. A fine performance. Many crawl up from sick beds to vote. We have fewer sick seeking pairs than the Tories. 10 to 15. Of the Liberals, 7 Simonites[1] vote with the Tories and 1, Edge, with us. The rest, according to Party decision, abstain. This is a high hurdle jumped. We breathe again and the spark of life within us, grown dim last week, glows brighter.

Friday 30th January
To West Leaze for the weekend. Ruth has been working like a black, with the workmen in and out and no maid. Very tired, poor little object, but she has made a great improvement inside. Outside all is still a chalky mess, and there is much to do. And water catchment and pumping are problems still. But inside is very charming and we have delightful peace and great fun.

On 17th January the Government published the text of an Electoral Reform Bill, in the hope of buying the support of Liberals who were threatening to

1 Increasingly, the Liberals were splitting three ways between followers of Sir John Simon, Lloyd George and Sir Herbert Samuel respectively. The Simonites were moving towards the Conservatives, and after the 1931 crisis formed the National Liberal Party which merged into the National Government majority. Lloyd George leant towards the Labour Party. The Samuelites held aloof from both.

force an election over the Trades Disputes Bill. The Electoral Reform Bill provided for the alternative vote in all parliamentary elections. It never became law.

Thursday 5th February

Electoral Reform Bill read a second time this week. A strong sense of Lab–Lib co-operation in the air again. People told today of our lasting two years and dishing the Tories at the next election. But sentiment may veer right round again tomorrow!

Friday 6th March

Leah Manning won by 2000 in East Islington in a four cornered fight. To have lost would have been a bad blow. She should be able to dig in there. Baldwin said to Ammon, the day after she took her seat, 'I have seen your new lady member. She reminds me of a line of Tennyson "Broad based upon the People's will"!'[1]

The Liberals went potty over the Trade Union Bill and amended Clause 1 with Tory aid in Committee, so as to make illegal any strike which endangers the health or safety of any substantial section of the community.[2] This would illegalise any national strike in an essential industry – mines, railways, docks, banking, electricity, etc. What price slave labour?

The Bill is, therefore, dropped. The T.U.C. is furious with the Liberals, and not too trustful of us. But, on the whole, Jowitt has done well, and won their confidence. The Lab–Lib agreement is a little shaken, but Electoral Reform looks like going through. And we are gathering external prestige in Europe and India. And the Liberal poll is slumping very badly in by-elections.

The Lords have thrown out the Education Bill, and are mangling the Land Utilisation Bill.

The Tories are squabbling badly about their leadership, but I don't think Baldwin will be dislodged yet awhile.

Uncle has followed up the Geneva Council success, by his trip with Alexander to Paris and Rome, which has settled naval competition

1 cf. Tennyson's poem 'To the Queen':
   Broad based upon her people's will,
   And compass'd by the inviolate sea.
2 A Bill to amend the 1927 Trades Disputes Act was dropped by the Government, after a wrecking Liberal amendment (on the definition of an illegal strike) had been carried in committee on 24th February.

in the Mediterranean. This is a tremendous success. The World Disarmament Conference looks as though it might really succeed now. And I hope Arthur Henderson will be President.

Yesterday (5th March) Benn announced the terms of the 'Surrender to Gandhi'. Irwin[1] has worked a miracle. The results – for peace and world harmony and trade – may be immense. The river of history may now flow along quite another channel.

Meanwhile Trevelyan has resigned with a poor sort of letter (his stock has fallen to zero), and Arnold on grounds of health and Russell has died, and Mosley with four others has ratted and proposed to make a New Party. But the D.L.P.s [Divisional Labour Parties] are sound as a bell. We shall bomb the traitors out of their holes! They have made a complete mess of the details. Mosley has no judgment.

At Peckham yesterday Blake and Kaylor[2] were defeated for the L.C.C. This will illustrate how much Ruth and I did for them!

Mosley's New Party came into existence on 28th February. Apart from Mosley and his wife, only three M.P.s joined – Strachey, Oliver Baldwin and Dr Robert Forgan. W. J. Brown gave support, but held back from becoming a member. Strachey soon left, and the Party disintegrated after failing to win any seats in the 1931 election. In October 1932 Mosley founded the British Union of Fascists.

Tuesday 10th March
Meetings of National Executive at No. 10. Resolution expelling Lord Oswald for 'gross disloyalty' carried unanimously, and his New Party placed on the index.

It is a queer thought that this hateful fellow, whom I have always bitterly distrusted, should thus vanish from our Party, from our Conferences and Party Meetings, and from our platforms. The air seems cleaner already. But what amazing folly and miscalculation and mad pride! See Maurois's *Dizzy* p. 94 (French edition).[3]

1 Edward Wood, 1st Baron Irwin, later 3rd Viscount Halifax, 1st Earl of Halifax (1881–1959). Viceroy of India 1926–31. See Appendix.
2 J. Kaylor. Chairman of Peckham Labour Party. Member of the Executive Council of the A.E.U. Member of Labour Party N.E.C. 1930–37.
3 *'Dans un pays qui a une ancienne tradition parlementaire, dans un pays surtout qui, comme l'Angleterre, a le respect du loyalisme et le mépris des systèmes, il est à peu près impossible de se glisser entre les partis. On peut, à l'intérieur d'un parti, lentement préparer un essaimage: on ne peut imposer des idées nouvelles que sous une étiquette connue.'* (André Maurois, *La Vie de Disraëli*, Libraire Gallimard, Paris, 1927, p. 94.)

Wednesday 11th March

Alexander puts over his Navy estimates. Very successfully. He has done well lately. He is beginning to be spoken of as a future Prime Minister. By no means impossible.

Thursday 12th March

India debate. Baldwin v. Churchill, an open duel. Tories sit dumb and bewildered. Baldwin in his best form. Winston inconceivably diehard and mischievous.[1]

Saturday 14th March

Vernon Hartshorn[2] died suddenly yesterday. I have, after reflection, no ambition to succeed to a Cabinet job on the economic front.

Sunday 15th March

Bad mess on Electoral Reform Bill. Beaten by 4 votes (246:242) on abolition of University seats. Two of our Members, Wedgwood and Church[3] (B.Sc. *External!*) vote against and about 20 are away unpaired – some sick and unpairable, some slack, some at by-elections and unpaired through muddle with whips' office. Liberals let us down badly (nearly as many vote and pair against as for, and many absentees).

General fury. Lloyd George, having voted with us, goes home and finds Megan and Gwilym[4] sitting in front of the fire in their pyjamas! Neither had voted. It is said he spanked them both. Sinclair,[5] Liberal Chief Whip, resigns, as a protest against indiscipline.

1 On 27th January 1931 Churchill resigned from the Conservative Shadow Cabinet because of his opposition to Baldwin's support for the India policy of the Labour Government.
2 Vernon Hartshorn, q.v., had been Lord Privy Seal.
3 Major Archibald Church (1886–1954). Labour M.P. for Wandsworth Central 1929–31; Leyton East 1923–4. General Secretary of the Association of Scientific Workers 1920–31.
4 Gwilym Lloyd George, later 1st Viscount Tenby (1894–1967). Liberal M.P. for Pembrokeshire 1922–4, 1929–50. Conservative M.P. for Newcastle upon Tyne North 1951–7. Junior minister 1931, 1939–41. Minister of Food 1941–2, 1951–4; Fuel and Power 1942–5. Home Secretary and Minister for Welsh Affairs 1954–7. Son of David Lloyd George, q.v.
5 Sir Archibald Sinclair, 4th Bart; later 1st Viscount Thurso (1890–1970). Liberal Chief Whip 1930–31. Liberal M.P. for Caithness and Sutherland 1922–45. Secretary of State for Scotland 1931–2; Air 1940–45. Leader of the Parliamentary Liberal Party 1935–45. In fact, Sinclair stayed on as whip until August.

Thursday 19th March
Austin Robinson[1] to lunch, to discuss the possibility of his becoming
the Foreign Office Economist – if we can get this authorised. Very
pleasant and pretty capable, but not much character.

Monday 23rd March
Tom Johnston is to be Lord Privy Seal. He was my choice. Graham,
sitting beside me on the bench during debate on Russian timber, asks
me whether I have asked Uncle to press my claim to a Cabinet rank.
He thinks that I should have been considered before Morrison and
Johnston. I say I have no desire to shift from my present job. He says,
'No, but it is important to be in the Cabinet, and have a share in
directing policy.' He adds that there is a gulf between Uncle and
MacDonald and that he himself is not one of the latter's favourites.
This is a human unbending of Graham! He adds that he will himself
speak to Uncle next week about this point.

Thursday 16th April
A confidential talk with Uncle, initiated by him, on Cabinet reconstruction. He and Snowden are probably going to the Lords, in succession to Parmoor and Passfield. Snowden will never be the same
man again after his illness.[2] As to himself, he will have to be away
for some months next year at the Disarmament Conference[3] and he
will be seventy soon, and must keep his hold on Transport House.

To be relieved of the strain of the House of Commons and a constituency would be a great assistance to him. Van, he says, is very keen
he should take a peerage. (I think also he fears that he may lose Burnley
next time.) What do I feel about my own position? I say that I am the
only member of the late Parliamentary Executive who is not now
either resigned or in the Cabinet. I think I should now come in. Even
one of his Cabinet colleagues has asked me whether I have asked him

1 E. A. G. Robinson, later Professor Sir Austin (b. 1897). Economist. Lecturer,
  Cambridge University 1929–49. Fellow of Sidney Sussex College, Cambridge since
  1931. Government economist (Economic Section of the Ministry of Production,
  Board of Trade, Economic Planning Staff) 1939–48. Director of Economics at the
  Ministry of Power 1967–8.
2 Early in March Snowden fell ill with inflammation of the bladder. After a prostate
  operation, he retired for seven weeks' convalescence at Tilford. Graham took over
  some of the routine work of the Treasury, but Snowden continued from his sick-
  bed to exercise authority on important matters, including the preparation of the
  Budget.
3 The international Disarmament Conference, which opened in February 1932.
  Henderson was later appointed by the League Council to preside over it. See below,
  pp. 145–6.

to push my claims. If Graham succeeds Snowden, I think I have good claim to the Board of Trade.

He is very friendly and agrees that the time has come when my claims must be seriously considered. He thinks no one would question that. But, short of the Cabinet, would I care to succeed Pethick-Lawrence at the Treasury. That is a post which is always thought of as having next claim to Cabinet rank. I say no, certainly not. Then he paints the advantages of staying where I am with him in the Lords. I should then have charge of all Foreign Office business in the House. And prospect of succession later. I am not unattracted by this at first sight, but say that, if so, I should be a Privy Councillor. He takes the point, but says MacDonald is very chary of giving out P.C.s. As successor to me, he couldn't think of anyone but Phil [Noel-Baker], who has wonderful knowledge, but not perhaps yet much judgment. I agree that there is no one else in serious running.

The vote is amazing.[1] Government majority 54! And I had estimated a one in four chance of defeat. Now we should run on till autumn at earliest. And if only the unemployment figures will go on falling, everything will wear quite a different aspect then.

(Discussing the Cabinet reconstruction with Ruth, she is not keen on my staying at the Foreign Office and quite indifferent about the Privy Councillor. She thinks I should push hard for the Cabinet. I tell her I am afraid of the Board of Trade, with a coal crisis looming only two months ahead, and my coal constituency and, she adds, with possibly a disgruntled Shinwell[2] being disloyal behind my back.)

Tuesday 21st April
Start up another talk with Uncle, about the future. He is tired and sleepy and inclined to be peevish. So the talk is not superficially a success. But appearances are not all. I tell him that if there are to be two new vacancies in the Cabinet I consider that I ought to have one of them. I recall that I am now the only member of the Parliamentary Executive in the last House who is not either in the Cabinet or resigned. Also the Prime Minister's conversation with me when he offered me my present job. 'Several people thought you ought to be in the Cabinet but there are three or four of you very much on a level.'

Uncle is obviously disappointed at my not having been more

---

1 On a Tory censure motion on unemployment.
2 Emanuel Shinwell, later Baron (1884–1986). Parliamentary Secretary, Department of Mines at the Board of Trade 1924, 1930–31. Financial Secretary at the War Office 1929–30. Ruth's remark was prescient, in view of Dalton's difficult relationship with Shinwell during the fuel crisis of 1947, sixteen years later, when Dalton was Chancellor. See Appendix.

glamoured by taking charge of foreign affairs in the House of Commons. He says grumpily, 'Well, I don't want to stand in anybody's way.' I develop my 'claims to the Board of Trade'. He says, 'I shouldn't begin thinking of particular jobs. That only leads to disappointment.' He expresses doubts about Phil Noel-Baker. I say he has had a wonderful training inside the office 'for nearly two years'. He replies, 'Yes, but Phil is not you.' I say that I might be able to help him inside the Cabinet. He has sometimes complained that he got little support. He replies, 'Cabinets don't work like that. I have been in four now ......
I don't want to build up a force inside the Cabinet ...... if I can't get my way over disarmament, I shall go out.' So it ends rather inconclusively. I might have broken it off earlier, but, in his mood, could hardly have pushed it further.

Tuesday 28th April
Uncle says he has now succeeded in regularising weekly meetings between Cabinet leaders and Liberal leaders. They are to happen once a week, and afford an opportunity for discussing any current business and the Liberals informing their Party Meeting. Uncle has been trying to bring this sort of thing about for two years. Today there was MacDonald, Snowden, Uncle and Thomas; Lloyd George, Samuel, Sinclair and Lothian.[1]

Wednesday 29th April
Walked up Whitehall, with Hankey. He said of Van that he was 'very cultured for a civil servant'. Phil Noel-Baker heard from Rajchman,[2] who was at Chequers last weekend, that the Prime Minister asked who was being thought of for the Presidency of the Disarmament Conference. Rajchman said Uncle. A long silence. Then MacDonald said, 'Yes, a lot of people wanted me to take it, and I could have if the Conference had been in London. But if it is to be in Geneva, of course I couldn't spare the time.' And this to a foreigner and almost a complete stranger! Did he think that this wouldn't be passed on, or that, if it was, it would seem anything but childish jealousy!

Tuesday 5th to Tuesday 26th May
Sit on Selection Board for entrants for Foreign Office and Diplomatic

1 P. H. Kerr, 11th Marquess of Lothian (1882–1940). Secretary to the Prime Minister 1916–21. Chancellor of the Duchy of Lancaster in the first 1931 National Government. Ambassador to the United States 1939–40.
2 Ludwig Rajchman (1881–1965). Polish delegate to the League of Nations Assembly. Director of the League Health Organisation. Chief Bacteriologist at the Royal Institute for Public Health in London 1910–13.

Service exam. Entry of 76 (unusually large) including about 20 who are obviously quite good. More entrants than usual from the Universities other than Oxford or Cambridge – London, Birmingham, Manchester, Sheffield and University College, Loughborough all represented, though not very well. Of the 76, 3 or 4 don't appear, 9 are rejected. One referred back for a year and 3 or 4 allowed to go in for Consular only. One or more from London (King's), Birmingham, Manchester and Sheffield get through, so I hope this will encourage these new sources of supply. I have rather a fight for some of them.

Thursday 7th May
Norris[1] to lunch to explain about Ruth's annuity, which will have to pay both Legacy Duty and its share of Estate Duty, and will, therefore, not rise above about £880 gross, and be diminished further at the beginning. But we are on record as believers in the principle of death duties!

Tuesday 12th May
Lunch with Titulescu[2] at the Ritz in a *cabinet particulier*. He gives an amusing and accurate summary of the British political situation, and claims that he is one of the few members of the Diplomatic Corps who understand our politics, because he doesn't consort exclusively with duchesses. He also shows me a memorandum in Romanian (which he translates into French for me) written by Argetoianu[3] for the King,[4] advising a royal dictatorship and the suspension of Parliament. He has obtained it from a secret source and will publish it if necessity demands.

He keeps a sort of chancery in a suite of rooms upstairs at the Ritz. He is going to Geneva on the 14th. He won't travel on the 13th, because he is superstitious. He doesn't know who will be coming from Bucharest, but 'in any case I shall represent Romania'. I suggest that, perhaps, we will find Argetoianu there. He screams shrilly, as is his

---

1 Ruth's solicitor. Ruth's mother, Valentine Fox, had died on 19th April. The annuity came from money left to Valentine by her friend Sir Arthur Peterson, who had died in 1922.
2 Nicolae Titulescu (1883–1941). Romanian Minister in London 1922–6, 1928–32. Foreign Minister 1927, 1932–6.
3 Constantin Argetoianu (1871–1952). Romanian Minister of Finance and Home Affairs. Leader of the Agrarian Party (later allied to the Iron Guard). Prime Minister, following the murder of Calinescu by the Iron Guard, from 28th September to 23rd November 1939.
4 King Carol (1893–1953). In 1938 Carol set up a Government of National Union and abolished political parties by law.

habit, and says, 'Then I shall send him away. He would not dare to come.'

Thursday 14th May
I attend, in Uncle's absence, the Three Party C.I.D.[1] on Disarmament. A wretchedly inconsequent meeting. They all say whatever comes into their heads, and no one except Samuel wants to disarm. They wonder how good the French Air Force is, and whether the German evasions of the Peace Treaty are serious. Tom Shaw says he saw the Stahlhelm[2] drilling and thought they were very efficient. He isn't sure in which year. He thinks it was in 1926. Austen [Chamberlain] wonders whether we oughtn't to let the Germans reintroduce conscription. He thinks a mistake was made in prohibiting it at Versailles. Lothian says that the Germans at present have no security. They couldn't defend themselves if attacked. The problem is to give them security. Hoare[3] thinks we ought to have conversations with the French and also perhaps with the Germans, before the Conference meets. He asks the P.M. whether he would have been happy to go into the London Naval Conference without having had conversations with the Americans. The P.M. says No. A poor rambling discussion.

Monday 18th May
Uncle has been offered the Presidency of the Disarmament Conference. Phil [Noel-Baker] rings up from Geneva asking me to do what canvassing I can for a favourable answer from tomorrow's Cabinet. But it seems to me impossible to doubt an acceptance. I ring up Van, who will try to catch the P.M. tonight on his return from Buckingham Palace.

1 The Committee of Imperial Defence Sub-Committee on the Disarmament Conference (known as the 'Three Party Committee') was set up by MacDonald in March 1931. Its job was to advise on the policy to be adopted at the forthcoming Disarmament Conference. Dalton attended meetings on 14th and 21st May and on 16th July, in Henderson's absence.
2 The Stahlhelm ('steel helmet') was the largest of the German ex-servicemen's organisations. A bitter feud developed in the early 1930s between the Stahlhelm and Hitler's S.A., which eventually absorbed its rival at the end of 1933. The Stahlhelm was formally dissolved in 1935.
3 Sir Samuel Hoare, 2nd Bart, later 1st Viscount Templewood (1880–1959). Conservative M.P. for Chelsea 1910–44. Secretary of State for Air 1922–4, 1924–9, 1940; India 1931–5. Foreign Secretary 1935. Home Secretary 1937–9. First Lord of the Admiralty 1936–7. Lord Privy Seal (in the War Cabinet) 1939–40. Ambassador to Spain on Special Mission 1940–44.

Wednesday 20th May

Van tells me that he saw the P.M. late last night, who made all sorts of difficulties. How would the Foreign Office be run? etc. The Cabinet sent a message to Uncle saying that they left the decision to his discretion, since he would be in the best position to realise all the difficulties, from the Foreign Office and for the Party Organisation. Several were strongly against his acceptance. Jealousy, ignorance of the probable conditions of the Conference and a desire that Uncle should always be on top in London to take on everybody else's burden and get them out of the holes which they dig for themselves, combined in this 'decision'.

Uncle on receiving this message said it was no good to him, and if he was to accept it, he must have a warmer message, thanking on behalf of H.M.G. for honour conferred, etc. Selby on the telephone most of the day from Geneva. Van succeeded, with some difficulty, in getting this from the P.M. and Uncle duly made a public acceptance in suitable terms.

Thursday 21st May

Another Three Party C.I.D. Salmond[1] present to reply to questions. Admits that there is no defence, except counter-attack, against air attack. If, e.g., we were at war with France, the French would attack London and we should go for Paris. Someone asked whether our objectives in such a case would be purely military or not. Salmond said that on such a point, he would have to ask the Cabinet for instructions. The P.M. at this stage became very fidgety, and said he thought we shouldn't pursue this point any further; it wouldn't arise at Geneva.

Friday 22nd May

House adjourns for Whitsun recess. I go down to West Leaze and have a lovely uninterrupted holiday, with only two pouches for a week. Do a lot of useful chalk-carting, sodding, etc., and have some after supper walks with Ruth 'into our view'.

Thursday 4th June

In the evening dine, with Ruth, at the Belgian Embassy to meet Uncle and Aunt! I sit between Mrs Snowden and Lady Colefax.[2] The former

---

1 Sir John Salmond, later Marshal of the R.A.F. (1881–1968). Chief of Air Staff 1930–33. Director of Armament Production at the Ministry of Aircraft Production 1939–45.
2 Sybil, Lady Colefax, née Halsey. Political hostess. Married to Sir Arthur Colefax, a barrister and former Conservative M.P.

says that 'Philip would be lost if he retired', and that 'above his waist he is still a man of forty-five'.

We go on, killing two social birds with one stone, to the Austrian Legation, where a musical party is being given. It starts at 11.15. We leave about 12. Music not very good this time, bored faces, over rich women (only a few pretty), standardised men, uncomfortable chairs, and that wretched Tugendhat[1] hanging round all the time!

And thus do diplomats and 'Society' live!

Friday 3rd to Sunday 5th July
Uncle and Aunt for the weekend to West Leaze. Very hard work, but very successful. Weather not very good. ... He is very pet. Asks what is the name of this style of house. And which is the front. But they like the hot water laid on. Local Wesleyans come to ask him to take a service. He would like to next time he comes, if they will make 'suitable arrangements' with me!

He thinks MacDonald will retire from leadership when next we go into Opposition. I gravely doubt it. In another ten years our young men will have been trained, he thinks. Lloyd George and 20 Liberals or so may soon come clean over. And, if so, Lloyd George might have to come into the Government at once. His vitality is amazing and his recent speeches have made a tremendous appeal to our people in the House.

Tuesday 14th July
Harvey[2] to lunch, tête-à-tête. Still wants to be a Labour candidate as much as ever. But not inclined to leave the service till an election is imminent. Hopes to come back to the Office in the autumn and would like to be attached to Uncle somehow for next year's Disarmament Conference.

Phil Noel-Baker is not sure whether he likes Harvey very much. Nor am I. But he is, I think, competent and would be useful.

Thursday 16th to Friday 17th July
In the small hours of the 16th – all night sitting caused by I.L.P.

---

1 George Tugendhat (1898–1973). Austrian economist and banker. Former L.S.E. student.
2 Oliver Harvey, later 4th Bart, 1st Baron (1893–1968). First Secretary at the Paris Embassy 1931–6. Private Secretary to the Foreign Secretary 1936–9, 1941–3. Ambassador to France 1948–54.

opposition to Unemployment Insurance Anomalies Bill[1] – Thomas says to Ernie Hunter in the Bar, 'What folly it is to spend hours like this, when within a few hours we may have to declare a moratorium, and make big changes in the Government!' There have been rumours for some days, circulating among private members, of the formation of 'a National Government' to carry through moratoriums, etc., and a Treasury official (Fergusson)[2] has been running about saying that this is 'worse than 1914'! This is treacherous rubbish. Would Tories refuse to agree to emergency legislation, unless given a share of jobs in the Government? Then the sooner some of us come out and start to rebuild the Labour Party and its policy the better!

...

I catch the 6 p.m. train to Hungerford on Friday. Ernie Hunter boards the train to get a story. He has heard of my departure by this train. I give him a good deal. He says he gathers that the relations of Uncle and the P.M. are very bad. He adds that the P.M. has only three times sent for him since he has been lobby correspondent. Each time it was to try to get a paragraph in the *Herald* with some private whine – first, to complain that he hadn't been put on the Pilgrim Trust Committee, second, during the Round Table Conference to complain of prominence given to Reading's[3] speech and to insist that Mac-Donald was really in charge and directing everything, third – some other personal grouse, he forgets what about. But no such paragraph ever got in!

On Thursday night I dined with Ponsonby at the House, and he told me all about the sad case of Lord Beauchamp,[4] who has had a persistent weakness for footmen, and has been finally persuaded by

1 The Anomalies Bill was introduced in response to the Royal Commission on Unemployment Insurance, whose interim report in June recommended higher contributions and reduced benefits. The Bill gave the Minister of Labour powers to make alterations in the terms and amount of benefit. It was bitterly opposed by the Left, and nineteen I.L.P. members voted against it on the Second Reading. Though the Bill was passed, the all-night sitting of 15th July (when the I.L.P. group forced a total of thirty-three divisions) helped to make the split between the Maxtonites and the Labour leadership irreconcilable.
2 J. D. B. Fergusson, later Sir John (1891–1963). Private Secretary to successive Chancellors of the Exchequer 1920–36. Permanent Secretary at the Ministry of Agriculture 1936–45; Fuel and Power 1945–52.
3 Sir Rufus Isaacs, 1st Marquess of Reading (1860–1935). Foreign Secretary August–November 1931. Liberal M.P. 1904–13. Solicitor-General 1910; Attorney-General 1910–13; Lord Chief Justice 1913–21. Ambassador to the United States 1918–19. Viceroy of India 1921–6.
4 Sir William Lygon, 7th Earl of Beauchamp (1872–1938). Chancellor of London University 1929–31. Lord President of the Council 1910, 1914–15. K.G. 1914.

Simon and Buckmaster[1] to sign an undertaking not to return to England. The King didn't want a scandal because he was a Knight of the Garter!

Monday 20th July
Van tells me that he has never been so conscious of personal difficulties and frictions in any Cabinet he has known, as in this one. Baldwin used to have terrible trouble with Winston and Jix,[2] but it was only occasional and one knew when one was in for trouble. In this Cabinet one has to be on the lookout all the time. The rivalries and suspicions are always just below the surface, ready to burst out at any moment. Also the anti-French views are widespread and almost unreasoning – not only in the Cabinet but in all parts of the House of Commons, in the City and in the press. When he was going to Paris as a youth to learn French, an aunt threatened to cut him out of her will, and did. She thought Paris was a wicked place. The Victorian view was that the French practised all sorts of occult forms of sexual intercourse and were the wildest people on earth. The modern view was the same, only it had turned from the sexual to the political. If you went to Paris, you would catch some politico-venereal disease. They would infect you with their ideas and their guarantees. That was why the P.M. and Snowden had wanted to recall Uncle last week. But it was going better now. The City today was pale, but confident.

Phil Noel-Baker tells me that Laval[3] is a lawyer who earns a very large income, but never pleads. He always settles out of court. A good one! Uncle says Briand[4] is failing. He will go off suddenly one day. Even in the morning now he nods and loses grip, not only in the afternoon when he has had several glasses of wine at lunch.

Tuesday 21st July
King Albert and I are the chief speakers at a lunch organised by Dunnico[5] at the House for the Peace Society. King Albert full of buts

---

1 Sir Stanley Buckmaster, 1st Baron, later 1st Viscount (1861–1934). Liberal M.P. 1906–10, 1911–14. Solicitor-General 1913–15; Lord Chancellor 1915–16.
2 Sir William Joynson Hicks, 1st Bart, 1st Viscount Brentford (1865–1932). Conservative M.P. 1908–10, 1911–29. Junior minister 1922–3; Postmaster-General and Paymaster-General 1923; Financial Secretary to the Treasury 1923; Minister of Health 1923–4. Home Secretary 1924–9.
3 Pierre Laval (1883–1945). Prime Minister of France 1931–2. Socialist. Foreign Minister and Prime Minister several times 1934–44. Executed in 1945 for collaborating with the Germans.
4 Aristide Briand (1862–1932). French Foreign Minister 1926–32. Prime Minister eleven times 1909–26.
5 Rev. H. Dunnico, later Sir Herbert (1876–1953). Labour M.P. for Consett 1922–31. Baptist minister.

and ifs. I, following, speak of the Angel of Death in the Air ... and tell them of my early morning thoughts today. I receive many congratulations. The truth is that the comrades are refreshed to hear the old tale well told, stirring again propaganda memories and high hopes, from the lips of a member of a government that has grown befuddled with caution and indecisive self-importance.

Saturday 25th July
At Durham for the Miners' Gala. Maxton and Cook[1] the chief speakers. A downpour of rain, but crowds stood patiently, with or without umbrellas, listening for hours.

Tuesday 28th July
Stainer rings me at 7 a.m. to say that Canon D. died at 3.30. I go down to Windsor with Georgie,[2] who, egocentric as ever, weeps a little when she thinks she has 'never had a real father'. Mrs Dalton[3] surprisingly calm. ... For his own sake, it was well he lived no longer. His sight and hearing were failing and his nerves getting out of control. His disabilities were fast closing in upon him, and he was increasingly unendurable to those who lived with him. For me his affection continued quite unabated. ...

... [I] make arrangements for his cremation and for his funeral, and for his ashes to rest in St George's. This is obviously fitting, and the Dean[4] is immediately for this. But this latter is a queer, ill-bred man, though professionally a courtier-priest. When I call to see him, he tells me how difficult a colleague the old man was, how small a literary output he left behind, and how he lacked mental control and how he ran people and made favourites of them.

In August 1931, the Bank of England asked for an additional loan from the United States – in a desperate bid to save the gold standard, threatened by a

1 Arthur Cook (1885–1931). General Secretary of the Miners' Federation of Great Britain 1924–32. Spent twenty-one years underground. Jointly responsible for the Cook–Maxton Manifesto of 1928. Died 2nd November.
2 Alexandra Mary Forbes Watson, later Lady Forbes Watson, née Dalton (1891–1974). Hugh Dalton's sister. Married to J. B. Forbes Watson, later Sir John, Director of the British Employers' Confederation. She was called 'Georgie' after her royal godfather, Prince George, later King George V.
3 Catherine Alicia Dalton, née Evan-Thomas (1841–1944). Married Canon Dalton 1886. Mother of Hugh and Georgie.
4 The Very Revd A. V. Baillie (1864–1955). Dean of Windsor and Domestic Chaplain to the King 1917–44.

run on sterling. The New York Federal Reserve Bank replied that the British government should first show its intention of making economies, including a heavy cut in unemployment benefit. This was too much for many Cabinet Ministers. Twelve accepted a 10 per cent cut as necessary; but a minority refused to accept what seemed the negation of everything the Labour Party stood for. The Cabinet reached deadlock, and on 23rd August MacDonald went to the Palace ostensibly to offer the resignation of the Government. Instead, he announced to the Cabinet next day that the King was to invite 'certain individuals, as individuals, to take upon their shoulders the burden of the Government', and indicated that he, MacDonald, was to be one of these individuals.[1] Three ministers, Snowden, J. H. Thomas and Lord Sankey, were invited to join the new Cabinet and agreed to do so. Lord Amulree joined the Government later. All other Cabinet Ministers and most junior ministers lost their jobs and were replaced by Conservatives and Liberals.

Before the decision to form a National Government had finally been made, Dalton was summoned to a meeting of junior ministers at No. 10 Downing Street. This took place on 24th August. The Prime Minister tried to explain his actions. 'Christ crucified speaks from the cross', wrote Dalton bitterly. But he added, 'I go back tonight to West Leaze breathing cleaner air, happier than for many months.'[2] He did not return to office for nearly nine years.

Monday 17th August
From Windsor to West Leaze. Three unbelievable days in the study, looking through and destroying and sorting old papers and letters. He never threw anything away. Letters, all from men, except from members of the Dalton family. Some letters very affectionate. A strong homosexual strain is very clear. Men fifty and sixty years younger than he called him 'John'. The more interesting we put aside. Drawers stuffed at random with old newspaper cuttings, old bills (one for the repair of an umbrella two years before I was born), Royal letters, letters from protégés, all higgledy-piggledy. Dust, literally of generations, and, according to the faithful Ada, fleas also.

There is to be a great bonfire in the Chapter garden, and the dust-man will work overtime for weeks! ......

And so back to West Leaze and Peace.

Wednesday 26th August
My birthday. Happy, though weary. Finish at the Foreign Office.

1 PRO, Cabinet Conclusions, 23rd August 1931.
2 Diary, 24th August 1931.

Pay a round of visits with Gladwyn Jebb to the Departments and say goodbye to officials. A very nice lot these officials. Gladwyn and Van in a class apart so far as personal affections go and I shall miss my daily contacts with them. Arranged that Gladwyn shall go to Rome, an attractive post. He is quite pleased at this, and so is his wife. He and I have had great fun together. He tells me that he thinks I know by now where his sympathies are. He could not go on with my successor except very briefly, to tide over a week or two.

Shall I, one day, return as Secretary of State? It is not impossible, but politics are a queer uncertain business. The prospects of all of us 'younger' men are, however, much improved by the defections and the clearance at the top. ...

Rumour, later confirmed, puts Lord Reading at the Foreign Office. Precedents indeed are being broken. First a Secretary of State who has had no University education. Now one who has no foreskin.

A very wearisome joint meeting of National Executive, General Council and Consultative Committee. Poor old Uncle rather on edge and doesn't do himself justice allowing Cook and Burnley to rattle him. General Council very irritating and full of suspicion. Finally, after much palaver, *unanimously* agreed to offer vigorous opposition to new Government to approve action of ministers in declining to join and to recommend Parliamentary Party to become official Opposition. A small committee to draw up manifesto for tomorrow.

Frank Owen[1] to dinner. Ruth dislikes him as vulgar, untrustworthy and careerist. (She thinks he is the same type as John Beckett.) He is half inclined to come over, and will raise hell at Liberal Party Meetings. He thinks 10 will vote regularly with us. I doubt this.

Thursday 27th August
Tom Johnston to lunch. Awfully tired, but gives a very interesting account of some recent Cabinet history. He, Greenwood and Lansbury were against any dole cut throughout, others only joined up later. Uncle deliberately held back, while others did the fighting. But he never finally assented to anything. He always said he must see the complete picture. Then at the end he dug his feet in against the dole cut and then MacDonald saw the game was up. The resignations would be too numerous and important for replacements to be probable from the ranks of the Party. ...

Snowden had been very bitter at the majority of 15 to 6 for the revenue tariff and particularly bitter against Graham. He had said,

1 Frank Owen (1905–79). Liberal M.P. for Hereford 1929–31. Author and journalist. Editor of the *Evening Standard* 1938–42.

'William, there shall be a Free Trade candidate next time in Central Edinburgh.' He had refused to accept the majority decision, and even demanded that the vote should be rescinded. 'I can't stay in a Cabinet', he said, 'where 15 members are in favour of a revenue tariff.' And Uncle rubbed in afterwards on other issues the fact that a minority had a right to stand out and not yield to a majority.

In Paris last weekend Johnston had been told by Flandin[1] that Norman had twice asked the Bank of France to buy gold in London in order to maintain the price of sterling. Wigram[2] of our Embassy was present, and vouched for the settlement.

In the afternoon a good joint meeting agreed on the terms of a very good manifesto.

We shall give this 'National' Government the hell of a time in the coming weeks. But it would be a tactical mistake to defeat them too soon.

At a meeting of ex-Cabinet Ministers this morning, Uncle apparently agreed to accept the leadership, and Clynes will, magnanimous as usual, propose this himself tomorrow.

Those who voted for the dole cut are very angry with the *Daily Herald* for spilling the beans and showing them up.

MacDonald has been crawling along the hedgerows in search of Labour ministers these last few days. He offered the Ministry of Pensions to Malone (F. O. Roberts's[3] P.P.S.) and gave him an hour to make up his mind. He rang up me and Uncle and perhaps others asking advice. He got it!

Petica Robertson to tea. Very intelligent and quite on the right side. She has always hated MacDonald and was nearly sick when I took off his speech to the junior ministers.

Friday 28th August
An historic meeting of the Parliamentary Labour Party at Transport House. ...

Henderson, Sankey and Dalton were among speakers at this meeting. 'The first Labour Government had been destroyed by a Red Letter,' Dalton told

---

1 Pierre Flandin (1889–1958). French Conservative politician. Minister in several governments 1929–34. Prime Minister and Foreign Minister 1934–6. Foreign Minister in the Vichy administration 1940–41.
2 Ralph Wigram (1890–1936). First Secretary at the British Embassy in Paris 1924–33.
3 F. O. Roberts (1867–1941). Minister of Pensions 1924, 1929–31. Labour M.P. for West Bromwich 1918–31, 1935–41.

colleagues, 'the second by a Bankers' Order.'[1] Most M.P.s agreed. Only one was prepared to support the Prime Minister – MacDonald's son, Malcolm. After rejecting one Party Leader, the P.L.P. chose another. Arthur Henderson, the sole candidate, was elected, only a handful of M.P.s, all from the I.L.P. group, dissenting.

Afterwards Phil Noel-Baker and I have a talk and help to draft a talkie for Uncle. Then we walk back with him, and offer our services, if desired, as at Foreign Office. He seems pleased, and asks Phil to go on as P.P.S. 'Now I am going home for a wigging,' he says. But Aunt's wiggings, as Ruth says afterwards, aren't very serious.

Thursday 3rd September
Meeting on finance at Transport House. Also present Graham, Alexander, Greenwood, Lees-Smith, Pethick-Lawrence and Arnold. Discuss Uncle's speeches next week. Mustn't go into too much detail. They say that Snowden never gave them any real details of taxation proposals in the Cabinet.

This Committee to be the nucleus of a slightly larger one, to make financial policy. This will be very important.

To West Leaze in the evening, very tired.

Saturday 5th September
With Ruth to Cripps.[2] A jolly stone house and garden, but practically at Thames level and very dank. Cripps has been ill and Morrison too, who has been staying with him.

More light on the crisis. Cripps is the only lawyer in the House who has stuck to the Party, though he reports that Pritt[3] is sound too. Shows me letters from his father and from Beatrice Webb, his aunt, approving his attitude. The latter says that 'we' have never trusted MacDonald, that Snowden has been ruined by his wife, an 'out and out social climber', and that Thomas is a 'low liver', who has been allowed to do something for the railwaymen, in order that he may get a reputation as a T.U. leader, and then be used against other workers. ...

1 Diary, 28th August 1931.
2 Sir Stafford Cripps (1889–1952). Labour M.P. for Bristol East. Solicitor-General 1930–31. See Appendix.
3 D. N. Pritt (1887–1972). Labour, then Independent, M.P. for Hammersmith North 1935–50. Barrister (K.C.). Fellow traveller. Later a member of the Labour Party N.E.C. Expelled from the Labour Party in 1940 for writing in support of the Soviet invasion of Finland.

Cripps thinks that MacDonald was outmanoeuvred by the King, the Tories and the bankers. He understands that, when MacDonald offered his resignation on the Sunday night, Baldwin flatly refused to form a government. And then the King told MacDonald he must stay and form a 'National' government. I doubt this version. ...

Jowitt, he says, is quite broken and is retiring from politics. He feels he must stick to MacDonald, who had stuck to him and made a special friend of him, when he was ostracised and he and his wife insulted, when he joined the Labour Government as Attorney-General. I make an outburst at this and speak of giving hostages to rich society. My friends, I say, are poorer and simpler people. Mac-Donald long ago succumbed to the soft conditions and the flattery of the rich.

...

MacDonald, Sankey and Thomas all think they are coming back to the Labour Party. (Snowden is definitely retiring.) What a delusion!

Back at West Leaze feeling cold and dank. But dig with Ruth and feel much better!

Wednesday 16th September
Gandhi[1] at 5.30 and Keynes at 6.30! The former is impressive, so long as he keeps off economics and arms.

But as my friend Tout[2] said afterwards, 'bloody hopeless' when he comes to Lancashire cotton and the hand loom weavers. And on arms he has a terrible physical inferiority complex. He remembers with joy that two swords used to hang on his father's wall. He never drew one of them, and the sight of blood, he says, always makes him faint. But the British have 'emasculated the people of India' by not allowing them to carry arms, and by refusing to recruit them, unless of the 'martial races', for the Army. All Indians should be allowed to carry arms, and then he would appeal to them to make a voluntary surrender of them. ...

Ben Smith[3] reminds me of Bottomley's[4] attack on MacDonald in

---

1 Mohandas Karamchand, known as Mahatma, Gandhi (1869–1948). Leader of the Indian revolutionary nationalist movement. He had been imprisoned in 1930–31 after riots associated with his civil disobedience campaign.
2 W. J. Tout (1870–1946). Labour M.P. for Sowerby 1929–31; Oldham 1922–4. Former weaver.
3 B. Smith, later Sir Ben (1879–1964). Labour M.P. for Rotherhithe 1923–31, 1935–46. Minister of Food 1945–6.
4 Horatio Bottomley (1860–1933). Liberal M.P. 1906–12. Independent M.P. from 1918 to 1922, when he was expelled from the House of Commons. Newspaper proprietor.

155

1919, when he published his birth certificate, showing him to be the illegitimate son of one MacDonald Ramsay, a farm 'grieve' or bailiff, and how the T.U. Congress of that year cheered sympathetically for ten minutes, though most of them thought he had been all wrong about the war. Smith also says that Wing Commander Greig,[1] the Prince of Wales's attendant, had written to a Labour politician who had recently held a Court appointment, saying that he had been 'working for two years' to bring about a National Government. Others about the Court, Ben says, often used to tell them that there ought to be a National Government. Let them beware of being publicly caught *in flagrante delicto* of interference in our domestic politics.

Tuesday 22nd September
Gladwyn to lunch. Nothing much is happening in the Office. Reading seldom 'comes in'. Gladwyn hasn't seen him yet. His 'decisions' on paper look like those of an old man. Eden,[2] he says, has a good manner, and is open to argument. He himself expects to go to Rome in the autumn.

Tuesday 29th September
Graham tells me that Snowden would never tell the late Cabinet anything about his financial plans, because he distrusted Thomas, who, he believed, went out and used all information for speculation.[3] It was said that Thomas was in serious financial trouble, owing £30,000 to £40,000. When Snowden was ill, Thomas said that he was ill in the head as well as in the balls, and this came to Mrs Snowden's ears. She wrote Thomas a violent letter, demanding withdrawal and apology. Thomas wanted to succeed Snowden as Chancellor and also wanted a knighthood for his stockbroker. MacDonald was said to be sympathetic to both these aspirations.

Wednesday 30th September
The saying tonight is 'The Cabinet have been trying for a week to

---

1 Wing-Commander L. Greig, later Sir Louis (1880–1953). Gentleman Usher in Ordinary to the King 1924–36.
2 Anthony Eden, later 1st Earl of Avon (1897–1977). Under-Secretary of State for Foreign Affairs 1931–3. Conservative M.P. for Warwick and Leamington. See Appendix.
3 In May 1936, Thomas was forced to resign his office and his seat after a Tribunal had investigated allegations that he had leaked Budget secrets to a business associate, A. C. Bates, and Sir Alfred Butt, Tory M.P. for Balham and Tooting. Both Butt and Bates insured themselves heavily against rises in taxation which were included in the Budget. It was also disclosed that Bates had paid Thomas £15,000 as an advance for an autobiography which Thomas had not yet begun to write.

find a formula which Sir Herbert Samuel will not accept. So far they have not succeeded.'

Much running between Club and the House of Commons, but Lloyd George is inflexibly against an election.

Willie Graham tells me that he resigned a directorship of the Abbey Road Building Society (Stamp's concern) when he took office, on a written understanding that he should come back when he left office. But he now learns that he will not be reinstated. This means a loss of between £800 to £1000 a year. He finds also that many papers for which he used to write will take nothing from him now. Such is the bitterness!

Thursday 1st October
The Liberals are capitulating to the Tories. Anti-Labour Pacts are being arranged everywhere. Lloyd George is deserted, isolated, and impotent. MacDonald has arranged for *his* deserters all to stand their ground and fight their present constituencies with the aid of the Tory machine and a private fund supplied by 'certain friends'. This is the tale today.

MacDonald announced the dissolution on 2nd October – the first day of the Labour Party Conference in Scarborough. Preparations began for an election in which 'National' Labour and Liberal candidates were to be protected by inter-party arrangements in the constituencies.

Thursday 8th October
Back to London and dine with Gladwyn at house of George Wansbrough,[1] an Etonian Bolshevik who stroked the Cambridge boat, went on the stage, married a Roman Catholic Jewess, daughter of Sir George Lewis,[2] and is now in Bensons (Merchant Bankers). He thinks we ought to nationalise the Stock Exchange. We go to the Gate Theatre to see a play of Schnitzler's[3] – a cycle of fucking scenes. An amazing contrast to the politician's daily life!

1 George Wansbrough (1904–78). Banker. Labour candidate 1935. Joint Treasurer of the New Fabian Research Bureau 1936–7. A Director of the Bank of England 1946–9. Educated at Eton and King's College, Cambridge.
2 Sir George Lewis, 2nd Bart (1868–1927). Solicitor. His daughter, Elizabeth, was Wansbrough's first wife.
3 Arthur Schnitzler (1862–1931). Playwright. His work depicted the decadence of upper-class Viennese life. The play may have been *La Ronde*.

157

Sunday 11th October

After 1 a.m. Met by Joseph Jones[1] and his wife, who had taken a great liking to me. They put me up at their official residence (Yorksdown Miners' Association) near Barnsley. Jones is an intelligent little chap, and a great reader. He fears we shall lose Barnsley, which to me seems (at this stage) unduly pessimistic![2]

Monday 12th October

There is, incidentally, some evidence that, after Mosley faded out, MacDonald looked to Jowitt as his preferred successor. It was being put about that the latter was anxious to leave the Law Officers' Department and take a Secretaryship of State, so as to have a political, rather than a legal, career.

Arrive in the afternoon of this day at Bishop Auckland and start my campaign with three meetings.

Old Brian Bell has been chosen as agent, though I don't hear this till I get to Mrs Brown's. A good old fellow, but quite without knowledge. I have to watch over them at every stage, nominations, getting deposit money, issue of election address, arrangement of meetings, etc.

From the very beginning I am unhappy and uncomfortable in this campaign and I miss Ruth very much.

Wednesday 28th October

At the count it is soon clear that it is pretty close, and fairly early I formed the opinion that I was just out. And so it was.

Curry[3]	17,551
Dalton	16,796
Lib. Nat. Majority	755

I had dropped 1,042 votes as compared with 1929 and Curry had added 3,407 to the combined Liberal and Tory votes.

The crowd outside was largely Curryite. We got away, after a considerable interval, in a car to the Committee Rooms, and here I spoke pretty straight to a small gathering. I said that I had always left the organisation entirely to them; but that whoever fought the seat next time would be a fool to do so again. It was an unheard of thing that a

---

1 Joseph Jones. General Secretary of the Yorkshire Miners' Association. Member of the Labour Party N.E.C. 1926–31.
2 It was not unduly pessimistic. Though apparently safe, Barnsley was lost to the Liberal National candidate by 770 votes.
3 A. C. Curry, q.v.

3 'Congratulations, Mr MacDonald, on Having Got Your Free Hand', 31st
October 1931

Labour Candidate should not know, till he arrived for the opening
of his campaign, who the Agent was to be. But I thanked Brian Bell
and others very warmly for what they had done.

Dalton's unexpected defeat was not an isolated event. The 1931 election was
the greatest landslide of British democratic history. Labour was reduced from
288 to 52 seats, and there were 554 supporters of the Government in the new
House. Only one member of the old Labour Cabinet who was not now in the
National Government survived – George Lansbury, formerly First Commissioner of Works. Outside the Cabinet, the only ministers to hold their
seats were Clement Attlee, Sir Stafford Cripps and five former Under-
Secretaries.

3

Labour and the Slump
1931–7

The 1931 election pushed the Labour Party back to where it had been before 1922 – under-represented in Parliament, but strong and resilient in the constituencies, where local parties and trade union branches played an important part in working-class life. Meanwhile, the loss of seats left the Party leadership awkwardly divided. In the 1920s, the parliamentary leaders had dominated policy and enforced party discipline through their control of the National Executive. Now the direct link between Executive and Parliament was virtually destroyed. Only one N.E.C. member, George Lansbury, was still an M.P. As a result, the Party Executive became a powerful external body, watching its parliamentary rival with a jealous and critical eye. In this division, Dalton found himself on the Executive side.

Later Dalton would speculate that if he had held his seat at Bishop Auckland, instead of just losing it, he would have become Deputy Leader of the Party instead of Attlee, succeeding in due course to the Leadership and then the premiership. 'In the intense and self-regarding life of Westminster', he wrote ruefully in his memoirs, 'the absent are soon forgotten or left out of account.'[1] Yet the scale of the national landslide had advantages for him as well. By retaining his place on the N.E.C. just as this body came into its own, he was able to play a key part in the reformulation of policy. In Parliament, Attlee and Cripps were emerging as the leading figures of the coming generation. Outside Parliament, Dalton and Morrison quickly established themselves as directing influences on the Executive, steering it along a programme-making path that eventually bore fruit in 1945.

Dalton also used his freedom from parliamentary duties to broaden his horizons. In 1932 he visited the Soviet Union with a team of New Fabians – an experience that helped to shape his vision of Britain's socialist future.

1 FY, p. 20.

Later in the same year he made a trip to Italy, where he met Mussolini and was impressed by aspects of Italian corporatism. 'Planning' was much discussed in the early 1930s, and Dalton drew on Soviet and Italian models to develop his own proposals for state control of financial institutions and investment. His ideas appeared in his sixth book, *Practical Socialism for Britain*, published in 1935, which drew on the work of N.E.C. policy committees. *Practical Socialism* was closer to a blue-print for a Labour government than anything previously written, and a high proportion of its recommendations were implemented, in one form or another, by the post-war Attlee administration. The book was Fabian in approach, viewing the transition to socialism as a process of carefully considered administrative acts. The economic section was expansionist and semi-Keynesian. Dalton was implicitly hostile to the cataclysmic assumptions of some on the Left, yet envisaged a rapid programme of nationalisation and the central direction of industry. He also placed a strong emphasis on disinheriting the rich.

Despite the domestic preoccupations of *Practical Socialism*, Dalton's first interest remained foreign policy. When he returned to Parliament after the 1935 general election, he asked the new Party Leader, Clement Attlee, for shadow responsibility for international affairs. Attlee agreed. In the late 1930s, no brief was more important. Much influenced by first-hand observation of Nazi persecutions during a visit to Berlin in 1933, Dalton favoured a strong League policy, and gave full backing to calls for sanctions against Italy over Abyssinia. As spokesman on foreign policy, Dalton saw as his main task the need to persuade Labour – against its own traditions and instincts – to accept the need for collective security through the League, a formula which came to mean opposition to appeasement and support for rearmament. At first it was a lonely fight. Dalton was backed by some leading trade unionists, including Ernest Bevin and Walter Citrine, yet encountered passionate resistance not only from pacifists within the Labour Party, but also from Sir Stafford Cripps and others who argued that a capitalist government of the kind existing in Britain could not be trusted with the possession of arms.

In common with the N.E.C. majority and the leaders of the big unions, Dalton resisted Communist attempts to affiliate to the Labour Party. Though he was sympathetic and helpful towards attempts to democratise elections to the Party Executive, he regarded 'united front' and 'popular front' movements in Britain as Communist-inspired ploys. He was not greatly aroused by the conflict in Spain, focus of left-wing concern from 1936 to 1939. He regarded Hitler as a bigger threat to international peace than Franco, and security against Germany as a more urgent priority for the British government than aid to the Spanish Republic. Hence he had much in common with Léon Blum, the French Socialist leader. At the same time, despite his

161

suspicions of Communism at home, he was a consistent advocate of closer diplomatic relations with the Soviet Union.

Tuesday 3rd November

Perhaps we may say of the Labour Government that it perished of an excess of team spirit. And certainly they knuckled under far too much to MacDonald and Snowden at all stages.

Addison, for instance, told me that during the final discussions, when foreign loans to save the gold standard were under discussion, he asked whether it wouldn't be better and cheaper, and wouldn't get them out of many of their difficulties, to go off gold *then*. He said that Snowden was more insulting to him than anyone had ever been in his life before, and, no one else venturing to take up the point, the Cabinet passed on.

Again ... when Uncle proposed the temporary suspension of the Sinking Fund to help the problem of balancing the Budget, Mac-Donald and Snowden brushed it aside. But a few days later, when these two were in conversation with the Liberal leaders, MacDonald said, 'Samuel wants us to suspend the Sinking Fund. We shall have to consider this very seriously.' Snowden, moreover, during all the discussions, would never give them details of his proposed new taxation, so as to enable them to form any judgment as to how far it carried out 'equal sacrifice' (perhaps as Graham once said to me, because he suspected Thomas of going out and speculating on any confidential information).

And dear old Uncle saved Snowden, when he was in a minority of one in the Cabinet during the Land Values row, and could easily have been irritated into resigning on the spot, by suggesting he should take a night to think it over!

Thursday 5th November

Molly Hamilton[1] to dinner. She says that when the dole cut started in the middle of the election, the Blackburn Employment Exchange Manager expected a row, and asked for extra police, but not one murmur of complaint was heard, even from those who were told to go away and come back next day, because the Exchange had run out of coppers. Such meekness is a miracle. ...

... [O]f the anti-Uncle campaign Malcolm MacDonald had said to her, quite casually, some months ago, 'Of course, Henderson is making an awful mess of foreign affairs.' She had expressed sur-

1 Mary Agnes Hamilton, q.v., M.P. for Blackburn 1929–31.

prise and disagreement, but clearly it was his Father's Voice. He also put about the tale that, during the financial crisis, Uncle telephoned to Briand all the financial secrets Montagu Norman told the Inner Cabinet, so that Norman refused to say anything confidential in Uncle's presence. In fact, Uncle never telephoned to Briand, they having no common language. But the story shows how his close friendship with Briand aroused jealousy and ill-natured comment.

Also on Jowitt. She had met him at lunch with Wilfred Greene,[1] just after his return from the Continent when the First National Government had been formed. He told her that MacDonald had appealed to him as a friend and said, 'I count on you to stand by me.' They hadn't discussed the merits at all, and as we know from Uncle, Jowitt had made no attempt to hear the other side from him. At this lunch, he hadn't quite decided, so he said, and asked advice. He added, 'I have no convictions at all on the matter.' A feeble character, indeed, with all his good legal brains!

('O Molly, I wish to God I had some convictions.')

Tuesday 10th November
To West Leaze with Ruth for a real long spell, a delayed summer holiday of two months. ...

I read Jeans and Eddington, and McTaggart and Goldie's life of him, and Whitehead, and their economics.[2] And Ruth reads Queen Victoria's Letters and Journals, rather fascinating after some of our own Royal letters.[3] This is a beautiful and blessed place and though the making of it was a wise extravagance, it is cheap to run.

I reconcile myself, Ruth thinks, with a surprising lack of outburst, to the changed immediate prospects of my life. Four years out of Parliament, working at and thinking about economics, probably writing and, I hope, travelling. We think of the U.S., a lecture tour, and a visit to the Soviet Union and perhaps next summer Czechoslovakia and Vienna.

1 W. A. Greene, later 1st Baron (1883–1952). Barrister. Standing Counsel to Oxford University 1926–35. Master of the Rolls 1937–49.
2 Dalton may have been reading Sir James Jeans on astronomy; Sir Arthur Eddington on relativity theory; the writings of John McTaggart, the Hegelian philosopher, who had much impressed him at Cambridge; G. L. Dickinson's life of McTaggart (1931); and work by the mathematician and philosopher Alfred Whitehead.
3 Canon Dalton's papers contained letters from royalty (especially from George V) and these had passed into Hugh's possession. They are now in the Royal Archives.

Wednesday 9th to Friday 11th December

Phil and Irene Noel-Baker[1] for the weekend. He is going as Uncle's secretary to the Disarmament Conference in February. More evidence of MacDonald's intentions to form a National Government months ago. Passfield had been trying for months to resign and in June wrote to MacDonald insisting that he must be free by the autumn. And MacDonald replied in a letter, still in June, begging him to stay on a little longer. 'The truth is we have not got the men and I may soon take a decision that will surprise you.'

(I remember that Mrs Webb told me in 1924, when the first Labour Government was formed, that MacDonald had said that his difficulty was that there were so few of his followers who were capable of taking charge of Departments.)

Clifford Allen,[2] moreover, whom he had ignored for years, he suddenly invited to Chequers last autumn, and, having made a great fuss of him, suggested that he should edit a weekly paper to put MacDonald's point of view. This came to nothing, but when the crisis came, Clifford Allen was sent for again and was very busy indeed trying to obtain support for MacDonald within the Labour Party.

Irene asks me what office I should like when we come in again. She thinks the Treasury is terribly important. She thinks I ought to go to the Treasury, and Phil to the Foreign Office! So like her to put it so naïvely!

Friday 1st January 1932

Clifford Allen has been rewarded with a peerage! He wrote letters to *The Times* and other journals in a difficult hour, deploring passion in the crisis and, in appropriate organs of the Inside Left, comparing MacDonald to Lenin in purely strategic retreat. The first imprisoned Conscientious Objector who has been specially ennobled, I think. Ewer suggests Lord Conchie of Maidstone as his title.

The *Evening Standard* says I am really responsible because Allen went up to Cambridge a Tory and 'fell under Dalton's spell'.

But MacDonald will wish for at least one unconditional spokesman on the back-benches in the Lords. 'That queer vain simulacrum of a Statesman' (Wells). 'The greatest snob on Earth' (Winston). Two good summaries. The *Standard* also had a paragraph a week or two ago, reproduced in the *Statesman*, wherein the *Manchester Guardian*

---

1 Irene Noel-Baker, née Noel (d. 1956).
2 Clifford Allen, later 1st Baron (1889–1939). Writer and publicist. Chairman of the I.L.P. 1924–5. Chairman of the Next Five Years Group 1936–7. Dalton first knew Allen as an undergraduate in the Cambridge University Fabian Society.

said that MacDonald had left for the weekend for a destination kept strictly private, and the *Evening Standard* announced that he was spending it with the Londonderrys at their Rutland Seat (How many 'seats' have they altogether?) and had attended a meet of the Cottesmore Hounds. He will end up in a Pink Coat!

My own New Year Resolutions. (1) Never give the appearance of being cynical, (2) tell no one that I keep a Diary.

Wednesday 6th to Friday 8th January
Lionel and Iris Robbins[1] to stay. She has very little to say, and doesn't grow on acquaintance. But she is quite pleasant and has no positive faults. His intellectual development is a disappointment. He will do much distinguished work in economic theory. But he has stiffened in an old-fashioned *laissez-faire* attitude of approach to current problems. He is bemused by modern Viennese theory, and by the personality of Hayek,[2] in particular. He has no belief or interest in, or knowledge of, Planned Economy, such as in the Soviet Union. He over-cultivates his feud with Keynes. He thinks he is working out a diagnosis of our ills in terms of a monetary bacillus. He is exercising a powerful influence – for he has a powerful intellectual personality and much charm – on younger teachers and on students. He is still young enough to grow and change, but *this* phase is negative and rather tiresome. I foresee the possibility of intellectual friction at the School.[3]

Sunday 10th January
Tomorrow we go back to London, after two months at West Leaze. Strength has returned to us both, I hope. We have, at any rate, been quite consciously happy for a large part of the time. And that, in this mottled life, is a rare patch of rich colour.

Monday 11th January
Meeting of the New Fabian Research Bureau[4] to discuss project of a

1 Iris Robbins, née Gardiner.
2 Friedrich von Hayek (b. 1899). Austrian economist and political theorist. Tooke Professor of Economic Science and Statistics at the L.S.E. 1931–50. Director of Austrian Institute for Economic Research 1927–31.
3 Dalton had returned to his full-time teaching post at the L.S.E., with Robbins as his head of department.
4 The New Fabian Research Bureau had been founded in March 1931 by Douglas and Margaret Cole, q.v. The N.F.R.B. was in a nuts-and-bolts, Webbian mould, replacing the virtually moribund Fabian Society, with which it eventually merged. In the summer of 1932 Dalton joined a party of 'New Fabians' on a trip to the Soviet Union. On his return he wrote an essay about Soviet economic planning, published in *Twelve Studies in Soviet Russia* (ed. M. Cole), New Fabian Research Bureau, London, 1933.

Mission of Enquiry to Russia. My name is among those proposed. The chief problem is to find the money.

Dine with Lansbury and Cripps at the Cock. Both full of difficulties of working with Transport House. Cripps has rather wild views on money and foreign investments. Not a very balanced judgment, I fear, though great gifts of character and legal brains. Lansbury toying with idea of Lloyd George coming into the Party. Cripps and I both strongly against this.

Tuesday 12th January

Take Uncle for a walk in St James's Park. Not very well, I fear, and showing signs of nerviness not at all usual in him. Has a strange tale of allegations that Zilly[1] is a Bolshevik agent and may have been having his correspondence tampered with. I must enquire further into this.

Thursday 21st January

Will Henderson tells me that Quibell[2] told him that MacDonald said to him later in the lobby, just after the Palestine fuss, 'I want to put Malcolm in the Government. I wanted to do it when the Government was first formed, but I knew there would be opposition. But I shall do it now at the first opportunity. It is Malcolm who is really responsible for the settlement in Palestine, but Henderson has got all the credit. It's a shame!' More loyalty to colleagues.

Saturday 23rd to Monday 25th January

Ruth and I stay with the Webbs at Passfield Corner.

Mrs Webb is a good seventy-four. They haven't planted anything since I was last here, in 1927 or 28, and they are quite uninterested in the country, and they still talk a lot of 'the producers' and 'the consumers'. It is significant that they had *nothing* to say about Colonial Office problems, and his time there. But they are friendly, and more human than of old. And she full of gossip, much of it feline.

Clifford Allen (whose pamphlet is just out) asked Ponsonby to introduce him in the House of Lords, and seemed quite hurt when Ponsonby said he wouldn't unless Allen would sit with them and take their whip and oppose the Government.

1 Konni Zilliacus (1894–1967). Member of the Information Section of the League of Nations Secretariat 1919–39. Labour, later Independent, M.P. for Gateshead 1945–50. Labour M.P. for Manchester Gorton 1955–67.
2 D. J. K. Quibell, later 1st Baron (1879–1962). Labour M.P. for Brigg 1929–31, 1935–45.

Mr Webb says that MacDonald offered Peerages to Citrine[1] and Bevin[2] some months before the Labour Government fell. Citrine refused at once, and Bevin next day. Citrine keeps a diary of all his doings and conversations and keeps it in typescript.

The Webbs are both much interested in Russia and are going there in May and June. They hope for the success of this Socialist exemplar. They think that, when next we have the opportunity to form a Government, 'we must proceed at once to take over control of finance', etc., and that we should have an undertaking beforehand from the King that he will enable us to do this by creating Peers, if necessary, without waiting for the Parliament Act. They think the King would not agree to a restriction of his prerogative in this respect without an election. Also that MacDonald got from the King an undertaking that he might have a dissolution if the Tories pressed him with policies outside the National Mandate.

When Webb suggested to MacDonald that Ponsonby should lead in the Lords, MacDonald said reflectively, 'Yes, that was what Londonderry suggested to me.' When Webb had warned MacDonald several years before about the difficulty of going to Seaham[3] in view of Londonderry's being a symbol there, MacDonald said, 'That's very awkward. He and I are on Christian name terms.' And Ponsonby told me that MacDonald said to him, after the Lords had thrown out Trevelyan's Bill, 'Londonderry tells me you made a very offensive speech.'

Mrs Webb thinks that MacDonald's suggestion to Citrine of Mosley as Leader was designed to make them want *him* to stay on.

Similarly when in 1924 MacDonald had wanted to take the Foreign Office as well as the Premiership, he had told Brailsford (who rang up Webb in consternation) that Thomas was probably going to the Foreign Office. And he told Snowden in 1931, when he was inclined to give up, that Thomas would succeed him at the Treasury. Webb says it was practically agreed that Snowden should come to the Lords and take the Colonies when *he* retired.

Friday 12th to Sunday 14th February
At Bishop Auckland. Unanimously readopted on 13th February.

---

1 W. Citrine, later Sir Walter, 1st Baron (1887–1983). General Secretary of the Trades Union Congress 1926–46. President of the International Federation of Trade Unions 1928–45. Chairman of the Central Electricity Authority 1947–57.
2 Ernest Bevin (1881–1951). General Secretary of the Transport and General Workers' Union 1921–40. See Appendix.
3 MacDonald was M.P. for Seaham, Co. Durham 1929–35.

Stay with Will Davis.[1] Much activity is being shown now. If a small fraction had been shown before the election, I should still be an M.P. Thank God it wasn't.

During the summer of 1932 Dalton travelled to Russia, visiting Leningrad, Moscow, Sverdlovsk, Magnitorsk, Kazan, Stalingrad, Rostov and Kiev.

Saturday 8th October
For nearly eight months I have given this diary a rest, though I kept one during my visit to the U.S.S.R. in July and August.[2] In May I spent a week in Milan acting as *Rapporteur* in a discussion on 'The State and Economic Life' organised by the International Institute for Intellectual Co-operation. For the rest, I was kept busy by National Executive meetings, including many meetings of its Policy Committee and Sub-Committees, especially that on Finance, of which I was chairman. Uncle's absence at Geneva for the greater part of the year was much felt. He could not exercise influence from a distance and when he came back it was clear that he had lost touch a little with the home situation and had also lost, not unnaturally, a good deal of his old ascendancy over the E.C. The lack of 'coming leaders' is painfully visible. Against everyone, even in the longest line of possibles, there are tremendous objections.

A group got together by Cole meets at intervals to discuss policy. It ends by producing a 'Programme of Action' which it presents to the Executive. I refuse to sign this and have a difficult job in steering between non-co-operation with Cole's group (which includes Lansbury, Cripps, Attlee, Addison, Shinwell, Mellor, Laski and a number of others) and the charge within the Executive Committee of indulging in 'parallel discussion' on policy. Later in the year, owing to the disaffiliation of the I.L.P., a new Socialist League is formed, on the eve of the Annual Conference at Leicester, out of the anti-disaffiliationist section of the I.L.P. led by Wise and Dollan[3] and the S.S.I.P.[4] There

---

1 W. N. Davis. Secretary of the Bishop Auckland Divisional Labour Party. Dalton's closest friend and ally in the constituency. A teacher.
2 Not included here.
3 P. J. Dollan, later Sir Patrick (d. 1963). Chairman of the Scottish I.L.P. 1920–31. Leader of the I.L.P. minority in Scotland which opposed the decision of the July 1932 I.L.P. Conference to disaffiliate from the Labour Party. After this split, Dollan helped to set up the Scottish Socialist Party, whose activities parallelled those of the (purely English) Socialist League (see n. 4 below).
4 The Society for Socialist Inquiry and Propaganda. Founded by the Coles in 1930

is much suspicion of this new body in orthodox circles, at Transport House and on the National Executive, and some opposition within S.S.I.P. itself. The whole problem of personal relationships is increasingly difficult. The Parliamentary Party is a poor little affair, isolated from the N.E. whose only M.P. is Lansbury. Attlee is Deputy Leader of the Parliamentary Party – a 'purely accidental position' as someone puts it – and he and Cripps, who are in close touch with Cole, sit in Lansbury's room at the House all day and all night and continually influence the old man. With none of these are Uncle's relations close or cordial.

Cripps, who has many good points, including personal charm and political courage, breaks down unexpectedly. Though a first class lawyer, according to ordinary standards of judgment, he doesn't, as Wilfred Greene put it to Molly Hamilton, 'know a good point from a bad one'. On currency he runs after crank theories and his speeches are thought by many to be curiously 'irresponsible'. Attlee is a small person, with no personality, nor real standing in the Movement. ...

West Leaze is a lovely possession and a great source of health as well as happiness. We have let 5 Carlisle Mansions till next March and I have lodgings in Bloomsbury for mid-weeks during School term.

From Newcastle, whither at the beginning of September I go to attend an E.C. meeting concurrently with the T.U.C., I pay a night's visit to the Trevelyans at Wallington. I spend a day with Trevelyan on his estate, looking at his afforestation schemes. In the evening the family and visitors sit round and Lady Trevelyan reads aloud. On this occasion she is reading Wilkie Collins's *Woman in White*! There is a great discussion as to what notice should be put in the grounds to discourage visitors from leaving paper about. Appropriate mottoes have been invited and the two most favoured are 'Pigs make litters: why should you?' and 'When you make a litter, Lady Trevelyan has to clear it up after you'. The daughter[1] who has very recently married a German announced that she can feel the baby already inside her.

---

1 Katharine Götsch, née Trevelyan (b. 1908). Married Johann Götsch of Frankfurt in 1932.

---

with Bevin as Chairman, the S.S.I.P. was originally linked to the Coles' other creation, the New Fabian Research Bureau. In October 1932 many S.S.I.P. members joined pro-Labour I.L.P.ers (led by E. F. Wise) in forming the Socialist League, to take the place of the I.L.P. as a socialist society affiliated to the Labour Party. Soon the new League began to rebel against the official Party leadership, and this tendency increased after Cripps succeeded Wise as Chairman of the Socialist League in 1933. Although the S.S.I.P. and the ex-I.L.P.ers never formally united, the S.S.I.P. ceased to operate after the foundation of the League.

And Trevelyan gives it out, to all whom he meets, that he has made £8. 15s. 0d. by selling to delegates of the T.U.C. (who visited Wallington yesterday) copies of his eighteen penny book on the history of Wallington and the Trevelyan family.

We have a little political conversation. He has given up his old constituency, and doesn't feel inclined to re-enter Parliament (his wife is all against his doing any more politics). He is shouting for bold socialist policies, and Cole has recently visited him. (Remember that when asked at the first Cabinet of the second Labour Government, what would be the cost of raising the school leaving age, he couldn't answer!)

On 8th December 1932, Hugh and Ruth left London for Italy in order to study the Corporate State at first hand. The trip was also an opportunity for a holiday in a country they both loved, and a chance to see Gladwyn Jebb, Hugh's former private secretary, now at the Embassy in Rome. Hugh spent much of his time visiting libraries and talking to politicians, economists and other intellectuals. The highpoint of the visit was an audience with Mussolini, which Dalton found at the time a more exhilarating experience than he was later prepared to admit. He returned to England unconverted, but impressed by some aspects of Italian economic planning.

Saturday 17th December
Received by Guido Jung,[1] Minister of Finance, a businessman with a good brain and a sense of humour. ...

In the afternoon I spend several hours in his library, shown round by Lello Gangemi,[2] Librarian and Professor at Perugia. An excellent library and a *pompeggiante* librarian. Very Fascist. He asks me to a party at his house in the evening. Rather fun. Continuous conversation and light refreshment till 1.15 a.m. Sessa, a journalist who spent some years in Russia and brought back an ugly Russian wife. In central Asia the Bolsheviks have abolished high prices for wives and distributed women more fairly among the proletariat who are, therefore, very contented.

---

1 Guido Jung (1876–1949). Italian Minister of Finance 1932–5, 1943–4. Economist.
2 Rafaele Gangemi. Theorist of Fascism. Writer on public finance and political economy. Author of *La Politica Finanziaria de Governo fascista 1922–1928* (1929).

Wednesday 21st December

... [T]o tea with Marinetti,[1] who is married to Cappa's sister.[2] A dynamic little man, who talked very good sense on architecture, and sound sense. Youth and *La Guerra Vinta* are the two bases of Fascism. Mussolini[3] has accelerated the rhythm of Italian life. The natural tendency is to *pilgrizia* and *languore*.

Modern architecture should be functional. Marinetti was saying this many years ago, a pioneer. You can't make a baroque auto-strada!

Parliamentarism appoints Commissions. And talks. And puts up a case for special interests. The Duce gives orders.

Thursday 22nd December

Lunch with Kirkpatricks.[4] He tells Ruth that, when he wants to ask a Cardinal to a meal, he has to send to the Vatican a list of those whom he intends to ask, and if the list is approved, a special department of the Vatican arranges the table. On this are the pence of the Irish and Polish peasantry spent! Christian humility ... Princes of the church. ...

Dine at the Embassy. Graham[5] makes a good impression, very pro-Fascist as one had heard, but reasonable in his exposition. ...

At dinner tonight were the German Ambassador[6] (a sensible fellow with a mainly consular career) ... Lady Sybil Graham,[7] young, handsome and hard. Also very pro-Fascist. Thought party government was the curse of England. Not very tactful, I thought.

......

Mrs Leigh-Smith[8] at lunch said to Ruth, 'Which is better. To have a few professors put away in the Lipari islands and the people employed developing their country, or to have all the professors at large, and all the people out of work?'

1 Filippo Marinetti (1876–1944). Writer on art and politics. Founder in 1918 of the Futurist Party (later absorbed into the Fascist Party). His ideas helped to inspire Italian Fascism.
2 Benedetta Marinetti, *née* Cappa. Sister of Innocenzo Cappa, Republican leader.
3 Benito Mussolini (1883–1945). Prime Minister of Italy 1926–43.
4 I. A. Kirkpatrick, q.v., was First Secretary at the British Embassy in Rome 1930–32 and Chargé d'Affaires at the Vatican 1932–3. Married to Violet Kirkpatrick, née Cottell.
5 Sir Ronald Graham (1870–1949). Ambassador to Italy 1921–33.
6 Ulrich von Hassell (1881–1944). German Ambassador to Italy 1932–8. Executed as one of the civilian leaders of the 1944 July Plot against Hitler.
7 Lady Sybil Graham, née Brodrick (d. 1934). Daughter of 1st Earl of Midleton.
8 Alice Leigh-Smith, née Prebil. Married to Philip Leigh-Smith, First Secretary at the Foreign Office 1932–6. Italian by birth.

Shades of Lionel Robbins, etc. St Helena and Falkland Islands?
......

Kirkpatrick's food was better than the Embassy. Mrs K. is a good hostess, and not too bloody 'social'. She should be promoted.

Wednesday 28th December
I search the Ministry of Finance Library in vain in search of positive exposition of the Corporate State.

Thursday 29th December
Visit office of *Lavori Publici* in the afternoon. Bring away some more literature.

Friday 30th December
At 10.45 call at the Chancery, and so in to see Graham. A quiet, decent, not too protocolonic Ambassador this. He says that the Duce starts work at 8.30 and finishes at 11 p.m. But he takes exercise, unlike most Italians of eminence. He rides, fences and after lunch plays the violin, quite badly, but intensely enough to take his mind off the troubles of the moment. Four years ago he was a very sick man; today he is quite fit. Graham would like Simon to come to Rome. Uncle's visit was a great success. The Duce can't leave Italy. He would probably be assassinated. The assassins would count on a spectacular political trial and a great forensic assault on Fascism. And in Italy there would probably be massacres.

The Italians, Graham thinks, are more genuinely friendly to England than any other country except, perhaps, the Greeks.

I ask about the succession. Graham thinks Mussolini has made a political testament. There are versions of this in Ludwig's book;[1] different versions in different editions. The King[2] might reappear on the stage. He has great physical shyness, owing to his short legs. But he is full of wisdom and experience, says Graham. Perhaps there would be a triumvirate. Badoglio,[3] Grandi[4] and Ciano[5] have been mentioned. Balbo[6] is a very dangerous man. The Duce would like

1 Emil Ludwig, *Talks with Mussolini*, Allen & Unwin, London, 1932.
2 King Victor Emmanuel III (1869–1947). King of Italy 1900–46.
3 General Pietro Badoglio (1871–1956). Italian Army Chief of Staff 1919–21, 1925–8. Prime Minister and Minister of Foreign Affairs (after the arrest of Mussolini) 1943–4.
4 Dino Grandi (b. 1895). Italian Ambassador in London 1932–9. Foreign Minister 1929–32. Minister of Justice 1939–43.
5 Count Galeazzo Ciano (1903–44). Foreign Minister 1936–43. The Duce's son-in-law.
6 Italo Balbo (1896–1940). Minister of Aviation 1929–33. Squadrista and Quadrumvir of the 1922 March on Rome.

to be rid of him. The Duce is much steadier than he was. But there is still a danger that he may go off the lines. He has the country behind him now, as he had *not* a year or two ago. His recent receptions in Milan and Turin have been mass demonstrations of enthusiasm.

Then an hour with Gladwyn, without Cynthia. He is full of interest in things, and his specialisation on economics and finance has been good for him. His introduction to the so-called commercial secretary's report is a good bit of writing. ...

6.15 see the Duce. Approach through a long series of rooms in Palazzo Venezia. Many plain-clothes detectives including one who sits opposite me while I am waiting.

Finally ushered into an immense room, with marble walls. At the far end the Duce, standing, with upturned eyes reading a book. He advances to meet me, when I am half-way across the room, 'with a friendly smile' as the journalists say.

We spend half an hour together. I think I succeed in keeping my end up. My Italian is better than usual. He has charm and intelligence. Very small brown eyes. He turns them up and the whites show, like a clown at a circus. Less tall than I expected. But strongly built. Evidently, as I had been told, he likes seeing people. He adjusts himself well to what he conceives to be my prejudices.

Where did I learn to speak Italian? In the war on the Italian Front. He recalls that I have written a book about this. How long was I on their Front? A year and a half. From May 1917, on the Carso under the Duca d'Aosta. Ah, he says, the war on the Carso was '*duro*'. Was I an officer? ......

I am interested to see Rome again after fourteen years. What a change. Here and in the rest of Italy. He is proud of the embellishments of Rome.

I refer to Uncle's visit and say that he returned much impressed with Rome and with his contact with Mussolini. He doesn't rise at all at this. Then I praise the *slancio* and *energia* which I find in Italy. I wonder whether in England, where now there is so much impotence in face of the economic crisis, we could, though our traditions and institutions are different, catch something of this spirit.

He is very pleased at this, and smiles sweetly. Almost caressingly, he asks, 'Yes, why don't you?' 'Partly because we have too many old men in high places.' '*Ah, bisogna svecchiare l'Inghilterra, e gli altri paesi*'[1] ...... Pitt was Prime Minister at twenty-two ......

I say that England is often thought not to understand Europe and

1 'There is a need to rejuvenate England and other countries.'

to be remote from it. But we understood, I think, a little more than America. He agrees.

And then we come back to Rome, and its embellishments. The Via dell' Impero isn't finished. 2000 more houses must be demolished in the centre of Rome, and the people housed, much better, in the outskirts. I speak of the Mussolini Forum. He says they are going to build a new bridge to give access to it, and so it ends. He accompanies me to the door. Where have I been? ...... Subiaco. He has never been there. That's where S. Benedict went into a cave ...... when next I am in Rome, I must be sure to come and see him again.[1] And he walked me back arm in arm. Voice of Romagna where good opera singers come from. Yes, charm, intelligence, energy, and no play acting. That is for the gallery.

There is no other living man whom it would have thrilled me more to meet. Ruth thinks he has conquered my susceptibilities too much.[2]

Saturday 31st December
Finally succeed in getting some literature from the Ministry of Corporations!

Wednesday 4th January 1933
Back to West Leaze by 7.55 from Paddington! A jolly trip, but it's jolly to be here.

After returning from Rome, Dalton planned a visit to Germany, where one of his graduate students at the L.S.E., Brindley Thomas, was making a study of the German economy.[3] Before going to Germany, Dalton went to Switzerland, where the Disarmament Conference was foundering, despite the dedicated Presidency of Arthur Henderson.

Thursday 26th January
To Geneva with no great enthusiasm.

Friday 27th January
Stay with Zilly at 112 Route de Chêne, a large, rather untidy house. Very Slav, but very friendly. ...

1 For the rest of this conversation, see FY, pp. 34–5.
2 Later insertion: '(I could have held him to our side, but O Stresa! O Abyssinia!)'
3 Later included in a collection of essays edited by Dalton: *Unbalanced Budgets. A Study of the Financial Crisis in Fifteen Countries*, Routledge, London, 1934.

I see a lot of people at Geneva. Uncle several times. He had a bad time sacking people at the Head Office – the economy campaign's next stage. Still moderately hopeful and Phil [Noel-Baker] ridiculously hopeful about the prospects of the Conference. But while I'm there, both the French and German governments fall in one day. And in Germany ... a terrifying row of portents. Germany might go any whither now, civil war, foreign war ...... all very grim and tragic. ...

Matsuoka,[1] the Jap chief delegate, is reported to have said that Japan was isolated at Geneva, just as Christ was left alone on the Mount of Olives, and Japan was willing today to follow in Christ's footsteps. Also, after a visit to Mussolini, that this was a man who had walked with God. He had made a pilgrimage to the graves of his parents. (A new ritual this in store for diplomatists?) Madariaga[2] says that all posts – President, *Rapporteur*, etc. – in connection with the Disarmament Conference should be made hereditary. ...

Between two spectators. Question on hearing Matsuoka explain that Japan must take action against bandits in Manchuria. 'Why are all the bandits in Manchuria on the side of China?' Answer. 'I don't know. But why are all the bandits in Europe on the side of Japan?'

Dalton returned to England on 1st February 1933. The following month he visited Zurich to attend the Executive of the Labour and Socialist International. At the end of April he made his projected visit to Berlin, seeing at first hand the effects of the Nazi persecutions – in particular the fear and disruption caused in Jewish and academic circles.[3] 'Germany is horrible', he wrote when he got back. 'A European war must be counted now among the probabilities of the next ten years.'[4]

Friday 12th May
Citrine to lunch, with little Winter,[5] the Czech. Citrine is a sensible

1 Yosuke Matsuoka (1880–1946). Head of the Japanese delegation to the League of Nations, which withdrew in March 1933 after the League Council had condemned Japan over Manchuria. Japanese Foreign Minister 1940–41.
2 Don Salvador de Madariaga y Rojo (1886–1978). Spanish delegate to the League of Nations 1931–6. Ambassador to France 1932–4. Professor of Spanish Studies at Oxford 1928–31.
3 See FY, pp. 38–41.
4 Diary, 30th April 1933.
5 Gustav Winter (d. 1943). Czech journalist. London and Paris correspondent of *Pravo Lidu*, a Prague socialist daily.

fellow, with a wider range of interests than many. He says that in Germany the collapse of the socialist and T.U. movement is the more inexplicable, because there were said to be plans fully worked out, though known only to half a dozen inside people, for a General Strike and for destroying power stations, etc. if a Fascist Dictatorship was attempted. Local comrades, enquiring what to do, were told that everything had been thought out, and that, at the right moment, the call would be issued ...... And then something went wrong ....

Perhaps the Reichstag fire forestalled and frightened them. Anyhow, as Ruth says, it's like a steamroller going over a worm.

Citrine and I both very hot against the culminating latest number of the *New Clarion*,[1] which is Communism without the courage of its convictions. Citrine also said that German T.U. leaders begged him not to attack Nazis, because this would make it harder for them to make terms!

Thursday 18th May

Mary Sutherland[2] to lunch. She says that Cripps has 'an adolescent mind' on economics and politics.

Ponsonby, whom I meet walking by Westminster Abbey on the way to the House, says the Government will go to the country *as* a National Government, with MacDonald as P.M. in a safe Tory seat, in about two years' time, unless they become frightened of waiting so long, and will come back with a reduced majority, fighting the election on our unfitness to govern, and lack of good names. He discounts both Cripps's phantasy of a Winston victory on India next spring (and no election), and still more Hamilton Fyfe's[3] 'Capitalism won't allow an election in 1936' stuff.

1 The *Clarion*, a Labour paper once edited by Robert Blatchford, had been bought by the Victoria Printing House Company in 1932. It reappeared as the *New Clarion* in June of the same year, after the T.U.C. had invested £2,000 and Bevin had been made Chairman of the Board. Contributors included a number of leading left-wingers, such as Cole, Brailsford, Laski and Wise. The result was an uneasy relationship between the new paper, which looked increasingly like an organ of the Socialist League, and some of its trade union sponsors. The first public row occurred when Wise wrote in the issue of 13th May 1933: 'Free speech, a so-called Free Press, are no more part of the eternal verities than is Free Trade.' Citrine angrily accused the new League (of which Wise was Chairman) of advocating dictatorship. The League proposed, in particular, the immediate abolition of the House of Lords and the passing of an Emergency Powers Act to give a Labour government sweeping powers.
2 Mary Sutherland (d. 1972). Chief Woman Officer of the Labour Party 1932–60.
3 Henry Hamilton Fyfe (1869–1951). Political writer for *Reynolds' News* 1930–42. Editor of the *Daily Herald* 1922–6. President of the League Against Cruel Sports 1934–46.

He says Mosley has been carrying on with many women lately (Lady Cynthia died in a nursing home yesterday), including the daughter of Lord Moyne (Guinness) who is having a divorce ......[1]

Saturday 3rd June
With Ruth to Paris.

Thursday 8th June
Dine with Comert[2] ...
   Comert speaks of the menace of the German 'civil' air forces. They could destroy London and Paris in a night. And the lunatics in charge are capable of this. But, in a few years' time, especially with the relative growth of Polish and German population, France will be stronger. (I say this is contrary to the view I have often heard put that Germany is seeking a delay of five or ten years, because she will be stronger then.)

Monday 12th June
Ruth had tea today with Mrs Peake.[3] Awful picture of five tea parties in one afternoon that diplomats' wives think they must attend. French society women talking endlessly about clothes. English talking to each other in a corner. A futile life. Meeting no one who matters, or is interesting. Restless life. Getting little good out of Paris. Moving in a silly little groove, and living too expensively.

Tuesday 13th June
11.30 See Sir R. Cahill.[4] Not a gentleman and very reactionary. I don't believe he ever meets anyone on the Left. He says the Left really want inflation (this, I think, is just a lie); there is no will to govern at present. They should have reduced the pay of functionaries; the rentiers have to pay more to their cooks, etc. Bad impression of Embassy contacts heightened!

1 Diana Guinness, née Freeman-Mitford, was the daughter-in-law, not the daughter, of 1st Baron Moyne. She divorced her husband, Bryan Guinness, in 1934, and married Sir Oswald Mosley two years later.
2 Pierre Comert (1880–1964). Head of the Information Section of the League of Nations Secretariat in Geneva 1919–33. Chief of the Press and Information Service at the French Ministry of Foreign Affairs 1933–8.
3 Probably Catherine Peake, née Knight. Married to C. B. P. Peake, later Sir Charles, Second Secretary.
4 Sir Robert Cahill (1879–1953). Commercial Counsellor at the British Embassy in Paris 1921–39.

1.0 Delightful lunch with Viénots[1] in modern studio flat ... Longuet[2] also there. And Haas[3] now an *émigré*. Viénot very intelligent and right minded, and friendly to individual Germans. Very shocked at British government's refusal to agree to nationalisation of manufacture of armaments.

The Daltons returned to London on 14th June.

Wednesday 21st June
Tea with Phil Noel-Baker at New University Club. He is clearly near to parting from Uncle. The adjournment of the Disarmament Conference for three months, which Uncle has been persuaded to agree to (his promised talks with foreign prime ministers at the Economic Conference having come to nothing) he thinks disastrous.

Friday 14th to Sunday 16th July
Zilly at West Leaze. Very eager and affectionate, but rather too much about Japan and the inevitable failure of the Disarmament Conference. Has been seeing Labour intellectuals of various sizes in London, who tell him that I have 'dropped out', 'ceased to count', etc. By which, apart from wish father to thought, they mean that I've refrained from taking part in their silly bogey mongering publicity and vote-scaring hysterics about 'Dictatorship', etc. I tell him where my strength lies in the Party and where their weakness.

Friday 18th August
To Paris for L.S.I. [Labour and Socialist International] Conference, remaining till 22nd August. Rather a sad and ineffectual affair. The German Socialist collapse in the forefront. I speak for our delegation and am thought to have done well. I claim that democracy isn't beaten yet – nor even seriously threatened in the countries which knew it before the war. Disarmament plus control. Hitler should be hauled before the League for conduct towards Austria and secret rearmament. Economic sanctions against aggressors would make

1 Pierre Viénot (1897–1944). Socialist deputy. Under-Secretary of State for Foreign Affairs 1936–7. Escaped from France to join the Free French in 1943, and became de Gaulle's ambassador in London.
2 Jean Longuet (1876–1938). Leader of the minority wing of the S.F.I.O. Grandson of Karl Marx.
3 Robert Haas. French League of Nations official. Former professor at the University of Paris.

The Labour Party ?...... Defeatism and Inferiority Complex... Leaders forget its mission as the party of reconstruction and accept the status of a Nº 2 "Safety-First" Company, hoping and praying they do not get a majority at the next election.— *LOW'S SPY, bitterly.*

4 'Inspection of the Guard of Honour', 10th July 1935
Second row includes: Bevin, Morrison, Citrine. *Front row:* Bevan, Dalton, Addison, Attlee, Alexander, Greenwood.

military sanctions unnecessary, etc. British opinion practically united against Hitler. Poor old Lansbury[1] feels he's the odd man out in our delegation, and goes home early. He says the Allies are 100 per cent to blame for Hitler, and relapses into the old mood of vague non-resistance. No good!

The Labour Party Conference opened in Hastings on 1st October. Joseph Compton was in the chair.

Friday 29th September to Friday 6th October
At Hastings. The devil of a week! I am right in everything, including the preparatory work with the groups and standing orders committee.

1 George Lansbury, q.v., had been Leader of the P.L.P. since November 1931 and succeeded Henderson as Party Leader in October 1932. Lansbury resigned over the Party's policy on Abyssinia in 1935.

The Conference is very healthy and no first class discords develop. Some criticise the E.C. as weak, and too conciliatory, or too 'opportunist'. And if we had taken the other line, some of these same critics would have called us reactionary! Like Jellicoe at Jutland, we 'turn away' from the assault of the Socialist League, Lansbury undertaking that we will consider their ideas and report next year.

My luck was in this year and I had a great success. I was continually in the picture, and scored particularly full marks, in the general judgment of the delegates, every time. ...

My popularity is rather terrifying. I come out top of my section of the E.C. with a record vote. ...

There is only one change, Trevelyan for Jenkins. In the T.U. and women's sections no change, though Footwipe,[1] who has been half tight at several E.C. meetings and delayed and disturbed the proceedings, is only just in, Gooch[2] and Collick[3] running up.

In the other section:

Williams[4]	1,459,000
Laski	748,000
Kirkwood[5]	141,000

This is one in the eye for yideology (Eileen's[6] patent).

We elect Footwipe Vice-Chairman for the coming year, but his future is a little precarious, I feel. ...

I have a sense of strength as a result of this Conference.

......

School term peaceful owing to absence of Beveridge in U.S. Finishing off *Unbalanced Budgets* – mostly at West Leaze – set going Policy Sub-Committees, and numbers of persons making memoranda.

1 Apparently W. A. Robinson, q.v., General Secretary of the National Union of Distributive and Allied Workers, who came twelfth in the trade union section of the N.E.C. in 1933, and served as Vice-Chairman of the Labour Party 1933–4.
2 E. G. Gooch (1889–1964). President of the National Union of Agricultural Workers 1928–64. Labour M.P. 1945–64.
3 Percy Collick (b. 1897). Official of the Associated Society of Locomotive Engineers and Firemen. Assistant General Secretary 1940–57. Labour M.P. 1945–64. Junior minister 1945–7.
4 T. E. Williams, later 1st Baron (1892–1966). President of the Political Purposes Committee of the Royal Arsenal Co-operative Society. Member of the socialist societies section of the Labour Party N.E.C. 1931–4. Member of the L.C.C.
5 David Kirkwood, later 1st Baron (1872–1955). Labour M.P. for Dumbarton Burghs 1922–50; Dumbartonshire East 1950–51. Former I.L.P. Clydesider who broke with Maxton and stayed in the Labour Party in 1932.
6 Eileen Power, q.v., had been a colleague of Laski and Dalton at the L.S.E.

On 6th January 1934 Cripps delivered what came to be known as his 'Buckingham Palace' speech. 'When the Labour Party comes to power', he declared, 'we must act rapidly and it will be necessary to deal with the House of Lords and the influence of the City of London. There is no doubt that we shall have to overcome opposition from Buckingham Palace and other places as well.' The implied attack on the King caused uproar in the press, and anger on the N.E.C. Cripps was forced to assure the public that he was 'most certainly not referring to the Crown'.[1]

Friday 19th January 1934

Following on meeting of 16th January. Wigs on the green at the Constitutional Sub-Committee. Cripps's speeches, and a few less important speeches and writings by others, under consideration.

Cripps seems quite unable to see the argument that he is damaging the Party electorally. It is all 'misreporting', or picking sentences out of their context. He has become very vain and seems to think that only he and his cronies know what Socialism is, or how it should be preached. His gaffes cover an immense range – Buckingham Palace – League of Nations – 'compelling' Unions to declare a General Strike – prolonging Parliament beyond five years, unless ...... 'seize land, finance and industry' (without compensation?) – Emergency Powers Bill in one day, giving 'all necessary powers' ......

Attlee defends him, and so does Laski. On the other side, Citrine, I, Lees-Smith, Dallas[2] – (and little Clynes rather negatively in the chair). Walkden[3] wobbling.

I make a violent – perhaps too violent – speech – asking that this stream of oratorical ineptitudes should now cease, or some of us who are very reluctant to enter on public controversy with other members of the Party, will come to the limits of our tolerance. It is the *number* of these gaffes which is so appalling. Our candidates are being stabbed in the back and pushed on to the defensive. Tory H.Q. regard him as their greatest electoral asset. Many of the speeches are simply incompetent presentation of a good case. But remarks on General

---

1 See C. A. Cooke, *The Life of Richard Stafford Cripps*, Hodder & Stoughton, London, 1957, p. 159.
2 George Dallas (1878–1971). Chief Organiser of the Agricultural Workers' Union. Member of the Labour Party N.E.C. (Chairman 1937–9). Labour M.P. 1929–31.
3 A. G. Walkden, later 1st Baron (1873–1951). General Secretary of the Railway Clerks' Association 1906–36. Labour M.P. for Bristol South 1929–31, 1935–45.

Strike are most improper for a member of professional classes, who couldn't deliver his own section of the working class on the battlefield ...... and so on ......

Attlee says I am like a pedagogue addressing a pupil. I wish the pupil were a bit brighter.

Citrine said he had been urged to say publicly that Cripps had no authority to speak for the Trade Unions, had no knowledge of the T.U.s, and no standing in the T.U. world, but had hitherto refrained.

Lees-Smith told Cripps that he was a poor witness and hadn't really answered any of the points made against him ......

We passed to a consideration of the proposed E.C. statement on Democracy and Dictatorship, repudiating statements out of line with Party policy.

Laski objected to any reference to 'individual statements', even if 2000 names were given. Cripps suggested that he himself should be named. I asked, 'Haven't you had enough notoriety already?' Laski ended with a polysyllabic threat to diminish his interest in the work of the Party, if such a repudiation were issued. We decided to refer the matter back, with a verbal report to the E.C.

A wretched business, fundamentally so silly!

Monday 22nd January
Ruth thinks I've been less 'tactical' than usual and have made some enemies. Report of another outrageous speech by Cripps, saying that if, under Locarno, there were 'a capitalist war, in the ordinary sense of the term, the Labour Party would resist it, and organise a General Strike if it could.'!!! Every word wrong!

At the end of 1933, following the lead of the Comintern, the British Communist Party approached the various bodies of the Labour Movement on the question of a 'united front', based on joint action. The National Joint Council of the Labour Party and the T.U.C. turned down this proposal and the National Executive issued a Manifesto, 'Democracy versus Dictatorship', in which it declared that the task of British Labour was 'to uphold the principles of Social Democracy' against dictatorship of any kind. This was intended as a snub to Cripps, the Socialist League, and others within the Labour Party who favoured joint action with the Communists, or who advocated a constitutional dictatorship in order to carry out socialist measures when Labour came to power.

Wednesday 24th January

National Executive decide after much debate, by 18 votes to 4 (Uncle, Trevelyan, Susan, and I think, Lady Mabel Smith),[1] to publish a statement on 'Democracy and Dictatorship'. I have revised the draft, putting in a positive sentence on our views, adding a few strengthening epithets, and putting the 'repudiation' in the final sentence, conditioned by 'in so far as'. My revise, by arrangement, is fathered by Greenwood, who shows it, at the table, to Clynes and Roberts who approve it.

Uncle wants to issue nothing, but to have it all further discussed at a joint meeting of the three national executives.[2] (This couldn't, however, happen until the end of February, as Citrine won't move earlier.) But the feeling is strong and obstinate (except curiously enough from Morrison who thinks the issue may interfere with the L.C.C. elections)[3] in favour of publishing now and without essential modification. Trevelyan and Susan try to get the repudiation out, but unsuccessfully. So it is issued to an expectant world! I vote for it without any hesitation.

Uncle is very vexed. I lunch with him afterwards. He seems to have told Greenwood, whom he thought was the nigger-in-the-woodpile, that this was 'the most serious mistake which the N.E. had made during the past twenty-five years'. He fears counter attacks, including perhaps one from Lansbury. But he has been away and hasn't felt the rising pressure. Also he is chagrined, because many of the present N.E. won't accept his guidance. He says he will resign soon, if this goes on. I try to calm him down. He is feeling bad about Disarmament and so easily explodes on other things. Also he wants a short and simple election programme drafted by the Policy Committee. He doesn't really much like our Policy Reports!

Attlee mentioned the possibility of resigning at our Sub the other day, if there was any 'repudiation' which might involve him. This was mentioned at the N.E. and Dallas said audibly, 'Well, let him. If he does, he'll never get anything else!'

1 Lady Mabel Smith, née Lady Mabel Fitzwilliam (1870–1951). Member of the Women's Section of the N.E.C. 1930, 1932–5. Married to Colonel W. M. Smith. She was the sister of the 7th Earl Fitzwilliam.
2 'the three national executives': the Labour Party N.E.C., the P.L.P. Executive and the T.U.C. General Council.
3 In March 1934 Labour won the L.C.C. elections, for the first time gaining a clear majority of seats over all opponents.

Monday 29th to Tuesday 30th January

At Cambridge for by-election. Wood[1] is a strong candidate. Two
small meetings in schools on the first night; big and keen Guildhall
Rally on the second. ... Wood, off his own bat, has written to Cripps
telling him that he'd rather he didn't come and speak during the by-
election. Wilmot[2] very vexed with Cripps, and wrote to Lansbury
about his speeches. Canvass Milton Road, but no sniff of dictatorship
bombs on the doorstep!

Wednesday 31st January

Cripps has been complaining to Uncle about being warned off
Cambridge during the by-election. Uncle says that he had to do the
same with Keir Hardie in 1902 at Barnard Castle, with K.H.'s complete understanding and approval.

1934–5

Keeping a diary is a bore. In 1934 I dropped it. But, as the year turns,
I make a note or two. ...

... [A] wonderful summer and a wonderful drought. The bloody
book[3] and lack of water (I have to fetch it in two buckets by hand from
the Shepherds') limits our hospitality very severely.

Uncle is out of the Party Secretaryship. But he had practically to
be pushed out! He is losing his tactical sense, once so acute, pretty
badly. He first offered to resign, tying the question up awkwardly with
the Clay Cross verdict,[4] which he didn't like, putting his resignation
on the ground of health and suggesting a 'mutually convenient date'.
Clynes and two or three more were deputed to see him, and get the
two disentangled.

Then they found that, in spite of his health and a solemn doctor's
report, he wanted to drag on till the General Election, devolving some
of the work. They had to insist, in the interest both of his health and

---

1 Alexander Wood (1879–1950). Labour candidate for Cambridge in the 1929, 1931
  and 1935 general elections and the February 1934 by-election. Fellow and Tutor
  of Emmanuel College, and University Lecturer in Physics. In the by-election,
  Wood reduced the 1931 Conservative majority from 18,421 to 2,720.
2 John Wilmot, later 1st Baron (1893–1964). Labour M.P. for Fulham East 1933–5;
  Kennington 1939–45; Deptford 1945–50. Dalton's P.P.S. at the Ministry of Economic Warfare and then the Board of Trade 1940–44. Joint Parliamentary Secretary
  at the Ministry of Supply 1944–5. Minister of Supply 1945–7.
3 *Practical Socialism for Britain*, Routledge, London, 1935.
4 Bevin had complained to the N.E.C. about the selection of Arthur Henderson as
  candidate for a by-election at Clay Cross, in preference to the Transport Workers'
  nominee.

the Party, that the change over should come at the turn of the year. He was very sore at this.

Then he set himself to work Middleton[1] into the succession, in spite of all he had said and thought of him in the past, and Will[2] into the succession to Middleton. (The idea of new blood in the office he violently resisted.)

In the former he just succeeded, in the latter he failed. Middleton was chosen (in December) by 13 to 10 over Arthur Woodburn,[3] the runner up. (First vote, Middleton 10, Woodburn 7, Creech Jones[4] 5, Shepherd 1.) It was an awfully poor list. Cripps and Williams were away. Both would have voted against Middleton.

It was decided in January 1935 to close down the Assistant Secretaryship and give Luckhurst Scott[5] to Middleton as Principal Assistant. Uncle fought these two decisions violently. He thought he would stay in his own room as Honorary Treasurer (he had declined any pension or payment), with Scott and Miss Steel (£800 a year) to look after him. He had to be literally pushed up to a room on the 5th floor, keeping Miss Steel. Tenacity! Yes, but, now in his decline at the expense of dignity as well as wisdom.

Wednesday 23rd January 1935
National Executive. Cripps at luncheon interval. 'I can't come back this afternoon. It's cost me £120 to be here this morning and I might just as well have sent my typist.'

Tuesday 12th February
Accompany Anthony Mouravieff[6] [?] whom we call the Red Indian, to call on Sir Ronald Waterhouse.[7] This has been suggested via a certain Captain Beer, a low fellow, I judge, mixed up with Rother-

---

1 James Middleton (1878–1962). Secretary of the Labour Party 1935–44. Assistant Secretary 1903–35.
2 Will Henderson, q.v., Arthur's son, was an official at Transport House.
3 Arthur Woodburn (1890–1978). Labour M.P. for Clackmannan and East Stirlingshire 1939–70. Junior minister 1945–7. Secretary of State for Scotland 1947–50.
4 Arthur Creech Jones (1891–1964). Organising Secretary of the Workers' Travel Association 1929–39. Labour M.P. 1935–50, 1954–64. Junior minister 1945–6; Colonial Secretary 1946–50.
5 A. Luckhurst Scott (1886–1952). Private Secretary to Arthur Henderson 1918–34. Chief Assistant to James Middleton as Secretary of the Labour Party.
6 Not identified. Handwriting unclear.
7 Sir Ronald Waterhouse (1878–1942). Principal Private Secretary to the Prime Minister 1922–8. Former Lieutenant-Colonel in the 6th Dragoon Guards. Served in the War Office Intelligence Department 1915–18.

mere,[1] Tory diehards and Maundy Gregory;[2] apparently he met Waterhouse in the Secret Service.

Waterhouse, it was said, would like to return to No. 10 as Principal Private Secretary to the next Labour Prime Minister. He is acting, I feel, in a rather suspicious and undistinguished fashion in thus thrusting himself before the notice of small size intermediaries like Beer and the Red Indian to whom he appears to have blown his own trumpet, declared himself a high constitutional authority eager to help and smooth the path of the Labour Government, and claimed intimacy with many from the King downwards.

But I see no objection to meeting him. He has a sumptuous flat at the Albany. The Red Indian withdraws after 20 minutes. Waterhouse and I talk for $2\frac{1}{4}$ hours. He makes no positive offer of assistance, nor do I invite one. But the whole trend of the talk from his side is to emphasise his expertness and his willingness to serve another political master. Much patter about the King, 'rather a difficult person to handle' – Stamfordham, an old fashioned courtier, is a stickler for constitutional etiquette – Wigram, very different, much easier, 'much more democratic'. Waterhouse says that, not having been an official civil servant, he had greater freedom to do good work for his political chiefs. A long story about how he wrote to Willingdon[3] in Canada when Baldwin was going over, and secured Canadian government hospitality and a free passage on the liner. He shows me the bill, chiefly tips, which he sent in after the trip to the Treasury. MacDonald going to the U.S. in 1929 (after Waterhouse had left No. 10) was less well looked after. *That* trip cost £1,200.

Much talk about the dissolution of 1924. Ben Spoor, as Chief Whip, was 'all in the air'. Waterhouse had to arrange the dissolution with Stamfordham. He showed me a memorandum addressed to the Chief Whip, reporting the negotiations. He also showed me a letter, drafted for Baldwin to send to Stamfordham in July 1925, when the latter, writing nominally on the King's behalf, but Waterhouse thinks really on his own initiative, had proposed that the Speaker should be informed that the King was displeased at the lax manners of M.P.s during an all night sitting.

1 H. S. Harmsworth, 1st Viscount Rothermere (1868–1940). Chief proprietor of the *Daily Mail, Daily Mirror, Evening News*, etc. Air Minister 1917–18. Younger brother of 1st Viscount Northcliffe.
2 Maundy Gregory (1877–1941). 'Honours Broker' to Lloyd George, who used the sale of honours to boost the Lloyd George Political Fund.
3 1st Marquis of Willingdon, q.v.

This letter, rejecting the King's right to intervene, was not sent because Waterhouse persuaded Stamfordham to withdraw the first letter.

etc. ......

Baldwin, he said, advised MacDonald to take him on as Principal Private Secretary in 1924. And, in his presence, in No. 10 Baldwin told MacDonald that he would let him stay in, but for less than a year!

He recognised that Lansbury is our Leader, who would be sent for, if we won next time. But he thinks, in view of Lansbury's age, and the King's experience when Bonar Law[1] resigned, and he was 'left without a Prime Minister for three days', that he would want to know who was Deputy Leader. I say Attlee is now. He may or may not be after the election. Our Parliamentary Party makes such choices. He says we ought to have our Shadow Cabinet ready. I say this is not easy to prearrange. I also say I think the chances are against our winning a clear majority next time. He pretends to disagree. An odd evening!

But he may be a useful intermediary one day, though his eagerness stands in need of explanation. What is he up to?

I must try to draw Van about him.

Wednesday 13th February
Meeting on Priorities. Poor old Lansbury now terrified that we shall press things through too fast, and destroy the spirit of Parliament. Cripps, Laski, Citrine and I form an unusual combination on the other side. I get them to agree to having Heads of Bills drafted. I hope this will come off.

Saturday 23rd February
Finish reading Lockhart's *Retreat from Glory*.[2] Very good and appreciative on the Czechs. Has a love of beautiful country everywhere. But Oh what a weak, dissolute, spineless, sponger! Such opportunities of travel and experience, and such a boring apologetic tale of debts and night life!

---

1 Andrew Bonar Law (1858–1923). Conservative M.P. 1900–10, 1911–23. Junior minister 1902–6. Colonial Secretary 1915–16. Chancellor of the Exchequer 1916–18; Lord Privy Seal 1919–21. Leader of the House of Commons 1916–21. Prime Minister 1922–3.
2 R. H. Bruce Lockhart, later Sir Robert (1887–1970). Journalist with the *Evening Standard* 1928–39. Director-General of the Political Warfare Executive 1941–5. At various times author, diplomat and banker. *Retreat from Glory* (Putnam, London, 1934) was a volume of reminiscences.

Friday 31st May

... Charles Brook[1] this morning said that Attlee came to speak at Smethwick last week, when they expected an important pronouncement on current issues. And he talked about – 'The Sino–Jap dispute'! ... [I]nfinitely remote from the audience both in time and space. Little man, little head, little speech, little essay!

Monday 3rd June

Shocking news in the morning paper. *Knighthoods* for Citrine, Pugh,[2] C. Edwards,[3] P.C. for Attlee, *C.B.E.* for D. Grenfell,[4] Arthur Shaw,[5] *O.B.E.* for Annie Loughlin,[6] and three or four minor T.U. officials.

To take these bloody titles at all (I except the P.C.) is bad enough. But to take them from MacDonald!! Ruth is almost in tears, says we had better join the Communists! What the *hell* will decent people in the Movement think! Citrine is *by far* the worst case!

International Studies Conference opens. Meet Liddell Hart[7] at lunch at the School. Very interesting on air danger, vulnerability (England most vulnerable, then Germany, Italy, France, Soviet Union in that order). Dispersion of industry and population diminishes vulnerability.

Speak with Maisky.[8] He is worried by Labour Party attitude in Parliament on rearmament. He says, 'By all means talk with Hitler, and come to agreements and compromises. But talk to him with a rifle in your hand, or he will pay no regard to your wishes. We proved this with Japan.' He suggests that Labour Party should agree to let votes for larger armaments go through, on condition Government makes non-aggression treaty with Soviet Union. A little too simple!

1 Dr Charles Brook. Secretary of the Socialist Medical Association. Member of the L.C.C. Labour candidate for Smethwick 1935.
2 Sir Arthur Pugh (1870–1955). General Secretary of the Iron and Steel Trades Confederation 1917–36.
3 Sir Charles Edwards (1867–1954). Labour Chief Whip 1931–42. M.P. for Bedwellty 1918–50.
4 D. R. Grenfell (1881–1968). Labour M.P. for Gower 1922–59. Miner. Parliamentary Secretary at the Department of Mines 1940–42.
5 Arthur Shaw (1880–1939). General Secretary of the National Union of Dyers, Bleachers and Textile Workers.
6 Annie Loughlin, O.B.E. 1935, D.B.E. 1943 (1894–1979). General Organiser of the Tailors and Garment Workers' Trade Union 1916–48; General Secretary 1948–53.
7 B. H. Liddell Hart, later Sir Basil (1895–1970). Military historian and theorist. Military correspondent of the *Daily Telegraph* 1925–35; *The Times* 1935–9. Personal adviser to the War Minister 1937–8.
8 I. M. Maisky (1884–1975). Soviet Ambassador to Britain 1932–43.

5 'Another Ascent into the Stratosphere', 11th September 1935

Thursday 10th to Monday 13th October
Brussels. With Dallas, Compton, Gillies, Hicks,[1] Walkden. L.S.I. [Labour Socialist International] and I.F.T.U. [International Federation of Trade Unions]. Very sound and united on sanctions. Silly waste of time in L.S.I. on United Front with Communists. We all weigh in (Dallas, Compton and I) and assert our point of view. Dutch, Swedes, Danes and Czechs – the *real* parties – rally round us. ...

On the train back Walkden, so mild and once so captivated, denounces Cripps on his own initiative. 'This man Cripps', he cries, 'has done it again!' 'Done what?' I ask. 'Talked about "working class sanctions",' he says ...... 'strikes' ......

Tuesday 15th October
Speak with John Wilmot at Fulham Town Hall. He'll have a hard and difficult fight against the Astor money.[2]

1 George Hicks (1879–1954). General Secretary of the Amalgamated Union of Building Trade Workers 1921–40. Labour M.P. for Woolwich East 1931–50. Junior minister 1940–45.
2 Wilmot's Conservative opponent was W. W. Astor, son of Viscount Astor and Lady Astor, q.v. Astor won with a majority of 1,054.

189

Tuesday 22nd October
National Executive. Rough draft of Election Manifesto by Green-
wood. ... we improve it a good deal. I am left to draft the foreign part.
This is much better than farming it out to the likes of little Laski.

On 23rd October 1935 Baldwin announced that there would be a dissolution
two days later and a general election on 14th November. The campaign was
quiet, with foreign policy the main issue in the speeches of leading politicians.

Wednesday 23rd October
Settle draft of Election Manifesto in the morning. Then Joint Meeting
of three E.C.s and Parliamentary Party. Nothing much emerges.

Then National Executive, and we pilot through Election Manifesto.
No serious damage done, but fatiguing. Then Greenwood and I
finally clean it up.

Red Indian to see me – at my request, Morgan Jones having
bleated out something to the large meeting on conscription – and he
produces a statement by Beer on a Yorkshire country house discussion.[1]

Arthur Henderson died on 20th October.

Thursday 24th October
To Uncle's funeral at Methodist Church and Golders Green Crema-
torium. The Methodist Service is horribly ugly and undistinguished.
But I daresay he would have liked it.

Take Herbert Morrison to lunch and talk about the Red Indian's
document. Cautious and doubtful but interested. I shall leave him to
handle it while I'm in the North.

Friday 25th October
Memorial Service to Uncle in Westminster Abbey. Very beautifully
done. I sit by Lord Cecil in the stalls. Van beside Ruth just beneath
us. He weeps a good deal, as do I.

Speak at Braintree for Toynbee.[2]

1 See below, p. 191 and n.
2 W. F. Toynbee. Labour candidate for Maldon. Compositor.

Saturday 26th October

Red Indian to see me in the country. Sir Gervase Beckett,[1] Eden's father-in-law, is the missing name.

Speak at Wellingborough for Dallas. Round to George Wansbrough on my return to find out about Beckett. Not much known. Only Morrison, Wansbrough and Bob Fraser in the secret.

Monday 28th October

Arrive at Bishop Auckland for the duration. Surely we can't lose this time!

Adopted in the evening.

My estimate is that we shall have, if we can't use the Red Indian's bomb,[2] nearer 240 than 200. The Liberals less than 20.

If we can use the bomb, we shall be nearer 275 than 250. Any who are more optimistic forget that we reached our high water mark of 289 in 1929 with a multitude of *real* three-cornered fights. This time three-cornered fights will be a good deal fewer, and many will be merely nominal. Liberals polling too few to affect the result.

I assume that the Tories have no first class bomb against us.

Tuesday 29th October

Baldwin last night at Wolverhampton has made our bomb much less effective. Gordon Macdonald[3] has given him his chance. Damned fool!

(P.S. The bomb was never exploded, Morrison gave it to Hunter and Keir,[4] and they smelt round and found nothing, and at a ☐[5]

---

1 Sir Gervase Beckett, 1st Bart (1866–1937). Banker. Conservative M.P. 1906–29. His daughter, Beatrice, was married to Anthony Eden, q.v.
2 'the Red Indian's bomb': from diary references on the 23rd, 26th and 27th October, this seems to have been a document revealing conscription plans prepared by, or on behalf of, leading ministers. Dalton hoped to disclose the contents in order to embarrass the Conservatives, who equivocated on the issue of rearmament while claiming to be working for a general limitation on arms.
3 Gordon Macdonald, later 1st Baron (1888–1966). Labour M.P. for Ince 1929–42. Governor of Newfoundland 1946–9. Paymaster–General 1949–51. On the first day of the election campaign, Macdonald made a speech in Lancashire in which he challenged the Government to make clear its intentions on conscription. If it declared that conscription would not be introduced, 'then the Labour Party will not make use of [this issue] as a weapon during the campaign'. Baldwin replied in a speech at Wolverhampton on 28th October that rumours about conscription were completely unfounded.
4 Probably D. E. Keir (b. 1905), a journalist and former Labour candidate.
5 i.e. four-sided.

conference with Stevenson[1] and Vallance,[2] it was decided to do nothing. Too cautious!)

Sunday 3rd November
My left leg and back increasingly painful. I speak in pain and with discomfort and prop myself up, while speaking, against a chair. And climbing into and out of the car is painful. So, in the afternoon, after a meeting in Coundon Picture Palace, I go to see Will's Black Doctor Cherry. He says I have sciatica and a touch of lumbago and gives me some medicine and some ointment to rub in and advises me to take some loosening exercises, swinging my body round, and bending over to touch my toes.

In the evening motor to Gateshead, and make a good shouting speech, free from pain, to large audience for Jimmy Wilson.[3] Then back home in good spirits. When going to bed, do my prescribed exercises, and suddenly as I am bending down, something seems to crack in my left backside and I flop on to the bed in a state of acute pain ......

This turns out to be a tear in the tendons of a muscle.

Monday 4th November
Dress with very great difficulty and hobble down. Cherry summoned. Puts me back to bed. I have a sharp attack of lumbago and have, as it turns out, to stay in bed for a week. In the early days much pain and completely immobile. Cherry calls several times daily. The District Nurse is involved. I have to use a bed pan. Ruth has to make speeches at all meetings and explain. Also to nurse me! Also to see to press twice daily, *Gazette*[4] and *Northern Echo*, to give them advances. She is a heroine! ...

Friday 15th November
At the Count. ... Proud, the Returning Officer, in surprise, says it looks like 8,000. I am unwilling to believe this. But it turns out to be true.

Dalton	20,481
Curry	12,395
Majority	8,086

1 W. H. Stevenson. Editor of the *Daily Herald* 1931–7.
2 Aylmer Vallance (1892–1955). Editor of the *News Chronicle* 1933–6.
3 James Wilson (1879–1943). Labour candidate for Gateshead 1935. M.P. for Oldham 1929–31; Dudley 1921–2.
4 The *Evening Gazette*, a Middlesbrough newspaper.

We shake hands, both inside and out on the balcony, and I refer, with a little sarcasm, to the silly story, sedulously kept alive in the Division for four years, that I refused to shake hands with Curry in 1931. (Ruth has dealt with this at several meetings and Curry has had to deny it at a meeting, in answer to a question.) ...

Ask for police protection to prevent me from being smacked on the back. ...

Now focus on (1) the Leadership, (2) getting rid of this physical unfitness. As to (2) ionisation by Miss Wickstead. As to (1) many activities!

The result of the election was even more discouraging for the Opposition than Dalton had feared. With fewer candidates, Labour's total vote was almost as great as in 1929, and its share of the poll (37.9 per cent) higher than ever before. However, the arithmetic of the electoral system provided Labour with only 154 seats, while supporters of the National Government obtained 387, giving Baldwin an overall majority of 247. The Labour front bench was strengthened by the return of Morrison, Clynes, Alexander and Dalton. But few of the younger Labour candidates were successful.

The immediate problem confronting the P.L.P. after the election concerned the succession to George Lansbury, who had resigned as Party Leader on 8th October. Attlee had been chosen as Leader for the rest of the session, on the understanding that a proper contest would be held as soon as the new Parliament met. By this time, Dalton had already decided not to pursue the Leadership for himself, but to back Morrison against Attlee and a third candidate, Arthur Greenwood.

Early in October Dalton pledged his support to Morrison, making his own ambitions plain at the same time. 'I feel, though it isn't a job one would hold out glad hands for in the present state of the world, that I could do the F.O. better than anyone else in the Party', he explained. 'If the external world was quiet, perhaps I could do something big on the Home Front. But, as for the Leadership, I think it should go to someone who has *not* had exceptional opportunities.'[1] With the general election over, Dalton now went into action noisily, and ineffectively, on Morrison's behalf.

Tuesday 19th November
See Beveridge at the School, and arrange to terminate my connection at the end of the session. Very cordial! For about six months I shall draw School salary + Parliamentary salary and reduce my overdraft!

1 Diary, 5th to 6th October 1935.

Then a lump sum to wipe out all debts, and have a small balance over –
for West Leaze, etc.

Canvass Lees-Smith for Morrison. Successful.

Wednesday 20th November

Canvass Pethick-Lawrence for Morrison. Successful.

Write a number of letters to M.P.s. Mention Morrison to Whiteley[1]
and Jenkins. Party in the evening to meet Zilly. He acts as cover. To
dine Watkins,[2] Fletcher,[3] Bellenger[4] (this turned out to be a mistake!),
Parker.[5]

Come in afterwards, Kelly,[6] Viant,[7] Creech Jones, Chuter Ede,
Ellen [Wilkinson], John Wilmot (only non-M.P.),[8] Frankel[9] and per-
haps a few others whom I forget. Zilly had asked to meet new M.P.s.
He wasn't in very good form, but talked disjointedly. Of course, the
Leadership came up, and we were nearly all for Morrison. Bellenger
talked disconnected rot in a tiresome way, but didn't commit himself.
Creech Jones kept on asking, 'What if Morrison won't stand?' I knew
it was a foolish question but couldn't say so. (Tracey,[10] on behalf of
Greenwood, had been spreading the tale in Transport House and its
purlieus that Morrison couldn't give up the London Labour Party.)
Ellen pretended not to be keen. She wrote to me afterwards that she
was very keen on Morrison, but feared Bellenger blabbing. She turned
out to be right. He is a wretched little tyke.

A heavy evening. Rather tired and discouraged.

1 William Whiteley (1882–1955). Labour M.P. for Blaydon 1922–31, 1935–55. Chief
  Whip 1942–51.
2 F. C. Watkins (1883–1954). Labour M.P. for Hackney Central 1929–31, 1935–45.
3 R. T. H. Fletcher, later 1st Baron Winster (1885–1961). Labour M.P. for Nuneaton
  1935–42. Liberal M.P. for Basingstoke 1923–4. Created a peer in 1942. Minister of
  Civil Aviation 1945–6.
4 F. J. Bellenger (1894–1968). Labour M.P. for Bassetlaw 1935–68. Junior minister
  1945–6. Secretary of State for War 1946–7.
5 John Parker (b. 1906). Labour M.P. for Romford 1935–45; Dagenham 1945–83.
  General Secretary of the New Fabian Research Bureau 1933–9; Fabian Society
  1939–45. Junior minister 1945–6.
6 W. T. Kelly (1874–1944). Labour M.P. for Rochdale 1924–31, 1935–40.
7 S. P. Viant (1882–1964). Labour M.P. for Willesden West 1923–31, 1935–59. Junior
  minister 1929–31.
8 Wilmot, q.v., victor at the East Fulham by-election in 1933, lost the seat in 1935.
  He returned to Parliament at another by-election in 1939.
9 Dan Frankel (b. 1900). Labour M.P. for Mile End 1935–45.
10 H. T. Tracey (1884–1955). T.U.C. Publicity Officer.

Thursday 21st November
See Scott Lindsay. Against Attlee, but for Greenwood rather than
Morrison. The latter 'a bit too ambitious', Greenwood 'such a nice
self-effacing chap'.

Friday 22nd November
See Garro Jones. Very much all right for Morrison. Fought a bold
and skilful fight in North Aberdeen.

Saturday 23rd November
The *Daily Express* and *Evening Standard* have news of my meeting
here for Zilly on Wednesday. I am not named but fairly clearly
identified.
    All the anti-Labour press want Attlee continued – obviously
Bellenger has leaked!
    Bob and Betty [Fraser] to dine. They don't think it has done much
harm. Either one must remain inactive or one must run risks.

Sunday 24th November
A number of references in the Sunday press. In one I am named. But
so is Bevin as working on behalf of Greenwood.
    Great activity by enemy press on behalf of Attlee.
    Morrison rings up (a daily occurrence now) slightly bothered about
the degree of press. But I persuade him that the least said by either of
us the better.
    I guess that the press have been trying to get at me. But I'm not in
the telephone book, and am recorded in Labour Party publications
as living in Wiltshire!
    Bob rings up in the evening to say that he has put through a good
strong leader in the *Daily Herald* saying that anti-Labour press stories
are designed to hurt us, that all three candidates have been liable to
damage by these tales, and that vote on Tuesday should be without
outside interference and on grounds of merit alone. He also spoke
to Clynes on the telephone, who said, for publication, that he didn't
feel able to accept the Leadership, and privately that he would do his
best to help to secure a wise choice.
    I agree with Ruth that I *won't* accept nomination for Deputy
Leader, if proposed.

The Parliamentary Party voted on 26th November. Attlee led on the first
ballot with 58 votes, compared with 44 for Morrison and 33 for Greenwood;
on the second ballot nearly all Greenwood's votes went to Attlee, giving him

88 against 48 for Morrison. Morrison was bitterly disappointed and declined to accept nomination for the Deputy post, which therefore went to Greenwood. 'A wretched disheartening result!' Dalton wrote at the time. ' "And a little mouse shall lead them"!'[1]

Thursday 5th December
I make my first speech in this Parliament, opening the second main day's debate on the address, on foreign affairs. I have prepared it with a good deal of labour and don't do too badly – though I don't love speaking in the House much more than I used to do. I go on for forty-five minutes and cover a lot of ground. Most of our people seem to like it. And at least I give the impression of knowing something about the subject – a new sensation for the House after 1931–5! Far East – Egypt – Abyssinia – oil sanctions. Sanctions in general – Disarmament.

Government supporters don't like it much. They think it too superior and sarcastic. But why not? Grigg[2] very shocked because I comment tartly on Laval. But what's the use of being in Opposition if one can't speak one's mind more freely than when one's in Government?

On 8th December Sir Samuel Hoare, the Foreign Secretary, was persuaded by the French Prime Minister and Foreign Secretary, Pierre Laval, to accept a plan for ending the Abyssinian war (and thus removing the need to impose sanctions). The Hoare–Laval plan involved the cession of two-thirds of the territory of Abyssinia to Italy, while the rump Abyssinian empire would receive in return a corridor to the sea (the 'corridor for camels') at Assab. Details of the plan appeared in the French press on 9th December. Immediately there was a strong public and political reaction. On 18th December, just before a debate in the Commons arranged for the next day, Baldwin sacked Hoare and appointed Anthony Eden as Foreign Secretary in order to save himself and the Government. But the damage to Baldwin's prestige, and to the League of Nations, was permanent.

---

1 Diary, 26th November 1935.
2 Sir Edward Grigg, later 1st Baron Altrincham (1879–1955). National Conservative M.P. for Altrincham 1933–45. National Liberal M.P. for Oldham 1922–5. Governor of Kenya 1925–31. Junior minister 1939–42. Minister Resident, Middle East 1944–5.

Thursday 19th December
My second speech in the House, winding up on our vote of censure on the Hoare–Laval proposals. I want to practise the art of winding up. Pretty successful; a good deal of box-banging. Comrades pleased, though two thought I went rather far in calling Mussolini a lunatic. But two Tories privately told me that they thought this was good.

We have been having days of drama – for poor old Westminster. Hoare resigning. Baldwin much shaken personally. An amazing mail bag of letters protesting against the proposed 'exchange of half an Empire for a corridor for camels'. Very exciting while it lasted.

Friday 20th December
To West Leaze to join Ruth who has planted seventy-one subjects, including half a hundred whitebeams along the road in two days, all by herself!

Peace. Snow. Two days' clear blue sky and sunshine. Then thaw and wet, and too little gardening possible.

Saturday 28th to Monday 30th December
Bob and Betty for the weekend; we find them rather heavy, boring and irritating. He thinks the Labour Party is really pretty ill, and won't win any great confidence for years, nor power for three elections. Perhaps. To what purpose, then, are we wasting our lives!

Wednesday 19th February 1936
Two Liddell Harts, Delahaye[1] and Hugh Gaitskell[2] to lunch. Liddell Hart says that bombing planes now have a radius of 450 miles (+450 return). New type 'Post Douglas' have a radius of 1,000 miles. Our Rearmament programme won't be complete till 1939. 1937 will be a dangerous year.

On 7th March, German troops entered the demilitarised zone in the Rhineland, in blatant violation of the Treaties of Versailles and Locarno.

---

1 Probably Lt-Col. J. V. Delahaye (1890–1948). Former General Staff Officer. Labour candidate 1931.
2 Hugh Gaitskell (1906–63). Lecturer in Economics at University College, London. See Appendix.

Wednesday 11th March
Slight easing of strain. Locarno powers and League Council coming
to London. ... Soviet pressing for 'firm stand'. 'Hitler must be humiliated'. 'No negotiation till he leaves the Rhineland'. 'Sanctions if he
refuses'. Greenwood and I say the British public, including the Labour
Party, won't stand for this.

Later Boothby tells me that he nears from Paris that France, Soviet
Union, Czechoslovakia *and Poland* are determined to 'go through
with it', even if we won't join. They speak of air demonstrations over
Germany. This is madness, if true.

At lunch I told Kagan that the right tactics were to begin by asking
for 'strong measures' and, when we refused, to press us to join an
explicit All European Pact of mutual assistance, inviting Germans to
join.

Boothby said Oliver Stanley told him that Stanley had said that the
Cabinet's policy was 'Peace with as little dishonour as possible'.

The strain of these days is terrible! Nicolson said to me, 'Aren't you
glad you aren't Foreign Secretary?'

Thursday 12th March
I give an exposé to the Parliamentary E.C. on the International Situation, which is much approved. Don't condone Hitler. It is a very
serious shock to confidence. Case for going to P.C.I.J. [Permanent
Court of International Justice]. Germany freely signed Optional
Clause in 1928 and Hitler freely *renewed* in 1933. Versailles grievances
a bit flyblown by now. Our Rhineland occupation gone, Reparations
gone, unequal treatment in Disarmament gone. Only remain territorial grievances in Europe, which are insubstantial, and colonial
grievances which are to be met by mandating, etc., not by transferring
colonial people from one Imperialism to another.

There are five Treaties of Locarno, not one. Meanwhile, no military,
and probably no economic, sanctions can be justified, or would be
supported by public opinion or by Labour Party opinion in particular,
against Germany, unless she has actually attacked anyone. We should,
however, in view of the danger of this situation, press for an All
European Pact of mutual assistance against aggression, try to re-
galvanise Disarmament discussion and have conference on wide
agenda, on Colonies, markets, etc.

Sunday 15th March
Tom Johnstone and Molly [Hamilton] to lunch. Reminiscences of
1929–31, especially 1931. And of old Willy Adamson, who spoke out
at final Cabinet, 'I've never voted against the poor yet, and I can't

now.' MacDonald asked him next after Amulree,[1] who 'agreed with the P.M.'!

Monday 16th March
Zilly to dine, with Phil [Noel-Baker] (book not finished), Morrison and Grenfell. Latter and Tom Williams[2] are, I think, being educated by the Soviet Embassy and against the *Daily Herald* (Ewer).

Attlee and I had an hour and a half with Stevenson[3] and Ewer this evening. Disagreeable and unprofitable. Stevenson not there, except when I emphasise that the *News Chronicle* carried French Socialist manifesto and *Daily Herald* not. Ewer says, more than once, 'I'm not pro-German.' I replied, 'I haven't said you are.' I tell him I have complaints from the Soviet Embassy that he doesn't keep in touch, nor even put their political stuff in. He says, 'This is impertinence.' He keeps drawing the subject away from his conduct to the general situation.

When we part, he quite impenitent, I say, 'Well, we shall have to explain to a lot of our friends from abroad in the next few days that the *Herald* isn't a Labour paper.' He is very angry at this and replies, 'And many of the Parliamentary leaders don't follow a Labour policy.'

Bob Fraser tells me that he said later, 'Well at least Dalton's clever. But Attlee's just a bloody fool.'

That night with Morrison and Zilly to squash at Kingsley Martin's.[4] Edgar Mowrer[5] there. Very charming and talks well. Naturally impressed by his experience in Berlin. He had to run for his life after [publishing] 'Germany puts the clock back'. Also Toller,[6] Cockburn,[7] etc. Very much the Soviet line. Then come down to talk of boycott of Olympic Games.

---

1 Sir William Mackenzie, 1st Baron Amulree (1860–1942). Barrister. Chairman of Joint Committees of both Houses on Consolidation of Bills 1934–9. Secretary of State for Air 1930–31. Member of first National Government 1931.
2 Thomas Williams, later 1st Baron (1888–1967). Labour M.P. for Don Valley 1922–59. Junior minister 1940–45; Minister of Agriculture and Fisheries 1945–51.
3 W. H. Stevenson, q.v., Editor of the *Daily Herald*.
4 Kingsley Martin (1897–1969). Editor of the *New Statesman and Nation* 1930–60.
5 Edgar Mowrer (1892–1977). Berlin correspondent of the *Chicago Daily News* 1923–33. Expelled from Germany after writing an anti-Nazi tract.
6 Ernst Toller (1893–1939). Expressionist writer. Communist. Left Germany after Hitler came to power. Committed suicide.
7 Claud Cockburn (1904–81). Communist journalist. Editor of the *Week*, an iconoclastic political news-sheet. Diplomatic correspondent of the *Daily Worker*. Formerly worked for *The Times*.

Tuesday 17th March

Lunch with Attlee and Greenwood at Soviet Embassy. Litvinov,[1] Maisky and Rosenberg[2] – once of the O.G.P.U.,[3] now Assistant Consul General at Geneva – a small slightly hunchbacked Jew, with a cruel mouth. Gives me a wink early. Zilly had told him of me. Litvinov is impressive. He has grown authoritative without losing his twinkle. But they are pitching it less high now than last week.

Election Sub. We decide to let Silkin rip in Peckham.

In July 1936 Dalton had tried in vain to persuade the P.L.P. to abstain on the Service Estimates, rather than vote against, as was its usual practice. The following year he succeeded, and the decision marked an important change in the Party's attitude to foreign policy and deterrence.

Monday 27th July

I leave tomorrow for Sweden, following Ruth and her W.E.A. Party. It has been a tiring and unproductive session. Apart from the Derby by-election, which has brought back Phil, there is no evidence of any movement in our favour in the country. Our leadership is small and uninspiring. The Government go on doing badly, but we do not appear as an alternative. We made a very silly decision, by 57 to 39 (60 either absent or not voting) to vote against all Service Estimates under closure of supply. Only Alexander, Lees-Smith (not very emphatic-ally) and I were against this in the Parliamentary E.C. (Clynes was away, as usual, or might have supported us). In the Party Meeting our support was proportionately greater. The other view was to move amendments, to reduce by small sums and then to abstain on the main votes. I shall exercise the conscience clause and abstain tonight. So will an uncertain number of others. A lame 'get out' statement has been issued to the press, saying that a vote against the Estimates doesn't mean a vote for Unilateral Disarmament. Hopeless! We shall be out for the rest of our lifetimes which the coming war may shorten or render even more unimportant and unhappy than today. Will it come?

1 Maxim Litvinov (1883–1951). Soviet Foreign Minister 1930–39, 1941–6.
2 Marcel Rosenberg (d. 1937). Soviet Ambassador to Madrid 1936–7. Recalled to Moscow and executed.
3 Unified State Political Directorate (Soviet political police).

In October 1936, Dalton began a year of office as Chairman of the Labour Party. Unlike many of his predecessors, he chose to interpret this role positively, and undertook three major tasks: to defeat the Crippsite Left, which he saw as a threat to Labour's electoral credibility; to alert public opinion to the plight of the Distressed Areas; and to shift Labour attitudes on foreign policy and rearmament.

The most pressing problem was provided by the challenge of Sir Stafford Cripps and the Socialist League. In the summer of 1936 plans had begun for a so-called Unity Campaign, to be based on an alliance of the Communist Party, the I.L.P. and the Socialist League, which, alone of the three, was an affiliated organisation of the Labour Party. The campaign was ostensibly 'against Fascism, Reaction and War', and arose partly from left-wing dissatisfaction with the inertia of the Labour Party leadership, partly from passions aroused by the Spanish Civil War, and partly from the desire of the Communists for closer links with the rest of the Labour Movement. The Unity Campaign was launched in January 1937, and held some big meetings. However, the Labour Party N.E.C. and Conference had forbidden joint action with Communists, and so the Campaign led rapidly to the disaffiliation and disbandment of the Socialist League.

Meanwhile another campaign of a more effective kind had been organised: the Constituency Parties Movement, which aimed to give local parties better representation on the N.E.C. Although backed by the Left and resisted by some trade union leaders, this rank and file campaign succeeded in convincing the Party Chairman that a desire for constitutional reform was widely felt. During 1937, Dalton used his influence to ensure the success of proposals for the direct election by local parties of the N.E.C. constituency parties section, and the expansion of its membership to seven. (Hitherto a section of five had been elected by the whole Conference, which meant, in practice, by the trade union majority.)

Wednesday 11th November[1]
Ernest Bevin lunched with me alone. I said I would like him to arrange for me to lunch with him and Elias.[2] I had never met Elias. This was

---

1 This entry, entitled 'Minute', is in the Dalton Papers 3/1 (4–5).
2 J. S. Elias, later 1st Viscount Southwood (d. 1946). Chairman of Odhams Press Ltd. In 1929, Odhams had bought a 51 per cent holding in the *Daily Herald* on the understanding that Odhams should run the paper but not control the politics of what was to remain Labour's official organ.

an example of the lack of contact between the *Daily Herald* and our Parliamentarians. Bevin said he would be glad to arrange such a meeting *à trois*.

He asked me whether I thought a weekend, e.g. at Lyme Regis at the W.T.A. [Workers' Travel Association] hostel, to be attended by, say 30 or 40 people, including a few of the professional non-co-operators – e.g. Cripps and Bevan – and also by selected members of the Parliamentary Party, the National Executive, and the General Council, would be useful. There should be no press notices but very frank discussions on policy and modes of co-operation between different sections. He would frankly face up Cripps to the question, 'Do you want us to win or not. What are you playing at? We have had MacDonalds, and Mosleys. We do not think you are another, but your conduct is inexplicable and unhelpful.' This, of course, would be only one of the topics to be discussed.

I said that such a weekend, if the members were well chosen, would be very useful. Bevin suggested that we should have a consultative conference from time to time, e.g. once a quarter at Transport House with representatives of County Federations and Borough Labour Parties. The G.C. organised similar conferences three times a year with representatives of Trade Councils; three members of the G.C. attended, and answered the questions and noted suggestions. These had been very useful. The G.C. paid delegates' fares and the Councils paid their own expenses.

As regards our National Conference he thought that the Block Vote should be allowed to fall into desuetude except on big issues on which the big Unions felt strongly. He thought habit had grown up for the N.E. and the Chairman of the Conference to call for a Card Vote on many occasions on which this was neither necessary nor generally desired by the T.U. delegates. An outstanding example of this was the vote on the Labour League of Youth at Edinburgh. He thought that in five cases out of six on which Card Votes were now taken delegates would be quite content to accept a decision based on a show of hands. But it was essential to organise the Conference more efficiently. At Edinburgh people were on the floor and holding up their hands who were not delegates, e.g. M.P.s and other ex-officio members of the Conference. Only delegates should be allowed in the body of the hall. Ex-officio members should be in the gallery or segregated behind a rope barrier. The Chairman should call on the Secretary on the first day to announce the number of delegates present, and the total voting power represented. It was also important to support the stewards at the doors in refusing admission to all persons without admission cards. At the T.U.C. this was very strictly observed. At the Labour

Party Conference it had become very loose. Many unauthorised persons found their way in.

By way of counter-attack we might cite the methods of voting at the Tory Conference, regarding which Ernest Hunter and Peter Howard both knew and had already said a good deal.

6 'Hopeful Funeral', 19th May 1937

National Executive Elections

Bevin said that on this he thought the Unions had a very open mind. There were a number of possibilities, only a few of which had been properly discussed or considered. I said that I personally was in favour of abolishing all separate panels for nomination and letting the Conference as a whole vote for 24 candidates, while retaining the rule that no affiliated organisation can nominate more than one. I added that this point had been suggested (not by me) at a meeting I had recently held in Romford division, one of the most militant and dissatisfied D.L.P.s in the country, and that it had been generally welcomed by the delegates. Such a change might lead to the displacement of one or two of the candidates who now get on at the bottom of the T.U. panel, and also of one or two women, in favour of some of the candidates who polled well in the D.L.P. section, but now failed to get a place.

Bevin was rather taken with this idea and said, 'Yes, I like that. Why the hell should I have to vote for —— and —— ?' We agreed that it was a strong argument in favour of this change that it left the Conference to vote as a whole and avoided further sectionalisation.

He also liked the suggestion, which I said I found was popular with D.L.P.s, that the votes of D.L.P.s who cannot now for one reason or another be represented at the Conference might be carried by the delegates of the County Federation or Borough Labour Party, as the case might be.

On 28th May 1937, Baldwin resigned as Prime Minister, and was succeeded by Neville Chamberlain.

Tuesday 15th June 1937

Dined with Alexander and Noel-Baker to meet Titulescu, who demanded to be fed on roast beef, cheese and claret, and to have all windows in the dining room closed. ...

He told a story about Baldwin. On the occasion of George V's funeral, King Carol was in London and Titulescu persuaded Baldwin to meet him at lunch (generally Baldwin cannot be persuaded to lunch with foreigners). 'My King behaved very badly. In the middle of lunch he turned to me and said, "Titulescu, can't I do what I like in Romania? Aren't I the King?", and I saw a frightened look come into Mr Baldwin's face. He had a sudden vision of what your Edward VIII[1] might turn into when he was a few years older. Carol is rather like Edward. I think it was at my luncheon that Baldwin decided he must get rid of Edward. He has a queer sort of insight into the future.'

He also said, 'As soon as this country stands up to Hitler, then Neurath and Schacht[2] and Blomberg[3] will join in getting rid of him. They don't think he is safe, but at present his prestige is so high that they cannot do anything with him. If, on the other hand, you let him

---

1 Edward VIII, later Duke of Windsor (1894–1972). Came to the throne on 20th January 1936 and abdicated on 11th December. The coronation of George VI took place on 12th May 1937.
2 Dr Hjalmar Schacht (1877–1970). German Minister for Economic Affairs 1934–7; President of the Reichsbank 1933–8.
3 General Werner von Blomberg (1878–1946). German Chief of Staff 1933–8.

get stronger and stronger, one day he will speak to this country in a very unpleasant tone which will be quite new to you. At present he is still polite to you, but that is not because he is friendly to you. The Germans are a *peuple élu* and they will not tolerate any equal, much less any superior.'

Titulescu wears pretty well, though I am not sure whether he can work his way back to effective control of Romanian foreign policy. In the Byzantine political framework of that country I fear the effects of Nazi propaganda by word and bribe. He is a wonderful wangler and has long been very sensible about the Soviet Union. It would be good if he went back into power. I hear that Churchill, in a speech at a luncheon in his honour, said, 'In Romania, as in England, many good men are at the present time outside their government. I understand that the head of the present Romanian government is a gentleman named Tatarescu.[1] I hope that before long our guest of today will give his opponents Tit for Tat.'[2]

Wednesday 16th June

Dined at the House of Commons with Bernstorff,[3] Fletcher and Nicolson. The latter told us of a farewell dinner to Baldwin by Parliamentary Private Secretaries, etc. at which Nicolson was present. Baldwin, asked to give the young men some good advice, said, 'Never try to score off the Labour Party, or to be smart at their expense. Never do anything to increase the sense of bitterness between parties in Parliament. Never go out of your way to irritate or anger the Labour Party. Remember that one day we may need them.'

Nicolson also said that at the final crisis of his talks with Edward VIII at Belvedere, they came in from the garden and Baldwin asked whether he might have a whisky and soda. Edward VIII poured this out for him with trembling hands and then burst into tears. Someone to whom Baldwin was telling this, asked, 'And what did you do then?' 'I cried too.'

Bernstorff, looking formidably fit but not less sly than of old, spoke as usual very freely against Hitler, who, he said, was getting madder, more cruel and less predictable every day.

1 G. Tatarescu (1886–1957). Prime Minister of Romania 1934–7. Minister of Industry 1933–4.
2 Titulescu, q.v., had been dismissed as Romanian Foreign Minister in August 1936.
3 Albrecht Bernstorff. Former Counsellor at the German Embassy in London. Left the diplomatic service 1933. Banker.

Hostility between Arabs and Jews in Palestine grew during the 1930s, partly because of an increase in Jewish immigration caused by the Nazi persecutions. In July 1937, after a wave of Arab violence and rioting, a Royal Commission recommended the partition of Palestine into Arab and Jewish states, leaving Britain with a mandate for Jerusalem and Bethlehem. However, Arab pressure proved too strong for this to be carried out. A White Paper in May 1939 promised that Jewish immigration would end when an additional 75,000 had arrived in Palestine.

Friday 18th June
Lunched with Namier. I thought he was still a don at Balliol but it seems that he has been for a number of years now the Professor of History at Manchester. He is also very close to Weizmann.[1] He showed me, in great confidence, a letter from the latter to Ormsby-Gore,[2] in which Weizmann is prepared to accept partition provided certain conditions are satisfied, notably, a sufficient area for the new Jewish State, complete sovereignty of the Jews therein after a brief transitional period, acceptance of a special regime in Old Jerusalem and Haifa, the suburbs of New Jerusalem to be included in the Jewish State, and the reservation of the Negeb under British control to be made available later on for Jewish settlement and then to be incorporated in the Jewish State. During the transition period there should be a great increase in Jewish immigration, and the frontiers should be so drawn as to contain, not a Jewish majority now but a Jewish majority at the end of the period, say three to five years hence. The chemical works on the Dead Sea should also be included in the Jewish State, and Akaba should be developed as a Jewish port, (a) for export of chemical products from the Dead Sea and (b) for imports from India, Australia, etc., thus furnishing, with overland communication to Tel Aviv or Haifa, an alternative trade route to the Suez Canal.

Namier claimed that he had drafted this letter. Weizmann was running a great risk in accepting, even thus conditionally, the idea of partition, which would be violently opposed by many Jews. It would be an essential condition that the Jewish State should become a British Dominion and that immigration should from henceforth rise

1 Chaim Weizmann, q.v., was Reader in Biochemistry at Manchester University.
2 W. G. A. Ormsby-Gore, later 4th Baron Harlech (1885–1964). Colonial Secretary 1936–8. Conservative M.P. for Stafford 1918–38; Denbigh 1910–18. First British representative on the Permanent Mandates Commission 1932. First Commissioner of Works 1931–6.

sharply and continue at a new high level for many years. Namier thought that relations with the new and enlarged Transjordan could be quite friendly, provided British officials did not create difficulties, e.g. as regards proposals for resettling any Transjordan Arabs from within the borders of the Jewish State. He blamed very bitterly for past mis-handling, Passfield, the Colonial Office officials, and the British administrators in Palestine. The latter always favoured the Arabs at the expense of the Jews, whom they did not understand and found antipathetic. He quoted two sayings illustrative of this. A British official had said to him, 'When I give an order in a Jewish village, they argue; when I give an order in an Arab village, it is obeyed.' The wife of a British official had also said to him, 'When an Arab is dirty he is picturesque; when a Jew is dirty he is filthy.' He thought Wauchope[1] was completely discredited. He had been very weak and had failed to maintain order. He hoped that he would not be continued during the Transition Period. It would be a bold step, but much the best solution, to appoint a Jewish Governor straight away and to make a number of Jewish appointments in the higher ranks of the Administration. He had heard that Weizmann had been at a dinner given by Sir Archibald Sinclair some ten days ago, at which Sinclair, Churchill and Attlee had been present and had all argued against the acceptance of partition. In spite of this, Weizmann was prepared to negotiate with Ormsby-Gore on the basis of partition. But the conditions put forward in the letter he had shown me were an absolute minimum. I said that many of my colleagues who were very friendly to the Jews would be inclined to oppose partition in the interests of the Jews themselves. He said that this would do no harm. He thought that Snell[2] was the best informed man in our Party on this subject, but Passfield had always refused to listen to him. Mussolini had been making Weizmann most wonderful offers, including the setting up of an Independent Jewish State, on condition that he broke all British connections. But Weizmann had not been attracted by the idea of Italian protection. Namier said, 'After all, the Italians would not be content unless their Black Shirts had a ceremonial march under the Arch of Titus, and you know that no good Jew ever walks under that Arch, through which the Roman conquerors dragged our priests as captives. They will only walk under it again when a free Jewish State has been re-born.' ...

1 General Sir Arthur Wauchope (1874–1947). High Commissioner and Commander-in-Chief, Palestine and Transjordania 1931–8.
2 Henry Snell, 1st Baron (1865–1944). Leader of the Labour Party in the House of Lords 1935–40. Labour M.P. 1922–31. Under-Secretary for India 1931. Former L.C.C. councillor. Fabian.

That evening Ruth and I met the two Weizmanns at dinner. We did not like her[1] – hard, rich, no taste – but were greatly impressed by him. He is a born leader, a natural statesman, as well as a great scientist. We talked at great length on Partition. He is clearly for it, thinking that he has a good prospect of getting from H.M.G. conditions which would make it workable. In particular, he thinks he has now got all Galilee intact. There was danger that the northern tip would not be included in the Jewish State. He is prepared for an international regime in Jerusalem, but hopes that some political arrangement might be made whereby the Jewish population, which predominates in the new suburbs, might be 'associated' with the new Jewish State. If this were done and if, conversely, the Arab population of Haifa were similarly associated with the enlarged Transjordan, a Jewish majority would be secured at once within the limits of the proposed Jewish State. Failing this, there would be a very even balance of Arabs and Jews, which could only be offset by a large Jewish immigration during the Transition Period. This he insists upon in any case, and attaches importance to the replacement, during this period, of a number of the present very unsatisfactory British officials by Jews. Quite definitely, the new Jewish State must be a British Dominion and British control should be retained over the Negeb. He believes there are great possibilities of future settlement there, particularly along the coastal strip, which is potentially very fertile right up to the Suez Canal. He thinks that the Jewish State, once established, and the Mandate liquidated both there and in Transjordan, they could bargain with the Arabs and give financial inducements for Arabs within the Jewish State to sell out and settle in Transjordan. This would be agreeable to both governments. He says that the author of the Partition scheme is Coupland,[2] who sought him out for a long private talk just before he left Palestine. He will have difficulty in persuading some of the Jews to accept Partition in any case, but he will clearly try his best if he can get the conditions he hopes for.[3]

1 Mrs Vera Weizmann, née Chatzman.
2 Professor R. Coupland, later Sir Reginald (1884–1952). Beit Professor of the History of the British Empire at Oxford 1920–48. Member of the Palestine Royal Commission (Peel Commission) 1936–7.
3 This was one of several important meetings between Dalton and Weizmann. Dalton's own view became official Labour policy when he wrote a long Party document on the International Settlement in 1944, containing a crucial paragraph which presented the case for partition of Palestine and the transfer of population. Dalton claimed later that he had written this passage without any close consultation with the Zionists. But he acknowledged that 'over a long period I used to see Weizmann from time to time and Lewis Namier occasionally, and some of my pupils ... had been, and still were, keen Zionists' (FY, p. 426).

The Italian conquest of Abyssinia was completed by May 1936 with the occupation of Addis Ababa. In July, the failure of an army coup in Spain precipitated the Spanish Civil War, which aroused fierce passions on the British Left. During 1937, backed by Italy and Germany, General Franco made rapid advances. In June 1937 a Popular Front government was formed in France under the socialist leader Léon Blum, who sympathised with the Republican cause. However, with his own government divided and the British government hostile, he resisted pressure to send aid and instead proposed that all countries should agree to 'non-intervention'. Britain, Germany, Italy and Russia were among the states which signed an agreement to this effect at the end of August. A Non-Intervention Committee, charged with enforcing the agreement, held its first meeting in London on 9th September. The failure of 'non-intervention' became apparent by the end of October.

In June 1937, purges in the Soviet Union were extended to the army. Over the next few months, an estimated 35,000 Soviet officers were arrested and executed, including more than half of all officers of general rank.

Thursday 24th June
Saw Vansittart[1] in his room at the Foreign Office at 5 p.m., and Maisky in his room at his Embassy at 7. Curious how these two very dissimilar witnesses corroborate each other's evidence on many points.

I had asked to see Van to do my duty to Sheila Grant Duff[2] and the Czechs. Van denied, as I expected, any pressure by the Foreign Office on the Czechs to take Henlein[3] into the Czech Coalition Government. What we had done, he said (and this, of course, I knew already), was to take every opportunity of urging the Czechs to do everything possible to remove reasonable grievances entertained by the German Minority, in particular as regards schools, contracts, and jobs, whether for officials or manual workers. There was no doubt that

---

1 Sir Robert Vansittart, q.v., was Permanent Under-Secretary at the Foreign Office 1930–38. Dalton saw him frequently from 1937. The two men shared strong anti-Nazi sentiments, and a bitter hostility to the appeasement policies of the Government.
2 Sheila Grant Duff, later Mrs Newsome (b. 1913). Dalton's secretary.
3 Konrad Henlein (1898–1945). Leader of the extreme right-wing Sudeten German Heimatfront. Later appointed Reichsstathalter of the Sudetenland by Hitler, following annexation.

the German Minority in Czechoslovakia was even now much better treated than any other Minority in Central Europe, e.g. than Germans in Poland or Poles in Germany. He thought Hodza[1] was a wise man and doing his best, but the agreement lately reached between the Czech Government and the German Activists, though good on paper, was very slow to come into operation and was, no doubt, sabotaged by any local Czech officials. As to Henlein, Van had had him to lunch some years ago and formed the view that he was a small man, but might be dangerous in certain conditions. He had then denied any dependence on German Nazis, or any desire either for revision of frontiers of Czechoslovakia or domination of Czechoslovakia by Germany. Of course, one should not believe too readily such protestations, and, even if true then, in the meantime, through the growth of Nazi power, Henlein's mind might have changed. Van's view was that Czech ministers and politicians should cease to treat Henlein as a social and political outcast. To take him into the Government would, no doubt, be going much too far, but to establish friendly personal relations, to listen patiently to his grievances, and to try to remove as many as possible, would be sensible and prudent. Van feared that there might be some element of truth in Germany's allegations of mal-treatment of Weigl and Staubner in Czech prisons.[2] Gross exaggeration, no doubt, in Nazi Press, but Czech police methods were not very civilised, though much less barbaric than those of most of their neighbours, especially Germany. The danger was that the Germans had some colourable grievances connected with Czechoslovakia and, given the personalities and moods now prevailing in Germany, there was a constant danger of violent explosions in this direction. He suggested that in tomorrow's debate in the House, whoever spoke for the Opposition should refer to present conditions in Central Europe and emphasise our concern. This would enable Eden[3] to say something, when replying, which might have a reassuring effect, not only in Czechoslovakia, but in Austria and elsewhere. The Government had already declared that they could not undertake any more specific military commitments in Central Europe but that did not mean that we were disinterested in events there.

He said that Hitler had never been so 'hot under the collar', so hysterical and dangerous to the peace of Europe as during the past week. He had been keeping vigil alone with the dead from the *Deutsch-*

1 Milan Hodza (1878–1944). Czech Prime Minister 1935–8.
2 Earlier in June, the German press had alleged that Reich citizens Weigl and Staubner had been arrested and tortured by the Czech authorities.
3 Anthony Eden, q.v., was Foreign Secretary 1935–8.

land (thirty-one corpses of German sailors). Left unrestrained, he might have ordered wholesale onslaughts by sea and air on 'Red' Spain. Some of his advisers had succeeded in controlling him. Goebbels[1] was always his evil genius, urging him towards violence in word and deed, but it was believed that Goering and the professional heads of the Fighting Services were at present, at any rate, for moderation. Van himself was extremely doubtful whether any torpedo had been fired at the *Leipzig*. So was our own Admiralty. But the personal factor of Hitler was incalculable.

Corbin[2] had called this morning and was extremely jumpy, especially at the prospect of the debate in the House tomorrow. He feared that words might be used which would set Hitler off again. And indeed, Van added, the German press campaign, directed, of course, by Goebbels, had been turned furiously against the British during the past few days. He begged me, and several times repeated this, to use my influence to moderate the language of any who might be speaking in the debate. I said that this was very difficult, if not impossible, particularly as regards speeches from the back-benches. I also thought that Ambassadors and Foreign Office officials were inclined to be unduly nervous about Parliamentary debates. After all much had been said, both in recent debates and in daily questions on foreign affairs, which would give Hitler any excuse which he wanted. None the less, I promised to repeat what Van had said to Attlee.

As to Spain. Van said that he was satisfied that arms had been going in in great quantities in recent months to both sides. He believed that our intelligence reports on this subject were very good. Large consignments had been reaching Valencia and Barcelona, principally from Black Sea ports, but also by round-about routes from some of the smaller European countries and also from across the Atlantic. A good deal had also been going in over the French frontier. I said that Bevin and Citrine, at a private meeting held at the House of Commons last night, had reported that Mounsey had made this same assertion. I added that most of those present had not believed this. Why, one asked, if this were true, had the War in the Basque country been so one-sided, and why had there been no military movements by government forces on any of the other fronts? Van said that the Spanish government had, in fact, sent a number of aeroplanes to help the Basques, but that these had been destroyed on the ground in their aerodromes by German and Italian bombs. This fact had not been published by either side. Each thought they had an interest to conceal

1 Joseph Goebbels (1897–1945). German Minister of Propaganda 1933–45.
2 Charles Corbin (1881–1970). French Ambassador to London 1933–40.

it. On the Madrid and Aragon fronts, offensives had been delayed because of (a) internal trouble in Catalonia, and (b) the slow progress made in training both ground troops and air personnel. He said that the Spanish government were finding very great difficulty in persuading the Catalans to get into military uniform. They had great disinclination to become soldiers. They preferred either politics or work in the factories.

There was still danger that Germany and Italy would declare a blockade of the Spanish government coast. This might produce very grave incidents immediately, e.g. they might begin to stop, or even sink, British or French ships. Meanwhile, rumours that the German fleet was concentrated in the Mediterranean were not true. On the contrary, their ships were going west through the Straits of Gibraltar. But they might, of course, suddenly return.

We spoke of the export of arms from this country. I said that we had been surprised by answers given in Parliament showing the magnitude of such exports recently. He said that he, personally, wished we had been able to export more to those countries which were our regular clients for arms. We had to supply Iraq and Egypt, with whom we had special treaty arrangements. We were also supplying certain quantities to Scandinavian and Baltic States. We were also still supplying something, though much less than some years ago, to Portugal. Germany and Italy were trying to take our place in Portugal. The supply of arms generally carried with it a supply of trained instructors and political influence. If we ceased to supply Portugal, our political influence, already much diminished, would vanish altogether. At this moment it was generally believed that our new types of aircraft were the best in the world and this view was widely held abroad. Although our exports of arms had, to some extent, been maintained, the requirements of our own arms programme had obviously operated to diminish them.

As to Russia. He had been very sceptical about the earlier blood baths, but he was satisfied that the Generals were guilty; that they had been in close relations with Germany and were planning a military dictatorship and the elimination of Stalin and Voroshilov.[1] For the moment, no doubt, the Red Army had been weak and this was very dangerous both for the obvious reason that it might encourage the Germans to take risks, and for the more subtle reason, not generally appreciated, that, personal links between the German and Russian High Command having been broken, the German soldiers would no longer be restrained through this channel from contemplating an

1 Marshal Kliment Voroshilov (1881–1969). Soviet Commissar for Defence 1934–40.

attack on Czechoslovakia. (I did not pursue this point, but I infer that the basis of the German-Russian military friendship was not so much Russian indifference to a German attack on Czechoslovakia, as Russian indifference to a German attack on France and Britain.)

I saw Maisky alone, as I generally do, but I daresay there was an unseen listener to our conversation. I began by saying, 'It is some time since we met and a lot of things have been happening in your country which have disturbed us a good deal. I should like you to give me some information about them. I hope that they have not seriously weakened the Red Army.' He replied, 'Let us put that down as No. 2 on our agenda. I should like first to speak about Spain.' He urged that in tomorrow's debate there should be what he called 'an outcry in advance' against further German and Italian action against the Spanish government. For the moment there was a lull, but he was sure that they were preparing something, probably a blockade of the Spanish government coast, and perhaps even more violent action, e.g. bombardment of Valencia and Barcelona. They were determined to secure a victory for Franco within the next few months. Otherwise the superiority of forces at the disposal of the Spanish government would lead to Franco's defeat, not indeed immediately, but within measurable time. It would also be a serious consequence of a German–Italian blockade that the supplies of arms which were now reaching the Spanish government would be seriously interfered with. I asked whether, in fact, the government had been getting large supplies. He said, 'Yes, certainly. From many quarters.' I asked whether he thought they had been getting as much as Franco. He replied, 'Probably yes.' I asked how this was done in spite of the 'control'. He smiled and said, 'It is very easy. When the Italians send men and arms to Franco in Italian ships they fly the Italian flag until they come to Spanish territorial waters and then they hoist the Spanish flag. There is no control over Spanish ships. It is just the same on the other side.' He added that the production of arms in Catalonia is now proceeding on a large scale. A few months ago this production was utterly disorganised. 'The Anarchists', he said, 'are the criminals.' They had insisted on a forty-hour week in the arms factories and this had completely disorganised production. But now things had changed. I made the same point as to Van. If the Spanish government have all these arms, why have they not been using them lately to relieve pressure on the Basques? He said that there had been great difficulties in the organisation of the government armies, lack of unified control, lack of competent commanders, the need to train large masses of civilians. But in the next few months there would be a great change. He used, as in previous conversations with me on this subject, the analogy of the Russian Civil War in which, for the first year, the Red Army hardly existed as a military force, 'and then', he said, 'we gradually gained the upper hand over the Whites and were able to bring our reserves of manpower into action.' I said that conditions in Russia, both geographical and as regards material and human resources, had been much more favourable to the Red Army than were conditions in Spain today to the Republican Forces. He admitted this, but still pressed the analogy. He urged that, in tomorrow's debate, we should declare that any further German and Italian action, by way of blockade or bombardment, against the Spanish government would not be tolerated by this country. A clear and emphatic warning would have its effect. Nothing else would. We should also declare that, unless the 'volunteers' on both sides were all speedily withdrawn, the non-intervention agreement should be denounced. I said that the attitude of our Party now was that, in view of Plymouth's[1] admission that the non-intervention agreement had completely broken down and become a farce, it should be ended forthwith, independently of action for the withdrawal of volunteers. He said that he did not quarrel with this. He added that Plymouth, at the meeting of the Non-intervention Chairman's Sub-Committee, after making the statement which I had just quoted and which had been published in the press, had gone on to suggest a 'symbolic' withdrawal of an equal number of volunteers from both sides. This had not been published. It was a preposterous suggestion which showed the state of mind of the British government. Franco had at least 150,000 Germans and Italians on his side. The Spanish government had, at the outside, 20,000 non-Spaniards helping them. To withdraw equal numbers would therefore operate entirely to Franco's advantage. He asked whether I thought that the stiffer attitude apparently adopted yesterday by the British and French governments was due to the replacement of Baldwin by Chamberlain. I said that on this particular point I did not know, but that I thought, in general, that Chamberlain would be in favour of a firmer policy than Baldwin when he thought British interests were directly threatened. Whether he would take a wider view of British interests, e.g. that these would be threatened very seriously, even indirectly, by a victory of Franco in Spain, I was not so sure. Maisky said that it was very unfortunate that Delbos was going on as Foreign Minister in France. He was a very weak man. Before taking any decision he always asked, 'What does Mr Eden think?'

1 I. M. Windsor-Clive, 2nd Earl of Plymouth (1889–1943). Parliamentary Under-Secretary of State at the Foreign Office 1936–9. Conservative M.P. 1922–3. Junior minister 1929, 1931–2.

We then passed to Item 3 on the agenda. He gave a long explanation, largely on familiar lines, of the recent trials and executions. He said that the Generals, particularly Tukhachevsky[1] and Putna,[2] who had been Military Attaché here for some time, were definitely pro-German, anti-French and anti-British. When Tukhachevsky had been over here for the funeral of King George V he had spoken openly and contemptuously of Britain and France, both as regards their Parliamentary institutions and their armed forces. He was a great admirer of the efficiency of Germany. Putna was the same. There was no doubt that they were plotting a military dictatorship in Russia, close friendship with Germany, the re-establishment in some measure of Capitalism in Russia, and the cession to Germany of part of the Ukraine, including Odessa, in return for the re-absorption of the Baltic States into the Soviet Union. They were willing, on these terms, to let Germany have a free hand in the West. I said that I found the story about ceding even part of the Ukraine almost incredible in view of (a) the importance of this area to the Soviet economy, and (b) the obvious fact that the Germans, if they got part of it, would soon want the whole and much more besides. He said that I must remember the immense area of the Soviet Union. I might think that the analogy was for this country to cede Scotland to Germany. In fact, the analogy was rather to cede Trinidad. I told him that I still did not find this part of the story convincing.

As I was going away, he said that he hoped I did not resent his making suggestions to me about the line we should take in Parliament. I said, 'Certainly not. I have been very interested to hear your suggestions. Many of these are not new and we already have been thinking on the same lines; and I have made suggestions to you before on other questions, for instance, that you should convey to Mr Dimitrov[3] that he should take steps to liquidate the Communist Party in this country and let its members join the Labour Party as individuals. This would get rid of many difficulties and would improve relations between your country and the Labour Movement. I am sure that you have already passed on that suggestion of mine.' He laughed a little uncomfortably; perhaps at this point he was more acutely conscious

1 Marshal M. N. Tukhachevsky (1893–1937). Soviet general shot with seven others in June 1937 after a secret espionage trial. Former chief of Soviet military academy. Commanded Russian forces against Poland in 1920.
2 General V. Putna (d. 1937). Shot with Tukhachevsky. Also a veteran of the Polish campaign. Military attaché in London 1936.
3 G. M. Dimitrov (1882–1949). Secretary of the Executive Committee of the Communist International (Comintern) 1935–43. Former Bulgarian revolutionary. Accused by the Germans of trying to burn the Reichstag in 1933, but acquitted. Prime Minister of Bulgaria 1946.

of the unseen listener, and he said, 'I cannot interfere in such matters. I have no authority to do so.'

It is, I think, conclusive that Vansittart and Maisky, relying on their different sources of information, corroborate each other, (1) on the supply of arms to the government of Spain, (2) on the guilt of the Red Generals.

Tuesday 14th September
Paris
Blum.[1] With Ruth and Gillies by car to Les Mesruels. Blum and his wife, as last year, in this remote little house in a small village, but fewer telephones in the living room ...

Spain. He had bad accounts of internal divisions – and bitter hatreds – on the government side. The hatred between Prieto[2] and Caballero[3] was intense, and of long standing. Caballero was not resigned to loss of power. The Communists were aiming at getting on top, and were already suppressing some opposing elements – not only the P.O.U.M. [Partido Obrero de Unificación Marxista][4] – with great cruelty. The Republican Army was now capable of small, but not of great, offensives. Negrín[5] and others claimed that next year they would be able to produce all their own arms – even aeroplanes – with the exception of heavy guns. But the danger that the Republic would be destroyed by internal strife was real.

In reply to a question by me, he said that we should not now, as a year ago, embarrass him by denouncing the non-intervention agreement. There was a great movement of opinion in France on this subject. A year ago they had been paralysed by Radical Opposition. Now Daladier[6] in particular, and others, had changed their attitude.

1 Léon Blum (1872–1950). Vice-Premier of France June 1937–March 1938 in the Chautemps Government. Leader of the French Socialist Party. Prime Minister at the head of the Front Populaire Government 1936–7. Imprisoned during the war. Prime Minister briefly in 1946.
2 Indalecio Prieto y Tuero (1883–1962). Leader of the reformist wing of the Spanish Socialist Party. Minister of Defence under Negrín 1937–8. Ambassador to Chile 1938–9, remaining in exile after the Civil War.
3 Francisco Largo Caballero (1869–1946). Leader of the left wing of the Spanish Socialist Party. Prime Minister and Minister of War 1936–7, when he was replaced by Negrín. Secretary-General of the socialist trade union, the Unión General de Trabajadores.
4 Revolutionary communists.
5 Dr Juan Negrín Lopez (1889–1956). Prime Minister of Spain 1937–9. Socialist. Formerly Professor of Physiology at the University of Madrid.
6 Edouard Daladier (1884–1970). Prime Minister of France 1933, 1934, 1936, 1938–40. Radical Socialist. Imprisoned by the Vichy regime 1941–5.

I said that the Labour Party had now, as he knew, declared against non-intervention, but we should not move the Government. He was not sure. He thought he had noticed, a few days ago, a distinct change in the attitude of Eden, and also in Vansittart. They were much stronger against Italy. And Admiral Chatfield[1] was very determined. ...

Blum said that he thought the most serious situation of all was today in the Far East. He thought that Japan intended, in the very near future, to attack Russia as well as China. It was a sinister fact that she was calling up against China her oldest classes of reservists. She was keeping the younger classes in reserve against Russia. The maritime pursuit of Russia was indefensible. If Russia became involved in war in the Far East very grave things might happen in Europe. (I think he meant, not only that Germany might attack Russia, but alternatively that Germany might feel free, with Italian help, to strike westward.) Events were repeating themselves, as before 1914. Attempts had been made to get common action in the Far East between Britain, France and U.S. The U.S. were very suspicious, particularly of Britain, remembering how Simon had let them down in 1932.

He had no doubt that Tukhachevsky was in very close touch with Germany. He was for Russia having no westward entanglements, and he was planning a military coup d'état to get rid of Stalin.

I asked, following Comert's cue, whether he found co-operation with the Russian government becoming easier or more difficult. He replied, rather unexpectedly, that the most essential thing in Europe was to improve British–Soviet relations. ...

In France, the Communists, like Communists everywhere, were a mystery. The relations of the Socialists and Radical Parties were not easy. In the Cantonal elections the Communists would gain heavily – they were starting from zero – and the Radicals would lose heavily. The Socialists might gain slightly. In the Socialist Party there was a strong feeling against continuing in the Chautemps Government.[2] If at the Radical Congress at Lille, immediately after the Cantonal Elections, there was any resolution passed, reflecting ever so slightly on the Socialists, this feeling might become uncontrollable. He was for going on in the Chautemps Government. There was no alternative

---

1 Admiral Sir Ernle Chatfield, later 1st Baron (1873–1967). First Sea Lord and Chief of Naval Staff 1933–9. Minister for Co-ordination of Defence 1939–40.
2 Camille Chautemps (1885–1963). Prime Minister of France June 1937–March 1938. Radical Socialist. Chautemps succeeded Blum after the collapse of the Front Populaire Government, in which Chautemps served as Minister without Portfolio. The Chautemps Government fell, in turn, when the Socialists appeared to be withdrawing their support.

majority in the Chamber for any Government except Front Populaire, and an early dissolution required the consent of the Senate. But many Radicals were only held to the Front Populaire like a dog on a lead. He himself had had to struggle very hard, at the National Council, at the Marseilles Conference and in the Parliamentary Group, for a majority for going on in the Front Populaire. He was like a man who, during the past twenty years, had built up a big balance at the bank, of confidence in himself by the Party. And now he was having to draw cheque after cheque against this balance, so that it was dwindling. He did not wish to be Prime Minister again unless he could bring in another large and rapid series of reforms. And this was not possible in present conditions.

As we were going, he said that François-Poncet[1] complained that he could not get the same intimate relationship with Nevile Henderson[2] which he had had with Phipps.[3] He thought Henderson leaned too much towards the Nazis. Poncet was not a man of the Left, but he was one of their best Ambassadors and knew Germany very well.

The Labour Party Conference took place at The Pavilion, Bournemouth, on 4th to 8th October. Dalton was in the chair.

Thursday 21st October
Saw Peter Howard[4] in the smoking room at the House of Commons. Congratulated him on last week's *Sunday Express*, comparing the Bournemouth and Scarborough Conferences. He told me that he had asked Cripps for an interview, to get a line but not for straight publication. He had, he said, been most graciously received by the great man in his chambers in the Temple. Cripps had told him that he had no desire to be the Leader of the Labour Party; he did not think that Attlee would 'put difficulties in my way'; he thought that Morrison will 'come our way before very long'. This was all Peter would tell me at that moment, as others joined us.

---

1 André François-Poncet (1887–1978). French Ambassador to Germany 1934–8; German Federal Republic 1949–55.
2 Sir Nevile Henderson (1882–1942). British Ambassador to Germany 1937–9.
3 Sir Eric Phipps, q.v., Ambassador to Germany 1933–7.
4 Peter Howard (1908–65). Political columnist for the *Sunday Express* 1933–41. Author, playwright and former rugby international. Moral rearmer.

George Lathan[1] tells me that Cripps has now sent £250 to the Campaign Fund with promises of three further sums of like amount to follow at due intervals. He is curiously rash and ill-judged in many of his political contributions. I recall that he blurted out to me, immediately before the final row over the Socialist League,[2] when I had him alone in my flat, that in the last Parliament, when Lansbury was out of action, he had subsidised Attlee, it 'having been decided' (? by whom) that it was better that he himself should not lead the Parliamentary Party. This revelation somewhat embarrassed me at the time, as Cripps and I were then supposed to be fighting each other on the United Front and other issues.

Thursday 4th November

Had a letter from Van suggesting that we might have a short talk. (I had told him, through Clifford Norton[3] who was at the House last week, of Henderson's onslaught on my political innocence.)[4]

I went round to the Foreign Office about 12. Nothing very new or topical from Van's side. He said that the drive against him was going as strongly as ever. Londonderry, Lothian, *The Times* ...... it was worse now because lots of people were frightened and thought that by giving things away right and left to Germany they could buy our own peace and security. I said I was frightened too, but I did not say so in public, nor did my fear make me act like that. He said, 'So am I, but it is one thing to have fear in one's heart and quite another to show funk and run away from these people. That won't help at all.' The dictators were now getting more and more openly abusive, not merely, as a little while ago, to Red Russia, but now to all the 'reactionary democracies'. The barrage against this country, both in the German and Italian press, was mounting. The Germans might change their list of

1 George Lathan (1875–1942). Labour M.P. for Sheffield Park 1929–31, 1935–42. President of the National Federation of Professional Workers 1921–37. Member of the Labour Party N.E.C. (Chairman 1931–2).
2 The Socialist League (of which Cripps was the most prominent member and leading financial backer) had been disaffiliated in January, and had dissolved itself in May in order to avoid the expulsion of its members from the Labour Party. At the Bournemouth Party Conference in October, with Dalton in the chair, motions to 'refer back' N.E.C. rulings on the Socialist League and the Unity Campaign were heavily defeated with the aid of the trade union bloc vote.
3 C. J. Norton, later Sir Clifford (b. 1891). Private Secretary to Sir Robert Vansittart as Permanent Under-Secretary 1930–37. Counsellor at the British Embassy in Warsaw 1937–9.
4 Sir Nevile Henderson, q.v., the new British Ambassador in Berlin, visited Dalton at Carlisle Mansions on 28th October and spent an hour trying to persuade him of the merits of appeasement (Diary, 28th October 1937; FY, pp. 105–9).

priorities. They might alter the order of their dishes, but the menu remained the same. Today, probably, it was No. 1 Austria, No. 2 colonies, No. 3 Czechoslovakia, but it might be changed tomorrow. He agreed with me that it would be almost impossible to stop the Nazification of Austria if the change came through an engineered internal explosion.

As to Czechoslovakia, he saw Henlein for the second time a little while ago and thought that he was losing his head. He was putting his demands higher and higher. Van had said to him that he really should show more moderation, since if war came in Central Europe all the areas in which the Sudeten Germans lived would be smashed to pieces first and worst of all ... Russia, he thought, was in a terrible state of disorganisation after all these purges and shootings, but he repeated that he was satisfied that some of the Red Generals had deserved all they got. ... In the Far East they were thoroughly frightened and had not even said 'peep-peep' to the Japs. Meanwhile, *Izvestiya* and *Pravda* were daily full of leading articles attacking the 'supine British' for doing nothing to stop Japan. This weakness of Russia was most unfortunate, encouraging Hitler and Mussolini. The latter seems to have lost all powers of cool calculation such as a few years ago he undoubtedly had. He was very much the junior partner on the Berlin–Rome Axis. He had plunged in 100 per cent into the German embrace. If he had only gone in 40 per cent he would have retained valuable power of manoeuvre. He had apparently been persuaded, quite literally, to sell Austria to Hitler. Van reminded me that some time ago he had said that neither he nor anybody else could guarantee what would happen in Europe after the end of 1937.

4

The Umbrella Man
1938–9

Dalton's year as Chairman strengthened his position in the Party, and increased his reputation for effectiveness in Parliament and in the country. He had led the way in reforming the Party Constitution, in conducting an N.E.C. inquiry into conditions in the Distressed Areas, and in stiffening Labour's foreign policy; he could also take much of the credit for the rout of Cripps and the Socialist League. In October 1937, Dalton relinquished the Chairmanship, and for a while he was out of the limelight. In December he set out on a five-month trip around the world – ostensibly to represent the Labour Party at the 150th anniversary celebrations of the foundation of Australia. He spent a month in Australia and a fortnight in New Zealand, before sailing home via the Panama Canal. He returned to the Old World mentally refreshed, deeply committed to the Commonwealth idea, and increasingly gloomy about the future of Europe.

When the Germans entered Vienna in March 1938, Dalton's ship was still in the Pacific Ocean. He made no immediate comment in his diary, but over the next few weeks his sense of foreboding grew. 'When I left [England] there was an unspoken question in my heart', he wrote shortly before disembarking on 5th April, ' – but to whom would it have profited to speak it? – "Will IT begin before I come back?" IT is the NEXT WAR, not some little War in a Corner – China, Abyssinia & Spain. But War in the Open, all over Europe, perhaps all over the world ... "Time is on our side", some say. I doubt it, whether as to arms, or economic strength, or allies.'[1]

Hitherto, Dalton had focused on the problem of how to prevent a European war. Now the issue was ceasing to be whether there would be a war – but when, and what would be the outcome. It followed that steps must be taken to ensure not only that German aggression should be challenged, but that if war came, Germany would be defeated. In holding these views, Dalton was

1 Diary, April 1938.

221

ahead of many of his Labour colleagues, who continued for some time to believe that collective security, without the need for rapid rearmament, could restrain the Dictators. Meanwhile, Dalton's position was close to that of Winston Churchill and L. S. Amery. Thus, when the Tory dissidents looked round for allies, it was natural that they should turn first to Dalton.

The scope for a cross-bench arrangement of some kind had been growing during the winter months, while Dalton was away. In February 1938, Eden resigned as Foreign Secretary, objecting to the Prime Minister's personal diplomacy and in particular to Chamberlain's pursuit of an understanding with Italy. After the *Anschluss* in March, discontent on the Tory back-benches grew. On 16th March, Churchill told Harold Nicolson that he was thinking of refusing the whip, and that he might take fifty people with him.[1]

Nothing came of this, but inter-party alliances were the subject of continued speculation and gossip. On the one hand, there was talk of a broadened National government, bringing in independent Liberals and Labour. On the other, there emerged various schemes for an anti-Government combination, within Parliament or outside it. The most widely voiced proposal was for a 'Popular Front', uniting all anti-Chamberlainites on a limited range of foreign or defence issues. But the Labour leadership was cautious and the trade unions were hostile: the dangers of taking up a proposal whose main inspiration seemed to come from the Communist International seemed to outweigh other considerations. Early in April an Executive statement declared that 'there can be no association in any way whatever with either "United Front" or "Popular Front" Movements.'[2] The N.E.C. admitted, however, that a sizeable rebellion on the Government side might cause it to revise this decision.

Such a rebellion seemed about to occur in the autumn of 1938, after Chamberlain had given in to Hitler's demands at Munich. During the Commons debate, Harold Macmillan approached Dalton on behalf of Tory anti-appeasers and asked for help. This was the first of several discussions, and some early co-operation was achieved. But hopes for a full-scale alliance between Tory rebels and Labour never materialised. Such a possibility was finally destroyed at the beginning of 1939, when Sir Stafford Cripps launched a personal campaign for a Popular Front (from which Tories were to be excluded), turning the issue of inter-party alliances into a bitter wrangle within the Labour Party.

At the end of April 1939, the Government introduced a limited form of compulsory National Service. The Labour Party and most Liberals were opposed. Though privately uncertain, Dalton voted with his Party. This incident has been used as evidence of the strength of Labour's pacifistic

1 N. Nicolson (ed.), *Harold Nicolson: Diaries and Letters 1930–39*, Fontana, London, 1969, p. 325.
2 *Daily Herald*, 14th April 1938.

sentiments right up to the outbreak of war. In fact, opposition on conscription was no more than a symbolic gesture, an echo from the past. The issue quickly ceased to be contentious, and on all major defence and foreign policy matters in the summer of 1939, Labour and Tory critics of the Government stood side by side. It was in these final months of peace that the basis of agreement was established which made possible the successful anti-Government combination a year later.

During this period, Dalton was closely in touch with East European diplomats and politicians. He also received unofficial, and sometimes illicit, information from sympathisers within the Foreign Office and Air Ministry. Dalton's detailed exposure of the inadequacies of Britain's air defence in May 1939, based on leaked statistics, caused Aneurin Bevan, not usually an admirer, to write of the 'deep sense of unease' the Shadow Foreign Secretary had created in the House.[1] On foreign policy, Dalton's best informant was the Government's Chief Diplomatic Adviser, Sir Robert Vansittart, who had been ousted as Permanent Under-Secretary and replaced by Sir Alexander Cadogan at the beginning of January 1938. As a result, Dalton was as well informed on British defence capabilities and on the details of British diplomacy in Europe as anybody outside the Government inner circle – and better, perhaps, than some within it.

Wednesday 6th April

Returned yesterday and saw Nield[2] at the House tonight. I rowed him for habitual indiscretions and hoped that he took it in. He told me of the progress of the sub-committee of three on the Research Department and seemed very satisfied with progress so far. The sub-committee's report will not be finished till Laski returns from the U.S. He has seen a lot of Laski and found him receptive and constructive. Nield had also seen Morrison who was still suffering from a persecution mania traceable to his failure to get the leadership in 1935. He had, however, incited Morrison, at my suggestion, to operate on George Ridley[3] who, we thought, was being drawn too much into Greenwood's orbit, probably by flattery and special attention. Nield told me that Grant McKenzie[4] had put in a most bitter and highly documented

1 *Tribune*, 27th May 1938.
2 W. A. Nield, later Sir William (b. 1913). Official in the Research and Policy Department of the Labour Party 1937–9. Post-war Civil Service career. Permanent Under-Secretary of State at the Department of Economic Affairs 1968–9. Permanent Secretary at the Cabinet Office 1969–72; Northern Ireland Office 1972–3.
3 George Ridley (1886–1944). Labour M.P. for Clay Cross 1936–44. Member of the Labour Party N.E.C.
4 Grant McKenzie. Assistant to Arthur Greenwood in the Labour Party Research Department at Transport House.

memorandum which, by its excessive bitterness, had damaged the author but had also convinced the sub-committee that something drastic must be done. Many efforts had been made to prevent Nield from speaking freely before the sub. He had been spoken to by ... Willie Hall,[1] and by two M.P.s, friends of Greenwood, whose names he did not know. Also by Greenwood himself, who said that, of course, McKenzie had always been a viper in his bosom but that he hoped that Nield, as a decent and promising young man, would not be led away and get into bad company. Nield also showed me a document of some interest. It was a summons to a special meeting of the New Welcome Lodge, dated four days before the meeting of the Parliamentary Party at which Attlee was re-elected Leader after the last election. This Lodge is masonic and appears to cater especially, though not quite exclusively, for Labour M.P.s. The secretary summoning the meeting was Scott Lindsay. He canvassed me for Greenwood at the time and, in reply to my obvious point of doubt, told me that Greenwood had promised that, if elected Leader, he would never be out of control on important occasions. A full list of members of the Lodge was on the back of the summons. The list included Sir Robert Young, Joe Compton, A. Short, Major Milner, J. W. Bowen, Rev. H. Dunnico, Colonel L'Estrange Malone, Colonel H. W. Burton (a Tory M.P. and the only one in this *galère*), Jack Hayes, F. J. Bellenger, Willie Henderson, F. O. Roberts, Greenwood himself (these two appear to have joined about the same time), W. Dobbie, Ben Tillet, George Hicks, Lord Kinnoull (now dead).[2]

This is a surprisingly large number, and some of the names are very surprising. I recall that I unwisely invited Bellenger to the 'private meeting' in my flat designed to win support for Morrison. And then we wondered who leaked to the press, and suspected poor little Ellen Wilkinson, probably quite innocent. Nield told me that he had shown this document to Morrison, who said, 'I have got a copy locked up in

---

1 W. G. Glenvil Hall (1887–1962). Labour M.P. for Colne Valley 1939–62; Plymouth Central 1929–31. Financial Secretary to the Treasury 1945–50.
2 Labour M.P.s and ex-M.P.s: Sir Robert Young (1872–1957), Labour M.P. for Newton 1918–31, 1935–51; Joe Compton, q.v.; Alfred Short, q.v.; Major James Milner, later 1st Baron (1889–1967), Labour M.P. for Leeds South-East 1929–51; J. W. Bowen, later Sir William (1876–1965), General Secretary of the Union of Post Office Workers, Labour M.P. 1929–31; Rev. H. Dunnico, q.v.; Col. L'Estrange Malone, q.v.; J. H. Hayes, q.v.; F. J. Bellenger, q.v.; W. W. Henderson, q.v.; F. O. Roberts, q.v.; A. Greenwood, q.v.; William Dobbie (1878–1950), Labour M.P. for Rotherham 1933–50, former President of the National Union of Railwaymen; Ben Tillett (1860–1943), Labour M.P. 1917–24, 1929–31, dockers' leader; George Hicks, q.v. Also: Col. H. W. Burton (1876–1947), Conservative M.P. for Sudbury 1924–45; G. H. H. Kinnoull, 14th Earl (1902–37).

my drawer. Someone sent it to me a few days after the election.'

Thursday 7th April
Cartland[1] spoke to me at some length in the library, continuing till midnight after the House had risen. He said that they had now a Führer in the Conservative Party. The P.M. was getting more and more dictatorial. It was astonishing how the bulk of the Party followed him blindly, though there had been great perturbations both at the time of Eden's resignation and when Hitler took Vienna. The inner ring in the Cabinet consisted of the P.M.,[2] Simon, Hoare, Swinton,[3] and Kingsley Wood.[4] He supposed that Halifax, now that he was Foreign Secretary, was in the ring part of the time. Eden had been got rid of as the result of activities pursued over many months. Swinton, possibly under the influence of drink, at a male dinner party soon after Whitsuntide, had declared that our foreign policy must be entirely remodelled, that Vansittart must go and that a group of four, namely the P.M., Simon, Hoare and himself were going to run foreign policy for the future. Someone had asked, 'What about Eden?' Swinton had replied, after some abuse of his colleague, 'He will either have to do what we tell him or go.' A member of the party had made a note of all this and taken it round to Van, who had taken it to Eden, who had taken it to the P.M., and demanded explanations. Van, to some extent, and Eden still more so, were greatly upset. The P.M. had merely replied, 'How foolish of Philip Swinton to think that he would be put on any committee dealing with foreign policy.'

There had been several occasions on which Eden might have resigned,[5] e.g. on the Chamberlain–Mussolini correspondence, or on

1 Ronald Cartland (1907–40). Conservative M.P. for King's Norton 1935–40. Progressive Tory. Killed in action. Brother of Barbara Cartland, the novelist.
2 Neville Chamberlain (1869–1940). Prime Minister 1937–40. See Appendix.
3 Sir Philip Cunliffe-Lister, 1st Viscount Swinton, later 1st Earl (1884–1972). Secretary of State for Air 1935–8. Conservative M.P. 1918–35. Junior minister 1920–22. President of the Board of Trade 1922–4, 1924–9, 1931; Colonial Secretary 1931–5. Minister Resident, West Africa 1942–4; Minister of Civil Aviation 1944–5. Chancellor of the Duchy of Lancaster and Minister of Materials 1951–2; Secretary of State for Commonwealth Relations 1952–5.
4 Sir Kingsley Wood (1881–1943). Minister of Health 1935–8. Conservative M.P. for Woolwich West 1918–43. Postmaster-General 1931–5. Secretary of State for Air 1938–40; Privy Seal 1940; Chancellor of the Exchequer 1940–43.
5 Eden had resigned as Foreign Secretary on 20th February 1938, after being humiliated by Chamberlain in the presence of Count Grandi, the Italian Ambassador. The immediate issue was the Prime Minister's desire for an understanding with Italy; the background was Eden's exasperation at repeated interventions by Chamberlain in foreign policy, especially over Roosevelt's proposal for an international conference, which Chamberlain rejected without consulting the Foreign Secretary. Eden's successor at the Foreign Office was Lord Halifax, q.v.

the Halifax visit to Berlin. But in each case it would have seemed a question of personal pique. I said that the right time for him to have resigned was on Abyssinia. Cartland agreed but said that it was always very difficult to judge the right time for resignation. When Eden did resign, the old gentlemen in the Government and the sly people in the Conservative Whips' Office put round the story (1) that it *was* personal pique, and (2) that poor Anthony was completely exhausted by strain in the Foreign Office and had lost his grip and judgment. The second explanation, in particular, had infuriated Eden. Now they were trying to treat him like the Duke of Windsor and persuade the world, and particularly the Conservative Party, to forget all about it. But this would not be possible, because he had just come back from a holiday in France by all accounts very full of fight.

I asked who really influenced Chamberlain. Cartland said not much any of his colleagues in the Cabinet. But there was a queer figure, Sir Joseph Ball,[1] now in the Conservative Head Office, who had been in M.I.5 during the war, in whom the P.M. had great confidence.

Ribbentrop[2] had been lunching with the P.M. and Halifax the day before Hitler took Vienna. He had told them nothing about it. It was not clear whether he knew what was coming. In any case the P.M. had taken grave offence, regarding it as a slight upon his dignity that Ribbentrop had told him nothing.

The Conservative Party had had some very excited meetings in Committee Rooms upstairs during my absence. Nicolson had been forced to resign the vice-chairmanship of their Foreign Affairs Committee because he had taken a strong and persistent line against the P.M.'s policy. (From another quarter I heard that during one of these discussions Lady Astor had said to some colleague, 'You must be a bloody Jew to say a thing like that', to which Winston had replied, 'I have never before heard such an insult to a Member of Parliament as the words just used by that bitch.')

Friday 8th April

Lunched with Kingsley Martin at the Savile Club, of which he is now a member. I told him that I intended for some time to listen rather than to speak, in view of all that had happened during my absence. He said that Chamberlain had at last got a coherent foreign policy,

---

1 Major Sir Joseph Ball (1885–1961). Director of the Conservative Research Department 1930–39. Chamberlain used Ball as an intermediary in his attempts to win over Count Grandi, the Italian Ambassador.
2 Joachim von Ribbentrop (1893–1946). German Foreign Minister 1938–45. Ambassador in London 1936–8.

whether right or wrong. He took the view that this country was so weak in arms, and London so indefensible, and France so weak, that we could not afford to antagonise in any degree a German–Italian combination. (This explained why *The Times* and *Telegraph* had both refused, in consequence of official guidance, to print any accounts of atrocities in Austria since they did not wish to offend Hitler.) Chamberlain, therefore, was striving to detach Mussolini from Hitler, believing that Mussolini was really, though he did not admit it, very vexed at having Hitler on the Brenner. Chamberlain's policy included letting Spain go and recognising Italy in Abyssinia, although there was much very good evidence, some published in the *New Statesman* this week, that the Italian hold on Abyssinia was badly shaken.

One of the great difficulties was to get to know the technical facts. It was being said that Chamberlain had told the General Council of the T.U.C. that Germany was now stronger in the air than ourselves and the French combined. Martin was convinced that there was shocking inefficiency at our Air Ministry and that our production programme was very far from being fulfilled. On the other hand, rumours were going round that we had made new discoveries which would make London much more defensible.

Martin spoke at some length of the state of mind of politicians and public after Hitler's march on Vienna. The idea of a new coalition government was very much in the air. Churchill was to be Prime Minister and Eden Foreign Secretary. The Labour Party and Liberal Party would both be strongly represented in the Cabinet. It was said that Bevin would be willing, if offered the Ministry of Labour. It was calculated that there would be so large a breakaway from Chamberlain in the Tory Party that this breakaway plus Labour plus Liberal would command a majority in the House of Commons. It was said that five Cabinet Ministers – Hore-Belisha, W. S. Morrison,[1] Oliver Stanley, Ormsby-Gore and Elliott – were prepared to resign from the present Government and join such a new one. Martin had been very active in running as go-between at this time. He had seen Attlee, who, at the beginning, had been not unfavourable to the idea. Later, he had changed his mind. Greenwood had been much interested; Herbert Morrison even more so. Such a government would have sought allies everywhere and made a definite commitment to Czechoslovakia. It

---

1 W. S. ('Shakes') Morrison, later 1st Viscount Dunrossil (1893–1961). Minister of Agriculture and Fisheries 1936–9. Conservative M.P. for Cirencester and Tewkesbury 1929–59. Financial Secretary to the Treasury 1935–6. Chancellor of the Duchy of Lancaster and Minister of Food 1939–40; Postmaster-General 1940–42; Minister of Town and Country Planning 1942–5. Speaker of the House of Commons 1951–9.

would have actively explored the possibility of bringing the Russians right into a scheme of mutual guarantees. But the idea died away within a few days. By the following Monday there was nothing left of it.

Monday 11th April
Lunched with Citrine at Thames House ... He gave me some account of events since last December. He thought that there was still great confusion of mind both on the General Council and on the political side regarding the international situation. Our own people were passionately concerned about Spain, but the great mass of the public were not. This might be deplorable but it was true. He had had some rows with Attlee, who had sworn at him in front of several others – 'Does he often swear?' he asked: 'Not very efficiently,' I replied – because Citrine had pressed for information on Attlee's conversations with Chamberlain and Halifax ...

The G.C. had taken the view that any question of speeding up armaments, e.g. by demarcation changes – he thought that it was these rather than dilution that the Government wanted – was purely an industrial matter in which politicians should not interfere. The A.E.U. [Amalgamated Engineering Union] were always a difficult crowd, squabbling openly among themselves as well as squabbling with the other unions concerned. Personally, he did not see how you could draw a logical distinction between producing armaments at present and agreeing to a speed up of arms production. He said that immediately after Hitler took Austria there had been wild rumours. The House of Commons, he said, was always full of rumours. It was the most unreliable source of information in the country. He knew nothing of approaches, except by quite irresponsible people in our own Party, to trade union leaders with a view to the formation of any coalition government. In particular, he did not believe the story, which I quoted to him, of Bevin having been willing to become Minister of Labour in such a government. He said that Bevin's health was bad. He was retiring from various committees and should really take a good rest. He was more difficult than ever to do business with, being very cheerful one day and unaccountably morose and suspicious the next.

The same evening I talked to Attlee, who had had very bad accounts of aircraft production. He heard that aeroplanes had been exported to Finland complete with all the latest gadgets which we could not get ourselves. Cripps had arrived with a story that workmen at Bristol were being told to paint swastikas on newly completed fighting aeroplanes for export to Germany. I said that this seemed almost unbelievable. It should be carefully checked or we should make public

fools of ourselves. On the other hand, if it was true, we should raise
public hell about it.

I impressed on Attlee, and later in the same evening on Alexander,
both of whom were quite receptive, that this failure of the Air Ministry
and of private enterprise to give us aircraft was the biggest single issue
at the present moment, and that we should concentrate our minds on
this to the exclusion of less important matters.

The Spanish Republicans suffered serious reverses in the spring of 1938. A
Republican Aragonese offensive at the end of 1937 achieved an initial success,
but Franco's counter-attack regained all the lost territory, preparing the
way for a major Nationalist advance which cut the Republican zone in two,
pressing southward towards Valencia. By the end of April, the Nationalists
seemed close to victory.

Tuesday 12th April
Lunched at House of Commons with Attlee, Greenwood, Alexander,
Wedgwood Benn and Phil [Noel-Baker] to meet Julius Deutsch,[1] fresh
from Spain, and Gessner, acting as interpreter. A gloomy, desperate
business. Deutsch said he had been sent over to find out whether (1)
more arms could be got for the Spanish government, and (2) whether
anything could be done to raise the morale of the government forces.
As to arms, he said that there was a preponderance of planes on the
Rebel side of 12 to 1 and of artillery of 6 to 1. A number of Russian
planes had recently arrived via Bordeaux, but the Rebel spy service
was so good that whenever more arms came for the government an
even greater addition was soon made on the Rebel side. The morale
of the government troops had become very bad immediately after the
second battle of Teruel. Two Catalan Divisions had broken up and
run away. There were now a number of Castilian troops on the Catalan
front and these were better soldiers. None the less, there had been
great discouragement, although he alleged that the morale of the
civilian population was still high. He suggested that morale might be
maintained if further 'pronouncements' were made, or resolutions
passed, by the I.F.T.U. [International Federation of Trade Unions]
and L.S.I. [Labour and Socialist International]! (What pathetic drivel
and self-delusion this is. It nearly makes me sick.) He also thought

1 Julius Deutsch (1884–1968). Austrian politician. Led the Social Democrat militia
  in the fighting of February 1934. Fled to Czechoslovakia in the same year, and later
  became a Republican general in the Spanish Civil War. After the Second World
  War he returned to Austrian politics as Secretary of the Socialist Party.

that we might have an important debate on Spain in the House of Commons. I said that I understood there had been thirteen such debates in the past nine weeks. If all they wanted were friendly quotations from Labour leaders' speeches they had more than enough material already. Moreover, there had been an enormous Hyde Park demonstration last Sunday, at which a long resolution (he said they liked resolutions!) had been carried.

Passing now quite clearly beyond his official mission, Deutsch said that he did not see how, unless very large supplies of arms were sent to the government, they could continue to hold out for more than a few weeks in Catalonia, or for more than a month or two in the rest of Spain. The question, therefore, arose whether we should not make the French admit that they could not send great supplies of arms, and that we could not either, and that, this being so, it would be better for the Spanish government to seek mediation to negotiate terms of peace. I was shocked at the reluctance of several of those present to pursue this line. Phil has transferred all his eager enthusiasm and credulous optimism from Geneva to the Spanish front. 'Barcelona may turn out to be a second Madrid'; 'It will be very difficult for Franco to keep up the pressure for very long'; 'The government have now to defend a shorter line so they need less arms'; 'What terms could they hope to get if they did negotiate now?' Attlee made typical motions of going into his shell and said that 'We could not think of anything of this kind unless it was authorised by the Spanish government'. Alexander and I, on the other hand, thought the possibility should be pursued (in any case it will be, because Deutsch saw Citrine this morning and told him what he now tells us, and Citrine is going to Paris on Thursday for a joint meeting of L.S.I. and I.F.T.U.).

Deutsch said that Negrín[1] believed that if the Spanish government resisted a bit longer there would be a general war in Europe which would 'relieve the pressure by Hitler and Mussolini on Spain'!!!

I left this party before it broke up, to see Vansittart. He is still in the same room at the Foreign Office, but no longer has a male secretary. He was very doubtful whether to accept his present position,[2] which is largely humbug. Clearly he has no great influence on policy now and often only hears of decisions already made. Sometimes, he said, he was able to intervene before decisions were taken. Obviously a most unsatisfactory status, both for himself and for Cadogan.

He was quite catty about Eden, who, he said, had been trying to edge him out for a long time. Eden had pressed him very strongly to take the Paris Embassy but he had firmly refused. Eden had been

1 Juan Negrín Lopez, q.v., the Spanish Prime Minister.
2 i.e. as Chief Diplomatic Adviser.

jealous of him, thinking that he had too much of the limelight. I said, 'Surely you had very little compared with Eden himself.' Eden had brought back Cadogan from China with the object of making him Under-Secretary. He wanted a tame and colourless civil servant with less character, less knowledge and less persistence in arguing with politicians when he thought they were wrong. At the end, Eden had resigned on what he thought a most inadequate pretext, and had never discussed it with him or given him any warning of his intention. One night when Van was down at Denham, Eden had rung him up on the telephone and said, 'I've finished.' Van said that he thought of Eden as a man with whom he had often had to go out tiger shooting and who, at the end, had shot him in the back. The French had never had much confidence in Eden. They thought him young, inexperienced and ambitious. They had never thought that their case was properly presented by him. Van had been reluctant to go altogether, because it would have been regarded as a triumph by the Germans and a setback by all our friends in Europe and by his personal friends in particular, such as Prince Paul of Yugoslavia.[1] The Cliveden set[2] had, of course, worked very hard to get him out. They had influenced Chamberlain early and in the end even old Stanley Baldwin had thought Van ought to go because he was 'inclined to be too pessimistic.' Van observed that Cadogan went to Cliveden and that even Eden had once been there for a weekend.

Van disagreed with Eden on the merits of the Anglo–Italian negotiations. He had long thought, and his view was strengthened by events in Austria, that it was possible to detach Mussolini from Hitler. In Austria Mussolini had certainly been duped, and though he did not say so in public, was very angry. In Spain it was likely that he would be duped again. It was Germany and not Italy who would secure lasting and material advantages from intervention on behalf of Franco. The Spaniards despised the Italians but respected the Germans. I said that, even though Mussolini might be vexed with Hitler, I thought that he would calculate that he would gain more by hanging on to Hitler than by leaving him. Van admitted that this might be so, if Mussolini thought that Germany was the predominant power in Europe and the only one who was ready to fight.

1 Prince Paul of Yugoslavia (1893–1976). Regent (1934–41) for his cousin's young son, King Peter II. Married to Princess Olga of Greece. The successful coup against him in 1941 was backed, and partly organised, by the British Special Operations Executive, for which Dalton was then the responsible Minister.
2 'The Cliveden Set' was a term coined by Claud Cockburn, q.v., in his scandal-sheet the *Week*, to describe the pro-appeasement house parties of the Astors, which supposedly determined British foreign policy.

I said that I was deeply disturbed by the failure of the British air rearmament programme. He did not deny that it was most unsatisfactory. 'After all,' he said, 'we are not a nation of organisers. It always takes us a long time to get things in order.' I also questioned him on the French Air Force and asked him whether he was sure that the adverse reports which he got were objective and not from tainted reactionary sources. He said that he was quite satisfied that things were very bad, but he hoped they might soon improve. The French army remained the best army in the world, but with the passage of time it could not maintain this superiority over the Germans. Moreover, if the Germans penetrated further and further east and acquired wheat, oil, etc. the value of our navy as a blockading force would disappear.

I questioned him closely about Russia. It is clear, I think, that they really do not know much. He had little to add to what I had heard from him before. But he was very anxious that we should not cold-shoulder the Russians, nor drive them into isolation. He was sure that it was knowledge of Russian weakness and disorganisation that had loosed the present war in the Far East. If Russia had been stronger, Japan would not have dared.

He quoted an American journalist who said, after the capture of Austria, 'Next time I hear anybody say, "It is the method I object to", I shall scream.' Also Corbin, who had said, 'What I find requires most self-control is to hear people, a week or two after some German coup, saying encouragingly, "I think the international situation is a bit easier now, don't you?".' The Germans went on and on and would be content with nothing less than the domination, first of Europe, and then of the world. The reduction of all the rest of Europe to vassal states, and the destruction of all liberty and democracy as we know it. It was no satisfaction to Van to be able so often to point out that the correctness of his view was being justified time after time. The Germans would not discuss anything with you on terms of equality if they thought that soon they would be stronger than you. I said that I recalled many instances when, the British government attempting to speak with them, they simply walked away.

Sunday 5th June
Douglas[1] and Peggy Jay[2] at West Leaze, she very radiant at being a London County Councillor, he rather dissatisfied over recent *Daily*

1 Douglas Jay (b. 1907). City Editor of the *Daily Herald* 1937–41. Author of *The Socialist Case* (1937), the first systematic attempt to combine socialist and Keynesian doctrine. See Appendix.
2 Peggy Jay, née Garnett.

Herald experiences. He says that Southwood[1] has been sent for several times by Halifax and flattering appeals made to him as a great press magnate. There has been some reflection of this in pressure to prevent too critical a line on foreign policy.

'No gloom' has become an Odhams slogan. Therefore you may not talk of a slump or emphasise statistics indicating that it has already begun. One weekend when Douglas was away 'they' tried to get his sub-editor to put in a quantity of statistics of recent high profits which were supposed to show continued prosperity. His sub stood firm.

'Budget surplus'. Douglas had great difficulty in preventing this from being boosted. He had to say that he knew the Party in the House would, quite rightly, maintain that the Budget was in fact badly un-balanced and showed a large deficit.

Dead millionaires' fortunes. He put in, a few weeks ago, a note on some recent instances, regretting that the State had not taken more. This called forth a protest from Mr Cook, the business manager of Odhams, who wrote a minute to Lord Southwood saying that this para was bad for advertising, and was also unfair, since if men could not leave money to their families they would not make it. This minute reached Jay via Francis Williams.[2] He wrote, 'Surely Mr Cook does not suggest that my statement is contrary to Labour Party policy.'

A note on working-class savings also caused trouble. Jay gave some figures and argued that, though large in the total, such savings were small per head, and were much less than was often alleged, since e.g. the rich held shares in Building Societies, etc. This produced another memo from the egregious Mr Cook. 'Very bad for advertising'. Here, he said, [we had] been telling advertisers that our readers had plenty of money to spend, and this note suggests that they have not. 'Nothing should be printed in a paper unless it either helps advertising or interests the readers. This does neither.'

Row with Lord Wardington (Beaumont Pease).[3] Jay had com-mented on his Chairman's speech in which he said that municipal expenditure should be restricted. Jay had said that such expenditure was chiefly for slum clearance and housing, and had noted that the recent L.C.C. loan was not taken up, perhaps through political prejudice. He added that Lord Wardington had not criticised gamb-

---

1 1st Viscount Southwood. J. S. Elias, q.v., proprietor of the *Daily Herald*. South-wood had formerly been a subscriber to Conservative Party funds.
2 Francis Williams, later Baron Francis-Williams (1903–70). Editor of the *Daily Herald* 1936–40. Controller of News and Censorship at the Ministry of Information 1941–5. Adviser on Public Relations to the Prime Minister 1945–7.
3 J. W. Beaumont Pease, 1st Baron Wardington (1869–1950). Chairman of Lloyds Bank 1922–45; Bank of London and South Africa 1922–48.

ling in gold shares which had been taking place on a large scale just before Lord W. had addressed his shareholders. Lord W. had then asked to see Jay, who suggested that if His Lordship would send the *Daily Herald* something in writing it should be published in the City column. Lord W. refused and pressed for an interview. This was acid and disagreeable. Lord W. complained of unfair comment. He had not made any political statement. He was not against housing and slum clearance. He had always believed in good relations with the press. That was why his Bank advertised in the press, not because it paid them. The interview, after some further argument, ended badly.

Then Lord Wardington got on to Southwood. It was indicated that Odhams banks with him. Then memos began to circulate. It was emphasised that Lord W. advertised a good deal in the *People* and *John Bull*, though not much in the *Daily Herald*. This row was still running. Jay was not disposed to make any recantation.

He was afraid that one day a resolution might be passed by the directors saying that there must be 'No more politics in the City column.' Francis Williams has a very heavy time, fighting many battles. Jay doubts whether any of them on the staff are really secure. I told him not to do anything drastic or melodramatic without consulting me again. He has never met Citrine. To approach him direct might seem to be going behind the back of Williams. I say that if things become much more difficult I will arrange for him to meet Citrine none the less.

Wednesday 15th June

Nield has just finished a very good piece of work on air 'defences'. Attlee, Greenwood and I only have copies. Nield I hope talks less about leading people to others than he does to me. Me he tells that he has been pressing Morrison to concentrate much more on the House and to earn the right to the leadership. He thinks that pressure by him and others is having effect. (I agree. Morrison has been much more regular at Parliamentary Executive lately. I was also much interested a few days ago when, at Parliamentary Executive, the question of votes on the defence services was raised, and Morrison, Shinwell and Johnston, all in the beaten minority last year, said that they thought that we could not chop and change from year to year and, having decided not to vote against last year, could not vote against next month. If we have broken the back of this folly I am well pleased. It will save me much time not to have to canvass and mobilise my troops and make a strong speech in the Party Meeting, antagonising some poor softies.)

Nield also told me that little Laski had been suggesting to Morrison that Attlee's leadership was intolerable, equally Greenwood's deputy leadership. His suggestion was that Morrison should be Leader and Cripps Deputy. Cripps apparently was present when this suggestion was made.

I said that it was very difficult for anybody outside the cage of the Parliamentary Labour Party to measure up the inclinations of the inmates. But I was sure that for this particular ticket the votes were not there. Nor would they be, I thought, after the next election.

Thursday 7th July

Noel-Buxton came to see me at the House this afternoon ... [He] wanted the Labour Party to issue a declaration urging the Czech government to make large and speedy concessions and to hint that, if they delayed much longer or offered too little, they would lose the support of British public opinion. He wishes this particularly in order to bring pressure on Beneš.[1] Hodza he thought was much more reasonable but not allowed a free hand by 'Czech Chauvinists'.

I said that we had already issued a declaration with a somewhat different emphasis and that I could hold out no hope that the Party would act as he wished ...

On parting Buxton said, 'I hope you do not regard me as utterly pro-German or being a Nazi agent.' I said, 'I know you have always been more pro-German than most of the Party and I think that you are less shocked than most of us are by the internal regime in Germany.' He replied, 'I am very shocked by much that is going on and I am doing my best to help the refugees.'

I heard later that he had been to see Attlee who had snubbed him rather vigorously.

In mid-August, the threat of a German invasion of Czechoslovakia led the British government to put increasing pressure on President Beneš to make concessions over the Sudetenland. On 4th September Beneš conceded almost everything the Sudeten Germans wanted. Nevertheless, the fear of an imminent invasion remained. All awaited with trepidation Hitler's speech planned for the Nazi rally at Nuremberg on 12th September.

---

1 Edouard Beneš (1884–1948). President of Czechoslovakia 1935–8, 1945–8. Foreign Minister 1918–35. Prime Minister 1921–2. President of the Czech government-in-exile 1938–45.

Monday 5th September

Lunched with Van alone. He was more disturbed than I had often seen him. He said that 'perhaps because of advancing years' he had been sleeping badly lately, last night only four hours. He did not want to become dependent on drugs for his sleep.

He thinks that the big pronouncement at Nuremberg will not come before next Monday, 12th September, when Hitler makes his final oration. Beneš is much to blame for not having produced already for publication a clear statement of what he is prepared to do for the minorities. If he did this and it was as reasonable a plan as has been suggested, then we could all say, 'Now Czechoslovakia has made a very fair proposal and anyone who refuses to discuss things on this basis is in the wrong.' Beneš, however, has frequently gone back in one interview on what he offered in the last and has refused to make things clear. Van has been pressing Jan Masaryk[1] constantly in the sense suggested.

There is certainly a strong war party in Berlin. They simply do not believe that, if they attacked the Czechs, we or the French or the Russians would do anything effective. They are playing with the idea of a sudden and overwhelming attack upon Czechoslovakia and then the offer from conquered Prague of a wonderful Peace Plan, including, perhaps, air pact and limitation, the abolition of the bombing of civilians (look at Spain!) and the voluntary evacuation of Prague and other non-German conquered areas. They count on a delay due to France having to obtain from the League of Nations an assurance that she would not be an aggressor in going to the help of the Czechs, also on our doing nothing until France did something. These are the calculations of the war party, of which, in fact, Hitler is the head. There is also a more moderate party, but weak. If the above plans succeeded, the moderate party, already discredited by past events, would simply disappear. So would all remnants of resistance to Germany in Middle and South-East Europe. A great number of Germans are thoroughly disconcerted and frightened at the idea of war, but, if the Blitzkrieg comes off, they will say, 'Hitler was right again.'

The Siegfried Line is now very strong. It is doubtful whether the French, even though their army is still the best in Europe, could force it without enormous losses. If, on the other hand, they fly over, the German Air Force is much more powerful than theirs and would retaliate. The Russians have purged their military forces so thoroughly

1 Jan Masaryk (1886–1948). Czech Minister in London 1925–38. Foreign Minister 1945–8. Foreign Minister in the government-in-exile 1940–45; Deputy Prime Minister 1941–5.

that they are undoubtedly much weakened at the moment. They have also lent a good deal of material to Spain and China. Some think that they might send 100 aeroplanes to Czechoslovakia, but this would be a very small factor. It is possible that the Romanians would raise no objection to Russian aircraft and, more doubtfully, Russian ground troops, crossing through their country. The present rulers of Romania, including the King, now realise the danger which they would be in if Czechoslovakia fell. The Yugoslavs are much less satisfactory. Stoyadinovitch[1] would gladly wash his hands of the Czechs. Until recently the Polish attitude was most unsatisfactory. It seemed that they were merely anxious to share the spoils of Czechoslovakia with Germany. Lately there has been a slight improvement here. Goering,[2] as minister in charge of the Four-Year Plan, realises better than most the damage which a British blockade would do to Germany. But he is not for this reason to be counted in the peace party. All really depends on Hitler, whom it is very difficult to reach. In so far as he is reached by Ribbentrop he is misled, for Ribbentrop saw too much of Londonderry and Mayfair and too little of England.

Henderson is not the man to put over on the Germans an effective threat that we should come in early and heavily. He has too long talked to them in tones of sympathy with their projects. His inclination is to be defeatist and pro-Nazi. It was a disastrous innovation that he should have been present at the Cabinet the other day. Any request, e.g. from the T.U.C., to the Government for a statement of their policy would probably draw only very cautious formulas, adding nothing to what has been published.

The U.S.A. is much more full than in 1914 of anti-German feeling. Dictatorships are amazingly unpopular in the U.S. at present.

Italy is completely unpredictable. The French are inclined to think that Mussolini would join the Germans if war came in Central Europe, but the Germans are very far from sure of this and are probably making their plans on the assumption that he will remain neutral.

Cadogan has been away on leave during the past month. Among those much to blame is Tyrrell who, in spite of his great knowledge, long experience and known views, has said nothing publicly either in the House of Lords debates or, e.g. in a letter to *The Times*, to stem the flood of blind pro-Nazi sympathies.

Hitler's speech on 12th September was aggressive – but vague. Next day,

1 Milan Stojadinović (1888–1961). Yugoslav Prime Minister 1935–9. Serbian Radical.
2 Herman Goering (1893–1946). German Air Minister and Commander-in-Chief of the Air Force 1933–45.

the French Cabinet decided not to mobilise, and Daladier asked Chamberlain to seek a settlement by conference. Meanwhile Chamberlain, on his own initiative, had sent a telegram to Hitler declaring his readiness to fly immediately to Germany. Hitler, delighted by the success of his intimidation, responded by inviting Chamberlain to meet him at Berchtesgaden.

On 15th September the British Prime Minister saw the Führer. Three days later Daladier and Bonnet came to London, and Chamberlain persuaded them to agree to the destruction of Czechoslovakia – not so much giving in to Hitler's demands as anticipating them. Meanwhile Labour's attitude had been hardening. The National Council of Labour (which included representatives of the General Council, T.U.C. and Shadow Cabinet) issued a manifesto on 7th September which declared: 'The British Government must leave no doubt in the mind of the German Government that they will unite with the French and Soviet Governments to resist any attack upon Czechoslovakia.' On 17th September, while the Cabinet was still discussing Chamberlain's plan for the immediate transfer to Germany of all districts with more than 50 per cent of Germans in the population, the National Council of Labour sent a delegation to the Prime Minister, consisting of Citrine, Morrison and Dalton, to present the views of the British Labour Movement. Before this meeting, Dalton received a private briefing from the Government's Chief Diplomatic Adviser, Sir Robert Vansittart, who was so concerned by the drift of events that he was prepared to pass on secrets to the political opponents of the Government he nominally served.

Saturday 17th September

Van came to see me at my flat at 9.30. I told him we were going to see the P.M. He said he did not know how much the P.M. would tell us, but he hoped he would speak frankly. Van said that the French were weak, especially Bonnet,[1] but this must on no account be mentioned to the P.M. as it would suggest that we had knowledge of what was in F.O. telegrams, and this might rebound against him. It was clear to me that he is having a terrible tussle with ministers and getting very little of his own way. His fixed view is, as it has been for years, that this move against Czechoslovakia is only the beginning of a process. Hitler is determined to destroy Czechoslovakia as a stepping stone to further conquests. In itself, the Sudeten German question has only a demagogic value. The first diplomatic trench, said Van, which we should still hold if possible, is along the present frontiers of Czechoslovakia.

1 Georges Bonnet (1889–1973). French Foreign Minister 1938–9. Radical Socialist. Appeaser. Many ministerial posts 1926–38. Supported Vichy during the war. Re-elected a deputy 1956–8.

Within these frontiers a negotiated settlement on the lines of the Fourth Plan might still be possible if a sufficiently strong front were presented to Hitler. But it looks as though this line is already lost, and he is now trying to think out a second trench line. This might include cession, as preferable to a plebiscite, of some Sudeten areas and then a direct guarantee of the new Czech frontiers in which this country would join with France and Russia. Van attached enormous importance to Russia being kept in, but it was clear that he feared our Government would take a different line. 'After all,' he said, 'Russia is at least half a European power with enormous reserves of force, and it is madness to try to push her out of Europe in order to please Germany. From the most material point of view, if war should come who but a lunatic could wish the whole power of the German Air Force to strike westwards instead of being divided between East and West.' I infer that this is a point on which he is making a stiff but unhopeful fight. I said that it was amazing how some people, otherwise intelligent, had a mad fixation about Russia and seemed almost to prefer that this country should be defeated in war without Russian aid rather than win with it. He did not disagree, and added that no sane person could suppose that Russia was any threat to this country. The Anti-Comintern stuff of Hitler and Co. had, however, had surprising success in Mayfair, though he now heard that Mount Temple,[1] for example, was becoming frightened and changing his line.

I said I hoped the Government was doing all it could to get the U.S.A. to interest itself publicly in the Czechoslovakia question, e.g. to suggest a conference at which there might be a U.S. observer. Van said that he had strongly urged, some time ago, representations by us to Washington in this sense, but I gathered that nothing effective had been done. I said that I hoped there was no danger of a Four Power Conference – Germans, Italians, French and ourselves – leaving out Russians and Poles. It has been freely rumoured that a Four Power Pact is one of Chamberlain's objectives. Van shrugged his shoulders, was unable to say much, but evidently shared my apprehensions. He added that one danger of any big power conference was that economic concessions might be made to Germany which would strengthen her without changing her intentions. As to Italy, he pointed out that there might be certain advantages to Germany in Italian benevolent neu-

---

1 W. W. Ashley, 1st Baron Mount Temple (1867–1939). Conservative M.P. 1906–32. Minister of Transport 1924–9. Chairman of the Anti-Socialist Union. He resigned as President of the Anglo-German Fellowship following reports of the Jewish persecutions of November 1938. (See R. Griffiths, *Fellow Travellers of the Right*, Constable, London, 1980, pp. 338–9.)

trality during the first stages of war, as distinct from direct intervention. Such neutrality would tend to nullify a British blockade and we should have the same sort of difficulty with Italy as we had with the U.S.A. in 1914–16. But Mussolini was now 'very axis'. He must earn his keep as Hitler's hired servant. Even on the most hopeful assumptions the Poles might remain neutral for months before coming in on our side. I asked him about the Soviet attitude. He said that all he could say was that their declarations were clear, repeated and recent, but general. They were not bound to move unless France moved; they said that if France moved they would move; but it might be that their movement would be limited to air resistance and that not on a very great scale.

Waiting all day, in touch with Citrine and Morrison by telephone, for time to be fixed for interview with P.M. Long Cabinet meetings. I urge Citrine to use emphatic, though not necessarily discourteous, language to Horace Wilson demanding that our interview shall be today, no matter how late, and before anyone else other than the P.M.'s Cabinet colleagues.

At 6 message that our interview is fixed for 6.30. By taxi to Transport House and a quarter of an hour's conference with Cripps, Morrison, Dallas and Middleton. Drive in Citrine's car – a better looking vehicle than Herbert's and hence more dignified – to No. 10. Moderate crowd at bottom of Downing Street. Swarm of press men and photographers in Downing Street itself. Inside, wait five minutes, then spend an hour and a half in Cabinet room, we three sitting facing P.M. across the table, he having Halifax on his right and Horace Wilson on his left. Only we six.

After the meeting,[1] Dalton wrote: 'The best that can be said of the P.M. is that, within the limits of his ignorance, he is rational, but I am appalled how narrow these limits are, and it is clear that Hitler produced an enormous impression upon him, partly by hustling intimidation and partly by a few compliments and words of courtesy. If Hitler had been a British nobleman and Chamberlain a British working man with an inferiority complex, the thing could not have been done better.'[2]

---

1 Described fully in FY, pp. 176–82.
2 Diary, 17th September 1938; see also FY, p. 183.

Sunday 18th September
At Attlee's request, I made a pilgrimage to his little Victorian villa
at Stanmore, which I have never been inside before, to meet Nečas,[1]
Czech Socialist Minister of Social Welfare who is paying a flying visit
to London, though he is seeing no ministers, and Kosina[2] who came
to interpret. I had met Nečas in Prague some years ago. He is a tall
man, finely built, and full of courage, very Slav looking, with a small
beard. Alexander joined us for part of the talk before lunch, but did
not stay long. Nečas began by laying out the familiar Czech case with
aid of maps and statistics. We know all this by heart, but it would
have been unkind to cut it short. He said, 'We would sooner die and
be drowned in our own blood than become Hitler's slaves. Every man
in our country knows what is coming, every woman, even every child.
We shall all be massacred, but we shall fight to the last, rather than
give in.' Kosina said, 'People in this country don't understand Hitler
is like a shark. When he tastes blood he wants more. The more he eats
the greater his appetite becomes.' The circle of mountains round
Bohemia has stood as the frontier for nearly 1,000 years. Once that
frontier is given up, all the defensive strength of Czechoslovakia dis-
appears and the economic losses would also be fatal to the future life
of the State.

Monday 19th September
9.45. Twenty minutes with Van at his house. He had been up till the
small hours of the morning in connection with the Anglo-French Plan.
He said, 'Since we last met I have been upbraided for holding views
which are not those of the Government.' He said that his position had
become very difficult and that he could not go on indefinitely. But he
thought it was his duty to hold on for a time. If he resigned now it
might seem that he was moved by personal resentment or ambition,
which was not the case; his elimination from the scene would also give
great delight to the Germans and 'Nevile Henderson would go through
the roof with joy'. But there was need for even greater care in the
arrangement of meetings between him and me. (For some time past
we had agreed that we could not meet at the Foreign Office.) He did
not think that he was suspected by ministers of contact with the Labour
Party, but they knew that he and Winston were old friends and that he
sometimes saw some of the more active critics in the Conservative
Party. I asked him to have a word with me before finally deciding to

1 Jaromír Nečas (1885–1945). Czech Minister for Social Welfare 1935–8. Socialist.
  Member of the governing body of the International Labour Office. Fled to Britain
  1940, and served in the Czech government-in-exile.
2 J. K. Kosina. Czech diplomat.

clear out. I said that I thought I might have some useful things to say on some aspects of such a decision. I asked whether he thought that the time had come for us privately to urge the Czechs to give way rather than make a hopeless and heroic fight against overwhelming odds if they were to be deserted by all the Great Powers. He said this would be going too fast as there were important factors in the case which he could not tell me now without grave breach of secrecy, but which perhaps a little later he could explain. For the moment, he counselled great reserve both in public utterances and in anything said privately by us to the Czechs ...

Alexander has it on good authority that Kennedy,[1] the American Ambassador, is profoundly shocked at the failure of our Government to consult the Czechs before producing a plan to dismember their country. He felt so strongly on this point that he went down to Downing Street and protested against this procedure.

Tuesday 20th September
Our N.C.L. [National Council of Labour] declaration reads well in the press this morning. It is not too long, the epithets are right, and it avoids more than one tempting pitfall. Attlee tells me that Winston rang him up this morning and said, 'Your declaration does honour to the British nation.' Attlee apparently merely replied, 'I am glad you think so.' I hear later, via Balogh[2] and Nield, that Winston intended this to be an overture for some form of concerted action and that he was huffed that Attlee did not make a warmer response. My view is that openly concerted action between our Party and other critics of the Government is less useful at this stage than outwardly separate action. We have been visibly and constantly active for days. Others have done practically nothing, so far at least as outward signs go. It would not strengthen any appeal of ours if it were associated with Winston or Eden or the Liberals, even if they would join, and I doubt whether it would strengthen any appeal of theirs for us to be associated with it. But it is possible to be too cautious, as well as too rash, towards any suggestion for conversations. Alexander, more than any of us, has been itching for more contacts with other critics of the

1 Joseph Kennedy (1888–1969). U.S. Ambassador in London 1937–41. Anglophobe. Cadogan wrote in his diary for 22nd and 23rd September: ' ... I have to hold Corbin and Joe Kennedy at arm's length. The latter makes little secret of what he thinks of us!' (D. Dilks, ed., *The Diaries of Sir Alexander Cadogan 1938–1945*, Cassell, London, 1971, pp. 102–3).
2 Thomas Balogh, later Baron (1905–84). Hungarian-born economist. National Institute of Economic Research 1938–42. Oxford University Institute of Statistics 1940–55. Fellow of Balliol College, Oxford 1945–73. Economic Adviser to the Cabinet 1964–7. Consultant to the Prime Minister 1968. Junior minister 1974–5.

Government, but, when he put his point of view to me, I warned him of some of the difficulties, particularly of the possibilities that we might upset a large number of our own Party and destroy our credit in our own home market. I heard last night that Winston had said privately, 'The Government had to choose between war and shame. They have chosen shame and they will get war.' I hear today that he is flying to Paris to try and stiffen the French government. This is an attempt which he can make but we can't.

When Chamberlain returned to Germany on 22nd September for a second meeting with Hitler at Godesberg, Hitler raised the stakes: he now demanded the immediate occupation of the German-speaking areas. Late in the evening of 23rd September, Hitler presented an ultimatum – stipulating deadlines for the proposed occupations.

Friday 23rd September
At 9.30 p.m. Liddell Hart rings up about A.A. guns. The word 'go' has not yet been given. It will take 48 hours to get everything ready. In Berlin already the guns are out and the crews manning them. Visible on high buildings. Pile[1] is desperately anxious to get on. He is being stopped by an intermediate sandbag at the War Office. Liddell Hart intends to work on Geoffrey Dawson[2] to speak to Halifax tonight.

After some consultations, I decide that it is best for me to work on Morrison, and ring him up. He is apparently away in Cornwall! Meetings! I write a letter in case he is back late, emphasising that this 'specially concerns your London' and that it is his job to hustle the War Office.

Bob [Fraser] reports on telephone that Halifax told Greenwood – though this is at third or fourth hand – that he thought the odds today were 51 to 49 against peace. De la Warr[3] was told to confer with

1 Major-General Pile, later Sir Frederick, 2nd Bart (1884–1976). 1st Anti-Aircraft Division, Territorial Army 1937–9. General Officer Commanding in Chief, Anti-Aircraft Command 1939–45. Director-General of the Ministry of Works 1945.
2 Geoffrey Dawson (1874–1944). Editor of *The Times* 1923–41. Although Dawson was a committed appeaser (and supposed member of the 'Cliveden Set'), on 26th September *The Times* supported a strong stand against Hitler's latest demands.
3 H. E. D. B. Sackville, 9th Earl de la Warr (1900–76). Lord Privy Seal 1937–31st October 1938. President of the Board of Education 1938–40. Junior minister 1929–31. Supported MacDonald in 1931, and served in the National Government, again in junior posts, 1931–7. First Commissioner of Works 1940. Postmaster-General 1951–5.

Litvinov at Geneva. (This is the first direct Anglo-Soviet diplomatic contact since 7th September!!) Press says that parts of conversation were confidential, but general impression favourable. Bob says they say that last night Hitler threw himself about like a lunatic, and, at 11.15 p.m., Prague [ordered] full Czech mobilisation.

Saturday 24th September

See Salmon,[1] Gater's[2] deputy, at County Hall and put Liddell Hart's point about A.A. guns. Morrison is in Cornwall but coming back, we hope, today. Both Gater and Attlee have so advised him by telephone. Salmon, very quick and efficient, says that Government departments have been desperately slow all round. L.C.C. officials have gone to extreme limit of pressure upon them to quicken up. Gater, meeting Ruth and me on Westminster Bridge, says that at last we have an evacuation plan, at any rate for school children, which has been communicated today to every head teacher. Salmon says, 'A week ago we were all keyed up to face a war; then we felt the fear had gone; now we have to key ourselves up all over again. It is not easy, particularly for those who in the last war were in the front line trenches and who had been counting on a base job this time, and now we find that here in London we shall be in the front line.' This man and Gater give one a sense of assurance and calm competence.

......

Van to see me at flat at 12.30. Already he has been rung up by several M.P.s who are furious at Chamberlain's reported statement at Godesberg that 'It is up to them now', i.e. to the Czechs. I say that Ruth, much more intelligent than the average and much braver, said to me last night, 'Are we really to decide between peace and war on a mere question of procedure?' Van said that this morning several junior officials at the Foreign Office had put the same point to him. Perhaps Hitler is counting on this new proposal once more to weaken the will of France and England. Van has no confidence in the advisers of the P.M. on the Rhine. It is a disaster, he says, that Horace Wilson has 'usurped my functions', and that with him is Henderson. Van fears, though we must await the Prime Minister's return before we know, that Hitler has played his cards well. 'Unless you start from the assumption that you are dealing with a semi-lunatic with a streak of

1 E. C. H. Salmon, later Sir Eric (1896–1946). Deputy Clerk of the L.C.C. 1934–9; Clerk 1939–46.
2 Sir George Gater (1886–1963). Clerk of the London County Council 1933–9. Permanent Under-Secretary of State for Colonies 1939–47 (seconded to Home Secretary and Minister of Supply 1939–42).

low cunning, you get everything wrong.' He has been putting this point of view for years, and is now rebuked by ministers for being incurably anti-German. I tell him what P.M. told us, that Hitler said, 'All right, I am prepared to face it. If there must be a world war I would rather it came soon, for I am forty-nine now and I want to lead my people to victory.' Van said that this had not been on any of the Foreign Office papers, but was most significant. He also shared my view that Chamberlain's idea that 'there was another side' to Hitler, as illustrated by his remark that he would have liked to come to London rather than put an older man to so much inconvenience to come to Germany, was perilously gullible. This last proposal for a 'symbolic cession' nine miles deep all along the frontiers would, he hoped, be rejected by the Czechs, and he hoped that the British government would not press it upon them. I said that as I read the map, the Germans had already a symbolic cession of the Eger–Asch triangle. Behind this and elsewhere along the mountain tops ran the first Czech defensive line; within a nine-mile belt the second and third lines were also found; therefore a nine-mile-deep symbolic cession meant the abandonment both of strong defensive lines and, if enforced speedily, the surrender of large numbers of guns in fixed emplacements, etc. It was like pulling the shell from the crab's back. He said he thought that this was right. But Hitler, his cunning for the moment gaining an ascendancy over his lunacy and blood lust, might be calculating that by such a proposal he could weaken and disorganise British and French will to resist. I quoted my East Anglian batman in the war: 'This 'ere Kaiser, he's like a man who has gone up to the top of a hill and looks round the world and says "This is all mine".' Van says, 'Yes, like Greta Garbo who, offered £40,000 down and £40,000 on completion of a contract, said, "I want the bunch now".'

I said I had seen Phipps yesterday in Paris. I said his bedside manner was getting better and better. Van shrugged and said, 'He was a better man when he was in Berlin.' I referred to the Lindbergh report,[1] and Van said, 'He has flown the Atlantic but what does he know about military air forces? He just had a scamper round, and he is in with the Astor group.' ...

---

1 Col. Charles Lindbergh (1902–74). Special Adviser on technical matters to Chief of Staff, U.S. Air Force. First solo flyer across the Atlantic 1927. Lindbergh arrived in London from France on 21st September and warned Kennedy, the American Ambassador, of the vast preponderance of Germany's air forces over those of all European Powers combined, including Russia. Kennedy passed on this report to the Prime Minister. (See J. W. Wheeler-Bennett, *Munich: Prologue to Tragedy*, Macmillan, London, 1948, p. 159n.)

7 p.m. To Masaryk by arrangement. Horrified to find not only Attlee and Greenwood, but Dallas and Middleton, already sitting there ... Talking to diplomats in front of office boys is difficult. When Masaryk says to me, in front of the other four, 'Would you like a copy of this?' (meaning the Hitler memorandum) I say, 'Thank you very much', and put the copy he offers me in my pocket. Whereat, Middleton, 'Clem, you ought to have a copy'; then, being ignored, again, louder, 'Clem, you ought to have a copy.' Whereat, I say, 'Shut up, and don't keep on about matters we all understand.' Then Dallas, seeking to save the situation, says to Masaryk, 'You might send us a copy round to Transport House to put on our file'!!!

Attlee and Greenwood to see the P.M. again tonight. Masaryk says they cannot accept, but the P.M., before leaving the Rhine, said to the press, 'It is up to the Czechs now', and he supposes that since they accepted the Anglo-French Plan under duress it can now be said that this is only a scheme for carrying it out; that the P.M. has saved them from invasion, and 'are we to have a war over a mere question of procedure?' Then he supposed that there will be more Anglo-French pressure, and the Czechs will either give way again or fight alone and be smashed. (I am conscious of the sense of immediate relief at the prospect of six days more of sure life. How weak we democrats are!) Masaryk to me criticises Phipps, who had reported back all the scare stuff about the French Air Force and believed it.[1] Masaryk says that Eden, when Foreign Secretary, ordered Horace Wilson out of his room because he tried to teach him how to conduct foreign policy. The only important thing, to be friends with Germany. Nothing else, he thought, mattered. It is most sinister to think of Chamberlain on the Rhine with Horace Wilson on one side and Nevile Henderson on the other.

Sunday 25th September

... Masaryk, asked by me on the telephone whether he thinks the British and French governments are getting a little more firm, replies, 'Firm! About as firm as the erection of an old man of seventy.'[2]

---

1 Cadogan noted in his diary on 18th September: 'Reports on French Air Force coming in – too frightful. They have 21 machines (not in squadrons) equal to modern German machines!' (*Cadogan Diaries*, p. 100). This was the day Chamberlain saw Daladier and Bonnet, and strengthened the determination of the British government to persuade the French to accept peace on any terms.
2 The typescript reads: ' "Firm! About as firm as ...... " (there follows a lively metaphor which I could not possibly dictate).' The metaphor is inserted in longhand.

On 24th September Daladier had ordered a partial mobilisation. On the 25th the British Cabinet rejected the German demands. By 27th September, it was widely expected in Britain that the country would be at war within days. Chamberlain, however, was determined to buy peace at any price. On the 29th, he flew to Munich to make further concessions – and returned next day having given the Germans what they wanted, thereby destroying the structure of European defence.

The shock of this capitulation encouraged the Government's opponents on both sides of the House to come together. 'Thus, for a fleeting moment,' Dalton wrote later, 'it seemed possible that a large-scale Tory revolt against Chamberlain might change the whole scene.'[1] On 3rd October, Macmillan approached Dalton, and there followed a meeting between Dalton and a group of Tory rebels including Churchill and Eden, which in turn helped to bring about a sizeable Tory abstention in the vote on the Munich debate. Cripps wanted to follow up this initiative, and at his prompting there was a series of secret meetings between Labour leaders and Tory dissidents. But the Tories were divided among themselves, and the Labour leaders were cautious, fearing the attitude of the unions and of the constituency parties towards any open fraternisation. The chance for a serious cross-bench alliance of Government critics – perhaps even for Macmillan's dream of a '1931 in reverse' – soon passed. Nevertheless, private contacts and gestures of co-operation across the floor of the House continued until the beginning of 1939.

Tuesday 18th October

Duncan Sandys[2] came to see me at his own request. He raised various points in the course of an hour's conversation. He asked what action we were going to take about air defence. Were we going to demand the appointment of a special enquiry? He had had some recent evidence which showed that things were even worse than he had supposed. His figures did not wholly tally with Liddell Hart's over the weekend. He was seeing the latter to check up. Did we intend, when the debate on the report of the Select Committee came on, to emphasise the air

1 FY, pp. 209–10.
2 D. E. Sandys, later Baron Duncan-Sandys (b. 1908). Conservative M.P. for Norwood 1935–45; Streatham 1950–February 1974. Ex-diplomat. Married to Diana, daughter of Winston Churchill (marriage later dissolved). Political columnist of the *Sunday Chronicle* 1937–9. Junior minister 1941–4. First Commissioner, then Minister, of Works 1944–5. Minister of Supply 1951–4; Housing and Local Government 1954–7; Defence 1958–9; Aviation 1959–60. Secretary of State for Commonwealth Relations 1960–64; Colonies 1962–4.

defence deficiencies as distinct from personal responsibilities dealt with in the report? He hoped we should. He drew my attention to the fact that in the last paragraphs the Select Committee had nailed responsibility for breach of privilege upon Belisha. I said that our minority had whitewashed him (Sandys) as assiduously as the majority had whitewashed the Attorney-General.

He tackled me also on possibilities of co-operation between anti-Chamberlain Conservatives and our Party. Could propaganda based on a common platform be started? He left a rough note on the lines on which this might be done. Likewise on colonies. He was against any concession to Hitler and hoped that we should stand with dissident Conservatives on this. He expected that within a week or two this matter would become actual. Further, as regards his own constituency. Attempts were being made in this, as in all the others, to displace dissident Members. He had a meeting of his Executive tomorrow at which a pistol would be pointed at his head and he would be asked to promise to give whole-hearted support to the Government in future. He would consider the possibility of resigning and facing a by-election if he could be assured that there would be no Labour opposition. I said that he had better not contemplate this possibility.

Emphasised that I was not able to be very encouraging to particular projects for united action but encouraged him, if he felt inclined, to come and have another talk with me later on. We both agreed that it would be undesirable to let people know that we were meeting.

Thursday 8th December
Lunched at house of General Spears[1] to meet the King of Greece[2] 'incognito'. Also present Amery, Hudson,[3] Cranborne,[4] Boothby and

1 Major-General E. L. Spears, later Sir Louis, 1st Bart (1886–1974). Conservative M.P. for Carlisle 1931–45. National Liberal M.P. 1922–4. Churchill's special representative to the French Prime Minister, Paul Reynaud; brought General de Gaulle to England May 1940.
2 King George II of Greece (1890–1947). After reigning briefly (1923–4) and being deposed, King George II returned to the throne in November 1935, following a plebiscite. In August 1936, he granted full dictatorial powers to the right-wing Prime Minister, General Metaxos (see p. 249, n. 3).
3 R. S. Hudson, later 1st Viscount (1886–1957). Parliamentary Secretary at the Department of Overseas Trade 1937–40. Conservative M.P. for Whitehaven 1924–9; Southport 1931–52. Ex-diplomat. Junior minister 1931–5. Minister of Pensions 1935–6; Shipping 1940; Agriculture and Fisheries 1940–45.
4 R. A. J. Gascoyne-Cecil, Viscount Cranborne, later 5th Marquess of Salisbury (1893–1972). Conservative M.P. for Dorset South 1929–41. Parliamentary Under-Secretary for Foreign Affairs 1935–8 (resigned with Eden). Paymaster-General 1940; Secretary of State for Dominion Affairs 1940–42, 1943–5; Colonies 1942. Lord Privy Seal 1942–3, 1951–2; Secretary of State for Commonwealth Relations 1952; Lord President of the Council 1952–3; Acting Foreign Secretary 1953.

another Tory. The King is not very impressive but brighter than Royalty as revealed in certain letters which I have lately been re-reading.[1] He is a small man with a round head, a small voice (some say he has cancer of the throat) and a lot of gold stoppings. His younger brother was picked by Venizelos[2] as being the more intelligent, but unfortunately died of a monkey bite. This man is said to be now much under the influence of Metaxos.[3] He said that his people were now very much more united, the sort of silly banality one expected. ...

Pertinax[4] told Spears that Daladier was drunk at Munich during the most important parts of the discussion; that, as announced in the press, they all had a 'light buffet lunch', but that the Germans deliberately plied Daladier with drink, with the result that he only focused when the final terms were being read out. He then rose and began a long, indignant speech, declaring that the terms were impossible, but then went out of action again. Spears also says that in the days preceding Munich, large numbers of Soviet aeroplanes flew over Romanian territory and landed in Slovakia. The Romanian Prefect of their northern Province telephoned day after day to Bucharest reporting that this was going on. Bucharest seemed uninterested. Finally, he went to Bucharest and said to the Minister of the Interior, 'Whenever I look up into the sky I see Soviet aeroplanes flying over.' The Minister replied, 'Mr Prefect, why need you look up?'

Friday 9th December
Lunched with Lord Rea[5] at his house, 6 Barton Street, Westminster. It is almost a year since he first tried to engage me in a conversation about allotting seats between the Labour and the Liberal Parties. This was on the boat between Bombay and Colombo. I recall that I found

---

1 Probably letters from members of the Royal Family to Canon Dalton. (See p. 163, n. 3 above.)
2 Eleutherios Venizelos (1864–1936). Prime Minister of Greece 1910–15, 1915, 1917–20, 1928–32, 1933. Liberal. Following the restoration of George II in 1935 he was forced into exile in France, where he remained until his death.
3 General Ioannes Metaxos (d. 1940). Pro-German dictator of Greece, who had helped to engineer the restoration of the monarchy in 1935.
4 'Pertinax': pen-name of the French journalist André Géraud. Diplomatic correspondent of *France-Soir*. Contributor to the *Daily Telegraph*, New York *Foreign Affairs*, and other newspapers and journals.
5 Sir Walter Rea, 1st Bart, 1st Baron (1873–1948). Liberal M.P. 1906–18, 1923–4, 1931–5. Government whip 1915–16, 1931–2.

him rather tedious and changed the conversation to that of rival methods of disposing of the dead by Hindus, Parsees and Mahommedans. This seemed not an inappropriate theme to develop with an old Liberal politician now relegated to the House of Lords. He had approached me twice since then, but each time I had been unable to meet him.

Today, he developed the suggestion that 'here and there we should keep out of each other's way' at the next election. He said that he realised that nothing could be guaranteed or even formally arranged. Public talk of popular fronts and electoral pacts only did harm. He also recognised that there were many constituencies where it would be to our interest that a Liberal candidate should run, especially in the North of England. In many cases, the utmost that he would suggest would be that, even if a Labour candidate was in the field, and could not be withdrawn, we should not unduly encourage him, e.g. by sending down any of our leading speakers. He said that the Liberal Local Associations were very jealous of interference from the centre, but, although the Liberal central funds were now not large, they could still exercise some influence by either offering or refusing financial assistance in particular cases. I said that if he told me that they were going to run 200 Liberal candidates at the next election I should think that he was bluffing; I should guess that they would not run more than about 120. He replied that they would very much like to run as many as 200 but were doubtful if they could manage it. He, however, would be very disappointed if they did not run more than 120. I said that we already had, including sitting Members, well over 500 in the field. There was, of course, a hard core of absurdity beginning with the City of London, which we should not attempt to touch. But it had been our practice in recent elections to fight the maximum number of constituencies where local parties were, or could be made, willing. There was, however, a possibility that, in order to make the best use of our financial resources, we should leave certain very difficult seats unfought next time. ...

I am doubtful whether much will come out of this, but if I can head off Liberal candidates in even half a dozen constituencies where a Labour win in a straight fight is likely, it would be worth while. These people must, however, be handled very gingerly. Rea is rather like a little sparrow. His butler stared at me rather hard when I gave him my name. I told Rea that I thought his butler might be a political spy. Most of our conversation was done alone upstairs after lunch.

Thursday 22nd December

Had a short talk with R. S. Hudson in the Lobby. He says he will not resign unless the P.M. asks him to ...

... [V]ery gloomy on international outlook. February or March will be a very dangerous period. Hitler may threaten to attack us unless we promise not to intervene in Eastern Europe. The Soviet Union alone won't resist, being much weakened by the shooting of officers. This, at any rate, is our military information.

The French Air Force is still deplorable. More crashes than new machines. *All* flying officers would be killed in a fortnight of war. This is bad for morale ...

[Hudson] is one of the most vigorous and live members of the Government. He should certainly be in the Cabinet in preference to most of the duds there now. I hear from Gladwyn Jebb[1] that he is one of the few ministers who can set civil servants running about in pursuit of his hares.

Gladwyn, who looks in on us at West Leaze early in the new year,[2] also says that February or March will be a very dangerous time. He thinks it possible that Mussolini will attack France. Also possible that the French may not wish us to intervene on their behalf, thinking that they can defeat Italy alone, and hoping to keep Germany out. Mussolini has been cultivating his nuisance value so assiduously that he is now becoming quite indignant that nobody is offering to give him something. On the other hand, the Italian Air Force is suffering very severely in Spain and the economic position of Italy goes from bad to worse. In September, Mussolini never mobilised and only began to make violent speeches when he knew that war was off.

Disappointed by the failure to get a parliamentary alliance with dissident Tory M.P.s, Cripps tried a new tactic. In January 1939 he launched a campaign for a Popular Front. This differed from the 1937 Unity Campaign in that Liberals were invited to join. It also differed from the post-Munich cross-bench negotiations, because Churchill and his group, now accused of 'reactionary imperialism', were to be left out. On 13th January Cripps put his proposals (the 'Cripps Memorandum') to the N.E.C., which rejected them. In a gesture of open defiance, Cripps thereupon circulated local parties, calling for support. Summoned to explain himself to the N.E.C. on 18th January (as indicated below), he failed to appear. On Morrison's proposal,

1 Jebb, q.v., was Private Secretary to Permanent Under-Secretaries of State at the Foreign Office (Vansittart and then Cadogan) 1937–40.
2 Clearly this entry was dictated some time after the date heading it.

the Executive finally decided to refer the matter to the N.E.C. Organisation Sub-Committee, to make a report which could be discussed by the full N.E.C. on 25th January.

Thursday 19th January 1939

Two special E.C.s within a week! The first, on Friday, the 13th, summoned at Cripps's own request, with him present, to advocate matter contained in his memorandum. This was rejected by 17 to 3 (Cripps, Pritt and Wilkinson). ...

Second special E.C. summoned for Wednesday, the 18th, at 4.15, to consider Cripps's action. He wrote that he regretted he had a legal consultation with the Midland Bank which would prevent his coming. This is pretty cool, as the meeting was fixed after 4 p.m. so that his rare presence might be got after the Courts had risen. Middleton, should, however, have taken the precaution of ensuring his presence before summoning the meeting. A typical slip.

At this meeting, which lasted more than three hours, so that I was prevented from speaking for Crawley[1] in North Bucks, various proposals were made, ranging from a proposal for Cripps's immediate expulsion to action limited to the issue of a new manifesto. On the former proposal, made by Mrs Gould,[2] Pritt raised legal arguments and hinted at legal proceedings by Cripps against the Executive, in view of their failure to give him notice of the intention to expel him, and the grounds for such action. Pritt also said that there might be legal proceedings against the B.B.C. for issuing an alleged untrue statement regarding last week's Executive decision. All this lawyer's bluff has more effect on some of my simpler colleagues than it should.

Pritt's tactics were obviously to obstruct and waste time and he made much heavy weather over leakages in the press of our last meeting. On the issue of expulsion, the general feeling was that, legalism apart, we should not take such action until Cripps had had an opportunity of hearing the case against him. Clynes's proposal to do nothing but issue a manifesto and to allow the controversy to run on till the Whitsun Conference, found no support. ...

After the meeting, I got reactions from various quarters. Windle[3] is most anxious that we should take strong action. Otherwise, the

1 A. M. Crawley (b. 1908). Journalist. Labour M.P. for Buckingham 1945–51. Junior minister 1950–51. Conservative M.P. for Derbyshire West 1962–8. Chairman, then President, of London Weekend Television 1967–73.
2 Barbara Ayrton Gould (d. 1950). Member of the Labour Party N.E.C. (Women's Section). Chairman 1939–40. Labour M.P. 1945–50.
3 R. T. Windle (1888–1951). Assistant National Agent of the Labour Party 1929–46; National Agent 1946–51.

decent people all over the country are discouraged and the trade union leaders increasingly irritated. He thinks that if we expel Cripps next week there will be a few squeaks and protests, but nothing comparable to the trouble we are in for if we let him go on. Windle sees the case both for and against a special conference. The case against is that you give Cripps something you never gave MacDonald: a wonderful new run of publicity and limelight. I feel that the attractiveness of expelling him is so great that one must be on one's guard against accepting it too eagerly. None the less, the choice still seems to lie, as I thought it lay last week, between (1) expelling him now and having no special conference, and (2) having a special conference quick, and taking powers to expel him and others if they go on agitating. I am still not quite sure which is best.

The case against him includes (a) the agitation before Bournemouth, (b) the use of the *Tribune*, and (c) this last performance. If immediate expulsion is contemplated, he should, I think, be given the option of this or some impossible condition, e.g. the withdrawal of his memorandum. Since this was an individual effort, we could, if we expelled him now, concentrate on him only. In the other case, we might have to treat a large number of other people as equally blameworthy with him, which would be a great nuisance.

Behind all this folly, lies the chance of (a) a General Election, which it would be convenient for Chamberlain to precipitate while we are squabbling, and this may be an argument against a special conference, even a few weeks hence; and (b) the danger of another stiff international crisis next month or in March. ...

Why did Mr J. S. Elias become Lord Southwood? I am told by X that he was told by Y that he had heard from the secretary of Lord Southwood that the latter had contributed substantially to the National Government's Party Funds. I have no means, at present, of checking the truth of this report.

......

J. K. Kosina came to dinner. I had last seen him at the Empress Stadium after our demonstration during the Czech Crisis. He had then been going off to join his regiment on the Czech Maginot Line.

He says that the Germans are pressing the Czechs –

(1) to pass anti-Jewish laws, which they are very disinclined to do because it is quite contrary to the Czech tradition.
(2) to build two main roads: (a) from north to south, Breslau to Vienna. This road would be German territory and would be fenced on both sides and controlled by German police; (b) from

west to east, right through Carpatho–Ukraine, to facilitate subsequent German troop movements eastwards.

(3) to build an Oder–Danube canal through Czech territory.

The Czechs want neither these roads nor the canal, which are intended only to serve German purposes, but it is impossible to refuse. There is also strong pressure to bring Czechoslovakia into a customs and currency union with the Reich.

A press censorship has been set up in Prague by German instigation, and now, if they negotiate for coal – and they must import much from the transferred area, especially lignite – the Germans say, 'You want some more coal, but isn't it horrible that such and such a newspaper should have printed such and such an article?' In this way, constant pressure is exercised.

Hitler is now asking for 100,000 Czech workers to go to Germany, as he has a shortage of labour, and it will be difficult to refuse this. The Skoda Works are now surrounded by Germany, who wishes to obtain all aircraft and A.A. guns produced there and, in addition, to take over some of those now in the possession of the Czech army.

When the new two-party system was formed, 'we feared that the Labour Party would be stronger than the Government Party'. This is a paradox. But it would have given a pretext to Hitler to invade the country and occupy it. So, too, in Slovakia. Dérer[1] and others could have overthrown the Hlinka Guard, but then Hitler would have marched into Bratislava. The Hlinka Guard receive money from Hitler and give a salute practically the same as the German.

The Czechs have now to be very cautious, to watch and wait for their opportunity. They are accustomed to this; this was their fate for centuries before their liberation in 1918. But personal liberty still exists in Czechoslovakia. Men are not victimised because they are trade unionists or socialists. Fascism is contrary to the deepest democratic instincts of the Czech people. The Slovaks are different, but 'there are only two million of them and we could easily deal with them if the situation changed'. Here a clerical pro-Hitler minority has got control.

Many forest villages, purely Czech, have been seized by the Germans because they want the timber. When they have cut down all the trees they will probably return these villages to Czechoslovakia. ...

Kosina is still in touch with the military, and trusted by some of the High Command, having worked in military intelligence and won their

1 Dr Ivan Dérer (1884–1973). Slovak Social Democratic leader. Minister of Justice in Czechoslovakia 1932–8.

confidence immediately after the Crisis. He took British naval ob-
servers round the Frontier when the Germans were taking over. He
told me that there were many cases of suicide, both among officers
and men, when the retreat was ordered. One officer in command of a
fort, when ordered to retire, said 'A living soldier must obey orders,
a dead soldier cannot', and shot himself. There was another officer
holding a strong post with machine guns. When the Germans advanced, he opened fire upon them until he had exhausted all his
ammunition, and then shot himself before they took over.

In its report on Sir Stafford Cripps, the N.E.C. Organisation Sub-Committee
accused the M.P. for Bristol East of 'organising and preparing' a campaign
to change the direction and leadership of the Party.

Monday 23rd January[1]
We have several alternatives, all open to grave objections. Some want
to expel Cripps right away. The temptation to do this and to get rid of
him is overwhelming, but we must carefully examine consequences.

Others incline to an early special conference to decide the matter.
This, it is objected, looks weak and gives Cripps what we never gave
to MacDonald. I am not much moved by these arguments and am
quite sure that such a conference would turn Cripps down by an
overwhelming aggregate majority. There is, however, a danger of an
appearance of division between the T.U.s and D.L.P.s [Divisional
Labour Parties] although I do not accept the view that the latter, if
the conference were really representative, would show a majority for
Cripps.

I am inclined to ask him whether he will give a very definite undertaking, if we summon a special conference at very short notice, to
accept the decision of that conference and thereafter to cease entirely
from this propaganda, including propaganda in the *Tribune*. If he
says Yes to this, I would have the conference very quickly. If he says
No, or gives some hedging reply short of a clear undertaking, I would
then have no hesitation in voting for his expulsion from the Party and
publishing to the world his refusal to accept in advance a special
conference decision. If we can manoeuvre him on to this ground, we
shall, I think, avoid much of the outcry which would be raised if we
now simply expelled him for his conduct up to date.

1 The entry for 23rd January 1939 and part of the entry for 19th January 1939 are
 headed 'Note', and are in the Dalton Papers 3/1.

This conduct is, however, utterly intolerable. The broadcasting of the opinion that we cannot win the next election will tend to spread a miasma of defeatism and discouragement all over the country, particularly in constituencies where the fight is difficult. The article by Cummings[1] in this week's *Tribune* is a perfect example of fouling the nest.

What is not understood by some of Cripps's well-intentioned supporters who do not know the Labour Party is that (a) you cannot carry such proposals through a conference, and (b) that there is a serious danger of splitting the Party merely by continuing the controversy. The practical proposal is not What could you add to a Labour Party kept intact, but What would you lose from the Labour Party to balance even that hypothetical addition?

If this thing were to be countenanced, a great number of individuals holding key positions in D.L.P.s, in addition to a number of strong organisations, would simply pack up.

To start this hopeless campaign just at this moment is to invite Chamberlain to take an election while the Labour Party is engaged in a bitter and weakening controversy. The thing is perfectly timed to create the maximum embarrassment and weakness in the Party.

The Cripps memorandum itself is full of weaknesses. Its electoral calculations are slipshod, in addition to being grotesquely defeatist. ...

The idea that there is an enormous body of opinion which would come in on the Cripps proposals and won't come in now is, I am satisfied, sheer illusion. In some areas, e.g. round Oxford and in the South-West, it might be advantageous in certain constituencies for Liberal or Labour candidates to stand down. But the scope of such arrangements is very limited. Morrison and I have been advocating greater 'elasticity' in handling such cases, and I have also emphasised, more than once, the desirability, on financial grounds, of limiting the number of Labour candidates at the next election. Any action along these lines, however, would need to be taken quietly and unostentatiously. The possibility of doing anything at all of this kind is ruined by such moves as Cripps's.

The man has the political judgment of a flea.

On 25th January, the N.E.C. asked Cripps to reaffirm his allegiance to the Labour Party, its Constitution, Programme, Principles and Policy, and to

1 A. J. Cummings (d. 1957). Political editor and chief commentator of the *News Chronicle* 1932–55. His *Tribune* article ('Labour and the Rebel Tories') appeared on 20th January.

withdraw his memorandum by circular to the persons and organisations to whom it was addressed. When he refused to do so, he was expelled.

Dalton wrote in a separate, undated, note:[1]

I tried to save him from expulsion (a) by interviewing him privately before the first of the three E.C.s. His wife was present and we got nowhere; (b) by sending him a hint, through Ellen, that if he would accept the verdict of a special conference he might get it, though she said that from his talk she knew he would not accept; (c) by putting three questions to him at the end of the third E.C. before the vote. Any clever lawyer could have found a way out then. I asked him –

(1) Whether he did not think that a prolongation of this controversy would assist Chamberlain and weaken the Labour Party.
(2) Whether, in view of the evidence now available, he had any hope that he would carry a Party Conference.
(3) When we were to reach finality in this controversy.

He need only have replied (1) yes, (2) yes and (3) I will accept the decision of a special conference, and the road would have been clear, though I was not quite confident that I could carry a majority of my colleagues in favour of a special conference even then, but I would have tried. In fact, he answered –

(1) He did not think he was strengthening Chamberlain
(2) He believed he could carry a Conference, but
(3) He could give no pledge as to finality!

On 15th March 1939, German troops entered Prague, and 'Bohemia–Moravia' was declared a German Protectorate. On 18th March the Soviet government proposed an international conference to discuss means of resisting possible future aggressions. Chamberlain rejected this initiative, and suggested instead a declaration by Britain, France, Russia and Poland that they would act together in the face of any new German move; Poland, fearful of Russia as well as of Germany, refused. Meanwhile, on 21st March, the Germans demanded changes to the status of the Polish Corridor and the cession of the Free City of Danzig.

Friday 24th March
Saw Van at his house (we avoid F.O.) for forty minutes this afternoon. This was my first talk with him since Munich. He is still trying to urge

1 Dalton Papers 3/1 (30).

the Government to [make] clear and definite commitments for mutual assistance. He says the Russians are now very willing to come in. Maisky used to tell him that he thought Hitler would go West rather than East. Van says that lately Maisky has not been so sure, particularly since the occupation of Czechoslovakia which, as Van said to him last week, instead of being, as the Germans used to allege, a pistol pointed westwards at their hearts, has now become a pistol pointed eastwards at the Ukraine. The Russians and French will now, Van thinks, sign anything with us, no matter how definite. But the Poles are still not quite sure whether we would go through with them to the end. It is most urgent that they should not continue to delay, as is Beck's[1] nature. Let them raise objections or points of detail about the proposed declaration. Let them speak freely. But don't let the present mood in this country to be more firm evaporate through Polish indecision.

Romania, greatly discouraged, has now not quite sold out but has gone a long way towards surrender to Hitler. ...

Mussolini will speak on Sunday. Probably he has not even yet made up his mind what to say. Van thinks it is about even chances whether he will pitch his claims so high as to indicate a willingness to face war now, or so moderately as to invite negotiations. But, if the former, a strange situation will arise, since Germany has now got all that she can comfortably digest for some time to come. No German, however enthusiastic a Nazi, would be disappointed if he had now to wait till 1940 for the next triumph. Therefore, it might well seem that, if Mussolini pitches his claims very high, the Germans were required to go to war in support of a purely Italian quarrel.

Van thinks our broadcasts in German are doing good, but we must not much strengthen the dose or it will all be stopped.

On 31st March, Chamberlain officially abandoned appeasement, telling the House of Commons that Britain would defend the independence of Poland. On 6th April, the Government reached an agreement with Poland which completed the policy of reversal, taking it even further than some critics might have wished: in the words of one Tory rebel, 'never before in our history have we left in the hands of one of the smaller powers the decision whether or not Great Britain goes to war'.[2] On 7th April, Mussolini's troops

1 Colonel Josef Beck (1894–1944). Polish Foreign Minister 1932–9.
2 See Duff Cooper, *The Second World War: First Phase*, Jonathan Cape, London, 1939, p. 320.

invaded Albania. On 11th April the British government decided to offer a guarantee to Greece, and on the 13th to Romania. Negotiations with the Soviet Union began on 15th April.

Monday 17th April
Saw Maisky, who is leaving tomorrow for Moscow for consultation. He expects to be away about ten days, perhaps more if, he says, he can arrange to stay for the great May Day Parade in Moscow. It is quite a different Maisky today, much more cheerful and less carping. He thinks that last Thursday's (the 13th) debate was very useful. He was particularly delighted at Simon's reply to my question – that H.M.G. had no objection in principle to an Anglo–French–Russian military alliance. He wonders, could this reply have been unpremeditated? Is Simon that sort of man? (Rothstein, the press attaché, whom I saw in the hall, was also full of glee and said that on Friday all Fleet Street was saying that Simon and I had concerted this question and answer beforehand. I tell him that Fleet Street is quite wrong.)

I said that, in the light of his attitude at our last meeting, when he feared that there would be no British guarantee to Romania and that this was to be interpreted as an invitation to Hitler to go East along a selected route, I supposed that the Romanian guarantee had made a lot of difference. He replied very warmly that this was so and that it had removed much, though not yet all, of the distrust in Moscow and the doubt whether, even now, H.M.G. 'really means business'. Until he heard the P.M.'s speech last Thursday, he was inclined to bet that there would be no Romanian guarantee. He spoke, as he came into the Diplomatic Gallery, to Tilea[1] who likewise did not know the guarantee was coming.

He agrees that British opinion on Anglo–Soviet relations has moved with a rush. He lunched today in the City with a number of bankers and financiers who were all very angry with Germany and declared their desire for close collaboration with the Soviet Union. I said, 'What a tribute all this is to your skilful propaganda. You will be able to boast, when you get to Moscow, of the resounding success of your diplomatic mission in London.' He was rather pleased, I think, at this very obvious flattery, and no doubt intends to speak somewhat on

---

1 Virgil Tilea (1896–1972). Romanian Minister to Britain 1938–40. Tilea had regarded the German terms, in the Germano-Romanian talks, as an ultimatum. On 10th April, he asked Cadogan for a provisional guarantee for Romania.

these lines. To me, however, he said that he thought perhaps Hitler too had helped. ...

Maisky says that Romania is thought in Moscow to be more crucial than Poland, (1) because she is militarily weaker, (2) because she is internally more divided, containing some pro-German elements, (3) because Hitler on the Black Sea would be only thirty miles from Odessa, and (4) because Germany would then have her oil. Also Romania is more willing than Poland to accept Soviet aid, especially aeroplanes and fighting material.

Sunday 23rd April
Dine at Romanian Legation to meet Gafencu[1] who has just arrived from Berlin and Brussels. ...

Gafencu is very friendly to me; he expresses much gratitude at my part in obtaining the guarantee, as to which I think that Tilea has told him a great deal. Arthur Henderson, jnr, who is one of the guests, met him in Bucharest a few months ago and is on good personal terms with him. (A hard-working and creditable, if not very clever little man this.) Gafencu has been an airman, economist, journalist, newspaper proprietor, Parliamentarian – member of the Peasants' Party – and Under-Secretary before being made Foreign Minister. He is good looking, especially in profile, and, as Raczynski[2] says to me tonight, 'It is so seldom that a man is both good looking and a good worker.'

Gafencu says that he was received with respect in Berlin and that they did not try to bully him, 'thanks to your guarantee'. He saw Hitler, Ribbentrop twice, and Goering. King Carol has replied to the German enquiry, whether Romania fears German aggression, that such a question is a quite new diplomatic procedure and that he does not understand its significance; that he has no fear of attack by any of his neighbours, but that Germany is not a neighbour.

All the high Germans said to Gafencu in Berlin, 'So you have got the English and French to fight for you? But they cannot help you.' But they added that they had no objection to British and French guarantees, but they would interpret a Russian guarantee very differently. Hitler, he says, gave him an indication of the speech he will make on Friday, the 28th. He will declare that he never had any

1 Grigore Gafencu (1892–1957). Romanian Foreign Minister December 1938–May 1940. In March he had signed an agreement which gave the Germans extensive control over the Romanian economy.
2 Count E. Raczynski (b. 1891). Polish Ambassador in London 1934–45. Foreign Minister in Polish government-in-exile 1941–3.

intention of attacking Holland, Belgium or Switzerland, nor of attacking the colonies of Holland, Belgium or Portugal. He will hint that France and England have suggested this. He will say that he wants *his own* colonies back, and base this claim on the grounds of justice and right. Gafencu hopes that our reply will be strong. If changes are to be based on justice and right, then, we might reply, let Hitler first leave Prague and then we could talk of other changes.

He says that Hitler worked himself up into great excitement about war, declaring that he himself desired only peace. He said, 'If the British want war, they may have it, but it will be a far more terrible thing for them than they imagine.'

He then went on to speak of the immense power of the German Air Force and of all the new and terrible inventions of their chemists and scientists. He said that very soon many great cities of England would be completely destroyed. But then he added, 'So, I know, would many cities in Germany and other countries which were at war. And what would be the good of this?' Gafencu said that Hitler worked himself up into a great passion and 'cried' at this point. Then he suddenly quietened down again and went on to speak of economic questions, and the German 'Living Space'.

I am sorry to find that Gafencu is still very shy about Russia, even of an Anglo–French–Russian agreement formally detached from guarantees. If war came, he says, of course Romania would accept any help, but he does not wish to say so beforehand. Russian troops in Romania would certainly do Communist propaganda. Russia, he thinks, has not the will to peace, as Britain and France have. He suggests that we might also lose American support if we come too close to Russia. I say that I think this is no longer true. I ask, 'Have you any objection to a triple alliance, or at any rate a triple declaration, against aggression by London, Paris and Moscow?' 'If your country chooses to make it, I have no right to object. Your guarantee to my country is unilateral, and I am very grateful for this, but I would prefer that you and the French made a military arrangement, which would not be published, with the Russians, rather than a political arrangement, which would be published.' He thinks that in any case Russia would not do very much to help if war broke out. She would prefer war to peace in Europe.

Raczynski, to whom I speak afterward, takes much the same line. He thinks that such a triple alliance would give Hitler a further pretext of encirclement and might precipitate a war. Raczynski says that he has for some time been pessimistic. He thinks the odds are perhaps 3 to 2 in favour of war. A triple declaration, he thinks, would increase the risk of war still further. I say that he will have seen that the desire for a triple pact has now spread far beyond the Labour Party. He agrees this is so. Poland, he says, was opposed to the original proposal which was made by H.M.G. to have simultaneous and reciprocal pacts with Poland and Romania. This would have looked too much like encirclement. I reply both to Raczynski and Gafencu that there is another possibility, namely, that if we are able to display to the Germans an overwhelming potential force arrayed against them in the event of aggression, it will make such aggression less likely. Both take the line, in reply, that Germany knows that Russia would do something against her if war came, and that nothing is gained, and much might be lost, by aiding Hitler's propaganda inside Germany, by such a declaration.

Wednesday 3rd May
Saw Van at his house at his suggestion. Before he came in, I had five minutes with her.[1] She is full of indignation against Sir Horace Wilson who, she says, still has as much power as ever at No. 10. Years ago he used to come quite often to see Van but now has not seen him for a year. She says that Cadogan is also jealous of Van and never initiates any discussion with him or suggests that he should be called in to conferences. Van himself has always to 'muscle in', as he puts it, on his own. Halifax, she thinks, is friendly to him and can be influenced a good deal, but he is subject to the Inner Cabinet, which contains some bad men. All very womanly! She says that Cadogan, and also some Cabinet Ministers, have never forgiven him for not being willing to take the Paris Embassy, when it was urged upon him.

Van says that, as far as he knows, Horace Wilson and Nevile Henderson are still where they were, incredible as this may seem in the light of Munich. *The Times* and the rest of Hitler's Fifth Column in London – I tell him that *I* called them that in the House of Commons the other day – are still active and ready at any time to start up appeasement again and to sell the Poles as they sold the Czechs. Wilson now is always present at Cabinet meetings, which is an innovation. Van has never had a private conversation with the P.M. on foreign affairs, nor, for a long while, has he spoken to Simon, who never liked him. On the other hand, Hoare is, and has been for a long time, very sound on Russia. It is a mistake to put him in the same group with P.M. and Simon. Halifax, likewise, understands the position well. (According to all this, two out of four of the Inner Cabinet are not too bad, but

1 Sarita Vansittart, née Ward. Vansittart's second wife. Widow of Sir Colville Barclay, a diplomat.

of the other two one is P.M. and the other the snakiest of them all.)
Van shares my great impatience over the slowness of the Russian
negotiations. He says – and this is a new way of putting it – that he
finally lost his reputation as a trustworthy expert on 18th September
when the French ran out and sacrificed the Czechs. He had always
been labelled as pro-French and had been telling everybody that the
French would stand firm over Czechoslovakia, if only we did. Then
the French, not much encouraged by us to stand, ran away. ...

Hitler *may* understand a show of biceps; he will certainly understand nothing else. This is why a firm stand by the Poles has such
importance, and why an arrangement with Russia should both be
made and proclaimed. It is time now to tell the Germans that, having
got 100 per cent of their demands in Austria, Czechoslovakia, etc.,
they must not in future expect to get more than 30 per cent at the
outside, and that only if they will negotiate, behave decently, and give
evidence by way of deeds, not merely promises. He agrees with me
that the Poles are thundering bad propagandists for themselves. They
should long ago have made a full and reasoned statement of their
position as regards Danzig and the 'Corridor'.

On 26th April, the Prime Minister announced that the Government would
introduce a limited measure of conscription.

Thursday 4th May
First day's debate on Second Reading of Conscription Bill. P.M.
incredibly inept and said to have upset even his own Yesmen. Two
major blunders are (1) a shilling a day for conscripts – he should have
said that they would get so many pounds a week of which, however,
so much would be for splendid food, so much for first-class accommodation, so much for well-fitting uniforms, and on top of this something more for luxuries and fun – and (2) reference to N. Ireland,
which is so 'loyal' that he trusts it to furnish, without conscription,
its quota of volunteers. This makes, very naturally, great uproar on
our Benches. ...

In corridor find Eden, Winston and J. P. L. Thomas[1] very excited
against Government. Winston says, 'Fancy having thrown away the

1 J. P. L. Thomas, later 1st Viscount Cilcennin (1903–60). Conservative M.P. for
  Hereford 1931–55. Junior minister 1940–45. First Lord of the Admiralty 1951–6.

Czechs, a gallant and democratic people, and now we have to do the best we can with the Poles. I cannot defend many things the Poles have done, but we must make the best of it now. If the Cabinet had a plan and weren't simply bumping about in a panic they would have a perfectly clear, though unpublished, understanding with the Poles about the point at which the Poles would fight.'

Sunday 7th May

From Hyde Park demonstration to Soviet Embassy. Have not seen Maisky since the eve of his departure for Moscow ... I say that I have a feeling that for the moment war is at least postponed. Maisky says that Hitler thinks that he will die within two years and therefore he must do big things quick. For the moment the Axis has a military superiority, but this may not last and would be quite removed by the triple alliance. ...

He says he thinks the real obstacle here to acceptance of the Russian proposal is the Umbrella Man (Maisky and I always refer to him thus). Also Simon. I tell him I hear that Hoare is, and has for some time been, in favour of a Russian alliance or something very near it. He says that this is so, and that Halifax, he thinks, would also like to go much further than the P.M. and Simon.

Sir Horace Wilson is as well entrenched as ever, he thinks, at No. 10. He suspects that it was he who instigated Rushcliffe[1] to write an appeasement letter to *The Times*. Chamberlain, like Beck and Bonnet, is personally quite unreliable and always looking for a hole in the hedge. This snag can only be removed when we get a new P.M.

As I am going away, he asks how many members there are in the Parliamentary Executive. Is it about 24? I say the full membership is 15 plus one or two Lords. An average attendance is about a dozen. He says that some of my colleagues have been indiscreet and have been talking outside, and even writing in letters, about what he has told to Attlee, Greenwood and myself. He hints that we should say less, particularly where he is involved, in the Executive. I try to get names out of him without success, but he assures me that he knows I am always most discreet. ... Maisky adds that 'at No. 10 Downing Street they think that I am an arch plotter. I do not mind that, but I hope you will ask your friends to be careful.' I say that I thought Phil [Noel-Baker] was a little indiscreet in Parliament on Friday in mentioning 15th April as the date of the arrival of the last Soviet Note. Clearly he could only have got this either from Maisky or the Foreign Office.

1 Sir Henry Betterton, 1st Bart, 1st Baron Rushcliffe (1872–1949). Conservative M.P. for Rushcliffe 1918–24. Junior minister 1923–4, 1924–9. Minister of Labour 1931–4.

Wednesday 24th May

Bellenger engages me in conversation on the Terrace and asks whether I have ever considered becoming a Mason. I say no. He then explains how useful this association is and tells me that there is a Lodge at the House of Commons, called the New Welcome Lodge, to which a number of Labour M.P.s belong. 'Greenwood', he said, 'is a member.' He assured me that there was no politics in Free Masonry, but that there was a wonderful sense of fellowship, etc. I thanked him for his suggestion but said that I did not feel that I would care to join. I added, 'There is a good deal of talk going round about this Lodge.' 'There ought not to be,' said he, slightly embarrassed I thought.

I don't know whether he just blurted this invitation out without consideration, or whether he had been deliberately sent to try to buy me off. Anyhow I now have part of the story direct from another source.

Sir Stafford Cripps's expulsion from the Labour Party in January was followed by what Dalton later called 'a fight to the finish'.[1] Cripps launched a 'National Petition Campaign' in support of his position, and Aneurin Bevan, G. R. Strauss and Sir Charles Trevelyan were expelled by the N.E.C. for backing it. On 16th February, Dalton wrote to Sir William Jowitt:

> Cripps is the hell of a nuisance, but not, in my view, much more. In spite of intrigue, misrepresentations, and the lavish expenditure of money on his latest stunt, I am confident that his expulsion will be approved by the Conference at Whitsuntide and the Popular Front decisively rejected. I do not think that my colleagues are in any mood to make what might appear to be concessions either to him or to his point of view before the Conference at Southport has taken the decision. Since he has challenged us, he must be defeated, and law and order re-established in the Party. That, I think, is the general view.[2]

Cripps was permitted to make a speech defending himself at the Southport Party Conference held in May, but the big unions were against him and all the N.E.C. decisions on the issue of the Popular Front and the expulsions were overwhelmingly endorsed. As a result, Cripps – still in Parliament – spent most of the Second World War as an Independent M.P., free of party entanglements.

---

1 FY, p. 213.
2 Dalton Papers 5/2 (29).

Friday 26th May to Friday 2nd June

Southport Conference. Hard work but quite a success. As usual, the first day of the Conference is the most difficult. Owing to coyness of many colleagues, I was given the job of dealing with Cripps. Wisely, though after many hesitations and discussions on procedure, precedence, etc., it was decided that he should be allowed to address the Conference 'on behalf of himself and other expelled members'. He did very badly. He said nothing on behalf of his colleagues, except to dismiss them in a sentence as 'the others', whose case, he said, was different from his own and therefore he could not deal with it. For the rest, he put up a legalistic argument, reading his whole discourse from typescript and upsetting many delegates by a tactless reference to his private wealth and the attempt to 'create class prejudices' by reference to it.

I astonished myself by my power of self-restraint in reply and by the sense of regret at having had to get rid of him which I think I managed to convey. He gave me an opening to let out the three questions I had put to him at his last E.C. These, and his answers, impressed the Conference. It was an easy victory on the vote, more than 5 to 1 in favour of the expulsion, and among the Constituency Parties alone, more than 3 to 2. ...

There was evidence of a pro-Cripps bloc vote among the D.L.P.s, 100 of whom, practically all represented at Southport, had sent us resolutions protesting against his expulsion. The voting strength of this bunch was very nearly the vote recorded for Mrs Strauss[1] for the Executive: 142,000. She had never been at a Conference before and is completely unknown outside Crippsite and *Tribune* circles.[2] It is clear that some sort of string was run by Crippsites for the Executive. They tried to turn votes away from Morrison, Dallas, Wilmot and myself. Wilmot unfortunately missed re-election by one vote (200,000 as against 201,000 for Griffiths[3] who, I think, though not a member of the string nationally, got some of its support regionally). Special steps were taken to see that George Dallas was saved, particularly through the Agents. Morrison and I were safe in any case, having a wide,

---

1 Patricia Strauss, née O'Flynn, later Lady Strauss (b. 1909). Author and journalist. Later a prominent London County Councillor. Married to G. R. Strauss, q.v.
2 *Tribune*, initially financed by Cripps (Chairman of the editorial board) and Strauss, had been launched to accompany the Unity Campaign in January 1937. The editor from 1938 to 1940 was H. J. Hartshorn. For most of this period *Tribune*'s analysis closely reflected that of the Communist *Daily Worker*.
3 James Griffiths (1890–1935). Labour M.P. for Llanelli. See Appendix.

diffused support which the Crippsites could not hope to undermine. Clearly, however, the Crippsites, having a grudge against the four above-named members of the E.C., gave their votes to the other three – Laski, Noel-Baker and Pritt – and thereby a little disturbed what would have been a natural order.

When we came to the Popular Front on Thursday, their opposition had crumbled, and only 70,000 D.L.P. votes were in the minority. The D.L.P.s, therefore, voted against the Popular Front by more than 6 to 1. Morrison spoke very well on this.

In private session, things were said both by Bevin and Francis Williams concerning the weakness of Attlee's leadership. He, poor little man, has been ill and is going into a Nursing Home for an operation (prostate gland). I hear that the view is now taken both by Citrine and Bevin that a change in the leadership must be made. Also that they have no confidence in Greenwood either.

Ellen Wilkinson has an indiscreet article, not under her signature, in *Time and Tide*, and another, signed, in the *Sunday Referee*. To shift anybody from anywhere in this sheepishly loyal Movement of ours is a Herculean task. The fact remains that at Annual Conferences, when Morrison and I are the principal performers, we can build up the self-confidence, unity and morale of the Party in a most surprising way ...... and then, a few weeks later, others having resumed their feeble sway, down it all sags again!

I tell Francis Williams a few things, e.g. about the Masons, which he did not know, on the last morning of the Conference. I say that I am prepared to go to all lengths to get the right sort of change, provided there is reasonable chance of pulling it off. Otherwise what is the good?

......

There were some humorous little incidents, e.g. when the Crippsites [started] cheering their hero when he came to the rostrum in the Conference Hall, others started to boo. Little Mrs Lathan said to me afterwards, 'I was sitting in the gallery and the people round me began to clap when he came in, so I booed like anything.' Mrs Walker, Jim's wife, also booed from behind the platform and seemed quite proud of it. I think that, as Crossman[1] says in an article in the *Statesman* in which I recognise signs of my own inspiration, Cripps has now bored and irritated most of our Party to sheer distraction.

1 R. H. S. Crossman (1907–74). Leader of the Labour Group on Oxford City Council 1934–40. Assistant Editor of the *New Statesman and Nation* 1938–55. See Appendix.

Wednesday 14th June
Party Meeting, at which a vote of sympathy with Attlee in his illness, and of personal confidence in him, is passed nem. con. This is the climax of some well-meant but maladroit and most ill-timed publicity. The peg on which a rather disagreeable discussion at the Party Meeting was hung was an article by Ellen Wilkinson in the *Sunday Referee* of 4th June. ...

The Masons had been actively going about, swearing that they would have Ellen's head on a charger and alleging an immense and far-tentacled intrigue to impose Morrison upon a reluctant and indignant Parliamentary Party ... The Masons, though no doubt hoping that Attlee will come through his operation all right, would like him to retire on grounds of health in a month or two and Greenwood to get the leadership, but for the moment they concentrate on indignation at this attempt to stab a sick man in the back. (*And, indeed, these articles are most untimely*. Attlee is due to have his second operation for prostate within ten days of the first ... It is by no means sure that he will come through. Maurice Webb,[1] indeed, told me some days ago that he had heard he had no better than a 2 to 1 chance. From what I hear elsewhere, I think his chance is much better than that, but he may well be out of action for some months afterwards.)

Having heard the Masonic rumblings, I have some words on Monday 12th June with Ellen and Morrison. I think we are not observed together, meeting, after the House has adjourned, in the little room behind the Speaker's Chair. I urge her, if attacked, to counter by spilling some Masonic beans. She says that Scott Lindsay, with Greenwood – the latter not wholly sober – have been threatening her tonight with votes of censure at the Party Meeting. I say that whereas Attlee is quite virtuous, in spite of all his inadequacies, Greenwood and the Masons are a scandal, and this is a chance to expose them. She agrees to this idea and says that Jagger,[2] generally very cautious, is now encouraging her to fight, particularly because he is infuriated at the activities of W. A. Robinson, who is the Masons' drummer in chief. Morrison thinks that it is very unfortunate that all this has been raised when Attlee is sick, but thinks that there should be some day an open discussion on the leadership in the Party Meeting. In 1935 we took a silent vote after, as he says, 'two smart questions put to me'.

---

1 Maurice Webb (1904–56). Journalist on the *Daily Herald* 1935–44. Propaganda Officer for the Labour Party 1929–35. Labour M.P. 1945–55. Chairman of the P.L.P. 1946–50. Minister of Food 1950–51.
2 John Jagger (1872–1942). Labour M.P. for Manchester Clayton 1935–42. General President of the National Union of Distributive and Allied Workers 1920–42.

Webb tells me on the same evening that Shinwell has been raging to him against Morrison who, he says, was a MacDonaldite in 1931 and whose capacities have been enormously exaggerated by well organised propaganda. Shinwell thinks that on the whole Attlee is the best available Leader. If he should fall out, Shinwell says that either Greenwood or I would be better than any other alternatives. This is interesting, because I was not sure where Shinwell stood, and suspected that he might be in favour of Alexander as Leader. There are faint rumours, which I cannot verify, that there is a minor campaign in favour of Alexander running at this moment.

On Tuesday night I walk home down Victoria Street with Alexander and ask him whether he is coming to the Party Meeting tomorrow. He thinks not, as he is very busy. He regrets the press reflections on Attlee, though, as I know, he has little use for him as Leader. I mention to him the Masonic matter, of which he seems ignorant – I suppose he is not a Mason himself in some other Lodge? – but he agrees with me that it would be a scandal and an impossibility for Greenwood to lead the Party. He says, 'Has not Greenwood got the T.U. vote?' This is an astonishingly ignorant question. I say, 'Of course, there is no T.U. vote on this issue. They are all split up.' We both cautiously avoid making suggestions to each other, though, checking up our memory of the events of 1935, I recall to him, casually and in passing, that on that occasion we both supported Morrison.

Webb also told me this evening that Greenwood's state of mind was (a) that he was terrified of the leadership, particularly if the international situation got bad, but that (b) he could not bear to serve under anyone else, except to continue under Attlee. ...

At the Party Meeting, after some non-contentious business, Greenwood raises from the Chair, 'with regret', the question of Ellen's article, but does not give detailed information about it, saying only that the E.C. thought it very wrong that at such a moment such an article should appear in effect expressing lack of confidence in our sick Leader. The discussion that followed was angry and confused. Ellen is not popular with most of the men at the best of times, and on this occasion she had infuriated (a) the Masons, (b) all the loyal little Attleeans, and (c) a number of Members who rallied to the side of a sick man. She did not make a very good defence and she did not counter-attack the Masons. Perhaps it was best that she did not, for this might have been resented by some non-Masons as a red herring, and she is so unpopular at the moment that she would not have been a good person to spill these beans today. Shinwell moved a resolution of confidence in Attlee's leadership which, as already noted, was carried nem. con. Ellen did not vote. All the rest voted for it. Francis

Williams, challenged, though not very aggressively, by Shinwell, made a short statement on his article, saying that he had no such intention as his critics alleged. ... No more was said on his part, fury being concentrated upon Ellen. ...

This has all been an unfortunate and miscalculated affair. There is nothing more to do at present except to wait and see the result of poor little Attlee's major operation. Morrison whispered to me later in the day on the Bench, 'That was a queer double-meaning debate we had this morning.'

Stokes[1] has a party to meet Nash[2] at the Savoy. I sit between Nash and Holland Martin[3] of the Bank of England, spoken of as a possible successor to Montagu Norman. I did not like the man. He is a thin-lipped, monocled, money lender. I start by rallying him half jovially about the Czech gold. He says, 'All the difficulty has arisen because we are not politicians.' He went on to defend the B.I.S. [Bank for International Settlements] as a place where bankers who were not politicians could meet without publicity and discuss the good of the world. I said that many of us politicians thought that it was high time the B.I.S. was wound up. I then devoted myself to Nash and did not speak to Holland Martin again until we were nearly through the meal. I then talked to him about America and then slid him on to Old Etonian shop. In the discussion which followed the meal, in which Nash was very clear and effective, Holland Martin took no part, and I very little; but at one stage I said to Nash, 'I think your mistake has been not to restrict imports enough, so that you have lowered your sterling balance and enabled people like this' – and here I indicated Holland Martin – 'to push you about.' Even then Holland Martin did not react, except by some faint murmur of denial.

Among those present was Kirkpatrick, whom I had known at the Foreign Office and who came back from Berlin at the end of last year, after a period first with Phipps and then with Henderson. He thinks that Hitler is the most wicked, treacherous, false and evilly ambitious man alive. Last December he was seriously contemplating an air attack on us just out of the blue, not necessarily immediately, but as

1 R. R. Stokes (1897–1957). Labour M.P. for Ipswich 1938–57. Minister of Works 1950–51; Lord Privy Seal 1951; Minister of Materials 1951.
2 W. Nash, later Sir Walter (1882–1968). New Zealand Labour Party politician. Minister of Finance 1935–49. Deputy Prime Minister 1940–49. Leader of the Opposition 1950–57. Prime Minister and Minister for External Affairs 1957–60.
3 R. M. Holland Martin (1872–1944). Director of Martin's Bank. Chairman of the Southern Railway. Old Etonian.

his next big move. After Munich, in spite of all his gains, he had been gnashing his teeth, disappointed then of his easy little war and his armed occupation of Prague. He had said to Goering after Munich, 'Next time I shall move so quick that old women like you won't be able to intervene to stop me.' I asked Kirkpatrick whether he thought that speedy agreement on the Anglo–Soviet Pact would halt Hitler or hasten his next offensive. Kirkpatrick thought it would probably halt him, though it was impossible to be sure. On the Anglo–Russian negotiations, he said, evidently critical of the way in which they had been conducted from this end, 'At the beginning our Government thought they were inviting the Russians to join the Turf Club and that they would fall over themselves with delight. The Russians, on the other hand, felt that they had a valuable oriental carpet to sell and were dissatisfied with the price offered.' He was hopeful that agreement would soon be reached. Molotov[1] was something of a suspicious peasant and was finding new and unintended meanings in some of the British formulae.

Wednesday 21st June

After lunch, talk with Van in his room, Kirkpatrick on the stairs, and Gladwyn in his annexe to poor fish Cadogan.

Gladwyn, recently returned from Poland, says the Poles will certainly fight. Their calculation is that they will have to retreat on their western frontier, but will hold up the Germans for two months and perhaps overrun East Prussia as well. At the end of two months they think the German regime will collapse from within. They are prepared for a rough federation, including Lithuania, Romania and the Czech and Slovak lands, with friendly relations with Hungary. They are very romantic, but also very determined. He does not think there are any severe internal strains. The Nortons,[2] he says, are being a great success in Warsaw, and so is the Ambassador, Kennard,[3] so long as his wife is away. But when she is there, she nags at him and he is less good. ...

The Italians, he thinks, are more and more in a blue funk, and don't quite know where Hitler is taking them to. A general war would certainly mean the early collapse of the regime in Italy. Musso, he says, 'sees fewer papers' than he used to do. He has now been furnished with a phlegmatic German blonde, partly to symbolise the Axis and partly

1 Vyacheslav Molotov (b. 1890). Soviet Foreign Minister 1939–49, 1953–6. He succeeded Litvinov in March 1939. Deputy Chairman of the Council of Ministers 1953–7.
2 Noel Norton, née Hughes, later Lady Norton. Married to C. J. Norton, q.v.
3 Sir Howard Kennard (1878–1955). Ambassador to Poland 1935–41. He was married to Harriet, née Norris.

because the very exciting dark Italian lady whose place she has taken was thought to be exciting him too much.

Abyssinia is a mess. Ciano is stupid, conceited, corrupt and pro-German. Starace,[1] who has never been out of Italy, was, during the war, the officer commanding the brothels of Brindisi. (This is very Italian! *Ricordi di vent'anni fa.*)[2] ...

Van, Gladwyn and Kirkpatrick all take an optimistic view of the Russian negotiations, though they say that Russian rigidity is a bit bothering.

The British negotiations with the Soviet Union, broken off on 14th May, were resumed on 27th May. Britain remained suspicious of Soviet intentions in Eastern Europe, and the Russians doubted whether the British had anything solid to offer. 'The Russians are impossible', Cadogan wrote in his diary on 20th June, expressing the Foreign Office view. 'We give them all they want, with both hands, and they merely slap them. Molotov is an ignorant and suspicious peasant.'[3]

Sunday 25th June
It is all very well that optimistic rumours should flow week after week both from the Soviet Embassy and the Foreign Office about the Anglo-Soviet pact negotiations. I am less and less inclined to believe them and, therefore, arrange to see Maisky at noon today. (I have not seen him for some weeks, partly because things were said to be going well, partly because I thought I had been seeing him too often for my own dignity, partly because I was conscious of jealousy of some colleagues at my frequent reported visits to him and did not wish to stir this needlessly.)

I began by telling him that all this optimism ... has kept me away from him, but that a fortnight ago I was 'very offensive' to the P.M. in the House and got a large mail, chiefly favourable, in consequence, and thought that perhaps the time had come to do it again, though these things could not be done too often or they lost emphasis. I asked what was really the trouble. Was it (1) a question of *naming* the Baltic

1 Achille Starace (1889–1945). Secretary-General of the Italian Fascist Party 1932–9. Secretary of State 1937–9. Arrested by the Badoglio Administration in 1943, and executed in 1945.
2 'Memories of twenty years ago': Dalton had served with the Royal Artillery in Italy 1917–18. See above, p. xiv.
3 *Cadogan Diaries*, p. 189.

States, or (2) the fact that H.M.G. would only undertake to *consult* in certain cases, or (3) difficulty about getting staff talks started. He said that on (3) he thought there would be no difficulty. Moscow would probably want dates fixed for these to begin and finish, but he thought this would be conceded. The difficulty was a combination of (1) and (2). The Soviet Union wanted the three Baltic States to be guaranteed and eight guaranteed States to be named – Belgium, Poland, Romania, Turkey, Greece, Finland, Estonia and Latvia. The British and French did not wish to guarantee the three Baltic States. He had suggested to Halifax two days ago the precedent of the Monroe Doctrine declaration, in which the U.S.A. had declared, without consulting the South American States, that any interference with their independence by an outside state would be a cause of war with the U.S.A. Halifax had complained to Maisky about the slowness of the negotiations, and Maisky had replied 'with a few figures'. He had pointed out that the negotiations had now lasted for 67 days, of which 17 had been occupied by the Soviet Union considering their replies to British proposals, and 50 by the British considering their replies to Soviet proposals (by Monday, 26th, when I put my next question in the House, it will be 70 days, i.e. 10 weeks, of which the British will have occupied 53; by Monday, too, Strang will have been in Moscow for 11 days).

Cadogan wrote in his diary for 28th June: 'As regards Soviet, we are going to the furthest limit without any very sure hope – on my part – that the dirty sweeps will respond.'[1]

Wednesday 28th June
Citrine, Morrison and I, appointed by the N.C.L. [National Council of Labour] to seek an interview with the P.M. on the international situation, with special reference to the Anglo-Soviet Pact, the Danzig danger and the Far East, spent two hours in P.M.'s room at H. of C. this evening – 6.15 to 8.15 p.m. We had a preliminary talk of just over half an hour in Attlee's room, and it was agreed that Citrine should open, taking in turn (1) Anglo–Soviet Pact, (2) Danzig, (3) Propaganda, and (4) the Far East. Citrine, though very reasonable and an excellent team man, is still inclined to be sufficiently anti-Russian to see, perhaps a little more clearly than is necessary now, the difficulties of H.M.G. over the Pact. But he never lets colleagues down publicly when facing the other side.

1 *Cadogan Diaries*, p. 190.

P.M. has with him Halifax, and Rucker,[1] his new principal private secretary from the Ministry of Health. ...

Citrine says we are much disturbed at long delay in getting Pact and urges its immediate conclusion; expressed fears as to possibility of early German aggression over Danzig, and suggests that H.M.G. should consider a rather clearer and more definite public warning to Hitler; on propaganda, he says that Perth's[2] appointment 'commands no support at all' in the Labour Movement and urges that there should be more drive and definiteness in our propaganda, though B.B.C. broadcasts, apart from a few technical defects, are good; finally, he asks for information as to the Far East, and especially what is being done to bring U.S.A. and Soviet Union into effective co-operation against latest Jap activities.

I speak briefly, limiting myself to the first two points ... Morrison then gives him quite a good lecture on how to conduct propaganda ... Morrison tells Halifax that he ought to be more cocky in his speeches. Sometimes to make a few jokes about the Germans, and to boost our success as regards social services, local government, etc. ...

P.M. – after the usual understanding that we shall all speak freely and discuss at the end how much can be passed on – leaves propaganda to Halifax and speaks at some length on the other three matters. In the Far East our position is very difficult. We cannot send a large enough fleet to the Pacific to have any influence on the Japs – much less a fleet large enough to win a major fleet action – without evacuating the Eastern Mediterranean, which the French would not be able to take over. This would create a situation in which Hitler would say to Mussolini, 'Come on now and drop all these hesitations.' (I infer from this that there is good evidence that Hitler has been pushing Mussolini towards a joint aggression, but that the latter has been hanging back. This accords with other evidence.) In the Far East the attitude of the U.S.A. is decisive. If they were prepared to threaten to use their fleet or take joint action with us for economic or financial boycotts, that would certainly stop the Japs, but the Americans are not at any such point yet. They are friendly to us and encourage us to take a firm line, promising that, if we do, they will consider what they should do next, and they are speaking behind the scenes to the Japs, warning them not to risk American displeasure. But this is all, and damage has been done by the speech of Bonnet, in which he said that

1 A. N. Rucker, later Sir Arthur (b. 1895). Principal Private Secretary to the Prime Minister 1939–40. Deputy Secretary at the Ministry of Health 1943–8.
2 Sir Eric Drummond, 16th Earl of Perth (1876–1951). Ambassador to Italy 1933–9; Chief Adviser on Foreign Publicity to the Ministry of Information 1939–40. Secretary-General of the League of Nations 1919–33.

if America would make it clear that she would be in the war from the first day, the war would not happen. The sure way, said the P.M., to lose the Americans is to run after them too hard. Moreover, just at this moment, with the Neutrality legislation going through Congress, it is most important to do nothing to strengthen the isolationist and anti-Roosevelt elements in the Senate.

It is true that our Concessions cannot be defended against real Jap attack, and even Hongkong 'could not hold out for very long'. It would be necessary, if things got really bad, to withdraw all our ships from the North China waters to the shelter of Singapore. (I gather that the Japs have ten capital ships in the Pacific, and we nothing stronger than cruisers.) ...

As to Danzig, I did not think him very satisfactory. He repeated our undertaking to the Poles to come to their help 'if there is any threat to Poland's independence and if Poland decides to resist.' 'And so', he said, 'if Germany commits an act of aggression in Danzig and the Poles resist, we shall be in it.' I took him up at once on this, and said that I was glad to hear him so definite, in view of stuff put out by *The Times* etc. some months ago, even though this had been repudiated by Simon in reply to me in Parliament. He then began to hedge. There were many different possibilities. The Danzig Senate might merely proclaim that Danzig was now part of the Reich. Nothing more might happen. If then the Poles occupied Danzig, the Germans might describe this as aggression. If we only had to deal with a reasonable Germany, it would be very natural and open to no real objection that Danzig should form part of the Reich. Some people, he said, were always warning him about the Poles, as being romantic and excitable people. Hence the difficulty of making a very precise declaration of warning to Hitler. It would be dangerous to say either too much or too little; too much, so that Hitler should feel he had no alternative but war, and the Poles be unreasonably encouraged; too little, lest Hitler should think there were some steps which he could take with impunity and then find out that he had been wrong. He praised Burckhardt,[1] the Swiss League Commissioner, who has apparently been flitting about between Ribbentrop and Beck, suggesting a possible solution whereby Danzig might be a Free City within the Reich, with a German–Polish guarantee of its new status, to remain unfortified, and Polish economic and financial rights to be maintained. It was possible, the P.M. thought, that some such arrangement as this might be acceptable. I said that I thought such a declaration as I had suggested might, none the less, be framed so as to have a restraining influence on Hitler

---

1 Carl Burckhardt. League of Nations High Commissioner in Danzig 1937–9.

and to reassure the Poles that we were not going to leave them in the lurch. (I did not say, 'As you did the Czechs', since I desired to get as much information as we could out of him.)

As to the Soviet Pact, I gathered two impressions, first that the P.M. makes more of the difficulties than Halifax, who once intervened to correct him regarding the attitude of the Baltic States, but, second, that, none the less, the P.M. realises that now a failure of the negotiations would be very damaging to him and to the Government and would be a great encouragement to Hitler. He told us a long story about how difficult it was to deal with the Russians, how full of suspicion they were, how they studied all our phrases under a microscope and read into them all sorts of sinister meanings which we had never intended. This was particularly so with Molotov, and the P.M. said that one of their difficulties had been that 'the Russians changed their Foreign Secretary just at a critical time. They got rid of Litvinov who, after all, was a man of the world. Negotiations with Molotov are not at all easy. He has never been out of Russia in his life. He sits up on a higher chair than the rest when negotiations take place, and this does not create a very friendly atmosphere. He only makes curt statements, rejecting or objecting to this or that proposal of ours. There is no real discussion.' ...

P.M. says that the latest instructions to Seeds,[1] which have been co-ordinated with the French instructions to Naggiar,[2] should give full satisfaction to Molotov, if he really desires to be satisfied. We have re-stated our objection to naming and guaranteeing the three Baltic States – namely that they are most unwilling to be named and guaranteed (the P.M. makes a slip here, saying 'Finland and Estonia have even told us that they would regard such a guarantee as an act of aggression', whereupon Halifax intervenes to correct him, saying, 'I don't think they went quite as far as that; what they said was that the entry of Russian troops under a claim to guarantee their independence would be regarded as an act of aggression') – but are telling Molotov that, if he still insists, we agree, provided that we also name Holland, Belgium and Switzerland, and the Soviet likewise guarantees them. Hitherto, H.M.G. has not guaranteed Holland and Switzerland, though we have privately informed the French that a German aggression against either would be regarded by us as an act of war. Further, it is understood that just as we and the French would be the judges of whether Holland, Belgium and Switzerland were victims of Nazi aggression, direct or indirect, so the Soviet Union would be judges

1 Sir William Seeds (1882–1973). British Ambassador to the Soviet Union 1939–40.
2 Paul-Émile Naggiar. French Ambassador to the Soviet Union 1938–40.

of whether or not aggression had been committed against any of the Baltic States. (If this is really in the instructions, it should remove yet another snag, mentioned to me by Maisky, namely that we were insisting on 'consultation' in respect of the three Baltic States, although claiming 'automatism' in other cases.) Further, said the P.M., we had agreed, although he greatly disliked it, to the insertion of a clause demanded by Molotov that if we were engaged in war, none of the three of us would conclude a separate peace. The objection to this was that circumstances might be such that the Russians would desire a war to continue whereas we and the French might believe that it should be concluded, and the Russians might be doing relatively little fighting. Further, although H.M.G. had originally proposed that there should be a reference to Article 16 of the Covenant of the League, we had now consented, in view of Russian objections, to eliminating any such reference. As to staff talks – we had asked whether any difficulty had arisen on this head and whether there was any unwillingness on our side to enter into such talks – the P.M. said that H.M.G. were perfectly willing to enter into staff talks as soon as the agreement was signed, and had so informed the Russians. At an earlier stage the latter had demanded that the agreement should not come into force until the staff talks had been held and completed, but we had pointed out that this was quite illogical and was contrary to what we had already done with the French, the Poles and the Turks, with all three of whom there had been staff talks following the signing of an agreement. The P.M. also told us – and this squares with information from Maisky – that Molotov had proposed, as an alternative to a more elaborate agreement, the conclusion of a simple Triple Pact of mutual assistance against direct aggression. I asked, 'Would not this be excellent, and a good beginning?' The P.M. said no, because it was so drafted by the Soviets as to exclude Soviet assistance to us if we became involved in war with Germany by reason of a German aggression against Poland, Romania or any other guaranteed State. (I am not sure either that this interpretation of the Soviet offer is correct, or that, assuming it to be correct, it could not have been modified and the obligations extended so as to cover any case in which any of the three Powers found themselves at war in Europe.)

We discussed the practical value of Russian assistance, and on this the P.M. was sceptical. He said they had from many quarters poor accounts of the efficiency of the Russian Army. Pressed by me as to the Russian Air Force, he admitted that many of the machines were very good, and likewise the pilots, but expressed doubt as to whether, given the enormous initial wastage which everyone expected would take place in the early stages of a war, the Russian power of production of aircraft and of organisation generally could long be maintained. In other words, Russian aid would not only be doubtful at the outset, but difficult to maintain even at its initial level. (I am very sceptical of all estimates on such matters. The hope is that all, including the Germans, will realise that there is a large element of doubt about the whole business, and that it may turn out worse for them than they think.)

I think, as stated above, that the P.M. realises the danger and damage of letting the negotiations now break down. None the less, when pressed by us as to his view of the consequences of such a breakdown, he said, in his flat, obstinate way, 'Well, I don't think that would be the end of the world.'

Thursday 29th June

Alexander tells me that he has had a telephone message from Chatham House regarding tonight's Annual Dinner at which Halifax is to speak. The message is that Halifax has been 'much concerned' at some of the things that were said by the N.C.L. deputation yesterday and that, in consequence, he has revised his speech considerably. A revise is being sent to Alexander, who later tells me that all the stiffest passages, which evoke much comment and general praise in our press next day, were new insertions in the second draft. I suspect that others, in addition to us three, had been at work on him, and that the message to us was partly soft soap.[1] None the less, I think we had at least a little to do with it. ...

Call on Raczynski ... I ... asked [him] what his latest information was about the situation in Danzig, and whether the attitude of his Government in this matter had changed at all since we had last spoken. He replied that he did not himself think that there was an immediate danger of war, i.e. not within the next few weeks. Beyond that it was hard to see. The German press had exaggerated the numbers of 'tourists' and other Germans who had come into Danzig from outside. The tactics of Hitler were the familiar 'psychological massage' which he applied to those who stood in his way. ...

I told him that we were still pressing our Government strongly to conclude the Soviet Pact, and asked him how this was now viewed in

---

1 The main direct influence appears to have been Vansittart. According to Cadogan (29th June): 'Dined at Chatham House for speech from Halifax that had been the bane of our lives for days. At last moment Van said we must put teeth into it. That quite right I think. So I sat down and wrote 2 pages – a moving paraphrase of "we don't want to fight, but by jingo if we do" &c.' (*Diaries*, p. 190.) In his speech Halifax declared that the threat of military force was holding the world to ransom, and the Government's immediate task was 'to resist aggression'.

Warsaw. He replied that, when Beck was in London, he was averse
to any direct arrangement between Warsaw and Moscow and also
somewhat discouraging to H.M.G. when they proposed negotiations
between themselves and the Russians. But this, said Raczynski, was
because Beck still wished to give Hitler the benefit of every possible
doubt and still hoped that, if Hitler saw that Britain and Poland intended to stand together, this would have a moderating effect on him.
Beck, therefore, was unwilling at this time to see the Russians brought
into the picture at all. Since then, however, 'things have gone from
bad to worse', Hitler having denounced both the Anglo–German
Naval Agreement and the German–Polish Peace Pact merely on the
ground of the Anglo–Polish arrangement, and having now intensified
his agitation in Danzig. Beck, therefore, today feels no objection to
an Anglo–Soviet Pact, though – and here Raczynski again quoted
from a telegram – he has warned the British not to expect too much,
by way of material aid, from the Russians even if the Pact is signed.
There still exist grave doubts in Poland as to Russian capacity, as
distinct from will, to bring help on a large scale.

Monday 10th July
Come back in the morning from West Leaze, having been sorely
tempted to stay down there another day, but have a Parliamentary
Question to Chamberlain on Anglo–Soviet negotiations. Speak to
Maillaud[?][1] in the morning, who says that latest formula of Molotov
is, the French think, 'not unacceptable'. The French, as usual, are trying to bridge gaps between us and the Russians, thinking us both unduly sticky. Corbin has been continuously active in this direction. The
latest formula relates to 'indirect aggression'.[2] I do not put any
Supplementaries to P.M. We are in a dilemma. Either we press the
Government or not. In the first case, we may encourage the Russians
to be more difficult and be represented by ministers here as impeding
the negotiations (Kirkpatrick has told Stokes that 'if only your Front
Bench would keep quiet for a little while, we could get an agreement');
in the other case, we are taken to be acquiescing in H.M.G.'s conduct
of the negotiations and make our supporters in the country impatient.

1 'Maillot' in the typescript. Probably Pierre Maillaud (1908–48), acting manager of
the Havas Agency in London and a well-known French journalist. Founded the
Free French *Agence française indépendante* in 1940. He became Secretary of the
Radical Socialist Party in 1947, using the name of Pierre Bourdan, and served in
the Ramadier Government as Minister for Youth, Arts and Information.
2 'indirect aggression'. Should the Soviet Union be given *carte blanche* to interfere
with smaller states if they became the victims of German pressure or attack? This
was one of the sticking points in the negotiations.

P.M., clumsily and curtly, in reply to V. Adams[1] who asked whether it was intended to send Halifax to Moscow, replied merely, 'No, sir.' Maillaud, whom I saw again in the afternoon, said that this was typically clumsy; it might well give the Russians further cause for offence.

The long statement by the P.M. on Danzig sounds fairly good. If one did not so distrust the man, one would be satisfied with it, but it does contain a possible get-out in referring in successive sentences to 'raising grave issues affecting the independence of Poland' and 'if Polish independence were clearly threatened'. Greenwood and I think, however, that no Supplementaries would help, particularly since the statement is a joint draft and P.M., if questioned, might do less well.

Raczynski is in the Gallery and I afterwards ring up Polish Embassy and ask Balinski to tell Raczynski that we thought the statement pretty satisfactory and, for this reason, sat tight and silent.

On 12th July, Dalton and Greenwood saw Halifax alone. 'Unless he was a much better actor than I suspected, he at least sincerely desired an Anglo-Soviet Pact', Dalton wrote later. 'But I doubted whether he asserted himself sufficiently against his colleagues.'[2]

Wednesday 12th July
Greenwood was less soft this afternoon than on previous occasions when I have been with him to see ministers, and began by putting the point that there was great concern, not only in our Party but in much wider circles, at the long delays over the Pact. I put it all a good deal more bluntly, and told Halifax that I thought it was a great mistake that he and Molotov had not yet met. I had suggested it before Whitsun in a P.Q. but the idea had been brushed aside. I appreciated that, if they met now for the first time with nothing settled, and after their meeting there was still nothing settled, this would be worse than not meeting, but I strongly urged that if only *something*, however partial, could be agreed and announced, a meeting would then both be good news and might, by diminishing mistrusts and misunderstandings, ease the next stages. Halifax did not disagree, though he said it would be very difficult for him to go to Moscow. He wondered whether

1 Vyvyan Adams (1900–51). Conservative M.P. for Leeds West 1931–45.
2 FY, p. 254.

Molotov would like to be invited here; he thought probably not, particularly for negotiations, since it seemed that he too had to refer everything back to a group of his own colleagues. (I thought, 'You like to suggest to us that he is tied by the leg just as tight as you!') I said, 'What about meeting at Geneva?' and Halifax said that he would be very glad to go if Molotov would go, but the next Council meeting was not till September. I said that we could not possibly avoid a debate before Parliament rose, but if there was still a real chance of pulling off an Anglo–Soviet agreement, it would be better to have the debate after this had been done. But I added that we were under very heavy pressure to have it all out in the House now. Halifax said that he quite understood this and thought that we had treated the Government very well in Parliament. He would be delighted to see us again at any time and tell us how things were going on. If a debate became necessary and no agreement had been reached, perhaps a ministerial statement, so phrased as to make the best of a bad job, could be drawn up and shown to us before the debate. He did not ask for an answer on this now, but perhaps we would think it over.

On the possibility of falling back on a simple Three-Power Pact for mutual assistance against direct aggression, Halifax said that the French were wholly against this. It would be a plain confession of defeat, would encourage Hitler, and would not cover any of the most dangerous cases, e.g. a German attack on Poland or Romania. I said, 'If that is to be ruled out, do try and think of some other partial agreement which could be announced and which would do something to restore confidence while further discussions were going on.' He said he was already turning this over in his mind.

As we were leaving, he said that he had seen Raczynski who reported that the Poles were in a very confident mood. Beck was quite satisfied with the P.M.'s declaration on Danzig. H.M.G. was sending General Ironside[1] to Poland to talk to Smigly-Rydz.[2] This would not be officially announced but would certainly leak out. I said, 'You should also send British bombers on training flights over Poland as well as over France, and let that leak out too.'

---

1 General Sir William Ironside, later Field-Marshal, 1st Baron (1880–1959). Inspector-General of Overseas Forces 1939; Chief of Imperial General Staff September 1939–May 1940. Commander-in-Chief Home Forces 1940.
2 General E. Smigly-Rydz (1886–1941). Pilsudski's successor as Inspector-General of the Polish Army 1935–9. Marshal of Poland 1936–9. Commander-in-Chief of the Polish forces at the time of the German invasion.

Friday 21st July

Maillaud says that, in their latest instructions to Moscow, the British now accept the principle of simultaneous political and military agreement, but still reject the Russian definition of Indirect Aggression as being too wide. The French government have pressed the British to give way on this last point also, being most desirous of getting the Pact signed and regarding it as vital for the peace of Europe. I said that I feared that some of our Cabinet wanted to break with the Russians and to break most plausibly.

As to the financial negotiations with Poland, Maillaud says that Leith-Ross[1] has sent a most rude and curt note to the Poles, rejecting their demand that they shall be free to spend the proceeds of our Loan where they like, and insisting that they shall only have credits to be controlled and expended here, in spite of the fact that they need many things which we cannot at present supply. Maillaud says that he has seen many diplomatic notes in the past, but none so rude as this. On these negotiations also the French have been urging us to give way, since it is urgent to reach agreement.

The third stage of the Anglo–Soviet negotiations, the military talks, ended inconclusively on 21st August. Late the same day, it was announced that Ribbentrop, the German Foreign Minister, had been invited to Moscow. Two days later Ribbentrop and Molotov signed a non-aggression pact between their two countries – sealing the fate of Poland.

Tuesday 22nd August

From Aldbourne to London, as news in the morning papers seems bad. German pressure against Poland is increasing and there is news of the projected German–Russian Pact. Our family *mot d'ordre* is 'no wobble'; Ruth fears that I may find some colleagues wobbling, but in fact it is not so.

Some time making any contacts; Citrine out of London; Greenwood out of touch till after 3 p.m. He, however, is doing pretty well – better than poor little Rabbit[2] ever did – seeing the P.M. and Halifax

1 Sir Frederick Leith-Ross (1887–1968). Chief Economic Adviser to the Government 1932–46. Director-General of the Ministry of Economic Warfare 1939–42. Deputy Director-General of the United Nations Relief and Rehabilitation Administration (U.N.R.R.A.) 1944–5.
2 'Rabbit': Dalton's private name for Attlee.

frequently, taking notes after his talks, and reporting pretty fully to colleagues.

Thursday 24th August
At Parliamentary E.C. this morning I raised the question of any of our people joining a mixed bag government. I say that I assume no one is committed, nor will commit himself, to this without authority from the Party. Greenwood, rather nervously I thought, said, 'Of course not; I haven't heard of anyone being approached.' Snell said, 'I hope that will apply to Trade Union leaders outside Parliament as well. There are rumours about some of them.' The meeting was, however, unanimous in my sense, it being understood that administrative work, such as Johnston and Alexander were already committed to, was not banned.

At Party Meeting immediately after, this question was raised and Rabbit, from Chair, said that no one had been approached and no one would accept unless Party so decided. 'We have our own constitution', he said.[1]

On 25th August Britain and Poland signed a treaty of mutual assistance. On 1st September German troops crossed the Polish frontier. A British ultimatum was issued on 3rd September at 9 a.m. and expired two hours later. During these last days of peace, Labour leaders did what they could to stiffen the Government's resolve, and to anticipate any possible weakening which might lead to a new exercise in appeasement. Between 25th and 30th August, Dalton and Citrine occupied themselves with a furious row over the refusal of the B.B.C. to broadcast a Labour Message to the German People. This dispute, irrelevant to last-minute efforts to prevent war, helped to establish ground rules for the treatment of the Labour Party and trade unions by the B.B.C.

Friday 25th August
Same question raised at meeting of Three Bodies. Marchbank[2] spoke violently in semi-revolutionary language, as I have heard him often

1 In 1933 the Labour Party had decided that, to prevent a repetition of 1931, a decision about whether or not to join a coalition government should be referred first to a special conference. In May 1940, the N.E.C. ignored this decision, Labour leaders accepted ministerial posts, and the Labour Party Conference (which happened to be in session at Bournemouth) overwhelmingly endorsed these actions.
2 John Marchbank (1883–1946). General Secretary of the National Union of Railwaymen 1934–42; President 1922–4.

283

before, against 'this Government'. Some wanted to pass and publish a resolution declaring that, if asked, we should refuse. But this was not done, when Citrine pointed out that we should make ourselves ridiculous; and Lees-Smith that we should give Goebbels a bull point.

These ventilations have, I think, done good. My present feeling is that we should decline participation in government if war comes – at least at the beginning. I remember how Arthur Henderson fared in the Great War, and it is not as if our present 'leaders' were supermen capable of exercising vast influence though in a tiny majority.

At meeting of the three Executives it was decided, on my proposition, to send a final Message of friendship and warning to the German people. It was left to Laski and myself, with the Chairmen and Secretaries, to make a draft. This we did in the afternoon, and, its terms having been finally agreed, I took steps with Will Henderson, from his office, for its broadcasting. Copies were sent to the B.B.C. (including additional copies to its Foreign News department); also to Vansittart's Private Secretary and to G. P. Young,[1] Perth's secretary at the F.O. Laski had spoken to de Margerie[2] at the French Embassy asking him to get it put over in German from Strasburg and Luxemburg. De Margerie had expressed approval but told us that the practice now was for the British Foreign Office to pass through all requests to the French for the use of these two stations. This is why, having failed to get Van on the telephone as he was deeply engaged, I sent two copies to his secretary. Copies were also sent – though not, apparently, delivered, owing to some error by the messenger – to the Polish Ambassador[3] to be put over in German from Polish stations.

On Laski's proposal, which I supported, it was agreed that we should ask the B.B.C. to let Citrine, in his dual capacity of Secretary of the T.U.C. and President of the I.F.T.U. [International Federation of Trades Unions], himself deliver the Message in English on the short-wave length. It was felt that this would make the Message more impressive and personal to the many Germans who listen in to British news. (The Message was only some 450 words long and would have taken only some three minutes to read.) I speak to Ogilvie's[4] secretary, a little before 5 p.m., conveying this request, and she promises to let me have a speedy answer.

---

1 G. P. Young, later Sir George, 5th Bart (1908–60). Second Secretary at the Foreign Office 1938–40.
2 Possibly Roland de Margerie, *chef de cabinet* to Reynaud as Prime Minister.
3 Count Raczynski, q.v.
4 F. W. Ogilvie, later Sir Frederick (1893–1949). Director-General of the B.B.C. 1938–42. Professor of Political Economy at Edinburgh University 1926–34; Vice-Chancellor of Queen's University, Belfast 1934–8.

I am, however, kept waiting for nearly an hour by the B.B.C., being told more than once, when I have rung up to ask whether a decision has yet been reached, that 'there is a consultation going on now about it', and that 'there are some difficulties which are being gone into'. Finally, about 6 p.m., Ogilvie rings through and says that some points have arisen which are difficult to discuss on the telephone, but would I come round and see him. I reply that I will come with Citrine.

At Broadcasting House we see Ogilvie and Graves.[1] Ogilvie begins by explaining, in opposition to our proposal that Citrine should deliver the Message, that it is the B.B.C.'s experience that messages are less effective when delivered personally than when reported as news. We do not accept this view, but admit that it is a technical question on which the B.B.C. are entitled to their opinion. I then say, 'Very well then, I take it that you will put over our Message as news, both in your English bulletins tonight and in your translations, especially the German.' Ogilvie replies that he 'hesitates' to give any undertaking on this matter. Both Citrine and I take him up very sharply at this point. We ask whether he is suggesting that what the Labour Movement has to say at such a time is not news. I tell him that 'We are not nobodies'; this message is spoken in the name of many millions of Trade Unionists and electors, and by the representatives of the alternative Government in this country. Citrine says that he has had previous experience of mutilation of important material submitted to the B.B.C. Ogilvie shows signs of being very uncomfortable; he tries to take back his words and regrets that we have put the interpretation upon them that we have. He also expresses the hope that our conversation has been quite confidential. After some further exchanges, I say, 'I am now going to ask you a question to which, I give you notice, I am not going to treat your answer as confidential. The question is, do you or do you not undertake to put over tonight, both in the British and the foreign bulletins, a reasonably full version of our Message?' He declines to give a straight answer to this question and says, 'You must wait and judge by results.' We warn him that if our Message is not properly put over, he will hear more of this, and Citrine tells him very frankly that he is not fit for responsibility. We then leave, Ogilvie accompanying us to the ground floor in the lift and endeavouring to make friendly advances on other matters. It is now 7.40 p.m.

I arrive at a friend's house a little before 8 p.m. and find two tele-

---

1 Capt. C. G. Graves, later Sir Cecil (1892–1957). Deputy Director-General of the B.B.C. 1938–42; Joint Director-General 1942–3.

phone messages, one from the Polish Embassy to say that our copy of the broadcast has not arrived, and the other from the Foreign Office. I take the second first, and find that Butler[1] wishes to speak to me. He says that our Message has been considered by Halifax himself and by 'all our experts'. Their view is that it would be inadvisable to send it over from Strasburg and Luxemburg tonight. I ask why, and he replies, first because a long new message has just come in from Nevile Henderson, which is even now being deciphered, and second, because the Foreign Office has evidence that 'in many parts of Germany where your Message would normally have made a strong appeal', such as Saxony and many of the mining areas, the workers are so delighted with the Pact with Russia that they are walking about with the swastika in one hand and the hammer and sickle in the other. I do not enter into any debate with Butler on the telephone, but tell him that there may have to be further considerations of this whole question by us, and that we have already this evening 'had words' with the B.B.C. on the subject. He says, 'I am not surprised to hear that.' I say that I presume he realises that our Message will be published tomorrow by the press, as it has gone some hours ago to all the agencies. I understand that he is only speaking to me about Strasburg and Luxemburg, and that the Foreign Office is not proposing to try to prevent publication by the newspapers. He says, 'Oh no, of course not.' I finally ask whether the opinion which he expressed to me that the Message should not go over the air in France would apply also to the air in Poland. He says, 'Yes, certainly, I think that would be even more dangerous.' I say that I take note of his opinion but that I am not going to enter into any argument with him at this stage. He offers to see me tomorrow if I should wish. ...

I listen in to the 9 o'clock news in English. Only two sentences are picked out of our Message and reported. I listen in also to the B.B.C. news in French, German and Italian between 10 and 11 p.m. In all these three foreign languages it is stated, 'The British Labour Movement has today sent a Message to the German people'. That is all, no hint of the contents of the Message and not a word of quotation. Ogilvie asked us to 'wait and judge by results'. These are the results!
......

---

1 R. A. Butler, later Baron (1902–82). Parliamentary Under-Secretary of State for Foreign Affairs 1938–41. Conservative M.P. for Saffron Walden 1929–65. Junior minister 1932–8. President of the Board of Education, then Minister of Education 1941–5. Minister of Labour 1945. Chancellor of the Exchequer 1951–5; Lord Privy Seal 1955–9; Home Secretary 1957–62; Deputy Prime Minister 1962–3; Foreign Secretary 1963–4. Master of Trinity College, Cambridge 1965–78.

I do not think that the matter can be allowed to rest here, particularly at a time when the Government are trying to enlist our aid in connection with propaganda and Ministry of Information. What has happened is that they have deliberately censored our Message.

Monday 28th August
Citrine writes to Halifax a long and strong letter on the treatment of our Message. He sets out the facts, emphasises that, in our interview with Ogilvie, we were 'treated like children', and that Ogilvie tried to make us believe that his 'consultations' were to be entirely with his subordinates on technical matters. We, on the other hand, realise quite clearly that it was the Foreign Office whom he had to consult.[1] Citrine goes on to say that he is instructed by the N.C.L. to state that they took a very grave view of this incident and of the management of the B.B.C. They were determined not to let the matter rest where it was, and he himself was disposed to advise the General Council of the T.U.C. to take no further part in any form of co-operation with the Ministry of Information. The Council desired to send a deputation – him, me and Phil Noel-Baker – to see Halifax, and would be glad if he would telephone, on receipt of the letter, what hour that night he could see us.

Later, Butler came on the phone to Citrine and said that Halifax was very much concerned over the whole matter and was most anxious that it should be fully investigated and that nothing should be said or done which would prevent the full co-operation of the N.C.L. with the Government in publicity and other ways.

Tuesday 29th August
When the House meets this afternoon, Butler engages me in conversation, and I go alone to his private room ... Butler said that there had been 'a difference of opinion' in the office on the subject, and it had undoubtedly been very much mishandled. Halifax and he were most anxious to create some machinery – none now existed – to prevent any repetition of such an incident ...

7 p.m. Interview at Foreign Office. Halifax, Butler and Perth; Citrine, Phil [Noel-Baker] and I. Citrine states the case very clearly and forcibly. Says that, in his view, Ogilvie is not fit for his job and that Graves, his deputy, seems to try to impersonate Napoleon, who walks up and down the room as impressively as he can with his hand

1 The real reason for Ogilvie's refusal to broadcast the Message was a telephone call from the Prime Minister's Office (B.B.C. Written Archives File R 51/600/1 1A. Record of Telephone Conversation 25th August 1939, 5.15 p.m., Prime Minister's Secretary to the B.B.C.). I am grateful to Jean Seaton for this reference.

inside his coat, and gains a reputation for strength and wisdom by saying nothing. Citrine also says that our people are getting pretty fed up with being expected to shout with the Government one day and being treated like a lot of children or nobodies the next. Both Citrine and I completely repudiate Ogilvie's allegation that he told us it was the F.O. whom he was to consult. I ask Halifax for more information regarding the reasons why our Message was suppressed. He can only repeat that it was felt that appeals today were not effective, nor were attempts to divide Hitler from the German people. I ask if this is all. He says, so far as he knows, yes. He repeats what Butler had told me, that neither of them knew of the decision; nor did Perth; it was taken on the judgment of his officials, for whom, of course, he must accept responsibility. 'Then', I say, 'I venture to remark that whatever officials advised you on those grounds to suppress our Message never attempted to apply their intelligence to the question at all. These are most superficial and trivial considerations. In so far as they have weight, they can be met by a few minor drafting amendments. I know many of the officials in this office. For some I have a high regard; for others a less high regard. I do not ask you which of them was responsible for giving you this advice, or rather taking this important decision without consulting either yourself or Butler, but I do say that whoever it may have been, you have been ill served. Phil weighed in a bit and said that this had a great bearing upon our future co-operation with the Ministry of Information. He was quite sure he could not co-operate if we were to be treated like this. Here Perth, making himself almost excessively affable, sought to pour gallons of oil upon the troubled waters; placed himself unreservedly at the disposition of any of us at any time; said that it was his dearest wish to have the very closest contact with the representatives of the Labour Movement in all phases of the work of his Department; trusted that we should exercise a great influence upon this work, and paid a tribute to the many sources of information which we had, both here and abroad, of which he hoped that we should allow him, in consultation with us, fully to avail himself. He almost, but not quite, said that if we refused to help him he would chuck up his job in despair. Citrine ignored most of this, merely saying that if Perth or the Government thought that we should be satisfied in having one member, who would count for nothing in an Advisory Committee of twenty, they were much mistaken. Perth replied that he hoped, on the contrary, that we should exercise an influence not less than that of any other section of the community. Halifax then tried to defend Ogilvie. He said that when he had been one of a group of young Tory M.P.s who 'used to rag Lloyd George', Ogilvie had devilled for them and collected their material. He knew him to be a first-rate man. Citrine said, 'He might have been good enough to collect material to help you to rag Lloyd George, but that doesn't satisfy me that he is fit to be Director-General of the B.B.C.' Halifax said, 'I can only say that I know you are mistaken about Ogilvie.' ...

Finally, just as we were breaking up, I said, 'And now, what about our Message? Would it not be helpful now that, perhaps with a few modifications, it should be broadcast after all?' I repeated that nothing I had heard this evening had suggested to me that anything more than minor amendments would be required. Halifax, I think, was rather vexed with me at this point, and said, 'Perhaps you would like to have a talk with Lord Perth about that.' I asked Citrine whether he saw any objection to such a talk from our point of view. He said no, and it was therefore fixed that we should meet next morning.

I raised this point at the end, partly because I was anxious to make them broadcast after all, thereby publicly admitting they had been wrong, and also because I also wanted to make contact with Perth at this stage and find out what he was up to.

I was amused to see how this incident had given rise already to a fat dossier. Both Perth and Butler had a thick lump of papers in their hands. ...

At 6 this evening the N.C.L. meets to hear reports, including that of the deputation – Citrine, Morrison and Mrs Gould – who have been to Chamberlain to urge immediate evacuation of priority classes from London and other evacuation areas. Greenwood this afternoon urged this point in his speech, and yesterday the N.C.L. had authorised Citrine to write to the Prime Minister on the subject.

It appears that the transport system could not complete this measure of evacuation in less than three and a half days. Morrison says that, having at first been sceptical, he has gone into the details and is satisfied that this is the shortest practicable period. Marchbank, speaking as a railwayman, says that he thinks the schedule is too optimistic, particularly as it would be necessary to move great quantities of goods traffic for military needs in the first days of a war. In other words, evacuation may take longer if you wait till war is started than if you do it now, quite apart from the dangers of interference with the process by air attack.

The deputation reported that Anderson[1] had been with the P.M.

1 Sir John Anderson, later 1st Viscount Waverley (1882–1958). Lord Privy Seal 1938–9; Home Secretary and Minister of Home Security 1939–40. Independent National M.P. for the Scottish Universities 1938–50. Lord President of the Council 1940–43; Chancellor of the Exchequer 1943–5. Civil Service career: Permanent Under-Secretary at the Home Office 1922–32; Governor of Bengal 1932–7.

It is known, from a report by Greenwood, that Anderson had wished to start evacuation on the morning of Monday 28th. He had told one of our people on the Sunday afternoon, 27th, that he was asking the P.M. 'to give me the word go'. On the other hand, the P.M. and, it is rumoured, Simon, were against it. The P.M. had told the deputation that it was a most difficult matter to decide and he admitted that the balance of argument was nearly level, but it was still the view of the Government that the moment to begin evacuation had not come. He then produced a series of snag-hunter's arguments, typical of the Civil Service mind at its most obstructive. 'If you sent the children away, and there was no war, when would you bring them back again?' 'If you kept them away some time, their mothers would become very discontented, and there would be strong demands either that the children should be brought back, or that the mothers should be allowed to go and see them. In either case, this would lead to great discontent and inconvenience.' 'Would there not be great dissatisfaction in the receiving areas, if all the inconvenience of reception continued for some time and there was still no war?' 'Would not the evacuation of the priority classes cause serious panic in the rest of the community?' 'Would not business men and others then wish to move, even though it was in the national interest that they should stay?' The P.M. added that he fully realised his responsibilities. After a sentimental reference to the 'young children who are always in our minds', he told the deputation that he was a grandfather himself. When someone said that many of the children had a grievance against Hitler because he prevented evacuation last September, Anderson, trying to be bright and pawky, said, 'I should have thought they would have had a grievance against the Prime Minister.'

The N.C.L. felt that nothing more could be done at present but that we had done our duty in putting the case strongly, and that our action would now be on record for the future. ...

Butler told me tonight in the House that Nevile Henderson was now doing very well in Berlin, though 'about three months ago Halifax was on the point of sacking him'. He had now recovered his health and was putting our point of view very effectively. Last night, when Hitler had dwelt upon the kinship of Germany and England, Henderson had replied that Hitler, he was sure, would agree that it would be neither a German nor an English act to break one's word to a friend (i.e., in our case, to Poland).

Wednesday 30th August
As arranged yesterday, see Perth at the Foreign Office this morning.

Phil also arrives – late – and Kirkpatrick is brought in halfway through. Perth explains that Kirkpatrick had no responsibility for the treatment of our Message. Perth suggests at an early stage that he would be prepared to recommend Ogilvie to broadcast tonight in the German news our Message, with only a few changes. ...

We leave it, therefore, that Perth will advise Ogilvie. Perth explains elaborately that of course Ogilvie is the final arbiter. I merely observe that if Ogilvie refuses his advice we shall take our own measures, both by publicity and otherwise. ...

10.15 p.m. Listen in to the B.B.C. News in German. Our 'Message', transformed into a 'Statement', and with one or two very unimportant omissions, exactly as agreed between me and Perth this morning, was put over with great gusto and licking of lips by B.B.C. spokesman. ...

At the end of talk with Perth about Broadcast, Kirkpatrick – who was for some time Counsellor in Berlin – says that Hitler is 'a very odd man', but he is not a madman and in some ways is supremely shrewd. Kirkpatrick believes him to be at bottom a coward, but just for this reason it is very rash to charge him with cowardice or he will try to disprove the accusation. Kirkpatrick hears that Hitler is suffering from *le petit mal*, which gives rise to *mild* epileptic fits. He does not, often at any rate, roll on the ground losing all control, but he is apt to have 'brain storms' which, when he is over-wrought, tend to become more frequent and more serious. ...

The Russians, he thought, were leaving every door ajar. There had been tremendous disillusion among the more doctrinaire Nazis at the Pact with Moscow. Rosenberg,[1] for instance, did not know what to say now. I said I hoped that the photographs of Stalin grinning and Ribbentrop looking solemn had been widely published in Germany. He said they had.

He said at parting, 'I think we have just about a 20 per cent chance of avoiding war.'

Thursday 31st August
Soon after noon, Loxley,[2] Butler's Private Secretary at the Foreign Office, rings up to say that Butler had wished to speak to me but has just been summoned by the Secretary of State. He wishes to tell me that the B.B.C. have decided to repeat our 'Statement' in German today in their midday bulletin. I express satisfaction and say 'We are doing quite well in the end.' ...

---

1 Alfred Rosenberg (1893–1945). Nazi ideologist. Minister for the Occupied Eastern Territories during the war. Executed for war crimes against the Russian people.
2 Peter Loxley (1905–45). Diplomat (First Secretary) seconded to the Ministry of Economic Warfare 1939–40. Private Secretary to Sir Alexander Cadogan 1941–5.

Friday 1st September[1]

I called on Raczynski soon after noon today. I told him that yesterday Greenwood had told Halifax that he had found Raczynski gravely uneasy, and that in his view Raczynski had some grounds for concern. Raczynski expressed to me his thanks and deep gratification at this action by Greenwood.

Raczynski gave me further particulars based on the latest information from Warsaw of the number of Polish towns already bombarded. He said that it appeared that every open town of any substantial size in Poland, except perhaps Lvov, had already been attacked. He had had illusions, he said, that perhaps the Germans would not begin bombardment of civilian populations, but these had now vanished. It was clear to him that they had intended to terrorise the Polish population everywhere.

I asked him whether he was fully satisfied with his latest contacts with ministers. He said yes. Immediately on hearing from Warsaw this morning, he had sought an interview with Halifax and said to him that, in his view, the Anglo-Polish Treaty had now become applicable, since Germany had committed an aggression against Poland. Halifax replied: 'I have no more doubt on that point than you have.' He had then thought it necessary to see the Prime Minister, but had not seen him as the Cabinet was just assembling. He had, however, met Simon in the passage, and the latter had said: 'Well, we are in the same boat now. England never breaks her word to her friends.' Raczynski then said to me that, as he had always regarded Simon as the most unsatisfactory of all British ministers, he thought this was specially significant.

He thought that Hitler's latest reference to Italy was clever. It was intended as a last effort to intimidate England and France. He felt sure now that when we moved, Italy would come in. I said that in this case Mussolini would soon fall. He said that all these things took longer than one anticipated at the beginning.

I asked him what he thought about Russia's intentions. He said that he was, and would for some time continue to be, very apprehensive on this point. But he was surprised that Hitler's references to Russia were not warmer. He thought this meant that Hitler had not yet got the full German–Russian military alliance which he wanted. He added that Hitler would now be quite prepared to make any promises, however extravagant, to the Russians if thereby he could win them to his side. 'He might, for instance,' he said, 'offer them the greater part of Poland, and Hungary, and Romania, and Constantinople,

1 'Note by Hugh Dalton' in Dalton Papers 3/2 (1), (2).

and the Straits. But I do not know whether that sort of bait would tempt the present rulers in Moscow.'

He said that, looking back now over more than a year, he had consistently felt that Hitler's policy must inevitably lead to war. None the less, he had always believed that a miracle was possible, but now this belief had been shattered. He showed, as always, great calm and dignity.

5

Phoney War
1939–40

War came as a relief to Labour leaders, who suspected the Government of preparing another Munich. The mood was summed up in a brief exchange outside the Foreign Office building, in the early hours of 3rd September. 'Can you give me any hope?' Dalton asked Lord Halifax. 'If you mean hope of war I think I can promise you a certainty for tomorrow,' replied the Foreign Secretary. 'Thank God,' said Dalton.[1] What had been feared for so long was now embraced as the only alternative to another round of betrayal and submission.

Nevertheless, Labour refused to join a war ministry headed by Chamberlain. There was no retreat from the decisions of 24th and 25th August, when the Three Bodies of the Labour Movement (Parliamentary Executive, N.E.C. and T.U.C. General Council) had resolved that nobody should join the Government without authority – a stance designed to prevent the Prime Minister from making selective pickings among Labour leaders in order to give his administration a more 'National' appearance, as MacDonald had done in 1931. The Labour Party disliked and distrusted Chamberlain. It also believed that to take a few offices would be to accept responsibility for the conduct of the war without the power to alter its direction.

Labour's attitude had major consequences. Without the support of the Opposition, the Prime Minister was unable to present himself as the leader of the people. At the same time, Labour politicians could dissociate themselves completely from the Government's failures. Labour's decision also made it more necessary for Chamberlain to guard his own flank by bringing into the Cabinet the two most influential anti-appeasers on the Conservative back-benches, Churchill and Eden. Finally, by holding aloof from this particular Government while supporting the war effort, Labour made the

1 The Earl of Halifax, *The Fulness of Days*, Collins, London, 1957, p. 270. For Dalton's version of the same incident (based on his diary entry), see FY, p. 267.

creation of a broad patriotic front seem the *sine qua non* of military victory.

During the first eight months of the war, Labour bided its time, consenting to an electoral truce. It was decided to maintain a special liaison with leading ministers. Since Attlee was sick in hospital, Greenwood, as Deputy Leader, was detailed to keep in touch with the Prime Minister and Foreign Secretary. Alexander agreed to liaise with the First Lord of the Admiralty, Lees-Smith with the Secretary of State for War, Pethick-Lawrence with the Chancellor of the Exchequer, and Dalton with the Air Minister and the Minister of Economic Warfare. The War Cabinet accepted this arrangement, permitting Labour front-bench spokesmen to keep up informal contacts while refusing to let them have information as of right.[1]

In addition to regular meetings with Kingsley Wood at the Air Ministry and Ronald Cross at the Ministry of Economic Warfare (M.E.W.), Dalton visited Churchill at the Admiralty, and frequently saw foreign politicians and diplomats, especially among the defeated Poles. One of Dalton's most useful sources of inside information was Hugh Gaitskell, now working as a temporary civil servant in the Economic Intelligence Unit at M.E.W. Gaitskell encouraged him to believe that the Government was faint-hearted in its pursuit of the economic blockade, and helping to shape his attitude as Minister a few months later.

For the moment, Labour made no attempt to displace Chamberlain, largely because this seemed impossible. It was also true that despite Labour's hostility towards Chamberlain personally, little now separated Labour M.P.s and Chamberlainites on the central issue of the day. Both hoped that the war would somehow go away without the necessity of having to fight it. Labour stuck to the official belief that the German working class might yet provide a solution. 'Victory for democracy must be achieved', declared a statement of War Aims in February 1940, 'either by arms or economic pressure or – better still – by a victory of the German people over the Hitler regime, resulting in the birth of a new Germany.'[2] All the same, the electoral truce did not please the Labour rank and file, and by the spring of 1940 many Party leaders were looking for an excuse to break with the Government completely.

Such an opportunity was provided by the Norway campaign. The humiliation of British forces at Namsos and Åndalsnes suddenly changed the political situation at home – and determined the future course of the war. Under pressure from the Opposition, the Government agreed to a debate, to be held on 7th and 8th May. Now at last the great pincer movement – Tory dissidents and Labour combined, Harold Macmillan's dream of a '1931 in reverse' – came into operation. Some Labour leaders, including Dalton,

1 PRO, War Cabinet Conclusions, 6th September 1939.
2 Labour Party Annual Conference Report (1940), pp. 188–9.

wondered whether the moment to strike had yet arrived. At a meeting of the P.L.P. Executive on 3rd May, Dalton argued that 'a vote at this stage was likely to consolidate the Government majority and that Chamberlain and Margesson[1] would like us to have one'.[2] But the majority disagreed, and the full Parliamentary Party endorsed an Executive decision to divide the House on the unusual motion of an adjournment for the Whitsun recess. The debate that followed proved to be one of the most dramatic in parliamentary history.

In the crucial division, forty-one M.P.s who usually supported the Government voted with the Opposition, and sixty-five were absent unpaired. This was seen as a massive blow to the Prime Minister's authority. Nevertheless, the Government had not been defeated, and its future still hung in the balance. What settled the issue, and put Churchill in power, was Labour's continued refusal to join an administration of which Chamberlain remained head. The Prime Minister raised the question one more time. Attlee replied bluntly, 'The fact is our party won't come in under you. Our party won't have you either.'[3] Chamberlain resigned forthwith.

The expected successor was the Foreign Secretary, acceptable to the Labour Party and to Chamberlainites alike. But Halifax did not want the job, and so Churchill was called to the Palace instead. The new Prime Minister kissed hands at 6 p.m. on 10th May 1940. The new Government was erected over the next few days, while Labour leaders met in Bournemouth in preparation for Party Conference. Discussions in London between the Prime Minister and Attlee and Greenwood (Leader and Deputy Leader of the Labour Party) were reported, as they took place, to the N.E.C. in Bournemouth. Attlee spoke to Dalton on the telephone, and Dalton relayed messages back and forth. Presented with the offer of two Labour ministers in a War Cabinet of five, the N.E.C., the National Council of Labour, and finally Party Conference, agreed that Labour should enter a Coalition.

Apart from its account of machinations to remove Chamberlain from office, the diary for the phoney war period is of special interest because of the impression it conveys of British indecision and inaction, as Hitler prepared his onslaught on the West.

---

1 Captain H. D. R. Margesson, q.v., Government Chief Whip.
2 FY, p. 305.
3 Francis Williams, *A Prime Minister Remembers*, Heinemann, London, 1961, pp. 32–3.

Wednesday 6th September

David Keir, and later Maurice Webb, ask me about our liaison arrangements. I tell them that our attitude towards the Government is one of 'cold, critical, patriotic detachment'. Alternatively, we shall act as patriotic gadflies on ministers. We shall still be free to criticise if we think fit in the House, and the so-called 'political truce' whereby no contested elections take place for the time being, is subject to termination at any time at our discretion.

......

I speak to Butler in his room and warn him that if Ogilvie does not hurry up and arrange his broadcasts in Polish, Czech, Serbo-Croat, Romanian, etc., I shall name him in the House. I ask Butler to let him know that we are greatly dissatisfied. The other incident, however, about the broadcast, is now handsomely closed, though no credit for this belongs to Ogilvie. ...

He asks why we decline to join the Government. I tell him that I will answer this question quite frankly. Having regard to our frequently expressed views of the P.M. and Simon, we could not enter a Cabinet in which these two were Numbers 1 and 2. Moreover, we should require the influence of Sir Horace Wilson to be eliminated. If we read that he had been appointed Governor of the Windward Islands and had already left England in order to take up this most respected position, we should be favourably impressed. (He asked whether we really attached as much importance to Wilson as this. I say, 'Yes, certainly, and I have so told a member of the War Cabinet, and one of my colleagues has so told another.') Continuing, I point out that if, for instance, members of the Labour Party were given, say, one seat in the Inner Cabinet, plus the Postmaster-General and the Secretaryship of State for Latrines, we should not only be uninfluential within, but we should lose most of our power to exercise influence from without, since we should be continually referred to 'Your Mr So-and-So, who is now a Secretary of State'. Further, we should lose much of our own credit amongst our own people, who would be filled with suspicions at our official participation. He said that he agreed that these were weighty arguments.

Sunday 10th September

Meet Gaitskell and Postan[1] at lunch. Both are at present in very

1 M. M. Postan, later Sir Michael (1898–1981). Head of Section, M.E.W. 1939–42. Professor of Economic History at Cambridge 1935–65. Lecturer at University College, London 1927–31, where he was a colleague of Gaitskell; L.S.E. 1931–5, where he was a colleague of Dalton.

subordinate positions in the M.E.W. [Ministry of Economic Warfare], but no doubt will be promoted later. The only other economists are Hall,[1] who has charge of a Section, Benham[2] (the only member of the L.S.E. staff to be taken on), who is supposed to know facts about Turkey and neighbouring countries, and Peggy Joseph,[3] who is said to be able but is only a name to me. Postan says that there is nothing to be bought by the Germans from Russia, but this is the end of his optimism. He is apprehensive of large leakages through Italy and, to a lesser extent, Yugoslavia. He says that Italy is importing large quantities of oil from Romania and Russia, though at the outbreak of war she was completely without stocks, and this was the real reason why she could not come in. She had 'emptied all her oil tanks' into Germany. He thinks she would be better as an enemy than as a leaky neutral.

Both Gaitskell and Postan are inclined to be pessimistic by nature, but I tell Gaitskell that I hope he will keep me regularly informed of what is going on in the Ministry.

Monday 11th September
Saw Kingsley Wood at 2.30 p.m. I told him that I took my duties in relation to him and his Department quite seriously. It was understood that all he told me I should tell Greenwood. To others I should tell some, but not all. ...

See Raczynski, who is much disturbed at relative passivity of French and British in the West. He thinks that telephone conversations to the Embassy will now be tapped as a normal war measure. He is anxious not to get into unnecessary trouble with the Government; hence the need for caution on the telephone, particularly at his end. Bracken, he says, rings him up regularly, but Churchill has become, naturally, less accessible since he entered the War Cabinet. Lloyd has not been in touch with him for several days. ...

---

1 N. F. Hall, later Sir Noel (1902–83). Director of the National Institute of Economic and Social Research 1938–43. Seconded to M.E.W., where he was in charge of the German Intelligence Section, and later in 1939 became Director of Intelligence. Joint Director of M.E.W. 1940–41. Lecturer, then Professor, of Political Economy at University College, London (where he appointed Gaitskell to his staff) 1927–38. Principal of Brasenose College, Oxford 1960–73.

2 F. C. C. Benham (1900–62). Cassel Reader in Commerce at the L.S.E. 1931–9; Professor 1945–7. Research Professor of International Economics at the Royal Institute of International Affairs 1955–62.

3 Margaret Joseph. Co-author (with Nicholas Kaldor) of *Economic Construction after the War*, English Universities Press, London, 1943.

The Polish general who has come over here on the special mission had seen the General Staff. Raczynski regrets that he was not present at the interview, as he doubts whether the generals completely understood one another. His general reported that the British said that there will be large-scale and persistent ground fighting in the West, and that this has already begun; that, in the air, the British and French Air Forces are now acting in support of the ground troops. But whether, as regards the separate air arm, long-range air attack is to be undertaken, is still in the balance, the decision not yet having been taken by the War Cabinet.

Raczynski feels that this is most unsatisfactory. To sacrifice an Eastern Front altogether is a tremendous price to pay for whatever advantages are supposed to result from air inactivity in the West. Ciano is saying in Rome that the British and French are fighting a purely defensive war; they don't do anything to help their friends in the East of Europe. This is having a most discouraging effect in the Balkans. ...

At the beginning of our conversation, Raczynski had said, 'It is like a shooting party; we are the partridges and they are the guns.'

Wednesday 13th September
I am with Winston at the Admiralty from 7.40 to 8 p.m. ... He speaks in a very encouraging way of naval operations. He is quite satisfied that we are beating the submarines. 'Many of them are corpses at the bottom of the sea and others have had a very rough ride home.' He speaks of the shattering effect of depth charges on submarine crews. Nothing in war inflicts a greater shock on human beings – suddenness, concussion and claustrophobia. If, he says, a depth charge exploded as far away from the Admiralty as the House of Commons, it would break every pane of glass. In the early days, German submarines were all well placed and did great damage, comparable to the worst days of the last war, but the convoy system is now rapidly coming into full operation, and for the past forty-eight hours no British ship has been sunk. Just before I go, he asks for the latest news: there are no new sinkings announced; now, therefore, there have been none for fifty-four hours. He says, 'I sit here waiting for news, and I only get bad news, of ships sunk. I don't get the good news, when submarines are sunk, because we never know for certain.'

We speak of Italy. He is sure it is wrong to urge that we should push Italy into war on the German side. At the same time, the Navy in the Mediterranean is quite ready for action if Italy should come in, and confident of the result, though it is never wise to underestimate one's adversary. The Italians have 100 submarines. I say that it is indispensable that we should stop her from being a leak in the blockade. He most emphatically agrees, and says that this is being done. He adds that 'The French think that she may pass, in time, from neutrality into an alliance with us, and this would open up new fronts against Germany.'

Thursday 14th September
Spoke to Boothby who said, rather sadly, that Winston had always had a one-track mind. Just now, all his energy was devoted to suppressing submarines. This followed on my remark that I had got the impression that he was quite on top of his job with regard to the Navy, but that he did not seem to me to have focused the problem of the Eastern Front. The *Pravda* article tonight has a very bad smell, and seems to suggest that the Russians intend to occupy Eastern Poland and so make a new Partition. Then they may take Bessarabia and some Baltic States. And then?

Friday 15th September
Maillaud comes to see me at his own request. Wants me to try to prevent the Treasury from making difficulties if it is decided to help Romania to form an Eastern Front. Polish resistance won't last for many more days. Romania fears an ultimatum from Germany, couched in friendly terms, demanding all her export surplus of oil, wheat, fats, etc. This would be followed, in case of refusal, by German armed attack. King Carol and his P.M.[1] say they will fight if equipped on a sufficient scale and given a loan of at least £12 million. If not, they will give in. ...

Were the Russians ever sincere in their negotiations for a Pact with us and France? It is difficult to say. They always thought that Chamberlain wanted the war to go East, and that the British would wriggle out of any commitment. And up till April, anyhow, Chamberlain did want the war to be German versus Slav. (Van said to someone two days ago that the first he heard of Strang's mission to Moscow was from the papers. He could have told them that *that* was a mistake and would be regarded in Moscow both as an insincerity and an insult. Clearly, though he did not say so, if no minister was to be sent, he himself should have gone.) Maillaud thinks that the Russians will, right at the end, come in against Germany, give her the *coup de grâce* when we and she and the French are all very tired, and aim then at dictating

1 Armand Calinescu (d. 1939). Minister President of Romania since spring 1939. He was assassinated by the Iron Guard on 20th September.

the peace and dominating Central Europe. (This may be French optimism.) ...

The British and French Staffs are quite unshaken in the belief that no help to Poland can prolong Polish resistance more than a week or two at the outside, and would, by starting war in the West, destroy much valuable war potential. But Maillaud wonders why the British did guarantee Poland if they did not mean either themselves to concert plans with Poland or to press her to take Russian help or at least to make a good job of the Anglo–Franco–Soviet Pact. British conduct, as seen from Moscow, was throughout most suspicious and unsatisfactory.

Unless there can be an Eastern Front, the war will be a stalemate. The attack in the West can only be slow and methodical. The Germans have filled the earth with minefields. These, if incautiously crossed, might lead to ten or twelve Divisions being blown into the air. Hence Gamelin's[1] scientific caution. As to whether the Siegfried Line, or bits of it, are built of unset concrete, this is be:ng tested by bombardment now.

The German conquest of Poland was completed within three weeks. On 17th September Soviet forces entered Polish territory from the East.

Monday 18th September

Last night, after a good day with the Wilmots on the High Weald of Sussex, heard of Russian invasion of Poland. First effect of this news very shattering; then got out the map and wondered whether a Russian elbow round Romania would now shut off Germany from that country. Romanian flurry of last week has now to be reconsidered. I mentioned this to Greenwood this morning on the telephone. He is to see the P.M. this afternoon. I urge that Russia should not be publicly slanged too much at present.

See Greenwood in the early afternoon and discuss pretty frankly the future leadership. A fairly early prorogation is desirable and I tell him that, in my view, as things are, I am in favour of his being Leader. Attlee at no time, and much less now, having been ill, and out of touch, is big enough or strong enough to carry the burden. I am quite

---

1 General G. M. Gamelin (1872–1958). French Commander-in-Chief. Succeeded by Weygand in May 1940 after the German invasion of the Low Countries. The British Expeditionary Force was placed under Gamelin's command.

frank about my past support of Morrison, but tell Greenwood that, having regard to all the circumstances, I should advise Morrison not to stand for the leadership now. I also tell Greenwood that sometimes in the past, in my view, he has 'sacrificed major things to minor things'. This is deliberately vague, but perhaps enough.

He says that Dulanty,[1] obviously speaking for De Valera,[2] said to him at lunch (a) that the Irish attitude would be benevolent neutrality underneath, though a little less than this on the surface, and (b) that Eire would be willing to supply food, but that they were having difficulties about prices at this end. Dulanty then went on to ask whether it would not be possible to make peace when Hitler offered it after the destruction of Poland. Greenwood said no; it was impossible to trust Hitler and the gang round him; it would merely be a breathing space for them before they made their final attack on us. ...

With Kingsley Wood from 5 to 5.50 p.m. What does the Russian move mean? I ask whether they had not foreseen it, and he said yes. We agreed that it might not be as bad as it seemed at first sight. The worst hypothesis of all was that Russian planes might be made available to the Germans, but this was mere hypothesis. There was, at present, no evidence whatever to support it. I recalled that I had several times proposed that Russian planes should aid the Poles. I also told him that, some time, there will be many questions to ask as to what H.M.G. had done between April, when they guaranteed Poland, and 1st September, when Hitler attacked, to plan and consolidate the defence of Poland. Kingsley Wood confesses that Ironside, when we went out in August, discussed only the Danzig question and took hardly any staff. Kingsley Wood says that Ironside and Smigly-Rydz both agreed at that time that each of us would have to do the best we could if Hitler attacked. Kingsley Wood says that half the German Air Force, both good and bad, was used against Poland.
...

He advocates the principle of conserving our forces in the West. If the Germans did all the attacking in the air, and we did none, their present superiority would soon disappear, for their losses would be very heavy. In fact, he realises that we should have to make some reply. I said that when I last saw him I asked when something more was going to happen. He replied that we have told the French that whenever they decide to make a really big push in the West, we will attack military targets in the rear of the Front. Our current production,

1 J. W. Dulanty (d. 1955). High Commissioner for the Irish Free State in London 1930–50.
2 Éamon De Valéra (1882–1975). Irish Minister for External Affairs 1932–7. President of the Irish Republic 1919–22. President of Ireland 1959–73.

plus that of the French, is now probably a bit larger than the German, but they still have a large advantage in the total. ...

Call on Butler at F.O. at 6 p.m. This is the first time that I have done this, but it may be useful as an occasional alternative approach. On the way in, I have a word with Gladwyn who says of the Russians, 'It's wonderful how these peasant diplomats get the better of everyone' (I recall Pritt's report of Chilston's[1] saying to him in Moscow, 'You know Pritt, it is very remarkable, they are all *working men*'). I say, 'We all remember that the best Foreign Secretary we have had here was the one who had the least formal education.' Butler's Private Secretary, a young man named Harrison,[2] asked whether he has ever met me before, says, 'I remember meeting you in 1930 at a Commem. Dinner at King's.' I say, 'I remember that dinner very well. I got so drunk that they have never asked me again.' He says, 'It was a very good evening anyhow, wasn't it?', to which I assent.

With Butler I take a tour of the horizon. I strongly urge that Russia should not be treated with high pique. He says he agrees, and that they are trying to keep relations as good as they can with the aid of the French and the Turks. The French, he says – though it would be very premature to say anything about it – are considering the possibility of sending some 'high personality', e.g. Herriot,[3] to Moscow. He realises that the Russians don't trust us, not any of us. He has heard that they mistrust Hoare less than the rest. I say that it was a first class blunder not to send Halifax to Moscow. He agrees that the failure to do so, or to send anyone else of importance, has greatly contributed to suspicion, resentment and recent events. ...

Of the dangers in the West, the gravest, Butler thinks, would be a German invasion of Holland, the Dutch having very poor defences. The significance of this would be that they could then bomb us from Dutch aerodromes, and this would greatly shorten distances – in both directions.

Wednesday 20th September

Saw Kingsley Wood on two points: (1) the scale of his future construction programme, and (2) the interpretation to be placed on Hitler's

---

1 A. Akers-Douglas, 2nd Viscount Chilston (1876–1947). Ambassador to the Soviet Union 1933–8.
2 G. W. Harrison, later Sir Geoffrey (b. 1908). Private Secretary to the Parliamentary Under-Secretary at the Foreign Office (R. A. Butler) 1939–41. Ambassador to the U.S.S.R. 1965–8.
3 Edouard Herriot (1872–1957). President of the French Assembly 1936–44. Radical Socialist. Prime Minister 1924–5 and for one day in 1926. Prime Minister and Foreign Minister 1932. President of the National Assembly 1947–54.

reference at Danzig yesterday to some new secret weapon.

As to (1), Kingsley Wood says that he hopes within a year to double the output in this country ... As to (2), there are several alternatives, and they have been discussing the matter at the War Cabinet this morning. Hitler has for some time talked in private interviews of some new and secret weapon. (I said that soon after Nevile Henderson went to Berlin he had told me that Goering used the same vague and threatening language about new and secret weapons to him. This is not, therefore, a new German boast.) Kingsley Wood says that the possibilities are:

(a) Just bluff and lies, designed to frighten us.

(b) Some new weapon to be used against ships, for only this could really fit in with Hitler's statement that the weapon could not be used by us against him.

(c) Mere indiscriminate bombing on a large scale.

(d) Some new gas; but as to this, our chemists think that they know all the possibilities and that there can be no important chemical surprise. They may, of course, be mistaken in this, but whatever new compound might be used against us could clearly, after an interval, be used in reprisal against Germany.

(e) Some mere new development of ingenuity with regard to bombs, e.g. some new development of delayed action.

I press Kingsley Wood as to the efficiency and persistence of our research. He says that he is now chairman of a committee which co-ordinates research for all the Service Departments. He is satisfied that they are making good progress in many directions, and that we have many inventions which the Germans have not, particularly in the air. On the other hand, much research is disappointing in that it leads to no results of immediate utility. Sir H. Tizard[1] has for years been organising a large staff of scientists for the Government, and Kingsley Wood thinks that I might like to meet him.

Plans are now being worked out for further development of balloon barrage-curtains, suspended bombs, etc. Increasing importance is attached, in all spheres of the war, to driving up enemy aircraft and preventing low-flying attack.

I tell Kingsley Wood that some of my colleagues say that the people at the top of the War Cabinet are hopeless, but that there are others, including himself, whom we might recommend for promotion later on!

1 Sir Henry Tizard (1885–1959). Rector of Imperial College of Science and Technology, London University 1929–42. Chairman of the Aeronautical Research Committee 1933–43. Permanent Secretary at the Department of Scientific and Industrial Research 1927–9.

Thursday 21st September

Maillaud tells me that Corbin has yesterday made a démarche to Halifax and also to Chatfield, expressing the French government's concern at our slow tempo. British troops are proceeding very slowly to France. Only one complete Division and parts of a second have yet landed, and they are still concentrated in the neighbourhood of the ports and have not moved up to the front line. The French would also like to see more British aircraft in France, and hold the view that we are keeping an excessive number for home defence in this country. Nor are they satisfied with our rate of expansion in arms production. Maillaud says that it seems to them that we are preparing, not for a war to last three years, but for a war to begin at the end of three years. He says that we seem to be slowly building enormous palaces which one day will, no doubt, be magnificent arms factories, but the French are not satisfied that we are making full use of our existing manufacturing capacity. ...

I thought there was an under-current of uneasiness in Maillaud's talk. He said that whatever the Germans did, even if they assaulted the Maginot Line in great force, or violated the neutrality of Holland, Belgium, Luxemburg or Switzerland, the French Army would be able to hold them up, but the losses might be very heavy, and it was felt that the British were not yet in a position to take their fair share, nor, he felt, were they hurrying to do so.

Monday 25th September

Go, on my own initiative, to see Eden at the Dominions Office. After some preliminaries on Australia and New Zealand, I speak to him about Russia and urge that the Government should not be too passive nor cultivate any sense of moral rectitude or bruised pride as regards Moscow. He says that 'the colleagues' are quite alive to the importance of this. When Russia attacked Poland, Halifax at once proposed to the Cabinet that we should not break off diplomatic relations, though there was a clear legal and moral case for doing this. His proposal was at once accepted by the Cabinet. Last weekend Halifax saw Maisky and formed the impression that he was very uncomfortable and ill-informed about the intentions of his Government. He could not answer any questions about the future.

For the moment, Eden thinks that our best line to Moscow is through the Turks. He said that Aras[1] had been to see him that very afternoon and left only a short time before I arrived. Aras is still very optimistic, and Eden told him that he had pledged his own credit,

1 Dr T. R. Aras (1883–1972). Turkish Ambassador in London 1939–42. Former Foreign Minister.

whatever that was worth, to his colleagues in the Cabinet that the Turks would not go back on us. ...

Eden said that Winston was playing a very active part in the Cabinet. I asked whether he was not at present very much concentrated on naval questions. Eden said, 'You can't imagine his remaining silent, and thinking only about submarines, when a general conversation develops!'

Thursday 12th October
Dine at Polish Embassy – rather like a funeral – to meet Zaleski,[1] whose features and manner at no time diminish such an impression. Sit between Lord Lloyd, who says that he bears me no grudge over my part in his dismissal from Egypt, and that he has lately been much more in sympathy with the Labour Party than with the Prime Minister over foreign policy, and Clifford Norton, who has a most vivid tale of retreat and bombing in Poland.

German aircraft unquestionably and continually bombed and machine-gunned undefended towns and villages of no military significance. At one of the last places where Beck and the diplomats stopped before going into Romania – it was, he said, a pleasant little semi-University town in a well wooded and undulating country – German planes dropped a series of bombs right up the main street, and when people were seen running, fired at them with machine guns as though they were rabbits. Biddle,[2] the American Ambassador, 'a rich young man in the middle forties', was magnificent and rallied all the other diplomats.

Wednesday 18th October
Lunch with Van at Coq d'Or. He hopes we shall keep an eye on the leaders of the Link,[3] namely Admiral Barry Domvile, Carroll,[4] an

---

1 August Zaleski (1883–1972). Served in Polish government-in-exile 1939–44. Foreign Minister 1926–32. Graduate of the L.S.E.
2 A. J. D. Biddle (1896–1961). U.S. Ambassador to Poland 1937–40. Accompanied the Polish government in forced moves from Warsaw to other cities and eventually to Angers, in France. Interim Ambassador to France 1940.
3 The Link was an Anglo–German friendship association, founded by Admiral Sir Barry Domvile, q.v., in July 1937. In June 1939 it had 4,300 members. In March, the Home Secretary had told the House of Commons, in answer to a question: 'I understand that this organisation is mainly for the purposes of pro-Nazi and anti-Semitic propaganda. More than that I do not know.' (See R. Griffiths, *Fellow Travellers of the Right*, Constable, London, 1980, pp. 309 ff.)
4 C. E. Carroll. Editor of the *Anglo-German Review*. Leading member of the National Council of the Link. First World War hero. Interned in 1940 under Regulation 18B.

Australian [and his] wife and Professor A. P. Laurie.[1] Van understands that all these have now joined the Council for Christian Settlement in Europe (I hear later that John Beckett is Secretary of this body!). He says that Mosley is also being active.

There is a danger of a Peace Push by the same people, including Horace Wilson, who were Munichois last year, if, as is possible, Goering takes Hitler's place. Goering, however, is just as bad as Hitler. He is an expansionist and a bandit, and just as great danger to us. Perhaps more dangerous, since he is full-blooded and enjoys high living, and therefore gets on well with Londonderry and other rich people, whereas Hitler can only drink water and is not a pleasant social companion. (Riddle: What is Hitler's secret weapon with which he has been threatening us? The one he showed to the American film lady, only it would not work.)

If we patched things up with Goering, there would simply be a waiting period and then a Western Blitzkrieg with no Eastern Front. At least Polish resistance prevented this last month, and allowed time for French mobilisation. Those who have great possessions find it hard to believe that these and their comfortable ways of life are really in danger. They won't face the facts. Hence Ribbentrop's conviction that Mayfair will never fight.

Others believe that there is always a 'good old Germany' just round the corner. They hope for just a small change, a Government of Generals, or even a Monarchist restoration and then all danger will be passed. This, too, is an illusion. There is no 'good old Germany' just round the corner. Until the leaders of the Nazi Party have been physically exterminated, and until the German military class has been broken, there can be no hope of steady peace in Europe. But it is much too soon to say this, or anything like this, in public, or we shall simply drive together these two dangerous classes.

On 28th October, Dalton flew to Paris with a small delegation of M.P.s from the British section of the Anglo–French Parliamentary Committee.

---

1 Professor A. P. Laurie (1861–1949). Chemist. Principal of the Heriot-Watt College, Edinburgh 1900–28. Leading member of the National Council of the Link. Author in May 1939 of a pro-Nazi tract, *The Case for Germany* (with a preface by Domvile).

307

Visit to France with party of M.P.s 28th to 31st October

Saturday 28th October

Party, led by the admirable General Spears, consists of Dai Grenfell, Phil [Noel-Baker] and I; Leopold Amery, Wardlaw-Milne,[1] Sir Robert Bird,[2] Harold Nicolson and Rothschild.[3] The last of these crossed yesterday. The other eight of us reach Heston just after noon. It is very rough and windy and Spears says that it is very doubtful whether the plane (Air France) will start. If not, we might cross tonight from Newhaven to Dieppe. I urge Spears to tell them that the plane *must* fly; it will be much better to have a short and unpleasant crossing than to lose a day. He agrees, and after some hesitation the pilot consents. It is indeed pretty rough and we have to fly low, so as to be visible all the time from the ground – otherwise we might be shot at or chased by fighters – and today the clouds are very low. We bump a good deal and one has the illusion that only the engine is fixed and the rest of the plane blowing about in the wind. Phil is very discreetly sick, and one or two other passengers less discreet. A woman behind me fills the air with eau de Cologne. I succeed in drowsing and arrive without more than the mildest premonitory sensation of discomfort.

Met at Le Bourget at 2.30 by group of French deputies, including Delbos,[4] Grumbach,[5] Taittinger,[6] Moutet[7] and Delattre. We drive in military cars driven by soldiers wearing the very becoming and utilitarian French tin helmet, to the Ritz Hotel in the Place Vendôme, where Spears has arranged for relatively cheap rates.

1 Sir John Wardlaw-Milne (1878–1967). Conservative M.P. for Kidderminster 1922–45.
2 Sir Robert Bird, 2nd Bart (1876–1960). Conservative M.P. for Wolverhampton West 1922–9, 1931–45.
3 J. A. de Rothschild (1878–1957). Liberal M.P. for the Isle of Ely 1924–45. Junior minister 1945.
4 Yvon Delbos (1885–1956). Radical Socialist. Foreign Minister 1936–8. Detained by Vichy forces in June 1940.
5 S. Grumbach (1884–1952). Socialist. Later with the French Resistance.
6 Pierre Taittinger. Member of the Chamber of Deputies Army Committee. Founder of a paramilitary right-wing organisation of streetfighters, the *Jeunesses Patriotes*. In March 1940 Taittinger was to make serious criticisms, ignored by the High Command, of 'Maginot Line' fortifications around Sedan.
7 Marius Moutet (1876–1968). Socialist. Joint Vice-President of the Franco–British Parliamentary Committee. Minister of Colonies 1936–8. Interned by the Vichy regime.

On 29th October, the British party was taken to inspect the Maginot Line. After travelling by train to Nancy, they were driven to a château just outside the town and given a lecture by a staff officer who told them of the French conviction 'that the Maginot Line cannot be forced, though the Western Section of it behind Luxemburg and Belgium is much less elaborate than the sections which face Germany.'[1]

Sunday 29th October
Drive back through Nancy, Pont à Mousson, Metz, Thionville, to the nearest point of the Line at Sierck ... at the western end of the zone in which fighting has been taking place. (The British troops are in the Line a little west of this, behind part of the Belgian and Luxemburg frontiers.) I travel in the same car with Delattre and Nicolson, who has a bad cold and coughs all the time. Probably I catch his germs. Very few signs of war until quite near the Line, though some anti-aircraft batteries near the road are pointed out to me, and a number of machine guns and other posts in the field. At Thionville blast furnaces are working continuous shifts, and beyond there are lines of barbed wire, including wire to be thrown across the road which, we understand, is also mined at many points.

We spend more than two hours inside the *ouvrages*. It is an amazing experience. We go down in a lift more than 130 ft, which seems equivalent of about five storeys. Lofty underground passages with electric railways to carry supplies and persons, central heating, formidable electric power plants, laboratories to test for the presence of all known kinds of gas if any should get in. We are shown the arrangements for the direction of fire on the surface from a chamber in the lowest stratum of this subterranean world – some say it is like a great subterranean battleship. On the wall of this chamber are maps, taken from the air, of the ground immediately above us, and an 'exercise' is arranged by the lieutenant in charge who reports the receipt of news that some German tanks have appeared at a certain point on the map against which a fire of anti-tank guns from a number of casements [is] to be directed. All the 'elements' of the fire are to be worked out very quickly and quietly down here below and the orders sent up after only about forty seconds from the receipt of the information. We are shown also the men's sleeping quarters, the cook houses – our party is being led here by a general who picks out a piece of meat in his fingers from the saucepan and pronounces it to be good – a barber's

1 Diary, 29th October 1939; FY, p. 285.

shop, the electric plant, etc. Then, ascending, we go into a casemate in which are four anti-tank guns which amongst them cover 300 degrees. I look out towards German lines, but there is nothing visible nor audible. The Germans have the sky line, but that is more than 6 km. – the width of no-man's-land – away. I am told that they are just beyond a nearer ridge and that their line is out of sight here. In the foreground [are] French barbed wire and tank traps. They have had very satisfactory results with their anti-tank guns, the shells from which will pierce the armour of German tanks, though French tanks have in many cases withstood the German anti-tank guns. We see also a casemate containing French 75 mm, and these also do an 'exercise', though not actually firing, for our benefit.

In all passages of the *ouvrages* there are at short intervals heavy iron gates which can be quickly closed, and arrangements permitting hand-grenades to be thrown through small openings in these. If, therefore, some Germans got into any part of the *ouvrages*, they could be isolated by the closing of these gates.

The troops here below ground give an impression of youth, intelligence – they are all specialists of different kinds – and self-assurance. They are a distinct corps, having a *roulement* among themselves so that in normal times a certain fraction of them are always on leave, but living, when on duty, always in the *ouvrages*. It is noticeable that their faces, and also their hands, look very pale. On the other hand, we are told that there is very little sickness indeed among them. These defenders of the *ouvrages* receive extra pay compared with the infantry outside, but one might well prefer their lot. It is indeed a queer new troglodytic life.

On 30th October, the British M.P.s returned to Paris.

Monday 30th October

Grenfell, Phil and I dine that night with Blum alone in his flat on the Île Saint Louis. (He has a soldier and a detective always on guard outside, ever since the assault upon him some years ago.) He was, I thought, in very good physical and mental form, and hopes to come to London in a few weeks' time with colleagues, for a consultation with us. He says that the Paul Faurists[1] are in a comparatively small

1 'Paul Faurists': followers of Paul Faure (1878–1960), former General Secretary of the French Socialist Party. Thereafter, Blum led the Socialists inside Parliament, and Faure (with Zyromski, q.v.) those outside.

minority in the Party now, and their pacifism is partly due to the exaggerated patriotism of the Communists, which affronted them. The Communists, e.g., had accused Blum of treachery because, when he was Prime Minister, he permitted Schacht to call upon him.

He regretted a little, but not much I think, the action taken against the Communists. Thorez[1] and several others who were in the army deserted and were thought to have escaped to Holland where they were waiting for a train to take them to Moscow. The conduct and pronouncements of the Communist leaders had alienated almost all their working-class following, and the *désagrégation* of the Party had gone very far.

Wednesday 1st November
Fly back in the morning. Relatively smooth crossing. Even Phil does not misbehave.

November 1939
A further ineffectual fidget about the leadership. It was felt by a certain number of Labour M.P.s that Greenwood did much better during Attlee's absence through illness than the latter would have done, particularly in the last days of August and the beginning of September. I myself was strongly of this opinion. On Attlee's return, however, although he was obviously ineffective and much below even his own normal par, this idea rapidly evaporated, and there was some resentment at rather crude efforts to popularise Greenwood in the non-Labour press.

With the ending of the Parliamentary session, a contest for the leadership became possible. I myself took the view that the only possible change was Greenwood for Attlee, and, on this narrow choice, I was for Greenwood and frankly told him so, nor did I wholly conceal this opinion from some others. I thought that Morrison, who had been doing real positive work of high value for London, while the rest of us had been doing mere critical negative quack-quack, would not at this stage be in the running. My view was that, once we loosened the earth and got the leadership moving, it would be much easier to bring Morrison in later in place of Greenwood, if, as was indeed possible, the latter did not wear well. Moreover, I felt that the present Parliamentary Party, pending a substantial change of personnel at a General Election, would not back Morrison.

1 Maurice Thorez (1900–64). General Secretary of the French Communist Party 1930–64. Joined the army at the outbreak of war, but deserted to the U.S.S.R. after the Comintern's condemnation of the 'Imperialist war'. Received an amnesty from de Gaulle in 1944. Minister of State under de Gaulle 1945–6.

Greenwood was, as usual, dilatory in decision, and no one else of any prominence in the Parliamentary Party took any decisive attitude in his favour. Days passed with nothing much being done, and even an attempt to get signatures to a request to him to run for the leadership petered out.

Then Alfred Edwards[1] wrote a letter to Attlee, Greenwood, Morrison and myself. This was not really a very helpful or sensible procedure. Only Morrison replied in writing to Edwards and *this*, I thought, was not a very helpful letter either.

On 9th November Edwards had written to Dalton: 'I have good cause for feeling that yourself and Morrison and Greenwood will be nominated, and I am writing to ask you, in order to avoid the development of any further unpleasantness on this question of election of Officers, to allow your name to go forward.' Morrison, receiving a similar letter, replied on 11th November declaring laboriously and at some length, his reluctant decision not to stand. '. . . I feel that as the health of Mr Attlee is still in process of recovery it would not be a kindly or generous action for the leadership to be contested this year,' he wrote, 'nor do I gather that there is a general or substantial desire in the Parliamentary Party to reconsider the matter at this juncture.' Morrison sent copies of this letter to Attlee, Greenwood and Dalton.[2]

On Wednesday, 15th November, at the Party Meeting, it was announced that, as threatened in Edwards's letter, all the four of us had been nominated. There was a queer, desultory discussion, full of expressions of gentlemanly good will (the Labour Party is apt to be dangerously good at this sort of thing). Attlee, directly asked by Edwards, said that he would never resent or regard as 'disloyal' nomination of any colleague for the leadership. We were a democratic party. And then Greenwood rose and declined nomination. He gave very poor reasons, his chief point being that it would encourage Hitler if we now had a contest for the leadership. Morrison then rose and merely read out his letter to Edwards. I then also declined, saying (which was true) that in no other political party could we have had such a discussion, so full of expressions of good will. I said that when Lindsay had told

1 Alfred Edwards (1888–1958). Labour M.P. for Middlesbrough East 1935–48; Independent, then Conservative, M.P. 1948–50.
2 Dalton Papers 5/6, (3), (5).

me last night that I had been nominated, I had told him that I did not propose to be a candidate, and that nothing had happened in the meeting this morning to make me change my view. I added that one of the most striking statements made this morning was that by Attlee from the Chair, which made it clear that if, in the future, the Party desired a contest, no resentment would be felt in any quarter.

As we dispersed after the meeting, Tom Smith[1] said to me, 'Well, you all did the big thing this morning. But there will have to be a change one of these days.'

When the elections for the Parliamentary Executive took place a week later, it was quite clear that a bunch of Members, between 20 and 30 in number, were indignant with me, and a not much smaller number indignant with Morrison. The common factor in both cases was that we had even been nominated. In addition, there was some further indignation against me for having espoused Greenwood's candidature. These feelings were reflected in a drop in the votes for both Morrison and myself. Tom Johnston was actually pushed off the Executive – rather stupidly, I thought – on the quite different ground that since he had been Scottish Regional Commissioner, he had been little in Parliament. In his place we have Jack Lawson, with no other change.

Morrison, meanwhile, was not very pleased with me, saying that I had 'deserted to the enemy'. This can, I think, be put right without much difficulty, but the whole thing is pretty feeble.

On 6th December, when Morrison made a good speech in the debate on the Address, I passed him a note along the Front Bench conveying compliments and adding, 'The way of earth shifters is hard in this political allotment and I am not attracted to do any more digging at present. Yours, with undiminished regard.'

Wednesday 15th November
See Kingsley Wood ... He is puzzled by the comparative inactivity of the Germans. I gather that the War Cabinet for some while have been expecting some big move, either by air attack on our ships or on targets in this country, or an invasion of Holland and Belgium. (He thinks that if they go for Holland they will go for Belgium as well.) German prisoners all emphasise that they have the very strictest orders only to attack our ships and, if attacked by fighters, to disengage and return to Germany. He thinks there is evidence that some of the German planes are disappointing. He fancies that the Germans are

1 Tom Smith (1886–1953). Labour M.P. for Normanton 1933–49; Pontefract 1922–4, 1929–31. Junior minister 1942–5.

313

much afraid of air attack by us on the Ruhr, where, if we seriously damaged their industrial apparatus, their war production would be very badly hit. Also they may be saving up oil, having used a great deal in Poland, and not being very sure of future supplies. He does not think they are getting much from Russia.

I ask whether, if nothing much happens till next spring, the War Cabinet have in mind any decisive operations. He says, rather guardedly, that if we have then got the air supremacy which he hopes for, the Air Ministry would be in favour of undertaking large operations against German targets, but they would wish these to be accompanied by some operations by ground troops, because, otherwise, large numbers of German aircraft would be liberated from co-operation work with the army and would be available for independent fighting. He adds that Gamelin is very cautious and does not wish to risk anything or undertake any large operations at present. On the German side, none of the present generals held commands above that of colonel in the last war. They are now all promoted Nazis and may, therefore, be prepared to accept rash and adventurous projects from their Master.

Saturday 18th November

Dine at Polish Embassy to meet Sikorski[1] and Zaleski. Sit between Layton[2] and Colonel Gubbins.[3] Layton thinks that the Reichswehr are urging Hitler to do nothing this winter, saying that France and Britain will get tired, that the blockade is making little impression, that Germany should conserve her oil supplies. He says that Liddell Hart has had a nervous breakdown and that he would not pay any regard to anything written by him just now (this helps to explain the two very defeatist memoranda sent me by L.H.). Gubbins is pro-Pole, pro-Czech and intelligent. Smigly-Rydz was unimpressive and conceited.

---

1 General W. Sikorski (1881–1943). Commander-in-Chief of the Polish Army 1939–43. Polish Prime Minister 1922–3. Prime Minister of Polish government-in-exile 1941–3.

2 Sir Walter Layton, later 1st Baron (1884–1966). Chairman of *News Chronicle* and *Star* newspapers. Editor of *The Economist* 1922–38; Director-General of Programmes at the Ministry of Supply 1940–42. Head of Joint War Production Staff 1942–3. Liberal.

3 Col. C. M. Gubbins, later Major-General Sir Colin (1896–1976). General Staff Officer (Second Rank) War Office 1935–9. Gubbins had led a British Military Mission to Poland in August 1939. In November 1940 he was appointed by Dalton to take charge of Operations and Training for the Special Operations Executive (S.O.E.) in Europe. Deputy Head of S.O.E. 1942–3; Head 1943–6.

Sunday 19th November
Beneš and his wife come to tea with us. Also present Phil [Noel-Baker], Lathan, Kalina[1] and Gustav Winter. He says, 'The Russians have big eyes; they are psychologists.' They are doing a good deal of propaganda in Slovakia, the Slavs being more impressionable than the Czechs. They hope for a Communist Poland. He is quite sure that next spring Stalin will press Hitler to re-establish an independent Poland and Czechoslovakia. (If this is true, it is very important.) The Russians say to themselves, 'If Hitler wins, he will attack us. Therefore we must occupy now strong points in the Baltic and Central Europe. If Hitler loses, the Western Powers will attack us, or instigate other people to do so.'

On 8th November Attlee defined Labour's war aims in a speech which was published as a pamphlet. 'We have no desire to humiliate, to crush, or to divide the German nation ... ' he declared. 'We wish the German people to know that they can now secure, if they will, an honourable peace.' On 30th November, the international situation took a new turn when the Soviet Union invaded Finland. A week later, the National Council of Labour issued a Manifesto condemning the Russian attack, and demanding that 'every practicable aid' should be given to the Finns.[2]

Saturday 16th December
In Edinburgh for a Peace Aims Conference. Communists, near-Communists and pacifists present in force, but have nothing to say against my statement of peace aims except that it is Utopian and that we should make peace with Hitler now, express no condemnation of Russia in Finland, and cease 'collaborating' with Chamberlain. Some ask whether France is not as Fascist as Germany, and others whether Hitler is treating Poles and Czechs any worse than we are treating Indian and African natives. One man asks why his son, who is in the Air Force, should have to 'defend British capitalism', to whom I reply, 'My good man, he is defending you.' Poor mental stuff, but not representative of more than an insignificant fraction of the 'rank and file' always invoked by such folk. (Next day, a similar Conference at Motherwell for Lanarkshire, though containing a few of these ele-

1 Probably Dr Othmar Kallina. Leader of the Czech National Party.
2 See G. D. H. Cole, *A History of the Labour Party from 1914*, Routledge & Kegan Paul, London, 1948, pp. 376, 378.

ments, is very much steadier, as one would expect from a mining area.)

Tom Johnston spends two hours talking to me at the Railway Hotel at Edinburgh on Saturday evening. He is thoroughly enjoying his job as Regional Commissioner, and potential dictator, for-Scotland, and, I judge, doing it very well. He says he has solved the problem of the forests by offering 3d. a pound for all venison delivered, cleaned and in good condition at the nearest rail head. This is turned into venison sausages which, he says, the butchers are falling over one another to sell. It is being offered a good deal cheaper than ordinary sausages to the public, and the taste for it is growing. He also thinks that he has put sheep farming in this country on its feet, and also saved the need for large bacon imports, by his new discovery of mutton-bacon. He says that that fool Macquisten[1] nearly spoilt the market by calling it 'macon', which sounds silly. Mutton-bacon sounds much better. They are making experiments in curing it which he thinks will be wholly successful. At present it looks a little darker than the ordinary bacon, but it is hoped to make it look and taste just the same soon, and to sell it cheaper. This will be a much more profitable way of selling sheep. ...

'This hotel is being watched,' said Johnston to me, and explained that attempts were being made to spread demoralising rumours among the population by the following cunning device. In a public room, where two dozen people might be sitting, someone would say, 'Let's turn on the German wireless and listen to Lord Haw-Haw.'[2] The wireless would then be turned on and his Lordship, in the course of his remarks, would give a number of local warnings, e.g. that there was an ammunition dump at X which might at any time be blown up, so people should get away from it; or a firm at Y were really making poison gas, although not even the workers realised this, and that there might be a serious accident there one of these days, so that the workers were advised to look out. (This last rumour, he said, had disorganised the work of this firm for several days, because a lot of girls, being frightened, stayed away.) These stories were, of course, repeated and passed on by people who had heard them in the hotel. What was happening was that an accomplice of the person who suggested that they should turn on Lord Haw-Haw, and who in fact set the wireless just a fraction to the right or left of the correct wave-length, installed himself in a bedroom somewhere in the hotel with a transmitter which

1 F. A. Macquisten (1870–1940). Conservative M.P. for Argyllshire 1924–40; Glasgow Springburn 1918–22.
2 'Lord Haw-Haw': William Joyce (1906–46). Broadcast propaganda for Germany during the war. Executed for treason.

was attached to an electric wire, and himself talked what purported to be Lord Haw-Haw and was heard by those in the room below.[1]

Tuesday 13th February 1940
Dine at Nathan's[2] invitation, with Greenwood, Morrison and a few others, to meet Sir W. Seeds, still nominally British Ambassador in Moscow. He tells me that the Embassy there is in the charge of le Rougetel,[3] a man from Rossall to whom I gave a very black mark when I was at the Foreign Office because, though he had been in Vienna for two years, he had met no Socialist leaders and seemed to know no way of meeting them. Seeds is not impressive. His case is all rather *ex post facto*. He says the Russians always work on rigid plans prepared for the Politburo by various so-called experts. Once accepted by the Politburo, these plans cannot be varied. Hence there was never any 'negotiation' in the ordinary sense with Molotov, and it would have been useless, he thinks, for Halifax to have visited Moscow. He would have had to sign on the dotted line or go away empty handed. (This seems to me to be nonsense, particularly if Halifax had gone out at a fairly early stage of the talks.) I ask whether at the end it was not a formula defining 'indirect aggression' which was the stumbling block. I understood that the Foreign Office, or rather Strang, prepared four alternatives, of which one Molotov would certainly reject, one certainly accept, and two were doubtful. Seeds says that formulas did not matter at all. We knew quite well what the Russians wanted, and to that we could not agree. (I do not believe this; it does not square with what we were told from both sides at the time.)

I say that it was to me a shocking muddle that Poles and Russians were never confronted by British or French representatives to discuss ways and means of co-operation. He says that 'It would have been no good.' (Damned fool!) He also says that it was the Labour Party in the House of Commons who continually roused the suspicions of the Russians against Chamberlain. I say that since it was I who regularly put one or two questions a week to him on the progress of the negotiations, I suppose he regards me as especially responsible for the breakdown of the talks. He says, with a smile, that he is afraid he does. I say that I do not think it needs my questions to infuse distrust of our

---

1 This implausible story, apparently believed at the time, indicates the prevalence of the 'fifth column' scare during the phoney war period.
2 Col. H. L. Nathan, later 1st Baron (1889–1963). Labour M.P. for Wandsworth Central 1937–40. Liberal M.P. 1929–35. Junior minister 1945–6; Minister of Civil Aviation 1946–8.
3 J. H. le Rougetel, later Sir John (1894–1975). Counsellor and acting Chargé d'Affaires in Moscow 1940.

Prime Minister into Stalin and Molotov. He says that Molotov frequently used to show him, when they met, translations of statements
by Labour leaders on Chamberlain, and ask, 'How can you expect *me*
to believe that that man is sincere?'

He says that of all the Russian leaders, he disliked only Zhdanov.[1]
He is a really bad man and a gangster, he thinks.

I doubt whether this poor mutt could do any good by returning to
Moscow.

In February an N.E.C. document entitled 'Labour, the War and the Peace'
replaced Attlee's November speech (called by Dalton 'the Rabbit's Peace
Aims') as the authoritative Labour statement. The main change was in
emphasis. The new declaration was less apologetic about the war, more pro-
French and more punitively anti-German – reflecting the changing popular
mood and the sentiments of the document's draftsman, Dalton. The revised
statement opposed any peace negotiations 'except with a German Government which has not merely promised, but actually performed, certain acts
of restitution'. It stressed the common aims of Britain and France, and the
need for a new international authority. It recognised the French right to
'security'. And it informed the French: 'Henceforth, in resistance to any
German aggression, our two peoples must be not merely allies for a season,
but brothers for all time.'

Middle of February
I have had a number of interesting talks during the last ten days,
several with a Professor,[2] whom I introduced to Morrison (on the
5th) and Attlee (on the 6th); also one with Van on the 6th and with
Halifax on the 8th. I have also got through, at last, 'Labour, the War
and the Peace'. Finally, only Attlee and Pritt would not vote for it,
and only Pritt voted against it. Jim Griffiths would have made trouble,
and wrote stupid letters, but was away ill. Attlee 'doesn't like the
balance of it'. He thinks there is too much about France and Germany! In the classic entitled 'The Rabbit's Peace Aims', the only
reference to France is near the end, when it is stated that his Vague

---

1 A. A. Zhdanov (1896–1948). Head of the Soviet Agitation and Propaganda Directorate (Agitprop) 1944–8. Secretary of the Central Committee of the Russian
  Communist Party.
2 Not identified. Apparently a German dissident with anti-Nazi contacts in Germany.

New World would be equally acceptable to the Chinaman, the French-man, the Dane, the Belgian and the Javanese. I broadcast on the following Wednesday and get a large fan mail, with some hearty abuse. ...

With Halifax. I leave a copy of our Declaration (as we left 'Labour and the Nation' years ago).[1] I say I think he will agree with much of it. This leads him, at the end, to raise the question of joint political meetings. I say we had better not reopen that till after Whitsun, when we shall put the thermometer into the water to feel the temperature of the Labour Party. In any case, I say, the P.M. is the greatest obs-tacle; we are much more disinclined to co-operate with him and some of his colleagues than with certain others, of whom Halifax is one. Halifax says, 'Isn't it a bit easier now?' and adds that the P.M. was 'touched' by Morrison's tone last week in the House in the Economic Co-ordination Debate. I say that I should not advise the P.M. to read too much into that (in fact Morrison is as violent against Cham-berlain as any of us) ...

Directly questioned by me, Halifax denies all peace feelers officially. I mention P.M., Horace Wilson and Montagu Norman.[2] He says, of course, that he cannot speak for the City. I say that there will be an explosion if anything of this kind turns out to be true. I refer to Nevile Henderson's remarks in public trying to distinguish Hitler from Goering. He says he has not it before him (I think he will look it up when I go). I press him not to believe that we should not speak against the Nazis publicly. He says he is inclined to attack the Nazis but not Hitler personally, so as not to rally Germans round him.

Sunday 25th February
Barbara Gould and I with two Poles, a man and a woman. He has scars on his face from the Gestapo. She is the sister of Alter, of the Bund,[3] who, I hear later, has been shot by the Ogpu. She does most

---

1 In 1929, Arthur Henderson had told Dalton to circulate copies of Labour's election programme, 'Labour and the Nation', among Foreign Office officials.
2 According to the 'Professor', Hitler had been telling his generals that he had re-ceived peace feelers from Britain, mentioning Chamberlain, Horace Wilson, Montagu Norman and Londonderry in this connection. Dalton did not believe the story, but was evidently glad of a chance to pass it on (Diary, same entry).
3 Victor Alter (1890–1941). Formerly a prominent leader of the Bund, a radical Jewish party in Poland, affiliated to the Second International. Alter was arrested after escaping from the German to the Russian zone of Poland following the invasions of September 1939. But he was not yet dead: he and an associate in the Bund, Henryk Erich, were executed in Kuibyshev on 4th December 1941.

319

of the talking. They were both in Warsaw when it was bombarded. The *élan* of those days was tremendous. They felt they were really defending something, on behalf of all Europe. They thought that the Socialist International would come to their assistance. Then came a terrible disillusionment. She slept in passages and cellars during the bombardment. He shows me a photograph of twelve Polish hostages demanded by the Germans when they entered Warsaw. ...

She says that three million Poles, including Jews, are now nomads. How can these ever be restored after the war? What can ever give back to the Poles their enthusiasm again? She went from Warsaw to the West of Poland and there saw in Poznan and other towns people being turned out, whole streets at a time, old people and children included, at a quarter of an hour's notice, generally in the middle of the night, being allowed to take with them only ten zlotys (i.e. a few shillings), food for two days, and small hand luggage. They were then marched off to the railway station and packed tight into trucks. They were dumped down, after a journey of five, six, seven or ten days, during a large part of which the trucks were shunted into sidings, with no sanitary arrangements, no heating and no additional food. After being dumped down, they were told to disappear within a quarter of an hour or they would be shot. Vast numbers of these destitute people have now crowded into Warsaw, Cracow and other Polish cities. They have to be supported somehow by charitable funds raised by the Poles themselves. German authorities contribute nothing. In the homes from which these people are expelled, the Germans take over everything, including furniture, linen, food, etc., and either carry these things off to the Reich, or hand them over to German tenants. Thus, German dentists, barbers, etc., from the Baltic States, or from inside the Reich, are given possession of the homes, offices, shops, etc., of Polish dentists, barbers and so on.

In one Polish town she saw fifty people rounded up into the square and shot for no reason at all. The Germans then stripped their corpses naked and said that their relatives could fetch them away, as no doubt they would be able to distinguish them even in this condition.

The man said that one day in Warsaw a Polish policeman – these are compelled to go round in pairs with German policemen – was shot while walking in the street from a high window in a block of workers' flats. Nothing happened till next day, when the Germans came at midday and searched this block from top to bottom, dragging out fifty-three men who happened to be inside at the time, though some of them did not live there. All these fifty-three were then shot down in the street, on the ground that they did not help the police to catch the murderer the previous day. Their bodies were left lying in the street for days, the Germans forbidding their removal.

Heavy fines were imposed all over Poland, on the slightest pretexts, on towns and villages.

Tuesday 5th March

Saw Kingsley Wood for one and a half hours ... [He] said that, as to plans for counter-attack, we have not bombed the Ruhr, etc., yet because it might antagonise U.S. and because the French don't want it, thinking German reprisals would probably be against them and not us. But all plans are minutely worked out, pilots allotted, and each with his special objectives, which he has studied so closely from photographs that he should know them as well as his own village. There would be no limitation in the Ruhr to air fields as targets. Industrial plant, railway stations, viaducts (these very important in the Ruhr), etc., would be included. The attack, to be effective, would need to be repeated by day and night for several days in succession. Our losses might be heavy, running up to even 20 or 25 per cent. It is the knowledge of this, and corresponding knowledge on the German side, which has hitherto discouraged mass air offensives. It still remains to be proved how far such offensives in any case can be decisive in war. He feels that the air weapon is, after all, one which might break in one's hands and be finally discredited by one or two spectacular failures. So far, the Germans have made tremendous gains merely by threats and bluff. ...

He says finally that he still cannot understand why the Germans did not go for us heads down at the start. He can only think it was because they did not quite trust the efficacy of their much-vaunted air arm.

Thursday 7th March

E. H. Keeling,[1] who is at the A.M. [Air Ministry] in uniform, draws me aside and tells me that the Germans have 1,750 heavy bombers, and we only 270. Of these totals, 1,250 and 160 may be regarded as immediately available at any given time. Of good fighters, Spitfires and Hurricanes, we have only 750. This, he says, is a catastrophic situation. He is not including our bombers in France, which are medium or light. He says that a number of people at the A.M. should be sacked, and also Ludlow-Hewitt,[2] C-in-C, Bomber Command, who is most unenterprising. He thinks that Kingsley Wood is not on

1 E. H. Keeling, later Sir Edward (1888–1954). Conservative M.P. for Twickenham 1935–54. Served in the R.A.F. 1939–45.
2 Air Chief Marshal Sir Edgar Ludlow-Hewitt (1886–1973). Air Officer Commander-in-Chief, Bomber Command 1937–40. Inspector-General R.A.F. 1940–45.

top of the job and never has been. Keeling would like a three-party secret meeting upstairs, where Kingsley Wood could be cross-examined. He says that he long wondered whether it was consistent with his duty to speak to me about these matters, and has finally decided that it is. I undertake to keep in touch with him.

Monday 11th March
Talk to Jowitt, who is Chairman of Air Sub-Committee of National Expenditure Committee. He says that what he hears, by way of casual and unpremeditated remarks by R.A.F. High-Ups, does not bear out Kingsley Wood's statement to me that British plus French current production is now greater than German. He gathers that it is only between one-half and two-thirds of the German. It still takes two years from the drawing board to a real flow of production for a new type of plane.

Thursday 14th March
Kingsley Wood comes, by invitation, to our Supply Committee, where there is a good attendance. He speaks chiefly about liaison ... following the main points raised by me in the Estimates Debate. He makes a good general impression on the Committee, and there are no tremendous revelations, nor man hunts, as Garro Jones had hinted to me there would be. Garro Jones himself does not put many, nor penetrating, questions. At the end I ask whether it is the case that we are heavily outnumbered in heavy bombers. He does not deny it, but hints that, particularly for attacks by night, there is no real defence against heavy bombers, and that a few may do as much damage as many. He thinks it likely that the Germans will not use their Air Force in the west except as a last resort if things are going very wrong with them. We may well have, he says, a similar situation in the air in this war as at sea in the last. The main fleets will be fleets in being rather than fleets in action, exercising influence at a distance through their possibilities, not through their positive actions.

Friday 15th March
Lunch with Maisky at Soviet Embassy. This little man has lately shown signs of coming to life again socially, and Strabolgi[1] and R. A. Butler have both been to lunch with him recently. Ruth, on the other hand, who is also invited, says she would sooner be found dead than in his Embassy, and Butler tells me that his wife took the same line. ...

1 J. M. Kenworthy, 10th Baron Strabolgi (1886–1953). Liberal, then Labour, M.P. 1919–31.

Madame Maisky, advancing upon me with rather too red lips, says she is so sorry that my wife is in the country. She adds, rather malaprop, 'So many people's wives seem to be in the country just now.' I say, 'Yes, it is such beautiful weather, isn't it.' Little Korj[1] sidles up to me holding a glass of sherry, which he lifts as though in salutation. I say, rather coldly, and in the hearing of several, 'I don't know what you think we are celebrating today.' I then ask him, 'Do you remember when we last met?' He says no. I say, 'It was on 22nd August. Do you remember now?' (This was the day that Greenwood and I came round to demand explanation of Maisky of Ribbentrop's announced flight to Moscow to sign the German–Russian Pact. On this occasion Korj spoke most offensively in the ante-chamber, saying, when I asked what was the meaning of all this, 'This is to teach your Government and the French a lesson.') Korj then slunk away. ...

I deliberately outstay the rest to talk with Maisky alone in his study. I am very frank and say that he and his Government are always letting us down, first over the Pact, then over Finland, where their aggression was disgraceful and indefensible. What next? I ask. Do they intend to push on to Narvik? He says no, certainly not. They have shown evidence of their good will by not occupying more than necessary strategic points in Finland. They could, in another two months, have overrun and occupied the whole country, but have preferred to make peace. I say that we are unpleasantly reminded of Hitler's action in the Sudetenland, which was followed, only a few months after, by the conquest of all Czechoslovakia. He says there is no parallel. I say, 'We shall watch and judge you by results.' I ask whether it is not true that I did as much as anyone to try to get the Anglo–French–Soviet Pact last summer, that I visited him as often as anyone else in Parliament and persistently pushed Chamberlain towards the Pact. He says Yes, that is all true. I ask, 'Why then am I singled out by name for abuse and attack in your press and wireless? Do you not report back to Moscow who are your friends and who are not?' He says, 'It was only after the Finnish War began and the Labour Party took up such an unqualified anti-Soviet attitude that these criticisms were made.' I say, 'This is not true. I was attacked long before the Finnish War.' ...

I say, 'We don't want war with you – I repeat that our purpose is to kill Hitler – but if you force us into it, we shall not run away, and if unhappily it should come to that, I don't think the principal scene of operations would be in Finland or Scandinavia.' 'Moreover', I add, 'I think I know the mind of the Labour Party, and don't rely too much

1 O.G.P.U. press attaché.

on my colleague Pritt,[1] who is a light weight in the Party and of little account.'

He says nothing in reply about Pritt, but assures me that he and all in Russia share my view that they do not want a state of war between our two countries. And he says, 'There is no reason why it should come provided your Government does not make mischief in the Middle East.' I ask what is meant by 'making mischief' and he says, 'If you were to attack us or encourage others to do so.' ...

Note. I endeavoured to strike a note of frank and friendly intimidation throughout this talk.

Sunday 17th March

Hugh Gaitskell spends some hours with me and gives a pessimistic appreciation of the conduct, or rather the non-conduct, of the war. He is now in charge of Intelligence for Enemy Countries at the M.E.W. Naturally his mind is almost wholly focused on the problem of his Department. He does not think the blockade is doing much at present ...

According to Gaitskell, the Germans were getting supplies of oil from Romania, oil and metals from Russia, fats from the Balkans and iron ore from Sweden.

I asked how Germans were paying for their imports. He said they paid with exports which were diverted from sea routes we had stopped, principally with machinery of various kinds. This suited the Russians very well.

The other smaller neutrals were still supplying Germany to an important extent. We did not ration them properly. I said I heard from Cross[2] that there was 'a Cabinet decision in favour of trade

---

1 D. N. Pritt, q.v., fellow-travelling member of the N.E.C., was in trouble with his colleagues for supporting the Soviet attack on Finland in two books (*Light on Moscow* and *Must War Spread?*). On 23rd March, the Executive expelled him from the Labour Party, only Laski, Ellen Wilkinson and Susan Lawrence dissenting.

2 R. H. Cross, later Sir Ronald, 1st Bart (1896–1968). Minister of Economic Warfare 1939–40; Shipping 1940–41. Conservative M.P. for Rossendale 1931–45; Ormskirk 1950–51. Junior minister 1938–9. High Commissioner to Australia 1941–5.

agreements rather than forceful rationing'. He said he was afraid that this was true. He said, 'What can we do? The Foreign Office won't let us bully any of the neutrals and the Treasury won't let us bribe them.' He said that Treasury officials, notably Waley,[1] were disastrous. They put up objections in detail at inter-departmental conferences to many positive proposals of M.E.W. The Foreign Office attitude was illustrated by the sale, without conditions, to Romania of a quantity of light alloys for the manufacture of aircraft. This had horrified him. Within the Department Cross was amiable and able, but too much inclined to speak optimistically in public, notably his speech in the House and his broadcast at the end of January. He was also too much impressed by Leith-Ross, who undoubtedly had great ability but who, Gaitskell thought, was three-quarters pacifist. When one said to him that the blockade was not working well, he seemed to think that the only conclusion was that we must make peace. Mounsey was useless and had obviously been handed over to M.E.W. by the Foreign Office because the latter knew this. Morton[2] and Noel Hall were both very good and tough. So was the Intelligence Department of the Ministry as a whole, as distinct from the Political Relations Department, which was very weak, compliant and reflecting the Foreign Office. Ingram[3] and Stirling,[4] both from the F.O., were weak as water.

Gaitskell thinks that what is needed now in public speeches in Parliament and outside is a cold analysis of the situation, without personal attacks on Chamberlain and Co., but rather a courageous and reasoned pessimism which will convert public opinion to the view that these old gentlemen, with their optimistic twaddle, cannot win the war, and that a Coalition Government is necessary. He says that the speeches of Paul Reynaud[5] in France are just the kind of thing he has in mind.

1 S. D. Waley, later Sir David (1887–1962). Principal Assistant Secretary at the Treasury 1931–46; Third Secretary 1946–7.

2 Major D. J. F. Morton, later Sir Desmond (1891–1971). Principal Assistant Secretary at M.E.W. 1939–40. Personal Assistant to the Prime Minister 1940–46.

3 E. M. B. Ingram (1890–1941). Diplomatic Adviser to the Minister of Economic Warfare 1939–41.

4 C. N. Stirling, later Sir Charles (b. 1901). Head of Southern Department, M.E.W. 1939–42.

5 Paul Reynaud (1878–1966). Prime Minister of France March–June 1940. Minister of Finance 1938–40. Moderate Conservative. Interned by Vichy, and then by the Germans, 1940–45.

On 9th April the P.L.P. Executive discussed the possibility of entering the Government, and remained opposed to serving under Chamberlain. Nevertheless, the prospect of a coalition had an increasing appeal, and Dalton's diary shows how strong was the desire to get rid of the Prime Minister, before the crisis which precipitated his resignation. ' ... [M]ost think that we should keep an open mind, as events develop', Dalton recorded, 'and that if Chamberlain disappeared, as a result either of rapid physical decay or of a bad turn in the war, we should again seriously look at the question.' There was discussion about procedure: should a special conference be called before accepting an invitation, or should Annual Conference be asked for freedom to make whatever decision seemed appropriate? Dalton felt that Annual Conference might turn down such a request. Attlee argued that the best tactic might be to accept an invitation first, and get a special conference to approve afterwards.[1] As Dalton wrote later, this was very nearly what happened – and sooner than any of them expected.

Wednesday 10th April
Denmark and Norway invaded. Hear Halifax speak at one of Nathan's lunches at the Dorchester. He is pretty good, and a civilised man, though today he thought it necessary to drag in his religion and talk of man's 'immortal soul' and 'responsibility before his maker'.

I warn that rabbit Franckenstein, who is at my table, against Habsburg propaganda. He querulously complains that Otto[2] (pudding face) had a great reception in U.S.A. but that none of this was reported in our press.

From this lunch I go straight to Maisky, who has been very pressing for an interview. His chief point is that he wants Trade Talks to be started at once and thinks that he could begin them in London with a representative of H.M.G. Any proposals put by us could be reported by him to Moscow (he clearly has no definite and detailed instructions at present) and then, if things went well, someone could go from here to Moscow to complete an agreement. I said that I should welcome such talks if they are likely to lead anywhere, but the big question was did the Russians intend to help or hinder us in killing Hitler? Every-

1 Diary, 9th April 1940; FY, p. 297.
2 Prince Otto of Austria (b. 1912). Habsburg pretender to the throne of Austria–Hungary. Son of Emperor Charles IV, with whom he was forced into exile after the First World War.

326

7 Ernest Bevin, General Secretary
of the Transport and General
Workers' Union, 1930

8 Sir Oswald and Lady Cynthia
Mosley with George Lansbury at
the Trade Union Club, Oxford
Street, December 1930

9 1935 Labour Party Conference at Brighton. Dalton with John Wilmot, M.P. (*left*) and H.B. Lees-Smith.

10 In the garden at West Leaze, August 1937

11 Political exile: Sir Stafford Cripps, with Lady Cripps, at the 1939 Party
    Conference

12 Maynard Keynes and Lydia Lopokova at home in Gordon Square, Bloomsbury,
    March 1940

13 Labour backs a Coalition. Card vote at the Bournemouth Party Conference, May 1940.

14 Major Denis Healey and Captain Roy Jenkins at the Blackpool Party Conference, June 1945

thing else was subordinate to that, including the question of the arrest by us of ships making for Russian ports in the Pacific, of which he had complained. He said that they did not want Germany to win the war but that he doubted whether we could win it ...

Gaitskell to dine. Waley said to him, 'Dalton is going about blaming the Treasury for obstructing economic warfare.' This was rather marked, and Hugh thinks that he is suspected of telling me things. It will be well therefore that I should make a parade of hearing my stuff from Einzig,[1] the City, etc.

Thursday 11th April
After Winston's statement on the naval fighting along the Norwegian coast, ending with a declaration in favour of 'vigour', X[2] tells me in the Corridor that the Air Force is furious because (1) they are still forbidden to bomb any targets on land, including aerodromes in Norway which are 'lousy with German machines'; (2) C.A.S. [Chief of Air Staff] has just succeeded, after much difficulty, in getting C.O.S. [Chiefs of Staff] Committee to agree to our bombing German coaloil plant; these are superb targets, much better than Sylt or ships, and 15 out of 24 are within 150 miles of the Western frontier; this proposal is now bogged in the War Cabinet, and the excuse is put out that the French are against it; the French are a little reluctant, for fear of reprisals, but even more so are some of our old women.

X wonders whether I could not do something about this. I suppose that publicity would do more harm than good; he agrees. He thinks I might see Winston.

Later this evening, at 10.15 p.m., I see Sendall,[3] Winston's P.S. – the latter being, quite naturally, up to the neck. I tell Sendall that this is only the second time I have sought Winston out since the war began, the previous time being when I wanted him, in the first week, to urge for action to help the Poles. This is rather the same case, and now Winston is also Chairman of the Defence Committee and has more responsibility. He is, I say, our one white hope in that black flock. I say that many of us are most restive at the failure to fight war with both fists. If Winston will push his colleagues that way, he can count on

1 Paul Einzig (1897–1973). Financial and political journalist. Political correspondent on the *Financial News* 1939–45; *Financial Times* 1945–56. London correspondent of the *Commercial and Financial Chronicle* (New York) 1945–73.
2 Not identified. One of Dalton's secret informants within the Air Ministry or R.A.F.
3 B. C. Sendall (b. 1913). Principal Private Secretary to Churchill as First Lord of the Admiralty 1939–40. Principal Private Secretary to the Minister of Information 1941–5. Deputy Director-General of the Independent Television, then Broadcasting, Authority 1957–77.

much support. If not, we must reserve the right to make a row in whatever seems the most effective way. Sendall hints, pretty broadly, that both he and Winston quite agree with my point of view, and undertakes to transmit my message. He adds, 'And most of those targets are not defended.'

Sunday 14th April

I decided yesterday that the time had come to read the Riot Act over Bastianini.[1] Rumours had reached me from many quarters that Mussolini had once more been bemused by Hitler on the Brenner, persuaded that a German victory was imminent and that he must fling in Italy soon; also that he was feeding furiously on old anti-British grievances and notably on memories of Eden; also that Italy had now been allowed by our economic non-warfare to pile up large stocks. It was also reported that the Italian press was twisting all news from Norway and being violently pro-German and anti-British. Having, therefore, an empty Sunday, I fixed to call on the Ambassador just after noon.

I spent an hour and a quarter with him and I think it was worth while. I began by reminding him that I had been for many years a friend of his country and that two of my proudest memories were of my right to wear above my heart an Italian *Medaglio al Valore* won on the Carso,[2] and of my most interesting conversation with Mussolini in Rome in December 1932. I had called to see him because I had noticed with great surprise the apparent lack of information in these last days in the Italian press, usually so well-informed, realistic and clear-eyed. It did not seem to be known in Italy that we had now sunk nearly all Hitler's fleet, and this was a fact of the first order of importance for the future of the war, since an even greater part of our great naval power would now be available for use elsewhere as might be needed, and since the naval action off the Norwegian coast, and in particular the ridiculously small losses suffered by the British fleet, showed what poor sailors these Germans were and how they were no match for ours. ...

On the blockade generally, I said that our intention was to starve Hitler of all war supplies, and I was urging the strongest possible action to this end. There was no desire to starve Italy of her own requirements, but certainly I could not agree to permitting the transit of war

1 Giuseppe Bastianini (1899–1961). Italian Ambassador to Britain 1939–40. Vice-Secretary of the Italian Fascist Party 1921–4.
2 During the Italian retreat after the battle of Caporetto in 1917, when Dalton was serving with the Royal Artillery.

supplies to Germany through Italy. He said that no supplies went through (that, thought I, is a whopper!) since Italy was a debtor country and was not in a position to buy from America (that, thought I, is just economic nonsense) ...

Bastianini warned me that it was impossible to try to divide the Italian people from Mussolini; just as impossible as to divide the German people from Hitler. Mussolini, he said, could in two days, by a strong speech, turn the whole mind of the Italian people in a new direction. I said, 'It may need some hard blows to divide the German people from Hitler, but we shall do it. On the other hand, I recognise, of course, the great influence of Mussolini over the Italian people.'

Bastianini then – and no Anglo–Italian conversation can ever be complete without this element – began to abuse the French. ...

Reverting to my statement that our intention was to defeat Germany, he laid his hand upon my arm and said, 'Ah, here is a *bonne bouche* for you. If you win the war – and I will concede that you will win it' (his English is not yet very strong, and I am not sure whether he meant 'I will assume for the sake of argument', or 'I do, in fact, assume') ' – you will have to make peace either against Germany or by discussion with Germany. In the first case you will soon be back where we are now, for you will have a resentful Germany which will soon give birth to another Hitler, or two or three more Hitlers. So what will be the use of that? If, on the other hand, you are prepared to make peace by discussion with Germany, you can have that discussion with her now and make peace now.' I recognise this as the formal Italian thesis which has been put about by their spokesmen, desirous of being seen as peace-makers, for many months. I replied, 'I rule out absolutely discussion with Hitler and his gang. One cannot trust a word they say, and their signatures are worthless. But I will answer your question. We will make peace with Germany and we will discuss with Germany, but only when we have pulled her teeth out.' He seemed to have no answer ready for this.

Bringing our talk to a close, I said that I often recalled Salandra's[1] phrase '*sacro egoismo*'. There was today a *sacro egoismo* of Italy and also a *sacro egoismo* of England. We must find practical means of adjustment between them. He said, I thought rather weakly, 'Yes, I have not come to London to make any trouble.' I said that I hoped

1 Antonio Salandra (1853–1931). Prime Minister of Italy 1914–16. Salandra used the phrase in October 1914, in a speech to mark the death of the Foreign Minister, San Giuliano. He declared that the good Italian's mind must be liberated from 'every prejudice, from every sentiment, save that of exclusive and limitless devotion to our fatherland, and of a *sacro egoismo* for Italy'.

in days to come we could rebuild the Stresa Front.[1] He said, with great vehemence, 'Ah, that accursed Eden spoilt all that. Had it not been for sanctions, we should not be in these difficulties today.' I said that we must work on to a new phase, and we parted, I recalling my many happy memories of Italy, of persons and places, of beauty and of battlefields, and he saying, 'I hope that some day I may be able to accompany you as a friend and a visitor in my country.'

Monday 15th April
A Mrs Phillimore[2] lunch to meet Scandinavian journalists. Easier to find things to say to a Norwegian who is fighting than to a Dane who has allowed himself to be squashed or to a Swede who is waiting and wondering. I am eagerly itching for news that we have landed troops in Norway.

Walk away from lunch with Alexander to whom I report my call at the Admiralty on Thursday last. He attaches some importance to the French objection to opening up the air war in the west, but warmly agrees that any prohibition on our bombing German air fields in Norway would be outrageous. Evidently, as repeated raids on Stavanger show, this prohibition is at least partially off.

He says that he is quite satisfied with, and very confident of the success of, our naval plans. The Admiralty are going steadily on, refusing either to halt or to hurry, and are going to mop up all German elements in Norwegian waters from the north southwards. They have begun at Narvik and will go steadily along the coast.

Winston, he says, has been very furious for a long time at Scandinavian neutrality. He wanted to mine Norwegian waters and stop the iron ore in the second week of the war, and has unsuccessfully been pressing the War Cabinet ever since. At the beginning of February King Haakon[3] made a special appeal to our King to use his personal influence to prevent this [violation] of Norwegian neutrality. 'Serve him right', I said, 'if the Germans are hunting him now with bombers!'

1 'Stresa Front': in April 1935 Mussolini met the British and French Prime Ministers at Stresa, on Lake Maggiore, to declare jointly their disapproval of Hitler's intrigues and rearmament. They pledged themselves to 'close and cordial collaboration' to maintain existing treaties. Mussolini's invasion of Abyssinia shattered the Stresa Front, and put an end to the hopes of Italian co-operation and understanding which it had embodied.
2 Lucy ('Lion') Phillimore, née Fitzpatrick (d. 1957). A prominent Fabian and political hostess, whose carefully arranged parties at the Ritz Dalton often attended during the war.
3 King Haakon VII (1872–1957). King of Norway 1905–57. Forced into exile when the Germans invaded.

I told Alexander that I was going to spend much time and effort now in continuing to binge up the blockade. A Finnish journalist said to me at lunch that, in the rush of events, it had almost passed unnoticed and uncommented that Germany had herself been violating Norwegian territorial waters by transporting through them armed forces hidden in iron-ore ships.

At this moment we see a poster, 'B.E.F. [British Expeditionary Force] in Norway: official'. I buy a paper with a song in my heart. I am half inclined to ring up Bastianini and ask him to let the Italian press get the news!

Friday 19th April
At his own request I visit Hoare. This is my first call at the Air Ministry since Kingsley Wood went.[1] Hoare is most anxious that we should maintain the liaison arrangement. ...

They are handicapped, he says, by very bad weather, by melting snow and tremendous winds. It is amazing what the R.A.F. and the ships have done in these adverse conditions. At Narvik a few German guns are still causing trouble, and small scattered German detachments in strong positions, but he hopes that all this will be finished soon.

Monday 22nd April
Mrs Phillimore lunch with Romanians – Tilea, Mateescu and Dumitrescu,[2] with Attlee, Greenwood, Alexander, Phil [Noel-Baker] and I. The Romanians are, for the moment, a little reassured by our success in Scandinavia and our intended trade talks with Russia, which, they seem to think, will postpone any attack on Bessarabia.

I ask Tilea whether it is not very dangerous to bring back the Iron Guard who have been, and probably still are, in Hitler's pay. Can the Romanians be sure that they will not act as traitors, like Sundlo[3] and Quisling[4] in Norway? Tilea not very happy, says that he is on the black list of the Iron Guard, and due to be murdered. Therefore, he can say frankly that he thinks it was wise to liberate them from gaol,

---

1 Sir Samuel Hoare replaced Kingsley Wood as Air Minister on 3rd April 1940. Wood became Chancellor of the Exchequer on 12th May.
2 Major G. Dumitrescu. Romanian Military and Naval Attaché in London 1936–41.
3 Colonel Konrad Sundlo. Norwegian Staff Officer and leading collaborator with the German Nazis.
4 Vidkun Quisling (1887–1945). Leader of the Norwegian Fascist Party. Puppet Prime Minister of Norway after the invasion 1940–45. Executed by the Norwegians in 1945.

so as to increase the sense of national unity in Romania.

Wednesday 1st May

Norway looks bad. Yesterday evening there seemed a tide in the House of Commons against the P.M. 'He must go now', many were saying, including some of his own. Attlee tells me he thinks we shall have to face up to it. Clearly he is in favour of going in, on certain conditions. I say one must be that Chamberlain packs up. Attlee says that a member of the Government has been urging him that we should come in. 'We want your tough guys in,' he says. I mention to Attlee, Campbell Stuart's[1] proposal that Halifax should be P.M. and Attlee lead the Commons.

Thursday 2nd May

P.M. announces that Åndalsnes has been evacuated ...

Talk at length later in the afternoon with Alexander who gives me an account of his conversations at the Admiralty. Churchill seems very subdued. Some even say, 'Winston has lost his nerve.' There is great conflict of evidence as to who wanted to do what. Churchill said last week, 'I can only speak for the Admiralty'; on another occasion, 'I had some very unhappy experiences in the last war when my naval advisers, after the event, said they had differed from me all along.' Someone has said that, remembering the Dardanelles, Winston in this war is like a singed cat. But Alexander had said to him some days ago, 'I thought you were not only First Lord of the Admiralty now, but Chairman of the Fighting Services Committee.' And now, Alexander understands, Winston has attained the right to take the Chair at meetings of the Chiefs of Staff.

Now follows Alexander's narrative to me.

Our force for Finland was dispersed because ships were scarce and wanted elsewhere. Our Intelligence Service failed to discover in advance the prospect of Norwegian treachery: nor did they detect the use of the Norwegian 'Covered Way' for the transport of armed Germans under hatches in iron-ore ships returning, nominally, empty. This, Alexander thinks, is our first bull point for criticism.

Winston wanted to mine the Covered Way last November. At that time there was some opposition from Dominions, who, feeling far

---

1 Sir Campbell Stuart (1885–1972). Director of Propaganda in Enemy Countries 1939–40. Deputy Director of Propaganda in Enemy Countries 1918. Managing Editor of the *Daily Mail* 1921; Managing Director of *The Times* 1920–24. Chairman of the Imperial Communications Advisory Committee, and its successor, the Commonwealth Communications Council 1933–45.

away, feared effects on their public opinion of violations of International Law. Winston, therefore, was overruled. In January he tried again, more insistently. The Dominions were now reconciled, but Attlee and Greenwood, when consulted, are reported in government circles to have advised against mining, though Sinclair was in favour. And King Haakon wrote a personal letter to King George, who, acting quite correctly, passed it on to his ministers, strongly against mining. So Winston for the second time was overruled, and, if we say too much, we may be confronted with Attlee and Greenwood, though they said what they did to ministers without consulting colleagues. Winston tried a third time at the end of March, and this time he won, but it was very late. ...

We spoke for a moment of alternative Prime Ministers. I said I was inclined to favour Halifax, and mentioned to him the suggestion of Campbell Stuart. Leadership in the Commons, I said, would give us a status otherwise not easily to be arranged. But he and I both shrugged our shoulders comprehendingly at Attlee in that role. None the less, I do not dismiss this possibility. Alexander, I think, would rather like Winston to be P.M.

Saturday 4th to Sunday 5th May
Conference in London with Blum, Zyromski[1] and Roucayrol.[2] Held at Victoria Hotel, Northumberland Avenue. Quite a convenient meeting place. We have a fair-sized representation of National Executive members. Dallas presides.

Saturday 4th May
We begin with exchange of information on Norway. Blum says that French public opinion was shocked by the very rapid change, within twenty-four hours, in the Norwegian situation as revealed by official British communiqués. ...

There was evidence of lack of preparation and of co-ordination between the French and British governments. It had been agreed, when operations in Finland were under discussion, that all these, including the land operations, should be under British command. This agreement, together with details of the forces to be supplied by France and Britain, were embodied in a Protocol. Since the command was to be British, Gamelin, when criticisms were raised in Paris, said that he could not intervene. The French did all the British asked, though not,

1 J. F. M. M. Zyromski. French Socialist leader. Representative on the Executive of the Labour and Socialist International 1936–40. Editor of *Le Populaire*.

perhaps, 'with zeal', since they held that all force withdrawn from the Western Front might be wasted on subsidiary expeditions.

Blum thinks that the plans made in February and March for Finland were still applied in April in Norway. (I don't think much of this argument.) Jules Moch[1] was at Scapa Flow on 7th April when the first news came that the German fleet were out. The British fleet went out within a few hours, hoping to meet the Germans in the North Sea and bring them to battle. In accordance with a pre-arranged plan, the British ships scattered over a wide circle in the North Sea and then converged upon a rendezvous. It was hoped that they would thus drive the Germans in front of them and catch them, as it were, in a net. But no German ships were caught, and the British and French only met themselves at the rendezvous. While they were thus sweeping the North Sea, the German transports and warships were in the Norwegian fjords, from Oslo up to Narvik. ...

After this exposé by Blum, Greenwood gave our French colleagues the following account.

Much remains to be explained. Why was the Force, said to consist of 100,000 men, for Finland dispersed? It appears that the British government did not know of the German plans for Denmark and Norway and were not prepared for the speedy success of these, as a consequence of Norwegian treachery and weakness. The French, he understood, came to the Supreme War Council quite opposed to the idea of withdrawing from the Trondheim zone. The original British plan was for a frontal attack on Trondheim, as being the strategic point of the campaign. This was accepted by the War Cabinet but was later modified on the advice of the Chiefs of Staff. (Greenwood is not clear, when questioned by me at this point, as to whether the Chiefs of Staff were unanimous or only two to one, the Admiralty dissenting.) Churchill, who had wanted the big bang, was driven to 'acquiesce' – this was his own chosen word – in the decision of the War Cabinet. A fortnight ago he was in a most indignant state of mind, but was now prepared to take his share of Cabinet responsibility.

At the Supreme War Council the French pressed the argument against evacuation. But the British said that the German forces were so strong and were advancing so fast, that effective defence was impossible. The French, having put their case very strongly, in the end agreed with the British view. Greenwood understood that this included

---

1 Jules Moch (b. 1893). Naval engineer on a French cruiser with the British fleet. French Socialist. Member of the Popular Front Government of Léon Blum. Minister in successive governments 1946–58.

agreement by the French that there was no point in holding Namsos if a big attack on Trondheim was no longer practicable. The French, however, insisted that we should [stay] on at Narvik. Greenwood understands that yesterday, 4th May, a landing was made by us at a point between Namsos and Narvik; also that our attack on Narvik was to be speeded up. The Germans will, however, probably destroy the railway to the Scandinavian frontier. He doubts whether Blum's estimate of the loss of one British warship a day is not excessive. On the other hand, it has been stated that 20,000 German troops were drowned in the crossings to Norway.

The P.M. had told him that the Germans might have anything up to 100,000 men now in Norway. The advance guards of these, running into thousands, had been landed, over a period of weeks, if not months, at various Norwegian ports from German ships, mostly the ore ships returning 'empty' to Narvik. These men, disguised as German merchant seamen, stayed in sailors' doss houses at the ports. All this pointed to a grave failure of British Intelligence Service in Norway (or to neglect or stupid discounting by those at home of Intelligence reports). If we can take and hold Narvik, together with the strip of Norwegian coast lying to the south of this, and if we can secure a good air base for our fighters, this will transform the situation in Norway. So, at least, the P.M. had told Greenwood!

When Edouard Daladier, the 'French Chamberlain', resigned as Prime Minister in March, President Lebrun had called on the more combative Paul Reynaud to form a government. Lacking a firm party base, Reynaud was forced to accommodate his former rivals and opponents in the Chamber. Thus he included Daladier as Minister of Defence in his Cabinet, but felt unable to bring in his personal friend Léon Blum, for fear of antagonising the Right. Reynaud's Cabinet nevertheless included six Socialists (S.F.I.O.) as well as Radical Socialists and left-of-centre moderates.

Sunday 5th May
Blum gives us today the following account.

The French Socialist Party had been very definitely in opposition to the Daladier Government. Not only was there no participation, but there were no contacts, such as we had. He thinks that perhaps we have all the advantages, both tactical and moral, of influence and information without responsibility. He does not know how long we shall be able to continue in this state of beatitude! In France the situation was quite different. They had no influence or contact as regards either the conduct of the war or domestic policy. There was great discontent in Parliament against the Government –

(1) owing to the personal character of Daladier, who was *solitaire* and *farouche*.
(2) because Daladier had too many jobs: he was P.M., Foreign Secretary, Minister of War, Minister for the Co-ordination of Defence, Minister of National Economy, and also in charge of the Service of Information and Propaganda! '
(3) Daladier was always adjourning his decision – not surprisingly in view of (2).
(4) Daladier last September said that he would create a separate Ministry of Information. When he fell from power he had not yet done this: this was typical.
(5) As regards Finland, he incurred very grave criticism. On this occasion all the critics and the discontented combined against him. At the Tribune he gave figures and details regarding the aid to Finland which were later proved, in one of the Committees, to have been seriously incorrect. He had made very energetic declarations in favour of an armed entry into Finland, but he did not persuade the Chamber or the Senate that his preparations had been complete. In the votes which followed his statements, there were large numbers of abstentions. People said, 'It's the same thing again: promises made; nothing done.'

The new Government under Reynaud was then formed. A majority of the French Socialist Party was in favour of going in. The chief argument used on the other side was: 'We refused in October to go into Daladier's Government, he being the leader of the Radicals. If now we go into Reynaud's Government, he being a very moderate Republican, this will upset the basis, electoral and political, of co-operation between parties of the Left. There has for many years been an understanding, even if unspoken, between Socialists and Radicals as against the forces of the Centre and the Right.' But most took the other view. Blum had been six weeks without any contact at all with Daladier, even by telephone, and this illustrated the state of personal relationships. Blum said that he himself would not enter Reynaud's Government. His presence would increase the violence of the attacks of the Right and Centre against Socialist participation. His name symbolises, for such critics, the Government of 1936. He thought he could best help the new Government, both in the Chamber and in the press, from outside.

Georges Monnet[1] had entered the War Cabinet, and Sérol[2] and Rivière,[3] both well liked in the Parliamentary Group, were to be Ministers of Justice and Pensions. Under-Secretaries were Février[4] at Information, Albertin[5] at Public Works and Blancho,[6] who was a Trade Unionist and a metal worker, at Munitions under Dautry.[7]

How solid was the new Government? The Socialists were its only really solid support! They had already saved the Government from defeat on the first day. Laval, Flandin and Marin[8] were all violently opposed. Reynaud and Flandin had hated each other for years. Reynaud and Daladier are, to put it mildly, not very intimate. The Radicals as a whole are jealous and doubtful. Daladier would like to be P.M. again. There is no obvious third choice. There has been some reaction in France from the events in Norway, since the first impression given was that the Germans had been caught in a trap!

Roucayrol added that when Daladier was in power things didn't go well but a majority of the Chamber wanted to cover him. With Reynaud in power, a majority wanted to destroy him. The Radicals think they have a right to hold the key positions in every French Cabinet. From them there is likely to be a permanent and jealous hostility.

1 Georges Monnet (1898–1980). Minister of Blockades in the Reynaud Government March–June 1940. Socialist. Opposed the armistice with Hitler, but abstained in the vote giving Pétain full powers. Minister of Agriculture in the 1936–7 Popular Front Government.
2 Albert Sérol. Minister of Justice in the Reynaud Government March–June 1940. Deputy President of the Parliamentary Socialist group 1937–8. Minister of Labour in the Blum Government March–April 1938. President of the Legislative Committee Chamber 1938–9.
3 Albert Rivière (1891–1953). Minister of Pensions (March–June 1940) in the Reynaud Government and Minister for the Colonies in the first Government of Marshal Pétain. Minister of Pensions under Blum 1936–7. Socialist.
4 André Février (1885–1961). Member of several governments 1937–40. Voted for Pétain 1940.
5 Fabien Albertin (1879–1950). Under-Secretary for Public Works in the Reynaud Government 1940. Voted for Pétain.
6 François Blancho. Served in Blum Cabinets 1936–7 and 1938 and in Chautemps Cabinet 1937–8. Under-Secretary for Armaments in the Reynaud Government 1940. Voted for Pétain but in 1941 was arrested by the Germans.
7 Raoul Dautry (1880–1951). Minister for Armaments in the Reynaud Government 1940.
8 Louis Marin (1871–1960). Leader of the Fédération Républicaine, the main conservative grouping in the Chamber of Deputies. Opposed the armistice in June 1940.

Refugees in France[1]

At our Anglo-French Conference, Blum, replying to enquiries by Laski and others, said that this question had been much exploited by Communist propaganda in England, and masked Nazi propaganda in U.S.A. It should be remembered that neither England nor the U.S.A. had taken in any large number of refugees, whereas France had received wave after wave since 1933. The first great wave, of those who fled when Hitler came to power, went nearly all either to France or Czechoslovakia. The English took quite insignificant numbers. France then received a wave from the Saar, and from Austria; then an immense wave from Spain after Franco's victory; then two waves from Czechoslovakia, one largely Sudetens after Munich, and another of Czechs after March 1939.

Among this immense army of refugees there is a considerable proportion of Nazi spies. When you think of what has happened in Denmark and Norway, you will not be surprised at this. Do not, therefore, be surprised if the first measures taken against refugees entering France, from the point of view of public safety, are severe. On the other hand, they have never been cruel. It has been a question of satisfying ourselves that individual refugees are not working for Hitler. It was our experience that a number of refugees, who had been innocently vouched for by British Socialists and other persons of good will, were in fact spies. In addition to the problem of public safety, there was, by reason of the numbers of the refugees, an immense problem of administration. Camps on a great scale had to be improvised. Of course, conditions there were not irreproachable. But the French Socialists have been most active as regards all this, and the headquarters of all the exiled Socialist Parties, German, Austrian, Czech, Polish and Spanish, are in France. Eight days ago some of them went to see Reynaud himself on these matters, and every day individual injustices are being redressed. But there are still in France 500,000 Spaniards, including a very large number of suspect individuals whom we simply cannot allow to live, and to move about freely, in France. It is very easy to excite sensibilities on this question, but critics should make an effort to put themselves in the place of Frenchmen. Risks of injustice to individuals are, in these conditions, inevitable. Two or three French Socialists are specially dealing with such cases, and the service of the French Parliamentary Group is also being used.

As regards the Communists, British Socialists should also make an effort to realise the difference in French and in British conditions.

1 Note dated 5th May 1940 in Dalton Papers 3/2 (45–7).

French Communists suddenly changed in 1935, after the conclusion of the Franco–Soviet Pact, from an attitude of revolutionary defeatism to an extreme nationalism and chauvinism. During the summer of 1939 they were most intransigent against Hitler and were demanding that not the slightest further concession should be made to him either in Poland or anywhere else. This attitude continued over the outbreak of war, and then suddenly, in a day, on orders from Moscow, they returned to revolutionary defeatism. This double change, at short notice, was carried out on orders from abroad. The question which French Socialists had to ask themselves was 'Can you tolerate, in time of war, a group of seventy-five members in the Chamber when you know that their action is wholly determined by a foreign power which today is very nearly an ally of Hitler?' ...

There has been much misrepresentation of the alleged death penalty for possession or circulation of Communist literature. In French law the death penalty has always existed for treason. The recent decree, concerning which so much has been said, gives certain further definitions of treason in wartime, and includes 'deliberate and conscious attempts' to undermine the national defence. It must be proved that any person charged has been deliberately plotting against the security of the State. Sérol, the present Minister of Justice, is a Socialist ... He will certainly administer this decree reasonably. Innocent persons who merely possess or even innocently circulate Communist literature, will not be subject to it. But, in time of war, the need to defend liberty sometimes requires restrictions on some liberties in order that any liberty at all shall survive.

Following the evacuation of troops from Åndalsnes and Namsos, the Government gave way to demands for a parliamentary debate on the failure of the campaign. When the debate opened on 7th May, it rapidly became clear that the real issue was not the Norway operation, but the whole conduct of the war.[1]

Wednesday 8th May
This is the second day of our House of Commons debate on the conduct of the war. Yesterday Chamberlain was unimpressive and Oliver

1 Dalton gave a full account of the events of the next week in his memoirs, which drew heavily on his diary for this period. Entries are included here in full because of important omissions and changes in the version that appears in *The Fateful Years*, and because of the special historical significance of Dalton's contemporary account. See FY, pp. 304–18.

Stanley mild and feeble. The most striking speech was that of Keyes[1] on the failure to go in and take Trondheim in the first twenty-four hours after Hitler moved. Hugh Gaitskell, who came to breakfast with me this morning, says that he has it from a Foreign Office source that Halifax threatened to resign unless an attack were made against Trondheim: that Sargent[2] and Collier[3] of the Foreign Office are both leaking very freely and saying that Cork and Orrery,[4] the Admiral at sea, asked for permission to go right into Trondheim and that this was refused by the Admirals in Whitehall. Cork and Orrery said afterwards, 'In the first twenty-four hours I could have taken Trondheim with my bare hands.' Hugh also reports that the attack on Trondheim was ordered and counter-ordered three or four times. As to Narvik, he says that people in the M.E.W. are saying that we shall be 'out in a fortnight, or in a month at the most'. He wonders whether we have any preparations of any kind in the event of Hitler going for Holland and Belgium. He thinks that, unless we really pull ourselves together, we shall literally lose the war.

At 10.30 this morning Parliamentary Executive meets and we discuss whether or not to take a vote tonight on the adjournment. A better discussion than usual. A majority, including Morrison and Lees-Smith, is for taking a vote: a minority – Tom Williams, Pethick-Lawrence, Wedgwood Benn and I – against. My view is that there are strong arguments on both sides, but that a vote at this stage is likely to consolidate the Government majority and that Chamberlain and Margesson[5] would like us to have one. At the Party Meeting later in the morning the Executive recommendation to have a vote is accepted, though with some doubts and dissentients. Later events prove that this was quite the right decision, and that my judgment was wrong.

Today's debate is very dramatic. Morrison opens very well, though somewhere in the middle of his speech he lost grip for a while, but he has lots of detail and is very definite. He again names Chamberlain,

1 Admiral Sir Roger Keyes, 1st Bart, later 1st Baron (1872–1945). Conservative M.P. for Portsmouth North 1934–43. Admiral of the Fleet 1930. Director of Combined Operations 1940–41.
2 Sir Orme Sargent (1884–1962). Deputy Under-Secretary at the Foreign Office 1939–46; Permanent Under-Secretary 1946–9.
3 L. Collier, later Sir Lawrence (1890–1976). Counsellor at the Foreign Office 1932–41. Minister to Norway 1941; Ambassador to the Norwegian government 1942–50.
4 W. H. D. Boyle, 12th Earl of Cork and Orrery (1873–1967). Commander of all forces in the Narvik area. Admiral of the Fleet 1938.
5 Captain H. D. R. Margesson, later 1st Viscount (1890–1965). Government Chief Whip 1931–40. Secretary of State for War December 1940–42. Conservative M.P. for Rugby 1924–42; West Ham Upton 1922–3.

Simon and Hoare as men who must go. He ends up by saying that we shall vote. Thereupon, when he sits down, up jumps the Old Man, showing his teeth like a rat in a corner, and says, 'I accept the challenge.' (Ruth says next morning, 'What else could the silly old fool do if we said we were going to have a vote?') 'No Government can continue unless it has the support of Parliament and the public. I ask my friends – and I still have some friends in this House – to support the Government tonight in the Lobby.' He then sat down and Hoare began to speak about the Air. The Old Man's intervention was gawky in its appeal to his 'friends', as Lloyd George and others rubbed in later on. I had thought for a moment that he was going to announce a general election, a course which had been hinted at in the *Evening Standard* of the night before, in the event of our insisting on a vote, and which had been put to me by Frank Owen in the Lobby when I had asked his opinion. Though I had not mentioned this to colleagues, and had thought it a very remote possibility, I had kept this idea at the back of my mind and it had influenced my view in the Parliamentary Executive this morning. I had judged that in a general election campaign the Old Man would win hands down and we should be wiped further out than in 1931.

Lloyd George made a violent attack, but, as always now, without much constructive in it, but with one superb retort to Winston: 'I hope he is not going to allow himself to be used by the others as an air-raid shelter.' Lloyd George ended by recalling the P.M.'s appeal for 'sacrifice'. He added, 'I say solemnly that the Prime Minister should give an example of sacrifice, because there is nothing which can contribute more to victory in this war than that he should sacrifice the Seals of Office.' The debate continues to run very badly for the Government, only a few third-raters defending them, while Duff Cooper[1] and Commander Bower,[2] ostentatiously in uniform, denounce them, and the former states that he will vote against them. (Keyes, who is today in mufti, appeared yesterday in uniform with his breast covered with ribbons, and said in the opening sentences of his speech that he had put on uniform in order to show that he spoke for a large number of naval officers who were deeply critical of the Government's handling of the naval side of the war.) After Lloyd George had

1 Duff Cooper, later 1st Viscount Norwich (1890–1954). Conservative M.P. for Westminster St George's 1931–45; Oldham 1924–9. Junior minister 1928–9, 1931–4. Financial Secretary at the Treasury 1934–5; Secretary of State for War 1935–7; First Lord of the Admiralty 1937–8. Minister of Information 1940–41; Chancellor of the Duchy of Lancaster 1941–3. Ambassador to France 1944–7. Cooper had resigned in 1938 over Munich.
2 Commander R. T. Bower (1894–1975). Conservative M.P. for Cleveland 1931–45.

spoken, Winston was heard to say to Kingsley Wood on leaving the Chamber, 'This is all making it damned difficult for me tonight.' It is also reported that he was heard to say to Elliot of Lloyd George's attack on the P.M. 'absolutely devastating'. A good deal of riot, some of it rather stupid, developed towards the close of Winston's final speech, and then we voted. When I went into our Lobby it seemed to be full of young Conservatives in uniform. Earlier in the day I had not thought that, at the outside, we should get more than a dozen to fifteen Government supporters in with us, although many would no doubt abstain. In fact, we had between forty and fifty. My eyes filled with tears. Many of them giving the last vote they would ever give, for their country and against their Party.

Terrific buzz in Lobby afterwards. People asked, 'What is the next step?' I say, 'The Old Man must go along to Buckingham Palace and hand them in.'

Earlier in the evening I had seen Butler and said to him that I was not authorised to speak on behalf of my colleagues, but that in my view, provided Chamberlain, Simon and Hoare disappeared from the Government altogether, we should be prepared to discuss the question of entering the Government. I said that there were difficulties connected with this, but that, subject to the condition I had mentioned, they could be hopefully explored. I added that, if I was asked who should succeed Chamberlain as Prime Minister, my own view, which I thought was shared by a number of others, was that it should be Halifax. In time of war I was not concerned with the fact that he was in the Lords. Indeed, this had some advantages in relieving the strain upon him. Some might think of Winston as P.M., but in my view he would be better occupied in winning the war. If one passed beyond these two one arrived in the outer circles of Anderson,[1] etc., and no one there seemed to stand out. I told Butler that I did not wish him to keep what I had said entirely to himself, but should be glad if he would pass it on to Halifax. He said that he was much interested, and thanked me for speaking, as on other occasions, so frankly. He asked whether we would not consider the possibility of Chamberlain continuing as P.M. if certain other changes were made. There was, he said, a great loyalty to Chamberlain in the Conservative Party. I said there could be no question of this. In our view Chamberlain and Simon had failed so often, both in peace and war, and had such long crime sheets, that they must go. I did not myself put Hoare in the same class, but most of my colleagues, I thought, would insist on his going too.

1 Sir John Anderson, q.v., Home Secretary and Minister of Home Security 1939–40.

I had said much the same, the night before, to Assheton,[1] Under-Secretary to the Ministry of Labour, with whom I had found myself alone in the Newspaper Room after the House had risen. So they can't say that they are getting no guidance from us! On the other hand, it would be a mistake to say this kind of thing publicly, particularly as one is on the eve of the Bournemouth Conference, which is perfectly synchronised with this crisis.

Thursday 9th May
10.30 a.m. Ivor Thomas[2] tells me on the phone that posters now announce 'Premier sees the King'.

House in a buzz. Boothby says most of the 43 of last night met today and decided not to join or support any government which did not contain members of the Labour and Liberal Parties; also to serve under any Premier who could create such a government. He asked would it help us to publish this? I said yes, certainly; no member of our Party would serve under Chamberlain, nor, I thought, with Simon or Hoare. With these three out, on the other hand, we should be prepared to discuss, and to accept our full share of responsibility on proper terms. Later, I saw him surrounded by the press. The Old Man was telephoning personally from 8 a.m. onwards, trying to conciliate opponents of yesterday. He seems determined himself to stick on – like a dirty old piece of chewing gum on the leg of a chair, as someone said – but is offering to get rid of Simon, Hoare, and, if need be, Kingsley Wood, if this would propitiate critics. It will not. Last night's division, and especially the large number of young men in uniform in our Lobby, has shattered them. Wise[3] said to me today, 'I have come straight back from Namsos to vote against the Government. I voted on behalf of my men. We were bombed by German aeroplanes and had nothing with which to reply, not even a machine gun. When I went back last night to the Mess, everyone, from the Major General downwards, said Well done!' That, I believe, is the spirit of the fighting services. Lloyd George has seen Attlee and said that Chamberlain should resign and might then advise the King to send for Attlee. What should he do then? I told Attlee that I thought he could not possibly

---

1 Ralph Assheton, later 1st Baron Clitheroe (1901–84). Parliamentary Secretary at the Ministry of Labour and National Service 1939–42. Conservative M.P. for Rushcliffe 1934–45; City of London 1945–50; Blackburn 1950–55.
2 Ivor (Bulmer) Thomas (b. 1905). Fusilier with Royal Fusiliers 1939–40. Recruited into S.O.E. end of 1940. Labour, then Independent, then Conservative, M.P. for Keighley 1942–50. Junior minister 1945–7. Journalist and historian.
3 A. R. Wise (1901–74). Conservative M.P. for Smethwick 1931–45; Rugby 1959–66. Lieut-Col. in the Queen's Royal Regiment (West Surrey).

be P.M. in this situation. He quite agreed. The P.M. *must* be a Ministerialist. He agrees with my preference for Halifax over Churchill, but we both think that either would be tolerable.

We go tomorrow to Bournemouth, and the timetable is unpredictable. There may even be a new offensive by Hitler. Opinion in our Party is, I think, steadily hardening along the lines which I have held for some time. They will go in with both feet if necessary personal demolitions are effected. Trade Union common sense will insist on this.

Friday 10th May
This morning Hitler violated Holland, Belgium and Luxemburg. Should Parliament meet? Alexander telephones from Manchester suggesting it should. I hold strongly that it should not, for this would give the cheer-leaders and crisis-exploiters a chance to rehabilitate the Old Man. All N.E. members due to leave for Bournemouth by 11.34 a.m. train. I go round to House of Commons at 10 and see Attlee who arrives about 10.30. Greenwood also comes in later. We all agree that we should not ask for Parliament and should go to Bournemouth. Attlee and Greenwood had seen the Old Man last night, when he had once more begged them to enter a Government under his premiership. They had told him bluntly that this was impossible and that the mood of the country required a new premiership. He then asked would we serve under a new Premier. They said they could give no answer to this before consulting colleagues. He asked for an early and definite answer to this last question and also to the first which he had put, namely, would we serve under him. He had also asked whether, pending an answer to these two questions, we would not send a message saying that the Labour Party supported the Government at this grave crisis of the war. This old man is incorrigibly limpet and always trying new tricks to keep himself firm upon the rock.

This morning, therefore, I drafted a message which Attlee and Greenwood accepted and issued over their two names (reported in the press on Saturday, the 11th): 'The Labour Party, in view of the latest series of abominable aggressions by Hitler' (Attlee in the first draft had said 'In view of the present critical war position': I said this lacked punch; he agreed!), 'while firmly convinced that a drastic reconstruction of the Government is vital and urgent in order to win the war, reaffirms its determination to do its utmost to achieve victory. It calls on all its members to devote all their energies to this end.'

And so to Bournemouth. I share a taxi alone with Attlee from the House of Commons to Waterloo Station. In the course of this drive

I say to him, 'For myself I am not rushing or scrambling for any job. I should not be interested now in any job which had not got a very close relation to the waging of the war. Nor would I wash bottles for anyone. I am through with that phase. I should prefer the Ministry of Economic Warfare. That is on the border line of economic and foreign policy. Those are the two fields I know best. That is all I am going to say about myself.' He said, 'Of course it would be quite out of the question to suggest that you should play second fiddle to anyone in any Department. You are entitled to a Department of your own. A member of the Government said to me the other day, "We shall want all your tough guys"; and', said the little man, with rather an engaging smile, 'you are one of those.' At the station Herbert Morrison came to see us off. He said that he felt at this moment his job was in London in case things began to happen. It would look bad if he was down at Bournemouth when the first bombs fell. (In fact, he came down later, though he left early.)

Arrived at Bournemouth, the N.E. met and without too long discussion, even though many were more talkative than usual, being in a state of excitement, decided *unanimously* that we were prepared 'to take our share of responsibility in a new Government which, under a new Prime Minister, would command the confidence of the nation'. We also decided that Attlee and Greenwood should go forthwith to London to carry on any negotiations necessary to implement this decision, and that it *was* a decision and not merely a recommendation to the Conference on the following Monday, it now being Friday. This, we said, is a time when we must act swiftly and show leadership. As Attlee and Greenwood were about to leave, the P.M.'s Secretary rang through to enquire whether we yet could answer his questions. It was now about 5 p.m. Attlee communicated our resolution on the telephone. Then they left. When they reached London, Chamberlain had already resigned, and Attlee and Greenwood were asked to go to the Admiralty to see Churchill. It is thus clear that the last blow which dislodged the old limpet was struck by us at Bournemouth this afternoon.

Saturday 11th May
It soon became clear that the big Unions would stand up well to the crisis. The Miners, with 100 delegates, decided by 98 to 2 to support our decision; others followed suit. All through this day I am doing liaison on the telephone between the National Executive and Attlee and Greenwood in London. They report the progress of their talks with Churchill and I ask various questions for elucidation. At about 5.30 p.m. they ask for N.E. authority to accept

(a) Two seats out of five in a new War Cabinet; these to be filled by themselves.
(b) One out of three of the Defence Ministries.
(c) A reasonable number of other offices, including several key positions, for members of our Party (but details not settled yet).
(d) Chamberlain to be a member of the War Cabinet but to have no Department (it had previously been proposed that he should return to the Treasury) and not to be Leader of the House of Commons (this was being pressed for by his supporters and had been hinted at in the *Daily Telegraph* and other papers).

Attlee and Greenwood strongly urged acceptance of these terms. To get Chamberlain out altogether was impossible. Moreover, it would create such embitterment among his friends as to make the life of the new Government 'brutish and short'. Simon was to go to the Woolsack. There, said Attlee, 'He will be quite innocuous'. Hoare was to have nothing.

The N.E. boggled a bit at some of this, and Morrison was rather awkward, saying that this didn't sound like a government that would stand up any better than the last one, and that it would not impress the public. He was inclined to think that he would stay outside. (I had told him on the platform at Waterloo the day before that I thought he ought to take hold of Supply. He had not been very pleased at this, and obviously would have preferred to be in the War Cabinet without a Department. Later this evening at Bournemouth I and several others urge him to go right in and take this job if offered it. I think he will.) Several of our N.E. members are apprehensive as to whether the Liberals and the Tory Rebels are working closely with us. One or two, moreover, are very solicitous that Lloyd George should be in the new show! I have a further conversation on the telephone with London and bring back the news that the Liberals are in and satisfied, Sinclair having one of the Defence Departments; that the Tory Rebels, whose number has been growing – now that the tide is visibly flowing in their favour, a cynic would say – have been in the closest touch with Attlee and Greenwood, have been very firm, and are also to get a number of their men in key positions. After some more chit-chat, I am authorised by the N.E. to go back to the telephone and tell Attlee and Greenwood that they can accept so that Winston can publish the five in the War Cabinet plus the three Defence Ministers tonight. Attlee says to me, 'We are getting several more very important offices and you are well in the picture.'

Later that evening, after the N.E. decision, the N.C.L. meets. There is a little, but not much, difficulty in getting their agreement, when I have given a chronological statement of events. Citrine, who did not get back from France till Friday night, when our first decision had already been taken, gives us his warm support. I gather that he definitely does not wish to be in the Government, though, if he did, no doubt this could be arranged. He thinks he can be most serviceable remaining in his present post. Lately, relations between him and Bevin have been bad, and as Bevin is to be in, there may be some malicious forethought in Citrine's staying out. One of the points which I was instructed to put to Attlee and Greenwood on the telephone today and yesterday was our desire that 'some industrial leaders outside Parliament' should be in the Government. Attlee tells me that they have this much in mind and that Winston wants it. At our N.C.L. tonight it was decided to call a meeting of the Three Executives for tomorrow, so that there should be as much consultation (after the event!) as possible.

Sunday 12th May
Further meetings of various kinds, but nothing vital. The sun and the sea are more than usually beautiful – tragic, tense, ironic beauty. We hold two demonstrations in the evening, at one of which, in the Pavilion, a first-class hall with splendid acoustics, I speak. I tell the story of the happenings last week in the House, and of the young Tories in our Lobby. I read out the two declarations of Friday, the first by Attlee and Greenwood and the second by our N.E. I say, 'I am completely confident that tomorrow our Conference, the supreme democratic authority of our Movement, will endorse the unanimous decision of the N.E. by an overwhelming majority. In leisurely times of peace we should have had further consultations before we took our decision, but these are not leisurely days. In these days History goes past at the gallop. The Four Horsemen of the Apocalypse – War, and Pestilence, and Disease, and Death – are riding again across the plains of Europe. We are in the midst of the most tremendous struggle that the world has known for many centuries. We must be mentally prepared for everything except one thing, and that would be to lose the war. It is unthinkable that the world, under the impact of these Nazi hordes, should crash down into slavery and black darkness.'

That night Attlee and Greenwood arrive from London. They give a long account of their doings to the N.E., which endorses them. The case for keeping Chamberlain somewhere in the Government is overwhelming. This is generally recognised. Laski says to me, with characteristic malice, afterwards, 'Not very impressive. I felt as though the cook and the kitchen maid were telling us how they had sacked the butler.' Laski also tells Attlee that there is increasing concern because

347

so far I have not been appointed to anything. Attlee comes across and whispers in my ear that 'It is all right. I have told the new P.M. that you ought to be at M.E.W. and he is quite in favour. It is as good as settled.' He repeated the same thing to me next morning, but I replied, 'If it is as good as settled, why the devil isn't it announced?'

Monday 13th May

Attlee has to leave at 10.30 a.m. in order to reach London in time for the meeting of Parliament. He must know before the House meets how we have decided. Therefore, the vote must be taken at 1 o'clock. The debate is a ragged affair with a lot of freaks talking pathetic rubbish. The only big speaker from the floor is Will Lawther for the Miners, the biggest card vote in the Conference and always, in a crisis, our storm troops. He speaks forcibly and to the point in favour of going in. Greenwood winds up, and the majority for the Executive is 2,450,000 to 170,000. To say we won by 25 to 2 would flatter the minority.

Tuesday 14th May

Still no news, and I am becoming very irritated in having to parry friendly questioners. Just before lunch John Wilmot tells me that journalists who were in London last night and have returned today after yesterday's sitting of the House report that 'a great battle is going on over Dalton's body'. It is said that Montagu Norman is trying to veto my appointment, but that Attlee and Greenwood are sticking to their guns. This creates some sensation among my colleagues, who contemplate various forms of emergency action, e.g. a special meeting of the N.E. or a special telephone message by a few of them to Attlee. But none of this is either done or necessary, for I receive a message at four o'clock that a personal call will come through for me between five and six.

At six the P.M.'s Secretary rings me up and Winston himself comes to the phone. The following dialogue ensues:

W.C. Is that Dalton? I want you to help me.
H.D. Why, of course.
W.C. I want you to take a post in my Government.
H.D. I should be very proud to accept if you offered me a job which I was confident I could do well. (I had previously told Attlee that of the jobs now left I would only take M.E.W. Failing this, I would stay outside.)
W.C. Your friends tell me that you have been making a considerable study of economic warfare. Will you take that Ministry?

H.D. I should be very glad. I think I *could* do *that*.
W.C. Well, if you will excuse ceremony, I will have that announced
      tonight. Time is pressing and it is a life and death struggle.
H.D. Very good.
W.C. All right. That is agreed. You will take the oath tomorrow.
      The Privy Council will tell you when.
H.D. All right. Good luck, and I am very proud to serve under *you*
      (this last word with great emphasis).
W.C. Thank you very much. (Rings off.)

I return by train, having telephoned the news to Ruth and told her to
order Hugh Gaitskell to attend in my flat before midnight, where I
discuss with him the question of his becoming my Principal Private
Secretary.

II

Practical Socialism

6

Dreams
1945-7

Dalton served as a leading minister, outside the War Cabinet, throughout the Churchill Coalition. In August 1940, the Prime Minister added to his responsibility for the blockade of Germany by placing him in charge of the new Special Operations Executive (S.O.E.), concerned with black propaganda, sabotage and aid to resistance movements in occupied countries. In February 1942, he was moved from both jobs to become President of the Board of Trade, a post which he held until the break-up of the Coalition at the end of May 1945. Here, he took a special interest in the pre-war Distressed Areas. His Distribution of Industry Bill, the precursor of post-war regional policy, received the Royal Assent on 15th June, the day Parliament was dissolved. Like most people, Dalton expected the Conservatives to win the election that followed. All the same, he took the precaution of telling Attlee where his interests lay in case the improbable should happen. In private conversation, and then in a letter, he made it clear that he wanted the Foreign Office.

Polling took place on 5th July. Because of the delay in counting the Service vote, it was not known until 26th July that Labour had won by a landslide. With 393 seats against 213 Conservatives, 12 Liberals and 22 others, Labour had an overall majority of 146, and was able to take power for the first time without minor-party support. As soon as victory was certain, Attlee accepted the King's invitation to form a government, pre-empting a move by Morrison to have the question of the premiership discussed by the new P.L.P. On the morning of 27th July, the new Prime Minister told Dalton that he would 'almost certainly' be Foreign Secretary. Later the same day, however, Attlee changed his mind. Dalton was disappointed to learn that he would become Chancellor of the Exchequer instead.

He had little time for regret, and was soon immersed in the testing problems presented by his new department. The first of these was presented by the abrupt end to Lend–Lease. When the Labour Government took office, it

353

was still widely believed that the Japanese war would continue for another eighteen months, and that the Americans would agree to an extension of the Lend–Lease Agreement when hostilities ceased. The dropping of the atomic bomb on Hiroshima and Nagasaki in August upset both calculations. The early end to the war forced the new Chancellor to seek an American Loan in order to save Britain from bankruptcy and (as some believed) from poverty, social disorder and political collapse. The negotiating team in Washington was led by Lord Halifax, British Ambassador to the United States, and Dalton's Economic Adviser (and former tutor), Lord Keynes. On 6th December 1945 a Loan Agreement was signed – but on terms that were to have disastrous effects twenty months later, when the Agreement's 'convertibility' clause came into effect, precipitating a run on the pound.

In the 1954 edition of his pre-war book on public finance,[1] Dalton recalled the six urgent problems he faced on his arrival at the Treasury. First, the reconversion to peaceful purposes of industry, manpower and expenditure. Second, a smooth transition, maintaining full employment and avoiding industrial unrest or inflation. Third, honouring Labour's pledge to extend social services. Fourth, changing taxation in order to cut the total, and also to reduce the gap between richest and poorest. Fifth, the carrying out of nationalisation pledges. Sixth, finding a way to pay for the imports necessary to prevent mass unemployment and starvation. The last, he wrote, was the most difficult and immediate. As it turned out, it was also the one which, directly and indirectly, undermined many of the Chancellor's other policies and destroyed his reputation. Yet it is arguable that acceptance of the onerous terms of the American Loan was a necessary step, providing a crucial breathing space that allowed Labour's programme of domestic reforms to be pushed ahead.

Indeed, more than any other Labour Chancellor, Dalton sought to relate the direction of financial policy to socialist objectives. Some of his measures were less radical than he liked to imagine. Thus, the nationalisation of the Bank of England at the end of 1945 actually changed little and offended few, and did nothing to strengthen Treasury influence over Bank decisions. On the other hand, Dalton's taxation policy was governed by egalitarian principles, as well as by a concern to avoid a post-war boom followed by a slump. Although there was no capital levy (Dalton's pet scheme for dealing with the rich), death duties were raised, and income-tax reductions benefited the poor proportionately more than those paying high rates. These measures – though scarcely revolutionary – were accompanied by a Jacobin rhetoric that delighted Labour back-benchers and helped to make Dalton the best-hated minister in Tory and City circles.

1 *The Principles of Public Finance*, Routledge & Kegan Paul, London, 1954 edn, p. 229.

Dalton's most controversial policy was one on which there was at first a wide measure of agreement. ' ... [B]y the end of the war, cheap money was an unquestioned, and bipartisan, orthodoxy', as one economic historian has written.[1] Dalton's campaign for lower interest rates, which had the backing of Keynes and other Treasury advisers, at first aroused little comment. Criticism began in the autumn of 1946, and the Chancellor's policy became the subject of widespread derision in the financial press after the launching, and collapse, of a $2\frac{1}{2}$ per cent undated stock early in 1947. This stock, soon dubbed 'Daltons', became a symbol of the supposed failure of the cheap-money policy, and many purchasers never forgave the man who encouraged so unwise an investment. Nevertheless, cheap money probably played little part in the 'convertibility' crisis later the same year.

Arguably, problems over convertibility were always inevitable, given the insistence of the Americans on including in the original Agreement a provision for the free exchange of dollars and pounds. That the crisis was so swift and extreme, however, certainly owed much to the fuel shortage during the preceding winter. In February, Shinwell, the Minister of Fuel, suddenly announced severe cutbacks in electricity supply. Unemployment rose temporarily to two million, and £200 million of exports were lost because of disruption in production. This, in turn, exacerbated a growing dollar deficit, and when sterling was made freely convertible in July, under the terms of the Loan Agreement, the 'dollar drain' became a torrent. With the Loan virtually used up, convertibility was suspended on 20th August. Pilloried by the press, exhausted physically and mentally, Dalton was compelled to prepare an emergency Budget – inaugurating a period of deflation and rigid austerity in economic policy, over which another Chancellor, Sir Stafford Cripps, was to preside.

Dalton's resignation as Chancellor, following the inadvertent leaking of Budget secrets,[2] brought to an end an important transitional phase in the conduct of British economic policy. In one sense, the 'Keynesian Revolution' had been achieved in Sir Kingsley Wood's 1941 Budget, and consolidated in the 1944 White Paper on Employment Policy, whose declaration in favour of keeping up the level of employment through the maintenance of total expenditure had been accepted by all political parties. However, under wartime conditions, direct controls had become increasingly important as a means of holding back demand, and budgetary policy had been given, in practice, a comparatively minor role. Dalton's period of office was marked by a gradual reassertion of Treasury power. In the immediate aftermath of war, the need for economic planning through demand management (as opposed to the

1 J. C. R. Dow, *The Management of the British Economy 1945–60*, Cambridge University Press, Cambridge, 1970, p. 21.
2 See below, p. 423.

control of inflation through physical controls) became more apparent, and the eagerness of the Treasury to combine financial and economic powers under one authority – its own – increased.

The solution eventually adopted, a simple extension of Treasury powers, came about accidentally rather than by design. All the same, during 1947 the Government inner circle was much exercised by the problem of the location of planning powers. Should these remain with the Lord President, Herbert Morrison? Or should they be given to an independent minister, perhaps Ernest Bevin? Behind the intrigues that surrounded the position of the Prime Minister lay the question: how, and by whom, could policy on the domestic front best be co-ordinated? In this debate, Sir Stafford Cripps was ahead of his colleagues, first demanding that the Foreign Secretary be brought back to the home front to take charge of production, and then seeking to make Bevin Prime Minister in place of Attlee. In the autumn of 1947, Attlee diverted this challenge to his authority by giving the key planning job to Cripps himself, with the title of Minister of Economic Affairs. However, the experiment of an economics minister (Cripps) and a finance minister (Dalton) working side by side lasted only a few weeks. Dalton's resignation in November 1947, and Cripps's succession to the Treasury, without losing the planning brief, enabled the new Chancellor to combine financial and economic spheres. Thus the departure of Dalton and the arrival of Cripps completed a process begun by Wood in 1941, and set a pattern of economic management for at least a generation.

The following entry, undated, was dictated after polling day, but some time before the results of the election were known.

July 1945

I take no further interest in the last weeks of this Parliament, except to watch this precious Bill[1] of mine go through. I begin, thus early, to make speeches for Labour candidates and become more and more immersed in electioneering – mostly in the North as far as Teesside – for there is nothing to hold me in London now. The election is very long drawn out, going on for nearly six weeks until the Polling Day – in all except twenty-four constituencies where it is postponed owing to local holidays on 5th July. I am totally tired by the end of it, especially of hearing myself repeat the same old arguments and phrases night by night. ...

In addition to this I addressed, I suppose, nearly fifty meetings in my

1 The Distribution of Industry Bill (see p. 353 above).

own division, and kept my engagement with the Miners at Blackpool, made some months before, to speak to their Annual Conference – the first of the new National Union of Mineworkers. It is, on the whole, quite a quiet election, though there is evidence of a serious mind among the electors and intelligent interest in many questions. Going around, I am very pleased with the showing of a number of our candidates. We have certainly never had a better team in the field than this time. In a number of constituencies, where it would be a close thing any- how, the personality of our candidate will just make the difference. e.g. Grimsby and, perhaps, Watford. On the other hand, but for the personality of the P.M., we should undoubtedly have trampled the Tories underfoot and got a large majority. 'You can't trust the Tories' has been a difficult slogan for them to shout or argue down. The Laski affair was most irritating.[1] I don't think it will have turned over very many votes and I only once – at Grimsby – got a question on it in all my meetings, but it was worked up into a mild scare which will have brought out a certain number of old women who otherwise would not have voted. Laski should not have intervened, in the first instance, on the invitation to Attlee to go to Berlin. He was not in touch with the Parliamentary leaders or would have known that they had been consulted and agreed; nor could there have been any question of us being 'bound' by decisions reached in Berlin, now that we are no longer in the Government; nor, on the other hand, is it very likely that we should wish to line up against anything agreed to, not only by Churchill, but by Stalin and Truman; nor should professors use words loosely – in this case the word 'observer' which, in relation to con- ferences, always means a dumb person at the conference table, obviously an impossible position. But this silly little intervention gave the Tories just what they had lacked till then. A plausible new bogy. It is a pity his name was Laski, and not Smith, and that he was not a Member of Parliament. The question of the relationship of the National Executive to the Parliamentary leaders is, in fact, slightly delicate, though there is nothing new about it. It is not a thing the public discussion of which brings any gain to us. A further fuss, as to whether the little fool said that in any circumstances we should 'use violence' – I always find it rather comic that this contingency should be discussed by this puny, short-sighted, weak-hearted, rabbinical- looking little chap! – has been stopped for the moment by the issue of writs, a very sensible move. But I have a sort of suspicion that here too he said something he should not.

1 Early in the campaign Harold Laski, Chairman of the N.E.C., caused a storm by declaring that Attlee should go with Churchill to Potsdam only 'as an observer'.

In my own division everything went quite well. Maurice Mason proved a very level-headed and reasonably competent agent, after a slightly uncertain start, and dropped no large bricks at any stage. Will Davis, with whom I stay, and was very comfortable and well looked after – despite the clamour of the dogs and chronic excess of farinaceous food – was more than ever a tower of strength. He told a great story, I hear, at meetings while I was not present, about my doings for King, Constituency and Country, and there is just enough to show now, in the way of new factories etc., to make an impression, though there is some agitation against Jews[1] and it is most important that we should have only Gentiles now, in addition to the three pioneer firms, at St Helen, and not too many Jews on the new Estate at Shildon. The switch over of Spennymoor and Aycliffe from R.O.F.s [Royal Ordnance Factories] to Trading Estates for Peace production seems [to be] going pretty well and, after a month or two of transition, I hope that there will be very little unemployment in the area, especially as West Tool should have got going by then.

The last minute opponent produced against me was a Lieutenant Tily[2] from Dorsetshire. He had apparently been a Military Policeman and had returned from Italy to offer to fight an election for the Liberal Gnats. He had never been in the division before. The official Tories were quite lukewarm about him, though old Thompson spoke twice for him, and the official Liberals sat on the fence and took no part in the election. He brought with him an elderly agent from Tynemouth. On the day of their arrival they went into the Clerk's Office at Bishop Auckland to ask what were the boundaries of the constituency. It is said that he had never made a speech in his life before and he had very few regular meetings during the campaign – never more than one a night. His wife and daughter went around in a car with a loudspeaker, exhorting anyone who might hear to vote for him, and also, apparently, calling out, 'What about Dalton in 1938?' But neither I nor anyone else knows what this meant. ...

I grew very weary as the fight went on, though several times I got a second and then a third wind. On the eve of the Poll I addressed eight meetings. On most other nights in my own constituency three, or four, or five, and sometimes a visit to a neighbouring constituency thrown in. I stayed most of the day at Manor House, paid very few visits to

1 Several of the owners of new factories on the trading estates in Dalton's constituency were ex-German Jews.
2 Lieut. W. J. W. Tily. National Liberal candidate for Bishop Auckland in the 1945 election. Insurance inspector. He obtained 11,240 votes against 20,100 for Dalton in a straight fight.

15 Herbert Morrison asks Barbara Castle to dance, 1945 Party Conference

16 Cardiff victors, July 1945. *Left:* Hilary Marquand. *Second from right:* George Thomas. *Right:* James Callaghan.

Opposite, left: 17 Richard Crossman addresses Coventry businessmen, September 1945

Opposite, right: 18 John Strachey, Minister of Food, 1946

Opposite, below: 19 Attlee with his press officer, Francis Williams, at No. 10 Downing Street, 1946

Right: 20 Chancellor of the Exchequer. Dalton at West Leaze, April 1947.

Below: 21 At Le Donon, Vosges, August 1950. *Seated:* Dalton, a Belgian woman, Callaghan. *Standing, left:* Crosland. *Right:* Healey.

Above, left: 22 James Griffiths, *c.* 1950

Above, right: 23 Harold Wilson as President of the Board of Trade, 1949

Below: 24 Attlee the orator, 1950

the Committee Rooms and did practically no personal canvassing. They gave me my breakfast in bed and I generally did not get up till about 11 a.m.

On the day of the Poll I started out with Davis and Mason, though we left the latter in the Committee Room during the afternoon to make sure we had checkers at all booths in Bishop Auckland town and we covered that day 108 miles, all inside the constituency. Practically everywhere, except in Bishop Auckland town, things looked very good. At the great majority of booths we had checkers and Tily had none, and our people had broken all the rules, e.g. by sticking up bills and chalking 'Vote for Dalton' close outside the entrance to the polling station, and sometimes the checkers themselves sitting inside the booths. The only blot before lunch was that at three of the four polling stations in Bishop Auckland town we had no checkers, but this was corrected in the afternoon. When, however, having been everywhere else, we landed up at about 7.15 at the Cockton Hill schools, we found thirty enemy cars concentrating on this ward and depositing their loads of voters. This was the first and only place during my tour when I was slightly booed. Inside the yard our checkers stood with very long faces. They said, 'This has been giving us the creeps for the last hour.' We told them that all the 'outsides' were looking quite healthy, and that obviously the Tories were concentrating on the most Tory ward in Bishop Auckland. Afterwards we checked up and found that, out of a total electorate of 42,000, those who polled at Cockton Hill numbered 4,500. If we assume that 80 per cent of these voted and that, of those voting, 90 per cent voted for Tily, this would only give them just over 3,000 votes. Nearly everywhere else in the division, including Shildon, where there is also a heavy electorate, there was very little to be seen of them, either cars or committee rooms, though one of our people at South Church was slightly panicked because, wearing no colour, he had been taken for a Tory and the man in charge of the Tory car had said, 'I think, if we get all our people up, we may just win if there's a lot of apathy on the other side.' But I think the Poll will turn out to be about 75 per cent, which will give us a total vote only a little less than last time, when I won by 20,000 to 12,000. Curry,[1] moreover, had then been the sitting Member for four years and was well-known in the area. It is difficult to think that Tily can poll as well as Curry, so that, if there is a general swing our way in the country as a whole, there will not be something of a swing here too. And so, to sum it up, I shall regard it as a bit of a blow if I don't get a five figure majority. Ten thousand is the target.

1 A. C. Curry, q.v., National Liberal M.P. for Bishop Auckland 1931–5.

My general estimate of the election is – I am quite conscious – queerly influenced by that last scene at Cockton Hill. If I had gone round the place the other way, and seen my own supporters pouring in during the last hour in some of the strongholds, including Shildon, I might have felt quite different. So, when I say my hunch is that we have won about 80 seats, giving us about 240, with 30 for the odds and ends, including the Liberals, and 370 for the Government, giving them a majority of about 100, I dare say I am a bit of a pessimist. Much depends on how heavily the Liberals poll, broadly the heavier the better for us. Anyhow, 300 triangular contests must help us a lot as compared with an election mostly of straight fights. ...

And so back to London on 6th July, feeling in need of a few 'days of silence' à la Gandhi. I hope to get these in the country in the next few days – provided Durbin[1] doesn't make me talk too much!

Wednesday 25th July

After a lazy fortnight at West Leaze I go to Bishop Auckland for the count tomorrow. ...

Thursday 26th July

Labour gains begin to pour through and the defeat of Bracken,[2] coming early, gives me a tremendous thrill. By 1 p.m. it is established that we shall have a clear majority over all parties, and, as the day goes on, the size of the majority grows. I go to two workers' meetings in Bishop Auckland and Shildon and then travel by night train with David Hardman,[3] who has had a great win at Darlington. Not much sleep! We have made a clean sweep in Durham, our narrowest win being at The Hartlepools where D. T. Jones[4] has a majority of 275.

Saturday 28th July

The King hadn't much to say, but seemed quite resigned. (I hear that

---

1 E. F. M. Durbin (1906–48). Labour M.P. for Edmonton 1945–8. P.P.S. to Dalton 1945–7. Former economics lecturer at the L.S.E. Writer on political ideas. Economic Section of the War Cabinet Secretariat 1940–42; Personal Assistant to the Deputy Prime Minister (Attlee) 1942–5. Junior minister 1947–8.
2 Brendan Bracken, later 1st Viscount (1901–58). Conservative M.P. for Paddington North 1929–45; Bournemouth 1945–50; Bournemouth East 1950–51. Minister of Information 1941–5. First Lord of the Admiralty 1945.
3 David Hardman (b. 1901). Labour M.P. for Darlington 1945–51. Junior minister 1945–51.
4 D. T. Jones (d. 1963). Labour M.P. for The Hartlepools 1945–59.

later, when he met Truman[1] at Portsmouth, the latter said, 'You've had a revolution.' The King said, 'Oh no! we don't have those here.' I heard from John Wilmot and others that when, a few days later, they were sworn in and took the oath, the King said, looking at Wilmot, Bevan etc., 'Well the Prime Minister has had a very difficult time, I'm sure. What I say is "Thank God for the Civil Service".')

Tuesday 31st July
National Executive. All very pleased! Nearly all, including all the women, are now M.P.s. A preliminary meeting of the newly appointed ministers on the King's Speech. I press for, and obtain without difficulty, a place for my banking legislation in the first session – Bank of England, a hybrid Bill, and a second Bill on other points.[2]

Wednesday 1st August
International Sub-Committee of National Executive. I tell them I can't carry on in the chair now. Laski takes it *pro tem.* until we see who else are ministers.

Today the new Parliament assembles. What a sight! Song and counter song. The Tories sing for Churchill, 'For He's A Jolly Good Fellow', and we reply with the 'Red Flag'. But we are not yet a Parliament, the Speaker not being elected. I also speak today to Morrison on behalf of Wilmot. He is a little doubtful. He recommends Strauss[3] to me for F.S.T. [Financial Secretary Treasury]. I say I don't like him and I don't trust him. He's always intriguing against me. I say that, if Wilmot is not available, I want Willie Hall.

Thursday 2nd August
Attlee back from Potsdam. We greet him on his return to No. 10. Cabinet meeting later. I speak to him again about Wilmot. He says he has decided to make him a No. 1 minister. He is to have Supply plus M.A.P. [Ministry of Aircraft Production] – exactly what he and I thought would suit him best. A string of eager people calling at No. 10 all day.

I have a great fight with Pethick-Lawrence for Willie Hall, who had first been asked for by him to be Under-Secretary for India. I win the fight, Attlee backing me, and Pethick is consoled with Arthur Henderson.[4]

1 H. S. Truman (1884–1972). President of the U.S.A. 1945–53, having succeeded to the Presidency on Roosevelt's death in April 1945.
2 Handwritten insertion: '(Contract of Investment and of Foreign Exchange)'.
3 G. R. Strauss, later Baron (b. 1901). Labour M.P. for Lambeth North 1929–31, 1934–50; Lambeth Vauxhall 1950–79. Junior minister 1945–7. Minister of Supply 1947–51.
4 Handwritten addition: 'having refused Woodrow Wyatt'.

15th August was V.J. Day.

Friday 17th August

For a fortnight I have kept no diary notes. I am now moderately well settled in at the Treasury and am sleeping at No. 11 Downing Street. I have a bedroom on the second floor and shall have an office, as Kingsley Wood had, on the ground floor. Morrison will have the first floor for an office and a bedroom as well. All this is very convenient, particularly the inter-communication between Nos. 10, 11 and 12. ...

We have had a number of Cabinets and no doubt I shall shake down gradually. Meanwhile there is great volubility by many.[1]

By an incredible coincidence the Jap surrender exactly coincides with the eve of the opening of Parliament. These events are too tremendous to be clearly apprehended by us who are a bit tired and preoccupied.

I am conscious of having some mountainous problems in front of me, especially with 'overseas financial liabilities'; Lend–Lease may be stopping any time now and the resulting gap will be terrific.

I have already had preliminary talks on Heads of the Bill (i) to nationalise the Bank of England and (ii) to control investment and continue certain other controls. Today I have had a most successful talk with Catto[2] who is taking everything very well and said that he would like to go on as Governor under the new regime. He is a splendid little asset.

Work in these last few days has been much interrupted by Victory celebrations. I have been receiving good advice, in addition to pep pills, from Horder.[3] I have sometimes felt pretty tired, but seem as well to have a good deal of resilience.[4]

1 Handwritten insertion: '5 out of the 20 of us sit for Durham seats (plus Whitby) and 5 out of the 20 are miners'.

2 Sir Thomas Catto, 1st Baron (1879–1959). Governor of the Bank of England 1944–9. Financial Adviser to the Chancellor of the Exchequer 1940–44.

3 T. J. Horder, 1st Baron (1871–1955). Physician in Ordinary to the King. Consulting Physician to St Bartholomew's Hospital.

4 Handwritten insertion: 'I intervened, successfully, with Attlee to get Ivor Thomas into the Government. The latter came to see me, very damped, when the main list was out, and he not in it. He had tackled Attlee who had said, "You've no judgment." Attlee said to me, "No one has asked for him." I said he was a bit unpopular, but young and very clever – "much cleverer than you or me", I said. I suggested Civil Aviation. He got it, with the speaking part in the House.

'My first speech as Chancellor on 21st August. Ten days at West Leaze with Betty, Rosalind and Bob Fraser for weekends.'

After Potsdam, East-West relations cooled, as the Soviet Union tightened its political and economic control of the countries occupied by Russian troops. At a conference of foreign ministers in London in September, the expansionist aims of Soviet foreign policy became more than ever apparent. Bevin likened Molotov's tactics to those of Hitler, and in the parliamentary debate on 7th November, the Foreign Secretary accused the Soviet Union of trying 'to come across the throat of the British Commonwealth'.[1]

Wednesday 17th October
Following the breakdown of the Foreign Ministers' Conference, Bevin told me this. There had been a big reception at the Soviet Embassy, to which I and many others had gone and also Bevin who, however, arrived very late, just as I was leaving. I had a few words with Molotov in the inner room into which the Select had been shepherded. He had, I think, been told that I was a comparatively friendly native, for he was effusive and cheerful. He said to me in English, 'I agree, I agree, I agree. Am I not learning English very well?' I said I had heard of the great success of the evening at Chequers and of how we all thought that more Russians should come to this country. He asked, 'Do you want a football team or some ballet girls?' I said, 'Both.' There was nothing more serious than this in our conversation. What Bevin told me later was that, just as he himself was going – and this would have been perhaps three-quarters of an hour after I had left – he was in the outer hall with Molotov, Gusev[2] and Madame G. Molotov was 'drinking all his toasts as usual' and, Bevin thought, had by now drunk rather much, even for him. Molotov then said, 'Here's to the Atom Bomb!' And then he added, 'We've got it.' Gusev, at this point, put his hand on Molotov's shoulder and hurried him away.

A few of us have discussed all the larger implications of this and are inclined to think that the least risk would be to tell the Russians all we know, and have a new Three Power Meeting solely for this. Only so, we think, is there any hope at all of breaking down their growing suspicion. And certainly they know a lot already and have good scientists. Meanwhile, President Truman is said to be terrified

1 H.C. Debs [416], col. 1342; see also B. Jones, *The Russia Complex*, Manchester University Press, Manchester, 1977, pp. 115–16.
2 F. T. Gusev (1904–73). Soviet Ambassador to Great Britain 1943–6. Deputy Foreign Minister 1946–55.

lest the decisions on all this should get into the hands of the Senate Foreign Affairs Committee.

Meanwhile, Raymond Blackburn,[1] Michael Foot[2] and others are getting much worked up about it, and the former wanted to raise it on the Adjournment, but has, with great effort, been dissuaded from doing this. He has been talking to an Australian scientist (Professor Oliphant)[3] who has, I think, been telling him a lot of things which are not true, but which are designed to show that we sold out everything completely to the U.S.A. (this being the fault of Churchill at the Quebec Conference) ... and that the U.S. are within only a year or two of other large peace-time applications on railways, etc.[4]

'A week ago today it looked as though the Washington talks might break down', Dalton recorded at the beginning of his entry for 7th December 1945. The talks, whose aim was to secure a substantial American Loan to Britain, had begun on 13th September. Keynes's early optimism was gradually worn down as the talks proceeded, and when the British government finally

1 A. R. B. Blackburn (b. 1915). Labour M.P. for Birmingham King's Norton 1945–50; Labour, then Independent M.P. for Birmingham Northfield 1950–51.

2 M. M. Foot (b. 1913). Labour M.P. for Plymouth Devonport 1945–55; Ebbw Vale 1960–83; Blaunau-Gwent since 1983. Acting Editor of the *Evening Standard* 1942. Editor of *Tribune* 1948–52, 1955–60. Secretary of State for Employment 1974–6; Lord President of the Council and Leader of the House of Commons 1976–9. Leader of the Labour Party 1981–3. Biographer of Aneurin Bevan. Son of Isaac Foot, q.v., and brother of Dingle Foot, q.v.

3 Professor M. L. E. Oliphant, later Sir Mark (b. 1901). Professor of Physics at Birmingham University 1937–50. Assistant Director of Research, Cavendish Laboratory, Cambridge 1935–7. Returned to Australia (University of Canberra) 1950.

4 Handwritten insertion: '(Raymond Blackburn was more right than I knew at this time. See later)'. In addition to material included here, the diary entry for 7th December contains details of the Quebec Agreement of August 1943. It concludes: 'This astounding sell-out puts it in the power of the United States to refuse us any rights in the industrial application of atomic energy, even though all other nations in the world would be free to exploit it. This would indeed be an Atomic Bomb on Churchill's reputation. And, indeed, it seems inevitable that it should, at some stage, be revealed. Meanwhile, Attlee will have to try in his talks with Truman to get it cleared out of the way. Even now the thing is not wholly secret, for Professor Oliphant, an Australian scientist who has been in on the research, told Raymond Blackburn a good deal about it, and the latter is liable at any time to let it out, being also, as Morrison would say, "a bit highly strung".' For the rest of this entry see HTA, p. 62, where it is mistakenly dated 1st November.

authorised the signing of an agreement on 6th December, it accepted far more strings, for a much smaller loan, than had been contemplated at the outset. Greatest hostage to fortune was the so-called 'convertibility clause': the requirement that Britain should restore convertibility for current transactions (that is, the free exchange of sterling and dollars) after a period of a year. which meant, in practice, in July 1947.

Friday 7th December

Rab Butler said to me today that he was enjoying a rest from office and that, speaking frankly, he was delighted at the strength of the Socialist Government. And indeed a number of us are making, it is clear, a very good impression of confidence and competence. If we don't play our cards badly, we and our successors should be in office for many years.

Winston is becoming rather a pathetic spectacle. The barber's shop downstairs at the House was all through the war decorated with pictures of Churchill in every possible pose. When the new Parliament assembled all this had been taken down and, the day after my Budget Statement, the old boy went in to get his hair cut. The barber, so I am informed by one who was present, said to him, 'Sir, why don't you go right away? That would be much better than hanging about this place like you're doing.' And in the country his stock has fallen right down. And the Tory Party whom we face now is totally bereft of the prestige which, at the last election, he gave it. ...

My worst headache still remains the Washington Talks. These have now dragged on for seven weeks and we are not yet in sight of a tolerable outcome. Keynes is becoming rather sulky and it is clear that, as must always be the case, following these long negotiations, those who represent us out there and we here at home have drifted into a condition of mutual incomprehension.

Tube Alloys have also been much on the map. Attlee is going to see Truman. We have had several meetings of an Inner Cabinet on this, and the outcome is that the only possible course, if the world is to be saved from further and greater disasters, is to put all our force behind a real United Nations Organisation, with power and determination to smash any aggressor by every means, including Atom Bombs. It is quite idle, most of us feel, merely to make rules designed to secure that war, if it comes, shall be conducted without the use of this new weapon. ...

It is thought by some that it was Churchill who intervened on the famous Friday, following our election victory, with Attlee in the luncheon interval to persuade him to change round Bevin and me. I have often thought, in these last weeks, that I should be most grateful to him for this intervention. While I have been proceeding with my tasks at the Treasury, Bevin has been badly bogged in his talks with the Russians. I feel inclined to say to him, regarding Auntie Molotov, what Bevin said to Stalin at Potsdam regarding Hess.[1] When Stalin in a long speech had protested against our not bringing Hess to trial as a war criminal and had developed a long theme of suspicion of our motives, Bevin rose to his feet and simply said, "Ess, you can 'ave him!'

On 5th March 1946 Winston Churchill made his celebrated 'Iron Curtain' speech at Fulton, Missouri, in the presence of President Truman. This aroused anger on the British Left, still hoping for co-operation with the Russians.

Monday 25th February 1946
Back from West Leaze in time for 11 a.m. Cab. This is a bad Monday morning institution. Some of the colleagues are exceptionally loquacious, especially this morning the Minister of Health.

Churchill has sent a telegram from Florida that he is seeing Byrnes[2] and Baruch,[3] who seem to get on badly with one another, but that the latter persists that he is most anxious to help us and not to jeopardise the Loan. On the other hand, he is obviously disgruntled at not having been consulted and says that Keynes mismanaged the negotiations. I am to send Churchill some material for future use, including [for] his forthcoming speech at Fulton. ...

1 Rudolf Hess (b. 1894). Deputy Führer of Germany 1933–41. Hess flew to Scotland in 1941 on a private mission to persuade Britain to combine with Germany in a common fight against the Soviet Union. He was later tried at Nuremberg and imprisoned at Spandau.
2 J. F. Byrnes (1879–1972). U.S. Secretary of State 1945–7.
3 B. M. Baruch (1870–1965). American financier. U.S. representative on the Atomic Energy Commission 1946–51. Economic Adviser to successive Presidents, from Wilson to Roosevelt.

Last Friday (22nd) I lunched with Bruce Lockhart. He says that David Garnett[1] is writing the history of P.W.E.[2] with its various war-time forerunners, but that the latter is, he thinks, making a mistake in wanting to go into too much detail and to bring out all the differences between ministers – and how acute they were! – and to comment on various mistakes made. ...

In the first week of Bevin, Lockhart said that Cadogan and Sargent both thought they were out. But, as I thought but did not say to Lockhart, Bevin's weakness necessarily was that he would not have known by whom to replace them since he really knew nothing of any of the higher personnel of the Foreign Service either at home or abroad.

Meanwhile, I said that I had originally thought the Treasury would be more difficult than the Foreign Office. I had since quite changed my mind and was, on personal grounds, much relieved at being here and not there.

Lockhart also spoke of Eden's passionate eagerness to become the first Secretary-General of U.N.O. He knew a good deal about Eden's efforts to get this job. The truth was that Eden was not now at all sure whether, or when, he would get the Tory leadership and still less sure when, if ever, this would make him Prime Minister. None of the Tories knew when Winston would resign the leadership, there were growls against him now that he was away but if he came back and said he wanted to go on Lockhart did not think that they would put him out. And meanwhile, Eden was not doing very well as acting Leader. Many of the rest didn't like him and several, including Macmillan[3] and Butler, were trying to oust him.

On 19th February, Lord Pethick-Lawrence, Secretary of State for India, had announced that a Cabinet Mission consisting of himself, Cripps and Alexander would visit India to discuss with Indian leaders the constitutional settlement by which power would be passed to Indian hands. Meanwhile, Anglo–Soviet tension was rising over the Iraq–Azerbaijan dispute. On

1 David Garnett (1892–1981). Bloomsbury writer.
2 The Political Warfare Executive was set up in 1941 under the joint control of the Minister of Economic Warfare, the Minister of Information and the Foreign Secretary. Bruce Lockhart had been the official representative of M.E.W. on the Executive.
3 Harold Macmillan, later 1st Earl of Stockton (b. 1894). Conservative M.P. for Bromley 1945–64; Stockton-on-Tees 1924–9, 1931–45. Junior minister 1940–43. Minister Resident in North-West Africa 1942–5. Secretary of State for Air 1945. Minister of Housing and Local Government 1951–4; Defence 1954–5. Foreign Secretary 1955; Chancellor of the Exchequer 1955–7; Prime Minister 1957–63.

21st February, Bevin enraged some Labour left-wingers, and pleased the Opposition, by questioning Soviet good faith and indicating his intention to defend Anglo–Iranian oil interests. Early in March, the Iranian government appealed to the U.N. Security Council, complaining of the increased Russian military presence. In the face of strong Anglo-American pressure, the Russians agreed to withdraw on 4th April. The crisis was an important watershed in establishing the diplomacy, and the battle-lines, of the Cold War.

Friday 22nd March

In domestic politics we are in a good patch, though the international scene is a bit speckled and one can't be sure how India will go. Our Mission of Three Wise Men left this week. Pethick-Lawrence and Cripps flew off together – someone suggested to me that their cross-talk would probably be a bit boring for third parties! – and Albert Victorious [Alexander] went off on his own. The P.M. having explained in the House that, if the Indians wanted 'independence' they could have it, there is quite a shrill scream of welcome from the Congress, though Jinnah[1] seems still to be grizzling. We now have more room, physically, in the Cabinet, and, in particular, there is now nothing to separate me and Shinwell.

The Russian attitude is still very difficult. A fortnight ago I ran into Bevin in the evening and found him in a great state, saying that the Russians were advancing in full force on Teheran, that 'this means war', and that the U.S. were going to send a battle fleet to the Mediterranean. I said we couldn't go to war with the Russians about Persia, and next day told the P.M. of this incident and said that I thought Bevin was – no doubt quite naturally – in a strung up state. The P.M. quite agreed with me and is indeed pressing on the Chiefs of Staff and the Defence Committee a large view of his own, which aims at considerable disengagement from areas where there is a risk of us clashing with the Russians. This would mean giving up any attempt to keep open the passage through the Mediterranean in war-time, and to pull out from all the Middle East, including Egypt, and, of course, from Greece. We should then constitute a line of defence across Africa from Lagos to Kenya and concentrate a large part of our forces in the latter. We should face the prospect of going round the Cape in war-

1 Mohammed Ali Jinnah (1876–1948). Leader of the Muslim League Party. President of the All-India Muslim League 1934–48. Governor-General of Pakistan 1947–8.

time and, the future attitude of India being somewhat uncertain, we should concentrate a great part of the Commonwealth defence, including many industries, in Australia. We should thus put a wide glacis of desert and Arabs between ourselves and the Russians. This is a very bold and interesting idea and I am inclined to favour it.

Bevin is rather fascinated by the Middle East and doesn't want to move troops further out than the Canal Zone. On the other hand, he is very much attracted by the Lagos–Kenya idea and wants to build a road linking them right across Africa, passing through the top of French Equatorial Africa and enabling us, if need be, to protect the deposits in the Belgian Congo. He also thinks great trade developments might come between East Africa (including Natal), India and Australia. This would be a triangular ocean trade. He has lately been more and more friendly with me and is constantly putting the Treasury point of view, both in my presence and in my absence, to foreigners and to our own Chiefs of Staff, etc. In these last weeks he has seemed sometimes much less self-confident and self-sufficient than he used to be. Sometimes, indeed, he has seemed to be clinging for support to me and one or two other colleagues. He has also put up an important paper on the future of Germany, in which he sticks firmly to the view that the industry of the Ruhr should be taken over and owned by an international consortium of governments including ourselves, the French, the Americans, the Russians and any smaller Allies who want to come in, and that the Ruhr should be permanently occupied by an international force but that it should not otherwise be politically detached from Germany. I have backed this as being the most helpful and least difficult of many alternatives.

On 9th April 1946, Dalton introduced his second Budget. The Chancellor reaffirmed his cheap-money policy, announced remissions in income tax, and increased death duties. He also launched the National Land Fund, which was intended to make it easier for great houses and estates to be handed over to the nation in lieu of duty. 'The Tories are very chagrined to find how well we are doing', Dalton noted, 'and amazed that we shall be next year, as I put it last night, within striking distance of a balanced Budget. And, as for cheaper money, things are moving perfectly just now ... [I]t is very good to see the smiling faces of one's political friends and be told that one has achieved a great personal, as well as Party, triumph.'[1]

Meanwhile India was moving rapidly, if unsteadily, towards indepen-

1 Diary, 12th April 1946; see also HTA, p. 122.

dence. Early in April the Cabinet decided to accept the partition of India into Pakistan and Hindustan, on the grounds that the only alternative was a breakdown of negotiations and subsequent chaos. Nevertheless, on 9th May, Cripps secured the agreement of Nehru and Congress leader Maulana Azad to a three-tier federation, in an effort to preserve the unity of the sub-continent.

Wednesday 15th May

This morning we spend half an hour more on the declaration on India, framed by our Cabinet Mission and Wavell,[1] and amended as a result of messages from the Cabinet here. They have accepted some of the amendments we suggested, but are strongly resisting others and re-fusing to accept responsibility if we don't give them the 'All clear' today, since already everything is leaking out there. I spoke with great emphasis in favour of giving them the 'All clear'. We have sent out three good men and they have soaked in the atmosphere and all that divides us is a few forms of words. The important thing is to get the Indians to accept the new proposals for Constituent Assembly, etc. No doubt we shall be charged with giving away essential British interests, but the Cripps Declaration,[2] when Churchill was Prime Minister, is both an historical reality on which there can be no going back, and a good debating point against the Tories. It would be wonderful to see India self-governing within a year or two. Mean-while, however, many millions, even though this be only 1 or 2 per cent of their total, seem likely to die of hunger. The world famine lurks behind all our talks. It comes down to my Departmental level in losing me £48 millions of beer duty owing to the cut in brewing, in order to save barley to be shipped to the western zone in Germany. Morrison is in Washington talking to Truman and the American public. Ben Smith, I hope, won't last much longer. Indeed, Attlee

1 Field-Marshal Sir Archibald Wavell, 1st Viscount, later 1st Earl (1883–1950). Viceroy of India 1943–February 1947. Commander-in-Chief, Middle East 1939–41; India 1941–3. Supreme Commander South-west Pacific 1942.

2 In 1942, Cripps had been sent to negotiate with the Indian leaders on behalf of the British government. With the authority of the Cabinet behind him, Cripps announced the British intention to set up a constitutional assembly immediately after the war, in order to bring about 'the complete transfer of responsibility from British to Indian hands'. On hearing the contents of this declaration Gandhi is supposed to have remarked 'the British proposals form a post-dated cheque on a crashing bank' (cited in E. Estorick, *Stafford Cripps: A Biography*, Heinemann, London, 1949, p. 307). Although the Indians rejected the declaration, it was a remarkable advance on what had previously been offered.

told me the other day that he was only waiting for Stansgate[1] to get back from Cairo in order to arrange for Strachey[2] to become Food Minister and be succeeded by de Freitas.[3] This would be a good move.

Meanwhile there is a start in breaking the block on promotion with three junior ministerial changes announced last weekend. Jennie Adamson becomes, most suitably, Vice-Chairman of the Assistance Board and is succeeded by Arthur Blenkinsop,[4] quite a nice young man, though not, I think, with much force. But this will raise morale in the Whips' Office from which he is promoted. Foster[5] having resigned from Fuel and Power, Hugh Gaitskell has taken his place. He may find personal relations difficult with Shinbad,[6] but, on the other hand, he is very skilled at handling such things and will find, if he can get a personal *modus vivendi*, that they have more nationalisation and post-nationalisation work in this Ministry than in any other in the next two years. Finally, John Parker has most deservedly been reduced to the ranks and his place taken by Arthur Bottomley.[7] This will certainly be a change for the better. ... A good deal more of this ought to be done. We must get our good young men on. I am always hammering at the P.M. on this.

Bevin is having a hell of a time in Paris at the Four Foreign Ministers' Talks.[8] It all looks pretty bad again and Byrnes is being encouraged to try to make Peace Treaties without reference to Russia. I tried, being

1 William Wedgwood Benn, 1st Viscount Stansgate, q.v., Secretary of State for Air 1945–6.
2 John Strachey, q.v., Parliamentary Under-Secretary at the Air Ministry 1945–6. Strachey became Minister of Food on 27th May 1946, retaining the post until 1950.
3 G. S. de Freitas, later Sir Geoffrey (1913–82). P.P.S. to the Prime Minister 1945–6. Labour M.P. for Nottingham Central 1945–50; Lincoln 1950–61; Kettering 1964–79. Parliamentary Under-Secretary for Air 1946–50; Home Office 1950–51. High Commissioner in Ghana 1961–3; Kenya 1963–4.
4 Arthur Blenkinsop (1911–79). Parliamentary Secretary at the Ministry of Pensions 1946–9; Health 1949–51. Labour M.P. for Newcastle upon Tyne East 1945–59; South Shields 1964–79.
5 William Foster (1887–1947). Parliamentary Secretary, Ministry of Fuel and Power 1945–6. Labour M.P. for Wigan 1942–7.
6 'Shinbad': Dalton's derogatory nickname (sometimes 'Shinbad the Tailor') for Emanuel Shinwell, q.v., the Minister of Fuel and Power.
7 A. G. Bottomley, later Baron (b. 1907). Parliamentary Under-Secretary at the Dominions Office 1946–7. Labour M.P. for Chatham 1945–50; Rochester and Chatham 1950–59; Middlesbrough East 1962–74; Teesside, Middlesbrough 1974–83. Secretary for Overseas Trade at the Board of Trade 1947–51. Commonwealth Secretary 1964–6; Minister of Overseas Development 1966–7.
8 Throughout May the Foreign Ministers of the United States, Russia, France and Britain argued in Paris over the European peace treaties. Reparations, and the treatment of Germany as a single entity, remained unresolved issues.

deeply desirous of seeing a Peace Treaty with Italy as soon as possible, to persuade the Cabinet to suggest to Bevin that he might give way to the Yugoslavs on Trieste if other things were reasonably settled. Since the Italians are now, happily, to retain the Alto Adige and there seems some chance of their getting at least Tripolitania back again, it would not, I think, be asking too much for them to let go Trieste. I am afraid that Bevin is getting rather obsessed with the 'Iron Curtain' and this was used in one telegram as an argument against letting Tito[1] have Trieste. But, as I pointed out, and other colleagues supported, as soon as you walk a mile outside Trieste, you are in Slovene villages, so the Iron Curtain hangs around the town, if not along the water front.

Crossman thinks that H.M.G.'s reaction to the Palestine report[2] was very bad and that it is absurd to talk of disarming the Hagana, which is only a Jewish Home Guard and quite distinct from the Terror Gangs. He complains of the presence of so many anti-Semites in H.M.G. and in the Colonial Office. He says we have nothing to fear from the Arabs, who have no arms. I find all this rather refreshing, but it is difficult at this stage to do much about it. The continued absence of Bevin in Paris is a great handicap to these discussions, though in other ways it is a great relief, since overburdened though he is with foreign affairs, he still tends to meddle over-much with the business of his colleagues. How I love a colleague-free day! Then I can really get on with the job. The greatest curse of ministerial life is the mass and multiplicity of ministerial committees and sub-committees.

Monday 20th May

Ruth and I spent the weekend (17th–19th) at Clacton – for the first time in our lives. It is not nearly so bad as I thought, and we stayed with some dozens of others in quite a good modern-architecture hotel now owned by the C.W.S. [Co-operative Wholesale Society] and run by the W.T.A. [Workers' Travel Association]. The occasion was an International Socialist Conference. I was in the chair for its duration and was rather relieved to find that we steered clear of a number of reefs. ...

On the Sunday we had a general discussion, and in the afternoon

---

1 Josip Brož, known as Marshal Tito (1892–1980). Prime Minister, then President, of Yugoslavia 1945–80. President of the National Liberation Committee 1943–5.
2 The report of the Anglo-American Committee of Enquiry into the Palestine problem (set up in November 1945 on Bevin's initiative) was published on 20th April, recommending the acceptance of the request for an increase in the number of entry certificates. Crossman had been a member of the Committee. A cool British response to the report was followed by a wave of Jewish terrorism against the British in the Mandate.

took certain decisions – to set up in London a 'Liaison Office', or 'Information Centre', to be run by us and to gather and distribute information on the course of events. This will mean that D. Healey[1] will need, I think, one more assistant and one additional typist.

Thursday 27th June
I am riding just now on a high tide of success. I must, therefore, cautiously watch my step!

Tuesday 10th September
Had a talk, alone, with Bevin this morning. He seemed in very good physical and mental condition. He said that lately he had changed his tactics and had 'worked things from behind the scenes' from his hotel in Paris, instead of plunging into constant public debate with Molotov and others. He complained that Phil [Noel-Baker] was always founding new organisations and that he had no minister in the Foreign Office, both Phil and McNeil[2] having arranged, independently of one another, and of him, to be in New York next week! He thought Cadogan was doing very well in New York because he 'works to instructions' ...

After forty minutes' conversation, in which, as usual and as I desired, he did much the most of the talking, he had to go to open the Palestine Conference. He was extremely friendly and said he would like to have a further talk before I go off to Canada and the U.S.A. He said that Stansgate[3] had been rather weak in Egypt – I said that I thought he was too old – and that three weeks' deputising in Paris had given Alexander 'quite a new view of the world'. He was less combative than before and was beginning no longer to see things simply from the point of view of the Admiralty. I told him of my proposal to the P.M. that the post of Paymaster-General should now be filled by Willie Hall and that I should be given a third minister at the Treasury, preferably Harold Wilson.[4] I also added that I heard that Morrison

---

1 Denis Healey (b. 1917). Secretary of the Labour Party International Department 1945–52. Labour M.P. since 1952. Defence Secretary 1964–70. Chancellor of the Exchequer 1974–9. Deputy Leader of the Labour Party 1980–83.
2 Hector McNeil (1907–55). Parliamentary Under-Secretary at the Foreign Office 1945 to 4th October 1946. Minister of State at the Foreign Office 1946–50. Labour M.P. for Greenock 1941–55. Secretary of State for Scotland 1950–51.
3 Stansgate had led a British Treaty Delegation in Cairo whose aim was to negotiate a new Treaty of Alliance with the Egyptians, to replace the Anglo–Egyptian Treaty of 1936.
4 J. H. Wilson, later Sir Harold, Baron (b. 1916). Parliamentary Secretary at the Ministry of Works 1945–7. Labour M.P. for Ormskirk 1945–50; Huyton 1950–83. Secretary for Overseas Trade 1947; President of the Board of Trade 1947–51. Leader of the Labour Party 1963–76. Prime Minister 1964–70, 1974–6.

had put forward an alternative idea for Paymaster-General. Bevin, having reacted automatically by abusive reference to Morrison and his mishandling of all our information services, said that he himself had wanted Gordon Walker as an extra Under-Secretary at the F.O., but that Attlee had said that Morrison wanted him for Paymaster-General. He hoped I wouldn't anyhow take Harold Wilson from Works, unless George Tomlinson could have a good man in exchange. He said that Hall had been doing very well in Paris. He said that no doubt I had heard that it was intended to move Phil. I said I had heard this. I suggested that he might find an occasion to support my proposal on Hall with the P.M. He said, 'I can't ever get Clem to say anything. Can you?'

I have cleared my Autumn Budget in outline, first with Attlee and then, separately, with Morrison and Bevin. The former says that he thinks it is 'skilful and well composed'. I have also quite an easy passage with the other two, though Bevin is full of ideas of his own on this subject. I am not going to tell any other members of the Cabinet until the Monday morning before the day when I introduce it. Otherwise they might leak.

On 18th September, Dalton visited North America for the first annual meeting of the Board of Governors of the International Monetary Fund and the International Bank for Reconstruction and Development. He flew first to Canada, visiting Quebec, Ottawa and Toronto, arriving in Montreal on 25th September and leaving for the United States next day.

Thursday 26th September
Leave Montreal very early ... At the Washington airport we are met by a swarm of representatives, including Gordon Munro,[1] stalking along like a general; Catto, trotting along like a small kitten; and a horde of attendant secretaries, statisticians, etc., with representatives of the State Department (rather spruce), and the Treasury (rather squat).

Catto and Munro in car with me. The former says that he has made three speeches to New York bankers and given nothing away. And he seems to have handled the press most diplomatically. Asked whether

1 R. G. Munro (1895–1967). British Treasury Representative in Washington 1946–9. Financial Adviser, U.K. High Commission in Canada 1941–6.

7 From *Let Cowards Flinch!* by Sagittarius (Vicky), 1946

he was here for the meetings – Fund and Bank – he said, 'No.' Asked why he was here at all, he said, 'At the request of the Chancellor of the Exchequer to give him advice on any subject on which he might require it.' Asked whether he was Governor of the Bank of England he said, 'Yes.' Asked how they should describe him he replied, 'You can describe me as a small man with grey hair and an Aberdeen accent.' Asked whether he could make a statement on the economic and financial situation in the U.K. he said, 'It would take me a day to explain that to you. But let me ask you a question. "Do I look depressed?" '

Having driven with Trend[1] and the others to the Embassy, I demand a drink which is furnished after the Ambassador[2] and I have gone together into the pantry and arranged this. Munro and I then drive off to see Snyder.[3] The Ambassador says that he is like a little white mouse and one can't hurry him. He is very keen on goodwill between our two countries, and is very close to the President, closer than anyone else now. But he does not understand much about anything, being a small-town banker from the President's home state, Missouri, and he will get very suspicious if anything is put to him in a pretentious or complicated way. I am told that my first talk with him will be most important.

Arriving at the Treasury and having shaken hands with all the elevator men and lady secretaries on the way up, I am ushered into Snyder's room and find also present Vinson,[4] his predecessor, now Chief Justice, a man from Kentucky, who was more accurate, Keynes used to say, at long distance spitting into a spittoon at the far end of the room than anyone else he had ever met. Will Clayton,[5] whom I had met in London, and Gardner,[6] Under-Secretary to the Treasury and ex-Governor of North Carolina.

We had a friendly introductory talk, they all telling rather long and

---

1 B. St J. Trend, later Sir Burke, Baron (b. 1914). Principal Private Secretary to the Chancellor of the Exchequer 1945–9. Secretary to the Cabinet 1963–73. Rector, Lincoln College, Oxford 1973–83.
2 Sir Archibald Clark Kerr, 1st Baron Inverchapel (1882–1951). Ambassador to the U.S.A. 1946–8; U.S.S.R. 1942–6.
3 J. W. Snyder (1895–1985). U.S. Secretary of the Treasury 1946–53. St Louis banker.
4 F. M. Vinson (1890–1953). Chief Justice of the U.S.A. June 1946–53. U.S. Treasury Secretary 1945–6.
5 W. L. Clayton (1880–1966). U.S. Under-Secretary of State for Economic Affairs 1945–7.
6 O. M. Gardner (1882–1947). Under-Secretary to the U.S. Treasury 1946–7. Governor of North Carolina 1929–33.

not very pointed stories, as seems the American habit, and I seeking to radiate beams of goodwill, fellowship and co-operation and then, after some quarter of an hour, the others are ushered out to another meeting and Snyder and I and Munro are left together. I then tell Snyder that it is with him that I have been instructed by our P.M. to make and keep contact; that we must clear everything together, and particularly any difficult points which may arise in this next ten days; that I know the State Department always take an interest in these matters, as do the Foreign Office in the U.K., but that Mr Bevin has told me that he is sure my straight line must always be to Snyder. He seems to like this and says that we must have a number of heart-to-heart talks together. ...

I then broach with him, just before leaving, the delicate question of our decision to cease to mint silver coins and gradually to replace them with nickel. In London there has been a great flap on about this, following a leakage in the *Daily Herald*, and I may be asked about it at my press conference.

Bridges[1] had proposed that I should tell the press that I had no statement to make, but I refused to do this, saying that it was not my style and would create much needless suspicion. Therefore I wished to 'inform', though not to 'consult', Snyder before making any statement here, but thereafter to tell the press quite frankly what we meant to do.

Snyder took it very well. He said he supposed this would not mean that we were going to give up 'hard money'. I said certainly not and explained that our silver had always been, and still was, a token coinage, but that we were most anxious to repay the silver which we owed the U.S. as soon as possible and gradually to substitute nickel for silver. He said this would be quite all right and offered me the additional argument that, after all, we were only doing what the U.S. themselves did in minting nickel.

So far so good and I come back to a late lunch at the Embassy.

Sleep a bit in the afternoon and later try on a thin suit, procured through the enterprise of Munro, which fits me surprisingly well, though the trousers are much too long and some two feet have to be taken off them. These trousers were built for an American with an immense paunch, but this doesn't matter at all inside a belt, a new illustration of the great superiority of the latter over our old world braces. I shall now be much happier and more efficient because much cooler.

1 Sir Edward Bridges, later 1st Baron (1892–1969). Permanent Secretary at the Treasury and Head of the Civil Service 1945–56. Secretary to the Cabinet 1938–46.

They are having an Indian summer in Washington and it is much hotter and more humid than usual at this time of the year. The first night I find myself waking up at 4 a.m., but soon go to sleep again. Blankets are quite out of place on a bed. The temperature has been around 90 and so has the humidity. I understand that 100 humidity is another way of saying that it is raining. So long as the air is in movement I don't mind it at all, but in order to avoid unnecessary perspiration I find myself tending to walk more slowly and with greater dignity.

The Ambassador, Catto, Trend and I dine at the Embassy in dressing gowns. I find the Ambassador as good as ever, a great sense of humour and no fussing. We drink some muscat white wine presented to him by King Carol when he went on a special mission, which had no success, to Romania. He has a Russian servant, whose arrival caused a great flutter in Washington (they are, of course, all frightfully Russophobe here). The American security people were inclined to raise objections officially but the Ambassador said, 'Oh! you can't do that, Uncle Joe gave him to me.' He also has a Scots piper who pipes outside our windows about 8 a.m. and also, I am told, on ceremonial occasions at dinner. It will be very comfortable being fixed here for a week on end, after rushing around in Canada.

Friday 27th September
I hold my first American Press Conference in the Embassy. It all went very smoothly, and was thought to have been a success. The press men were much less aggressive and asked much less troublesome questions than I had been led to expect. It was surprising how certain topics were not raised at all. Thus, no one mentioned Imperial Preference and I was asked nothing about silver. ...

Spend a good deal of today working on my broadcast for tomorrow. At the start everybody here seemed frightened out of their wits by my intention to say, among other things, that we had no strikes in England. They thought this might seem provocative and insulting to the Americans. They were also rather frightened of my telling the Americans that we had nationalised the coal mines, or that we had done this because the previous owners had made a mess of things. They thought perhaps, if I *must* say this, I should hasten to add that we were not going to nationalise many more industries and that even after we had carried out our programme, 80 per cent of our industries would remain in private hands. I refused to accept any of these suggestions. There is really no point in not telling these people the facts and gradually bringing them to a better understanding of who we are and what we are doing. ...

Snyder gave a large reception at the Wardman Park Hotel which is our meeting place for all Bank and Fund gatherings, and where we also have our office and where all those of my party who are not at the Embassy are staying. A great swarm of diplomats, officials, financiers, wives of all these, photographers and press men. A marine band in red uniforms nearly drowns all conversation, but the hot fried oysters are very good and there are a few drinks. After meeting and being introduced to the same people about three times I get rather bored and make my escape. The only man I meet whom I dislike at first sight [is] Harry White.[1] I hear that Snyder is likely soon to get rid of him. This would be a good thing from every point of view and would make our relations on the official plane much easier.

Saturday 28th September
Attend my first formal meeting of the Governors of the Bank and Fund. Snyder is in the chair and I am vice-chairman at the Procedure Committee ... Walking through the lounge on the way to the elevator, Meyer[2] said to me, 'Snyder isn't a bit colourful. I have done my best to put him over, but I can't make him photogenic.'

Monsieur Schuman,[3] French Finance Minister, lunches alone with me at the Embassy. He has practically no English so all the talk is in French. A very nice man and very reasonable in discussion, but looks very sad and is not, I should think, physically very strong. ...

He spoke of French political prospects and thought that the Communists had shot their bolt and would lose a little in the next elections. He said that, as a Frenchman, he always felt humiliated when French Communists showed themselves to be the slaves of a barbaric and backward Asiatic State like Russia.

He thought the Radical Socialists had no future. They were only a few generals without an army. They had, in the past, always profited from the second ballot, as a result of intrigues and combinations. The second ballot had now been abolished in the French constitution and [replaced by] a system of P.R. based on the Departments as the constituency units. He would like, he said, a government of the M.R.P. [Mouvement Républicain Populaire] and the Socialists without the Communists or the Radicals or the extreme Right. He seemed very

1 Harry Dexter White (d. 1948). U.S. Executive Director of the I.M.F. 1946–7. Assistant to the U.S. Treasury Secretary 1943–5.
2 Eugene Meyer (1875–1959). First President of the International Bank for Reconstruction and Development June–December 1946. Proprietor of the *Washington Post*; Editor 1940–46.
3 Robert Schuman (1886–1963). French Finance Minister (M.R.P.) in the Bidault and Ramadier Governments 1946, 1947. Prime Minister 1947–8; Foreign Minister 1948–53. Minister of Justice 1955–6.

conscious of the moral shock from which France was still suffering and was afraid that the Americans, as indicated in Byrnes's speech at Stuttgart, were in danger of further deceptions at the hands of the Germans. I said that I had always shared the French view of the Germans. ...

Mendès France,[1] who is here with him, is not, I think, very much *persona grata* to him and it would have been a great mistake to have had them both along together. Mendès France is said to be holding his present position precariously and may disappear from the Government after the elections. He is, of course, a Radical.

Sunday 29th September

I don't get up till after 10 a.m. and am then driven out by Munro some 45 miles to the Plains on the way to the Blue Ridge Mountains and the Skyline Drive ... We lunch with Ralph Lloyd Thomas[2] and his wife, who are living in an American farmhouse lent to them by Averell Harriman.[3] Before lunch Munro and I take a rapid walk for half an hour and perspire quite a pleasant lot.

We drive back in time to change and attend a large cocktail party given by Meyer, where I am made much of by many, including swarms of Slavs, especially Poles, and advised the Yugoslav not to overdo his objections to the entry of Italy into the Fund and Bank, since this entry is now quite certain to take place. I also met André Bonnet[4] whom I used to know at Geneva, now French Ambassador here, with his wife who used to be the wife of Aghnides;[5] also Walter Lippmann[6] who is much better looking and more attractive than I had expected and whom I am to meet again tomorrow. We then return and dine at the Embassy, the Ambassador having returned from New York. We

---

1 Pierre Mendès France (1907–82). Governor for France of the International Bank for Reconstruction and Development 1946–58. Head of French Financial Mission to Washington at Bretton Woods in 1944. Minister of National Economy 1944–5. Prime Minister of France 1954–5. Radical Socialist. Author.
2 Not identified.
3 Averell Harriman (1891–1986). U.S. Ambassador to Britain 1946. Secretary of Commerce 1946–8. President Roosevelt's Special Representative in Great Britain March 1941. U.S. Ambassador to the U.S.S.R. 1943–6. Special Assistant to President Truman 1950–51. Governor of the State of New York 1955–8.
4 Henri Bonnet (1888–1978). French Ambassador to the U.S.A. 1944–55. Married to Hellé, née Zavoudaki. Member of the League of Nations Secretariat 1920–31.
5 Thanassis Aghnides. Greek Ambassador to Britain 1942–7. Chairman of the Greek Delegation to the General Assembly of the United Nations October–December 1946.
6 Walter Lippmann (1889–1974). American journalist and author. Special writer for New York Herald Tribune Syndicate 1931–62.

dine out of doors and sit up rather late. The Ambassador tells a number of stories of his experiences in Moscow. He says the Russians were quite determined to make him drunk when he first arrived, but, having once completely succeeded, they afterwards treated him with greater respect and left him pretty well alone. He says that Molotov drinks a great deal and related one evening when Molotov pinned the Swedish Minister in a passage stretching out his arms on either side of him and leaning heavily against the wall and repeating several times, 'We don't like neutrals.' The Swedish Ambassador made a long speech explaining why his country was neutral, but Molotov only kept repeating, 'We don't like neutrals', and then, swinging his arm round, struck the Ambassador on the breast saying, 'We prefer men like this.' This incident was exaggerated by some of the onlookers into a story that there had been a most serious Anglo–Russian disagreement and that Molotov had struck the British Envoy!

Monday 30th September
We go this morning to the Wardman Park Hotel, as usual, and receive at successive meetings the first Annual Reports of the Fund and the Bank. There is no discussion whatever on either of these. It is amazing how purely formal many of these meetings are. The weather today is much cooler. There is a cloudless blue sky and quite a strong cool wind. I walk with Trend from the Hotel to the Embassy. This takes us about twenty minutes and it is quite difficult to find our way. Everybody seems to think that it is most eccentric to be walking at all.
...

The official car drivers, in particular, seem to think that something quite extraordinary has happened when we arrive at the Embassy on foot. I feel that we have created quite a Washington sensation.

Lieftinck,[1] the Dutch Finance Minister, who is rather a bore, is trying to fix up discussions with the Americans and ourselves about what he calls 'the German Problem'. I have told my officials that I would not join in any discussions on this subject with the Dutch, unless the French were there too. When Lieftinck spoke to me direct about this, I replied, 'The German problem is very simple, the problem is that there are too many Germans.' He did not seem very satisfied with this observation.

The Ambassador and I lunched today with Snyder at the Treasury. Also present Clayton and Gardner. Snyder is very friendly and quite quick to take and settle points ...

1 Professor Pieter Lieftinck (b. 1902). Dutch Finance Minister 1945–52. Governor of the International Bank for Reconstruction and Development. Executive Director 1956–71. Executive Director of the I.M.F. 1956–76.

After lunch the Ambassador and I had a few words alone with Snyder in his study. He showed us a picture of a party on board a yacht which had gone on a holiday cruise to Jamaica. The group included the President and Snyder but no other politicians. It was clear from this picture, as from much other evidence, that Snyder is very close to the President. The Ambassador said to me afterwards, 'The President never forgets his old friends and Snyder used to cash Harry's cheques when Harry was a young man.' The Ambassador thinks that the President is suffering a good deal from a consciousness of heavy burdens. He realises that he is not doing very well.

Later in the afternoon I get a message from Snyder that he and I and Clayton are to meet with the Italian Chargé d'Affaires, as we agreed at lunch, to have a word with him about the Italians' admission to membership of the Fund. ...

I go round to the Hotel and to Clayton's suite. The ante-room is full of a crowd who turned out later to be State Department officials and experts of various kinds. Clayton is in a room inside with the fat little Italian Chargé. I have only had time to say good afternoon to the lady secretary when Snyder walks quickly in through them all, quite unattended by officials, and enters Clayton's room, I following on his heel, without a word to any of the crowd in the ante-room. ...

Clayton has a wrinkled brow, but now Snyder who is calm and impassive, a man of few words and quick sentences. Trend says that he is puzzled to make up his mind whether behind this impassivity there is a 'good deal or nothing at all'. Nor am I yet quite sure.

Later in the afternoon I go to a large reception at the French Embassy. We are now beginning to meet everyone over and over again, but there were a few new faces here tonight, including Tirana[1] and his wife who kissed me most affectionately before this large crowd, and Madariaga. This evening the Ambassador gives a large dinner party at the Embassy. ...

I am now on Christian name terms with Snyder and also, though with faintly more hesitation on his part, with Clayton. Many of the English are rather slow at this, but the Americans like it. The Ambassador told an amusing story of Halifax having to be bucked up to call Sol Bloom 'Sol'[2] ... Labour Party politics are a much better training for this than the Civil Service or the Vice-Royalty.

---

1 Rifat Tirana (1908–52). Albanian-born U.S. official. Dalton had known him since the early 1930s, when he was on the staff of the League of Nations. He wrote under the pseudonym Thomas Reveille.
2 Sol Bloom (1870–1949). Congressman for New York. Chairman of the Foreign Affairs Committee 1939–46.

Wednesday 2nd October

Pay my first visit to the White House at a quarter to one today. I am accompanied by the Ambassador and Catto. The latter has been most eager to see the President, I think for the support of his own prestige with other Governors of Central Banks. I fix with Snyder that 'Lord Catto' shall, if I agree, come with me. We have exactly one quarter of an hour (all this is marked down with great exactness and each day the Press reports the list of the President's callers of the day before, with the times of their coming and going).

Mr Truman is alone in a not at all interesting office. He is not an interesting man. He has a slow amiable smile, but I doubt if he ever has very much to say. The conversation was completely platitudinous. We speak of the great goodwill prevailing between our two countries, the value of personal contacts as through these meetings, and Catto, whom I introduced to him as 'Our No. 1 Banker', brought the proceedings to their brightest point by relating that three of his four children had been born in the U.S. and were, when in America, U.S. citizens and could get in without passports. The President smiled and said that this must be very convenient.

As we three went out at 1 o'clock prompt, we were met in an ante-room by an impenetrable crowd of pressmen demanding to know what we had said to the President and he to us. I gather this is quite routine. I shake all the pressmen individually by the hand, asked them how they thought things were going, and told them that our interview with the President had been most friendly and agreeable, but that no matters of importance had been discussed. I also presented to them Catto who was trying to escape round the corner. ...

Return for the second time to the White House this afternoon for a reception of Governors of the Fund and Bank, etc. Not very interesting or impressive. Quite different, I hear, from Roosevelt's day when he used to sit in his chair and have people brought up to him in turn for short conversations. This President, having shaken hands with all on entry, seems to fade out unnoticed. ...

Gutt[1] gives a dinner party this evening and I am sat between Madame Gutt whom I rather like, and the wife of Harry White, who whines at me about the Fulton speech, etc., one of those – miserably ineffectual in their own country – pseudo-idealists.

Thursday 3rd October

Today the official business of the Bank and Fund finishes, a day ahead of schedule ... I have to make another short speech and then am

1 C. A. Gutt (1884–1971). Managing Director of the I.M.F. 1946–51. Belgian Minister of Finance 1934–5, 1939–45.

photographed with Snyder, taking over from him the Chairman's gavel, with Meyer and Gutt grinning away one on each side. This looks rather a good photograph and I am trying to get the original.

I send an indignant and rhetorical telegram to the Foreign Secretary, in reply to one from him proposing that we should pay more to the Americans for the keep of Germany. There is a bad pressure just now of claims on our 'improvident good nature'. This may mean a lot of supplementary estimates this year. The only gain would be if, by paying more this year, we paid less next. This might help towards that balanced Budget. Meanwhile, I telegraph to Bevin that 'the stability of our finances, the standard of life of our people and the reputation of our Government will be put in peril unless we make a firm stand now against demands that we should foot every bill which anyone presents to us.'

Tonight there is a final official dinner party at the Statler Hotel, with Snyder in the chair, and hundreds of governors, executive directors, officials attendant upon all these and as many wives as can be collected. It is all rather long and slow, and an American lady singer goes on singing song after song for hours on end. At one stage I am required to make a speech as the new Chairman. I tell them that all those who want money from the Fund will have to come to *Mrs* Gutt and all who want loans from the Bank to *Mrs* Meyer. This is thought to be extremely funny – it just hits the right level of the general sense of humour. And so we come to the end of the last official day.

It is difficult to size up the value of these sessions. As usual, one is tempted to say that the chief value is in the formation of contacts, and a reasonable degree of personal confidence off stage. But this, I think, has done a little more than that. In this next year I think that both the Fund and Bank will begin genuine operations, even though with caution.

There is a good deal of vague apprehension here of an American 'recession'. I can't find any real reason for this. Grigg[1] told me that the other day, asking an American businessman what was 'American business opinion' on this question, the man replied, 'American business opinion? There ain't no such thing. We're just a bunch of crooks.'

Friday 4th October
Fly to New York for a speech to the New York Chamber of Trade, followed by a lunch, and fly back to Washington for dinner ...

1 Sir James Grigg (1890–1964). British Executive Director of the International Bank for Reconstruction and Development 1946–7. Permanent Under-Secretary of State at the War Office 1939–42. Secretary of State for War 1942–5. National M.P. 1942–5.

I don't like New York. The skyscrapers are remarkable at a distance, close up, I find the whole thing repulsive, including, particularly, the overhead railway which crashes along above one of their main streets …

Dine at the Embassy – the Ambassador being out – with Trend, Young,[1] Bell,[2] and Anstruther.[3] Bell, whom I had not talked to much before, has a sense of humour and the right political approach.

The Ambassador, returning after taking part in some sort of Quiz or Brains Trust for the United Nations, which he had found very tedious, relates how at Yalta, Winston had been making a speech – translated sentence by sentence into Russian – in honour of 'Stalin the Great' as he used to call him and had said, 'I regret to inform you that in my country the people are beginning to turn rather pink', to which Stalin had instantly interjected, 'I am glad to hear they're getting a bit more healthy.' This had pushed Winston entirely off his perch and he had not found any good rejoinder.

I am given at dinner a first note of the long delayed ministerial changes at home. Some of these are as expected – the overdue resignation of Lawson[4] and Stansgate, but I am very sorry to find that George Hall,[5] although he has been wanting to go, is still being kept on with a peerage and moved to the Admiralty. Winster[6] has, after all, accepted the governorship of Cyprus, as I strongly urged him to do on the eve of my departure. The list of junior ministers is not quite complete, but I am very delighted that Chris Mayhew[7] and John Freeman[8] are

1 Possibly G. R. Young, Personal Assistant to Dalton as Chancellor of the Exchequer, and later Chief Press Officer in the Information Division at the Treasury.
2 W. F. Bell (b. 1909). Secretary to the Ambassador. First Secretary at the British Embassy in Washington 1946–8.
3 Personal Assistant to Inverchapel.
4 J. J. Lawson, later 1st Baron (1881–1965). Secretary of State for War 1945–6. Labour M.P. for Chester-le-Street 1919–49. Junior minister 1924, 1929–31.
5 G. H. Hall, 1st Viscount (1881–1965). First Lord of the Admiralty 1946–51. Colonial Secretary 1945–6. Junior minister 1940–43. Parliamentary Under-Secretary at the Foreign Office 1943–5. Labour M.P. for Aberdare 1922–46.
6 R. T. H. Fletcher, 1st Baron Winster (1885–1961). Governor of Cyprus 1946–8. Minister of Civil Aviation 1945–6. Liberal M.P. 1923–4; Labour M.P. 1935–42.
7 C. P. Mayhew, later Baron (b. 1915). Parliamentary Under-Secretary at the Foreign Office 1946–50. Labour M.P. for Norfolk South 1945–50. Labour, later Liberal, M.P. for Woolwich East 1951–October 1974. Assistant Private Secretary to Dalton at M.E.W. 1940–41. Navy Minister 1964–6.
8 John Freeman (b. 1915). Financial Secretary at the War Office 1946–7. Labour M.P. for Watford 1945–55. Parliamentary Secretary at the Ministry of Supply 1947–51. Editor of the *New Statesman* 1961–5. High Commissioner to India 1965–8. Ambassador to the United States 1969–71. Chairman and Chief Executive of London Weekend Television 1971–84.

now definitely in at the F.O. and W.O. respectively. The first of these two appointments will make a lot of jealousy among others. But that can't be helped. Nathan, though not a popular figure, will make quite a competent Minister of Civil Aviation, but I doubt if Lindgren[1] is really good enough to have the speaking part in the House of Commons. This looks to me like the weakest of the junior ministerial appointments, in which there is a gap, since no successor to Lindgren at the Ministry of National Insurance is announced. It will be very stupid if this post is not filled by one of the young trade unionists. But I think, in fact, that it quite certainly will be.

Saturday 5th October
Today I fly to Tennessee. But this morning I call, with Munro, on Clayton. Since it is a Saturday we have to enter the State Department through the back door and there is a general air of nobody being about. I have nearly an hour with Clayton, Munro being with us most of the time. I take him over a number of European–financial points and, on the whole, his responses are good.

Munro takes a careful note which I shall use in London. Clayton and I are agreed that U.N.R.R.A. [United Nations Relief and Rehabilitation Administration] must definitely stop, as arranged, in the next year and that, apart from the Germans, only. Italy, Austria and Greece should rank for further doles from either the U.S. or U.K. He welcomes my suggestion that we should press neutrals and he thinks Brazil could pay up towards this work of relief. He agrees with me that Italy should be urged, with the backing of U.S. and U.K., to go direct to Argentina and ask for a gift. Brazil should give coffee, the Swiss should give money and the Swedes give either money or food. None of these should be loans, thus keeping clear of reparation entanglements. He further agrees that next year (U.S. fiscal year runs from June 1947 to June 1948) must be declared to be the last year of all such doles. ...

The Ambassador does not think the Russians are planning world domination, but they are trying all the time for more security as they conceive it. They are a very difficult and bad mannered people; like a pup which is not house trained, they bounce about and bark and knock things over and misbehave themselves generally and the next

---

1 G. S. Lindgren, later Baron (1900–71). Parliamentary Secretary at the Ministry of Civil Aviation 1946–50. Labour M.P. for Wellingborough 1945–59. Parliamentary Secretary at the Ministry of National Insurance 1945–6; Ministry of Town and Country Planning, then Housing and Local Government (under Dalton) 1950–51. Junior minister 1964–70.

day are puzzled if one is still resentful. They still have a terrible sense of inferiority. They like, therefore, to be treated very nicely in public and it does nothing but harm to shout at them in public; on the other hand, shouting in private often does good ...

On 5th October 1946, Dalton flew in the company of several British and American officials to Tennessee to look at the work of the famous Tennessee Valley Authority, symbol of Roosevelt's pre-war New Deal.

We fly to Knoxville in a small, but most excellent, plane ... We are met at the airfield at Knoxville by Lilienthal,[1] an attractive quiet person, the principal inventor and presiding genius of T.V.A. [Tennessee Valley Authority] ...

Lilienthal and all his principal helpers regard the thing most idealistically. In these next two days I saw quite a number of them. They gave me an impression of devoted efficiency.

T.V.A. is not Socialism as we understand it. Except for the dams and the power stations, they seem to *own* very little and are actually selling off a lot of land to farmers. More than half the area is wooded, but mostly owned in relatively small private units, and T.V.A. is not acquiring any more than its present quite low proportion. They sell their electric current at wholesale and aren't entering into retail supply. On the other hand, they have filled a tremendous gap which private enterprise had left wide open.

I told Lilienthal next day that T.V.A. ran counter to the preconceptions both of the Right and the Left. Hayek and Co. would strongly disapprove of it – and probably prove to their own satisfaction that it couldn't exist – while to me, and still more to some of my more inflexibly-minded political associates, it seemed to make very poor provision for public ownership and planning-with-teeth-in-it. I was astonished to find they relied so completely on persuasion, education, etc., and took no powers to give orders to anyone to do, or not to do, anything – apart, of course, from the actual waterworks and power stations. On the other hand, they got a good deal of money from the Federal Budget and were assisted in various ways by the governments of the seven States which they served.

1 D. E. Lilienthal (1899–1981). Chairman of the Tennessee Valley Authority 1941–6. Chairman of the U.S. Atomic Energy Commission October 1946–50.

Monday 7th October

We had planned to sleep one more night at Knoxville and fly back tomorrow, but we are told there is a hurricane knocking about off the Virginian coast, so had better fly tonight. We take off against a terrific sunset, and, with a slight headwind, get back in 2½ hours reaching Washington at 9 p.m. ...

I find that Laski and Frankfurter are dining at the Embassy and join them with the Ambassador. The talk is mostly of Palestine, along anticipated lines. Both the Jews say that Truman isn't just electioneering in his endless repetition of the one hundred thousand,[1] but that this is part of the general outlook of Americans of both parties.

Some talk of Stalin, who, Laski says (but one can never be sure whether it isn't all lies!), told him that what was troubling the Russians was the doubt whether the British Labour Government would be durable, or whether the Tories would not come back and gang up against the Soviet Union. Stalin, Laski says, told him that he himself believes that an Agreement with the West is possible, but that Molotov is inclined not to believe this. He said that it would help if, once in a while, Bevin would say a kind word to Molotov. Polit Buro is said to be divided into three sections, (i) pro-Western, with Stalin, (ii) anti-Western, with a third section uncertain and holding the balance.

Dalton returned to London by air on the night of 9th–10th October.

Wednesday 23rd October

Our M.P.s still seem to like me very much and I get a remarkable cheer when first rising to reply to a Question after my return, and I have fun, which our chaps enjoy, with the Tories at Question Time ...

A special Conference of all No. 1 Ministers was held to consider the House of Lords and tactics towards them. The general view was that we should not attack them unless they first badly mauled one of our Bills, but that they might easily do this in the near future, e.g. the Compensation and Betterment Bill, and that, in that case, we should

---

1 On 31st August 1945, President Truman had asked the British government to issue 100,000 certificates for Jewish immigration into Palestine, as an emergency measure. Dalton wrote later: 'I would like to be able to assert that, when President Truman made his original request, I supported it, and urged it on my colleagues in the Cabinet. But I confess that I did not do this, nor, if I remember rightly, did any of my colleagues' (HTA, p. 150).

be ready with a short and drastic Bill to prune their powers under the Parliament Act.

Friday 20th December
There is a steady run of varied trouble about food, and the constant prospect of a shortage of fuel. 'Starve with Strachey and shiver with Shinwell' is one of the Tory slogans which is going around. On the other hand, one has, I hope, an occasional feeling that in twelve or eighteen months' time we should be through the worst of most of these shortages. But, as I constantly tell my colleagues, we shall be on the rocks in two years' time, if we have exhausted the Canadian and U.S. Loans, unless we have severely cut down our overseas expenditure (military and other) and built up our exports to a much higher level than now.

The more difficult troubles there are about, the less any particular one should rob one of one's sleep or peace. I have slept well, though short, having been up pretty late recently, including two 3 a.m.s in the last two days following Parliamentary activity. ...

This afternoon the P.M. makes a statement in the House about Burma to the effect that we are inviting their leaders to come to London to discuss how to quicken up the process of Burmese independence either inside or outside the Empire. Churchill, of course, attacks this and uses the familiar old word 'scuttle', but I don't think this will cut much ice with many. It is quite clear that we can't go on holding people down against their will, however incompetent they are to govern themselves, for the whole pace, as determined in the East, has quickened in the war years, and it would be a waste both of British men and money to try to hold down any of this crowd against their will. They must be allowed to find their own way, even through blood and corruption and incompetence of all kinds, to what they regard as 'freedom'.

Monday 27th January 1947
In the House I still find myself quite alarmingly popular and small embarrassing contrasts in more than one direction are being drawn.

At the beginning of 1947, the economic situation suddenly took a sharp turn for the worse. The winter of 1946–7 was the most severe for three-quarters of a century, and the coal industry could not meet the extra demand for power. 'We are having an exceptionally bad run of weather and the coal and electricity supplies are in a pretty poor way', Dalton recorded on 6th February. 'It will be a great relief to get through March and into the period when more coal is being produced, and then we shall have to make plans for stocking up well in advance of next winter. Shinwell is the most mercurial of ministers and according to all accounts a very bad administrator. His officials are in despair at his failure to settle down to a close and objective study of the facts, or to follow a steady line in regard to many of the very tricky issues arising in his Department.'[1] Next morning, Shinwell asked the Cabinet for permission to tell the House that all electricity must be cut off from industry in London, South-East England, the Midlands and the North-West, and from all domestic consumers for five hours each day. 'This is a complete thunderclap, following on the usual rather hopeful tales we have had from this man during the past week', noted the Chancellor.[2]

Monday 10th February

The next few days are full of Fuel. And I become more and more angry with Shinbad. He is by far the least attractive member of the Government, always looking round for someone to whom to pass the blame. He is always trying to pretend that it is Alf Barnes's[3] fault for not moving the coal. Barnes, on the other hand, has not done at all badly. A widely held opinion among Labour M.P.s is that [Shinwell] should be moved. He is a bad administrator. He will not face facts squarely. He is reported by Douglas Jay, who was present at the time when the P.M. put before him in the late summer certain figures about stocks, to have said, 'You mustn't let yourself be led up the garden by all these statistics.' He also said in the hearing of the same witness, way back in April, 'You'll only get Poles into the mines over my dead body.'

In mid-January, Morrison was taken ill with a thrombosis which moved from his leg to his lung. In February his condition was critical. The crisis passed and he left hospital on 25th March, but he was unable to resume official duties until the end of April. In the meantime, Dalton was obliged to serve as Acting Chairman of the Lord President's Committee.

---

1 See also HTA, p. 203.
2 Diary, 7th February 1947; HTA, pp. 203–4.
3 Alfred Barnes (1887–1975). Minister of Transport 1945–51. Labour and Co-operative M.P. for East Ham South 1922–31, 1935–55.

Monday 24th February

Morrison is now not expected to be back for a month or two, though, very foolishly, the other day they put forth a communiqué from the hospital saying that 'He is making very good progress'. I am not at all sure what sort of physical and mental come-back he will be able

8 'Budget Hike', 15th April 1947

to achieve. Bevin is in no fit condition to go on much longer. This afternoon he was in a state of total exhaustion, as a result of having to walk up two flights of steps at Great George Street. Just how he will fare at Moscow is anybody's guess. It is quite on the cards, I fear, that he may not come back. But it is terribly difficult to know what to do, since he won't think of giving up yet and at any rate he has a doctor always with him. He said today after the meeting that it was his heart that was wrong.

Saturday 24th to Thursday 29th May
At Margate for Labour Party Annual Conference. A wonderfully sunny week ...

A very fine spirit in the great majority of delegates, with the sense of solid satisfaction at the achievements of the Government and of steady support of the leadership on all major issues. The Executive, indeed, suffered two defeats both on resolutions demanding 'immediate' action: first on the abolition of the Tied Cottage and second on Equal Pay. But neither of these are to be taken very seriously. A very conservative vote for the Executive, no old member being unseated; the only new-comers are Mark Hewitson[1] in replacement of Tom Williamson who goes to the General Council and Miss Jones[2] – daughter of Tom Jones and the only woman Lobby Correspondent – in replacement of Jennie Adamson who did not stand again. In the Constituency Party Section I had a very good vote, second only to Aneurin Bevan, and in front of Morrison, Laski, Jim Griffiths, Shinwell and Phil [Noel-Baker]. The latter was not a good Chairman, too hesitant and indecisive. Crossman, who spoke three or four times, and shows increasing signs of disgruntlement and impatience, was the runner up.[3]

Quite a flutter over *Cards on the Table*.[4] This very brightly written

1 Captain Mark Hewitson (1897–1973). Labour M.P. for Hull Central 1945–55; Hull West 1955–64. National Industrial Officer of the General and Municipal Workers' Union. Member of the Labour Party N.E.C.
2 Eirene Jones, from 1948 Mrs Eirene White, later Baroness (b. 1909). Labour M.P. for East Flint 1950–70. Junior minister 1964–6. Minister of State at the Foreign Office 1966–7; Welsh Office 1967–70. Her father was Thomas Jones (1870–1955), former Deputy Secretary of the Cabinet, Secretary of the Economic Advisory Council, friend of Baldwin and Lloyd George, and distinguished diarist.
3 Dalton's footnote: 'Votes in thousands: Bevan 646, Dalton 624, Morrison 592, Laski 571, Griffiths 539, Shinwell 475, Noel-Baker 460. Then Crossman 334, immediately followed by Driberg, Mikardo, Zilliacus and Silverman, trailing down to 113.'
4 '*Cards on the Table*': a pamphlet calling for closer co-operation on defence with the U.S., to resist Soviet aggression. It angered the Left. Healey's version of this episode, as told to two young journalists nearly a quarter of a century later, was rather different: 'I showed Dalton *Cards on the Table* and said that I had just produced it for the Party, and did he agree that I should publish it. He said "Yes". Then there was a terrible row at Margate, and it was savagely attacked. The Executive held meeting after meeting, and it wasn't until almost the end of the last one that Dalton, under repeated prodding from Shinwell, admitted that he had cleared it for publication. Up to that point he let it appear that I had done this entirely off my own bat without consulting anyone.' (B. Reed and G. Williams, *Denis Healey and the Policies of Power*, Sidgwick & Jackson, London, 1971, p. 61.)

392

pamphlet by Denis Healey has caused a stir among our anti-Americans, though, in fact, it criticises the U.S. nearly as much as the Soviet Union. The history of this publication is that, about a month ago, Healey sent me – as Chairman of the International Sub – a draft. I was full of other work and read this quickly and thought it bright and interesting. He said that it was to be looked at by McNeil to make sure there was no political objection to it. I replied that, on this basis, I was quite content that it should forthwith be published. No other member of the E.C. saw it, nor any Sub-Committee!

When, therefore, I was suddenly asked at Margate whether the National E.C. was in agreement with it, I had to hedge. To have said 'Yes' would have been a plain untruth, since they had not seen it; to have said 'No' would have quite discredited the pamphlet and its author. Therefore I adopted a challenging tone and said that, as this question had been put, I would most gladly let them have a definite answer before the Conference closed. Then we had a long jaw in the National E.C., several members taking great objection to the pamphlet. I had to keep rather quiet as to my own individual role in the matter which was not, I think, known to all my colleagues. Finally, I got them to agree to my telling the Conference that – as I had already said two days before – this pamphlet had been issued as part of the regular activities of the Head Office in circulating information and stimulating discussion; that it was not a declaration of policy, but 'a contribution to its interpretation', that its issue had been duly authorised and that the E.C. 'while not necessarily agreeing with every statement in it, considered that it had been rightly published as etc., etc.' This little incident was submerged in the tidal wave of the Bevin speech on Thursday. He scored a very great personal success and swept away all opposition. He has a most astonishing – and unique – conference personality. There was no come-back.[1]

Friday 13th June
This week I have been taking my Finance Bill through Committee and we have had one late sitting – up to 5.30 a.m. It went, on the whole, quite smoothly, with never a closure motion. We shall have two more days next week.

Much more troublesome remains the Dollar Drain. This is rapidly

---

1 Marginal note: 'Crossman was obliterated, humiliated and deeply offended.' Crossman was one of a group of back-benchers calling for the adoption of a 'Third Force' or neutralist position between the two super-powers.

getting worse, not only in the U.K. but for all the world. We have drifted a bit waiting for the arrival of Clayton who was supposed to call in here on his way back from Washington to Geneva, but this morning our Big Five met, with officials, and agreed that we must at

9 'The Dollar Loan Is Running Out', 5th June 1947

once send some communications to Washington and that we must settle the import programme next week. The rush of the Gadarene Swine towards the precipice is quickening and I am anxious that we should not lead the charge. The timing of negotiations is troublesome, since the U.S.A. enters early next year into its political silly season. Marshall[1] gives the impression of wanting to do something big, but the Congress are completely illiterate in these matters.

I made, on Wednesday, a Parliamentary Statement about 'Equal Pay', accepting the principle but refusing to apply it now or to give any future date when it could be applied. This was taken surprisingly well in the House as, indeed, it had been at a Party Meeting held earlier the same day. I don't think there is much political steam behind the Equal Pay agitation, and people are becoming better educated to the dangers of inflation.

Friday 4th July
Bevin is just back from Paris and is, as always, full of hope, resource

1 General George Marshall (1880–1959). U.S. Secretary of State 1947–9. Chief of Staff of the U.S. Army 1939–45. Defence Secretary 1950–51. Marshall made a speech at Harvard on 5th June which led to the setting up of the Organisation for European Economic Co-operation and the provision of Marshall Aid.

and courage. He plans going to Washington at the beginning of August, nominally to discuss Germany and to try to get the Americans over here at the beginning of September. He asked whether I would like to go with him to Washington. I said that I thought this was unnecessary. It will be time enough for me to weigh in in September. He thinks it will make it easier to get the Americans to produce the dollars now that the Russians have behaved so unreasonably.

On 15th July, the free convertibility of dollars and sterling came into force. In the week beginning 20th July, the dollar drain reached $106 million. By the week ending 16th August, the drain had increased to $183 million per week. On 20th August, following British discussions with the Americans, Dalton announced the suspension of convertibility – a major humiliation for the Government and for the Chancellor personally. Meanwhile Dalton allowed himself to be drawn into a series of abortive moves to replace Attlee with Bevin as Prime Minister.

On 25th July he attended the annual Miners' Gala in Durham. His fellow speakers included the Foreign Secretary.

Friday 25th July
George Brown[1] tells me that the boys all talked, during the all-night sitting this week on the Transport Bill, about the lack of leadership. Most were in favour of substituting Bevin for Attlee; they seemed to think that these two could just swop jobs. Failing this, I was the only name mentioned as a possible new Leader! They thought that I was the minister who, until now,[2] had shown himself most obviously 'on top of the job'. Failing me there were no other strong candidates. It was generally felt that Morrison was now not at all fit and could not do it. No one else – e.g. Cripps or Bevan – was mentioned. I said to Brown, 'That is all right, but let them come and talk freely and kick up a row, if they feel like it, at the Party Meeting next Wednesday.'

---

1 George Brown, later Baron George-Brown (1914–85). P.P.S. to Dalton as Chancellor 1947. Labour M.P. for Belper 1945–70. See Appendix.
2 Marginal note: '(but I had a bad reaction within a fortnight)'.

After lunch today I brought in Edelman[1] who had been lunching with me and others at No. 10 with the French Parliamentary Delegation and said to him, 'It's no use sending abusive messages to ministers. You must all come to the Party Meeting and say what you think.' I had in mind a rude message sent to me from Crossman, via Kenneth Younger[2] yesterday evening, to the effect that I and others 'had no guts'.

On the way up to Durham in the train I am pondering shock tactics and the possibilities of threatening to resign unless the chaps will face the facts. It is not easy to see how this would work.

At Durham this evening Bevin and I had a short talk. He is all for 'fighting it out' and can't believe that the miners won't work harder and produce more coal. He will make a great appeal to them tomorrow. I am rung up tonight by Cripps who hasn't yet given up hope of fixing something with the Russians in spite of Harold Wilson's failure to get an agreement. He hopes that none of us will say, publicly, that the talks have broken down. (I hear from various quarters – Bevin the next day and Sir William Stephenson[3] on Monday – that Cripps is intriguing to keep open a door towards co-operation with the Russians rather than the U.S.A. Bevin says that Makins[4] was asked to lunch with Cripps, who was talking in this sense, and that Makins, very shocked, reported this to Bevin. Sir W. Stephenson says that in the U.S. Cripps is regarded as a dangerous half-communist for this same sort of reason.)

Saturday 26th July
Bevin made a magnificent address, speaking to the miners as only he can and appealing to them, in effect, to work an extra half hour. He makes several friendly references to me, which are well received by the crowd. Then back to lunch at the County Hotel. I sit next to Morrison whom I find a little distant and difficult. I wonder how far he suspects that moves are going on? He is still fidgeting about the

---

1 Maurice Edelman (1911–75). Labour M.P. for Coventry West 1945–50; Coventry North 1950–February 1974; Coventry North-West February 1974–5. Author and journalist.
2 K. G. Younger, later Sir Kenneth (1908–76). Parliamentary Under-Secretary at the Home Office 1947–50. Labour M.P. for Grimsby 1945–59. Minister of State at the Foreign Office 1950–51.
3 Sir William Stephenson (b. 1896). Director of British Security Co-ordination in the Western Hemisphere 1940–46.
4 R. M. Makins, q.v., was at this time Minister at the British Embassy in Washington.

organisation of his office, and bothering to have Plowden[1] and his Planners inside *this* office rather than in the Cabinet Secretariat.

I have arranged to drive back to London with Bevin, who never goes by train if he can help it. I am alone in the same car with him, and Bob Dixon[2] and some policemen in a second car. We have another detective sitting in front of us beside the driver. These Jews have made all this fuss necessary.[3]

Bevin is very long-winded and very vain. These are his two most obvious failings, though Brown says he is also very unfaithful to his friends. (I took Brown down to Dorchester and Tolpuddle the week before for the Agricultural Workers' celebrations and we had much talk about the matter in the car.) Bevin and I talk about all sorts of things and he seems to be most friendly. I think that, at least, it may be said that he is more friendly to me than to Attlee, Morrison or Cripps. He complains about all three of them – but I doubt whether he complains to any of them about me! He says that Attlee is very weak, he can't get him to make up his mind. He has made an awful hash of some of his appointments, especially Inman.[4] Why not Charlie Dukes?[5] I said that I had suggested the latter to Attlee who had replied that (a) he had very little Parliamentary experience, and (b) perhaps Bevin wouldn't like him being put into the Cabinet, since he might regard him as a trade union rival. Bevin, who was in Moscow when this decision was taken, is very snorty and says that he is always trying to get Attlee to appoint more trade unionists and would have liked very much to have Dukes in the Cabinet. Of Morrison he simply says that obviously he is a sick man and not much more good. Of Cripps he complains that he is more than half-way to Moscow, and that he and Lady Cripps have been intriguing to get jobs for their friends in the Foreign Service which Bevin has had to refuse. I tell him that Brown – whom I go out of my way to praise – has been telling me that a large number of Members want Bevin to become P.M. He

---

1 Sir Edwin Plowden, later Baron (b. 1907). Chief Planning Officer and Chairman of the Economic Planning Board 1947–53. Chairman of the Atomic Energy Authority 1954–9. Chairman of a committee of inquiry on Treasury control of public expenditure 1959–61.
2 Dalton's personal detective.
3 There was a fear of attack by Jewish terrorists.
4 P. A. Inman, 1st Baron (1892–1979). Lord Privy Seal April–October 1947. Former Chairman of the B.B.C.
5 Charles Dukes, later 1st Baron Dukeston (1881–1948). General Secretary of the National Union of General and Municipal Workers 1934–46. Labour M.P. 1923–4, 1929–31.

says that Percy Wells[1] has told him the same thing, but that he doesn't want to do anyone out of his job. I say that he has a gift which none of the rest of us have, that he can speak very frankly to the trade unionists everywhere and that, in this crisis of our fate, it may well be thought by many that he is the predestined Leader. We then leave this subject, and return to it some hours later. In the interval we talk of many things including his own staff at the Foreign Office. He does not think much of Sargent who is soon retiring. He proposes to put Strang in his place with Makins as No. 2. Dixon[2] is going as Ambassador to Prague – the office had wanted to send him to Mexico, but Bevin had said no to this. He will have, in his place, Frank Roberts,[3] who he thinks has done very well in Moscow. He is keeping on Duff Cooper[4] for a little longer, but intends to replace him in a few months by Oliver Harvey. He thinks Gladwyn[5] is 'too impetuous' and that 'his judgement is not always good'. He thinks that he might succeed Cadogan at U.N.O. I praise Gladwyn, but am conscious that many in the Foreign Office have been trying to fix Bevin's mind against him.

Near the end of the journey I return to the earlier question. I urge him not to put out of his mind the possibility of becoming P.M., and so we part.

It is a very hot night and I go to bed reflecting on these two major political events; the replacement of Attlee by Bevin and the possibility of my own resignation if they won't come into line. The time is short, both before we exhaust the U.S. credit and before Parliament gets up. There is a great campaign being run against us in the Tory Press and I hear on

Monday 28th July
that suggestions are being put to Barney Baruch and others on the transatlantic telephone that the Americans should insist on there

---

1 P. L. Wells (1891–1964). Labour M.P. for Faversham 1945–64. P.P.S. to Bevin as Foreign Secretary 1945–51.
2 Sir Pierson Dixon (1904–65). Principal Private Secretary to the Foreign Secretary 1943–8. Ambassador to Czechoslovakia 1948–50. Deputy Under-Secretary at the Foreign Office 1950–54. Permanent Representative at the U.N. 1954–60. Ambassador to France 1960–64.
3 F. K. Roberts, later Sir Frank (b. 1907). British Minister in Moscow 1945–7. Principal Private Secretary to the Foreign Secretary 1947–9. Ambassador to the Soviet Union 1960–62.
4 Duff Cooper, q.v., was Ambassador to France 1944–7. Sir Oliver Harvey, q.v., succeeded him, serving until 1954.
5 Gladwyn Jebb, q.v., was Assistant Under-Secretary of State and United Nations Adviser 1946–7. He succeeded Sir Alexander Cadogan, q.v., as Permanent Representative to the United Nations in 1950.

being a change of government here. This would be quite intolerable; hence my inclination to dig my feet in on the Balance of Payments.

This morning we have an inconclusive talk of the Big Five,[1] to be resumed this evening on the basis of my paper. Bevin is set against cuts and makes a number of quite useful positive proposals, but we don't really get down to my statistics. It would be a great bore if I were to be threatening to resign on some point on which I don't see eye to eye with him, while, at the same time, I were, even remotely, connected with some move to make him P.M.!

Sir W. Stephenson to lunch alone. He says that the Americans are very frightened of Communism here and of Horner[2] and Cripps in particular. On the other hand, he says, I have quite a good press on the other side. He is bringing Bill Donovan[3] to see me tomorrow.

[One] of the advantages of Bevin becoming P.M. would be that he could shift Shinwell into the outer darkness.

Bevin has been sending some very good telegrams to Washington including some explosions to Ambassador Douglas.[4] The latter has been dining a lot at the House of Commons with various groups of M.P.s and telling them all that there is no chance of Congress doing anything at all before March and no chance then of their doing anything special for the U.K. as distinct from Western Europe.

......

10.30 p.m. The hot weather continues and I prefer it to the cold. But tonight I am very hot, very tired and very angry, after a long discursive indecisive meeting of the Big Five. George Brown tells me that the movement to make Bevin P.M. has petered out. It is not now thought that there is any pressure left in this pipe. It is one of the ever recurrent Parliamentary miracles how great waves of opinion disperse themselves in broken spray! Tonight, in view of the seeming importance of getting my colleagues down to decisions, I am once more pondering the thought of resigning – or at least of threatening to resign in order to try to get things moving. After this a thought comes to me, purely of presentation, to speak not of 'cuts' around which

1 'the Big Five': Attlee, Bevin, Cripps (President of the Board of Trade), Morrison (Lord President) and Dalton.
2 Arthur Horner (1894–1968). General Secretary of the National Union of Mineworkers 1946–59. President of the South Wales Miners' Federation 1936–46. Communist.
3 W. J. Donovan (1883–1959). American lawyer and diplomat. Special missions for President Roosevelt in Europe 1940–41. Director of Office of Strategic Services 1942–5.
4 L. W. Douglas (1894–1974). U.S. Ambassador to Britain 1947–50. Former Arizona Congressman, and Principal of McGill University.

there is an aura of distaste and timidity, but that we should 'stop buying dollar foods'. The effect of this would be to emphasise that we are being rooked, and thus to raise a positive indignation against the Americans and also to leave the thing a bit indefinite so as to minimise the resistance here.

At the Cabinet meeting on 29th July Dalton explained that, at the present rate of drawing, the United States credit would not last beyond November at best and would probably be exhausted in October or even late September. Once the United States credit had been exhausted, Britain would have only the remains of the Canadian credit, which was not likely to amount to more than £100 million in November, and her final reserves of gold and dollars, totalling at less than £600 million, which had to serve not only the United Kingdom but also the other countries in the sterling area. The Chancellor argued, therefore, that there must be substantial reductions in the year 1947–8 both in government expenditure overseas and in expenditure on imports – especially food – and he proposed that for a limited period Britain should stop the purchase of a wide range of food imports.[1]

Tuesday 29th July
Cabinet this morning, without papers, to discuss Balance of Payments generally. Attlee opens briefly and then I speak. Morrison has now more or less come round to my side and Cripps is on my side, though playing no leading part at all in the discussion. I emphasise the urgency of it all and the need to take big, bold measures and I put over the 'stop buying' slogan. To my surprise Strachey takes this very well. (I see him after the Cabinet alone and tell him that his career and mine, of which his should last a bit longer than mine, will be totally ruined if we do not act boldly. It is agreed that our officials should look into the possibilities of dollar savings through 'stop buying' for a period and I take the precaution of dictating, in his presence, a note on what we are agreed. This, in view of his previous slippery conduct.) We have, as usual, full length orations from Shinwell and Bevan. The former is exceptionally rattled, suspicious, irrelevant and discourteous. He demands information on our gold and dollar reserves as though I had deliberately withheld it from him. He has by now wholly antagonised all our colleagues. The most severe criticism that any person with real knowledge could make of the P.M. is that he has allowed this man to continue for so many months of failure to be Minister of Fuel and Power.

1 PRO, Cabinet Conclusions, 29th July 1947.

It was agreed at this morning's Cabinet that I should prepare a paper with definite proposals for Friday's Cabinet. I do a first cock-shy this afternoon.

After dinner I have a considerable talk with the P.M. He has been dining with Strachey – apparently a long-distance date and not a short-term intrigue by the latter – and tells me that Strachey is quite reasonable. We go through the heads of his speech for tomorrow's Party Meeting. He seems stronger and less rattled now that he too, no doubt, has heard that any immediate threats to his position have evaporated. I again press him to get rid of Shinwell. I tell him that this afternoon Catto came to see me and was, as always, most reassuring and helpful. ...

Catto arriving meets Bill Donovan departing with Stephenson. This is the final act put on to impress Donovan! He and I had a very good talk in the course of which I told him a series of ancient stories about miners; their character, the record of the private mine *owners*, the personalities of the National Coal Board, the total *political* weakness of our Communists, their *relative* weakness industrially – with an excursus on Horner, who seems a bit of a bogey-man in the U.S., and Sam Watson's[1] introduction of him at the Gala last Saturday. I told Donovan that the one thing we wouldn't stand was any attempt by the U.S. to tell us how to run our politics. I praised our Labour majority and denigrated the Tories. I added that we knew that transatlantic talks took place between some Tories and Barney Baruch as to what sort of Government we ought to have. He scoffed at Baruch saying, 'That old boy still thinks he's a king-maker.' Then Donovan asked whether there was any truth in what was often being said in the U.S. now by some of our political opponents that if only Winston was out of the way the road to coalition would be clear. I said this was total rubbish and he might repeat this as widely as he liked. He spoke about Russia and said that they regarded the U.K. and West Europe as more and more a bastion of liberty. I said that, in this case, they would have to give it some substantial support in the next few years. The only danger of the growth of Communism here – and I did not rate it high anyway – was if, through total withdrawal of dollars, we were forced into a descending spiral.

The P.M. tonight told me that he was getting many reports of the conversations of Ambassador Douglas with groups of M.P.s. The P.M. was increasingly displeased with the *many* dinners which the Ambassador was taking at the House of Commons. This was quite contrary to the best tradition and he recalled what a row the Tories

1 Samuel Watson (1898–1967). Secretary of the Durham Miners' Association 1936–63. Member of the Labour Party N.E.C.

had made when Maisky, some years ago, had dined with some members of the Opposition at the House. It was quite a different thing for the Ambassador to entertain M.P.s of any party at his Embassy, or to meet him at a meal on neutral ground, e.g. in some hotel or private house. But Eric Fletcher[1] and other M.P.s had told the P.M. that at one recent dinner Douglas had said, when asked about the socialisation of the Ruhr mines, that there was nothing in this because we should be bankrupt in two months and should be handing it all over to the U.S. Fletcher further reported that next morning Douglas had rung up his host at the previous night's meeting and said, 'I hope I didn't go too far last night.' The P.M. thought that perhaps Douglas had had a bit too much to drink. 'In vino veritas,' he said! Bevin was getting increasingly vexed at these dinners. It was gradually undermining the confidence which, at the beginning, most of us had felt in Douglas.

The P.M. had been profoundly disturbed by Shinwell's conduct at this morning's Cabinet. I once more urged him to take a risk and sack him. We must return to this incessantly.

Wednesday 30th July
The much heralded and long awaited meeting of the Parliamentary Labour Party happened this morning. Committee.Room No. 14 was packed. There must have been at least three hundred persons sitting and standing. The P.M. made, of his characteristic kind, quite a good speech. He told them most of the facts, flicked a lot of cherry stones at our opponents, declared against a coalition, an early election or a May Committee.[2] He also put forth, in broad detail, our proposals to increase the production of coal, steel, textiles, export goods generally and home grown food. He spoke also of import reductions, though not with great precision. He had a good reception. There is no doubt that this sort of speech – which included, at the beginning, some figures about the U.S. Loan, our gold and dollar reserves etc. – will have had a good effect upon the morale of our supporters.

Then followed a long series of rather good speeches, with a large

1 E. G. M. Fletcher, later Baron (b. 1903). Labour M.P. for Islington East 1945–70. Minister without Portfolio 1964–6.
2 In February 1931 Philip Snowden had set up a committee, under the chairmanship of Sir George May, to consider the need for cuts in public expenditure. The true purpose of this committee, which included only two Labour representatives, was to provide ammunition against soft-hearted Government supporters. The committee obliged, and in July produced a report which painted so black a picture of Britain's economic plight that it frightened not only M.P.s but foreign holders of sterling as well – helping to precipitate the crisis in August. In 1947 some back-benchers feared the same tactics and the same results.

number of proposals, many of which are very familiar, and then I wound up. Bevin had arrived late and the P.M. opening had said that Bevin was arriving later and that he mentioned this because so many rumours ran about, and Bevin would not wish it to be thought he was deliberately staying away from the meeting. Bevin passed me a slip saying, 'I think it will be a pity if they are left under the impression that I led anyone to believe that the Marshall Plan was a solution.' I duly used this, with acknowledgments, in replying, and told them that, as Leah Manning had said in a bright little speech this morning, 'This was a totally different situation from 1931, now we had a majority and a five years' Mandate.' I repeated, with greater emphasis, the P.M.'s declaration against a coalition, an election or a May Committee. I said that, on the latter point, I was *disgusted* to hear that a member of our Party who ought to know better had been saying, only two days ago, that he believed that we might very soon have a May Committee. I said that this was a disgraceful and ignorant thing to say. It would never happen, so long as I was Chancellor of the Exchequer. Ministers would take their own responsibilities and we might have to rephase some of our building programmes, etc., but we had done a wonderful job in the last two years and there would be no going back upon this. The trouble we were in had practically no relation to our internal programme. If we had had Tories in office, pursuing quite a different domestic programme, the trouble would have come just the same, and probably a good deal sooner because the miners would certainly have been producing less, rather than more, coal if the mines had not been nationalised, and there would probably have been a good few strikes as well. Thus, having briefly recapitulated the P.M.'s principal statements and having emphasised that we could not let our 'Final Reserves' – which I took credit for having increased since the American Loan was granted – be run down much, I said that some lazy-minded people sometimes said to me, 'Why shouldn't we dip into these reserves?' I said that this was quite unthinkable because we should thus be putting ourselves at the mercy of the U.S. to dictate to us what sort of a government and what sort of a policy we should have. This was much applauded. Therefore ... the whole thing was extremely simple, and here I had a flick at those who try to complicate very simple situations by asking for more detail and more papers – and, I said, 'When any of you get into the charmed circle of the Cabinet, you will find that not only do you have to spend a terrible amount of time sitting on committees, but that when you want to take decisions you are constantly asked, instead of *decisions*, for more papers and more information.'

I then said that Socialism did best when it marched in step with the rules of arithmetic, and that Socialist projects did worst when they were based on the proposition that one and one make ten. We could do, and would do, a number of symbolical cuts – I then spoke of films, foreign travel, etc. – but said that it was quite impossible to close the gap in time unless we made large reductions quickly in dollar food imports. We were being rooked, I said, by the Americans and we had proved, in the case of tobacco, that the way to deal with them was to stop buying. Our tobacco buyers had been shrugging their shoulders at recent markets and going off for a holiday, leaving no address or telephone number. The result had been that tobacco prices of the sorts we bought had fallen heavily and all the farmers had gone squealing to Washington. (This was enjoyed by the comrades.) We must do the same thing with other dollar foods. We should tell them that we were going to stop buying and keep them guessing for how long. I was pretty sure that the result of this would be to bring prices down and also contribute to what – and it was not my phrase – had been called 'the education of America about England'.

I assured them that their valuable suggestions would be fully considered by the Cabinet at their next meeting on Wednesday, when we would make statements in detail in the Parliamentary Debate. Meanwhile, we had given them clear indications as to the lines on which we were moving.

In some ways this was a disappointing meeting. I had been promised a denunciation of Shinwell by some of the Members. This didn't happen. I had been told, in particular, that Jack Jones[1] would denounce him by name. Therefore, when, after the P.M.'s speech, a crowd of Members rose, of whom Jack Jones was one, I passed to the Chairman a note suggesting that 'Jack Jones would, I am sure, make a constructive and interesting speech. I hope you will call him.' The Chairman did, but Jones never mentioned Shinwell! The latter sat looking sourer than any milk could ever be, and at one stage it seemed as though he might be stung into rising to speak, when one Member said that he would like to hear from the M.F.P. [Minister of Fuel and Power] whether there was sufficient transport to move the coal. We, however, evaded this, the Chairman shaking his head at the Member and saying that this was not a time for questions to particular ministers.

Brown was disappointed at the whole thing and at the P.M.'s speech in particular. He will scout about today and find out what they feel now.

1 J. H. Jones (1894–1962). Labour M.P. for Bolton 1945–50; Rotherham 1950–62. Parliamentary Secretary at the Ministry of Supply 1947–50.

Big Five meeting at 10 p.m. with Bridges and Eady.[1] A most shock-ing performance. I put before them my draft of the paper for tomor-row's Cabinet proposing a variety of actions. Bevin, who had ob-viously had a very good dinner – he said next day that he had been entertaining the Afghanistan Minister – was at his worst. Morrison, after an hour of this, left the room in indignation, declaring almost audibly that he had 'had enough of this drunken monologue'. The P.M., Cripps and I – and, of course, both the eminent officials – showed infinite patience and good manners. Very late in the proceed-ings we got to the more important parts but discussion was, I thought, most inconclusive. Attlee showed no power of gripping or guiding the talk. We adjourn at half an hour past midnight, Bevin enquiring as he lurched toward the door (he always walks with a lurch whether drunk or sober), 'Where do we sleep tonight – in 'ere?' I brought Bridges and Eady with me to my room and commiserated with them. 'Anyhow it was often worse with Winston,' I said. But *this* is not the way 'to ride the storm' or even to conduct a serious Government at any time.

Thursday 31st July
I was, indeed, so angry that I slept very little. It is generally anger rather than any other condition which keeps me awake! I practically made up my mind that I would resign unless I got my way on a group of essential points, including:

(i) food cuts, substantially on the scale set out in my paper,
(ii) no more dollars for German civil supplies,
(iii) suitably large cuts in overseas military expenditures and in manpower in the Forces.

I went at 9.45 to see the P.M. and told him how I felt. He seemed startled and said that he thought that, though Bevin had been terribly long-winded, we had got on rather well last night and reached agree-ment on most things. I said I was not so sure!

Friday 8th August
We have been running at terrific pressure for the past week. It gets fiercer and fiercer – and it is largely unnecessary, only the Prime Minister in particular and certain others are so afflicted, some with indecision, some with infinite powers of loquacity and repetition and nearly all with so complete a lack of any sense of the value of time –

1 Sir Wilfrid Eady (1890–1962). Joint Second Secretary at the Treasury 1942–52.

so that what astonishes me most is that a substantial number of my colleagues do not simply drop in their tracks. What a good thing it would be if some of them did! We are, indeed, all very tired. Some of us have, as one of our Tory critics said, 'been clamped to the Treasury Bench since 1940'. We have had two immensely strenuous sessions and this heavy National Emergency quickly growing to gigantic stature within the last few weeks. But *I* have seen it coming, and said so, publicly and privately on innumerable occasions. I am asking Trend to collect together into one folder all my successive warnings. The trouble is that so many have not heeded until now.

Yesterday and the day before we had the Debate on The State of the Nation. The P.M. spoke for over an hour on the first day. It was, judged by its manner, a most disappointing speech. It had a good deal of substance in it – oh! and how painfully built up from a multitude of confused and ambiguous and imprecise Cabinet decisions! – but much of this was not recognised at the moment. On the second day, I opened with an immensely long speech lasting some two hours. It lasted so long partly because I deliberately went so slow in order to get a number of figures across. These at least were, as I can always claim to be, extremely clear. I tried further to put a sharper edge on what the P.M. had said the day before, and in particular had a long passage on the strength of the Armed Forces – overseas and at home. It is here that the greatest difficulties arise in our own Party. Not only the 'Keep Left Group'[1] – who have been in a state of perpetual hysteria during these last few days holding two or three meetings each day or night – but also a wide section of the Party feel that we should run down our Armed Forces much faster. And they are certainly right. And I said so to the P.M. as long ago as last February and wrote it in a letter, almost threatening to resign then. And I have said it again in these last days, but have been met with mulish resistance from Bevin and Alexander who have been half backed up by the P.M. himself. The simple point is not so much the money, as the number of people kept in uniform and out of production. I made the best play I could yesterday with all the cards in my hand and moved a number of chaps a bit, but the effort of getting these totals down is monumental, though I think we shall, with ever continuing pressure, have increasing success. But why the hell all this struggle to get something done which sticks out a mile? The truth is that we are all in this, as

1 In April 1947, Crossman, Foot and Mikardo published a pamphlet called *Keep Left*, demanding the revolution which voters had allegedly asked for in 1945. The 'Keep Left Group' of left-wing M.P.s who supported this document provided the nucleus of the Bevanites in the 1950s.

in other things, exhausting each other and wasting each other's time by stupid failures to give ground early which clearly must be given later.

Cripps made a very fine winding-up speech yesterday. I have never heard him better. He showed great vigour and energy and restored to our own ranks a much greater sense of confidence. Though my speech lasted over two hours and it had a mass of statistics and difficult argument in it I never felt for one moment in the least tired. This is due to some truly remarkable pills[1] which I have been taking for the last two days. Urwick[2] has been giving me various things to drink and swallow, the net effect of which on my morale and efficiency has been tremendous! But one can't go on living for ever like this on pills and potions.[3]

The Tories think, quite naturally, that they are on a good thing just now. It is very easy to say: 'Why didn't you tell us about this before? Why didn't you begin doing something about this before? Why aren't you more definite about what you are doing now?' And 'We are quite sure that what you are doing now is not enough.' All this is fair game enough and Eden made a very good speech on these lines yesterday. ...

I ... in these last weeks, have had serious thoughts of resigning if I could not get my colleagues to move further on cuts in imports and on forces. When I conveyed these thoughts to Cripps, as I did the day after the Cabinet when Bevan had made *his* resignation threat, Cripps clearly was thinking in terms of some new combination in which he and I and Bevan would be together. Personal manoeuvres apart – and these don't much interest me at present – I think the sensible decision *now*, in the first week of August, is to refuse to be bound as to what we shall put into the King's Speech in the third week in October. Much will have changed by then.

Tuesday 12th August
I hope I have now – at long last – finished all my immediate labours. They have been very heavy and prolonged and anxious, and I am pretty tired. Tomorrow afternoon I hope to escape to West Leaze and next Monday to Scotland, to be among the trees, until 4th September. The P.M. is also going away. He, too, seems quite wearied out. And so are most of the rest of us.

1 Marginal note: 'Benzedrine, which the German soldiers took before going into battle.'
2 Dr Desmond Urwick. Dalton's physician.
3 Marginal note: 'And Benzedrine makes one very insensible to others' opinion.'

10 11th August 1947. Dalton's dollar economies included an effective ban on American films.

Dalton left for West Leaze on 13th August. Two days later Bridges and Dalton's Private Secretary, Burke Trend, travelled down to Wiltshire to deliver bad news about the dollar drain: an early suspension of convertibility had become inevitable. Eady was immediately dispatched by air to tell the Americans. 'Maybe I'll fly to Washington. Maybe I'll resign! I'll just give up the ghost!' Dalton scribbled in his diary after the entry for 12th August 1947. 'It has been a wonderful summer. So was 1940!' At Cabinet on 17th August, Dalton told colleagues that drawings in the five days up to 15th August had amounted to $175.9 million, as compared with an average of $115 million a week in the previous six weeks and $77 million a week in the second quarter of 1947. To prevent the complete exhaustion of the credit, he proposed to suspend convertibility – after Eady had consulted with the Americans next day. The Cabinet accepted these recommendations.[1] Three days of Cabinet discussion and transatlantic negotiation followed, before agreement was eventually reached. Late on the evening of 20th August, the Chancellor made his short, formal announcement of the suspension of convertibility, while reaffirming that the 'full and free convertibility of sterling' was still 'a long-run objective'.[2]

Sunday 17th August
Quick return of ministers to London by rail, car and plane. The *Sunday Express* got wind of this, but no other Sunday papers. Gradually a large crowd gathers in Downing Street, friendly sightseers inclined to cheer anyone they know by sight. I arrange a series of interviews. Cripps to see me at 2.45. He is always very quick off the mark, and thinks that we ministers should at once fly to Washington. We cannot leave discussions, he thinks, in the hands of officials. He also says that, unless the Cabinet will face the consequences, in ration cuts, etc., of our latest move, he will leave the Government. He thinks *now* that we should bring in the Iron and Steel Bill next Session. He is, in any case, firmly in favour of what I want the Cabinet to decide tonight.[3] I am going on to see Bevin at 2.45, and suggest that Cripps should come too. He thinks Bevin has 'an inhibition' about him, but consents. My own personal movements were wonderfully cloaked throughout the day. We had driven up this morning from West Leaze through the Horse Guards Parade to the foot of the

1 PRO, Cabinet Conclusions, 17th August 1947.
2 See R. N. Gardner, *Sterling Dollar Diplomacy*, McGraw-Hill, New York, 1969, p. 323.
3 Marginal note: '(suspend convertibility)'.

steps leading up to Downing Street. The two ladies accompanying me went first, carrying some parcels, and I followed a few minutes later when they had the door of No. 11 open. A certain crowd further down Downing Street did not notice me. Later, when crossing to the Foreign Office, we rang across and arranged for the side door on Horse Guards Parade to be opened, and I went out through the gate in the garden wall of the garden of No. 10. Carter produced the key of this. It is very rarely that it is used!

Bevin was against a sudden flight to Washington. He had been working to a programme by which he – and others if necessary – went about the middle of September, when the European plan and all the others were equally ready. Cripps made a tentative approach to him to 'take over' from Attlee. He resisted this. He also was in favour of what I proposed to decide tonight. I left them and went across to see the P.M., just hurried back from his holiday in North Wales, still looking very tired. He also seemed in favour. Since the news of the ministers' meeting was out, and the press and photographers were already all around Downing Street, in which there was now a thick crowd, it was decided to bring the ministers across from Great George Street, where it had been originally intended to hold the meeting for greater secrecy, and have it at No. 10 after all. The P.M., Morrison and I had a few minutes together before the meeting. Morrison, as usual, was inclined to be critical of the Treasury and the Bank, on the basis of a brief supplied by Nicholson.[1]

Practically the whole Cabinet turned up, along, as usual, with Strachey who was mentioned in the communiqué as having 'also attended'. This put the press on some wrong clues, e.g. that we had met to discuss ration cuts. The meeting was long but surprisingly good. Shinwell said practically nothing and that little attacking something which Bevan had not said. The latter was friendly and helpful, and I passed a note to him after he had spoken to say so. None was against what I proposed. Some were in favour of quickening things up, and blocking on Monday. Bridges, who was there, twice intervened most usefully and persuasively.

I am to broadcast on Tuesday, after the 9 o'clock news. We hope our news will be held till then, but I am very doubtful, particularly after Eady opens the ball in Washington on Monday. On Wednesday I am to go with Morrison to his press conference. The P.M., Morrison, Bevin and I are staying in London for the moment. Most of the others will go off again, though prepared to be recalled at short notice. Much

1 Max Nicholson (b. 1904). Secretary of the Office of the Lord President 1945–52. Director-General of Nature Conservancy 1952–66.

more turns on how the Americans will react to Eady's statement. The temperature in Washington is said to be 110!

After dinner, fix with Bridges, Makins, etc., the text of the telegram to Eady. This will come as a bit of a shock to some of them. I do not feel that the statistics are being sufficiently quickly produced to show what is happening. This has for some time been the Treasury view. The Bank have not been very good at this. It is a new sort of demand on their staff. Catto saw me today, and thought we were inclined to move too fast. We are getting no very useful guidance from this nice little man in this critical hour.

Monday 8th September

In the afternoon I drove down to Southampton to meet Snyder, disembarking from the Queen Elizabeth.

I went to his cabin and found him very effusive but quite drunk. His staff were much embarrassed. They were afraid he might say something frightful to the press, who, with the picture man, were thronging outside. They wanted to send them all away. But Snyder thought he would like to see them. So we went up together to the sun deck, he pulling himself together a bit, and we shook hands in front of them all, and said only, I hope, a few harmless platitudes. I had intended to propose to bring him back in my car. But Overby[1] – and I agreed! – thought it best not. So he is dining with me alone tomorrow night.

All this was quite a new view of John Wesley Snyder! But, as he tried to embrace me this afternoon, I thought, 'That personal link I've forged so patiently is still holding.'

Maud,[2] who was, I think, an amused witness, said he had seen a lot of flasks lying about in the cabin and that 'after all, there isn't much to do on a liner'!

Moves to oust Attlee had been rumbling on throughout the summer, but no positive action had been taken. On 5th September, Cripps took the initiative, proposing that he, Dalton and Morrison should go to the Prime Minister and tell him to resign in favour of Bevin. Dalton did not discourage Cripps, but doubted whether Morrison would be prepared to join. This caution

1 A. N. Overby (b. 1909). U.S. Executive Director of the I.M.F. Special Assistant to the U.S. Treasury Secretary 1947–9.
2 Sir John Maud, later Baron Redcliffe-Maud (1906–82). Master of Birkbeck College, London University 1939–43. Permanent Secretary at the Ministry of Education 1945–52; Fuel and Power 1952–9. Master of University College, Oxford 1963–76. Chairman of the Royal Commission on Local Government in England 1966–9.

proved to be justified. When Cripps spoke to Morrison, the Lord President warmly supported the view of his senior colleagues that a new Prime Minister was needed. However, he was appalled at the prospect of elevating his old enemy Bevin – and indicated that he, Morrison, was the appropriate man to succeed.

Thus thwarted, Cripps tried an alternative tactic. On 8th September he told Dalton that he intended to see Attlee alone, and tell the Prime Minister to give up his post and allow the Foreign Secretary to succeed him. Cripps added that if this failed, he would himself resign and hold a press conference to explain why. 'Stafford Cripps at least has courage and clarity', Dalton wrote in his diary. Next day (9th September), however, Cripps showed more clarity than courage. Attlee listened patiently to the President of the Board of Trade, and then coolly bought him off. Instead of agreeing to resign, the Prime Minister offered him ministerial responsibility for economic planning. A reshuffling of posts followed, and it was ostensibly to discuss possible changes in the Government that Dalton saw Attlee, still imperturbably in charge, on 10th September.

Mid-September

On Wednesday evening [10th September] I had a long talk with the P.M. after dinner. We spoke of much reconstruction in the Government and re-arrangements, not only of chaps in jobs, but of our whole procedure. I said that I was quite utterly disgusted by the way in which, in recent months, I had never been able to spend enough time in the Treasury to do my work properly because I had to spend hour after hour, sitting with large numbers of persons, ministers and officials, at Fuel Committees, Lord President's Committees, and other Committees in addition to the Cabinet Committees, listening to dreary discussions of perambulatory detail which should all be settled outside, and too long tedious speeches by ignorant, egotistical and jealous men – notably Shinwell. I said that there were many matters on which I should like to consult a limited number of my colleagues, but that I simply refused to bring them before Cabinet, either by papers or orally, first because I was quite sure that the information would be leaked to the *Observer* or other papers and, second, because, quite literally, I would not tolerate having these things discussed at great length by ignorant fools, such as Shinwell and others. I told the P.M. that his own reputation would soon suffer most seriously unless he shifted Shinwell from the Ministry of Fuel and Power and, indeed, from the Cabinet altogether. Provided that he offered him another job and – we mentioned one such – he refused it, the P.M. would have a clear answer to any grumbles which this wretched creature might afterwards make. On other individual transfers I gave him my views as Morrison and Cripps and – no doubt – Bevin had already done, and he gave me some of his. He said that his mind was not yet finally made up on some of these matters, but I urged him to get moving quickly. I spoke also, once more, of the need to cut down vigorously the Armed Forces. He said, rather indignantly and defensively, that hardly a day had passed during the past few weeks that he had not been pressing this forward. We were in agreement with each other – and with Cripps – regarding Morrison. He is not a fit man in health, and he cannot handle these planning problems anyhow. He eats out of the hand of his twittering little bird-watcher,[1] and, as Attlee said, he reads out briefs in Cabinet without really understanding them.

I speak also of the need, in making new junior appointments, to have a good proportion both of P.P.S.s and of young trade unionists, and to get rid of elderly and unpromotable junior ministers. If he does all he has in mind, there will be quite a long list of present ministers, both senior and junior, who will be ministers no more. This, I am sure, will greatly invigorate the country!

Thursday 18th September
I am trying to get away for a fortnight to begin within the next few days. The difficulty is to find a moment when one can draw a line, and thereafter disengage oneself. We have been threatened with a Cabinet on Palestine, but this is being delayed because Creech Jones,[2] now in the West Indies, has been impeded by a hurricane which has been making hay of Palm Beach in Florida. Just possibly, therefore, I shall be able to escape on Friday night.

The reshuffling of the Government is proceeding much too slowly. The P.M. has been receiving lots of good advice, particularly from Cripps and me, but seems to be finding difficulty in acting on it, particularly because so many people are away. But it is high time the thing was pushed through. Cripps has been, in these last few days, in the North making speeches on the Export Drive. The P.M. has asked him to carry on with the co-ordination of our economic efforts at least until the end of the month when Morrison comes back. Cripps and I agree that this was not good enough but he will not raise the matter forcibly until the P.M. has had an opportunity of surveying

1 Max Nicholson, q.v., was a keen ornithologist and the author of books on birds.
2 A. Creech Jones, q.v., was Colonial Secretary 1946–50.

the rest of the field. Meanwhile, I find it quite impossible to meet anybody in the political world outside since they will all wish to ask me whether they are to be promoted or dismissed. Very embarrassing!

In September, the United Nations Committee on Palestine recommended partition, with Jerusalem remaining as an international city. The British government responded by announcing that the Mandate would end on 15th May 1948.

Saturday 20th September
Cabinet this morning on Palestine. Decide that Creech Jones shall say at U.N. that we will, as recommended, give up the Mandate; that we will implement any plan on which Arabs and Jews agree; but that we won't use force to impose on either any plan to which the other objects. Later we must be prepared to name a date, as with India, for withdrawals. There was no opposition to this general line, which was supported by Attlee, Bevin, myself, Cripps and Aneurin Bevan.

Three Service Ministers and Chiefs of Staff were waiting outside, but, on my suggestion, weren't asked in. This, I said, was politics and Alexander could speak for the Service Ministers. Phil [Noel-Baker] walked in by himself about five minutes later. ... He said the Air Staff wanted to stay in Palestine, but he thought they were wrong. Bevin said, 'Tell [them] that, if they want to stay, they'll 'ave to stay up in 'elicopters.' This, if we stick to it, is a historic decision. We are drawing in our horns in the East Mediterranean. But we have been terribly slow in Palestine. Bevin has no credit out of this. (My chances of resigning are always being snatched from me – first Armed Forces; now this!)[1]

At the Defence Committee on 18th September, Alexander, the Minister of Defence, proposed a cut in the total strength of the armed forces from 1,007,000 to 937,000, with a view to bringing the total down to 713,000 by 31st March 1949. He also proposed a military expenditure of £711 million for the coming financial year. Dalton said that this was too much, and it was agreed that 'further studies should be made' to see whether the rate of run-

1 At the Defence Committee on 18th September, Dalton had made some progress in persuading colleagues that projected spending on the armed forces was excessive (Diary, 18th September 1947).

down might not be increased. 'The Chiefs of Staff have not been co-operating together, in spite of successive directives from Alexander', Dalton recorded. 'I hear that Monty won't work with the other two. The Navy have been leaking to the press about the proposed cuts on them. The *Sunday Times* had a terrible tale of woe, with highly accurate details, which can only have come from one of the Sea Lords.'[1]

Thursday 2nd October

I am having a final, rather broken, week of 'rest' at West Leaze. I went up on Monday – after a pleasant, but not superlatively good, Forestry weekend with Robinson[2] in the Dean (staying at Symonds Yat), but I prefer *new* forests to *old*, and beech and conifers to oak – for a Defence Committee. Alexander has been pushing the Chiefs of Staff hard, and has got them to move a bit, but Monty[3] won't co-operate with the rest. We accept total figures – for uniformed man-power – of 937,000 for March 1948, and 713,000 for March 1949. I said it was disappointing that we couldn't get down to this last figure quicker, and I restated my position on money, and asked for further enquiries into static Forces and Civilians.

These conclusions were accepted at a Cabinet today – I went up from West Leaze in the morning and came down in the evening. Bevin inclined to growl, but didn't resist. I always seem to get just enough – here as [on] Palestine – to make it very difficult for me to threaten to resign! When *alone* now I always want to resign. But the company of my officials, and even of my colleagues, saps my will!

Sunday 12th October

It is finished – the Reconstruction of the Government. It was an-nounced on Wednesday, the 8th. I saw a final version of the list on Tuesday afternoon. I had a final word with the P.M. on Monday afternoon. He hadn't been able to fit Willie Hall with the Ministry of Pensions, as I had proposed. So he wanted to leave him as Financial

---

1 Diary, 18th September 1947.
2 Sir Roy Robinson, 1st Baron (1883–1952). Chairman of the Forestry Commission 1932–52; Director-General 1945–7.
3 Field-Marshal B. L. Montgomery, 1st Viscount (1887–1976). Chief of Imperial General Staff 1946–8. Commander, Eighth Army 1942–4. Commander-in-Chief, British Group of Armies and Allied Armies in northern France 1944. Commander, 21st Army Group 1944–5. Commander, British Army on the Rhine 1945–6. Chairman of Western Europe Commanders-in-Chief Committee 1948–51.

Secretary to the Treasury for the present. Hugh Gaitskell, whom I had asked for as F.S.T. if Hall was promoted, or if he himself didn't – as I had recommended to Attlee – get a No. 1 office, *was* going to Fuel and Power. Douglas Jay, my next choice for F.S.T., might, Attlee suggested, become my P.P.S. I said I agreed with this. He had finally moved Shinwell out of Fuel and Power and out of the

11 9th October 1947

Cabinet – this, I had insisted repeatedly, supported by Cripps and Will Whiteley, who was much in things at the end, was essential. Having refused the War Office with much temper and many blackmailing threats, he had finally accepted it *outside the Cabinet*. He didn't, I think, want to lose the ministerial salary. Towards the end of the Coalition, he had told someone who had repeated it to me, that he realised he had been a fool not to take office when Winston offered it him, even as No. 2 to Woolton,[1] in May 1940, and that he wanted

1 Sir Frederick Woolton, 1st Baron, later 1st Earl (1883–1964). Chairman of the Conservative and Unionist Central Office 1946–55. Minister of Food 1940–43; Reconstruction 1943–5. Lord President of the Council 1945, 1951–2; Chancellor of the Duchy of Lancaster 1952–5; Minister of Materials 1953–4.

a salary to save out of. But, having accepted, he came back twice in high indignation to Attlee – once to protest against Michael Stewart[1] as his No. 2 at the War Office and demanding Wigg[2] instead; and once to protest that, though he was out of it, the Cabinet was still so large, only reduced by one. He had understood a number of others were to be excluded too. In the *Daily Mirror*, I think of Thursday, was a furious attack, obviously his mouth speaking, on me. I had been wrong on the American Loan, wrong on convertibility, and *I* had been responsible for last winter's fuel crisis, because I had been Chairman of a Cabinet Coal Committee which never met. (I recall how he resented its meetings, and how I helped him with transport and with priorities of his mining equipment, so much so that on the latter, Cripps appealed successfully to the Cabinet against one of my decisions in the interests of exports to Finland.) So, though Shinwell had been sacrificed, the *Mirror* went on, I remained in office, in spite of all these 'massive mistakes'. It might suit people like me, finished the *Mirror*, not to have Shinwell any longer in the Cabinet – I forget just what frightful future was in store for the reconstructed Government. Francis Williams says Sydney Elliott[3] was probably responsible for this.

For the rest – in addition to Greenwood – Inman, Westwood,[4] Bellenger, John Wilmot, Hynd[5] and half a dozen elderly Under-Secretaries and Ivor Thomas drop out. Wilmot rang me up on Tuesday morning, and said, 'I'm out.'[6] I got him to come round. He had just seen Attlee with Whiteley as a witness. Attlee had looked very un-

---

1 R. M. M. Stewart, later Baron (b. 1906). Junior whip 1946–7. Parliamentary Under-Secretary of State for War 1947–51. Labour M.P. for Fulham East 1945–55; Fulham 1955–79. Secretary of State for Education and Science 1964–5; Foreign Affairs 1965–6; Economic Affairs 1966–7; Foreign and Commonwealth Affairs 1968–70.

2 G. E. C. Wigg, later Baron (1900–83). Labour M.P. for Dudley 1945–67. Paymaster-General 1964–7. Chairman of the Horse-race Betting Levy Board 1967–72.

3 S. R. Elliott (b. 1902). Political Adviser to the *Daily Mirror*. Managing Editor of *Reynolds' News* 1929–43. Editor of the *Evening Standard* 1943–5. General Manager of the *Daily Herald* 1952–7.

4 Joseph Westwood (1884–1948). Secretary of State for Scotland 1945–7. Labour M.P. for Stirling and Falkirk Burghs 1935–48; Midlothian and Peebleshire 1922–31. Junior minister 1931, 1940–45.

5 J. B. Hynd (1902–71). Chancellor of the Duchy of Lancaster and Minister for Germany and Austria 1945–7. Minister of Pensions April to October 1947. Labour M.P. for Sheffield Attercliffe 1944–70.

6 John Wilmot, q.v., was Minister of Supply 1945–7, and responsible for planning the future of the steel industry. His dismissal followed conflict and confusion in the Government over nationalisation plans.

comfortable, and had said that he must make a change at the Ministry of Supply, and that he was afraid he had nothing else to offer Wilmot 'at present'. Wilmot said he was very surprised. Attlee asked if he would like a peerage. Wilmot said 'No' and that was all!

This is the change which grieves – and angers – me. To move Wilmot from Supply was one thing; to put him out of the Government was another. I spoke to Attlee afterwards about it. He said that at the end, there had been the Air Ministry. It had lain between Wilmot and Arthur Henderson – and he thought the latter had done better than Wilmot. It is clear that Cripps had asked for Wilmot to go, and – this making it all the more bitter – for Strauss to succeed him. It had been plugged with Attlee that Wilmot was lazy, didn't concentrate, didn't follow things through, also that he was unpopular with the Party in the House. I think Wilmot should find his future now in some Public Board field. He has been long with and long close to me. Though I can help all my P.P.S.s into office, I can't ensure they stay there.

Meanwhile George Brown is at Agriculture. I told him that if he concentrated on it, and had luck, he might well be Minister of Agriculture in the future. Tom Williams wouldn't last for ever, and we had no one else both young and knowledgeable on this subject. Of new appointments six are trade unionists – Brown, Robens,[1] Jones, Callaghan,[2] Robertson[3] and Hobson[4] – and four not – Gordon Walker,[5] Younger, Rees-Williams[6] and King.[7] Phil [Noel-Baker]

1 Alfred Robens, later Baron (b. 1910). Parliamentary Secretary at the Ministry of Fuel and Power 1947–51. Labour M.P. for Wansbeck 1945–50; Blyth 1950–60. Minister of Labour and National Service 1951. Chairman of the National Coal Board 1961–71.

2 James Callaghan (b. 1912). Parliamentary Secretary at the Ministry of Transport 1947–50. Labour M.P. for South Cardiff. See Appendix.

3 J. J. Robertson (1898–1955). Joint Parliamentary Under-Secretary at the Scottish Office 1947–50. Labour M.P. for Berwick and Haddington 1945–50; Berwick and East Lothian 1950–51.

4 C. R. Hobson, later Baron (1904–66). Assistant Postmaster-General 1947–51. Labour M.P. for Wembley North 1945–50; Keighley 1950–59.

5 P. C. Gordon Walker, later Baron Gordon-Walker (1907–80). Parliamentary Under-Secretary at the Commonwealth Relations Office 1947–50. Labour M.P. for Smethwick 1945–64; Leyton 1966–February 1974. Secretary of State for Commonwealth Relations 1950–51. Foreign Secretary 1964–5. Minister without Portfolio 1966–7; Secretary of State for Education and Science 1967–8.

6 D. R. Rees-Williams, later 1st Baron Ogmore (1903–76). Parliamentary Under-Secretary for Colonies 1947–50; Commonwealth Relations 1950–51. Labour M.P. for Croydon South 1945–50. Minister of Civil Aviation 1951.

7 E. M. King (b. 1907). Parliamentary Secretary at the Ministry of Town and Country Planning 1947–50. Labour M.P. for Penryn and Falmouth 1945–50. Conservative M.P. for Dorset South 1964–79.

goes, very huffily, from Air to Commonwealth, and Woodburn to Scottish Office. John Freeman goes to Supply, so just escaping Shinwell and, as he wished, at last getting away from men in uniform, after more than eight long years.

It is a much better Government and a good deal younger in the tail, as it should be. It's a bet which of these younger men do well, and which don't.

Morrison has taken the change very well. Our Inner Cabinet is now called the Economic Committee, the old five plus Addison.

I am to have an Autumn Budget, now well advanced in its planning. Cripps and I have had some useful talks already.

I have made two speeches this week, my Annual at the Mansion House, and the Annual Meeting of the National Trust. So have I broken a long silence, on which comments were beginning to be made. And I can come out of purdah now, and move again among M.P.s and lunch at the House – now that the Government is reformed.

I am still a bit below my optimum. But I hope it will all come back! I hate selling gold. Our reserves are very thin for their task. And these sales work the wrong way on the gilt edged market. I am haunted by the thought of a people starving, unemployed and in revolt! And of the end of our Socialist experiment and of all our Dreams!

Saturday 18th October
Stayed in bed till 5 p.m. – making the most of the weekend! – but am visited by several Treasury pundits. Soon after 6 p.m. leave for Chequers by car for a special conference of the Big Five.

Sunday 19th October
Talk shop from 10 a.m. till lunch and with one short break, during which we walked up and down on the grass terrace outside, from lunch till tea, and after tea (very cold in the covered-in courtyard!) from tea till 6 p.m. when Bevin and, soon after, Cripps and his wife leave. I stayed to dine and go off with Morrison and his wife after. The wives were asked but neither Ruth who has Madame Halévy[1] staying with us, nor Mrs Bevin who is ill in bed, could come. ...

Though this trip to Chequers has been slightly uncomfortable and socially uninteresting, it has been quite good as a shop talk and I am afraid I must admit that it would do good to repeat it at reasonable intervals!

1 Madame Florence Halévy, née Noufflard. Widow of the French historian Elie Halévy. The Halévys had been friends of the Daltons since just after the First World War. Ruth often stayed with Florence Halévy in France.

Monday 20th October

A long Cabinet which, on the whole, goes well. We decide on the form of the Bill to amend the Parliament Act. This intention has been shamefully leaked to the press and Bevan has made a most tiresome speech at Hull proclaiming it as our intention. Attlee reports that there was no trouble at all at Buckingham Palace over this. He had said that he thought it was quite reasonable to make the further reduction in the powers of the Lords after thirty-six years, and the King had seemed to think that this was quite an ordinary and reasonable thing to do. Whether others will dissuade him later remains to be seen!

We get through the investment programme and also, after a long wrangle of Strachey against most of the rest of us, the guts of the import programme. Strachey has now been warned by Attlee following suggestions from Morrison and myself, that he is not entitled always to stay at all items of the Cabinet – as he had got into the habit of doing for some months – but only to come when food was involved. This is a bit of a setback for him. This morning he argued at great length and with much exaggeration against any reductions of dollar imports at all. In the end he irritated everyone, including Attlee, Bevin and Cripps, as well as myself. Several ministers, who do not talk much as a rule, weighed in most sensibly, including Chuter Ede who said that people were definitely expecting disagreeable news and that we had far better give it to them now than later, so that they might have some hope of later improvements.

At Cabinet this morning we put through the Dollar Import Programme – including food cuts, with only minor variations from what was agreed at Chequers.

Strachey was very obstinate and obstructive, and put everyone (except his ally, Aneurin Bevan) against him.

He is no longer a habitual attender.

Wednesday 22nd October

With Attlee met Lascelles[1] and Alexander at No. 10 to discuss the question of a new Civil List Bill and much more money for Princess Elizabeth and Prince Philip.[2] We – mostly I – explained the dangers

---

1 Sir Alan Lascelles (1887–1981). Private Secretary to King George VI and Queen Elizabeth II and Keeper of the Royal Archives 1943–53.
2 Princess Elizabeth (b. 1926) married Prince Philip (b. 1921) on 20th November 1947. Their engagement had been announced in July. She acceded to the throne in 1952.

and difficulties of action, and public discussion now. It would raise discord, and many awkward questions, and would impair the popularity of the Royal Family. Lascelles was very sensible, and saw it all, adding the American difficulty. Alexander stuck to his financial guns a bit more. Finally Attlee and I advised postponement of any new demand for the present – and a public statement to this effect. I said it might, perhaps, mean a moratorium, of say, two years; if we were out of the wood then, it would all look very different. Especially, said Lascelles, if there was a baby by then. Alexander admitted that he had a nest egg from surpluses on Civil List during war years – due to small amount of ceremonial and entertaining ... They both said that no one on the Household Staff had had any rise in salary since before the war. Alexander tried to get me to say that, apart from timing, I thought amounts proposed reasonable. I tried to evade this. I am to see the King[1] and explain on Monday. I mentioned Labour M.P.s' letter to Chief Whip, and added that nothing had yet come before the Cabinet. The talk went much better than I had expected.

Thursday 23rd October
Cabinet. Strachey now brings up, for the first time, a doleful tale about potatoes, and wants to reopen all the decisions of Monday. Bevan – obviously primed beforehand – repeatedly comes to his support. But in vain!

Cripps's speech is to be delivered this afternoon. He must make the announcements. (He does very well, though a bit too much peroration.)

Strachey says, most improperly and P.M. should have pulled him up, that Liesching[2] had explained to him how all the High Ups in Whitehall held that the workers would only work harder if you starved them a bit, and that it was on this theory that we were deciding food cuts. Bevin protested against this.

I said that if we didn't make these cuts now we should be starving slaves of the U.S. before long.

Earlier this morning a great demonstration of pundits, including Plowden, as well as my regulars pressed on me the need to reduce food subsidies to at most £300m. They were very earnest about it, and did, in fact, argue that, only by raising the price of food – while making clear that 'this must not be used as an argument in favour of higher

---

1 King George VI (1895–1952). Acceded to the throne in 1936.
2 Sir Percivale Liesching (1895–1973). Permanent Secretary at the Ministry of Food 1946–8. Second Secretary at the Board of Trade 1942–6. Permanent Under-Secretary at the Commonwealth Relations Office 1949–55.

wages' – could workers be made to realise the seriousness of this situation. Also this is essential to our credit, national and external. I listened to what they said interpolating doubts and questions here and there, and then, having to go to Cabinet, promised to tell my colleagues of their representations.

(At the weekend I made a short note on alternative cuts in expenditure.)

This evening I put the finishing touches to my speech for tomorrow on dollars, and where they went!

Friday 24th October

Deliver the speech – with masses of figures and a little chit-chat. It was a crashing bore to make. It took 67 minutes. I think it has cleared a good part of the field, though there will be a few consequentials. But now it's behind me! To West Leaze and the sun and the autumn tints!

This is the last entry before Dalton's resignation as Chancellor three weeks later.

7

The Politics of Austerity
1948–50

Dalton introduced his fourth Budget on 12th November 1947, in close consultation with the new Minister of Economic Affairs, Sir Stafford Cripps. The Chancellor was being forced to do what he said he would not do – namely, introduce deflationary measures that seriously curtailed the Government's programme. In retrospect, Dalton's final Budget can be seen as an important economic landmark, the first peacetime recognition of the principles of Keynesian economic management. Yet at the time, the need to have an autumn Budget at all seemed a humiliation and a defeat, giving satisfaction to the Cassandras whose prophecies Dalton had laughed off for so long.

The sense of political retreat was, however, soon overshadowed by a personal catastrophe, caused by a moment's inattention. As Dalton entered the Chamber of the House of Commons to give his Budget speech, he was intercepted by the lobby correspondent of the *Star*, a London evening newspaper. In the brief conversation that followed, the Chancellor revealed the main items in the statement that he was about to make to M.P.s. The reporter immediately telephoned his paper. Copies of the *Star*, with the incriminating details in the stop press section, were on sale minutes before Dalton had reached the relevant passage in his speech. The Chancellor was told what had happened at lunch-time next day. He immediately offered his resignation and the Prime Minister, after some hesitation, accepted it. Cripps was appointed his successor.

In reality, Dalton's indiscretion was merely a technical error. The journalist was a respected member of the lobby, and might have been expected to avoid embarrassing his source; it was reasonable to think that there was not enough time for any details to be printed before they were made public in the House; and no Stock Exchange movements occurred as a result. Today, with Chancellors habitually flying Budget kites weeks or even months in advance, such a minor slip would probably be overlooked. In 1947 the code was stricter. More important, Dalton's position had become dangerously vulnerable – weakened by the convertibility crisis, by sustained attacks in the financial press, and by his own involvement in plots to remove the Prime Minister from office.

For the same reasons, Dalton's departure was less mourned than it might have been at other times. While Cripps set about implementing what had become his predecessor's economic strategy, gaining the admiration of officials and press alike, calumny was heaped on the shoulders of the unlucky ex-Chancellor, who became the scapegoat for all the Government's misfortunes. 'Well I had had it, my personal high tide,' Dalton wrote later, 'all the rest, I thought, would now be anti-climax; cross-currents in the shallows.'[1] Dalton was sixty, not old by ministerial standards. But after this setback, personal ambition seemed to ebb away, and he never returned to the inner circle of the Government.

For a time after his resignation, Dalton felt only intense relief and looked forward to a period of rest and recuperation. He returned to part-time journalism, writing for the *New Statesman* and the *Daily Herald*. In Parliament he adopted the role of 'candid friend' of the Government, scrupulously supporting the new Chancellor in his speeches. yet allowing himself to become a rallying point for those who, in the words of the *Daily Telegraph*, 'complain that the realities have rendered the Socialism of Sir Stafford Cripps and others less Socialist than it was'.[2] At Party Conference in May, Dalton demonstrated his popularity with the rank and file – and strengthened his political position – by coming second, after Aneurin Bevan, in the poll for the constituency parties' section of the N.E.C.

At the beginning of June, Attlee made him Chancellor of the Duchy of Lancaster, a post that enabled him to take an active part in Cabinet Committees yet kept him free for other special assignments should these arise. In November 1948 he was asked to lead the British delegation to the Committee of Western Union Powers, charged with examining possible ways of increasing European unity.

The impact of the Budget Leak on Dalton's reputation had just begun to fade when it was compounded by another, nastier, scandal arising out of the Lynskey Tribunal inquiry into political corruption. In the course of the Lynskey hearings at the end of 1948, it was suggested that the ex-Chancellor had sought a lucrative part-time directorship through the mediacy of a businessman and 'political broker' whose affairs were under investigation. Dalton hotly denied the accusation, and indeed no impropriety was alleged. Yet the smear, and other rumours and allegations arising from it, preoccupied

1 HTA, p. 287.
2 9th April 1948.

Dalton for several months and the surrounding publicity did not aid his rehabilitation.

Nevertheless, as deputy leader and leader of British delegations to the new Council of Europe in 1949 and 1950, Dalton returned to a major role in foreign policy for the first time since 1931, helping to shape the pattern of post-war European institutions. In doing so, the Chancellor of the Duchy was on the side of caution rather than of rapid advance. Generally, Dalton expressed the views of the Foreign Secretary and Cabinet, showing a willingness to help create and then support the Council of Europe, but concerned also to limit its powers. On one issue, however, Dalton began to diverge from some of his more liberal-minded colleagues. A major purpose of the Council was to strengthen the Western democracies against what many believed was a Soviet ambition to dominate the whole continent. Dalton sympathised with this aim but was unhappy about one aspect of it – the proposal to involve West Germany in the new European political arrangements. Over the next few years, Dalton's opposition to moves designed to integrate Germany politically and militarily with the rest of Western Europe became his strongest political passion. In the short run, this helped to make him a particularly keen advocate of the Labour Government's so-called 'functional' approach at the European Assembly, favouring co-operation and consultation, but firmly set against any federal solution. Like Bevin, he was a keen internationalist but a reluctant European.

Meanwhile, as a member of the Cabinet Economic Policy Committee, Dalton was closely involved in the discussions that preceded the devaluation of the pound in August 1949. Though publicly Dalton gave Cripps his full support, the irony of the 1949 dollar crisis – so similar to the crisis over convertibility two summers before – was not lost on him, and his diary reveals a wry satisfaction at the problems of his successor. When the Chancellor asked colleagues to agree to a programme of public expenditure cuts, Dalton helped to lead a successful ministerial campaign against what he regarded as a Treasury and Bank of England ramp, while at the same time deploring apparent tendencies to give in to pressure from private interests in the City and elsewhere.

In late July. after the Chancellor had departed for Zurich to receive health treatment leaving Treasury policy in the hands of Hugh Gaitskell, Harold Wilson and Douglas Jay (the 'young economists'), Dalton was persuaded that an adjustment in the exchange rate was unavoidable. This was also now the view of leading Treasury officials. Dalton, however, favoured devaluation largely as a technical measure. He did not share the view of Treasury advisers that it should be accompanied by a further round of cuts and austerity measures. After devaluation had finally been accomplished, this issue – whether, or how far, cuts should be made to take account of the change in the value of the pound – dominated discussions in Cabinet, and led to the postponement of the general election until the beginning of 1950.

1948

In January 1948 I began making speeches again, and made well dispersed visits all over the country.

In these speeches I could, after a number of years in bondage to Cabinet decisions and the departmental sensitivities of colleagues, speak freely.

I did so, keeping well within the boundaries of the 'Party line', but looking forward to the Second Five Years.

My speeches were attacked by the Tories as Left Wing, and even frightened and disconcerted some members of the Cabinet. But my audiences, and the Party generally, liked them.

An ingredient of the new Cabinet policy was an attempt to control wages. *A Statement on Personal Incomes, Costs and Prices*, a government document issued in February, tried to limit wage increases while freezing rents and profits. This approach was endorsed by the T.U.C. in March, but there was strong opposition within many unions.

Wednesday 11th February

We have had published in the last week two White Papers, the first on 'a Statement on Personal Incomes, Costs and Prices', the second, out this morning, on 'the U.K. Balance of Payments, 1946 and 1947'. Tomorrow there is to be a debate on the former. Cripps and Attlee are to speak. The facts are very grim, the argument very strong, the tactics, perhaps not good. There has been some commotion in T.U. circles, and among our M.P.s. They think Cripps is aloof; they fear what he may be up to; with whom is he in touch? (not with them, they complain); will he 'do another '31'?; what about profits?

Bevin, with whom I had a few words at lunch today, said he'd been asked to meet the T.U.C. tonight with Attlee, Cripps, etc., and was going. He was very doubtful of the wisdom of making such pronouncements. He thinks they only irritated people, and made wage-claims and unofficial strikes more likely.

Thursday 12th February

Today's debate went very flatly. No 'revolt'! Cripps seemed curiously unemphatic in making his strong case. Anyhow he got an anti-profiteering opening out of it. Ruth and I lunched at No. 10. Nothing important was said, but the news was around the House like a bit of hot gossip!

The Communist coup in Prague in February 1948 was a serious shock to the West, evoking memories of Anglo–French capitulation over Czechoslovakia ten years earlier. For Dalton, there was the added blow of the suspicious death of Jan Masaryk, an old friend from anti-appeasement days.

Sunday 29th February
We are at West Leaze. We had lunch out! And worked in the garden, repairing barriers against invading cattle and rabbits ...

Ruth and I have been much shocked by Czech news. This was an unprovoked aggression by the Communists, under Moscow orders. Forty-eight hours ago I thought I saw WW III starting in six months or less. We should have to drag ourselves back in, behind the U.S.A. The country would be practically unanimous. We should have to line up with all the worst reactionaries, and the Catholic Church! Ugh!

Today, though this hideous vision hasn't vanished, it has receded. I think there is more likely to be a pause. It is difficult to think of the Russians preparing themselves to fight beyond their frontiers against forces of any strength. But they have Communist Auxiliaries organised, and especially in Italy – and in France – there may be early trouble. But this need not mean WW III. Meanwhile Marshall Aid should come quicker!

Sunday 4th April
I am alone here; Ruth went back on Friday (2nd) for the Annual Conference of the London Labour Party. But we had just over a week together here. The Easter sunshine was wonderful, and the peace I find here – and I hope and think she still does – is very deep. The buds of our white-leaved trees are breaking. The first flowers are out on one of the cherries. The rosemary has been covered with its little flowers, and spreads its scent. There are daffodils everywhere in the grass. The judas tree is beginning to break. The lawn, rather devastated by moles this year – though they seem to have gone and I have tried to repair the damage – is mown. I have been clearing the grass from around the flowering trees at the bottom right-hand corner, and from a few others, and erecting barricades – some of chalk and some of sods to make heaps, and some of loose earth to reinforce the cleared space round the trees.

427

I am feeling very well (and my bowels are a sign of this health – in my last months as Chancellor I was, for the first time in my life, constantly constipated!) and, I try to write this quite honestly, *I don't want to go back into the Government yet*. I feel almost cowardly in saying this. But the sudden relief from responsibility was immense, and it is continuing. ...

I am thinking forward now to the next election programme. I should like to write a Personal Contribution, like P.S.B. [*Practical Socialism for Britain*] only much shorter, and with a bit more freedom from Conference and Executive decisions. This is the most useful and constructive thing I can do outside this Government. And I must spend time this summer in my constituency – to be much enlarged and politically worsened, but beautified under Redistribution. It has been left very fallow, deliberately, but now we must begin to tackle both organisation and propaganda. I propose at Whitsun to descend on Middleton in Teesdale, with a party of M.P.s, to a meeting, and then hike for a few days along the Pennine Way northwestwards[1] – this in my capacity as President of the Ramblers' Association; then a few days in the constituency before Parliament reassembles, and then at least a continuous fortnight in the summer vacation.

Tomorrow Cripps will explain his first Budget to the Cabinet and the King. I shan't be there. I suppose I should feel sad and jealous, but I really don't. I expect to approve of his Budget, and have it in mind to speak next day ...

Ruth, I know, is much keener for me to get back into the Government than I am. If it doesn't happen by August, she will be very disappointed. Therefore, I hope it *will* happen by August, but I doubt if, in fact, it will, unless someone near the top cracks. For there is no hole at present!

Tuesday 13th April
After a meeting in P.M.'s room at the House this afternoon of Chairmen of N.E. and its sub-committees to consider what to do about Platts-Mills[2] and other fellow travellers, Attlee asked me to stay and

---

1 See p. 449 below.
2 J. F. F. Platts-Mills (b. 1906). Labour, then Independent Labour, M.P. for Finsbury 1945–50. Platts-Mills was the first of four left-wing M.P.s to be expelled from the Labour Party for rebellious acts and statements. Platts-Mills's expulsion (recommended at the meeting mentioned here) followed the celebrated 'Nenni telegram' affair a few days earlier. Thirty-seven Labour M.P.s had sent a telegram wishing electoral success to Signor Nenni, Left Socialist candidate in alliance with Italian Communists. Signatories of this telegram were reprimanded by the N.E.C. Most retracted, or gave pledges of future good behaviour.

talk. He then raised the question of my return to the Government. He would like it to happen soon, but the question was how. Would I be willing to take a Department which was now outside the Cabinet, if I were myself in the Cabinet and at the heart of things? I asked what Department he had in mind. He said Civil Aviation. I said I wasn't much attracted by this. I would prefer to come back as a non-departmental minister. We then discussed Chancellor of the Duchy. I said I thought I would like this, if I had enough to do. I didn't, of course, want Germany. He said he wanted me to be not only in the Cabinet, but on the Economic Policy Committee and the Defence Committee. I raised the question of status in the Hierarchy. He said, 'You would go back to your old place.' I interpret this to mean after Morrison, Bevin and Cripps. He said he wanted to make use of my 'experience and advice as an elder statesman'! I said I wasn't pressing to return, but would be very happy to do so when all the conditions were right. I mentioned Commonwealth Relations as a Department which attracted me, not so much the Indians as the White Dominions. But it looked as though a non-departmental re-entry would be best. (Ruth said it was just five months to the day since 13th November.)[1]

Thursday 15th April
I thought I should see the P.M. again before the weekend and after lunch at the House, went to his room, where I found only Arthur Moyle[2] and Tom Brown,[3] the latter gossiping. I asked Moyle whether the P.M. would be free any time tonight or tomorrow. He rang through to No. 10 and the answer was 'come now'. So I went in, as of old, just after 3. I saw Attlee alone in the Cabinet Room. All plans seemed cut and dried. I confirmed my first response. I didn't want to be Minister of Civil Aviation. It was a troublesome Department and I knew nothing about aircraft and it would seem very artificial to promote the Minister of Civil Aviation to a post among senior ministers. One of our younger up-and-coming chaps should clean this stable, I thought. I would prefer to come back as a non-departmental minister – Chancellor of the Duchy, if that was the easiest. But I repeated that I must rank high and suggested next after him, Morrison, Bevin and Cripps. I had always championed the status of the Treasury, I recalled, and wouldn't ask to rank above Cripps. He accepted all this, and said he thought it should be about Whitsun. 'Before or after the Party Con-

---

1 The date of Dalton's resignation.
2 Arthur Moyle, later Baron (1894–1974). P.P.S. to Attlee 1946–55. Labour M.P. for Stourbridge 1945–50; Oldbury and Halesowen 1950–64.
3 T. J. Brown (1886–1970). Labour M.P. for Ince-in-Makerfield 1942–64.

ference?' I asked, and suggested that there was a tactical point here. I should, I thought, have a sympathetic ovation at the Conference and there might even be demands from the floor for my re-entry into the Government. Attlee thought this pointed to doing it just before the Conference. 'Otherwise it might look like yielding to clamour.' And so we left it. I said I would like to go to Paris the weekend after next, which as a minister, I couldn't do. I said I would only want a small staff, a personal assistant whom Bridges must find for me, to boil down papers and deal, at the proper level, with other Departments, a private secretary and a typist. I might also take on Roy Jenkins[1] as P.P.S. He liked this. Jenkins has written his life, which is out next week.[2] I said I would be glad not to have to be always answering P.Q.s and guiding Bills through Parliament, but I could, I thought, usefully intervene occasionally. He said, yes, especially in support of junior ministers. There were no non-departmental ministers available for this in the House now except Morrison. (I don't think he forgets that I can carry the back-benchers better than most.)

We spoke of Ernie's health and Herbert's, and his and mine. Clearly neither Ernie nor Herbert is set up for a firm long run. I might have to succeed either at short notice.

I went on to see Stanley[3] at 4 Aldford House, Paul Lane. He is seeing Morgan Phillips[4] tonight. He subscribes to the Labour Party through various channels, for the T.U. anti-Communist Committee, for Maurice Webb Fund, etc. He sent eleven cars to Gravesend on Polling Day and six to Croydon. He wants me to join the Board of G.U.S. [Great Universal Stores]. They would pay me a large 'fee' (he suggests £6,000 a year to begin with) and expect very little of my time, knowing how busy I am. One or two meetings a month. If I went back into the Government – and he is sure I shall in about four months in succession to Bevin, who would like to leave the Foreign Office and

1 Roy Jenkins (b. 1920). Newly elected Labour M.P. for Southwark Central. See Appendix.
2 *Mr. Attlee: An Interim Biography*, Heinemann, London, 1948.
3 'Sydney Stanley' was one of the aliases of Solomon Kohsynzcky, a Polish-born businessman who became the central figure in public hearings on political corruption at the Lynskey Tribunal a few months later. Stanley was to claim friendship with well-known political figures, including Dalton and Bevin, and to suggest that Dalton had asked for a directorship of Great Universal Stores. Unknown to Dalton when they met, Stanley had a shady past. He had been declared bankrupt in 1927, and a Deportation Order had been served on him in 1933.
4 M. W. Phillips (1902–63). Secretary of the Labour Party 1944–59; General Secretary 1959–62. Secretary of the Research Department 1941–4.

become Lord President of the Council – I should, of course, leave the Board, but come back if I left office again.

He presses me to lunch with Isaac Wolfson[1] tomorrow. I am engaged, so he presses that I should come and see him at noon. I agree. It is all most amusingly timed! He talks a lot about dollars, making a British shop-window in New York, raising a large credit in N.Y., etc. He suggests that I might like to make foreign trips of importance on behalf of the firm. I find it difficult to evaluate this little man, but it is clearly an approach not to be too rudely repelled.

Friday 16th April

With Stanley to see Wolfson at Jay's in Regent Street, where their head office is. Wolfson tells me the story of their growth – G.U.S. absorbing Jay's and Drage's and launching forth into manufacturing as well as hire purchase trading, with an army of visiting agents. They are manufacturing furniture at West Churton, in the old Ministry of Supply building, which I had put there, next door to De La Rue. And they own Polikoff in the Rhondda. And do I know Sir Philip Warter[2] with whom they dealt at the Board of Trade?

No definite proposal is made to me, but a hint is made. Wolfson would so like me to dine with him; he is in Manchester next week. Stanley is clearly to discuss details tentatively. Stanley says when we are alone (on two previous occasions) that he is paying Arthur Greenwood's hotel bill at Brighton unknown to the latter, and is arranging to put him on one of his Boards. (It will be a test of his influence whether he does.) He says he hears that Greenwood 'hasn't a penny to pay the rent' of his flat at Dolphin Court. He has had a very expensive illness. He was, he thinks, very badly treated by Attlee.

He talks as though he knew well and saw often, both Bevin and Shinwell, as well as George Gibson[3] and a number of other public characters. It is all very odd, if true.

1 Isaac Wolfson, later 1st Bart (b. 1897). Chairman and Managing Director of Great Universal Stores since 1934. Financier and industrialist. Later set up the Isaac Wolfson Foundation for the promotion of health, educational and youth facilities.
2 Sir Philip Warter (1903–71). Controller-General of Factory and Storage Premises at the Board of Trade (under Dalton) 1942–5. Chairman of the Associated British Picture Corporation Ltd 1947–71
3 George Gibson (1885–1953). A Director of the Bank of England 1946–8. General Council of the T.U.C. 1938–48; Chairman 1940–41. General Secretary of the Mental Hospital and Institutional Workers' Union 1913–43. Gibson's name was to be mentioned at the Lynskey hearings.

I think Attlee and Morrison will have agreed that it would be safer to have me back inside. Otherwise my popularity in the country may keep on growing, and I may say some awkward things.

Thursday 6th to Wednesday 12th May

In Fitzroy House Nursing Home, on Urwick's and Jenner Hoskin's[1] advice for treatment to get rid of my Dog's Heart – irregular beat which set in – though I haven't been conscious of it, unless greater weariness is a sign of it – probably in that bad year 1947 or early in 1948. The place is quite comfortable and I have a room at 16 guineas a week, including board and normal nursing, looking out on tall plane trees in Fitzroy Square. The treatment consists simply of lying in bed and being dosed with quinidine. I react, apparently, quickly and after four days Hoskin, who calls with his cardiographic instrument, says I am regular again.

Thursday 13th May

I am off tomorrow to Scarborough for Annual Conference. P.M. wrote on 6th to say that the change in the Government, which he had mentioned to me, could not now come before Whitsun as he had hoped, but would come within the first fortnight after our return. (Whiteley[2] says this is because Nathan is pressing for an Honour on leaving Ministry of Civil Aviation to show he is not being dismissed! This means Birthday Honours. Attlee is always slow in making these changes.)

I don't at all mind waiting another few weeks. I am still dangerously popular. (I think I shall head the Poll at the Conference.) Lately I have been speaking, in general terms, of the next election programme, and inviting everyone to discuss. Morrison doesn't much like this, and said to me, 'You're always dangerous just before an Annual Conference.' I said, 'Read my article in today's *Daily Herald*. You and Willy Whiteley are the only two people I praise.' There is a *mot d'ordre* 'consolidation' going the rounds for the next Parliament. Windle said it. So did Morrison. Even Ruth is a bit disinclined to do any more Socialism! Of course, we must have a consolidation, but we must also have a programme. Ruth says, 'If you're back in the Government, you won't have time to talk about the programme.' Maybe some others think that too. Meanwhile, I am much attacked by the Tories.

---

1 T. J. H. Hoskin (1888–1954). Physician and cardiologist at the Royal Free Hospital.
2 William Whiteley, q.v., was Chief Whip from 1942–51.

Reading Beatrice Webb's diary. Quite fascinating, though this volume only goes to 1911.[1]

Friday 14th to Friday 21st May
Travel north on Friday 14th May 1948. Conference opens on Monday 17th May and lasts till Friday 21st May. A very good, solid Conference. 'The Party is getting more and more mature,' said Sam Berger, obviously impressed. There is a sense of closing the ranks in view of the coming election, and a sense of economic difficulties still to be surmounted. The platform was only defeated on a few minor issues. ...

I had a good vote for the N.E.C., running second to Nye (as last year), but both of us with increased votes. Shinwell polled disappointingly well. Michael Foot beat Phil [Noel-Baker] for last place, but the latter took it very placidly. Herbison[2] replaced Braddock[3] in the Women's Section, which will be an improvement. Sam Watson is to be next year's Vice-Chairman, and Chairman in election year. He was level on seniority with Bacon[4] and Openshaw.[5] The latter was also proposed, but Watson won hands down.

The sun shone all the week. I had diarrhoea for the first two days, but this cleared with the aid of a concoction from the chemist and caution in food and drink. I had Roy and Jennifer Jenkins[6] and Tony Crosland[7] at my table. It was a very enjoyable Conference and I was conscious of being very widely popular.

Wednesday 26th May
Arthur Moyle rings up just before lunch and says that 'the Governor

---

1 *Our Partnership (1892–1911)*, edited by Barbara Drake and Margaret Cole, Longman, Green & Co., London, 1948.
2 Margaret Herbison (b. 1907). Labour M.P. for North Lanark 1945–70. Junior minister 1950–51. Minister of Pensions and National Insurance 1964–6; Social Security 1966–7.
3 Elizabeth ('Bessie') Braddock (1889–1970). Labour M.P. for Liverpool Exchange 1945–70.
4 Alice Bacon, later Baroness (b. 1911). Labour M.P. for North-East Leeds 1945–55; South-East Leeds 1955–70. Chairman of the Labour Party 1950–51. Junior minister 1964–70.
5 Robert Openshaw (1891–1962). Official of the Amalgamated Engineering Union. President 1954–6. Served on the Labour Party N.E.C. 1941–8.
6 Jennifer Jenkins, née Morris, later Dame (b. 1921). Worked for Political and Economic Planning (P.E.P.) 1946–8. Chairman of the Consumers' Association 1965–76. Married to Roy Jenkins, q.v.
7 C. A. R. Crosland (1918–77). Fellow of Trinity College, Oxford and Lecturer in Economics 1947–50. Dalton first met him in 1946. See Appendix.

General would like to see you at 3 o'clock' at No. 10. I lunch at the House and Labour M.P.s are all very cordial about the walk, which seems to have had even greater publicity in press and B.B.C. than I had realised. The Tories in the Smoke Room looked sour and distant. Just lately there has been a steadily rising howl against me in the Tory press. All my recent speeches have been strongly objected to! And there are constant references to me in Tory speeches in the House on both likely and unlikely occasions. We must, of course, expect a rising tide of political passion and bitterness from now on till the next election, and I am regarded as a specially dangerous man, as well as a traitor to my class. Meanwhile, the Eton College Chronicle this week publishes a little article of mine, requested by the editor, on *Eton and Politics* – beautifully non-controversial.

At 3 I see Attlee and we spend an hour together. He is not quite so warm as last time, and this, I sense, is partly due to someone having told him that I have been criticising Stafford. He says that, with me back in the Government, 'this might make things difficult'. I say that it is completely untrue. As he will recall, when I was in the Government Cripps and I were steadily in agreement, often against others. He says he remembers this. I say that nothing has changed in my attitude since then, though I don't, of course, know the latest details of 'the gap',[1] etc. The enemy press, of course, have been persistently trying to make trouble between Cripps and me, but any statement that I have been criticising Cripps is quite untrue. Where does it come from? He says it has been reaching him both through Parliamentary and Party channels. I say it is a bloody lie and I should like to know who told him. But he won't be drawn further. (And it *is* a bloody lie. Cripps is worth most of the rest of them put together. I am inclined, on a hunch, to suspect Morrison or Bevin, neither of whom, perhaps, is keen to see me back in the Inner Circle.)

I revert to this again at the end. I say that if people told him I had been criticising Shinwell, that would be true. Attlee says he did well at Scarborough, and the generals like him at the War Office. I agree as to the first, but say that what angers me is the way he drops bricks all over other people's Departments. But there may be less of this now he is no longer Chairman of the N.E.C. I then praise Jim Griffiths and Sam Watson. As to Cripps, I remind Attlee that I was quite willing that he should take my place at Scarborough in the Profits debate and, when it was decided otherwise, I asked Cripps to give me some notes of what he would have said, he did so and I used some and was careful

1 i.e. the dollar gap.

in the rest of my speech to say nothing to cut across his line. (I am, indeed, the arch-co-operator among ministers.)

He said he wanted now to make the changes 'about the weekend'. He half asked me to take Civil Aviation, but I repeated that I wasn't attracted by that. ... So we discussed it on the basis that it *was* to be Chancellor of the Duchy. He said I should have a Council, mostly over seventy, but could always overrule them. I had to appoint magistrates, and clergy to livings, and owned land in forty counties, and was a good landlord.

I suggested that, when I returned to the Cabinet, I should sit opposite to him, beside Bevin, so that we could look across the table at him like two owls.

He thought the Government, as distinct from the Party, should be thinking of the next election programme, and I might take charge of some of this. I said I gladly would, if Morrison wasn't jealous. Morrison's idea of having no new socialistic measure in the next Parliament would never do. There should be a study of various possibles, in industry, trade and finance. He thought we should look into wholesale distribution. I agreed. There might be trouble with the Co-op, but less now that Barnes was a minister. I also mentioned heavy chemicals, cotton (spinning board and merchanting), land (selective further acquisition), discount houses, industrial assurance (life insurance generally). He wondered about Smithfield and Covent Garden. We both praised Harold Wilson, and the style of his statement yesterday on clothing coupons. He said he might also ask me to do some overseas trips. I said I should like to do this, if other ministers affected were agreeable. And so we parted, he still just a little defensive, I thought. Someone in the last week or two has been sowing a few tares among the wheat!

Tuesday 1st June

'The glorious first of June' says Mrs Green, wife of the Chief Messenger at the Ministry of Health – who looks after us so well. 'I hope you'll be Prime Minister soon ...... They can't keep a good man down.'

I return to the Government and the Cabinet today. It has been a bit awkward for the last few days with the thing impending – unless Attlee should have had second thoughts, following the campaign, evidence of which appeared in our last talk, to make a breach between me and Cripps – and with a semi-leak in Sunday's *Observer*. I have had to keep away from the House and the journalists! ...

The press are surprised; not unfriendly on the whole; some saying that Attlee has done it to get me inside and so make me less dangerous. They play up my speech at Scarborough and my popularity there.

435

The *Express* says I am to have some special role in Empire talks.

Frank Pakenham[1] is to take Civil Aviation. Nathan resigning for business reasons, rather elaborately! And this is the only other change at present.

Wednesday 2nd June

Visit Buckingham Palace and receive the seals – alone with the King and the Clerk to the Privy Council, after other P.C.s have left the presence. This is an old procedure. The King would wish to talk about rents or other estate matters. No Royal comment on my appointment. He only asks, 'You haven't been in London all the time, have you?', i.e. since last November.

The comrades, in the House and outside, are delighted. I am still formidably popular, and this has been encouraged by the Tory hate. I have an office, a large room in the Privy Council office overlooking the Horse Guards. I interview two possible P.S.s and select Mason,[2] Ministry of Labour, a Geordie who took B.Sc. (Econ.) from Durham University. Had an accident, throwing him from a bicycle, which limited him to Army Pay Corps in the war, and to about eight miles walking. A smiling and, I think, sufficiently efficient young man. (I think I have hooked George Preston[3] to be my P.A. Harold Wilson is very good about this.)

Sunday 11th July

At West Leaze after three weekends of speech making – Yorkshire miners at Doncaster, Ramblers' Rally, between 2000 and 3000 at Cave Dale in the Peak District, and a run round Mansfield, Lincoln and Chesterfield. (Following visit to Duchy farms and forests.) During this last week I have had a boil in the ear, my first since I left the Treasury, but my resistance is much better now.

Having been back in the Cabinet and its Committees for just over a month, I find my colleagues – as I may have noted before – in surprisingly good mental and physical condition – Bevin, most of all. But the Chairmanship is terribly slow. This [is the fault] of Attlee –

1 Francis Pakenham, 1st Baron, later 7th Earl of Longford (b. 1905). Minister of Civil Aviation 1948–51. Chancellor of the Duchy of Lancaster and Minister in Charge of the Administration of the British Zone in Germany 1947–8. First Lord of the Admiralty 1951. Lord Privy Seal 1964–5, 1966–8. Colonial Secretary 1965–6.
2 W. H. Mason. Assistant Private Secretary, then Personal Assistant and Private Secretary, to Dalton at the Duchy of Lancaster 1948–50.
3 G. E. Preston (1910–59). Board of Trade official. Personal Assistant and Private Secretary to Dalton at the Duchy of Lancaster 1948–9. Principal Private Secretary to Dalton as President of the Board of Trade 1942–5.

worse in Cabinet Committees than in full Cabinet – and Morrison. Sitting for too many hours in Committees is still the great error of this Government. But I am impressed once more with the freshness following a break, with the efficiency of the Higher Civil Service, making crisp sense of ministerial wavering diffuseness, and preparing admirable papers making it as easy as possible for ministers to choose between clear alternatives.

Friday 6th August

Ruth and I have been at West Leaze for a week. A most peaceful August compared with last year, when our dollar crisis spilt over into Parliamentary debates after August Bank Holiday, when I was keeping going on Benzedrine, and then a recall for deconvertibility after I had just got down here. Parliament got up according to plan, this year at the end of July. Berlin, and the wider question of our relations with the Russians, hang heavy in the sky,[1] and there is always the cloud in the background about the Balance of Payments. But it is very difficult to believe that the Russians are ready to risk war now, though, since none of them have any direct knowledge of other countries, a sheer ignorant blunder can't be ruled out. (And what about ten years hence or less?) ...

I have read Winston's *Gathering Storm*[2] – I spent three solid days on it. It is a magnificent achievement. Nowhere can you say that he was wrong. ...

It was new to me that Winston had been struggling for months inside the War Cabinet for agreement to mine the Norwegian corridor, along which Swedish iron ore flowed from Narvik to Germany. He only got agreement when it was too late, the day before Hitler invaded Norway. I had been pressing for this, in the House and outside. This must have pleased him, and explains the terms of his invitation to me to be Minister of Economic Warfare. The only reference to me is p. 666, one of those 'whose services in high office were immediately required'. There is a fine finish. 'Facts are better than dreams.'

Sunday 22nd August

Last Tuesday, the 17th, I attended a small Cabinet. Morrison loved being Acting P.M. for three weeks![3] I took John Freeman out to

---

1 In July the Soviet Union had imposed a ban on all traffic from the West to Berlin, except by air. The Berlin blockade and the Western air-lift lasted 324 days, ending in May 1949.
2 The first volume of Churchill's war memoirs, published by Cassell, London, in 1948.
3 While Attlee was in Ireland, in late July and early August.

dinner. He is very attractive and intelligent. The first impression doesn't fade. He thinks the Tories don't expect to win the next election. (Gaitskell thought the same, a week before, or they wouldn't attack the Boards so much!) Freeman heard Hudson say that five years hence would be the time to begin fighting. 'Now it's hopeless,' he'd added. Forbes,[1] the two employers, and Barlow[2] – very doubtful propriety on the part of the latter – have sent in their resignations from the Steel Board, as from the introduction of the Bill in October. Freeman will have the rest of Ministry of Supply to run, while Strauss and Jones[3] are doing Steel. Only Sir G. Turner[4] and Mike Williams Thompson[5] of the officials are in favour. I am trying to get Williams Thompson a job in Gas. Freeman says Monty gave Bevan's fight with the B.M.A. as the way to win a battle to high British and American staff officers.

Saturday 11th September

See Cripps at my own request. I had had no tête-à-tête with him since my return to the Government more than three months ago, nor indeed since my resignation nearly ten months ago. I am not sure how far, if at all, he may have been influenced by the persistent propaganda distinguishing my policy from his, and suggesting that I am hostile to him personally, and working against him. I remember Attlee's mention to me of tales to the latter effect, when I was on the point of returning to the Government.

Our conversation today was friendly but, I felt, not exceptionally cordial. I said I thought he was doing a very fine job. He said he was doing his best, and that the latest figures were very good, except that coal output might be better. He complained bitterly of Harriman, who muddled all the channels to Washington and U.S. press. When Cripps saw the U.S. correspondents in London, they took and passed on the story of what we were doing – and it was a fine story – but their papers wouldn't print it. They took their line from Harriman. The

1 Sir Archibald Forbes (b. 1903). Chairman of the First Iron and Steel Board 1946–9; Iron and Steel Board 1953–9. President of the Federation of British Industries 1951–3. Chairman of the Midland and International Banks Ltd 1964–76.
2 Sir Alan Barlow, 2nd Bart (1881–1968). Joint Second Secretary at the Treasury 1938–48. Member of the Iron and Steel Board 1946–8. Principal Private Secretary to MacDonald as Prime Minister 1933–4.
3 J. H. Jones, q.v., Parliamentary Secretary at the Ministry of Supply 1947–50.
4 Sir George Turner (1896–1974). Second Secretary at the Ministry of Supply 1939–48. Permanent Under-Secretary at the War Office December 1948–56.
5 R. B. ('Mike') Williams Thompson (1915–67). Chief Information Officer at the Ministry of Supply 1946–9. Dalton first met him during the war, when he served on Lord Mountbatten's staff in the Far East. They became close friends.

latter was piqued because he had to deal with Hall-Patch,[1] instead of a Cabinet Minister. Cripps had said that, whenever Harriman wanted to see him, he could always come to Paris or see Harriman in London. It was only an hour by plane. But this wasn't good enough. Harriman was vain and said frightful things against us when he saw the press in Paris, or the French. Alphand[2] was a very bad influence on him, very anti-British ...

I broached P.M.'s health. He said he thought it wasn't at all good. Anyhow it would be a disaster if he led us in the next election. He didn't like the Parliamentary Party, and said they did not like him. Cripps said Morrison couldn't lead either the Cabinet or the Party, or the country. So there we left it! 'We shall just have to leave it to fate,' I said, but one day a general decision will have to be made. Cripps said he didn't know how he could explain to the Americans about nationalisation of iron and steel in Washington on his coming visit. I said I thought he should stress the monopoly point. He agreed. The choice was between private and public monopoly. He thought that many of the arrangements in the Cabinet were unsatisfactory. I said I was underworked, but was spending a good deal of time on Labour Party Committees and the next programme. He urged that we should 'take the lead' in U.S. Europe Movement.[3] Winston would be willing

1 Sir Edmund Hall-Patch (1896–1975). Chairman of the Executive Committee of the Organisation of European Economic Co-operation (O.E.E.C.) 1948–52. Deputy Under-Secretary at the Foreign Office 1946–8. British Executive Director of the I.M.F. and International Bank of Reconstruction and Development 1952–4.
2 Hervé Alphand (b. 1907). French Ambassador to O.E.E.C. 1948. Director of Economic Affairs for the French National Committee in London 1941–4. Ambassador to the U.S.A. 1956–65. Secretary-General of the French Foreign Ministry 1965–73.
3 'U.S. Europe Movement': Since January, Bevin had been exploring the possibility of American participation in a new organisation of Western European nations. The key issue was strategic: the British regarded progress towards closer unity in Western Europe as impossible without adequate assurances of American support for European defence. Meanwhile, moves towards Western European economic and military co-operation were accompanied by a political movement with an idealistic dimension. Partly inspired by the speeches of Churchill, a non-governmental 'International Committee of the Movements for European Unity' had been set up in December 1947, receiving cautious encouragement from Bevin and Attlee. When the Committee organised a Congress of Europe at The Hague in May 1948, the American State Department gave its blessing, declaring the United States to be in favour of 'the progressively closer integration of the free nations of Western Europe'. A combination of military necessity and political inspiration led to the setting up of the Council of Europe in May 1949, a month after the ending of negotiations which led to the establishment of the North Atlantic Treaty Organisation.

to withdraw, if others came forward. I said this was not easy, with Mackay[1] and Co. making themselves so busy.

I told him that I had heard last night – I did not say from Crossman – that juniors at U.S. Embassy were complaining of Hall-Patch. He said this was Harriman. In the war Harriman used to meet Churchill and Beaverbrook and Lyttelton[2] and drink all night with them. He resented not being made an equal fuss of now. Bevin was going to speak to Marshall about him next week, and try to shift him.

Wednesday 15th September
Make my first speech at the Box since last November, and my first since returning to the Government. Rather a boring occasion – winding up the general debate on the first stage of the King's speech discussion – with no vote and nothing much to answer, except departmental points I can't take.

Ruth left yesterday morning for France, and I am alone in the flat, and spending most of my time, for the moment, in the House of Commons. Bevin at lunch today was alarmist about Attlee. 'His mind's gone. It isn't eczema he's got, it's shingles.' Bevin's doctor had said to him some months ago, 'Has the P.M. got a good doctor? I've been watching him tonight. His nerves aren't right.' The King had said to Bevin yesterday, of Attlee, 'He sits opposite me, but I can't get him to talk.' This was bad because it would circulate in Court and into Tory circles. No hint, however, about succession.

We spoke of each other's periods of strain. I said I had been feeling it just over twelve months ago. He said, 'Yes, and didn't we all know it?' I said that a week after I had shed responsibility in November, I could both sleep and shit without pills, which I had had to take before, and had ceased to have boils. He said it was the same with him, when he could get away for a few days. It was wicked the way he was brought back from his holiday on the south coast after only four days in July. He hadn't had a real holiday this year. He was woken up last night every three hours by telegrams from Washington, and had to send quick replies, because the Americans were up then. His trouble was to stop the Americans doing something that would land us in war.

1 R. W. G. Mackay (1902–60). Labour M.P. for Hull North-West 1945–50; Reading North 1950–51. Former Organising Secretary of Common Wealth. Mackay was the only federalist in the Labour delegation to the Council of Europe at Strasburg in 1949.
2 Oliver Lyttelton, later 1st Viscount Chandos (1893–1972). Conservative M.P. for Aldershot 1940–54. President of the Board of Trade 1940–41, 1945. Minister of State Resident in the Middle East 1941–2; Minister of Production 1942–5. Colonial Secretary 1951–4.

Meanwhile queer things were happening in Russia. Stalin was ill again and down at Sochi on the Black Sea. He believed that Molotov had bumped off Zhdanov. The feeling against the Russians was growing in Germany and the 25-year sentences on the five Germans in Berlin yesterday would stoke this up. He had nearly pegged out at Moscow. '9th April was the day.' His detective had said afterwards, 'I thought you were due for a little box that day', and he had had a heart attack at the U.S. Embassy last March.

On 3rd September, Evan Durbin, Parliamentary Secretary at the Ministry of Works, drowned off the Cornish coast after saving the lives of one of his daughters and another child. 'He was one of the best young men in the Labour Party on whom I was eagerly counting for the future', Dalton wrote later. 'For years he had been one of the inner circle of my personal friends.'[1]

Thursday 16th September

Memorial Service for Evan in St Margaret's. He was a Christian, though knowing I was not, he never spoke to me of his beliefs. And so, for him, this would not have seemed a mockery.

I walked over from the House with Harold Wilson, who understands much. Vi Attlee,[2] in deep black, accompanied by John Dugdale,[3] sat on one side of us in the front pew, and Hugh and Dora[4] on the other. I wept a great deal, until the parson came in with the choirmen and began to speak in an uninteresting voice. This broke the spell for a time. The service, as usual, in the Church of England, was quite impersonal. But R. H. Tawney gave a beautiful and just and warm appreciation.

Marjorie[5] sat on the other side of the gangway, with another woman. She looked very small and frail, but wonderfully composed, with a far away look, as though a little bird, ethereal almost.

1 HTA, p. 307.
2 Violet Attlee, née Millar. Married to Clement Attlee.
3 John Dugdale (1905–63). Parliamentary and Financial Secretary at the Admiralty 1945–50. Labour M.P. for West Bromwich 1941–63. Minister of State at the Colonial Office 1950–51.
4 Dora Gaitskell (formerly Frost, née Creditor), later Baroness. Married to Hugh Gaitskell.
5 Marjorie Durbin, née Green (b. 1910). Widow of Evan Durbin.

Evan is the first casualty among the Young Victors of 1945. I shall miss him. He had a great gift for friendship, and he was a political scientist in a real sense. He loved West Leaze and we had a good many walks together. He was outstanding in his intellectual and moral qualities among the socialists of his generation. He had perfect intellectual integrity.

Friday 24th (evening) to Tuesday 28th September (morning) at Buscot Park
Very good informal conference. Crossman, Edelman, Crosland, Tom Cook,[1] Jack Bailey[2] (Co-op Party), Kingsley Martin, Acland,[3] George Brown (first day; he drove me down and was stopped by a rather truculent policeman for speeding for the second time in one day!), Callaghan, Davenport,[4] Mikardo[5] (one day), Young[6] and two secretaries. I had blackballed Balogh. He would have spoiled it all. I presided.

We discussed (1) restatement of Socialist doctrine, (2) administration of socialised sector, (3) extension of socialised sector, (4) Budget and the City, (5) central economic planning, (6) incentives – all with references to Second Five Years. Very good level, and very good social mixture. For me Jack Bailey was chief discovery. Very sensible, though idealistic, and an excellent mixer. For others Tony was chief

1 T. F. Cook (1908–52). Labour M.P. for Dundee East 1950–52; Dundee 1945–50. Junior minister 1950–51.
2 J. Bailey, later Sir John (1898–1969). National Secretary of the Co-operative Party 1942–62.
3 Sir Richard Acland, 15th Bart (b. 1906). Labour M.P. for Gravesend 1947–55. Liberal, then Common Wealth, M.P. for Barnstaple 1935–45. Supporter of the Popular Front movement and the Left Book Club in the 1930s; co-founder of Common Wealth in 1942.
4 Nicholas Davenport (1893–1979). Financial journalist. City Editor of the *New Statesman and Nation* 1930–53; Financial Correspondent of the *Spectator* 1953–79. Co-founder in 1932 of the XYZ Club, a semi-secret study group providing the Labour Party with inside information about the City. Member of the National Investment Council 1946–7. A personal friend of Dalton.
5 Ian Mikardo (b. 1908). Labour M.P. for Reading 1945–50, 1955–9; Reading South 1950–55; Poplar 1964–74; Tower Hamlets, Bethnal Green and Bow 1974–83; Bow and Poplar since 1983. Member of the N.E.C. 1950–59, 1960–78. Chairman of the Labour Party 1974.
6 Michael Young, later Baron (b. 1915). Secretary of the Labour Party Research Department 1945–51. Sociologist and writer. Director of Political and Economic Planning 1941–5; Institute of Community Studies since 1953. Chairman of the Consumers' Association 1956–65; Advisory Centre for Education 1959–76; Social Science Research Council 1965–8; National Consumer Council 1975–7.

discovery, and Bailey and Tom Cook, in particular, were delighted with his 'intellectual honesty' and 'courage', as well as with his ability and personal gifts.

Nicholas pleased them with his inner light on the City. We drove over to Hinton[1] after dinner on Sunday and had a number of drinks. Some of us walked vigorously on Saturday and Sunday afternoon. Notes of the discussions are to be circulated. I defended Fabianism – based on view that capitalism is inefficient and unjust, as against Christian Socialism and Marxism, and vigorously replied, in the light of 1931, to attacks. I said neither MacDonald nor Lansbury were fit to hold office in the present Government. This pleased Tony. Crossman has immense ability to argue any case. I think we should bring him into the Government on the Home Front.

Friday 15th October
Had an hour at Foreign Office with Bevin at his invitation. He thinks we may reach a balance with Russia, which will last a long time. We shan't reach any agreement, but we shall live together. He is trying 'to organise the middle of the planet' – W. Europe, the Mediterranean, the Middle East, the Commonwealth. He has told Liaquat[2] that Pakistan ought to take the lead in organising the Arab states.

If we only pushed on and developed Africa, we could have U.S. dependent on us, and eating out of our hand, in four or five years. Two great mountains of manganese are in Sierra Leone, etc. U.S. is very barren of essential minerals, and in Africa we have them all.

He told Marshall that W. Europe must have military Lend Lease, especially France, and it mustn't come out of Marshall Aid, or W. Europe would go Communist. Marshall has agreed to find equipment within a few months, for thirty French divisions. And the Republicans assent to this.

On 14th November, Princess Elizabeth gave birth to her first child, Prince Charles, later Prince of Wales.

---

1 Hinton Manor, near Oxford. The Davenports' country house.
2 Liaquat Ali Khan (1895–1951). Prime Minister of Pakistan from 1947 until his assassination in 1951. He had been Secretary of the All-India Muslim League, and represented Muslim India at the London Conference on the division of India in December 1946.

Sunday 14th November

Tonight at 9.15 an heir to the throne was born, a boy. The bells rang, and a man going down the street outside our flat called 'It's a boy' and the announcement was made on the air at 11 p.m. followed by the National Anthem. Queen Mary is a Great Grandmother. If this boy ever comes to the throne – and if we were defeated, or really badly knocked about in war, he wouldn't – it will be a very different country and Commonwealth he'll rule over. Our Cabinets are full, these days, of debates over Eire, determined to leave the Commonwealth, and India, whose leaders want to stay in, but on their own most awkward terms, so that the 'mystic' link of the Crown is being sadly strained, or broken.

Yesterday was the first anniversary of the Budget incident and my resignation. Ruth and I, who have been having a very happy weekend with no company or outside engagements, spoke of this. She thinks that, if it hadn't happened, I should have gone on getting more exhausted and less efficient. And that the only good way out would have been for Urwick to insist that I should resign on grounds of health – with the chance of coming back to the Government later when I was better. Also, she says, only my resignation made possible the co-ordination of the Treasury and the Planning Machine. But we agree that this is only possible, effectively, because Cripps is so brilliantly on top of his form. I am sure this set-up can't last. None of the Opposition could carry this double burden.

In November 1948, Bevin asked Dalton to lead the British delegation at a conference in Paris to consider the next steps to be taken towards closer union in Europe. Other members of the delegation included Sir Edward Bridges (Secretary to the Cabinet and Permanent Secretary to the Treasury), Lord Inverchapel (formerly British Ambassador in Washington), Sir Gladwyn Jebb (soon to be Permanent British Representative at the U.N.), Professor E. C. S. Wade (a constitutional lawyer) and Harry Gibb (a former Labour M.P.). Before the five-power 'Committee for the Study of European Unity' was a Franco-Belgian proposal for a parliamentary European Assembly. Dalton, as the *Daily Mail* put it, had been selected to head the British team 'to state the British case of "go slow" '.[1] He was happy to perform this role, strongly opposing moves towards European federalism.

---

1 15th November 1948.

Wednesday 17th November

I went down to Eastbourne on Wednesday 17th November to lunch and talk with Bevin about the forthcoming Western Union talks in Paris ...

Bevin and I have been steadily in agreement on Western Union policy and I anticipate no difficulty in maintaining this agreement during the Paris talks. More doubtful is the question whether the French and Belgians can be persuaded to be sensible.

Sunday 21st November
West Leaze

We have had a lovely weekend here. Sun yesterday and today. I have slept, shifted earth, and read Cabinet Papers on strength of Armed Forces (proposed to increase service from twelve to eighteen months for those joining on and after 1st January 1949. Chiefs of Staff say anything less than two years is very little good; they want N.S. [National Service] men, not so much to make a trained reserve as to meet current requirements, and they can only begin to do the latter after six months' training; we must, I suppose, accept eighteen months, but we must make a big effort to increase voluntary long service recruitment; this should draw on N.S. men, if the latter like their service and don't feel they are wasting their time.) ...

I had Retinger[1] to lunch on Friday (19th) ... He says – but he must! – that Winston likes me very much. Raymond Blackburn said the same to me last week, adding that Winston said I had 'Socialised M.E.W.' in the war, which he didn't like. I suppose this means my Black Brigade[2] – Crossman, Ivor Thomas, Hugh Gaitskell, Chris Mayhew, etc.

End of 1948

At our last Cabinet before Xmas, Bevin got approval for the new Ruhr authority and for a compromise, half-way to meet the Americans, on dismantling. But in the discussion, Cripps said we ought to make up our minds whether we regarded the Germans as still a danger, or

---

1 J. H. Retinger (1888–1960). Polish internationalist, whose second wife had been a daughter of E. D. Morel, q.v. Parachuted by S.O.E. into Poland during the war. Helped to set up the European League for Economic Co-operation and the Bildeberg Group. Dalton had known him since the 1920s.

2 'Black Brigade': As minister responsible for S.O.E. Dalton had been questioned by Churchill about allegations that there were 'many left-wing elements' among staff responsible for the organisation of 'black propaganda' at Woburn Abbey (Diary, 2nd March 1941).

as an ally in building W. Europe. Bevin said he was trying to steer a middle course. Aneurin Bevan said we ought to build them up as much as we could. They were a better barrier against Communism than the French. I was very angry that morning anyhow (in view of proceedings in my constituency, reported to me the day before)[1] and spoke sharply of the German danger; greater than the Russian, and greatest in combination with Russia. We should *aim*, I said, at a strong Atlantic Pact – with strong U.S. and Canadian contribution, a strong U.K., a strong France, a strong Benelux and a weak Germany. Tom Williams[2] flared up at this, and said I reminded him of what Austen Chamberlain used to say. Jowitt said he was nearer to Bevan than to me, but Addison backed me up. A bad presage for the future!

Tom Williams, I recall, not only voted against all arms, but wanted, on the (literal) eve of our entry into war in 1939, to issue a declaration to the world, in the name of the Parliamentary Executive, that we wouldn't go to war, unless France did!

He'd best stick to his spuds!

No wonder, after all this, I get a boil on my left cheek to celebrate the New Year. ...

Archie Inverchapel told me some good stories in Paris. He is living among his memories – as I suppose we all shall when we retire ... Archie relates how, soon after his appointment to Moscow,[3] he was in London trying in vain to get a clear directive from Winston for his Russian policy. On the eve of his return to Moscow, they lunched alone. Nothing. And then, just as he was leaving in despair, Winston called him back and said, 'You want a directive? All right. I don't mind kissing Stalin's bum, but I'm damned if I'll lick his arse!' 'Thank you, P.M.,' said Archie. 'Now, I quite understand.'

Wednesday 12th January 1949

I win a victory on Census of Distribution.[4] It is not to take place early in 1950, just before the general election, as proposed by Cripps and Wilson – a gratuitous political blunder – but is to be postponed till

---

1 Dalton had been exonerated by the Lynskey Tribunal after giving evidence in person. There was, however, an unpleasant aftermath. The publicity surrounding the affair fuelled local rumour, and the Attorney-General ordered an inquiry after receiving a letter about the issue of building licences in Bishop Auckland. As a result, two Scotland Yard detectives began an investigation in the ex-Chancellor's constituency.

2 Tom Williams, q.v., was Minister of Agriculture and Fisheries 1945–51.

3 Lord Inverchapel, q.v. (as Sir Archibald Clark-Kerr), had been Ambassador to the Soviet Union 1942–6.

4 'Census of Distribution': the redistribution of constituencies.

1951. Cripps, Bevan and Tomlinson were for going ahead; Phil [Noel-Baker] didn't speak; all the rest, including Harold Wilson when he saw how the debate was going, though some after a good deal of hesitation, supported me.

Did I put down, in earlier notes on our chit chat in Paris, Inverchapel's good saying that Eden now looked like 'an ageing rabbit'.

Sunday 20th March

At West Leaze for the first time for a month. In moments of moral weakness I think of retiring here and slowly living or dying on capital!

Last week North Atlantic Pact finally published; likewise National Parks Bill. And we hold Sowerby [by-election] – after South Hammersmith, Batley and North St Pancras ...

National Parks Bill has had a pretty good initial press.[1] The Ramblers won't like the composition of the Park Committees, and the Access provisions. But it is a good Bill on the whole. It wouldn't have been half as good, but for me, and Christopher Addison.

Sowerby, following the three others, shows that we are very strong in the country at the moment, and Morrison and Jim Griffiths have both been playing with the idea of a quick general election. But the Chief Whip, who has heard of this, has put his foot down, and said we must make no mistake either about the Parliamentary Bill or the Steel Bill. And so many others would say. We are children of the instant, and the Tories are in a very low state today. But they will gain seats in the municipal election and the Budget may be cold comfort for all.

Tuesday 29th March

Jenner Hoskin, heart specialist, whom I visit on Urwick's suggestion ... says that my weight has gone up from 13.10 to 14.7, but this is not excessive for my bulk, and that I *now* have a quite irregular heartbeat ... He says it is just a sign of wear and tear following a period of heavy strain and severe worry, but it might be worth trying to get it regular again. There is a drug which might do that, but it would involve going into a nursing home for a week or ten days. This I might manage say in second half of July. All this is rather a bore. It casts shades of age upon me. I don't feel I could run a Department effectively now!

---

1 This became The National Park and Access to the Countryside Act 1949. Dalton had become President of the Ramblers' Association at the beginning of 1948.

Tuesday 3rd May

Lunch for foreign ministers ... They are here to settle the Statute for the Council of Europe ...

6 p.m. We all reassemble at Buckingham Palace. The King is standing up – probably for too long – for $1\frac{1}{2}$ hours. He and Séan MacBride[1] have a very animated and friendly conversation, full of jokes and laughter. The foreigners, especially the French, are amazed at this example of our unwritten constitution! ...

Winston, either maliciously or thoughtlessly, put between Séan MacBride and Bech.[2] Very bored, but, having summoned the waiter to replenish his glass several times, he gets going with MacBride towards the end!

Tuesday 24th May

Talked again to Nye Bevan about the date of the next election. He is sure we ought to go to the country this year, and not wait till next spring or early summer. He says our Party in the House will be getting nervy and demoralised and there will be no more really interesting legislation. We shall be marking time, and lose our power of man-oeuvre. Next year's Budget will be even less popular than this one. And unemployment may go up. And the winter is always a bad time for morale. I think there is great force in this ...

I mentioned the possibility to Morrison, who said he had quite an open mind. Morrison's relations with Cripps and Bevan, especially the latter, are bad. They fratch in Cabinet. I said to Bevan, 'You have taken the Foreign Secretary's place, it is *your* relations with Morrison which are now so notoriously bad.'

Friday 3rd to Friday 10th June

Blackpool for Annual Conference. I speak with Nye at Sunday evening demonstration, with Herbert and Michael Foot next door. Good audiences.

The Conference is very easy. The Platform dominates the Floor, which is quite content to have it so. The programme goes over with little criticism. All E.C. speakers get long ovations – and have to rise and acknowledge – even I, who have only a minor part, to pick up the pieces at the end of the International Debate. Bevin, pretty tired, flies from Paris and makes an unusually short and kindly speech. No

1 Séan MacBride (b. 1904). Irish Minister for External Affairs 1948–51. Vice-President of the O.E.E.C. 1948–51. Active in the Irish independence movement, and imprisoned by the British. Assistant Secretary-General of the United Nations 1973–7.
2 Joseph Bech (1887–1975). Luxemburg Foreign Minister 1928–58. Prime Minister 1953–8.

serious criticism, even of him, great sense of unity in the Party, and of trust in leadership, which comes collectively very well out of the Conference. Cripps makes his standard speech, and this is received, though without the long ovation given to others, without resistance.

Driberg[1] is elected to vacant place on N.E. due to Laski's retirement. I am 5th as against 2nd last year, but then I wasn't a minister and got a special vote of sympathy. Foot goes up to 2nd. The top six, ending with Shinwell, get a very solid vote. Phil rather invites a rebuff in standing again. But Margate Conference of 1947 will repeat itself. Decisions will soon become largely irrelevant. The dollar gap will swallow all else! Pick up the hell of a cold at the Agents' Party on Monday night, and have little voice for last two days.

Starting in 1948, Dalton led a small band of Labour M.P.s and other friends on a series of annual Whitsun walks in areas of natural beauty. These expeditions combined pleasure with business, arousing great interest in the press.

Saturday 11th June

I had thought last night that I shouldn't be able to start on today's much publicised walk, and how the enemy press would jeer! But about 3 a.m. I wake in a fine sweat and with my head clear.

So we start as planned – Silkin,[2] who spoke with competence and effect last night at Ambleside, and today goes the first half hour's walk with us, and substantially last year's party – Geoffrey de Freitas, Barbara[3] and Ted Castle,[4] George Chetwynd,[5] Billy Hughes (new-

---

1 T. E. N. Driberg, later Baron Bradwell (1905–76). Labour M.P. for Maldon 1945–55; Barking 1959–74. Independent M.P. for Maldon 1942–5. Writer and journalist. Member of the Labour Party N.E.C. 1949–72. Chairman of the Labour Party 1957–8.

2 Lewis Silkin, q.v., was Minister of Town and Country Planning 1945–50.

3 Barbara Castle, née Betts (b. 1910). Labour M.P. for Blackburn 1945–50; Blackburn East 1950–55; Blackburn 1955–79. Member of Labour Party N.E.C. since 1950. Minister of Overseas Development 1964–5; Transport 1965–8. First Secretary of State and Secretary of State for Employment and Productivity 1968–70. Secretary of State for Social Services 1974–6. Member of the European Parliament since 1979. Leader of the British Labour Party Group in the European Parliament 1979–85. Diarist.

4 E. C. Castle, later Baron (1907–79). Journalist. Assistant Editor of *Picture Post* 1944–50. Editor 1951–2. Married to Barbara Castle.

5 G. R. Chetwynd, later Sir George (1916–82). Labour M.P. for Stockton-on-Tees 1945–62. P.P.S. to Dalton 1948–51.

comer), Fred Willey,[1] Tom and Madge Stephenson[2] and a number of pressmen and photographers – with Paul Wilson[3] and Acland (National Trust) part of the way.

From Grasmere up Far Easedale, Greenup, Ullscarf (glorious view of Derwentwater and Windermere, as well as of many peaks) and down to Watendlath, where we have a good tea, and Rushwaite, where we stay at the Scarfell Hotel. A very sunny day, and we all have red faces and heads where these are not well thatched.

With the balance of payments moving into surplus, the economy seemed much healthier during the first months of 1949 than in the previous year. However, a recession in the United States was putting pressure on sterling, and it gradually became clear that Britain's gold reserves were too small to provide an adequate cushion. By June, the City had begun to treat devaluation of the pound as inevitable. Cripps, on the other hand, remained obstinately opposed to such a step. By late summer the matter was no longer one of choice, and on 18th September the pound was devalued by 30 per cent against the dollar. There followed a further dose of deflation and austerity, provoking a sharp political reaction. Bevan, in particular, attacked the Chancellor over proposed cuts in the health service, providing a dress rehearsal for the 1951 Cabinet crisis.

Wednesday 15th June
First meeting of ministers (Economic Policy Committee) since Blackpool. Morrison and Bevin are away, but meeting includes Attlee, Bevan, Wilson, Isaacs and Strachey, and myself.

Very serious dollar situation. Gap widening and reserves running down. ... Cripps says that the danger is that, within twelve months, all our reserves will be gone. This time there is nothing behind them, and there might well be 'a complete collapse of sterling'.

We meet again in the afternoon, without officials, and Phil joins us. Cripps gets authority to stop *all* purchase of gold and dollars and

---

1 F. T. Willey (b. 1910). Labour M.P. for Sunderland 1945–50; Sunderland North 1950–83. Minister of Land and Resources 1964–7.
2 Thomas Stephenson (1889–1974) and Madge, née Bannister, his wife. Stephenson was Clerk of the Lieutenancy for the East Riding of Yorkshire 1940–61, and the pioneering figure in the Ramblers' Association.
3 P. N. Wilson (b. 1908). Prospective Labour candidate for Westmorland. Businessman.

will circulate a paper on other action proposed next week. He thinks – and we agree – that it is essential to announce *action taken* as well as *action proposed*, by 5th July, when periodical published statement on reserves will cause alarm. He is very calm. He says that he thinks we should have an early election. No one dissents, though we don't pursue this today. As we go out, Addison says, '1931 over again.' I say, 'It reminds me awfully of 1947.' Shall we never get free? ...

The danger now is of lower rations and less material imports leading to unemployment. (And other Western European countries in a pretty bad mess too.) Americans don't seem able to see the simple point about our reserves. Harriman, in particular, Cripps says, just can't see it!

He wants, also, an early Conference of sterling area countries, plus Canada. India is making immense demands for dollars. She may have to be put out of sterling area. But then she would charge us gold or dollars for what she sold us! 'We [didn't?] know about sterling area drawings till some time later.' How like 1947, when I was criticised for not moving sooner! Not much improvement since then.

We mustn't, it seems to me, be pushed into a corner. But we must have a bold, positive policy, and challenge Tories on it. There are all the makings of a panic here.

Thursday 30th June
Bevin says in Cabinet that all may be easier after July. That will be the difficult month. But 'others', i.e. Americans, 'don't want to be blown up' and he thinks they will see how much, for them, turns on backing us. All this in one of his hopeful asides, with a pretty confident smile.

Friday 1st July
Cripps was arguing in Paris till 2 a.m. then caught a plane and comes, looking tired and drawn, to E.P.C. [Economic Policy Committee] at 11.30. It goes on after lunch from 2.30 to 4. A big gathering, nearly all the Cabinet, with Gaitskell and Strachey and Strauss – and Oliver Franks,[1] Bridges and Makin as well as three Cabinet Secretaries. Bevan grumbles to me that it is P.M.'s weakness to have too many people for straight talk. Cripps got a pretty good agreement in Paris.

1 Sir Oliver Franks, later Baron (b. 1905). Ambassador to the U.S.A. 1948–52. Permanent Secretary at the Ministry of Supply 1945–6. Provost of Queen's College, Oxford 1946–8. Chairman of Lloyds Bank Ltd 1954–62. Provost of Worcester College, Oxford 1962–76.

He then expounds his paper. It is very bad in parts, as Jay had warned me. He gets no support from any minister on his proposal to cut food subsidies. Morrison leads off against it. It would cause a parliamentary revolt and won't do the trick anyhow. Bevin speaks against it, so do Bevan, Addison, Strachey and I. Cripps doesn't put up much fight for it. I insist that Budgetary [problems?] have no bearing on our difficulties at all. Our Budgetary situation – with a surplus of [£400m] – on revenue account is the soundest in the world.

I say, 'Montagu Norman walks again.' I thought we'd buried all this stuff about Bank Rate. Cripps says, 'You see I don't support it.' I said, 'I was surprised you even mentioned it. One gets a lot of advice one doesn't think worth mentioning.' ...

Morrison against food subsidy cut, thinks devaluation might be least of evils. P.M. inclined to agree. I argue the other way – support Cripps and on *this* point, the Bank. Bevin says neither devaluation, nor cutting food subsidy, will lead you anywhere in this situation. Only immediate action should be to stop purchasing. Tell workers they can't have increased wages now, but we aim to stabilise. In Western Europe we can't afford to run the risk of unemployment. If we do, all Atlantic Pacts in the world won't save us. Americans are playing with fire. They can't be settled on financial level. Must be taken on highest level. Try for temporary tideover with Snyder. (A good meeting!)

Tuesday 19th July
P.M. today held a council of war on the date of the general election, on which I had written to him before Blackpool. Also present Morrison, Bevin, Bevan, Whiteley and myself. Cripps, who left for Zurich today for his treatment, had written to Attlee who read part of the letter to us. Cripps wanted an election to give him and Bevin a fresh mandate for their talks at Washington at the beginning of September. He wrote that our Policy was not well received either by the U.S. or Canadian government, and that there was less co-operation in U.K. from various sections – I think he meant business and financial – who were in doubt whether we could win the election. Abbott[1] has said to him that it would all be so much easier if we had our general election behind us. But obviously Cripps's idea is quite impossible, since it would mean dissolution in a few weeks' time and an election campaign in the August holiday season. Attlee said it was clear that Cripps had been very much wrought up when he wrote this, and hadn't thought it out.

1 D. C. Abbott (b. 1899). Canadian Finance Minister 1946–54.

In subsequent discussion Morrison sat on the fence; he saw the possible advantages of an early election, but it was difficult at present to be sure how the public would react to an unexpectedly early appeal. Our Party Machine was not yet tuned up; it was in less good trim than the Tories. Printing was very slow. It would be necessary to speak, very confidentially, to Phillips and Windle.

Bevan spoke with his habitual force and warmth in favour of an election *this year*. Next Budget would be very unpopular, near the end of the financial year there would be heavy supplementaries, our Parliamentary [Party] would become demoralised in the last session, etc.

Bevin, who is just off for a holiday and is pretty tired, reacted against any election while the talks with the U.S. were on, and these might last till nearly Christmas. He was optimistic about the outcome of these. 'The Americans' – meaning the Administration and the military – didn't want our Government to fall. Foreign Secretaries (I remember Arthur Henderson) never want elections, for these disturb the next international negotiation!

I said – reminding the P.M. that I had written to him before Black-pool, before the dollar crisis had fully blown up – that I was more than ever convinced that we must not have another Budget in this Parliament. I had been shocked at the bad effect on morale of the last, inevitable though its policy was. Therefore we ought to have polling day at latest in February, and at earliest a dissolution at the end of September, when we saw how the Washington talks went. We should have to give up our preference for a spring or summer election this time.

Attlee said he quite agreed that he must dissolve before the next Budget, but was inclined to favour February, as agreed this year. Bevan argued at length for this year. Whiteley said that 'our people in the North' would be surprised if we did not go the full length, but that feeling might be different elsewhere. He did not think we could make up our minds at present. With this wise judgment we all agreed, but I think all are clear that February is the latest date, and that a strong case may develop for the autumn or early winter. I told Bevan afterwards that I thought we had made progress.

Some ten days ago (I may have noted this already) Cripps at an E.P.C. meeting, the officials having been asked to leave the room, said that he did not trust his own officials and advisers. They were all really, by reason of their training and their belief in a 'free economy', much more in agreement with the Americans than with British ministers. They would honestly try to carry out their instructions, but they would find it difficult. What should he do? I said, 'Use Douglas

Jay', and so he agreed to do. Jay went to Chequers for the talks with Snyder and Abbott, and also attended the Commonwealth Finance Ministers' Talks. But he told me, some days after the decision, that Bridges 'had other ideas', and was putting Wilson Smith[1] full-time on to these talks. I told Jay that he must get something in writing from Cripps. Jay thinks that not only are the officials not in sympathy with our policy, but that they are half expecting us to be beaten at the election, and are beginning to think in terms of a Tory Government and a Tory policy. They have many personal links, he believes, with the Tories – including Eccles,[2] Crowther,[3] etc.

No doubt the officials, or some of them, are writing minutes and papers for the record, to show to the Tories if they *should* win the next election.

End of July

Important discussions on the dollar crisis. Attlee is acting Foreign Secretary and acting Chancellor of the Exchequer.

Gaitskell and Jay come to see me at their own request to say they are now in favour of devaluation – and before Washington – chiefly to boost our reserves and to create a new and more hopeful situation. I say I'll think it over. I do, and agree, and see Attlee and tell him I have changed my view. I had also, I say, overestimated the effect and speed of action on cost of living. He says he is being served up from the Treasury and the Bank arguments which he thinks are fallacious on evil effects of our public expenditure. I say they *are* fallacious. He says he wants to have it all out at the Cabinet, I say I hope he will ask the young economist ministers to speak. He says he will.

Next day and the day after we discuss it at Cabinet, with Bridges and Franks present. General round discussion very satisfactory. Attlee calls on me to open, on a paper of Morrison's alleging that there is a 'close relation' between our high expenditure and our dollar

---

1 Sir Henry Wilson Smith (1904–78). Additional Second Secretary at the Treasury 1948–51. Permanent Secretary at the Ministry of Defence 1947–8.

2 D. M. Eccles, later Sir David, 1st Viscount (b. 1904). Conservative M.P. for Chippenham 1943–62. Dalton came to know him as Economic Adviser to the British Ambassadors in Madrid and Lisbon 1940–42. Minister of Works 1951–4; Education 1954–7, 1959–62. President of the Board of Trade 1957–9. Paymaster-General (with responsibility for the arts) 1970–73.

3 G. Crowther, later Sir Geoffrey, Baron (1907–72). Editor of *The Economist* 1938–56. Chairman of the Central Advisory Council for Education (England) 1956–60; Royal Commission on the Constitution 1969–72. Chairman of Trust House Forte 1970–72.

troubles. I say the relation isn't close at all; he must consider *how* we spend – capital expenditure, etc. Our Budgetary position is sounder than any other country's in the world, including U.S.A. We have a surplus on revenue account of between £400 and £500 millions. U.S. had a deficit of about this amount in year ending last June. Only backing Morrison gets is from Hector McNeil who, primed no doubt by Foreign Office officials, says we ought to 'meet half way' those in U.S. and elsewhere who haven't confidence in our policy. Devaluation isn't discussed, but is mentioned, approvingly by Morrison, myself, Bevan and Strachey. (Only Addison and Alexander were in the Cabinet in 1931.[1] How differently we ministers are reacting now!) No flicker of surrender.

Gaitskell and Jay come again to see me after this. Gaitskell says he'll resign if we commit ourselves again to convertibility. They say there is still very heavy pressure from all official quarters 'to have something else' as well as devaluation. We agree that we should reduce investment programmes and tell banks to reduce personal advances. Jay says Eady is obstructing this last. I say it can be done, if necessary, under my Bank of England Act. Jay says that even Helsby,[2] P.M.'s Private Secretary, said to him in car yesterday how dreadful it was that Cabinet wasn't in favour of 'anything else' in addition to devaluation. What they all want is a slash in public expenditure on social services.

Gaitskell and Jay both explain distrust of Wilson. They don't know what he's up to. They think he's currying favour with Bridges and Treasury officials. I, therefore, urge Wilson to come and see me. He said Cripps must have a Minister of State, to go to conferences, etc., for him. But this shouldn't be Jay who has a few sound ideas (e.g. Development Areas) buzzing in his head to the exclusion of all else. I say, 'You three young economists must work together.' He says Cripps reacted very strongly at the end against the very heavy pressure being brought to bear on him.

Sunday 7th August
From West Leaze to London (for one night before leaving for Strasburg).

---

1 Herbert Morrison, then Minister of Transport, was also in the Cabinet in 1931. Originally outside, he was given Cabinet status just before the crisis, in March 1931.
2 L. N. Helsby, later Sir Laurence, Baron Helsby (1908–79). Principal Private Secretary to the Prime Minister 1947–50. Permanent Secretary at the Ministry of Labour 1959–62.

It has been very peaceful at West Leaze with Ruth for ten days – all thoughts of the dollar crisis put away, a succession of lovely days, some quite hot, shifting chalk and planning a sorbarium, and the planting of some free-growing English yews.

One night we heard *Atalanta in Calydon* on the air. Quite moving! I love Swinburne still, and re-read most of the *Poems and Ballads* and Nicolson's very understanding and just book.[1]

I recall that on 4th June 1906 I recited a chunk of *The Triumph of Time* for speeches[2] – rather daring and original.

Monday 12th September

Back from Strasburg on Friday night (9th September) and slept most of the weekend. I had been sleeping very short at Strasburg. Today I asked Jay to come and see me. He was just back from a holiday in Devon. In the absence of Morrison and me at Strasburg – and Cripps in Switzerland[3] – the old fight had gone on. *In spite of all our Cabinet discussions and decisions*, the officials – Bridges, Wilson Smith, Makins (so the Foreign Office were in the game too), etc. – put up a brief for ministers immediately before they were due to leave for Washington, with all the old stuff about the 'need to restore confidence', and hence to make large reductions, including changes of policy, in public expenditure. The officials were so anxious for this that they almost changed their minds on devaluation, for fear that if this was done alone, it would be thought by the Government to be enough. (Of course it wasn't mentioned in the paper.)

Gaitskell and Jay fought this out. Jay praised Gaitskell most highly. He acted as 'Vice-Chancellor of the Exchequer' and attacked the officials, both on intellectual grounds and on tactics. Jay hadn't felt able to do so much, since he and Bridges had a balanced relation at the Treasury. But, under Gaitskell's attack, the officials retreated and a new first six pages were written, more in line with previous ministerial thought, which, in fact, ministers happily accepted. If Cripps had had the wrong paper put up, he might, having been out of touch and ill, have weakened (but it wasn't). If the P.M. had weakened on general proposition that transfer payments don't directly affect costs (but he didn't, remaining on the contrary, serenely set), all might [have] collapsed, and the Labour Party be breaking up as in 1931. Gaitskell

---

1 Harold Nicolson, *Swinburne*, Macmillan, London, 1926.
2 'speeches': a traditional public recital by senior boys at Eton.
3 On 18th July, Cripps went to Switzerland to get treatment for what later proved a fatal illness. His duties were nominally taken over by Attlee, in practice by a triumvirate of Wilson, Jay and Gaitskell. Of these, Gaitskell took the leading role.

and Jay saw eye to eye throughout. Wilson was away at this point but Jay doesn't trust him. He trims and wavers, and is thinking more of what senior ministers – and even senior officials – are thinking of him than of what is right. Jay wonders what he said to Cripps and Bevin when he took messages to them on the Continent?

Cripps, Jay thinks, is ill; not much improved by his time in Zurich. He is said still not to be sleeping and, Jay thinks, if he can't recover in a few weeks after his return from Washington, he will have to give up. (This would, indeed. be a bad blow – who could take his place, or even part of it?)

Cripps wasn't persuaded of the advisability of urgency in another matter, and Bevin only half persuaded. So nothing urgent was done. Clutterbuck[1] came over and persuaded ministers that Canada would go up in smoke if we proposed to pay her in sterling for her wheat, etc. So that is postponed. Jay fought alone and in vain against this at the last meeting of ministers. (Bevan wasn't there.)

Jay repeated several times that it is all due to my suggestion at E.P.C. when Cripps said he didn't trust the advice of his officials, that Jay should be in on the brief-making that has saved the situation. If he hadn't been in, nor would Gaitskell have been, and the officials would have had it all their own way.

Early in October, Dalton recorded a conversation in which Jay told him that on 29th September, 'Stafford Cripps gave one of his usual dinners with Aneurin Bevan, Harold Wilson, Hugh Gaitskell, Strauss, Strachey and Douglas Jay – the usual lot, leaving out, e.g. Isaacs, T. Williams and G. Tomlinson – and they were all, except Jay, now for a quick election, Cripps being "very emotional", and saying he "can't go on".'

Wednesday 5th October
I see Attlee in the afternoon, and we talk for $1\frac{1}{2}$ hours! ... On the [election] date he seems still against an early one. I tell him, as Morrison suggested, of the Cripps party. He says, 'Those are all the intellectuals.' On the other hand, he says, Addison, Ede, Tomlinson and Shinwell are all for waiting; Ede very strongly, because new registers, though due on 14th October, won't in fact be available till early November. This is, indeed, a strong argument. I say that I am inclined

---

1 Sir Alexander Clutterbuck (1897–1976). High Commissioner in Canada 1946–52. Permanent Under-Secretary at the Commonwealth Relations Office 1959–61.

to think very early in the New Year would be best. He says, looking troubled, that he fears Cripps's emotionally eager desire for a quick one is because he feels he can't go on carrying the burden. He says that he thinks Bevin will be against a quick one.

Monday 10th October

Douglas Jay to see me just before E.P.C. Cripps's paper is inspired by Plowden. This is another flank attack by officials. Cripps has it in mind to increase Health contributions by 1/- a head. This is a most regressive tax and would seem indefensible to the Party and the unions. Jay said to Cripps that the way to check inflation is to hold the wage line. Cripps said there must be 'no appeasement of the T.U.C.'! I said I wondered whether Cripps would demand an immediate election if we refused his proposals. Jay thought perhaps yes. He thought my influence, which had been decisive before against cuts in expenditure, might be decisive again. He knew I felt some personal difficulty in opposing Cripps, but perhaps this would be less now than a year ago. He thought many figures in the paper were bogus.

At E.P.C. we discussed Cripps's paper proposing, though without detail, that we should 'cut out £300m of consumption'. Morrison was silent, but the rest of us criticised the paper. In particular it was said by Wilson that, since the estimates were made, large trading profits by Departments, including his own, were expected to be realised. It was agreed that Departments should be asked about this, and any necessary corrections made. I felt that there was little chance that my colleagues would accept the sort of proposals that Jay said Cripps had in mind.

I drove Wilson afterwards to Board of Trade. He said that his man Cairncross,[1] a good Socialist, hadn't been at the meeting where this paper had been drafted. He said that Jay should still be vetting papers from the officials as in the summer. Since Cripps's return, this procedure has lapsed! I said the young Socialist economists must continue to work together and pull their full weight. He said, 'The trouble is that Stafford isn't an economist.' Healey brings me the draft of a very honest paper on Western Union for International Sub-Committee [of the N.E.C.]. I said he must add a more hopeful and co-operative finish.

1 A. K. Cairncross, later Sir Alexander (b. 1911). Economic Adviser to the Board of Trade 1946–9; Economic Adviser to the O.E.E.C. 1949–50. Professor of Applied Economics at Glasgow University 1951–61. Economic Adviser to the Government 1961–4. Head of Government Economic Services 1964–9.

Tuesday 11th October

I asked Bevan to come and have a talk this afternoon. He was effervescent, amusing and friendly. (Surrey Dane[1] told me at lunch that in the *Sunday Pictorial* last week [Bevan] had had a large majority in a readers' poll for P.M., beating Attlee, Cripps and Morrison, in that order, very easily. The poll had been taken a week before, just after his speech in the House.) Bevan said Cripps was in a very strained condition. He now had a persecution mania, and was taking very hard charges of dishonourable conduct over devaluation. I said that in public life men needed thick skins. Bevan said, 'Yes, either thick skins or an aristocratic temperament. Cripps hasn't got either.' Now, said Bevan, he was committed to producing proposals. But what proposals? He understood a reduction of housing and school building programmes – which was really a cut in the social services – and an increase in the National Health contribution. I then read Bevan part of the paper which I had dictated today, and he said he agreed. Cripps was exhausted, and under constant pressure, he said, by officials who were not our friends. I said it was embarrassing to discuss these things always with officials present. He said he had told Attlee this several times. I said that officials served ministers well, so long as they thought the Government would go on. If they had doubts on this, they wavered and were tempted to make minutes for the record, to show to successors. He had told P.M. that he should have a Minister of Health, outside Cabinet, to deal with health only. The rest of present Ministry of Health should be merged in one Department with Works and Town and Country Planning. Civil Aviation should go in with Transport (I told him how Swinton was appointed). Pensions should go in with National Insurance and its hospitals go over to Health. Chancellor of Exchequer should lose Economic Affairs, which should go under a separate minister. These changes would streamline government and make large savings. He thought Cripps would resign rather than give up his main proposals for economy. Others, including himself, would resign rather than agree. The catalyst was a quick election. We should accept Tory challenge. This couldn't be called 'running away'. Bevan said, 'The Tories are waiting now for the second stage of 1931.' We must not let them have it.

I said I would go to discussions with open mind. I thought that threats and counter threats of resignation might be the final argument for a quick one. ... He asked had I considered that a small Tory majority might be the best next stage. They wouldn't last long.

1 W. S. Dane (1892–1978). Joint Managing Director, then Managing Director, of Odhams Press Ltd (publishers of the *Daily Herald* and *Sunday Pictorial*) 1947–59.

Wednesday 12th October

Another E.P.C. meeting this morning, Gaitskell also being present. Inconclusive because we are still arguing about the amount of 'inflationary pressure', without any proposals before us for getting rid of it ... Cripps and Bevan, supposedly in close alliance, clash today. Each hints at resignation, if the other succeeds in preventing him getting his way. Attlee tries to bring us all together. We await the proposals impatiently, though I have heard unofficial accounts of what they are.

I take Hugh back with me afterwards. He is now very frightened of 'inflationary pressure' and says that if we don't deal with it, we shall have another dollar crisis in the spring. If this morning's clash came to a break, he would be with Cripps against Bevan, and so he thinks would the country, and most of the Party. Bevan, he thinks, should have been moved by the P.M. before now from a spending Department to, say, Ministry of Labour, where he would do very well. I think Plowden has been working on Hugh, for he quotes him to the effect that, when he went to see his doctor the other day, he found the waiting room full of women gossiping, with slight colds, coming for a chat and a free prescription. He finds Bevan very difficult. ...

Later I see Douglas Jay in my flat so as not to be observed. He has not moved as far as Gaitskell, and is very much against the proposed increase in national health insurance, a poll tax on healthy and sick alike 'to pay for free wigs for foreigners' as Tories will say. Much better make people pay something when they visit the doctor – you could exempt old age pensioners, etc. – and limit free prescribing. He finds Cripps very messianic and Bevan very ideological about what are practical administrative questions, not really lending themselves to either form of high emotion!

He says that Cobbold[1] and Eady have been urging an increase in bank rate, and in the short term rates on government debt, but that Cripps has withstood them. ... He says that Cobbold is authoritative and truculent. His proposal having been turned down, Jay referred to need for credit control by the banks and Cobbold said, 'I have made my proposal for that. It has been rejected; so I have no other way to propose.' I was against appointing Cobbold as Governor. I should not have done it.

Thursday 13th October

Cabinet this morning agreed to P.M.'s proposal that there should be

1 C. F. Cobbold, later 1st Baron (b. 1904). Governor of the Bank of England 1949–61; Deputy Governor 1945–9. Dalton felt that Cobbold had given him bad advice over cheap money in 1947.

no election 'this year'. Attlee gave strong lead for this, and was generally supported. Only Cripps, not with much punch, and Bevan were definitely against, though Wilson was half against, and Jowitt said, 'Either November or February, and I can't judge which.'

Sunday 30th October
Reflections at West Leaze after a day of sun and windless calm, shovelling chalk and sawing wood.

There is much truth in the last paragraphs of a *News Chronicle* leader on the 27th.[1] Ministers *are* tired. We have seen so many crises, and no lasting solution of any. ...

Birch[2] said to Willy Hall, 'Your first master was a knave, but we always knew where we were with him. Your second is a fool as well. I think now that he is the worst of the two.'[3] I looked up tonight my 3rd and 4th Budget speeches. They were certainly livelier and more confident than Cripps's.

Iron and Steel Nationalisation was the last major item on Labour's 1945 agenda. After much wrangling and amendment, the Bill was finally passed by the House of Commons in November, with the vesting date fixed for 1st July 1951, after the coming election. The Bill received the Royal Assent on 24th November 1949.

Sunday 20th November
So-called 'compromise' on Steel Bill having now been accepted – there were nervous objections to this at Party Meeting, but it went through all right in the House – we shall have this for our statute book this session, before Xmas, and all will be clear for an election early in the New Year if we want one. ...

Senator Patrick McCarran[4] of Nevada, chairman of 'Watchdog'

---

1 An article in the (pro-Liberal) *News Chronicle* of 27th October declared that 'Ministers are beginning to wear the air of beaten men ... There is a world of contrast between the ardour of 1945 taking the brave new world by storm, and the weariness of 1949 that seems to be retiring baffled before the dollar gap.'
2 N. C. Birch, later Baron Rhyl (1906–81). Conservative M.P. for Flintshire 1945–50; West Flint 1950–70. Junior minister 1951–4; Minister of Works 1954–5; Secretary of State for Air 1955–7; Economic Secretary to the Treasury 1957–8.
3 W. G. Hall, q.v., was Financial Secretary to the Treasury first under Dalton, and then under Cripps.
4 Patrick McCarran (1876–1954). Chairman of the U.S. Senate Judiciary Committee 1943–6, 1949–53. Democratic Senator for Nevada.

committee on expenditure, got into our debate on Monday, near the end. I was already speaking. He said next day that he had enjoyed it very much, and was 'so interested to hear Winston Churchill winding up'. No joke! These are the sort of people we have to do political business with.

Dalton wrote the following note, dated 26–27th November, in the margin of a copy he kept of a letter to Anthony Crosland:

Spoke, rather well, on 26th at 2 excellent meetings, at Staple Hill and Filton. Good spirit. Tony only spoke shortly and Alpass[1] more shortly still. I would have preferred to come last, but Alpass wanted it the other way. Motored back on 27th, lunched at Davenports', and Tony put me on the train at Oxford. He should be in next House, and do well, and this will be a little compensation for some of our losses of young men. He gave me a note on Disinflation, which I sent to Stafford and Douglas.[2]

Wednesday 7th December

4 p.m. Conference [at] No. 10 on When to Dissolve. Present Attlee, Morrison, Cripps, Addison, Whiteley and myself. Bevin is at Eastbourne, but has sent a message that he leaves the choice in our hands, since he feels that we know more about this sort of thing than he, who is no politician.

Attlee says the choice is between February and June, and he is inclined to favour February. Our men from the rural constituencies don't like the idea of February, because of bad weather, but he thinks this may cut both ways nowadays. All except Morrison, who hesitates and says he would like to have gone on till June, and 'faced a Budget', are for February. I say that bad weather is only argument against February, and it has a good deal of weight, but other arguments outweigh it. The indices – reserves, cost of living and unemployment – may go bad if we wait. We have nothing more to do in this Parliament. Our M.P.s will get more and more jumpy if we wait. We must have a new vote of confidence, a refreshment of our mandate and authority, if we are to deal with Big Business and Finance.

Cripps says he 'can't hold sterling beyond February'. Everywhere people are talking down sterling. The *Financial Times* in particular downs it every day.

1 J. H. Alpass. President of the South Gloucestershire C.L.P.
2 Dalton Papers 9/7 (62).

Saturday 10th December
If I were no longer a minister, I could spend more time at West Leaze, and begin to write my memoirs and make a new, and I hope lucrative, edition of my *Public Finance*.

I am very fit after a period of Part Time at the Duchy, but how long will some of these other chaps last? Or, if I took on another heavy Department, should *I* keep fit for long?

There would be some compensation, for most of us, in a Tory victory, with a very small majority. But it's better when you fight to win!

12 'Now Boys, Let's Watch and See that Nobody Comes to Wake Her Up', 14th December 1949

Wednesday 14th December
E.P.C. meeting. Cripps wants to put up interest rates – on part, at least, of Local Authority borrowing from Public Works Loans Board and of Public Boards of all kinds whether from the Exchequer or from the market – to $3\frac{1}{2}$ per cent. The advisers from the Treasury and the Bank kept on nagging at him over interest rates, and will never take 'no' for an answer. I have become convinced that it would be less of a disaster if the Foreign Office officials ran our Foreign Policy than if the Treasury and the Bank ran our Financial Policy. Very able most of them, but very dangerous without proper political direction. (I recall Arthur Henderson on Salter.) Bevan, surprisingly, wouldn't oppose higher interest rates, if he could have higher housing subsidies. I speak strongly against. You can't allow higher interest rates while resisting higher wage rates. You shouldn't accept $3\frac{1}{2}$ per cent as the best you can do. We shall have to have a showdown with the City if we win the election. ...

Morrison sent a note to P.M., being unable to come because ill, in which he swallows the whole Treasury case and says everything should go up to $3\frac{1}{2}$ per cent – on some crude general idea of being 'efficient' and having 'sound and honest finance' and 'not favouring public bodies'. *He* would be a complete disaster at the Treasury.

Thursday 15th December
Meet Berry in Whitehall – 'Sir Vaughan Berry'[1] now and British representative on the Ruhr authority ...

He says the feeling against H.M.G. is 'venomous' both among our own high ups in Germany – generals and admirals, etc., and their wives worse still – who ought to know better – and in the City of London. He was abused violently for twenty minutes by a bank mana-ger in a City shoe shop, where they were both trying to buy shoes. This man said, 'Why do you come to the City? You have no friends here now. You went over to the other side.' Berry hears that at the Bank of England 'Labour is out' and the Board is just an Old Etonian Club.

Sunday 1st January 1950
The Gallup Poll, published by the *News Chronicle*, suggests that the Tories will poll more than we, and the Liberals more than either of us, expect. But the authors confess that their generalisations are based on the replies of 1800 people only – truly, as they say, 'a diminutive sample'. I can't think that this is worth very much.

January 1950
On 2nd January 1950 from the peace of West Leaze to the constitu-ency, where I stay till 11th January ...

I am very uncertain as to the result ... I am inclined to expect us to come back with a smaller, but still workable, majority. If we don't do this, the next best is a small and unworkable Tory majority.

Thursday 19th January
Speak at Oxford Union. Motion condemning legislation of last Parliament carried by large majority, Tories and Liberals voting

---

1 Sir Vaughan Berry (1891–1979). British Delegate to the International Authority for the Ruhr 1949–50. Member of the Union Discount Company of London Ltd 1925–45. Full-time member of the Iron and Steel Corporation 1950–53. Berry had been a co-founder of the XYZ Club (see p. 442, n. 4, above).

together. Undergraduate speakers not very good. Strauss[1] opposes me at end. I have some moderately good fun, with a half solemn, half mock peroration on gladiators going into arena, some to live and some to die.

Friday 20th January
Lunch with Tony Crosland and walk in Trinity Garden, where we meet Weaver,[2] the President, a nice old thing who remembers entertaining Rupert [Brooke] and me and others in 1907. Talk about the garden trees – many good old yews and an ilex or two, and some newly planted beeches, judas tree and ginkgo. ...

Winston always speaks of 'Rabbit Butler'. What a happy family! I sense a clear majority of seats for us of just over 70.

Tuesday 24th January
Last week at E.P.C. Gaitskell, in agreement with Jay, put in a first class paper on Controls and Liberalisation. The first part is an admirable statement of economic doctrine. Don't rely mainly on financial controls to prevent inflation. Always keep demand just above supply, in order to hold full employment and rely on *physical* controls – especially on total imports, capital export, building, location and essential material – even when no longer 'in short supply' – to hold inflation. Really, therefore, though this is not the way anyone puts it – 'always have a bit of inflationary pressure, but use physical controls to prevent it breaking through.'

Cripps says, with a wan smile, that he supposes this is a vote of no confidence in the Chancellor. Of course, we all deny this. It is meant, we say, for guidance to official advisers, who keep on giving advice which runs contrary to H.M. Government's view of things. The principles of this part of Gaitskell's paper are approved. On 'liberalisation' we have gone about far enough. But we have done it for political reasons – U.S. and Europe. A great score today for the 'young economists'. ...

I am fighting my tenth Parliamentary election. The first five within thirty months, the second five within twenty-five years.

1 H. G. Strauss, later 1st Baron Conesford (1892–1974). Conservative M.P. for Combined English Universities 1946–50; Norwich South 1950–55. Junior minister 1942–5, 1951–5. Junior Treasurer of the Oxford Union 1914.
2 J. R. H. Weaver (1882–1965). President of Trinity College, Oxford 1938–54. Historian. In 1907 Weaver was an undergraduate at Keble College, Oxford.

Friday 27th January

Saw P.M. for the last time before starting on my election tour. He thought the result 'might be tight'. I risked 60 to 70, counting on Liberals just putting us in in a number of marginals.

I said, looking back over five years, it was amazing how well Cabinet and Government has worked – a few personal antipathies, Herbert v. Ernie and Nye v. Both – but bark worse than bite, and no real splits or resignation threats. This compared wonderfully well with other Administrations of which one has read and heard. Much of the credit, I said, was due to him.

He thought we had developed the Committee system very satisfactorily. Pre-war, it seemed, there was only one Standing Committee of Cabinet, and the rest was all ad hoc talks with P.M. and Minister concerned. Gain of Committee system was that 'No. 1 Ministers' outside the Cabinet could talk on a wide range of things outside their Departments, e.g. at Lord President's Committee, Ministry of National Insurance, Food and Transport. I said I thought Committee system was being a bit overdone in our first and second years, when a minister could hardly sneeze without getting colleagues' agreement. But this was better now.

I said that Cripps was absolutely irreplaceable as Chancellor. No one else could do it, until, in due course, one came down the line to the 'young economists'. At Treasury one needed not only quick intelligence, or bright ideas, or diligence or methodical administration, but power to resist high powered advice. One or two who were mentioned as possibles now would be quite impossible. (I had Morrison in mind.) But Cripps had much too much to do – old Treasury + new Planning + constant travelling abroad. I thought he should have a Minister of State, who could relieve him of some of this. Without it, the system would break down, and Cripps with it (no Tory could possibly handle all this). I thought Gaitskell was the man for this job. He agreed.

Generally, he said he was already discussing this with Bridges. But the new minister must have a defined sphere of responsibility – mainly perhaps in the 'old Treasury' field. We agreed that Gaitskell was better for this than Wilson (though he was doing very well), or Jay, who, though very able, had not always good judgment, and wasn't very personable.

I said Gaitskell had a great gift of concentration of clear thought and argument; his recent paper on controls, I said, had been quite masterly. In due course, he probably should be Chancellor of the Exchequer. He had done jolly well with the miners, who now much preferred him to his predecessor.

As to myself, I said I had wished for some time for a more active job, and hoped he would give me a suitable Department, if we came back. He nodded, and said half apologetically that there had been several changes he had had in mind, but it was difficult to make them at the end of a Parliament.

8

Teeth and Glasses
1950–51

Labour won the election held on 23rd February 1950, but the result gave ministers little cause for satisfaction. The Party in Parliament had an overall majority of 5, with 315 Labour M.P.s against 298 Conservatives, 9 Liberals and 3 others. Although this provided just enough margin to stay in office, there was scarcely any minor-party 'cushion' (as existed in 1929–31, and later in 1974–9) to allow the Government to pass laws by bargaining for the votes of non-aligned M.P.s. For the next twenty months the Attlee administration continued to govern, but under steady pressure from the Opposition and in constant danger of defeat.

In 1945, Labour leaders expected to lose but were full of ideas about how they would act if they should win. In 1950 the Government expected to win, but was gloomily aware that it had nothing new to offer. Hence the 1950 administration had the air of an inter-regnum. 'Austerity' remained, but many controls had been removed, and the nightmare of collapse and mass starvation that haunted economics ministers just after the war was forgotten. No controversial domestic legislation was introduced, and there were no major parliamentary debates on fundamental issues: only a guerrilla campaign by Tories against measures (such as the Steel Bill) that had already been decided in principle.

The problem was not just that the old men of the Government lacked ideas. It was also that Labour in power had lost its *raison d'être*. Since the war, Labour had ruled on two levels and with two sets of objectives. One was based on the policy discussion of the 1930s, and included a grocery list of commitments that were to be found in pre-war programmes: piecemeal nationalisation on the public corporation model, 'planning' loosely defined, social security for all and a free health service. The other derived from a new experience of economic management created by the war and by the post-war emergency. By 1950, the pre-war commitments had been achieved or aban-

468

doned. What remained was the broad acceptance of a new economic theory whose relationship with traditional socialism and the demands of proletarian politics was, at best, tangential.

The synthesis of Keynesianism and Fabian socialism, suggested by Douglas Jay in *The Socialist Case* in 1937, was still incomplete in 1950. Instead, what had occurred during Cripps's Chancellorship was a reassertion of the old identity of outlook between Treasury ministers and officials, though now on the basis of new principles of economic management. Influence had passed to younger politicians with greater knowledge and experience of Whitehall than of the Labour Movement, recent entrants to Parliament, who related more naturally to government economic advisers, and to leading civil servants, than to ministerial colleagues.

In July 1950 Cripps was incapacitated by illness, and in October he resigned. Gaitskell, already Minister of State for Economic Affairs and effectively 'Vice-Chancellor of the Exchequer', was appointed to succeed him. This appointment greatly pleased Dalton, who had pressed Attlee to make it. It was much less pleasing to some other ministers and M.P.s, and the animosities it immediately aroused, and those it later caused, developed into a sectarian conflict within the Labour Party that hardened over the years.

Controversy surrounding Gaitskell's Chancellorship can partly be explained in terms of personal rivalry. Aneurin Bevan, an ex-miner who had been in Parliament since 1929 and had performed brilliantly as Minister of Health, felt bitterly jealous of the young Wykehamist who seemed to have been promoted out of turn; Harold Wilson, with less cause, also felt slighted. But there was more to the conflict among Cabinet colleagues than resentment or hurt pride. Gaitskell's appointment, and the problems over the 1951 Budget that followed, gave constituency activists and an influential section of the P.L.P. further evidence of the managerial style of the Party leadership, and of indifference at the top to the aspirations of the rank and file.

International events brought the conflict between Gaitskell and his detractors to a head. Foreign policy had been the main interest of the Labour Left since the beginning of the Cold War. The conflict in Korea (which started in the summer of 1950) heightened the battle between those who favoured a non-aligned 'Third Alternative' approach to foreign policy, and Cabinet Ministers like Bevin, Morrison and Gaitskell who were almost unreservedly on the side of the United States. To the pro-Americans, communist advances in the Far East looked uncomfortably like a repetition of pre-war expansionism, and they feared the same consequences. A belief in the imminence of a Third World War was widely held, made more terrifying (to both Left and Right) by the atomic bomb.

Yet on the issue of rearmament, and more especially on the impact of increased arms spending on domestic policy, the Labour Party was far from united. Dalton's diary provides a unique account of the clashes of personality

469

and the divisions over socialism and foreign policy that led Bevan and two other ministers, Harold Wilson and John Freeman, to resign from the Government in April 1951. The immediate issue was the decision of the Chancellor to introduce charges for false teeth and glasses, a step seen by Bevan as an attack on the principle of a free health service. In the background were the conflicts over arms spending and foreign policy, and the sense of a coming struggle for control as soon as the veterans passed on.

Meanwhile, the Labour Left was on the march in the constituencies, where individual membership had almost doubled in five years. One by one, places on the N.E.C. constituency section fell to left-wingers: Michael Foot in 1948, Tom Driberg in 1949, Ian Mikardo in 1950, Barbara Castle in 1951. For the moment, Dalton held his seat – along with two other representatives of the old guard, Morrison and Griffiths. But the writing was on the wall.

In Cabinet, Dalton had already adjusted to a secondary position. As Minister of Town and Country Planning and then as Minister of Local Government and Planning, he was no longer in the main political firing line. Yet he retained more influence in Cabinet than these middle-ranking jobs in themselves provided. Attlee listened to him, and so did Gaitskell. With one of his protégés, Freeman, among the rebels, he sought to keep (as one Party official put it) 'a cloven hoof in both camps'. Though personally on Gaitskell's side, he was concerned to hold the Party together, and the diary records his anxious attempts to restore peace between the factions.

Saturday 25th February
Back from Bishop Auckland for breakfast at flat, with my good majority but very weary.[1] Cabinet at 11. Attlee says we should carry on, since we have a majority, even though a bare half dozen in new House. All present agree – Bevan, Tom Williams and Woodburn only absentees. Bevan seems to have been kept away by diarrhoea! Most think – and I most emphatically – that this Parliament can't last more than a few months. But Bevin thinks we should stay in and 'consolidate', and Phil [Noel-Baker] suggests playing of Liberals and carrying

---

1 Despite apparently adverse boundary changes, and the national swing against Labour, the result in Bishop Auckland was Dalton's best ever in a parliamentary contest. He received 25,039 votes, with a majority of 11,370 over his Conservative opponent (Lord Lambton), the Liberal losing his deposit.

470

on till May 1951! Cripps says cost of living is bound to rise and Budgetary position is very difficult. We all place our offices at P.M.'s disposal, following custom after an election. Creech Jones, only defeated Cabinet Minister, made a great fight at Shipley, ruined by redistribution, and only lost by 81. Wilson only got in by 824 at Huyton, and says R.C.s swung violently against him in last three days.

Return to flat and sleep. (But I caught no cold and kept my voice, and took no lozenge, and only four strychnine tablets all through the campaign!)

Sunday 26th February
Sleep again, nearly all day.

Make note on situation, which seems very gloomy. Worst possible situation. If we had lost 10 seats more, Tories would have had bare majority, and would have had to form a powerless government; if we had lost 10 seats less we would have had a majority between 20 and 30 and could have scraped along for a bit. As it is, we have office without authority or power, and it is difficult to see how we can improve our position. So strong in mining and industrial centres and in big cities, and yet so weak in House of Commons. The rural areas, with few exceptions, very disappointing.

Unless we can create some new issue, favourable to ourselves, every week we stay in office (without authority and without a working majority, and with events moving against us – prices, cost of living, unpopular Budget etc.) we lose ground. Therefore we should either dissolve as soon as possible, or put the Tories in, letting them beat us on the Address, e.g. on steel. Some of our colleagues are still living in a world of illusion – as though the Opposition didn't exist, or had no brains.

Monday 27th February
To the office. P.M. is reconstructing Government, but not very fast. I get a call for 10 p.m. He says we need a big drive on housing. Will I undertake this, along with Town and Country Planning? Housing will be taken out of Ministry of Health, where Nye will stay 'to clear up the mess he has made' over the Health Service. I agree, on condition I retain my present place in the Hierarchy, and get a decent allowance of money and materials. We then talk a bit about people. He is indignant with Silkin for not getting himself adopted anywhere, and says he won't send him to the Lords or, of course, keep him in the Government. He then adds, rather fiercely, 'And I can't do anything

for Creech.' The only defeated minister he is keeping is Soskice.[1] Solicitor-General needn't be in the House, but he hopes to get him back soon. He is thinking – in reply to question by me – of Griffiths for Colonies and Stokes ('We are taking a risk') for Works. He is giving Shinwell Defence. I raise my eyebrows at this, but he says, 'He has done very well at the War Office.' I say he is the one colleague I can't work with. Nye, he thinks, has lost us more votes than any other minister, by his vermin speech[2] and by his statement, during the election, that the middle classes don't really need domestic servants, they only want to be able to order someone about. He suggests Lindgren as my Under-Secretary; he has had useful local government experience. I make no objection, but am not wildly enthusiastic. And so to bed! Ruth is very surprised, and so am I, but not dissatisfied.

Tuesday 28th February
To the office, and write note to P.M. suggesting that he should put Jim Griffiths at Health and Nye at Colonies. I send this off just before 11 a.m. and go to Cabinet offices for King's Speech Committee. On arrival I get a message to go at once to No. 10. Attlee says that he has come to the conclusion that to take Housing out of Health at present would be too big a surgical operation. He, therefore, would like me to take the Colonies. I at once refuse. 'That is not my Kingdom,' I say. 'I have never studied Colonial questions. I would much prefer the Home Front.' (I had a horrid vision of pullulating, poverty stricken, diseased nigger communities, for whom one can do nothing in the short run, and who, the more one tries to help them, are querulous and ungrateful; of Malaya and a futile military campaign; of white settlers, reactionary and as troublesome in their own way as the niggers; of ineffective action at a distance, through telegrams to and from Governors, whom one has never seen; of all the silliness and emotion about the black man who married a white typist,[3] and Dr

1 Sir Frank Soskice, later Baron Stow Hill (1902–78). Solicitor-General 1945–51. Labour M.P. for Birkenhead East 1945–50; Sheffield Neepsend 1950–55; Newport 1956–66. Attorney-General 1951. Home Secretary 1964–5; Lord Privy Seal 1965–6. Having lost his seat in the general election, Soskice returned to the House following a by-election in April 1950.
2 There had been an outcry in the press when Bevan told a Manchester audience in July 1949 of his 'burning hatred' for the Tory Party, adding, 'So far as I am concerned, they are lower than vermin.'
3 The succession of Seretse Khama (1921–80), later Sir Seretse, to the Chieftainship of the Bamangwato tribe in the Bechuanaland Protectorate, had been blocked because of Seretse's marriage in 1948 to a British secretary, Ruth Williams. Pressure from the Regent (his uncle) and from the South African government led to a judicial inquiry, and early in February 1950 Seretse was forced into exile in England. Later he returned and became President of the Republic of Botswana.

Malan,[1] and the demand for the Protectorates; of friction over Trusteeship at U.N.O.; of irritating personal relationships with Ernie, and Phil [Noel-Baker][2] and Shinwell; of continuing difficulties over groundnuts;[3] of Parliamentary questions by pro-native cranks and anti-native capitalists – all this in a rush of a few seconds.) P.M. was a bit surprised and taken aback. Then he said, 'Of course you could be Minister for Town and Country Planning right away and perhaps we could bring Housing in later.' I said I would much prefer this, provided my place in the Hierarchy was maintained, and made clear. And he agreed to this. He had had my note just before I arrived. Clearly he wasn't willing to give Nye the Colonies, and Nye wasn't willing to give up Housing if he stayed in Health. Later, in the evening, Helsby[4] read over a formula, for publication, to the effect that I should combine departmental duties with the general responsibility of a senior minister of the Government. I agreed to this. He said that, in fact, I had moved up in the Hierarchy to 5th place – Attlee, Morrison, Bevin, Cripps and then I. ...

I am quite content, with these public explanations, to have a light departmental assignment – including National Parks, New Towns and the job of speeding up and simplifying Planning Procedures.

Morrison thought I had been very foolish in not taking Colonies. 'That Department wants shaking up,' he said. Well let someone else shake that one!

'Mr Dalton ... will hardly find his departmental duties onerous', commented the *Manchester Guardian* when Dalton's appointment as Minister of Town and Country Planning was announced. But Dalton was perfectly happy with his limited responsibility. He now assumed the role of energetic elder statesman: more interested in the activities of other people's ministries than of his

1 Dr D. F. Malan (1874–1959). South African Prime Minister and Minister for External Affairs 1948–54.
2 Philip Noel-Baker, q.v., had been Secretary of State for Commonwealth Relations 1947–50.
3 ' ... difficulties over groundnuts'. In 1947 John Strachey, as Minister of Food, had pressed ahead with a scheme for clearing more than three million acres in East Africa in order to produce 600,000 tons of groundnuts by 1951, thereby saving £10 million from Britain's food bill. However, technical problems and bad weather turned the project into a financial disaster. £37 million of public money was lost, and the scheme became a symbol in the Tory press for socialist incompetence. It was finally abandoned by Strachey's successor, Maurice Webb, late in 1950.
4 Laurence Helsby, q.v., Attlee's private secretary.

own. Meanwhile he scored one important victory. Following his advice to Attlee before the election, the Prime Minister made Gaitskell Minister of State for Economic Affairs, with a place on the key Economic Policy Committee.

Sunday 11th June

Our three week Whitsun recess ends tomorrow. It has been a week longer than usual, and no Labour Party Conference. I had three useful days in the constituency ...

(... The political prospect remains very bleak, and I can't see us doing much good in this Parliament or winning seats net at another election. Last night I dreamed that we had an election and that I lost Bishop Auckland! We are all stale and uninspired and uninventive.)

Following the constituency visit, I walked for three days in the Cheviots, lovely country, with long green shepherds' tracks, and most friendly shepherds with large families, loving the country and large flocks of sheep. We walked from Wooler to Yetholm, and from there to Alwinton, and thence, with a lift at the end, to Cambo, to stay the night with the Trevelyans. Charles, aged eighty-one, is bent, but very friendly and effusive. I look at Lake Hunt[1] photos. I was there in 1911, 1912 and 1913, and in each of the first two years caught George Trevelyan[2] – a great honour – and appear in two photos as a smooth-faced young man with hair smoothly parted in the middle. Our walking party was Arthur Blenkinsop, Geoffrey de Freitas, George Chetwynd, Barbara Castle, Fred Willey, John Philipson (local) and myself, with several pressmen and photographers. Still pretty good publicity. We walked fifty miles in three days, in addition to miles by car. Weather perfect. I had a very sore little right toe at the end, but all else sound, though I blew like a grampus going up hill with a pack on. But I raced ahead on level, or slight downward, slopes. Very good spirit!

In these four days, before being confined to Westminster Barracks, I've visited four more New Towns – Stevenage, Harlow, Hemel Hempstead and Crawley. Very encouraging, especially Harlow and Crawley. We shall have something to show in 1951 Festival Year.

Dalton's departmental duties were sufficiently light to enable him to take the job of leading the Labour delegation at the second meeting of the Euro-

1 See entry for 24th May 1928, p. 44, and note 1.
2 G. M. Trevelyan (1876–1962). Historian.

pean Assembly in Strasburg in August 1950. Before then, Dalton had helped to prepare a Labour Party policy statement on the Schuman Plan – the French proposal for the pooling of French and German coal and steel production under a joint authority. The federalist features of this Plan pleased neither the Labour Party nor Dalton, chairman of the N.E.C. International Committee. As Secretary of the Committee, Denis Healey prepared the first draft of a Labour Party pamphlet on the subject, called *European Unity*. When Dalton launched a modified form of this document at a press conference on 12th June, his strident anti-Europeanism caused a storm. The episode has sometimes been taken as the beginning of Labour opposition to closer European ties.

Thursday 15th June
Today P.M. was asked more questions in the House, and was forced into a statement that timing of publication was unfortunate. He refused, flushed and embarrassed, to say whether he had read it or not before publication. This was all thought by some of our boys to be very weak. I understand that he was being heavily pressed by Americans to repudiate the document!

I spoke to Ernest Davies[1] who said Bevin was quite happy about it all. He repeated that he had initialled and approved our final draft.

George Chetwynd, Fred Peart,[2] and others told me that 99 per cent of the Party thought the statement very good, and the P.M.'s line very weak. As to 'timing', *when* would it have been well timed? We couldn't have published it later. If we had published it a few days later, it would have been called a stab in the back for the P.M.

Friday 16th June
There has been a great fuss these last four days over 'European Unity'. It was on 24th May that the National Executive considered, and unanimously approved, and ordered to be published, as soon as possible, this pamphlet.

This statement had been on the stocks for some time. Bevin had several times asked me to get 'the Labour Party' i.e. the National Executive, to get a statement out. It would help him, he said, and

1 E. A. J. Davies (b. 1902). Parliamentary Under-Secretary at the Foreign Office 1950–51. Labour M.P. for Enfield East 1950–59; Enfield 1945–50.
2 Frederick Peart, later Baron (b. 1914). Labour M.P. for Workington 1945–76. Minister of Agriculture, Fisheries and Food 1964–8, 1974–6; Lord Privy Seal 1968; Lord President of the Council and Leader of the House of Commons 1968–70. Lord Privy Seal and Leader of the House of Lords 1976–9.

would be useful for Strasburg and for the education of public opinion. The Cabinet had several times agreed that this country could not lose control over its own Budgetary and financial policy, or over controls necessary for our planned economy. I had told Bevin in Cabinet that the N.E.C. would certainly take the same line. I had, indeed, put it on paper last autumn in a paper sent to General Affairs Committee of Council of Europe in my name, and that of Callaghan[1] and others. Bevin had seen this and expressed agreement with it. Before this the N.E. had approved the line of a draft by Healey, but had thought the presentation might be softened. This I had done in the later paper. The first draft of 'European Unity' was prepared by Healey for the International Sub-Committee. It was then modified a good deal and a second draft put up. The latter included several paragraphs on European Basic Industries, since the 'Schuman Plan' had been first launched on the world in the interval between the two drafts. I should add that Ernest Davies had sent Transport House a note, approved by Bevin, whose draft was being prepared, much stiffer and less compromising in language than anything put in the draft. I told Healey to keep in touch with the Foreign Office and I kept in touch with Davies during all this and later drafting.

Re-draft was passed by International Sub (with paragraphs on Basic Industries) with practical unanimity, and was ready for N.E.C. Bevin saw this re-draft and initialled it. He told Davies he approved it. He made no suggestions for amendment.

This re-draft was sent to *all* members of N.E.C. with other papers, as usual, some days before meeting on 24th May. At meeting on this day I presented the document. I expounded it for about ¼ hour, bringing out all salient points. I have a copy of note from which I spoke. Sam Watson and Morgan Phillips were away. Alice Bacon took the chair. All Ministers on Executive were present. Attlee, as usual, sat beside me. Morrison was there, and Bevan (the only other Cabinet Minister on International Sub) and Shinwell, and Griffiths and Summerskill[2] and Margaret Herbison. The document was unanimously approved, after a short discussion. Only suggestion made by Attlee was that a sentence should be added, after quote from Tory programme on horticulture imports, saying that he too has horticul-

---

1 James Callaghan, q.v., had been a delegate (as substitute for Morrison) to the first meeting of the Consultative Assembly at Strasburg in August 1949. He attended the second meeting in August 1950 as deputy leader of the delegation.
2 Edith Summerskill, later Baroness (1901–80). Minister of National Insurance 1950–51. Labour M.P. for Fulham West 1938–55; Warrington 1955–61. Junior minister 1945–50.

ture at heart. (This I put in.) This was practically the only amendment suggested.

I was surprised that it went through so quickly and easily. The N.E.C. then decided that it should be published as soon as possible.

This became a routine job for Transport House, and they found that it could be published on Tuesday 13th June, but not before. I was asked by Transport House (Morgan Phillips and Denis Healey) to take a press conference on it on Monday 12th June, and agreed. Parliament was to meet, after Whitsun recess, on 13th, and there were stories in the press that Attlee was to make a statement on that day on the Schuman Plan. But ministers had been scattered during recess. There had only been one Cabinet, on unimportant business, which very few had attended, and this was the Cabinet on Monday 12th. I was in London all the weekend, but had no communication from P.M. or any other minister. Nor did I particularly expect one. I, therefore, took the Press Conference on the Monday afternoon. I was anxious not to hit the headlines with any phrases of my own, and therefore concentrated on expounding the document itself, with a good deal of quotation. This meant that I was very unresponsive to questions, and refused, in particular, to say that, if there were more socialist governments in Europe, we should be more willing to enter into closer arrangements.

On Tuesday morning, 13th June, the Report did, indeed, hit the headlines! Many, of course, were sensational and inaccurate. But *The Times* had a pretty good leader.

Arriving at the office soon after 10, I had a message that the P.M. wanted to see me. I went to No. 10 and found him in a bit of a fuss. 'I don't remember ever seeing this before' he said, of the pamphlet. I reminded him that he had sat next to me at N.E.C. when it was passed, and of his horticultural comment. He then queried whether the paragraphs on basic industries were in. I explained that they were, and reminded him that Shinwell had asked whether we had taken account in this draft of Harry Douglass's[1] views. He then seemed to accept – and indeed he could do no other – the fact that he had seen, and agreed, it all before!

He then said it was very embarrassing to have it published that morning, when we had to make a statement that afternoon on the Schuman Plan. This was the first I had heard officially of any such statement. He showed me a draft. It was, I thought, rather flat. And

---

1 Harry Douglass, later Baron (1902–77). Assistant General Secretary of the Iron and Steel Trades' Confederation. General Secretary 1953–67. President of the International Metalworkers' Federation 1950–59. Member of Labour Party N.E.C. 1948–53.

we still seemed to [be] living in a world of make-believe, not stating clearly that we could not hand over our key industries to any supernational authority. He said Cripps had been very upset by it. He, therefore, summoned the latter, and Morrison, and Addison [was] also there, equally bothered because of what he might have to say to the Lords.

The discussion which followed was quite friendly. Morrison admitted formally his share of responsibility, but said he hadn't read the paper carefully – he had so many papers to read and, as this seemed to be about Strasburg questions, he had left it to me. Cripps said that it would make his job very difficult in future negotiations. He didn't disagree with the general line, but, if he had seen the draft, he could have suggested a few amendments, which wouldn't have changed the sense, but would have made it read more acceptably. I told them I had kept in close touch with Bevin and the Foreign Office and they agreed with the line. Cripps said he had always found the Foreign Office difficult from his point of view. I said I was sorry we hadn't shown him these paragraphs. This was the only slip in drafting which I felt had been made.

The afternoon (13th) the P.M. made his statement. Winston and others put a lot of supplementaries. But they didn't press hard on the N.E. statement; they wandered off on to the question of a Parliamentary debate.

I told Morgan Phillips of the point raised by P.M. that morning and he said that P.M. never came near them, or kept in touch with Transport House.

The press that day and the next ran this stunt very hard. It was suggested that neither P.M. nor Foreign Secretary had seen the document, or agreed to its publication.

A conference of European Socialist leaders opened in London on 16th June. Guy Mollet was the only representative from France, where socialist politicians were, according to Dalton, 'being a bit schoolgirlish' about the Labour Party pamphlet.[1]

Sunday 18th June
A morning talk at the Conference on general question of 'the authority'

1 Diary, 16th June 1950.

to run basic industries. Mollet[1] and van der Goes[2] again were alone. The rest were with us. We gave them lunch at St Ermin's and I had a talk afterwards with Morgan Phillips. He spoke to Bevin and so did I later, on the telephone. Bevin wanted to be assured that our declaration didn't commit us to a super-national authority. He was satisfied it didn't, though he would have liked a declaration definitely *against* such an authority. But he understood that the French and Dutch would not have agreed to this. He sounded very sleepy, and said he would like to see me tomorrow. Phillips very hot against Attlee for having no relationship with Transport House. [Attlee] had sent Moyle to see Phillips with a message about publications and conferences – which Phillips much resented. And he had fixed the Neepsend by-election[3] – and had tried to fix one at Leicester in July! – without any consultation either with Phillips or Windle. Phillips had put the Leicester one off till September.[4]

Monday 19th June
Saw Attlee after Cabinet and Bevin in London Clinic after lunch. Both very serene. Attlee says press has been monstrous and I need not worry. Bevin is only concerned not to hand over our industries and defence to a supranational body. We should attack Tories on this.

The Labour Government remained cautious about moves aimed at greater European Unity. In the debate in the Commons on 26th June, Cripps declared that political federation was not compatible with Britain's position as a Commonwealth, Atlantic and world power. 'Both Bevin and Cripps were as strongly anti-Federal as I was', Dalton claimed later. 'We were determined not to allow interference by a European Committee with our full employment policy, our social services, our nationalised industries or our national planning.'[5]

---

1 G. A. Mollet (1905–75). Minister of State in the Pleven Cabinet 1950–51, with responsibility for the Council of Europe. Socialist. Delegate to the Consultative Assembly of the Council of Europe 1949–56. Prime Minister of France 1956–7.
2 Marinns van der Goes van Naters (b. 1900). Dutch socialist politician and writer. Vice-Chairman of the Assembly of the Council of Europe.
3 Harry Morris, 1st Baron (1893–1954), Labour M.P. for Sheffield Neepsend February–March 1950, Sheffield Central 1945–50, was given a peerage in March 1950, thereby providing a seat for Sir Frank Soskice, q.v., who was duly elected at a by-election a few weeks later.
4 The Leicester North-East by-election (caused by the appointment of the Labour M.P. Sir Terence Donovan to the Bench) took place in September 1950, with Lynn Ungoed-Thomas as successful Labour candidate.
5 HTA, pp. 334–5.

Sunday 25th June

Tomorrow and next day we have debate in House on motion on
Government attitude to Schuman Plan. Our majority may be very
narrow, or even negative! We seem, as usual, to have a lot of sick.[1]
I have been heavily attacked in evening press for my share of responsibility for *European Unity* and shall no doubt be attacked again in the
debate. It is irritating not to be able to reply. But for the moment it
is clearly impossible for me to say anything publicly. I think I have
very solid support in the Party, and some sympathy on the ground that
some colleagues, especially P.M., seem to be trying to evade their
share of responsibility. Some clever commentators seem to think I
have been deliberately playing for such a strengthening of my personal
position. How wrong they are!

Should we not speak the truth as we see it?

I feel sometimes in these days as though I was living again through
the thirties. Who would speak out – on Hitler, rearmament, no air
force, etc. Who would hush it all up and muffle all the bells? Today
there is a mush of sentimental ambiguities over 'European Unity'. Our
European Unity has tried to clear some of this up – as usual *Tribune*
this week is very good – 'The Row about the Pamphlet'. But I am a bit
weary of it all. Release from responsibility sounds very attractive. We
have all been too long in office.

On 25th June 1950 North Korean troops invaded the South. The United
Nations (in the absence of the Soviet delegation) promptly condemned an
attack which many in the West saw as a curtain-raiser for a Russian attack
in Europe. The American decision to intervene (under a cloak of U.N.
respectability) received full British support. The war soon escalated, involving the mainland Chinese. Meanwhile the European political and economic situation was transformed in unexpected ways. There was a 'Korean
war boom' in the European economy; pressures for greater European co-
operation, especially in defence, were reinforced; and the British government
felt compelled to divert resources to armaments, at the expense of the social
services.

Thursday 3rd August

The war in Korea has begun to upset people. The fear of a Third
World War is becoming very real and widespread. But there is no

1 i.e. the Parliamentary Party had a lot of members on the sick list, thereby making
the Government vulnerable.

challenge to our policy of supporting the U.S., under the U.N. banner, in Korea. The Tories are critical about defence, but haven't any important new suggestions. Shinwell is doing very much better than I expected. And my personal relations with him are almost cordial! We say 'good morning' at the opening of Cabinet, and sit next to each other – this is quite new! –

Always something breaks the Peace of Summer. This year Korea! It is disconcerting that the North Koreans are so well equipped, and fight so effectively against the Yanks. ...

Attlee entertained Menzies[1] at dinner last month at No. 10, with Tory and Liberal leaders present. Menzies picked me out for reminiscences. I related the story of the dinner at the Athenaeum Club in Melbourne[2] when, at the end, he said, 'You're a most extraordinary phenomenon, a Socialist with wit', and I replied, 'You're a more extraordinary phenomenon still, a Conservative with intelligence.' I had swept through Melbourne, he said, like a tornado (he had been hired, yes literally hired, to entertain me) ...

When the ladies left, I was next to Winston. After a few exchanges about Strasburg, I challenged him on his story about my first Budget and Keynes, and 'Hate'. 'But you *do* hate, don't you?' he said. 'They say it's because you were unhappy at school. But I was very unhappy at school and I don't hate. And remember the rich are very useful, so long as you let them be rich, as revenue raisers.' I said I had been very happy in my last year at Eton. I had been captain of my House. I enjoyed it very much. (I didn't tell him Winterton's story, re R. Clarke,[3] nor that I had been a Tory democrat, with pictures of Joe Chamberlain on my walls in my first term at Cambridge. But this is only a Tory story to account for my position!)

Dalton's team at the second Annual Meeting of the Consultative Assembly

1 R. G. Menzies, later Sir Robert (1874–1978). Prime Minister of Australia 1939–41, 1949–66. Minister for Co-ordination of Defence 1939–41; Information and Munitions 1940. Minister for External Affairs 1960–61.
2 During Dalton's trip to Australia and New Zealand in 1937–8.
3 'Winterton's story, re R. Clarke'. See CBY, p. 18: ' ... I was reminded, more than forty years [after leaving Eton], by Lord Winterton, when he was Father of the House of Commons and I was a Cabinet Minister, of an occasion when, as Captain of my House, I beat the whole House, below the top four, because no one would own up to having scribbled some objectionable remarks on the wall of the lavatory. One of my victims on that occasion was, at this later date, a most blameless-looking Tory M.P. who had related this incident to Winterton.' If this was the story to which Dalton referred, the 'blameless-looking Tory' may have been Col. R. S. Clarke, later Sir Ralph (1892–1970).

at Strasburg in August 1950 included Callaghan, Crosland and (as economic adviser) Healey. For Dalton, the highlight of the visit was off duty. He recalled later: 'On 14th August, I led an expedition to Le Donon in the Vosges. I took with me Jim Callaghan, Tony Crosland and Denis Healey, three of the youngest, most intelligent, most amusing and most physically fit of my team … it had been a wonderful trip, which I shall long remember, in most agreeable company, seasoned with wit and wisdom, walking and wine.'[1]

13 'Your Winston Calls You', 16th August 1950

Saturday 2nd September

I am alone in the flat this weekend, writing up Strasburg and writing letters – to Bob Fraser, with whom I dined last night, and with whom my friendship, though I see him seldom, stays steady and firm and

1 HTA, pp. 330–3.

warm, as of old, with quick understanding on both sides (his little Rosalind is much stronger now) – to Nicholas Davenport, proposing to discuss with him which New Town he would like to be on – to Hugh Gaitskell, now out of town, about Full Employment at Strasburg and Service pay, etc., ending:

'And opportunity is carrying *you* forward on a great wave, and your future is taking on, more and more, the inevitable shape – subject to all mortal chances – that we spoke of, and that I spoke to the P.M. of, just before you took your present title. Good luck always!'[1]

I am feeling rather emotional, through these solitary days, about all my friends and particularly my young friends in the Party. What does the future hold for them? Death and terror and pain on a vast scale, or the opportunity to go on building that better world, and that Better Britain on which we have been labouring, with some substantial success, since 1945? I have never wanted, as some of my friends know, to be Prime Minister, but I enjoyed leading our team at Strasburg and, thinking of some of them, and of millions more in our Movement, I remember Arthur Cook's prayer 'God, make me worthy of the men I lead!' Someone said, 'As we grow older, we live more and more in the lives of others, and especially of the young.' Many will come up in politics. There's plenty of room near the top of the hill, though keen competition to get there. A very competitive profession is that of the politician.

I saw Bevin this morning. He is very quiet and has lost some weight, but has his wits about him. 'Neither I nor Churchill can last much longer,' he says. He has been working very hard on our relations with China, not believing at all that China is a Russian satellite. He has been in touch with Nehru,[2] and using his Ambassador in Peking, as well as our own, to assure them that we don't want to attack them or to deny them Formosa when the Korean trouble is over. He heard, through our own channels, two days beforehand of MacArthur's message to veterans about holding Formosa,[3] and sent Franks to

1 Dalton had repeatedly urged Attlee to consider Gaitskell for the succession to Cripps, who was now seriously ill.
2 S. J. Nehru (1889–1964). Indian Prime Minister and Minister for External Affairs 1947–64. President of the Indian National Congress.
3 For some time General MacArthur, commander of the U.N. force in Korea, had opposed the State Department's relatively cautious attitude towards the nationalist Chinese. On 28th August a message from the General was read to the Veterans of Foreign Wars, suggesting that Formosa (which Chiang Kai-shek still controlled) was essential to the American defensive system in the Far East: the fulcrum of an American island chain ringing the Asian mainland. 'If we hold this line we may have peace', he declared, ' – lose it and war is inevitable.' The message openly defied State Department policy, and Truman ordered its withdrawal – too late.

warn Acheson[1] and have it repudiated even if he couldn't prevent its delivery. He has communicated very frankly with Acheson about Formosa and at first got a very rude reply. But he came back with a long and argued letter about the awakening and resurgence of Asia, and on how fatal it would be for the future to antagonise the new China or to ignore the feeling of the new India. He told Franks to go and have, not one talk, but a series of talks on these lines at the State Department and he thinks he is having an effect. He wants, if the Cabinet agrees, to vote straight out at the start of the U.N. Assembly in favour of admitting the new Chinese government, even though this means voting publicly against U.S. He hopes there will be a landing soon, in force, on the East Coast of Korea, opposite Seoul, to cut the lines of the North Koreans ...

Ernie doesn't trust Lew Douglas any more. He thinks he sees too much of Churchill and tells him too much.

Friday 8th September
West Leaze
Ruth came yesterday. I have been rather lonely since my return from Strasburg, though I have done some simple manual work here, which is always a diversion of the mind.

But the state of the world is horrifying. Did an Arms Race ever stop a war? We have no choice, however, but to arm, and to join others in arming now. Maybe Russian atom bombs will make an end of us, or most of us, within a few years. I think much of the younger people, those I know and am fond of, and the young in the mass, in this country and in others, especially in Scandinavia and France and Australia and New Zealand and Canada.

Monday 11th September
Last week at West Leaze, Ruth and I discussed our Wills and other arrangements in the event of our deaths. When one is young, making a Will is an easy gesture, and Death is a romantic and remote idea. At sixty-three years old, and she at sixty, it is a closer and less romantic thing. 'To die will be an awfully big adventure', said Peter Pan. But now I reconstruct Arthur Symons's[2] poem 'It may be when this City of the Nine Gates'. We agree to streamline our Wills. I leave all to her and all, if she dies first, to the National Trust – subject to King's

1 Dean Acheson (1893–1971). U.S. Secretary of State 1949–53. Chairman of N.A.T.O. 1949–50. Adviser on foreign policy to Presidents Kennedy and Johnson.
2 Arthur Symons (1865–1945). Poet and literary critic.

having Rupert [Brooke]'s letters to me, and Georgie the Royal Letters, which my mother left to me. ...

I will ask [to be literary executors] Bob Fraser and, at Ruth's suggestion, Tony Crosland, whom she had hardly met but of whom I have spoken much. And she likes him for having written in defence of my term as Chancellor in the *Tribune*. Bob is forty-five and Tony thirty-two; so the age spread is about right. Bob was one of my favourite pupils at L.S.E. in the late twenties, and knows a lot about me and my life, both private and public, long before Tony became politically conscious. ...

Today Hugh Gaitskell and I lunched together. Cripps is resting in the country and is seeing no papers at all. Gaitskell, very fully, is acting Chancellor of the Exchequer. He thinks Cripps is a bit hypochondriac about his health. 'And he has such queer doctors.' Gaitskell says his own health is very good.

He is glad that Wilson Smith is soon leaving the Civil Service. He has been obstinate, resistant and almost disloyal. Plowden ... said he was no bloody good. Leslie Rowan[1] is to return from Washington to take his place. 'A bit too pi for me. School prefect type. Captained England at Hockey, etc.' But said to be very good. I say I think he is.

Gaitskell is going to Washington in October at his own request. He has never been to U.S. U.S. are very difficult about finance of our rearmament. Best would be if they would supply equipment free. This would reduce diversion of our own industry. He thinks some minister will have to take charge of Defence Production. Would I like that? I say No. I am not keen to move from my present Department and I am keeping fitter than some other leading colleagues and over the next years this may be important.

Gaitskell says Nye is absolutely fed up with Ministry of Health. They have the most frightful wrangles on the Cabinet Committee on finance of Health Service. Gaitskell is sure he ought to be moved. What about Ministry of Labour? He thinks Nye would do that very well, and Isaacs[2] isn't much use, but Bevin regards him as his Under-Secretary, and wouldn't like Nye there.

1 Sir Leslie Rowan (1908–72). Economic Minister at the Washington Embassy 1949–51. Assistant, then Principal Private Secretary, to the Prime Minister 1941–7. Permanent Secretary at the Ministry of Economic Affairs 1947. Second Secretary at the Treasury 1947–9, 1951–8.
2 G. A. Isaacs (1883–1979). Minister of Labour and National Service 1945–51. Labour M.P. for Southwark 1950–59; Gravesend 1923–4; Southwark North 1929–31, 1939–50. Minister of Pensions 1951.

I speak of curious situation on National Executive. The rising ministers, including Gaitskell, have no public face at Annual Conference. He agrees that he should do something about this, but can't this year. On Income Tax Royal Commission, Lord Justice Cohen[1] is to be chairman and of economists he proposes Kaldor,[2] Hicks[3] and Barbara Wootton. Not bad! Anyhow none of the really objectionable economists are to be on.

Tuesday 12th September
I ask Tony to be one of my literary executors, with Bob Fraser. He says he would love to be, though he hopes it may never be necessary. I am now very happy with these two, whom I must bring together. Dick Crossman, whom Tony regards as one of the great backbenchers of our time, makes his best defence speech so far. He can hold a House, even at teatime and after high excitements.

On 14th September, G. R. Strauss, the Minister of Supply, informed the Commons of the Government's intention to proceed immediately with the nationalisation of iron and steel. Strauss named the members of the new Iron and Steel Corporation, and stated that it would officially come into being on 1st January 1951. Churchill responded by tabling a motion which charged the Government with seeking to 'divide the nation'. A debate was arranged for 19th September.

Thursday 14th September
Cabinet has to decide whether to make a statement on Iron and Steel Board today, or put it off. John Freeman said to me last night that Strauss and he would both resign if there was more delay. I said I would speak to Nye, so we too could add *our* threats! But he was out of London ... But I said Bevin had always based it on defence, and that in his office he could rally great force. And Attlee said at the end he thought there was no alternative. But Morrison was ratty, though

---

1 Lord Justice L. L. Cohen (1888–1973). Chairman of the Royal Commission on Taxation of Profit and Income, established in January 1951.
2 Nicholas Kaldor, later Baron (1908–86). Fellow of King's College, Cambridge from 1949. Hungarian born. Formerly at the L.S.E. where Dalton knew him as a colleague in the early 1930s. Professor of Economics at Cambridge 1966–75. Special adviser to Chancellors of the Exchequer 1964–8, 1974–6.
3 J. R. Hicks, later Sir John (b. 1904). Official Fellow of Nuffield College, Oxford 1946–52. Former L.S.E. colleague of Dalton. Drummond Professor of Political Economy at Oxford 1952–65.

he didn't fight the decision. So Strauss rode that out. ...

The case to be put at the election, apart from Iron and Steel, is on Tory capacity to carry through rearmament with justice, as regards taxation and social expenditure, without rows with labour, without inflation and without precipitating us into war. 'You can't trust the Tories' in a different setting.

But till Tuesday we are all on the alert, and inclined to put aside hypothetical questions till we know the vote. This impossible Parliament must end some time, and I am not sure whether, if we hang on, we shall do better. But we may, in any case, do badly!

Friday 15th to Sunday 17th September at West Leaze
On Saturday (16th) I had diarrhoea and ate little. On Sunday it seemed all right. That night we travelled back to London and I worked very happily till 1 a.m. on

18th September
and then went to bed. But at 6 a.m. I had a furious bout of diarrhoea and went to the lavatory without a dressing gown. Coming out, I fainted in the passage and fell prone, 'a good weight falling from a good height', and hit myself heavily on the matting ... cutting my face and bruising myself on the jaw and right chest. I lay there groaning for five or ten minutes till Ruth, hearing my groans, came out and got me up – for another squitter and then to bed.

Urwick being away, a pessimistic young Scot called Macrae came to see me. And Hoskin the heart specialist. I said I *must* vote next day on the Steel censure motion of the Tories. Macrae, I heard afterwards, thought I was seriously risking my life. But Hoskin took a brighter view. 'I am a soldier ordered into battle,' I said, 'do you want to persuade me to be a deserter?' George Chetwynd came and fetched me in the car, and I walked weakly to the Chief Whips' room, where Cripps and Mackay also gathered, both invalids. My face was a picture of scars! I voted, being seen by few and very limp, and then went straight, as prearranged, to the Nursing Home at 16 Fitzroy Square, where I went for heart treatment in the spring of last year. We won by six votes!

Evening of Tuesday 19th to evening of Wednesday 27th September
I lay peacefully in bed, sleeping, reading, and receiving visitors – Mike Williams Thompson (twice), who left me his P.R.O. MS[1] to read,

1 Williams Thompson, q.v., published an account of his experiences in Whitehall (*Was I really Necessary? Reminiscences of a Public Relations Officer*, World's Press News Publishing Co., London) in 1951.

John Freeman, Bob Fraser, Maurice Edelman, George Chetwynd, Bill Piercy, Geoffrey de Freitas, Hugh Gaitskell, Douglas Jay and Ruth. Towards the end my brain began to work extremely well, and I wrote a good deal – a bit of memoir on my time at Eton, and a long note on Ian Little's *Critique of Welfare Economics*.[1] This with a coverer, and copies to Tony, I sent off the day after I came home, physically limp, but with my heart, which was racing furiously just after my bump, not well controlled but irregular. Tony wrote me a nice letter from Oxford, hoping I wasn't really ill and reporting on S.W. Regional Conference of last weekend. He is definitely leaving his rooms in Trinity on Saturday and bringing all his things away.[2] He will live in a hotel till Xmas and look round for something more permanent. He won't find life very easy now, without a comfortable base and on an M.P.'s salary. John Freeman, with whom he is great friends now, told me that he wondered whether Tony shouldn't have stayed at Oxford a bit longer as a Socialist don, influencing the young. Who would do it now? Also he thought Tony's speeches in the House sometimes lacked 'gravitas' and that perhaps he ought to be doing something part-time in business. I will speak to him about this, and, if he likes it, speak to Bill Piercy.

The Labour Party Conference was held at Margate during the first week of October. Sam Watson was chairman.

Friday 29th September to Friday 6th October
At Margate. I was very weary all the time. I ought not to have gone so soon, from the physical health point of view, and I was taking on doctor's orders some sedative drugs that further depressed me. I cut out all social events after dinner, and went to bed early. I hated sitting for long hours on the platform (and Jim Callaghan and others said I looked ill and tired) and I didn't like the running social intercourse as much as usual. But it would have looked very bad not to have gone. And I got a good solid vote for the Executive, though I had done nothing much to build it up (as compared e.g. with Morrison, who

---

1 I. M. D. Little (b. 1918). Economist. Fellow of Trinity College, Oxford 1950–52; Nuffield College 1952–76. Professor of Economics of Underdeveloped Countries, Oxford 1971–6. Little's *A Critique of Welfare Economics* was published by the Clarendon Press, Oxford in 1950.
2 Crosland had been elected Labour M.P. for Gloucestershire South in February 1950.

was only just above me). ... [I] had not to speak until the last morning (Friday 6th), when I accepted a resolution in favour of 'European Union' and our policy on the Schuman Plan, etc. It was a great effort making this speech but it went over fairly well – for the last morning – and then I drove wearily back to London, and went to bed for two days.

I helped Tony – and Roy Jenkins – to get in and make speeches which attracted some attention, particularly Tony ... He had a very cool reception, and was at first disappointed. But next day he got a good press and the impression grew that he had made one of the notable speeches of the week.

Wednesday 18th October
Douglas Jay told me tonight that Stafford had resigned. He had got this from Stafford's private secretary. He did not know who his successor would be. I therefore decided to go into action on Hugh Gaitskell's behalf. (I had, as I think is recorded in these notes, pressed strongly on Attlee, I think at beginning of August, that if Stafford couldn't go on no one (ruling myself out) could face this job who was senior to the Young Economists, and that, of these, Hugh was incomparably the best, far ahead of either Harold Wilson or Douglas Jay.) But I must tackle Attlee now, seeming not to know that Stafford has resigned, since it is supposed to be secret till Friday.

Thursday 19th October
I spoke to Attlee just before morning Cabinet and agreed to have a word after Cabinet before lunch. But Cabinet went on too late, and we both had lunch engagements, so I fixed to see him at 3.15, just before 3.30 Economic Policy Committee. Meanwhile colleagues waiting to go in to Cabinet had said how frightfully ill Stafford had looked in the Lobby last night and, as I went out to lunch, Douglas followed me and we drove together in my car, and he told me that Stafford had seen him that morning and told him that Hugh was succeeding him.

So I lunched at the French Embassy with a light heart. At 3.15 I saw Attlee, [and] said how ill I heard Stafford had looked last night. Was it still possible for him to carry on? Attlee said 'No', his doctors wouldn't allow it. I said, as indeed I felt, 'This is a hard blow.' I then reminded him of what I had said previously about Hugh. He said it *was* Hugh. I wrote to Hugh and Stafford and next day went to West Leaze.

Hugh will have a hard time and much jealousy to face.

Friday 20th October

The press has it all. Mostly pretty good reception for Hugh, as well as deserved tributes to Stafford. Several papers make reference to the horrors that were occurring and impending when I was Chancellor and Cripps took over. It was suggested that when he succeeded me, some great and beneficent change of policy immediately took place. In fact, of course, no such change took place. He and I had been, and continued to be, in close agreement on practical issues. His Budget surplus in April 1948 would have followed my ordinary Budget of 1947, and was, in fact, put up to very large dimensions by my autumn Budget of 1947. In that Budget I had wanted also to tax electricity, but couldn't get the Cabinet to agree, and before resigning, I had proposed a substantial cut – I think of £50m, and certainly of £25m – in food subsidies. This was countermanded by the Cabinet, led by Bevin, after Cripps took over, and was replaced by the White Paper on Personal Incomes. Some say Cripps changed my cheap money policy. In fact, by November 1947, the rate of interest had gone up seriously, and I had been too tired that summer and autumn to fight the Bank in favour of intervention. *I* had, in fact, given up that ghost, for the time being at any rate, though I might have split the Transport stock into 3 per cent and 2 per cent short, averaging $2\frac{1}{2}$ per cent. But Cripps did set up, on [combining] Treasury and Economic Affairs, a better scheme of expert and technical advisers than I had.

Monday 30th October

I spoke to Herbert Morrison and Willy Whiteley today about the hold up in the ministerial shuffle. I've heard no more from Attlee since I sent him a note on how Health could be split, and I take most of it into Town and Country Planning, eight days ago. But I've heard from others – including John Freeman – that Nye is being very difficult and behaving very badly and alienating many friends and sympathisers. He was offered Labour, but turned up his nose at it. He wants Colonies, but he couldn't be trusted there (a) not to waste money (b) not to be carried away by his colour prejudice, pro-black and anti-white.

Morrison said he couldn't make out why the P.M. was apparently afraid of him. He ought to tell him to take Labour. Whiteley said that the changes were postponed for the moment; that George Isaacs had told the P.M. some time ago that he'd be willing to go (to the Lords) at any time; that he had told the P.M. that he should say to Nye 'Labour or out', and that then he'd take Labour; if he resigned it wouldn't do anyone but himself much harm. I told them both that John Freeman should be a No. 1 Minister, e.g. at a new Health Service

Ministry, and I told Whiteley that Fred Peart should be the next junior minister.

Thursday 2nd November
Last night Bristol South-East chose, to succeed Stafford, Anthony Wedgwood Benn,[1] aged twenty-five, heir to old Stansgate – in preference to Arthur Creech Jones, for whom Windle had been doing his best, and Muriel Nichol.[2] Voting was 40:11:7. Very decisive!

Tony Crosland told me, in confidence, that he had worked this, by introducing Wedgwood Benn (whom he had known well at Oxford and thought the most impressive undergraduate speaker of his time, and who was very anxious to have a few years in the House of Commons before going to the Lords) to Rev. Mervyn Stockwood,[3] close friend of Stafford, and key man in the Bristol South-East Party. Windle told me, just before going down for the Selection Conference, that he thought he 'had it all salted' for Creech Jones, but that Transport House was sending down three names (– it was always safer to do that they said, and they had said they wanted a young man and a woman as well as Creech Jones); he was sending them Wedgwood Benn as the 'young man'. Tony laughed heartily at this. Obviously he had heard in Bristol that some of them wanted Wedgwood Benn.

Wedgwood Benn obviously swept the Selection Conference; he had since said to Tony, 'From my opening sentence I felt I had them.' And Bristol South-East was not a good place to send a rejected Cabinet Minister, thought, moreover, to be rather Right Wing and uninspiring. For they were a rebel party by tradition – expelled with Cripps in 1939, and again in 1942 when Jennie Lee[4] stood as an independent

1 Anthony Wedgwood Benn (b. 1925). B.B.C. producer. Labour M.P. for Bristol South-East 1950–60, 1963–83; Chesterfield since 1984. Son of 1st Viscount Stansgate (William Wedgwood Benn, q.v.), whose title he successfully disclaimed in 1963. Postmaster-General 1964–6; Minister of Technology 1966–70. Secretary of State for Industry 1974–5; Energy 1975–9.
2 Muriel Nichol, née Wallhead (b. 1893). Labour M.P. for Bradford North 1945–50.
3 Rev. Mervyn Stockwood, later Rt Revd (b. 1913). Vicar at St Matthew, Moorfields, Bristol 1941–55. Vicar at the University Church, Cambridge, 1955–9. Bishop of Southwark 1959–80.
4 Jennie Lee, later Baroness (b. 1904). Labour M.P. for Cannock 1945–70; North Lanark 1929–31. Junior minister 1964–7; Minister for the Arts (Minister of State, Department of Education and Science) 1967–70. Married to Aneurin Bevan. She stood unsuccessfully at a by-election in Bristol Central in February 1943 (not 1942) against the widow of the former M.P. whose death had caused the contest. The N.E.C., concerned to preserve the electoral truce, condemned her candidature, and several local councillors were expelled from the Labour Party for giving active support in the campaign.

socialist against Lady Apsley[1] in Bristol Central under the truce, and workers poured in from Bristol to help her. (It might be added that they had felt very neglected by Cripps latterly, and all but refused to readopt him last time: so they wouldn't be keen on a Cabinet Minister.)

Creech Jones had also been rashly saying a week or so before, that he would be very proud, as an old Bristol boy, to represent this Bristol seat. No doubt it's rough luck on Creech Jones – but he'll have to be fitted in in the final election rush. Dissolution Honours will make a gap or two.

Meanwhile it is fine to get this young man in, and on.

Saturday 4th November
I think we shall be beaten on Monday or Tuesday on the Address – most probably on the vote on the Liberal amendment on cost of living. And I'm afraid there's no doubt that in the ensuing election we shall be beaten rather badly. If we lose 50 seats we shall be in a minority of between 90 and 100. And we may lose more.

When we had our majority of 6 on Steel, Winston said that if only we had kept the University seats, we should have been beaten.

And if I hadn't intervened in Redistribution Debate in favour of additional urban seats – Battersea, Paddington, Hammersmith, East Ham, Reading, and Gateshead and one more in Bristol, Bradford, Leeds, Leicester and the rest – we shouldn't have had that small majority, and the Tories *would*. It's a pity I made that speech. ...

Tony has sent me, after an explosive prod on Thursday, his paper read to the Fabians at Oxford. It is awfully good. I've written him an appreciation and a few criticisms. His writing is very clear, firm, comprehensive and convincing, and touched with humour.

Sunday 5th November
I am in very much improved physical form these last few days. And time too! I can begin to do my fair share of political grind again, including a weekend of speeches in Lancashire next weekend.

But these last few days have been very disturbing. First, the odds seem to be that we shall be beaten in one or other of the amendments to the King's speech tomorrow or Tuesday. We have too many sick and that bloody Driberg is still away, unpaired and unashamed.[2] If we

---

1 Lady Apsley, née Meeking (d. 1966). Conservative M.P. for Bristol Central 1943–5.
2 See entry for 7th November 1950 below, p. 493. Driberg's journalistic trip to the Far East, at a time when other Labour M.P.s were being carried into the Palace of Westminster on stretchers in order to maintain the Government's knife-edge majority, was widely criticised. On 15th November Driberg was censured by the P.L.P. for 'gross neglect of his Parliamentary duties'.

lose one of these divisions, we shall go to the country at a bad time of year and at a bad political moment, and shall lose pretty heavily. Then, barring a war coalition, five years of Tory rule. And a lot of our best young M.P.s will go down in the battle (at the polls, and if war comes, more still in *that*!).

Tuesday 7th November

We have won all three critical divisions on the Address – housing, cost of living and permanent controls + steel and road hauliers. Majorities of 10, 15 and 10! 3 Liberals abstained on their own Cost of Living amendment. I made my first speech in new House winding up against 3rd amendment. I was in pretty good form, and our M.P.s were very pleased. Tories had as many sick as we. Driberg returned in time for *third* only of the three divisions. He has been away in Korea, Japan and Malaya for three months, and dodged the Party Conference at Margate. He should not have been allowed to stand for the E.C. There is great indignation among our M.P.s against him. Many think the whip should be withdrawn from him. He has certainly put the life of the Government in greater danger and has been absent, money making and having an interesting and no doubt enjoyable time, while others have been brought along on stretchers and from hospitals to vote.

Anyhow the Government will go on now for some months at least.

Monday 13th November

Last weekend I made three speeches in Lancashire – Bolton (delegate conference for region), Stretford and Liverpool ...

Alf Booth[1] at Bolton, praising me, said, 'The Right say he's Left Wing, and the Left say he's Right Wing, but I know he's in full flight towards Socialism on both his wings.'

I like that.

Britain had given more active support to the Americans in Korea than any other country (apart from Turkey). Before the end of the year, however, serious divergences between British and American policy had begun to appear: especially over the wisdom of extending United Nations operations to the North Korean frontier with China. On 1st October U.N. troops crossed the 38th Parallel into North Korea. By 24th November they had reached the Yalu River in the far north, and MacArthur launched an offensive 'to end the war'. Two days later the Chinese counter-attacked. By 30th November,

1 Alfred Booth (1893–1965). Labour M.P. for Bolton East 1950–51.

enemy troops had driven a deep wedge between the two main United Nations forces. On the same day, President Truman made comments at a press conference which were taken to mean that MacArthur might be permitted to use the atomic bomb at his discretion. European governments were deeply concerned, and so was European public opinion. After consulting the French, Attlee flew to Washington on 2nd December to urge restraint.

Thursday 30th November

After several bad days' news from Korea, and a general sense that the British point of view isn't sufficiently strongly put at Washington, we are in the second day of the Foreign Affairs debate. Morale of the Parliamentary Party very low. Then, this afternoon, it came over the tape that Truman had said that they were 'actively considering' use of Atom Bomb against Chinese Communists, and that use of weapons rested with Commander in the Field. This had spread consternation among our back-benchers, who began signing round robins in favour of withdrawing our troops from Korea, if A Bomb was dropped.

Nye and I spoke. He said he had told Clem he ought to fly out to U.S. to see Truman. He suggested that he and I should see Morrison about this. I said I didn't like this procedure. I would tackle Attlee direct. So I wrote him a note, and sat on the bench while he read it. We then spoke and he said he would see Ernie, and ran out of the House like a rabbit. At 6.45 Special Cabinet all unanimous that he should go, and *say so tonight*. Ernie full of rigmarole, and tried to stop his saying it tonight, because he didn't have Truman's agreement in time. But we brushed this aside.

Saturday 9th December

The Americans have been beaten by the Chinese in Korea. That is the deep fact that can't be shifted. Attlee's visit to Washington was clearly indispensable at this time, and I hope has done much good. But Europe is very dangerous and *West* Europe very weak, both materially and morally. The Russians, in view of this, and of the Chinese success, may decide that this is the time to strike in Europe or the Middle East. The arming of West Germans by us may be made a pretext, or even the announced intention to arm them. Kaldor sent me a long note by Myrdal[1] urging us not to. And Gladwyn, who has done his best with

1 Gunnar Myrdal (b. 1898). Swedish economist. Executive Secretary of the U.N. Economic Commission for Europe 1947–57. Swedish Minister of Commerce 1945–7. Professor of International Economics, Stockholm University since 1961.

Mr Wu[1] at lunch, puts on record that, unless everything is peacefully settled which looks most unlikely, his estimate is that Russia and her satellites will withdraw from U.N. and, with China, form a new International Organisation, counting at the start more than half the population of the world, and appeal to others, especially Asians, to join. This would be a very powerful magnet to many.

Wednesday 20th December

Saw Attlee tonight on eve of departure for Xmas. We spoke of my letter to him on rearming West Germans. He didn't disagree; indeed he agreed that situation was very dangerous and that Americans were dangerously hysterical and sure that war was coming. (I told him that Jim Callaghan who reads the *Herald Tribune* daily had expressed great concern to me about this.) ... We then spoke of redistribution of functions. (He will move Nye to Labour during the recess.) ...

I pressed John Freeman [for Minister of Health], but Attlee thought that, to maintain balance between Trade Unionists and others, since Isaacs would be leaving, it should be Robens. I agreed that he was very able and promising. Attlee and I both regarded George Brown as Tom Williams's successor, and agreed that it would be a mistake to move him from Agriculture. Tom Steele[2] might be worked in again somewhere, he agreed. But good young Trade Unionists were scarce.

Thursday 21st December

In continuance of yesterday, Jim Callaghan told me that he found many of his party members, particularly the older ones, very unhappy about our present international policy. They didn't want war with Russia, were now not at all sure that we ought to have gone into Korea, were upset by the atrocity stories there, had been still more upset by Truman on the Atom Bomb, thought Attlee hadn't been strong or outspoken enough at Washington, and generally feared that we had become a satellite of U.S.A. and lost our independence and were being dragged into war. For the first time he didn't feel he carried most of the meeting with him. Tony has said just this and more to me about a delegate meeting in his constituency. It's clear that dissatisfaction and concern are growing rather fast in the Party.

1 Wu Hsiu-ch'iian, otherwise Wu Xiuxhuan. Chinese Communist leader. Director of the Department of Soviet and East European Affairs in the new Chinese Republic 1949–52, and leader of a delegation to the United Nations in New York, presenting the Chinese case on the Korean War. Vice-Minister of Foreign Affairs 1951–5.
2 Thomas Steele (1905–79). Labour M.P. for Lanark 1945–50; Dunbartonshire West 1950–70. Junior minister 1946–50.

Attlee said yesterday that he thought Stalin would be very cautious in moving. He would like to see U.S. bogged down in war with China which is also rather a threat to him.

Thursday 4th January 1951

Hugh Gaitskell[1] came to my flat for a drink before dinner. He said he wasn't feeling too overworked; he was waiting for the 'acceleration programme' (arms) and couldn't decide much meanwhile. He had got Jay and Edwards[2] to take over a lot of work and relieve him of many minor decisions. Jay had been unhappy under Stafford, who had never let him decide anything; Edwards was already complaining of over-work – likewise a poor sign. ...

He [Gaitskell] said he despised the Bank and thought the Treasury did too. Cobbold was playing ball, but wasn't clever and often gave wrong advice. Mynors[3] was cleverer, but still disappointing. I said Cobbold had often given me bad advice. Hugh, with a smile, said he knew that.

R.P.M. [Retail Price Maintenance]. I said Harold Wilson was *very* weak and disappointing on all this. I hoped Hugh would back up a bold line in Cabinet. He promised. He said Wilson was weak, ambitious and overworked. The Board of Trade was an even heavier Department than when he and I were there in the war. I said, 'If he's ambitious, why doesn't he try to hit a headline against monopoly?' I said I was encouraging Edwards to be obstinate on Retail Rings.

Redistribution of functions. I told Hugh of my exchange of letters and talk with Attlee.[4] He said he was glad I had said I would take Housing. He was sure this was the right division. He supposed I would press him for more houses. I said no, I'd be content with 200,000 plus any more we can build for the same money – if he can speed up and cut cost. ...

---

1 Later insertion: 'my "ex-secretary and prize protégé" as *Sunday Express* called him a fortnight later'.

2 L. J. Edwards (1904–59). Economic Secretary to the Treasury 1950–51. Labour M.P. for Brighouse and Spenborough 1950–59; Blackburn 1945–50. General Secretary of the Post Office Engineering Union 1938–47. Junior minister 1947–50.

3 H. C. B. Mynors, later Sir Humphrey, 1st Bart (b. 1903). A Director of the Bank of England 1949–54. Deputy Governor 1954–64.

4 It had originally been proposed that Bevan should move from Health to Labour and National Insurance, and that Dalton should take on, in addition to his present responsibilities, the housing and local government functions that had previously come under Health. In discussing these changes with the Prime Minister, Dalton suggested that housing and local government should be dealt with by different ministers. Bridges, however, insisted that they should be kept together, and so Dalton took them both.

Hugh then asked whether I could tolerate having Strauss at Works. He knew I didn't much like him. I said, 'I hate the fellow' and this I would say of very few. A bit surprised at my vehemence, he asked why. I said he was a complete political fraud, a rich Tory pretending to be a Left Wing Socialist. He'd never wanted to nationalise iron and steel, and kept on trying to run away. We had had, more than once, to haul him back by the scruff of the neck, e.g. when he wanted to postpone vesting date by six months 'in case we had to introduce legislation under the Schuman Plan'. No one in Cabinet had backed him on that, not even Morrison or Addison or Jowitt. He had been a most reactionary Committee Chairman on the L.C.C.

And in the war, when Hugh and I were waiting for bombs at M.E.W., ... his wife [Patricia Strauss][1] ... wrote a book about British Labour politicians, in which she spoke of the 'depths of green insincerity' in my eyes. Hugh agreed that this was pretty bad!

I said why not promote Freeman to be Minister of Supply, and make Strauss something in the outer ring – Paymaster-General for instance. He said he didn't think Freeman had quite enough drive.

...

Freeman, I fear, has had a great fall since the first wonderful summer day in the 1945 Parliament. I am very grieved about this. But he's a bloody fool in his own interest, and what can he see in Driberg to justify *so much* public clinging?

Hugh and I agreed that Peart was one of the best of the non-ministers and should be considered for promotion. But Attlee had rather laughed at this, and spoken of his father. Poor Fred! But it's very natural.[2]

But the first step is to move Nye to Labour. Hugh has been pressing Attlee to do this in the Recess. Otherwise it will be too late, with the Tories attacking him again at Health.

---

1 Patricia Strauss wrote: ' ... in spite of his work for the Party, he is not trusted. A Labour M.P., commenting on Dalton's unusually pale eyes, once said, "they have a habit of looking at you intently and conveying unfathomable depths of insincerity." ' (*Bevin and Co. The Leaders of British Labour*, Putnams, New York, 1941.) Jokes about Dalton's eyes 'blazing with insincerity' often appeared in the press, and the phrase was repeated by Shinwell and other enemies.

2 See HTA, pp. 421–2: ' ... Tom Williams pressed hard for [Fred Peart] as Parliamentary Secretary and Whiteley's only reason for objecting was that he disliked Peart's father, who was a stormy petrel on the Durham County Council. If anything was given to the son, he said, it would make the father still more difficult ... '

Thursday 18th January

It is officially announced this morning that I am to be Minister of Local Government and Planning, taking over from Ministry of Health everything except the Health Service. This brings me Housing, Water, Sewerage, Local Authorities' finance and general oversight, Rent Control, and Local Government Reform. ...

Very acceptable and pleased letters of congratulations from a lot of my Young Turks, including Tony [Crosland], Mike [Williams Thompson] and Desmond [Donnelly].[1] There will be a lot of sorting out of officials, etc. to be done between the Departments concerned. Thus begins a new chapter, after long delays and slow negotiations. ...

On Wednesday afternoon, when Nye and I, of course, both knew, we had a short talk. He said he had had a 'tremendous row with Clem' over Gaitskell's appointment as Chancellor. These key positions should go to people who had some standing in the Movement. I said I knew Gaitskell very well, and thought very highly of him, and we went on to other things. Nye said Attlee should have made a lot of other changes, telescoping Health with National Insurance, Transport with Civil Aviation, etc. This would have made it all look more impressive. He heard Ince[2] had no sense of humour; this would make it very difficult for them to get on.

The other changes are dreary. Isaacs, instead of clearing out and going to the Lords, as first intended, takes over Pensions! And Marquand,[3] dullest of them all, takes Health Service. So no new blood comes in at all – not even Robens, because it's felt that he should stay at Fuel and Power. And I fear John Freeman's stock is badly down, because of Driberg. But we've reduced the Cabinet by one, from 18 to 17!

Ernie is being quite good and cautious over China and U.N. The Chiefs of Staff have advised most strongly and clearly against getting into a war with China. But the Americans are naturally upset by their reverses and casualties.

1 Desmond Donnelly (1920–74). Labour M.P. for Pembroke 1950–68. Independent M.P. for same constituency 1968–70. Donnelly won Pembroke from the Liberal incumbent, Gwilym Lloyd George, in 1950. Initially a close associate of Aneurin Bevan, Donnelly broke with the Left over German rearmament.
2 Sir Godfrey Ince (1891–1960). Permanent Secretary at the Ministry of Labour and National Service 1944–56.
3 H. A. Marquand (1901–72). Minister of Health 1951. Labour M.P. for Middlesbrough East 1950–61; Cardiff East 1945–50. Junior minister 1945–8; Minister of Pensions 1948–51.

Sunday 28th January
John Freeman comes for a walk with me from Ashley Gardens to Battersea Park, and back to tea with Ruth. He had been troubled by what I had told him of his backsliding in high favour because of his always being about with Driberg. He had been wondering whether this signified any doubts, at Supply of all Ministries, about his security. I said I was pretty sure it didn't. He said he would be quite willing – and from his constituency point of view would prefer – to go back to the back-benches. Strauss, he admitted, had given him no show at all, not even *one* Parliamentary Question to answer on a Monday during three years. But, very generously, he didn't speak ill of Strauss. ...

Freeman thought Ernie couldn't really go on as Foreign Secretary. Would I like the Foreign Office? I said, quite frankly, No – at this stage. I didn't want soiled bedclothes, and only for an hour. There must soon be either an election – which I was afraid we should lose – or a war. If I had had the Foreign Office since 1945, and had been able to handle a lot of things differently, though maybe not more successfully, it would be, for me, another story. But, at this stage, I preferred the Home Front.

I told Freeman, who asked what I proposed, that I was on the point of proposing to Attlee that, if Bevin couldn't go on, *he* should hold it, with the premiership, till the election. Freeman thought this was probably right. We both agreed that Shawcross wouldn't do, or suit the Movement at all. I said I would put this to Attlee quite strongly.

I like Freeman a lot, and would like to see him climbing. I'll try again at a good moment.

Wednesday 7th February
We win by 10 votes on Iron and Steel, with Liberals against us! A crowning mercy.

I thought we might easily lose, and had been holding everything in suspense, pending tonight. John Freeman wound up very well, and I hope has renewed a little his personal reputation. ...

After the division Winston was heard saying to Lyttelton: 'It looks as though these bastards can stay in as long as they like.'

Tony Wedgwood Benn made a very good maiden speech.

Thursday 8th February
We win again on Meat, by 8 votes, with the Liberals against us. I only hear the last half of Hugh's winding up – and most don't hear that – Tories yelling all the time. This is now normal in every Government

last speaker.[1] And Mr Speaker[2] makes no effort to check it.

After the vote Nye told off Dick Crossman in the Smoke Room, on German Rearmament. 'You never know when you've won ...... ' ...

Later Tony [Crosland] came in, bringing Tony Benn with him, and we had a very lively conversation, with Nye doing most of the talking. Tony kept his end up very well, (a) against Nye on location of steel plants (b) against me on Cambridge. My trouble, he said, was that all the people I admired, and who influenced me, at Cambridge were second rate – Rupert [Brooke], Belloc,[3] Pigou, Goldie [Lowes Dickinson], Moore[4] – and Cannan after. I liked his frankness in saying this – he had had a few drinks – we have, I hope, achieved the Principle of Total Frankness, even when sober. I said I would [not hold] an inquest on his second rate influences, beginning with Cole. He said Rupert came very badly out of the Keynes book.[5] I said Marsh[6] wanted to marry him to an Asquith. He said eagerly, 'Which Asquith? I'm very interested in them.' I said, 'Some old woman of sixty by now.' (Laughter.)[7] He said he was the only person there who'd read my book *With British Guns in Italy*. He said he'd read it at Lord's, during a dull spell of some match. His next door neighbour asked him what he was reading. 'Book by Dalton.' 'What Dalton? Not Devil Dalton?' I said the account of the Retreat [from Caporetto] was good. He said, 'No. Only Fifth Form stuff.' I said Toscanini's climbing Monte Santo was even better.[8] He didn't remember that ...

He asked me, if it wasn't too personal, why at King's I was called 'Daddy Dalton'. I said this name was never used in the vocative;

---

1 *sic.*

2 Douglas Clifton Brown, later 1st Viscount Ruffside (1879–1958). Speaker of the House of Commons 1943–51. Conservative M.P. for Hexham 1918–23, 1924–51.

3 Hilaire Belloc (1870–1953). Poet, satirist and critic. Liberal M.P. 1906–10. Brooke had introduced Dalton to Belloc's work at Cambridge, and Dalton became a keen admirer. After leaving Cambridge, Dalton and a friend founded a 'Belloc Club' in London.

4 G. E. Moore (1873–1958). Cambridge philosopher. His *Principia Ethica* (published in 1903) had a great impact on Dalton's generation at Cambridge.

5 Sir Roy Harrod, *The Life of John Maynard Keynes*, Macmillan, London, 1951.

6 Sir Edward Marsh (1872–1953). Author of a memoir of Brooke which he published in his edition of *The Collected Poems of Rupert Brooke* (John Lane Co., New York) in 1918. Assistant Private Secretary to Asquith (as P.M.) 1915–16. Brooke was a friend of the Asquiths and part of their circle.

7 Probably Lady (Helen) Violet Asquith, later Bonham Carter, later Baroness Asquith (1887–1969).

8 *With British Guns in Italy* (Dalton's account of his war experiences in 1917–18) described how Arturo Toscanini conducted a military band on the summit of Monte Santo after its capture in August 1917.

Rupert and I, e.g., were always straight Christian names. It was a name used in a small circle, including Keynes and Sheppard, because I was very solemn and earnest at that time (see Marsh's quote in the Memoir) about states of mind and socialism. Tony said, 'I'm glad you were earnest some time in your life.'

Friday 9th February
I lunched with Hugh at the Stafford Hotel (everyone seemed to know me; they had all been in S.O.E. etc!). He wanted to talk about Foreign Affairs. He felt we had been drifting apart on this in recent Cabinets. He was very much troubled by anti-Americanism of many. With Strachey it was pathological. After all the Americans were, in the last resort, our friends and the Russians weren't. He had been so much upset by the Cabinet decision on Thursday, 25th January, to tell Gladwyn to vote against the American Resolution at U.N., that he had been to Clem and said he would have to reconsider his position if this was adhered to. He thought that his stand on this had had some effect on Clem, and on the Cabinet revised decision next day. I said I thought that our decision of Thursday had also got Mike Pearson,[1] through Gladwyn, into action. I said I thought Franks put it right in one of his telegrams when he said that 'so long as U.K. and Canada are together against U.S., the situation is under control.' If we lose Canada, it may begin to be dangerous. I thought we must, short of a serious break with U.S., do all we could to put a brake on them, both as regards China and German rearmament. He said how miserable the Indians were, and how they neither would nor could fight. I didn't think, I said, that we were really far apart on all this now.

As to Russia and Germany he was very anxious that we shouldn't make a false deal. He didn't think German unity would be an advantage to us. The Russians would certainly try their hardest to get control of a united Germany and, if unarmed, they could just march into it. We agreed that it was better it should stay divided. I said this was A. J. P. Taylor's[2] view, the best writer on Germany, and the best contributor to the *New Statesman*.

He then asked whether I had said anything to Clem about the possible succession to Ernie. I told him what I had recommended and

1 Lester ('Mike') Pearson (1897–1972). Canadian Secretary for External Affairs 1948–57. Chairman of the N.A.T.O. Council 1951–2. President General of the U.N. Assembly 1952–3. Prime Minister 1963–8.
2 A. J. P. Taylor (b. 1906). Historian and journalist. Fellow and Tutor in Modern History at Magdalen College, Oxford 1938–63. Books published before 1951 included *The Habsburg Monarchy 1815–1918* (1941) and *The Course of German History* (1945).

501

February 1951   THE DALTON POLITICAL DIARY

why. He said he had had [a talk?] with Clem about this. There was no danger of Shawcross. He took a better view of McNeil than I, and a poorer view of Younger. I said Herbert couldn't do it. He wasn't so sure ... But he thought Herbert wouldn't want to lose control of the Party. Two other names, he said, which were being mentioned were Chuter Ede and Jim Griffiths. He had weighed in strongly against both. Chuter Ede was a most over-rated man and a shocking chairman. Griffiths was a timid man. Yes, I said, frightened of his followers. 'There go the people. I am their leader. I must follow them.' I strongly agreed that neither would do. McNeil, I said, was a Scots gawk, who talked too much in Cabinet.

By 22nd January 1951, the U.N. Command in Korea had been driven back to seventy miles below the 38th Parallel – a major humiliation for the United States. There was now strong political pressure in Washington in favour of withdrawal from Europe, and full-scale war in the Far East. To counter this pressure, Truman demanded that in return for maintaining a strong American presence in Europe, European governments must accept immediate rearmament, including the rearmament of West Germany.

In August 1950, the British government had announced an increase in defence spending of £1,100 million over three years. On 29th January 1951, Attlee told the House of Commons that the Cabinet had agreed to a further expansion from a total of £3,600 million to £4,700 million. Strauss and Wilson opposed this decision; Bevan initially gave lukewarm support, and made his commitment public in winding up the defence debate on 15th February. Dalton did not query the need for British rearmament: his main anxiety, and one which grew to an obsession over the next couple of years, was over the proposal for rearming Germany.

Meanwhile, Washington had been urging the United Nations to declare China an aggressor and to impose sanctions, tabling a resolution to this effect on 20th January. After the Americans had accepted a compromise Anglo-Canadian amendment, the British Cabinet agreed that Britain should support a modified American resolution. On 1st February the amended resolution was accepted by 44 to 7.

502

Mid-February 1951

CHINA, GERMAN REARMAMENT, RUSSIA

Over the past few weeks there has been great concern in the Cabinet, the Parliamentary Labour Party, the Labour Party in the country and in the nation at large over these international issues. And Ernie has been ill, and the question of a successor very difficult and debatable (I have advised P.M. to take it himself) and the Government has been in constant danger of defeat in the House, with an electoral defeat to follow.

I have been pretty active in discussions in Cabinet. I have tried to help to put a strong brake on American recklessness in Far East, which might land us in a major war with China; I have argued against German rearmament; and also against evading a Four Power Talk with Russia – and America and France – even though we must have no illusions about its outcome or fall into any traps.

It has been a source of immense confidence to have Gladwyn at Lake Success.[1] His telegrams have been first class, his handling of colleagues most skilful, and his speeches much better than those of most politicians. He is, since some time back, a Television Hero, with a million fans in the U.S.[2]

KOREA AND CHINA

Cabinet wobbles about on this. Very conscious, most of them, of danger of being landed in a major war in China, very vexed with MacArthur. But a few – Morrison and Gaitskell and McNeil particularly – very much afraid of being anti-American. Long arguments as to how we should vote at Lake Success on successive versions of American Resolution 'branding' China as an aggressor, and referring to study of possible sanctions. On 25th January Cabinet were for voting against, but next day, Hugh having told Attlee he might resign

1 Sir Gladwyn Jebb, q.v., was Permanent Representative on the United Nations Security Council 1950–54. The headquarters of the United Nations were at Lake Success, Long Island, New York, until the completion of permanent buildings on Manhattan in 1952.
2 The American media, and especially the rapidly expanding television network, had been taking a close interest in the workings of the Security Council after the Russians assumed the (rotating) presidency in August 1950, followed by the British (represented by Sir Gladwyn Jebb) in September. Lord Gladwyn later recalled that halfway through the Russian presidency, 'I became a sort of popular hero, out-shining most of the film-stars and receiving thousands of letters a week from all over the U.S.A.' (*The Memoirs of Lord Gladwyn*, Weidenfeld & Nicolson, London, 1970, p. 234.)

on this, and Gladwyn no doubt having been very active on telephone
to the Foreign Office and with Mike Pearson (first class chap!) to get
some new conciliation ideas put up, Cabinet retreats and agrees – I
still taking same view as yesterday, and having written to Attlee – to
vote for American Resolution as amended. But Gladwyn, on instructions, makes a *very* good statement on sanctions.[1] Feeling in the
Parliamentary Party on this is disturbed and unhappy.

In September 1950, the three Western foreign ministers, Acheson, Bevin
and Schuman, declared in New York that a German national army was still
undesirable, but the principle of German participation in an international
force should be considered. The French thereupon put forward the 'Pleven
Plan' for a European army with a German contingent. An international
conference met in February 1951 to discuss this proposal, and an interim
report on a European Defence Community (E.D.C.) was issued on 24th
July. Although an E.D.C. treaty was signed in May 1952, opposition from
many quarters ensured that the project would never get off the ground.
British aloofness on the whole question, which the election of a Conservative
Government did not diminish, helped to isolate Britain from moves towards
greater European unity.

GERMAN REARMAMENT

Against this there is increasing feeling in the Cabinet. Nearly all think
that, though 'Principle' can't at present be repudiated, application
should be delayed. At least until after Russian talks – when this could,
as Bevin always intended, be used as a bargaining counter. We are
encouraged by Eisenhower's[2] attitude – he seems to accept delay as
inevitable and wants no 'unwilling recruits' from Germany.

Feeling in the Party is very strong on this – stronger than on China.
Nye and I both encourage this. Morrison complains to me that 'it has
become known' that I am against German Rearmament. I talk

---

1 The amended American resolution had merely deferred sanctions against the
Chinese. Two days after the vote, Jebb emphasised British opposition to sanctions
at any time.
2 Dwight D. Eisenhower (1890–1969). Supreme Commander of N.A.T.O. 1950–52.
Supreme Commander of the Allied Expeditionary Force in Western Europe
1944–5. Chief of Staff of the U.S. Army 1945–8. President of the U.S.A. 1953–61.

frankly to a group of Labour M.P.s who dine together, the 1950 Club, on 1st February.

It looks as though the West Germans will make difficulties enough on their side, with impossible claims for 'equality', etc., to put all off for some time. Strachey is very active on our side, though not always helpfully, behind the scenes. ...

OUR OWN ARMS PROGRAMME

This is being accepted, in its modified but still very impressive form, without much opposition either in Cabinet or Parliamentary Party. China and Germany and Russia take precedence.

Strachey created some sensation by quoting in Cabinet, with Chiefs of Staff present, instruction 'War Possible in 1951, Probable in 1952'. This was half denied by Elliott,[1] but Strachey handed the paper to the P.M. who seemed disconcerted! At Cabinet on 8th February I spoke strongly against German Rearmament – it was decided to tell our people in Washington and also Kirkpatrick to go slow with negotiations, basing ourselves in part on Eisenhower.

Monday 19th February
Met Attlee in passage outside his room. I asked after Ernie. He said he was getting on very well, and would be able to carry on, for a time, at least, as Minister without Portfolio. This was first hint I had had that his retirement from Foreign Office was imminent, though I had, of course, written to Attlee on this hypothesis. I said I still thought Attlee should carry on.[2] He said he really couldn't. It was too much and it would look as though we hadn't got the men. I said it was necessary, in that case, to get someone who could fill the bill. It wasn't anybody's job, as he knew. I said I had heard Chuter Ede's name mentioned, but he would be quite out of his depth. Attlee said he agreed. Chuter Ede wasn't in the running. I said I doubted whether Jim Griffiths would be strong. He was too kind. (I raised these two names following my lunch with Hugh.) Attlee said Griffiths had a first class administrative record at both his Departments.[3] He listened to advice but he took his

---

1 Air Chief Marshal Sir William Elliott (1896–1971). Chief Staff Officer to the Minister of Defence and Deputy Secretary (Military) to the Cabinet 1949–51. Commander-in-Chief of Fighter Command 1947–9.

2 i.e. become Foreign Secretary as well as Prime Minister.

3 James Griffiths, q.v., was Minister of National Insurance 1945–50 and Colonial Secretary 1950–51.

own decisions. It was clear that he was Attlee's favourite. I said I didn't want it myself. (I didn't elaborate, but I had in mind the 'soiled bedclothes for one hour', and I didn't, in spite of my pretty sturdy health, forget that I was taking sleeping pills with a [fibrillating?] heart, and that the pressure of work and worry on a Foreign Secretary is *very* great. I couldn't afford to take on Foreign Office and fall short, physically or mentally.)

Attlee made no comment, but my remark clearly made the rest of the talk – still in the passage! – easier. He said some wanted Shawcross.[1] I declared violently against this; no lawyers at the F.O.! Remember Simon; anyhow the Party and the Movement would react strongly against Shawcross's appointment. He said he agreed; that McNeil was not mature enough, nor Younger; that Phil [Noel-Baker] couldn't possibly do it. I agreed with all this. I said that, of course, there was Herbert, but I thought Griffiths would be better. He said it was important to have a Trade Unionist. We couldn't give all the key posts to the middle class. He asked me to think it over and have another word with him.

Tuesday 20th February
Saw Attlee at 9 p.m. I said I'd thought it over and agreed with him that Griffiths was much to be preferred to other candidates for the Foreign Office, if he himself couldn't do it as well. He said he was sure he couldn't. Several others had suggested it. I repeated that I didn't want it, but said that, since I knew a good deal about it, and was Chairman of International Sub of N.E.C., I could and would help Griffiths all I could. I said his membership of N.E.C. was important. The Committee and E.C. would take things from him they wouldn't take from an outsider like Shawcross – and as they had taken from Bevin, whom they all regarded as very much one of us. My only fear about Griffiths was 'could he live above his officials?' as Arthur Henderson once asked me of Willie Graham. Foreign Office officials and ambassadors were, some of them, very impressive people. I said Attlee must warn him to be himself, and not their tool. He said he would.

I said it would please our Movement to have another trade unionist Foreign Secretary and to have, for the first time, a miner would satisfy many.

I then spoke of the succession at the Colonial Office. This gave a

1 Sir Hartley Shawcross, later Baron (b. 1905). Attorney-General 1945–51. Labour M.P. for St Helen's 1945–58. President of the Board of Trade, April–October 1951. Chairman of the Bar Council 1952–7; Royal Commission on the Press 1961–2; Thames Television 1969–74; Press Council 1974–8.

chance, I said, to bring on one of our young men. Did he think of putting up Dugdale? He said No; he liked him very much, but he didn't get on with people, e.g. admirals. I said I had heard this. Robens and Brown should stay on Home Front. But what about putting up Callaghan? He said he thought Callaghan wasn't quite balanced enough yet. He said what about bringing in Shawcross, and having him in the Cabinet. I argued strongly against this. I said he was vain and difficult ... I said he ought to go to the Bench. He had refused both Lord Chief Justice and Master of Rolls. The block in promotion, for over six years, in Law Officers Department was unprecedented and deplorable. I said I didn't think, anyhow, that he would be a good administrator. Attlee said he had been a good Regional Commissioner in war. I said he had made an awful mess of the Catering Wages Board.

I then returned to John Freeman, recalling his very remarkable speech last week; how he had been completely [wasted?] at Supply; how Strauss – though I added that Freeman had always, in conversation with me, been extremely loyal to Strauss – had given him no show at all, not one simple Parliamentary Question in three years! Attlee seemed shocked to hear this. I recalled Freeman's magnificent first speech on the first day of the 1945 Parliament. That was something I should never forget.

Then Attlee said he would like to put Freeman at the War Office and Geoffrey de Freitas at Air. 'That', he said, 'would be a bold stroke wouldn't it?' I said it would indeed, and I should welcome it tremendously. I knew, liked and valued them both very much. Of the two, I thought Freeman had something, in resourcefulness perhaps, that de Freitas lacked. If I was out tiger hunting, I'd be very happy to have either with me, but I'd prefer Freeman. He wasn't quite sure about this, but said Henderson[1] was no good. I agreed. He hadn't grown. I said it was very poor form to contradict C.A.S.[2] in Cabinet, as he sometimes did. I [reminded] Attlee that I remembered how, when there was only one Minister[ial] Chair left between Henderson and John Wilmot, he had preferred Henderson and I had told him at the time that I thought he was wrong. He said he would have nothing else to offer Henderson. He would have to go right out. I said he had no following. He said his brother Will was much better. I agreed. He said Strachey was a queer chap. I said he was always intriguing over a vast front. I sensed that Attlee might move him, but not drop him. But I didn't pursue that.

Then he said, 'What about Bottomley for Colonial Office?' I said that would be fine. He got on very well with people, including Colonial

1 Arthur Henderson, q.v., Secretary of State for Air 1947–51.
2 Marshal of the R.A.F. Sir John Slessor (1897–1979). Chief of Air Staff 1950–52.

people, and wasn't very well placed at Department of Overseas Trade. And it would be a good move for T.U. balance. I hoped he'd do it.

I said I doubted if Strauss was good enough for Supply in these times. I said he'd never done any real work in his life; only a sleeping partner in Metals. Attlee said, 'Sleeping partner! Not at all. Oliver Lyttelton told me he had wonderful judgment and used to know just when to plunge it, and make £20,000 or £30,000 on one deal.'

I then pressed Fred Peart for an under-secretaryship, and reminded Attlee of his good speech at Margate – and after a very thick night too, though I didn't tell Attlee so – he mustn't be penalised for his father.

Attlee half took this. Then said there were two who were always being recommended as knowing about industry – Mikardo and Albu[1] – but they both belonged to the Chosen People, and he didn't think he wanted any more of *them*. I said, 'Don't touch either of them.' Mikardo was conceited, disloyal and over-rated, and I didn't forgive Albu for having lost so much of Evan Durbin's majority.[2] He'd been a bloody bad candidate, and I didn't think much of him anyhow, though he was better than Mikardo.

Attlee then turned over the pages of Vacher[3] and seemed to find very little. Then he said, 'Crosland. That's an able chap.' I said, 'Yes, very', and briefly recalled Strasburg, and my report to him. 'But I think he'd better wait a bit,' said Attlee. 'Yes, I think so too,' said I.

I said to Freeman, 'If you are offered any move, accept it, and don't be choosy.' He said, 'I will.' I said, 'Discussions are going on.'

And I told Tony a bit more – but not *who* new Foreign Secretary was to be, nor *when* Freeman might move.

Friday 2nd to Sunday 4th March
At Cambridge. Spoke at Union for Democratic Socialism against W. Fletcher.[4] Only lost, in small house, by 140 to 112. Found one very promising young man – Brian Abel-Smith[5] of Clare – Haileybury,

1 A. H. Albu (b. 1903). Labour M.P. for Edmonton 1948–February 1974. Junior minister 1965–7.
2 In the November 1948 by-election at Edmonton, Albu was elected with a majority of only 3,327 – compared with Evan Durbin's 19,069 majority in 1945. However, the swing against Labour (16.2 per cent) was lower than in the Glasgow Gorbals by-election two months earlier (17.0 per cent).
3 Vacher's *Parliamentary Companion*.
4 W. Fletcher, later Sir Walter (1892–1956). Conservative M.P. for Bury 1945–50; Bury and Radcliffe 1950–55.
5 Brian Abel-Smith (b. 1926). Undergraduate at Clare College, Cambridge. Military Assistant to the Deputy Commissioner, Allied Commission for Austria 1947–8. Professor of Social Administration at the L.S.E. since 1965. Writer on social policy. Special Adviser to the Secretary of State for Social Services 1968–70, 1974–8; to the Secretary of State for the Environment 1978–9.

A.D.C. to General Winterton in Vienna, military-cum-City background, but good socialist, intelligent, good presence and personality, doing economics. I saw a good deal of him and other less outstanding young men.

Dined in Hall in King's with Kaldor. Oh, but against that tremendous background of my old college, physical, spiritual and memorial, he seems an in-comer – a small, slightly displaced person! He had first muddled the weekend, and then, this Saturday morning I went to his room, high in Gibbs Building, full of memories,[1] and he arrived late, sweating, breathless, untidy, only just in time for Hall. I knew none of the dons, except Adcock[2] and Pigou in the distance. But they looked a pretty good lot. From Hall we went to a party at Kaldor's house. I have described this in a letter to Tony. Balogh was there. There had been a great fuss and correspondence about this. Would I mind? Tony had begged me to be polite to all Hungarians. He had told Nicky [Kaldor] Etonians always have good manners in a crisis, but was keeping his own thumbs crossed.

I don't often want to go to Cambridge. All the dons I knew and loved are dead. And one can't be sure of meeting undergraduates with whom one will click at first sight!

Saturday 10th March
It is officially announced, at last, that Bevin leaves Foreign Office and that Morrison succeeds him. This has been pretty common knowledge for several days and Morrison has been walking about with a broad grin on his face.

So, since nearly three weeks ago, when Attlee and I talked, he has gone over from Griffiths to Morrison.

How will Morrison do? I am not at all confident. He did badly at Strasburg[3] and as Maurice Edelman said to me on Thursday night, in the course of a long talk, he doesn't seem to be interested, as I sometimes am, in individual foreigners, or to be able to remember their names. And his manners are terrible. I still remember his stalking round at Strasburg paying official calls and even being saluted by a guard of honour, with a pipe in his mouth – stuck in for the purpose.

---

1 One former resident of the Gibbs Building was Dalton's old friend and tutor Goldsworthy Lowes Dickinson, q.v.
2 F. E. Adcock, later Sir Frank (1886–1968). Professor of Ancient History at Cambridge 1925–51; Fellow of King's College from 1911.
3 Herbert Morrison had led the British delegation to the first meeting of the Assembly in Strasburg in 1949, with Dalton as deputy.

Edelman says he is not university educated, or trade union educated, but night school educated. His sense of relative values is very weak, and his outlook narrow. He is obstinate and ignorant. He may make an awful mess of it, and of his own reputation, and of international peace. This is the black side. On the other he is clever in a cocky fashion and very ambitious.

John Freeman, with whom also I had a long talk a few nights ago – late sittings help long talks – said he had been spoken to by Shinwell, with a hint that he might be wanted as a Service minister. He would like the War Office, but is a friend of Strachey and would be a little uncomfortable in replacing him. I said this was one of the inevitable occasional jars in politics.

He also told me – Mike Williams Thompson had put me on the track of this – that he had a definite offer from Kingsley Martin to take over the editorship of the *New Statesman* after a period as assistant editor. This offer would remain open for a reasonable time, allowing for the loss of his seat at the next election. Kingsley Martin wants to retire soon. The paper is very profitable and the directors would want this maintained.

I think John would do this very well.

Tony did an awfully good Week-at-Westminster broadcast. He is a first class broadcaster – voice and manner – (less Trinity Oxford than in ordinary talk) very rare in Labour Party. And very good and varied material. Ruth thought he was first class.

Monday 12th March

Bevin in Cabinet today seemed quite finished. Out of harness, he'll soon drop. We're in danger of seeming a Government of Pensioners.

Did I diarise this story, told me by John Freeman:

CLEM, having asked NYE to come and see him.
> You're the only member of the Government who hasn't advised me yet who should be the next Foreign Secretary.

NYE. Oh, I'd like it myself.

CLEM. I've been looking up the records, and I find that the Foreign Office has never led on to the Premiership.

NYE. Oh, then give it to Herbert.

George Brown tonight said that he'd advised Morrison last week not to take it, but he had replied, 'That other chap is getting all the publicity now. It's time I had a break.'

Brown thinks Morrison's health and reputation will both go on the job.

Jim Callaghan gave a very clear and confident and attractive Navy Estimates speech. I had to leave after ¾ hour. He is first class, though with no manners, and ruthless ambition.

Wednesday 14th March
Talk with Hugh. I say I would have preferred Jim Griffiths at Foreign Office. I understand Ernie wanted him. Hugh definitely of the other opinion. He says Jim is a pacifist and couldn't keep his end up with leading foreigners. He says that Willy Whiteley and Addison both wanted Shawcross. So, I think, did Morrison at one time. I say I was most strongly against. Hugh thinks Morrison is pretty cute. ...

I made a joke in the House in the small hours, when Horsbrugh[1] – dried up old spinster – was making a speech on sausages, 'What do we do with a sausage?' I said, 'The same as they do with bananas at Girton.' She only caught 'bananas' and said that unfortunately we had not got any now. ...

Community singing tonight in Tea Room. Morale of Parliament raised by pep talk by Ede at Special Party Meeting this evening. I couldn't get there, as I had to be on the Bench for Sheffield Extension Bill. But I found that fatuous Tory Charles Taylor,[2] in evening dress, hesitating to go in. So I took him round the waist from behind and just ran him in.

Thursday 15th to Friday 16th March
About 11 p.m. Labour Members invade Members' Smoke Room in overwhelming numbers, and sit and sing. Each new Labour arrival loudly cheered, and each Tory departure sung out to tune of 'Good night Tories!' Service of drinks stopped, because waiters can't circulate; crowd too thick.

Small groups of Tories encircled at far end of room – Macmillan, Brigadier Mackeson,[3] Crosthwaite-Eyre,[4] Jim Thomas,[5] Selwyn

1 Florence Horsbrugh, later Baroness (d. 1969). Conservative M.P. for Manchester Moss Side 1950–59; Dundee 1931–45. Minister of Health 1951–4.
2 C. S. Taylor, later Sir Charles (b. 1910). Conservative M.P. for Eastbourne 1935–February 1974.
3 Brigadier H. R. Mackeson, later Sir Harry, 1st Bart (1905–64). Conservative M.P. for Folkestone and Hythe 1950–59; Hythe 1945–50. Junior minister 1951–3.
4 O. E. Crosthwaite-Eyre, later Sir Oliver (1913–78). Conservative M.P. for New Forest 1950–68; New Forest and Christchurch 1945–50.
5 J. P. L. Thomas, q.v.

Lloyd[1] and a few others. I have never seen men look so angry. 'We'll reduce all the Tory Brigadiers to the ranks, when the Red Revolution comes.' 'We'll make Jimmy Hudson the Keeper of the Bar, when the Red Revolution comes.' 'We'll make little Crosthwaite-Eyre do his little sums, when the Red Revolution comes.' 'We'll make Florence Horsbrugh go a'hiking with Dalton, when the Red Revolution comes.'

Macmillan, not having been served with a drink by the waiter, got up to get one himself. A Labour M.P. at once sat down in his seat. Macmillan left, amid ironical cheers, through the Chess Room door. Only Tories who responded with any sense of humour were Walter Fletcher and Nigel Davies.[2]

This calculated affront to Tory amenities shows how high passions rise.

The Speaker has been the first casualty in this war of nervous exhaustion. He has clearly been ill and out of control of himself and the situation for several days.

Thursday 15th March
Sit at table in dining room with Tom Reid[3] and Ronny Williams.[4] Reid wants a Lab–Lib Alliance. He says Morrison has encouraged him to make enquiries about this; that Shawcross is in favour; that *all* leading Liberals are in favour, including Byers;[5] they would agree on a common programme and arrange to withdraw candidates; we would let them have a run in 50 seats.

I say that, merits apart, this is quite impossible – and the merits are heavily against too. Our Party wouldn't stand it.

But I note that Liberals are declaring against Tory tactics in the House.

Tuesday 20th March
Hugh and I talked. Following last meeting of ministers on Social Services, he has been fighting hard off-stage for improved pensions plus ceiling to Health Services, with some charges for teeth and glasses,

---

1 J. S. B. Lloyd, later Baron Selwyn-Lloyd (1904–78). Conservative M.P. for The Wirral 1945–76. Junior minister 1951–4; Minister of Supply 1954–5; Defence 1955. Foreign Secretary 1955–60; Chancellor of the Exchequer 1960–62. Lord Privy Seal and Leader of the House 1963–4. Speaker 1971–6.
2 C. N. B. Davies (b. 1920). Conservative M.P. for Epping 1950–51.
3 Thomas Reid (1881–1963). Labour M.P. for Swindon 1945–55.
4 R. W. Williams (1907–58). Labour M.P. for Wigan 1948–58.
5 Frank Byers, later Baron (1915–84). Chairman of the Liberal Party 1950–52, 1965–7. Liberal M.P. for North Dorset 1945–50.

but dropping prescription. He has got Ernie's support. And Morrison's, and he thinks Attlee's, but latter's economics are always so pathetically weak, he isn't sure. ...

I also saw Attlee today, just going into hospital. It is duodenal again, with a most boring diet and he has already given up smoking, which he dislikes even more. He hopes to be back in a week or two.

I say that I am still a bit sorry he didn't make Griffiths Foreign Secretary. He says there wasn't enough support for this, and Griffiths himself wasn't very keen. I said Morrison must give up all other work that took much thought or mind. Attlee agreed.

I said I hoped he'd bring some younger people into No. 1 jobs soon. ... I said Callaghan had done very well on Naval Estimate. He said yes, indeed, and Michael Stewart had been doing very well too. This rather perturbed me. I said, 'Yes, he's pretty good, but he hasn't got the gifts and the panache of Callaghan, Freeman or de Freitas.' But I didn't take it further. I hope this doesn't mean that Stewart is now being favoured for War Office rather than Freeman. Well, he'll have time to think about further Government changes in Hospital. I said I was sure we must go to the country this year. To drag on into 1952 would be a great mistake, and loss of by-elections might force our hand at any time. He said he agreed it must be in 1951. I said we wanted meat, sunshine, and, if we could, a better international scene. (That, in my mind, pointed to September or October.) ...

I shook Attlee's hand and said I hoped he'd soon be back and fit. He asked how my health was. I said I was a bit tired and sleepy, but otherwise all right.

American pressure to increase arms spending led the new Chancellor to propose economies for his 1951 Budget, including the imposition of charges for glasses and false teeth on National Health Service prescription. This particular proposal was first discussed in Cabinet on 22nd March.

Thursday 22nd March
Last Cabinet before Easter Recess. We shall all be the better for a break, though it will be only twelve days. (The Tories last night howled their heads off when we moved the adjournment just after 10, but this was perfectly in accord with the standing orders; Winston nearly assaulted the Sergeant-at-Arms, as he left with the Mace; all respect for the Chair, whether Speaker or Deputy Speaker, is rapidly going. This is doing Tories no good – though not perhaps much harm – in

the country. Eden and Butler are said to be against these tactics, but Winston encourages them.)

Great row in Cabinet today over Hugh's proposal, backed by Health Ministers and Summerskill, to charge something for false teeth and spectacles; to put a ceiling on Health Service Expenditure, and to make a series of increases in Old Age Pensions.

(Hugh had told me in private meeting two days before that he had squared Ernie, who had himself proposed the idea of a ceiling (as for food subsidies) and Hugh had advanced this from £393m to £400m and dropped proposal for prescription charge. Hugh said that he expected main opposition from Nye with support from Harold Wilson. I asked why Wilson? Hugh said he was always intriguing with Nye and was hoping to get Hugh's job if *he* had to resign.)

It went according to plan. Morrison in chair (Attlee having gone into hospital yesterday) announced that P.M. supported Gaitskell's proposals and hoped Cabinet would accept. Morrison also backed them. So did Bevin, already half asleep, although it is only noon. So did Marquand, McNeil and Summerskill, the latter speaking after Nye, and saying people would care much more about increased pensions than about a bit on teeth and glasses.

Nye, as expected, made very heavy weather. We were giving up a great principle of the Welfare State. We could no longer speak of a 'free health service'. American press would give banner headlines to our retreat. Improved pensions were not an improvement at all, only restoring what had already been lost. Why boggle at £23 million – the cost to be recovered for teeth and glasses – out of a total budget of £300m. His own personal position would be rendered impossible: his prestige would be undermined as Minister of Labour. It will be known that he has been over-ridden. When P.M. first asked him to be Minister of Labour, he refused. He won't give us reasons; that would only be personally irritating to some of those present. (I suppose, because he would have to say that he had wanted to be Chancellor, in place of Gaitskell!) But, when he did take it, he was assured by P.M. that there would be no going back on what had been established in Social Services. The truth was that this was the cost of rearmament. Why not cut £23m off the arms estimates. We knew we couldn't spend all the money we proposed.

Only Harold Wilson, rather ineffectively, backed Nye, though Jim Griffiths seemed half frightened of the whole situation – not, perhaps, a good Foreign Secretary after all? – and wondered whether it couldn't be all looked at again.

Addison spoke in support of Hugh, and so, very briefly, did I. I said that having held Gaitskell's position, I realised the pressures he was under and supported the ceiling. He must make a firm stand. I was sure that the Party and the country would *much* prefer better pensions to free teeth and glasses. Stopping teeth is still to be free, and teeth, after Wilson's order, will be cheaper, and children's glasses will be free.

When Morrison said the general view was in favour of Gaitskell's proposals, Nye said he must reserve his position, and could not usefully take part in any further proceedings of the Cabinet. He seemed on the point of leaving the room. But he was reasoned with sweetly, asked to think again, reminded that none of this will be public till Budget Day, three weeks hence. And Hugh added that he thought the tax changes, though he couldn't disclose that yet, will be popular. He said *he* couldn't go on, unless he got Cabinet support on point raised today.

I don't think Nye will resign. But he will be awkward, and will make all the trouble he can for Hugh. But Hugh will have very strong backing and I think his general picture will probably look pretty good.

Nye looked very evil this morning. ...

I got the Strasburg delegation through this week – at a meeting with Attlee, Morrison, Bevin and Whiteley.

They agreed to my main body, same as last year except that Callaghan and I, as ministers, fall out and Billy Blyton[1] and Tony [Crosland] move up and take our places. Billy makes good cover for Tony; I've played this one before.[2]

Sunday 25th March

I have the sense of a chapter soon to be ended. Unless there's a War first – and then, of course, a Coalition – I don't see how we can drag on beyond late summer or early autumn without an election. And if we *could*, we should be mad to try.

The Tories will win – perhaps handsomely – but we must fight our hardest and with all our brains and hearts, to minimise our losses. To regain our 'dynamic' will be much easier in Opposition. I can't pretend, in these conditions, to be able to get up a really driving interest in my new Department. Local Government and Planning is obviously the right combination administratively. And we are knitting it together pretty well. Sheepshanks,[3] who will never miss a catch and never hit a

1 W. R. Blyton, later Baron (b. 1899). Labour M.P. for Houghton-le-Spring 1945–64.
2 i.e. a working-class M.P. combined with a middle-class intellectual one.
3 Sir Thomas Sheepshanks (1895–1964). Permanent Secretary at the Ministry of Local Government and Planning, then Housing and Local Government 1951–5; Town and Country Planning 1946–51.

six, has Dame Evelyn Sharp[1] – best man of them all, with tremendous energy, first class administrative brains, and a capacity for trampling through and over obstructions of all kinds – and Wrigley[2] as his two deputies. Wrigley knows all about Housing, but won't delegate anything. A 'saintly figure' some say. I find him well informed, but a bit slow and set in his ways. He retires in about a year.

Sheepshanks agrees with me that we have a lot of ageing duds on the Local Government side – the Health Service took all the best in the old Ministry of Health, and they have gone to the new Ministry of Health. ... On the whole the personnel we bring from Town and Country Planning is better than what we take over at Local Government.

But what, in these conditions, can I as Minister do? Most of the exciting things are barred by the narrow Parliamentary majority – even apart from the probable early end of this Parliament. ...

The only important immediate things I can do are (1) to push Housing along, hoping that rival rearmament demands for labour and materials will be slow to arrive, and simplifying and cheapening design a bit, not sacrificing 'essential standards', but getting rid of second W.C. in a three bedroomed house, on which Nye insisted, and a few other small details.

(2) to push on building in New Towns. This is really on a rising curve at last.

(3) to push on designating National Parks.

Saturday 31st March to Sunday 1st April
I went to Plymouth for a Private Delegate Conference for Devon and Cornwall ... I had long talks ... both with Clem Jones,[3] who is retiring on 1st May, and with Ted Rees,[4] from Bristol, who is succeeding him.

Rees talked about Stafford Cripps. He had always found Stafford a very difficult chap. In 1945 when he was anxious to rejoin the Party, he and Windle went to see Attlee and Stafford[5] ... Attlee said,

1 Dame Evelyn Sharp, later Baroness (1903–85). Joint Deputy Secretary at the Ministry of Housing and Local Government 1951–5. Deputy Secretary at the Ministry of Town and Country Planning 1947–50. Permanent Secretary at the Ministry of Housing and Local Government 1955–66.
2 Sir John Wrigley (1888–1977). Joint Deputy Secretary at the Ministry of Health 1943–51; Local Government and Planning, then Housing and Local Government 1951–2.
3 Clem Jones. Labour Party Regional Organiser for the South-West 1924–51.
4 E. V. Rees. Labour Party Assistant Regional Organiser for the South-West. Regional Organiser 1951–65.
5 After Cripps's expulsion from the Labour Party in 1939, he had remained as M.P. for Bristol East, though as an Independent, until his readmission to the Party in 1945.

'We want Stafford back in the Party.' Windle and Rees said, 'He can come back at once if he'll sign this form.' Stafford said, 'I'm not signing any form' and walked out of the room. Attlee was annoyed with the two organisers!

Rees then went back to Bristol and set things in motion for the selection of a candidate for Bristol East since Stafford was still an Independent. Stafford came down and asked him if he was serious. When Rees said yes, Stafford signed the form at once, without any consultation with any of his old friends who had been expelled at the same time as himself. This reminded me of his independent line, regardless of associates, when we had to expel him.

Just before the 1950 election, he was almost not reselected. Rees told me this story in more detail than I had ever heard it before. Stafford hadn't been in the constituency for two years and had taken no interest in the Constituency Party. He didn't want even to come down for the selection conference. But Rees advised him that his seat was in danger. So he came by car with Isobel.[1] It was a very hot night. He took his coat off and spoke for ½ hour. Then a vote was taken on an invitation to him to contest the new S.E. Bristol Division. It was only carried by *one vote* with 120 delegates present. He had told them in his speech that he was a very busy man, and that national affairs must come first. Then, after the vote, he said he couldn't give them an answer that night, and drove off in the car with Isobel.

Then Rees had to get busy to get things right. Finally Stafford promised to come once a quarter and then, but still only by a majority, they selected him.

Wednesday 4th April

Long talk at House after dinner with Harold Wilson. I began, as usual, by asking when he would finish his anti-monopoly white paper. He said he hoped in a day or two. I then spoke of the need of a strong, fresh programme for an election in late summer or early autumn. ...

Wilson then said he couldn't hold Huyton and was thinking of moving.[2] Windle had advised him to wait till the last moment.

We then turned to immediate things. Wilson said Nye would resign, unless the Cabinet withdrew the charges. I said I hoped he wouldn't. I liked and admired Nye very much, but I thought he had this quite out of focus. Wilson said he agreed with Nye, and would have to consider his own position very carefully, if Nye resigned. I said that

1 Dame Isobel Cripps, née Swithenbank (1891–1979). Married to Sir Stafford Cripps.
2 Harold Wilson held Huyton with a majority of 834 in the 1950 election. Despite his fears, he won it again in 1951 with an increased majority.

wouldn't help him to find a better 'ole[1] with the aid of Transport House. I asked whether he thought anyone else would go. He said perhaps Strachey. Any junior ministers? He replied, 'What about John Freeman?' (This was a shot in the dark, see later note.)

I said it was a very narrow point on which to resign. He said it would soon be widened. Nye, once out, would attack on Foreign Policy, etc. He was young enough to wait for power and leadership. I said this was all very bad for the Party. Had he spoken to anyone else about it? He said Bevin. He would speak to Gaitskell. Also, perhaps to Addison, I suggested.

He said we seemed to be a long way now from our earlier talk on a programme for September or October. We went off and had a drink.

Harold Wilson is not a great success. He is a weak and conceited minister. He has no public face. But he is said to be frantically ambitious and desperately jealous of Hugh Gaitskell, thinking that *he* should have been Chancellor. He has disappointed me a lot.

Thursday 5th April

Saw Hugh this evening in my room at House, just before my dinner with Tony and Browaldh.[2] I told Hugh what I had learned of Nye's intentions, but did not tell him of my talk with Harold Wilson. I asked whether he had considered the consequences of Nye's resignation. He said Yes, and he was convinced that we must face these consequences. He was very firm and determined. He said we could not always be blackmailed and give way. If we didn't stand up to him, Nye would do to our Party what Lloyd George had done to the Liberals. It would, he thought, do us good in the country to make a stand on this. Nye's influence was much exaggerated. When the case was put, he would have very little support. He had himself accepted the prescription charge last year, which was much more objectionable than teeth and glasses, and people would think very little of these charges against the background of the Budget. He wouldn't much mind if the charges were carried with the help of Tory votes.

I said I was not proposing retreat on the charges. I had supported him on these, and would continue to. But I thought he seriously underestimated Nye and his potentialities for mischief. I thought that Hugh thought too little of the Party and too much, relatively, of the general body of the electorate.

He said Wilson had been to see him, and had talked very smoothly

---

1 'a better 'ole': this seems to mean 'a better bolt hole than Huyton'. See entry for 6th April 1951, below, p. 519.
2 K. E. Browaldh. Swedish economist.

about the difficulties of the situation. He had said he was in considerable difficulty himself, because he agreed with Nye.

I said I should do my best to stop Nye resigning. But I thought it
wasn't a bluff any more. On the charges I should support standing
firm. I said Strachey might go as well as Nye and Wilson. He said we'd
be well rid of the three of them!

Friday 6th April
I took John Freeman out to lunch, and asked him whether there had
been any group of ministers formed, to his knowledge, round Nye
to resign together, and what he thought of the latest crisis. To the
first he said No: Wigg had been spreading the story that Nye had
been very awkward.

He didn't know anything in detail about the latter. So I told him.
He thought that on the narrow issue – teeth and spectacles – Nye
would have very little support. But, on a wider issue, including Finance,
Rearmament and Foreign Affairs generally, he might have a lot. On
this wider issue, Freeman himself would have to consider his own
position very carefully. He was sure our Rearmament was an excessive
programme, could not, in fact, be carried out, and would, if attempted,
cause great dislocation and unnecessary shortages of necessaries. His
'rather illiterate Ministry' has unsuccessfully tried to put this ...

If Nye went, he thought the Government couldn't last more than
eight or ten weeks. He asked whether I had talked to Nye. I said not
since Cabinet. My special relationship to Hugh Gaitskell was known,
and how Nye hated him and was jealous of him. Freeman thought
that, none the less, it might be worth my seeing him. I fixed with
Freeman that he should see me on Budget Day and discuss again.
He said he would lose his seat anyhow next time but wouldn't run
away. He was very contemptuous of Harold Wilson, when I told him
he was asking Windle to find him a last minute bolt hole from Huyton.

Earlier, before lunch, I had talked to Addison, very wise and twenty
years younger than his age. He was afraid that Nye was only using
the charges as a pretext. He wanted to be out and irresponsible, and
to attack the Old Men in the Cabinet and to become the next Leader.
I suggested that Addison should see him. He said he would. He spoke
very nicely to me of my teamwork, and part played since 1947. He
deplored the mutual animosity of Herbert and Nye, and said so to
both of them.

In the afternoon, therefore, I asked Nye, who had been at a committee meeting in another part of the building, to come along and
see me in his old office.

He did, and we talked at length. The relationship, as between us two, was, as usual, 'perfectly friendly'. But he spoke very bitterly of Hugh, and to a lesser extent of Attlee and Morrison. He said again that he protested violently to Attlee when Hugh was appointed. He had no standing in the Party. Now he was trying to be a second Snowden, an Iron Chancellor, trying to please his friends in the Treasury; the whole Treasury business was out of date – and then much talk about surpluses, and balances, and tolerances. Hugh had blindly accepted an impossible Rearmament programme. He was wildly pro-American and anti-Russian. He was an amateur Foreign Secretary. He had tried a year ago to get Nye to agree to charges. He had resisted. He had always been 'against the Health Service'. I didn't reply at length to all this. I simply said that, as he knew, I knew Hugh very well, better than he did, and that he wasn't getting his picture right at all. I then spoke at great length on lines set out in my letter to him of the next day. But I couldn't move him. 'If it is such a small thing, why not give way? The compensation of giving way would be me. Is that a very small thing?' He clearly feels an effort is being made to drive him out.

He says of Attlee, 'He double crossed me. I didn't want to leave the Ministry of Health and go to Labour. I refused for some time. I only agreed, when he promised there should be no cut in the Social Services.' He said we couldn't pass the Bill imposing the charges. He couldn't vote for it, nor would a lot of others. I said it would be very disagreeable to carry it by Tory votes. He said the Tories would find a way, by some humbug, to vote against it. I spoke of splitting the Party, and how our young men would be mown down. He said it wouldn't be his fault.

I asked him what he intended. He said that, unless at Monday's Cabinet the charges were withdrawn, 'my resignation will be in the press at the same time as the report of the Budget Speech'. I urged him to reconsider and to work for an election in five or six months' time on a worthwhile programme, after we've had more meat and sun.

John Freeman, in our talk today, said that he had heard from his spies in the Foreign Office – he clearly meant Kenneth Younger,[1] of whom he has a very high opinion indeed – that Herbert wasn't reading enough or studying enough. He wasn't humble, as a new Foreign Secretary at such a time should be. It would be a very great mistake if he didn't use Younger fully. (And I guessed that Younger had said he didn't.)

As to Nye, Freeman is inclined to think it is the charges that move him, not wider issues – though he might, of course, soon bring these in.

1 Kenneth Younger, q.v., was Minister of State at the Foreign Office 1950–51.

On the morning of 9th April, Gaitskell informed the Cabinet of his Budget proposals. Morrison (in the chair in Attlee's absence) then moved the discussion to the question of the level of government expenditure on the social services. The Chancellor explained that, to meet his target of £400 million as a maximum expenditure on the National Health Service, the Health Minister had agreed to effect economies in hospital administration totalling £10 million and to introduce charges for glasses and false teeth which would produce £13 million. This statement provoked an immediate response from Bevan:

> Believing as he did, that such charges would involve a serious breach of Socialist principles, and having on numerous occasions proclaimed in public speeches his opposition to such a course, he did not see how he could be expected to vote in favour of such a Bill. If the Cabinet reaffirmed their decision that these charges should be imposed, he would be obliged to resign from the Government.[1]

Monday 9th April (Budget eve)
Two long Cabinets 10.30–1.30 and 6.30–9.15, on the Budget. Hugh's statement this morning, pretty good as a whole in difficult circumstances ... Then a long wrangle with Nye on Health charges, and a flood of arguments and appeals. Nye threatens to widen the issue to rearmament. We shan't spend all the money.

Hugh is very resistant. He offers to put off the Budget and resign. He promises, if he does so, to go quietly and not to attack the Government afterwards. This is a high moral attitude compared with Nye. If he had £23m to spare, he wouldn't use [it] to keep false teeth and spectacles free. He would rather spend it on improved family allowances or on more old age pensions, or on smaller income tax increase.

Could the imposition of charges be postponed? Tomlinson,[2] who has lost his courage, urges this. Hugh says no.

I make a strong short appeal to consider interests of Party, need to have election, not now, which would be a disaster, but some months hence, when we have had more sun and meat. So [do] Chuter Ede and Addison. Morrison reports that he and Chief Whip had seen P.M. in hospital. He said stand firm; a very heavy responsibility would rest on anyone who split the Government and the Party. The talk went on and on.

1 PRO, Cabinet Conclusions.
2 George Tomlinson (1890–1952). Minister of Education 1947–51. Labour M.P. for Farnworth 1938–52. Junior minister 1941–5. Minister of Works 1945–7.

At 1.30 I take the lead in rising to go. We are to meet again at 6.30 and I have Ian and Dobs Little[1] waiting for me to take them out to lunch. I told them I had one ticket for tomorrow, and hope to get a second. I said there'll be a 'spot of drama' tomorrow but didn't go into detail. I think, at this stage, that the odds are that Nye will resign but, though thinking this, I give them no hint of it, and they tell Tony afterwards that I gave them a wonderful lunch – at Josef's[2] – and was in cracking good form. We discuss Economic Theory, and modern Oxford Philosophy and Stock Exchange speculation, and Tony – 'I am an unconditional Tonyite', I say, and Ian says, 'I think I am too' – and my plan for directing big investors into gilt-edged.

And then I go back to the House and move the Second Reading of my Mineral Rights Bill.

Then I go out to the Smoke Room and see Nye and signal to him, and we go out together, and talk in his room and try again. No good! He attacks the Cabinet. 'Who are they? I didn't choose them. The P.M. chooses them. They are either old men or rootless men, like Gaitskell and Gordon Walker.' They are 'dismantling the Welfare State'. While I was with Nye, Wilson rang up. I said, 'Let him come up in ten minutes.' Then I went. I saw Strachey going up with Wilson.

In the second Cabinet the debate went on and on. Hugh looked very weary. It is his birthday, just forty-five. 'Many happy returns!' said someone. Nye's hatred of him glared out all the time, and of Morrison. We are slaughtering the Health Service. And what, I ask, would the Tories do on this, and countless other questions, if we put them in now with a big majority?

Finally the voices are collected, and all stand by the Chancellor, except Nye and Wilson ('Nye and the dog' I call them outside) and Tomlinson, who has lost his courage and wants to postpone decision. …

The only man who *looks* happy is Nye. But perhaps he isn't really. He had asked in the Cabinet today, 'Aren't I worth £23 millions?' (the revenue from the charges). He became very irritated at constant appeals to *him*. Why not appeal to others?

I saw Freeman later this evening. He said all Nye's friends were trying to persuade him not to resign before the Party Meeting on Wednesday (day after tomorrow, day after Budget Speech). He will do his best to stop him, but, if Nye goes, he must go with him. Freeman hopes that, if he and I are on opposite sides of the gulf, it won't end our friendship. He expresses a great regard and affection for me. I say

1 Doreen ('Dobs') Little, née Hennessey. Married to Ian Little, q.v.
2 A Soho restaurant much frequented by Dalton.

I feel the same for him. I read him my letter to Nye. He says it is a very moving letter.

Following the vote in Cabinet on 9th April on the issue of health charges, Bevan had informed his ministerial colleagues that in these circumstances he would have to resign from the Government. 'He would submit his resignation to the Prime Minister in the course of the following day; and he presumed that he would thereafter make a personal statement in the House of Commons, possibly on 11th April.'[1] The Cabinet asked him to reconsider.

Tuesday 10th April
Budget Day!
I ring up Tony's flat at 8.30. Ian answers the phone. ... I ask to speak to Tony – still asleep, as usual after late night. I tell him there is a very bad political situation. Nye, Wilson and Strachey are resigning, and perhaps Freeman (and someone also said Tom Cook,[2] but I only heard this later). We face an early election and a heavy defeat. Will come and discuss in my office. He comes at 11.30. He says he is very pro-Nye, but he is against him on this. I ask him to see Freeman with whom I have a date today, an hour after Hugh sits down. Tony says that, if Nye goes and the *Tribune* backs him, he will try to write an article putting the other side. He says Nye may be betting on coming out Leader in ten or even five years' time. These things are forgotten much more quickly than one thinks, e.g. Cripps, and they might be very quickly forgotten in Opposition. I said I didn't think Nye['s] was a very good life. He looked unhealthy. He said Freeman was a great Nyeite, but he'd certainly speak to him.

Tony goes off, and I take Ian, who has just arrived, down to the House and give him two drinks before lunch.

I then see Crossman in the Smoke Room. He says he sent Mikardo, rather unwilling, to breakfast with Nye this morning to dissuade him from resigning. Nye had kept it very quiet. Michael Foot knew nothing about it at midnight last night. Foot is passionately in favour of Nye resigning. He is almost the only one.

Hugh's Budget Speech is a tremendous success. He looks as fresh as paint, and wears a red carnation. Very lucid and lasts well. He is a much better economist than Stafford, who was very good at getting

1 PRO, Cabinet Conclusions.
2 T. F. Cook, q.v., Parliamentary Under-Secretary at the Colonial Office 1950–51.

up a brief, but didn't realise, as Hugh does, all the surrounding arguments. He gets a great ovation at the end. The Party are very pleased, and the Tea Room is full of his praises. I walk up and down outside the Tea Room with various companions and whenever any friend of mine comes out, I ask what is the feeling, and it is practically all one way. 'We can defend this.' 'The boys are very pleased.'

Nye kept off the bench and only came down to the Chamber to hear Hugh on the Health charges. He stood behind the Speaker's Chair. It was a great shock to him that there was no outcry when the charges were announced – hardly any audible reaction on either side of the House. Only Jennie [Lee], standing with him, said 'Shame!' just above her breath. Then she strode out into the passage.

After Hugh sat down, I went out into the corridors.

Six Under-Secretaries, headed by Jim Callaghan, had signed a letter to him, which Jim delivered.[1] The other signatories were Robens, Lee,[2] Michael Stewart, Blenkinsop and one other. They pressed him not to resign, and said that if he did, they would all lose their seats.[3] (I don't think Robens would.) Jim said that Nye, having read the letter, said to him, 'You are all putting me in a very difficult position'!! I hear that all his followers are now trying to persuade him not to do it. He will wait now for tomorrow's Party Meeting they say. This means he can't steal the top headline from Hugh, as he first intended, either in tonight's evening, or tomorrow's morning papers!

Hugh sat down at 5.45 and just before 6, as arranged, Freeman came to see me in my room. He says that Nye has definitely put off resignation till the Party Meeting. He has been working very hard at him – he was with me during the first part of the Budget Speech, till he went down to hear Hugh on the charges. So have many others, for hours on end, one of the most effective and outspoken being Stanley Evans,[4] who is an old buddy. I told Freeman of Hugh's moral attitude, in

1 The five junior ministers mentioned (there was no sixth) wrote to Bevan on 10th April: 'Any fragmentary resignations will split the Party in the constituencies, and we shall be not only defeated in the election but routed. In the Party's interest we urge you to wait until the Party Meeting has expressed itself tomorrow' (M. Foot, *Aneurin Bevan: A Biography Vol. II 1945–1960*, MacGibbon & Kee, London, 1973, p. 325).
2 Frederick Lee, later Baron (1906–84). Parliamentary Secretary at the Ministry of Labour and National Insurance 1950–51. Labour M.P. for Newton 1950–February 1974; Manchester Hulme 1945–50. Minister of Power 1964–6; Colonial Secretary 1966–7; Chancellor of the Duchy of Lancaster 1967–9.
3 None of them did.
4 S. N. Evans (1898–1970). Parliamentary Secretary at the Ministry of Food 1950–51. Labour M.P. for Wednesbury 1945–56.

offering to resign and say nothing. A snow peak compared to a steaming tropical swamp, I said. He still thinks that if Nye goes, he must go too. But he won't decide yet, and will see me first. I am trying to make him think less idolatrously of his idol! He admits he told me a white lie last Friday, when we lunched together. He *was* in a group considering joint resignation, but he was pledged to secrecy.

General MacArthur's outspoken and aggressive comments about the conduct of the Korean War and his demands for all-out force to drive back the Chinese had for some time disturbed the British government and embarrassed President Truman. Many shared General Bradley's fear that MacArthur would push America into 'the wrong war against the wrong enemy in the wrong place at the wrong time'. When MacArthur advocated the bombing of Manchuria and the transfer of Chinese troops from Formosa to Korea, the President finally dismissed him.

Wednesday 11th April
Party Meeting. Driving to the House I see a chalked newspaper notice 'Truman sacks MacArthur'. Just before the meeting starts, I get an evening paper with the news from Gunter,[1] and give it to Willie Hall, and suggest that he should give the meeting a good send off by announcing it. He does, and they cheer!

Going down from my room to the Party Meeting, I meet Harold Wilson, not very sure of his relations with me. 'Good morning, Mr Dalton. I hope we're still colleagues. I've been trying to persuade Nye not to resign.' I say, 'I've heard different.' He says, 'But why should I want him to resign?' I say, 'I'm sure I don't know.' Hugh opens with a short speech. Then Nye gets up and says that he and his friends won't take 'a certain step', but there is still time for further consideration. Party unity mustn't be imposed on one side only. Not a very satisfactory statement, but we gain more time and he loses it. Every hour makes it more difficult for the resignations now.

The general feeling in the Party is favourable to the Budget, though there is evidently a strong minority against the Health charges.

Nye and Herbert are almost in a personal clash. Nye has been warned not to develop an argument, and doesn't. But Herbert is on the edge of doing so. Nye jumps up to protest. And Herbert says his very next sentence was going to be 'Now I have finished with that'.

1 R. J. Gunter (1909–77). Labour M.P. for Doncaster 1950–51; Essex South-East 1945–50; Southwark 1951–2. Minister of Labour 1964–8; Power 1968.

Going out into the passage I meet Crossman and Strachey. To the latter I say, 'If there was an election now, you'd be down the pan good and proper, and with some better men than you and some worse ones.' He flares at this and says, 'You have got a simple and genteel way of putting things.' I say, 'Well, you've been psycho-analysed, you should [not] find any difficulty in plain speech.'[1] Crossman says that, if there was a break, he would go with Nye, and so would a lot more. I suggest we should all have a drink before lunch and we do. I gather that it had taken Nye a long time to see that he'd mass-murder the Party, if he went, including nearly all his own friends, and come back with a shrivelled Parliamentary Party, which certainly wouldn't wear him as Leader. (John Freeman says that he conveyed this point, which I had forcibly made to him, to Nye who hadn't thought of it like that before.)

As Crossman, Strachey and I have our drink, Crossman says that the division between Left and Right was never so sharp as now. Hugh, he says, is very doctrinaire and pro-American. He is giving an overriding priority to Defence. But Nye's mistake was not to break on armaments, when the programme [was] enlarged in February. I say he made no move. I asked Strachey why he didn't make a row then. He says it's very difficult for a Service Minister to do that. He recalls that I was the only one who backed him up when he read out Slim's[2] directive, 'War Possible in 1951, Probable in 1952'. I say we might review all that again. I say I want to keep the Party united and strong. Crossman says I'm a Transport House man.

Freeman, just after lunch, talks to me. We walk down passage leading past Foreign Secretary's room. He says he wrote a very strong letter to Nye last night, which he hopes has had a considerable effect this morning. While we are talking Morrison comes along, accompanied by Wigg. I said, 'Let's have a four at tennis.' Slight embarrassment!

Wigg was the first to spill beans of the crisis. He went round saying that Nye was being very awkward in Cabinet, obviously inspired by Shinwell. Nye was very cautious, fearing charge of disclosure of Cabinet secrets. Freeman said Nye would[n't?] resign on Bill, but wouldn't vote for it. I said that doesn't matter much provided he doesn't try to make all of you idolators abstain too. Freeman said he didn't think he would.

---

1 John Strachey underwent psychoanalysis for three years following his break with Mosley and the failure of his first marriage in 1932.
2 Field-Marshal Sir William Slim, later 1st Viscount (1891–1970). Chief of Imperial General Staff 1948–52. Commander-in-Chief of Allied Land Forces in South-East Asia 1945–6.

Douglas Houghton,[1] who took a very good line at Party Meeting, defending charges and adding that it would be disastrous to wobble back now, and would fatally discredit the Government, said that Jim Callaghan was seeing Nye at 3 and he didn't quite understand why Jim was being brought into these 'diplomatic exchanges'. He is a bit jealous of his old subordinate.

Nye going upstairs said to me, 'Clem says June for the election. So why try to pass this Bill now? If you try, the Party will be a rabble, and you won't carry it.' I said I wasn't sure about June. It sounded too early. But we certainly could look at the Arms Programme again if there was any new evidence. This evening the Nyeites are intriguing away hard. The aim now is to prevent the introduction of the Bill for charges. Lyttelton said yesterday that the Tories would support it. Nye and Wilson are spreading the story of the June election. I don't believe P.M. did say this.[2] I expect Nye said it ought to be June and Clem, in his usual way, said, 'Well perhaps that might be a good time.' (P.M. sent message to Thursday Cabinet saying he had never said election in June, in reply to telephone enquiry by Morrison.)

With Ede and Whiteley discussing movements, and individual attitudes. We spoke of Freeman. They said they had a report of a group meeting, attended by Crossman and Freeman, and that latter said that, if Nye went, he would go too. I said that I *knew* that Freeman was doing all he could to stop Nye resigning. They then spoke further of Freeman, whom I defended. Freeman told me later there had been no such group meeting.

Tony wound up debate tonight. He was disappointed with his speech, and felt he hadn't got the technique. He spoke too fast and without enough heavy emphasis. But it was, Hugh agreed with me, very good material. He must practise more.

Hugh told me he'd had a most amazing day yesterday. Up till noon he hadn't known whether he was going to make a Budget speech or not. He had twice offered to resign and not to attack the Government. Attlee – and even Morrison once – had cold feet and wanted him to drop all mention of the charges. He had finally agreed to leave one sentence out of his speech, in which he had intended to name a date

---

1 Douglas Houghton, later Baron (b. 1898). Labour M.P. for Sowerby 1949–February 1974. Secretary of the Inland Revenue Staff Federation 1922–60. Chancellor of the Duchy of Lancaster 1964–6; Minister without Portfolio 1966–7. Chairman of the P.L.P. 1967–74.
2 Attlee had been receiving treatment in St Mary's Hospital, Paddington, since 21st March. Bevan and Wilson had visited him on Budget Day, 10th April.

for the beginning of the charges. I said, 'Don't build yourself up too high. You've had a great triumph and every hour now makes it surer that they won't resign.' I said his broadcast had been a great success. He had that rare gift, a fireside chat manner on the air. But (here following a suggestion of Freeman) he ought to try to find some occasion for agreeing with Nye in Cabinet on some disputed issue, preferably when they would both be in a minority.

Thursday 12th April

Cabinet. Nye says to me, before we go in, 'It's not finished yet', rather gleefully. He said to me the other day, 'I should exert much more leverage outside the Cabinet than in it.' Megalomania and jealousy govern him. Shinwell to a group in Tea Room said, 'Some people must be made to toe the line.' He has not been a mollifying influence! I rang up Windle this morning before Cabinet as agreed with Morrison and told him this was a joint message from Herbert and me – Harold Wilson must not be helped to find a better seat; if Huyton was to be lost, let *him* lose it! Windle said he wasn't helping. I said Wilson had suggested to me that he was. Anyhow Windle took the point!

I try to get Nye into the right mood, just before we go in, and ask if he's seen the *Manchester Guardian* this morning on him and me and Lyttelton.[1] Very amusing! Then Wilson creeps out, and asks, 'Have you seen the *Daily Telegraph*? That's much more serious. That carries a full report of the Party Meeting.' I say, 'They always do. Nothing in that.' He says, 'But they say that Morrison said that it was time a certain person's bluff was called, and it would be this time.' I say, 'But nothing of that kind was said at the Party Meeting. Why are you always trying to stir things up? I'm trying to stir them down.' Nye, then a bit excited, as the little blighter intended, said, 'You must tell your friends in the Treasury to help.'

In Cabinet Ede mentions – as I and others had advised him to do – the two Bills to give effect to Health charges and Pensions improvements. They are to be presented formally next week, with Second Readings the week after, just before the Finance Bill.

Nye protests. Why bring in Health Charges Bill? He and Wilson saw P.M. yesterday,[2] and a date was mentioned for general election.

---

1 At the end of his entry for 11th April 1951, Dalton wrote: 'Today on bench, while Lyttelton was taunting Nye, who had come in to hear, and sat beside me, I tried to keep Nye amused, and to prevent his jumping up. This effort was successful ... '
The ploy was noted in the press.
2 In fact, 10th April, not the 11th.

This would mean Bill wouldn't come into operation. Don't provoke Party by bringing in Bill.

Everyone is rather tired of it all at this point and, apart from the Dog,[1] who monotonously affirms that he agrees with his master, there is no reaction, except from Shinwell who asks what is this date? Has P.M. told two ministers only? Then they say 'June', and Morrison says he has been in touch with P.M. who denies that he said there would be an election in June. Shinwell then becomes abusive of Nye. He says he has put his powers of vituperation into cold storage, but he is quite prepared to bring them out. (What a coarse-grained shit and low cur he is! I infinitely prefer Nye!)

Nye says that, if Bill is introduced, he can't vote for it. That's all. (No threat of further resignation.) He could [not] drag his feet into the lobby to support this.

I intervene quickly to say that this is all a fortnight hence and probably the Tories won't vote against it, as Lyttelton said yesterday in speech and broadcast. So very likely there won't be a vote. And anyhow need we discuss it further now? Tomlinson once more wants to put it off. All courage spent! But we decide to go ahead.

Hugh's speech and broadcast, and the Party's reaction in the House and Party Meeting, and the likelihood of Tory support on the charges, has made a new situation. Nye's resignation *now* would seem quite inexcusable and, if he did, he would get many fewer followers in House and country than a few days ago, and we *could* fight a not quite so hopeless election. But still pretty bad!

Talk to Tony, after Roy [Jenkins] has made a good speech in the House and just before he goes to entertain an Asquith at dinner.

Later talk to Freeman who hopes there's no truth in the rumour that Crossman with his 'illiterate brilliance' will replace Kenneth Younger, of whom Freeman thinks very highly, as Minister of State.

All over for the moment. But for how long? Nye, I fear, will try to make trouble again, and may pick a better pretext. Anti-Americanism won't have much appeal while Truman is fighting MacArthur and the Republicans. But he may campaign against Rearmament. He has a mixed lot of followers, and near followers, and they may be more serious in the press and in the country than in the Parliamentary Party, though he thinks arithmetic is such that even a few could wreck us. But Nye has shown great passion and hatred and a great lack of judgment, and this, I think, has shaken some of his worshippers.

---

1 'the Dog': Harold Wilson ('Nye and the dog').

Saturday 14th April

I am at West Leaze quite alone for the weekend (Ruth is pinned in London) writing up diary notes, and thinking, and digging.

Tonight on 9 o'clock news is Ernie Bevin's death from heart attack. The surprise is that he didn't die sooner. He had been no use, physically or mentally, for some time, and should have resigned earlier. ...

He did a lot of big things and, as Foreign Secretary, made some big mistakes. But on balance, he did a lot of good in his life. Stafford's latest news sounds pretty gloomy, so they may both be gone soon.

Who's coming up? Hugh Gaitskell certainly. And Nye is what and where he is – full of potentiality and uncertainty of touch, and danger to himself and the Party.

On 15th April, Dalton wrote to Attlee in hospital:

As to [Bevin's] successor, my first thought is that another Trade Unionist should enter the Cabinet, and a *young man*. Our average age is too high. The best all-rounder, in my view, is Robens, who has incidentally played a very loyal and active part during the past fortnight, backing Hugh Gaitskell, but doing his best to stop Nye from resigning. Unless you want to make other changes in the Cabinet now, would it not be simpler to make Robens Lord Privy Seal, but as the most junior member of the Cabinet, and give him enough work to do, including presiding over Committees of Under-Secretaries, or officials, until a suitable Department became available for him? ...

You will have heard only too much from too many about recent troubles. I did all I could, using all design and all human instruments I could, (a) to support Hugh, and (b) to stop Nye from leading a stampede. As you know, we were once or twice very close to the precipice. But we just didn't go over and smash the Party at the bottom.

Hugh's Budget Speech and Broadcast were both first class, and I felt very proud indeed of this young Chancellor, who was once my Private Secretary, and was one of my discoveries in the 1930s. ...

I have kept, I hope and think, the friendliest personal relations with Nye through all this – though I have not concealed a certain contempt for Wilson and Strachey, his two leading adherents in the Government – and I shall continue to try my best to hold Nye with us. The most dramatic danger point has been passed, but others remain, not far ahead. ...

I hear talk of the possibility of Crossman taking Younger's place at the Foreign Office. But Younger now knows a lot about it all, much more than Herbert as yet. Crossman, as someone has said, has an 'illiterate brilliance' in foreign affairs that might not combine well with the part of a new

Foreign Secretary. And he was declaring last week that 'if it comes to a break, I shall go with Nye', and criticising Hugh unfairly in this week's *Statesman*. He is a most gifted and attractive creature, and one of the best debaters in the House, and it is tempting to contemplate 'bringing him inside'. But would he stay inside in a crisis? I would have liked to see him in the Government long ago, but he always puts stones in his own shoes. As Willie Whiteley said once, 'He can't make up his mind what he wants to be.'

I hope you're really better and will be back soon. We miss you a lot. If you'd like me to come and see you, of course I'll come. But you may be having too many visitors.[1]

Tuesday 17th April

Letter from P.M. – no idea of throwing out Younger to make room for Crossman. Quotes the Warden of New College. 'Bad Judgment? No judgment at all.' Praise of Robens. I'm to see Clem this weekend.

Talk to Whiteley on coming ministerial changes. P.M. inclined to make Chuter Ede Lord Privy Seal and bring in Shawcross as Home Secretary. I say Shawcross has no judgment (common criticism!) and is very vain. He ought to have gone long ago to the Bench. Whiteley says Clem will bring in Robens, probably as Minister Without Portfolio, and give him material allocations, etc., to begin with. These changes should be made almost at once.

As to Service Departments, I say I hope he still means to get rid of Henderson and Strachey, and put de Freitas and Freeman in their places. Whiteley says he thinks so, and this should happen at Whitsun – when difficult Bills are passed, so as not to raise new troubles.

I will speak to Clem about all this at the weekend. Later I tell Freeman this. He says he would give anything to leave his present job. He would gladly move to another Under-Secretaryship, if he can't move up. He thinks he must tell Clem, if he offers him the War Office, that he would have gone with Nye, if Nye had resigned. I doubt the need for this, particularly if it isn't till Whitsun, and things have settled down by then. Freeman says he thinks he influenced Nye a lot at the end by writing to beg him not to split the Party, but to tell him that, if he *did* go, [he] would go with him.

I say Nye has lowered himself in my esteem by his recent conduct. Freeman says he has shown a lack of judgment (same old verdict). I say, still worse, he has been governed by personal hatred – chiefly against Hugh. I don't like this, or men who try to kick the ball through

1 Dalton Papers II, 9/18 (20), (21).

their own goals. I ask how far Freeman will follow Nye like a dog. Won't he, in future crises, recover his own judgment? He says yes certainly, and, if Nye were just to resign on the Charges Bill, he thinks he wouldn't go with him. He says Michael Foot and Jennie [Lee] – who is Opposition minded and doesn't like Nye being in the Government and has a guilt-complex about a Cabinet Minister's salary – have been pressing him to resign. He had been wrong earlier in thinking Jennie was a moderating force.

He shows me from Isobel Cripps a very sad photo of Stafford, lying on his face in bed, smiling but, we both thought, near death.

Wednesday 18th April
Chuter Ede comes in while I am talking to Whiteley to say that Nye said at the Welsh table tonight that he had much more support in the constituency parties than he thought. More trouble at Cabinet?

Coming back from Ernie Bevin's funeral at Golders Green, Willie Hall says that, when Hugh was made Chancellor, Nye told *him* that Stafford had told Nye that, if Stafford resigned from the Chancellorship, Nye ought to succeed him. Willie ... says that he wouldn't put it past Stafford to have said this.

When it was announced at a Cabinet meeting on 19th April that the Second Reading of the National Health Service Bill would be taken on 24th April, Bevan declared that, if there were a division, he would not vote in favour of the Bill and that if it was carried on the Third Reading, he would resign from the Government. In the course of the discussion that followed, Bevan indicated that his difficulties might be met by a statement that the proposed charges were only temporary, and no further charges were contemplated. Gaitskell, however, refused.[1]

Thursday 19th April
Douglas Jay says that, the day after Hugh was appointed, Nye said to him, 'I've been tricked, Stafford promised me that I should be his successor.' And he told me that he had made a violent protest to P.M. on Hugh's appointment. ...

When next week's business is raised, including Second Reading of Health Charges Bill, Nye says that he gives us notice that he will resign on the Third Reading and he wishes this to be recorded in the Minutes.

1 PRO, Cabinet Conclusions.

Morrison very properly says that this can't be done. Resignation is a matter between the minister concerned and the P.M.

Then comes a move, started by Shinwell of all people, to see whether we can't say that charges will be temporary, limited to one year. This follows a general impatience in the Cabinet with this continual nerve war – first [Bevan] threatened to resign before the Budget, then on Budget Day, then if the charges were brought in, then he wouldn't vote for Second Reading, and now this! At the end of one of these discussions in Cabinet, he said, 'Why should I have to put up with these bloody absurdities?' Glaring at Hugh. But Hugh said nothing, and the Cabinet dispersed.

Today I said I didn't propose to repeat my appeal to him not to resign, and not to divide the Party in the face of the enemy.

But after Shinwell's proposal, to which Nye said, 'Ah! that might make a big difference' – and threw across the table to Wilson a note saying 'We've got them on the run!' – a small group of ministers was appointed to try to find a formula, and report on Monday – Hugh, Nye, McNeil, Summerskill and Marquand with Chuter and Whiteley. Nothing came of it. A useless meeting was held.

Friday 20th April
I worked a bit in the office and then went over to the House.

Crossman, Harold Davies[1] and Baird,[2] on behalf of the West Midlands Group, saw Chuter and Whiteley this morning. They told me they thought it had not been too bad. They suggested something in the preamble to say the charges weren't permanent, something in the Bill to make them subject to annual renewal and a reduction in the charges from 50 to 20 per cent. They also wanted a Party Meeting next Wednesday to discuss it all! (But this is a National Executive day.)

I didn't think this sounded at all practical, but express no view to them, except that it was useful to keep friendly contact.

I saw Whiteley later. He said last night's meeting of ministers with Nye was no good. They had offered him a formula, to the effect that the charges were not necessarily permanent, and might be modified at any time by affirmative regulation.

He wouldn't take it, or propose any alternative, or agree to anything short of the withdrawal of the Bill. Later, with Jim Callaghan – who said he was a bit out of touch ... I was invited to go and see

---

1 Harold Davies, later 1st Baron (1904–85). Labour M.P. for Leek 1945–70. Junior minister 1965–7.
2 John Baird (1906–65). Labour M.P. for Wolverhampton North-East 1950–64; Wolverhampton East 1945–50.

Chuter. He shows us the formula offered to Nye last night. He swept it aside as 'a bromide', but made no alternative suggestion. It proposed that in the Second Reading speech the Minister should say that these charges were not necessarily permanent, but that, if the House approved, they could be removed or modified by affirmative order. Chuter and Co. had a longer – and I thought less good – statement which they were willing to show him, but in view of his complete rejection of the first, they didn't. I was glad, for the longer one contained some too stiff passages for agreement to have been possible. The first formula followed very closely the suggestion made in Cabinet yesterday by Shinwell – a surprising move, for he has been bitter and tactless towards Nye – much more so than anybody else in Cabinet ...

Chuter is now inclining to the view and so is Whiteley, that the time has come when the P.M. may have to tell Nye that he must either play with the team or go. I said, 'Be careful not to seem to be victimising him.'

Jim Callaghan afterwards talked to Foot, and reported that the latter had said that Nye must now spend a period on the back-benches. Foot has been pressing him, hardest of all of them, and against the views of most of them, to resign.

Today there is published a *wicked* Tribune attacking Hugh most outrageously, comparing him to Snowden, and his Budget to Snowden's in 1931, saying that he is the darling of the City and the Tories, with many supporting quotes from Tory papers. ...

It is becoming impossible to concentrate one's mind on anything except this odious war of nerves, which is becoming totally intolerable. See Clem in hospital in the afternoon. This visit was arranged some days ago ... I had not seen him since before he went into hospital.

He is having a conclave with Morrison, Hugh, Chuter and Whiteley when I arrive. When they come out, Morrison says to me, 'We must all keep a stiff upper lip now.' When I go in, Clem says, 'I've just sent Nye an ultimatum. He must either accept Cabinet decisions or go.' He added that Nye was a 'green-eyed monster'. Then we talked of other things. He was a bit flushed and a bit nervy, I thought, but who could wonder? He has been having trouble with his teeth. His former dentist was too old. He has to have part of his gum cut away. But he hopes to go down to Chequers for the weekend after next, and return to circulation the following week. He is strongly for the promotion of Robens. I say that, if Nye goes, Robens would make a good Minister of Labour. We agree that we must not think of Nye's resignation as forcing us to an immediate election. Let him, if he will, commit further acts of disloyalty to the Party, especially in the Division Lobbies. This will only make things worse for him. Meanwhile, I say, even a month hence would be better electioneering weather than now, though I would prefer September or October.

I deliberately don't mention any other possible moves, nor, in particular, Freeman. I say there's talk of Strachey resigning with Nye. P.M. says, with unusual animation, 'If I thought he'd take this line I'd have dropped him a year ago.'

Later in the afternoon talk to Hugh. This too was a talk fixed several days earlier. It was supposed to be about my departmental interest in investment programme. These details we settled amicably, and with give and take, subject to details being worked out by officials.

We then spoke of Government changes, whether Nye went or not. Hugh said should we try to bring in someone of the Left Group? We agreed Crossman was hopeless – always adding some bright little variation of his own to other people's intrigues. But what, asked Hugh, did I think of Freeman? I said I thought he was by far the most talented and interesting of the Under-Secretaries. He always did well when he got a chance, which was very seldom.

Hugh said he liked him very much, and knew that I did. And Dora liked his wife.[1] Hugh would quite like him as Financial Secretary to the Treasury if Douglas Jay went up – and he really *did* deserve promotion. He had been $3\frac{1}{2}$ years at the Treasury now. ... Hugh ... said that there was an idea now of having a special Minister for Raw Materials, and Jay might do that well – taking stuff away from Board of Trade and Ministry of Supply. Hugh said Freeman was also among those now being considered for that. I said he would be first class at either, or at the War Office. I told Hugh how angry I was with *Tribune*. Hugh said he had been much moved by a letter from Freeman. He hoped there was now no fear of his resigning. I said I hoped and believed not.

I went to bed, totally spun out and exhausted by this strain. I haven't felt so tired out, mentally and spiritually, for years.

Ruth is at West Leaze and I am alone in the flat.

Sunday 22nd April
Ruth being at West Leaze, I lunch with Bob and Betty [Fraser] and Rosalind[2] – now very short sighted and wearing glasses, poor little thing!

---

1 Margaret Freeman, née Kerr (d. 1957). Assistant editor of *University Quarterly*.
2 Rosalind Fraser, later Gilmore (b. 1937). The Frasers' daughter. Later career in the Treasury and National Giro Bank. Director, St George's House, Windsor, from 1986.

... [W]alk, after tea with Bob, on Heath again with John Freeman. I say I am very angry indeed about *Tribune* attack on Hugh. I have, as he knows, done my best to be nice to Nye, but this really marks him down as one unfit ever to lead the Party – egoism and jealousy beyond all tolerable bounds. I work hard to dissuade John from any thought of going with Nye. I think he must have heard of the Friday ultimatum. He says it's pretty clear now that Nye's going. He also admits he's going to a lunch tomorrow given by Mikardo. I press on him that Nye has almost completely lost caste by this *Tribune* performance. I tell him that Hugh was much moved by John's letter, and says how it is that people go on talking about this and only knowing half the facts.[1] I tell him that Hugh also speaks well of John's wife, and says Dora likes her. (I admit I don't much care for Dora, but John sticks up for her, and that helps the argument.) I tell John that his stock is quite high now with those who matter. ... I say that there are various possible ministerial changes now under discussion, quite apart from any question of Nye's resignation, which might be of great interest, at least as great as the War Office.

But, I say, I feel as though I am taking him to a high place and tempting him, as they tempted Christ, by showing him all the King-doms of the Earth (we are walking along the top of Hampstead Heath).

He laughs and says, 'You have too much sense of humour to keep on with *that* story!' But he says that he is *not* now committed to follow Nye. He will reach his conclusion quite calmly in the light of the whole situation. I ask him to promise to go and see Hugh before deciding to go. He promises. I go back and have a drink in his flat and meet his present wife. ...

I say as we part, 'I shall be *très déchiré* if you break.' He says, 'Don't let's discuss it again out here.' I say, 'No one will know what *déchiré* means. But your going would serve no useful purpose whatever.'

Back at the flat, I ring up Tony and urge him to work on John, especially in view of the *Tribune*.

I am a little vexed at John's obstinacy over all this. How can one go on being a Nyeite after this frightful exhibition of bad character?[2]

Monday 23rd April
Nye flopped in the House today on his resignation speech. No cheer when he entered, in the middle of questions, nor when he rose, at the

---

1 Later insertion: 'a clear enough hint to John to go and talk to Hugh'.
2 Later insertion: '(And, as it turned out, he never talked to Hugh!) John finally made up his mind to resign with Nye that night.'

end of questions, hardly any cheers while he was speaking, nor when he sat down. His attack on Hugh and his delighted confession of having tricked his colleagues by his manoeuvres[1] were not liked.

A most vicious speech, most quotable by the Tories. I spoke to Foot later in the corridor. I said, 'I shall never recommend anyone to read *Tribune* again. I was totally disgusted by it last week. I have never read such a shameful attack on another member of the Party as in your editorial. I'm through with you.' He said, 'I consider that all we said was thoroughly justified.' We parted, having been overheard by many. Roy Jenkins told me later that on the previous Thursday, when we were together in the Smoke Room, Foot had been most friendly and complimentary about me and my part in the affair up till then.

I saw John Freeman standing at the Bar listening to Nye. I tried to find him, and asked Tony to help. Later I noted, '5 p.m. I have tried to find him, and so has Tony. Without success. I have telephoned. He is not in his Ministry; not in his room, not with Nye, who is in the Tea Room.'

I was very much agitated. I said to Tony, 'Within five minutes I could get him promotion if I knew he would take it. But what does he want? He can't keep us all hanging about like this!'

Tony said later when the die was cast, that John is a *Statesman* Leftist, happiest in Opposition, and has been unhappy for a long time about U.S. and raw materials and rearmament.

I went down to see Willy Whiteley. He said John was out of the Government. Willy had asked him just before questions, whether he could tell the P.M. Freeman would accept promotion. (He might have gone to the Board of Trade as President, or to the Treasury as Financial Secretary.) John had asked for an hour to think it over. ...

Soon after 7 p.m. a messenger brought me this letter from John.[2] Then I saw him in the passage and brought him to my room, and was very sad. And then the telephone rang from No. 10, and a secretary asked if he would go and see the P.M. in hospital. And he said he would have to arrange about transport. But I said, 'Take my car' and went down with him into the yard, and put him in, and patted him

---

1 Later insertion: 'on prescription charges and housing programme'.
2 In a letter headed '23rd April 1951 7.15 p.m.', Freeman wrote to Dalton: 'I have decided after the deepest and most conscientious thought of which I am capable to take what you would consider the wrong decision. Nothing could have done more to influence me the other way than Nye's outburst this afternoon ... Tempers will be high and cruel things said for a time, but our friendship will always mean much to me.' A few hours earlier, Freeman had written to Whiteley as Chief Whip, informing him of his intention to resign 'which will preclude my accepting any suggestion of the kind you spoke to me about earlier this afternoon'. (Both letters are included in Dalton's diary.)

on the shoulder and said, 'Think again. Be prepared to change your mind.' And he went off. But later that night he wrote me another note, 'No change. So sorry!'

Oh Hell! I went home and wrote him a letter at midnight.

14 'Gone with the Wind', 24th April 1951

Tuesday 24th April
Party Meeting in Westminster Hall 9.30–11.30 a.m. Then Cabinet Ministers and some others go to the Abbey for Ernie Bevin's Memorial Service. Statement by Harold Wilson – quiet, but not very effective – and John – short and dignified, but not totally successful. Both say they won't do anything to bring the Government down.

Hugh makes a very good and calm defence. He answers points about the arms programme. Even if it can't be fully carried out – and that will depend on outcome of talks now going on in Washington – that won't make for an easier, but for a harder and more inflationary situation. He wanted this to be a popular Budget that would win votes. And it would have been a popular Budget if it hadn't been attacked, as it has been, in some quarters.

When he sits down, there is loud applause, and the clapping continues for several minutes. I help to keep it going. Nye glares. He wants to speak. He jumped up, and challenged Hugh on Cabinet decision. 'Publish the papers!' he shouts. Later, when he does get up, he is soon quite out of control. 'I won't have this ... I won't allow that.' I whisper to Morrison, beside me, 'This is Mosley speaking!'[1] He attacks Hugh. 'But for *my* Health Service he would never have been Chancellor of the Exchequer ...... I have served many more years in the Labour Party than he.' He had been a young man in 1931, when Snowden was Chancellor, and in this very room he had been howled down, when he warned the Party where it was going. He was sweating and screeching and seemed on the edge of a nervous breakdown. Once he said, almost as to himself, 'I think I had better sit down.' This makes a terribly unfavourable impression. (Roy Jenkins said to me later, 'Nye forgot that it is the Parliamentary Party not the constituency parties that elects the Leader.')

Then, after some unimportant interventions, Chuter winds up. Not very successfully and amid some confusion. As usual a cross between a schoolmaster and a sergeant major. He speaks of another meeting in this room and of scandalous attacks. Jennie Lee jumps up and he says, 'I mentioned no names, but the cap seems to fit.' Then he mentions Mosley. One of the speeches this morning reminded him of Mosley. Nye shouts, 'Now you've said it!' And so to the Abbey.

Part of the Party Meeting I was drafting an Executive statement in support of the Government and the Budget. After the Abbey, I went with Morgan Phillips to my office and finished the draft for N.E.C. tomorrow.

Wednesday 25th April
N.E.C. carries with four dissensions – Nye, Driberg, Mikardo and Barbara Castle – a resolution, much shorter than our draft of yesterday, backing the Government and the Budget.

These four write next day protesting that we have gone beyond our rights in making this declaration. (Quite a silly argument, which finds no support in our constitution or past practice.)

They *did* think of resigning from the Executive – in which case we

1 See entry for 20th November 1930, above, p. 130.

should have gained Phil [Noel-Baker], Emrys Hughes,[1] Mrs Jean Mann[2] and Miss Cynthia Martin – but think better of it.

I get John Freeman to come to my room and talk. I say I don't expect any more correspondence and he agrees. I say the one thing that bites me is that he didn't, as he promised, see Hugh.[3] I know Hugh had asked him. John says that on the Sunday, when he was with me, he had half intended to call in for a drink. But he had preferred my company. I say that in the real 1931 Jowitt only saw MacDonald and not Henderson. The latter said afterwards, 'If I had seen him, I might have persuaded him not to leave us.'

I said to John that he was a wonderful scalp for the uglies. I had heard Mikardo exulting over him in the entrance to a lavatory.

I said to John, 'Don't form a clique. Keep in circulation.' He said he had been told beforehand that everyone would be beastly to him, if he resigned. But they hadn't been. Perhaps, he says, his generation is kinder than mine. We speak of finance. He says he will have to live very quietly for a while.

Tuesday 1st May

Woodrow Wyatt[4] tells me that he is to be Under-Secretary for War, replacing Michael Stewart who takes John Freeman's place at Supply. Wyatt will do well.

I drive him home and meet his wife,[5] and we talk for some hours. I must have him to lunch some time. ...

Wyatt says that Tony (with whom he has been working closely for some time) and others think that my non-jealousy, especially since I left the Treasury, is very fine and a stabilising force in the Party. I say I am very happy that they think so.

Wednesday 2nd May

Health Service Charges Bill in Committee. A most shocking show! Our back-benches – 'all the rejects and the frustrates' – as someone

1 Emrys Hughes (1894–1969). Labour M.P. for South Ayrshire 1946–69.
2 Mrs Jean Mann (d. 1958). Labour M.P. for Coatbridge and Airdrie 1950–59. Member of Labour Party N.E.C. (Women's Section) 1953–8.
3 As a postscript to his letter to Dalton of 23rd April 1951, Freeman wrote: 'I have been unable – for administrative reasons – to see Hugh G, but shall continue my efforts this evening.' Beneath this Dalton scribbled: '(But what the hell's the good of that! I wanted him to see Hugh *before* he decided.)'
4 W. L. Wyatt, later Sir Woodrow (b. 1918). Parliamentary Under-Secretary and Financial Secretary to the War Office May–October 1951. Labour M.P. for Birmingham Aston 1945–55; Bosworth 1959–70.
5 Nora Wyatt, née Robins (m. 1948).

says[1] – keep up a furious attack on the Charges for several hours. Most bitter and abusive speeches are made. A vote is challenged on the First Clause, and though we win by 260 odd to 3 – with a few Tories and Liberals with us – some 30 of our chaps sit abstaining, and a lot more had left before the vote. Jam for Tories!

Crossman in Tea Room, white with passion, said, '*Now* you see. This is just a Tory Budget' ...... Now that he can't get into the Foreign Office with Herbert, he is a Nyeite.

All the publicists and columnists are Nyeites. And nearly all the televisionists and performers on other important broadcast series.

Earlier this evening, we had an XYZ and discussed the Inner Politics. Jack Diamond[2] thought Nye had gone right to the bottom of the pond last week. But now was climbing up. Jim Callaghan havered a bit, as usual, as to whether we could really achieve arms programme. Tony said most of our M.P.s were frightful cowards, watching which way the cat would jump. He himself has written both to *Tribune* and *New Statesman* this week. But he thinks very few others will have tried. He thinks Nye will carry constituency parties at Conference. I said I wasn't so sure. Tony also said that Transport House and the E.C. were such bloody fools that they always overplayed their hand ...

Friday 11th May
Roy Jenkins lunched with me, after meeting with Wilfred Fienburgh[3] in my office to discuss lines of a National Executive document on 'Towards Social Justice'. Fienburgh will write this up, and send copies to me, Roy and Tony to discuss after Whitsun recess.

Roy has hated recent atmosphere in House of Commons so much that he has only gone there to vote. Jennifer [Jenkins] is expecting a second baby in a week or so. ...

... Roy – and many others – have been deeply shocked by Nye and his 'sub-human' performance at Party Meeting. ... Roy hopes Clem will go on long enough to be able to hand over direct to Hugh. Under

---

1 Stanley Evans, Labour M.P. for Wednesbury, had accused Bevan of leading 'an uneasy coalition of well-meaning emotionalists, rejects, frustrates, crackpots and fellow-travellers, making Fred Karno's Army look like the Brigade of Guards'. (M. Foot, *Bevan II*, pp. 342–3.)
2 John Diamond, later Baron (b. 1907). Labour M.P. for Manchester Blackley 1945–51; Gloucester 1957–70. Chief Secretary to the Treasury 1964–70.
3 Wilfred Fienburgh (1919–58). Secretary of the Labour Party Research Department 1950–51. Labour M.P. for North Islington 1951–8. Author of *No Love for Johnnie* (1959), a novel about a Labour M.P. published posthumously and later made into a film.

Herbert, it would not be a happy Party. I said that Jim Griffiths should not be ruled out as a possible Leader. We agreed that Hugh had, as yet, no Public Face in the Labour Movement in the country, though he had it in Parliament and in public opinion generally. But this would come.

If we had a sharp reverse at the next election, most of Nye's friends would lose their seats. He was also afraid that Tony might go. ...

He criticised Dick Crossman's unreliability and inconsistency – even in the course of a single conversation. He said I seemed to do my departmental work pretty effortlessly, through long practice. He thought I was exceptional among ministers in wanting to read books, meet people and go to places unconnected with my Department.

Dick criticised Younger to me yesterday. He said he was only another civil servant at the Foreign Office and no real use to Herbert. He had hoped that Eddie Shackleton[1] would get Ernest Davies's job, but there had been some muddle somewhere. I said some thought that it wouldn't look well to have too many of Morrison's nominees in office.

Crossman had also told me that, when Winston offered Butler Education in 1940 and Butler accepted, Winston asked, 'Do you *really* want it?' And Rab said, 'Yes. It is the Department I would most like to have', and Winston snarled, 'That bears out all my worst suspicions of you!'

Dick says Rab is completely out now. He says Rab once said to him, he thinks at Woburn[2] in the War, 'I agree with nearly all your policy, except for one thing. I believe in inequality.' But this Me-too-ism didn't fit the Young Tories today.

Wednesday 16th to Monday 21st May
Whitsun Walk. Pembroke and Brecon.

Wednesday 16th May
Car from West Leaze to Thruxton airfield, near Andover, whence fly with Geoffrey de Freitas and Peter Ayles (spare pilot) to Withybush Airfield, Haverfordwest. Met by Desmond [Donnelly] and a crowd of local worthies.

1 E. A. Shackleton, later Baron (b. 1911). Labour M.P. for Preston South 1950–51; Preston 1946–50. Minister for the Air Force 1964–7; Minister without Portfolio 1967–8; Paymaster-General 1968; Lord Privy Seal and Minister in the Civil Service Department 1968–70.
2 Woburn Abbey, Bedfordshire, housed the propaganda side of the Special Operations Executive during the war. Crossman had worked in the German Section.

Sunday 20th May
Climb Brecon Beacon. Rain and near top of hill mist and strong wind.
But I make a speech to some sixty Ramblers and Youth Hostellers.
The *Daily Mirror* being represented, I tell them all to come and make
love, if they want to, in the lonely and beautiful high places – but not
on a day like this.

We are reduced to a small nucleus this year. Next year? An election
before then? Who will be left? I come back feeling very fit, though a
bit stiff. I went up hill on the Beacons slow and blowing, but I came
down at a hell of a pace, leading the band. Not bad! And rather
admired!

Tuesday 29th May
See Attlee and talk about election date and kindred matters. I say I'm
sure we oughtn't to go into another winter. My cold view is that,
barring something quite impressive, we shall lose. But we ought to
lose by as little as possible. If we wait till winter things will get worse
for us. Our best chance will be in September or October. Perhaps we
might dissolve as from the Conference at the beginning of October.

He says he agrees. (He often says this, and then slips.) Further
arguments are (1) that the King goes on his Australian tour in February, and the election ought to be over before then, and (2) the doubt
about the attitude of Nye and Co. I say I'm sorry Jim Callaghan wasn't
given a move up. He isn't very convincing on this. The resignations,
I fear, have put off the sackings – of Henderson, Strauss and Strachey.
(I think I noted earlier that Strachey went round to see Clem in
hospital to tell him that he *wasn't* going to resign with Nye – and then
said in some public speech that he agreed with Nye about the spectacles
and teeth, but wasn't resigning over it!)

Friday 1st June
Hugh to lunch alone in my flat. Very pleasant talk. He's still a bit too
much inclined to play safe and forget the Party. But he is very keen
to address next Annual Conference and I say this can certainly be
arranged.

Inclined to agree with me that we ought to have the election before
winter, especially if we could settle Korean war.

Thinks price control could be stricter – and might safely ruin some
of the highest cost producers. I denounce Shawcross as not a socialist
and too cocky to bear. Hugh defends him – moderately, but agrees
that on R.P.M. [Retail Price Maintenance] he's very weak, and will
try to buck him up on this.

543

Friday 1st to Sunday 3rd June

Weekend at Oxford ... I dine – and sleep two nights – at Littles'. First-class hosts. Raymond Carr,[1] his wife (very pregnant) and Nowell-Smith[2] to dinner. Very gay and lots to drink. Play croquet in failing light and after dinner and a lot of talk, poker, rules of which I had forgotten and have to pick up as I go.

I was particularly interested to see the famous Raymond Carr for the first time. I can picture him as a very gay and unrestrained companion on many adventures! He is, I hear from Ian, having difficulties in getting a Fellowship at any college, though he is a very good historian. And his All Souls Fellowship runs out next year. This seems bad luck.

Saturday 2nd June

Lunch at Trinity. Rediscover Philip Williams[3] – Labour, stayed at Evenwood with Bells,[4] follows Gallup Polls and knows a lot about French electoral law, etc. Nice man, but not a Fellow yet. Croquet after lunch.

Then Ian and I, at Landon's[5] suggestion, watch some cricket – University v. Free Foresters – but he didn't know which side was in, and brought back wrong information based on scoreboard. But it was splendidly sunny.

Tea with President, and Oh! his wife![6] I'm so glad I'm staying with the Littles and not with them.

Sunday 3rd June

Ian and Dobs [Little] and I drive to Nicholas and Olga [Davenport] for lunch. We find Tony's car there, and him sunning on the grass with Olga. He had slept here last night, coming from his constituency and a Youth Rally at Gloucester. Very pleasant company. Some played tennis. Tony and Olga drove back to London in her car, I in

1 Raymond Carr (b. 1919). Historian. Fellow of All Souls College, Oxford 1946–53. Fellow of New College, Oxford 1953–64. Warden of St Antony's College, Oxford since 1968.

2 P. H. Nowell-Smith (b. 1914). Fellow of Trinity College, Oxford 1946–57. Professor of Philosophy at the University of Leicester 1957–64; Kent 1964–9; University of York, Toronto 1969–85.

3 P. M. Williams (1920–84). Lecturer, Trinity College, Oxford 1946–53. Fellow of Nuffield College, Oxford 1950–53. Fellow of Jesus College, Oxford 1953–8. Official Fellow of Nuffield College, Oxford 1958–84. Biographer of Gaitskell, and author of books on French politics and history.

4 Jack Bell and his wife. Activists in Evenwood, a village in Dalton's constituency.

5 P. A. Landon (1888–1961). Bursar, Trinity College, Oxford 1921–51. University Reader in Criminal Law.

6 J. R. H. Weaver, q.v., President of Trinity, and Stella Weaver, née Acton.

mine which they took me into Oxford to pick up at Trinity, leaving Nicholas to drive Tony's car back on Tuesday.

A very good and sunny weekend!

Monday 4th June

... [D]ine, rather bleakly, with Morrison at Howard Hotel. Also present Morgan Phillips, Gordon Walker, Denis Healey and Wilfred Fienburgh. The idea was to discuss future policy. But we got on to the Annual Conference, and stayed there most of the evening. There was general gloom about the Conference. Strong support for Nye among constituency parties. His resignation and the resulting issues will be raised. There will be a claim by Nye and the rest to speak to Minority view, from the platform. If this is refused, they will resign, speak from the floor, stand for re-election and get back triumphant. Card votes needed to carry any major vote, and you can't be sure of big cards. Danger of Nyeites winning further seats on N.E. in C.L.P. [Constituency Labour Parties'] section. (On the other hand, if they try to run a much larger ticket, they may split each others' votes.) Can we concentrate on a *short* Party statement and get it agreed in N.E.C.? If it contains something on Rearmament, it might make it difficult for Nye to oppose it en bloc. When an election? Not before Conference, as this would be thought to be a trick. 'We must ride the Conference.' But how? Not a very bright evening!

Friday 15th June

Tony's motion on Monopolies. A most successful debate. Tony's speech was first class, though he had a very thin House. He spoke for forty minutes, and I passed him a note at the end. 'Your best so far.

$$\alpha + \text{in politics}$$
$$\text{economics}$$
$$\text{style}$$
$$\text{charm}$$

a very rare combination.'

Roy Jenkins said Tony had shown him this later. Roy was less enthusiastic than I about the speech. Shawcross, having been pepped up by me, made quite a good, though much too long, speech. Hudson for the Opposition fumbled irritably, and said it was clear that I had been telling Shawcross what to say.[1] This goes with the story in last

1 In the Debate on Monopolies on 15th June, R. S. Hudson, q.v., said, ' ... one of the most prominent persons today on the Government Front Bench was the Minister for Local Government and Planning. We could not fail to observe with interest that apparently he was instructing his Right Hon. Friend the President of the Board of Trade on what answers to give to the various points that were raised in the debate ... ' (H.C. Debs [488], col. 2,764.)

week's *Sunday Express* that I am being a ginger man and telling Shawcross to 'get tough with monopolies'.

Wednesday 20th June

I heard that Barbara Castle[1] had been asked to stand down from National Executive to make room for Harold Wilson. I encouraged her to refuse. They will, no doubt, try to run something of a ticket. But there is some danger for them – as well as for others of us – in this. They may trample each other in the vote, with wide spreads of voting by C.L.P.s, who are rather hard to organise to vote tickets.

Thursday 21st June

Saw John Freeman ... He is writing steadily for the *Statesman* now, but his succession to Kingsley Martin is less clear than I had thought from earlier talks with him. Nothing for two years, anyhow, he thinks. He and Dick, he says, act well on each other, Dick as a stimulant to him, he as a sedative to Dick. This week they say that Cabinet has been drained of personality, and is suffering from pernicious inertia. True, I'm afraid!

Friday 22nd June

Jack Ashley,[2] ex-President Cambridge Union, working engineer from Widnes, just back from U.S. debating tour, to lunch with me at the House. Very thrilled. We sit on the terrace after. He has got a II$_2$ in Economics, not bad considering how much else he has been doing. He asks me what I did when I went down from Cambridge, and is reassured when I tell him I did little or no politics for some years. He has been offered a job with Cadbury as Industrial Relations Officer. I advise him to take it – he was inclined to, but hesitating – and to aim at holding it for a year or two, but to keep in touch with the Fabians and the Birmingham Movement, where, I tell him, there is not much Parliamentary talent.

---

1 Barbara Castle, q.v., was elected to the Women's Section of the N.E.C. in 1950, successfully switching to the Constituency Parties' Section in 1951. A Bevanite, she had been closely associated with the Labour Left since before the war.
2 Jack Ashley (b. 1922). President of the Cambridge Union 1951. Radio producer 1951–7. Labourer and crane driver 1936–46. Television producer 1957–66. Labour M.P. for Stoke-on-Trent South since 1966.

Tuesday 26th June

Lunched alone with Hugh in the Treasury. We are both Octobrists. He says 'everything is getting too difficult' to go on being handled in this Parliament, with the narrow majority and the Bevanites.

Sunday 1st July

In nine days' time the famous *Tribune* pamphlet is due to appear.[1] There is still great dispute among the twenty-five as to its contents. The first half, on Foreign Affairs, by Foot was both very anti-American and very anti-Russian. Some want it toned down. The second half, by Mikardo, has hardly been discussed in detail yet.

Chiefly from Donnelly, and a bit from John Freeman and Dick Crossman, I hear about this unsteady progress. I think – as I may have noted before – that I seem to have had some influence through talks with Nye and Freeman both on the form of the document – not to be an itemised programme – and on the presentation ...

The group are

Nye, Wilson, Freeman, who will sign the foreword, Foot, Crossman, Mikardo, Barbara Castle, Driberg, Donnelly, Bing,[2] Bill Mallalieu,[3] Hale,[4] Acland, Jennie Lee, Delargy,[5] Bowles,[6] Tudor Watkins,[7] Cecil Poole,[8] Fernyhough,[9] Carmichael,[10] Harold Davies,

1 *One Way Only*, with an introduction by Bevan. This called for a cut in military spending, stabilisation of the cost of living, and an increase in taxation. Its publication was an important step towards the creation of a cohesive left-wing group centred on Bevan.
2 Geoffrey Bing (1909–77). Labour M.P. for Hornchurch 1945–55. Attorney-General of Ghana 1957–61. Adviser to the President of Ghana (Nkrumah) 1961–6.
3 J. P. W. Mallalieu, later Sir John (1908–80). Labour M.P. for Huddersfield East 1950–79; Huddersfield 1945–50. Junior minister 1964–9.
4 Leslie Hale, later Baron (b. 1902). Labour M.P. for West Oldham 1950–69; Oldham 1945–50.
5 Captain Hugh Delargy (1908–76). Labour M.P. for Thurrock 1950–76; Manchester Platting 1945–50.
6 F. G. Bowles, later Baron (1902–70). Labour M.P. for Nuneaton 1942–64.
7 Tudor Watkins, later Baron (b. 1903). Labour M.P. for Brecon and Radnor 1945–70.
8 Major C. C. Poole (1902–56). Labour M.P. for Birmingham Perry Barr 1950–55; Lichfield 1938–50.
9 Ernest Fernyhough (b. 1908). Labour M.P. for Jarrow 1947–79. P.P.S. to the Prime Minister 1964–7. Junior minister 1967–9.
10 James Carmichael (1894–1966). I.L.P., then Labour, M.P. for Glasgow Bridgeton 1946–61.

Baird, Lipton,[1] Manuel,[2] Griffiths.[3]

They meet on Tuesdays, but some don't come and a lot don't count.

I've been trying to be a bridge, and, looking a bit ahead, to make a programme that will be bold and yet make sense. Massingham,[4] who has a malicious fixation about me, has an amusing paragraph in this week's *Observer*, saying that my 'loving arms have recently been observed festively entwined around the shoulders of one mutineer after another'. I shall ask this chap to lunch.

Foot was reported at last XYZ meeting[5] to have told Jim Callaghan and Tony Crosland that I was their 'over-cover representative in the Cabinet'. I think it's mainly Foot that feeds Massingham, and Nye too no doubt.

Meanwhile I am making a fair number of speeches – I made one yesterday at Croydon – designed, as often at this season of the year, to strengthen my N.E. vote at the Annual Conference.

Yesterday Driberg was married, aged 45, to his 45-year-old widow.[6] Freeman – though twice married – was best man. Both Tshekedi[7] and Seretse Khama were there. And the chief Bevanites and Osbert Sitwell[8] and Tony Crosland. 'The most interesting wedding of the season' said the *Sunday Express*.

Ruth tells me that the Arts Council gave a cocktail party a fortnight ago to a mixed and rather distinguished company. Driberg came with a boy in a kilt. Sir Kenneth Clark[9] was vexed. An M.P. told me a boy in a kilt was at the church.

Monday 2nd July

... I saw P.M. Very friendly. I said we couldn't have Morrison trying to be Pam.[10] He said he agreed, and we must certainly keep in close

---

1 Marcus Lipton (1900–78). Labour M.P. for Brixton 1945–78.
2 A. C. Manuel (1901–76). Labour M.P. for Central Ayrshire 1950–55, 1959–70.
3 William Griffiths (1912–73). Labour M.P. for Manchester Exchange 1950–73; Manchester Moss Side 1945–50.
4 Hugh Massingham (d. 1971). *Observer* political columnist 1945–61; *Sunday Telegraph* 1961–71.
5 On 26th June.
6 Tom Driberg married Mrs Ena Binfield in 1951. The marriage was later dissolved.
7 Tshekedi Khama. Uncle of Seretse Khama, q.v., and Regent of the Bamangwato tribe in Bechuanaland.
8 Sir Osbert Sitwell, 5th Bart (1892–1969). Poet, novelist and critic.
9 Sir Kenneth Clark, later Baron (1903–85). Slade Professor of Fine Art, Oxford 1946–50, 1961–2. Chairman of the Arts Council 1953–60.
10 'Pam': i.e. a Palmerston-style gunboat diplomatist.

touch with U.S. Government. I said Morrison mustn't try to compensate himself for having been a Conscientious Objector in W.W.I. and against arms before W.W.II.

I said I was still an Octobrist. P.M. said so was he. Announce dissolution just before Annual Conference? I also urged that we should be much stronger on price control, and take a more aggressive posture against rising prices.

Sunday 15th July
Massingham to lunch with me at Josef's on Thursday (12th July). On the surface most frank and friendly. I tell him that, though I despise Wilson – 'bonfire of controls' and idleness over monopoly – I like and respect both Nye and John and tried to dissuade them both from resigning. 'Who thought I was anti-Nye?' I asked. 'I think Nye did,' he said. ...

We agreed that Jim Callaghan has been undeservedly passed over, and that it was bad to put him under Pakenham, who was his own age. To be under George Hall hadn't mattered. Massingham said that 'Attlee is hated' for such appointments as Pakenham and Ogmore – not only by Nyeites, but quite widely in the Party. ...

On Saturday (14th July) I go to Caxton Hall to sit and listen to John Freeman and Denis Healey at a Fabian discussion on Arms and Foreign Policy. Two of the ablest, most interesting and most attractive younger members of the party.

John has tremendous feline charm. He puts his case very brilliantly. And wins most of the audience – probably they were won before. But Healey is even better in reply – quite devastating and with some wonderful knock-about thrown in.

John says, 'Tony's at the White City' (AAA Championship) – probably with some very glamorous girl. I take John and Healey both to my flat for a drink. John says, in reply to a question by me, that he thinks it would be premature for Attlee to try to talk to Nye at present. All three of us agree that it would be good to postpone issue of a statement till just before the Conference.

Tuesday 24th July
Reporting to me this morning on conversation among Bevanites, Desmond Donnelly says that Driberg has a death wish, like a woman who wants to throw herself under a galloping horse; Mikardo doesn't take it all too seriously, he sits in a trench for some time and then gets bored and walks out to meet a hail of bullets. These two would like to resign from the N.E.C. Nye and Barbara [Castle] have more

of an eye to the main chance. But Barbara, worked up by Ted, is now talking about 'principle'. This is rather dangerous. Crossman doesn't help to prevent resignation. He spoke, at the meeting held at his house on Wednesday, where they gathered, of 'cold logic' and an 'inevitable clash'. If they thought there would be an October election, they mightn't fight. They know they won't be forgiven, if they can be shown to have split the Party.

Later the same day, at the Speaker's squash, Donnelly says they've met since his morning talk with me, and Nye not being there, advised that no decision should be taken to resign without the Group being consulted. Therefore there will be nothing precipitate at tomorrow's N.E.C. Nye is off to Yugoslavia on Thursday. John Freeman, Donnelly said, was very good and sensible in discouraging precipitate action.[1]

Friday 27th July
To Cambridge to stay with Walstons[2] at Newton Hall and address a Labour fête. Good hosts. Lots of dollars; heavy scores through devaluation.

Thursday 2nd August
Parliament adjourns till 16th October, but perhaps won't meet again till after a general election.

As always at end of July, people are tired and fractious. I go down to West Leaze tonight. Ruth went this morning. The Bevanites keep boring on about their differences with the Government, though Nye left last week for a month in Yugoslavia. Some say he'll embarrass Tito a bit. He was invited when still a minister. Now, as Low[3] says in a recent cartoon, he'll have to explain to Tito how he'll strengthen Yugoslavia by spending less on arms and more on social services. The

---

1 Scc Michael Foot's comment on 'the compulsive informer in our midst' who reported the proceedings of Bevanite meetings regularly to Dalton and thereby to the whips: 'His identity as Desmond Donnelly has been notorious for years but the full proof is contained in Dalton's unpublished diaries which record that the leakages to Dalton started on 30th November 1951' (*Bevan II*, p. 358n.). As this entry shows, the leakages actually started more than four months earlier.
2 Henry Walston, later Baron (b. 1912). Prospective Labour candidate for Cambridgeshire. Landowner and farmer. Counsellor to the Duchy of Lancaster 1948–54. Director of Agriculture, British Zone of Germany 1946–7. Junior minister 1964–7. Married to Catherine Walston, formerly Macdonald (d. 1978). The Walstons often entertained leading Labour politicians at their country house near Cambridge.
3 D. A. C. Low, later Sir David (1891–1963). Cartoonist and caricaturist.

25 Dalton among the workers. Canvassing in Bishop Auckland, February 1950.

26 With Aneurin Bevan, 1950

Above, left: 27 Greenwood and Attlee confer at the Morecambe Party
Conference, 1952
Above, right: 28 Anthony and Hilary Crosland after their wedding, November 1952

Below: 29 Bevanites: J. P. W. Mallalieu and Michael Foot at a football match, 1953

two Crossmans and the two Castles are also going, together, to Yugoslavia. So is a Fabian Party – John Parker, Roy Jenkins and two others.

Today Dick Crossman and I had a talk in the Smoke Room after lunch. (Bellenger came and butted in half-way through.) Dick said that last night he and I had had some acrid words. (We had. He and I and Nicholas [Davenport] together. ... I said I was *so* bored with everything being dragged back to that pamphlet, and so bored with all this personal animus and spite against Hugh. And Dick said he wasn't spiteful or jealous towards Hugh. And I said, 'Oh yes you are, like a lot of others. You're a Wykehamist Third Man' – I had Douglas Jay in mind.)

So today Dick said he didn't hate Hugh. And he didn't really hate anyone in politics. He didn't think *his* generation did, not like mine and the hatreds between leaders before the war. I said I didn't hate much either, though I sometimes got angry with people. And then we both agreed that Nye *did* hate people. Dick said, 'Yes, he personalises politics.' And now, said Dick, he hates Hugh much worse than Morrison. How silly of Nye, he said, to have driven Hugh into Morrison's arms. And how silly of P.M. to keep Nye stewing on at Ministry of Health instead of giving him a new creative job. I said I knew he wanted Colonies just after last election. And that would have enabled me to be Minister of Local Government and Planning right away. Dick said the great mistake P.M. made about Hugh was not in making him Chancellor, but in not making a real reconstruction of the Government at the same time to keep the balance between different sections. (I think he meant that *he* ought to have been brought in then.)

In reply to Bellenger, I said that Cripps and I had both strongly favoured Hugh as Chancellor. With Cripps and me out of it, I told P.M. there was no one else who could handle the job – and I knew something about it. Dick said he thought this was right, but then Nye might have been made Foreign Secretary.

We spoke of Harold Wilson without much enthusiasm. I said it was a pity he'd never had a back-bench life before becoming a minister.

Dick and I then recalled a dinner party I'd given, just after I'd been made Chancellor – 'The Young Victors' Dinner Party' I'd called it – at St Ermin's (Bellenger said he'd been there, but we both told him he was mistaken). The party had included Dick, Hugh, Evan [Durbin], Chris Mayhew, George Brown, John Freeman, Raymond Blackburn, Harold Wilson and a few others. Someone had said – 'Was it you, Dick?' – that some of them ought to go straight into the

Government. Dick said, 'No it was Evan. Only he would have dared to say a thing like that.' And I had said that I thought no new M.P. should go straight into the Government without a back-bench life. Dick thought I was probably right. 'But then they took Harold Wilson. If they *had* wanted to experiment with a new academic, they'd have done much better to take me.' Bellenger, 'But then you'd have been conditioned Dick.' Dick, 'Of course I should.'

A very revealing conversation. It *would* have been better to take Dick. He has terrific energy, and all the dynamisms, all at once, no matter how they clash! Great mental power, but no judgment. But that might have come through conditioning.

Tuesday 4th September
First Cabinet since Parliament adjourned ...

German Rearmament. I again speak strongly ... Morrison, as usual, irritated by my line, and Pakenham, as usual, reacts hysterically. But Chuter Ede and Robens speak on my side – Chuter says we'll create something we can't control; Robens dwells on enormity of arming Germans, which while our own troops, not to speak of French, etc., are short of arms and equipment. P.M., in his usual phrase, says, 'This should be played very slow.' Cabinet Minutes leave out all [the] row.

Morrison doesn't *work* at Foreign Office, and doesn't *know* about them. Strang, sitting behind him at Cabinet, nods vehemently when I develop an anti-German case, but I was displeased to see old Fraser,[1] First Sea Lord, grinning.

Two of my normal allies on this, Jim Griffiths and Hector McNeil, were absent.

Hugh – always very careful to balance between Morrison and me on this – seems to have done well at Blackpool. He tells me after that he had a very friendly personal reception and a long clap from the Congress when he finished. ...

See Attlee at my own request. Press the need for a quick election, preferably in October. To wait, I say, would be suicide for ourselves and massacre for our Parliamentarians. In the dark winter everything may go wrong – coal, electricity, rail transport, balance of payments – and we may be forced suddenly to go to the country by loss of by-elections. ...

---

1 Admiral of the Fleet Sir Bruce Fraser, 1st Baron (1888–1981). First Sea Lord and Chief of Naval Staff 1948–51. Commander-in-Chief, Home Fleet 1943–4; Eastern Fleet 1944; British Pacific Fleet 1945–6; Portsmouth 1947–8.

I was delighted to find him responsive to all this. I think he has already made up his mind. He was much impressed by risk of being let down by dissident abstentions. He was inclined to think in terms of polling on Thursday 25th October, with dissolution three weeks before this, and official announcement by himself a fortnight earlier; say about 20th September. Then we could rearrange Conference programme. We should hold Conference just the same. Windle, whose death, following an operation for cancer, is announced this morning, had told him that our solid Labour vote all over the country was holding; the only problem was getting it out. But Dick had added that he couldn't say how long it would go on holding.

I said Nye had wanted an October election and this should make him more amenable. He had said to me at the House, '*I* ought to be told.' Attlee hadn't seen him; 'he walked out on me; it's up to him to come and see me if he wants to.'[1] ...

I said I was very much against raising German Rearmament. I spoke of Kaiser's speech,[2] which I had sent him, demanding back the East. They are war-mongers I said. He said that they and the Americans, many of whom regarded war as inevitable, were a very dangerous combination. He said, 'We mustn't have Germans in uniform. We must back European Army.'

Sunday 16th September
P.M. having been out of action last Wednesday, I see him today at No. 10 at my own request.

He is in pain with lumbago and sciatica, not a very good opening to coming events. I come (a) to press again for a quick election, (b) to express concern at Morrison's handling of Foreign Affairs, particularly German Rearmament and Persia. On (a) all is well. I say, 'I hope your mind hasn't moved on this since we last talked.' He says, 'No.' He sticks to 25th October as Polling Day. The only doubt is whether to announce it this week or next. Morgan Phillips is for waiting till next week. I urge this week. P.M. is going to Scotland to Annual Conference of Scottish Labour Party next weekend. It would, I say, be an awful bore to have to speak there with the secret in his bosom. Also we must have time to rearrange Scarborough Conference business.

---

1 Marginal note: 'Tonight Desmond [Donnelly] dinner with me and we planned to denigrate Driberg for the benefit of Barbara [Castle]. (Beer and sex).'
2 Jakob Kaiser (1888–1961). German politician (C.D.U.) imprisoned during the Nazi regime. Federal Minister for German Reunion and for All-German Affairs 1949–57. Kaiser had addressed a youth rally in the Eastern Zone of Berlin on 17th August 1951 on the question of German unity.

Next week would give us too little time. Also we must draft an election manifesto. And, with press buzzing louder and louder, we can't keep on putting it off, or our own people will begin to be demoralised. Finally, if the new *Tribune* pamphlet is coming out this week, we'd better smother its publicity, as a public declaration would; if we delay till next week, it will look as though they've forced our hand. I think I persuaded him.

He now plans to see Phillips tomorrow; to call a Cabinet on Tuesday morning – for information; to see the King on Tuesday afternoon; to have the announcement in the press on Wednesday morning; to have an N.E.C. for information on Thursday. He should make, I suggest, a statement for Wednesday morning's press, and might invite Nye to see him on Wednesday, and suggest unity. Then at the weekend he can make a good election speech! And so can I at S.W. Regional Conference at Taunton.

I then spoke of Morrison, and said I was much shocked by his rashness and ignorance. P.M., to my surprise, quite warmed up, said he was *most* disappointed with Morrison as Foreign Secretary and, if we won the election, certainly wouldn't put him back at the Foreign Office. His ignorance, P.M. said, was shocking. He had no background and knew no history. He had pressed for the job, and most people whom P.M. had consulted had supported him. I reminded him that I had said I didn't want it – which was true – and had put forward Jim Griffiths. P.M. said he, Ernie and I were Jim's only supporters, and Jim himself was very unwilling, said he knew nothing about it, which was true, but he knew he knew nothing and Morrison didn't. Morrison, P.M. said, always read off a sheet of paper in Cabinet; he hadn't got any of it in his head. We spoke of Persia and I showed P.M. telegram in which Americans were restraining our little pseudo-Pam[1] from thoughts of military action against Persians to occupy Abadan.[2] I said I resented Morrison's attempt to rush the Cabinet into a false version of international law on this. We weren't as ignorant as all that. P.M. said, 'I am handling Persia; I've made it quite clear that troops are to go in only to save lives.'

1 See entry for 2nd July 1951, and note 10 above, p. 548.
2 The Iranian government had nationalised oilfields belonging to the Anglo-Iranian Oil Company in March 1951. Discussions about compensation broke down in June. Heavily criticised for his handling of the affair, the Foreign Secretary promised protection for all Britons in Persia, dispatched a cruiser, and contemplated sending in troops to seize Abadan. Morrison's sabre-rattling proved as ineffective as earlier attempts at negotiation, and the Iranian Prime Minister Mossadeq refused to be intimidated.

I said I'd wished Morrison well on his appointment, but warned him that this was a full-time job. My scouts told me [that the] Foreign Office were very uncomfortable. He treated it all so casually, and wouldn't work at it.

Tuesday 18th September
Am speaking a lot! Indeed I have the press almost to myself nowadays, with most other ministers abroad and Bevanites strangely silent ...

I want, a few years hence, to see a Young Turk landing on the beaches of Power and Fame – with my three companions at that unforgettable weekend at Le Donon – Jim Callaghan, Tony and Denis – in the van.[1] ...

Meanwhile I have been doing some good electioneering now for the National Executive at Scarborough. It'll be amusing to see the result.

Wednesday 19th September
Cabinet – but very thin attendance, only Attlee, myself and Ede, Albert Victorious, Hector McNeil and Douglas Jay (for Hugh) and Addison and Bob Taylor[2] (for Whiteley). Latter is rapidly breaking up – deaf, incoherent, repetitive and pathetic – a very quick and final decline. P.M. announces intention to dissolve. I warmly welcome and none present oppose. But Attlee says not all were agreed and it's clear e.g. from Morrison's comments from Ottawa, 'No Comment', 'still no comment', that *he* was furiously against.[3]

We discuss, at too great length, terms of P.M.'s broadcast announcement. The King is, I fear, very ill. ...

Attlee grins over storm I've raised over advice to housewives not to buy till prices fall.[4] No resentment! No one else capable of discussing this at this thin Cabinet. Perhaps the last Cabinet we'll have! No officials present. I stay behind and urge him to see Bevan. He says he will after tonight's broadcast – before he leaves for Scotland tomorrow. (But I don't think he did.)

This evening I dine, rather dully, at Australian High Commis-

1 In August 1950. See above, p. 482.
2 R. J. Taylor (1881–1954). Deputy Chief Whip 1945–51. Labour M.P. for Morpeth 1935–54.
3 Morrison was away on Foreign Office business for most of September, first in the United States, and then taking part in N.A.T.O. discussions in Canada.
4 Dalton had made a series of speeches demanding more rigorous price control, and urging housewives to bring down the cost of living by withholding purchases until clothing prices fell. The textile trade was predictably furious, and most of the Tory press shared the view of *The Economist* that this was 'an irresponsible piece of electioneering' (22nd September 1951).

sioner's. ... Then back to flat to receive John Freeman at 10.45. Rather ill, and overwrought – pain in his ears, very tired, going off for ten days' rest before election. Tony thinks he has become more and more emotional (a word of discredit in Tony's vocabulary) and confused about politics, though I'm glad that their friendship – politics barred – still holds.

I speak ill, and with knowledge, of Morrison as Foreign Secretary, doesn't know he knows nothing, cocky and reactionary. Wants to rearm West Germany, and put troops into Persia. John hears there's been a peevish exchange of telegrams across Atlantic – P.M. and Morrison.

I tell him I've pressed P.M. to see Nye. He suggests we put Dick Crossman on to broadcast, as best performer of the Bevanites. He's sure we're right to dissolve now, and not wait. We agree it's still pretty open, but we're likely to lose. He likes my campaign for cheaper textiles. I send him home to Hampstead in my car.

Thursday 20th September
I had lunch with Jim Callaghan and Tony at Josef's; all very cheerful. Jim thinks we may win the election; Tony doesn't. I tell Jim I've done my best for him with Attlee, and praised his 'energy and efficiency, personality and poise', and recommended him to succeed Tomlinson at Ministry of Education and in Cabinet, and commended him, on Strasburg basis, for speed in learning new stuff. But I'd met with some sales resistance ... Tony praised my loyalty to Hugh and his to me in a world where most spoke ill of all others. He didn't think Dick Crossman would be as good on the air as Tom Driberg. But I said, 'Out, out.' He thought Morrison's star had fallen heavily in the Party since 1945.

John Freeman told me last night that Shawcross ('Sir Peacock' I call him) had played up to Nye and Co. shortly before they resigned, and said he shared their view. Then he left them. John said that John Strachey, whom he liked, was a coward, but Shawcross was only a time-server. About right!

Friday 21st September
Poor little Liberals! I saw Dingle Foot[1] today at Megan [Lloyd George]'s request. He was pathetic. They have no foothold even on

---

1 D. M. Foot, later Sir Dingle (1905–78). Liberal M.P. for Dundee 1931–45. Labour M.P. for Ipswich 1957–70. Parliamentary Secretary at the Ministry of Economic Warfare (under Dalton) 1940–45. Solicitor-General 1964–7.

the lowest cliffs of power, and the rising tide will soon wash them away.[1]

Monday 24th September
After very successful weekend in South-West (Taunton and Bridgwater) I write to Hugh, just back from U.S., suggesting lunch, out of the wind, in my flat.

We drive round in my car (official) – which in a month's time I may cease to command – and, as I wait for him, I reflect how few of the passers-by are even faintly good looking. When I communicate this sad thought, as he comes out of the Treasury, he says, 'The Americans are much better looking, particularly the women.' He is, I'm glad to see, looking very fit and good morale. He enjoyed his visit to U.S. and Canada, and had some wonderful meals. Snyder got very drunk at a dinner and caused embarrassment by shouting that America couldn't go on paying out dollars for everyone and everything. Why didn't others put up money for the International Bank, and he turned to Danes, Dutch, etc., and repeated the question. 'It isn't a World Bank, it's an American Bank.' In his cups he became the Missouri small-town trader and isolationist once more.

Hugh thought he'd had some effect on Americans and others. As usual, Americans hadn't understood our present position; Administration is anxious to find a way to help, but is terrified of Congress, which is, in the mass, ignorant and unco-operative. ...

I asked if he was satisfied that it was best to have an election this month. He said, not quite. The earlier argument of this had been that, by now, we should have settlements in Persia and Korea. I said we might [not] get these for a long time. The risk of hanging on was much greater than the risk of going now. He didn't strongly disagree. He thought we should be beaten badly now, and one hated not to win, and to hand over power to the enemy. I said we should be beaten worse later. ...

I said Morrison was the worst Foreign Secretary in living memory. As an ex-Conscientious Objector of W.W.I he wanted to order troops into Persia. Hugh asked if P.M. agreed with me. I said, 'He'd say *very nearly* the worst!'

---

1 The Liberals, who retained nine seats in 1950, were reduced to six after the 1951 election. Megan Lloyd George, q.v., lost her Anglesey seat, but returned to Parliament six years later as Labour M.P. for Carmarthen. Dingle Foot also later came back to the Commons as a Labour Member.

The Labour Party Conference was held in Scarborough at the beginning of October. Alice Bacon was in the chair. In the election for the Constituency Parties Section of the N.E.C., there was a sharp swing to the Left. Barbara Castle, moving over from the Women's Section, came second, after Bevan, who increased his vote – as did the other two left-wingers, Driberg and Mikardo, both of whom overtook Dalton. Griffiths, Morrison and Dalton all lost ground, and Shinwell was pushed off. Dalton's vote dropped from 654,000 the previous year to 545,000, and he fell from fourth to seventh place.

Thursday 4th October

In the small hours at Manor House,[1] after making my election address – not a good one – with Will [Davis]. Tired and pessimistic.

Reflections after Scarborough.

National Executive elections. ... No tears for Shinwell, and he took it very badly, but he *was* Minister of Defence. For the first time since the present constitution was set up (in 1937) there has been a concerted attempt to organise the C.L.P. vote. Mikardo led this, and (assisted by Bing?) urged them, through contact men in each C.L.P., only to vote for four names. In one case told me by Callaghan, the delegates first decided only to support candidates getting more than 50 per cent of the delegates' votes. This, with careful lobbying, did the trick. The total vote was down, though the potential was up – sure evidence of deliberately wasted votes. Callaghan, George Thomas,[2] etc., as well as Herbert, Jim, myself and Shinwell, dropped as compared with last year. 'This is very provocative!' I'm very vexed at Driberg's and Mikardo's vote, but rather pleased at Barbara's. Driberg wasn't exposed anywhere – though, *since last conference*, he has been severely censured for neglect of duty by the Parliamentary Party, and this was published. Phillips mentioned it to one or two pressmen, and Donnelly told me he did the same.

There was a rowdy meeting of new N.E. at Scarborough, with suggestions by Bevanites, much resented by others, that manifesto was a 'compromise' ... There were T.U. threats to the Bevanites suggesting a change in the constitution and a return to old method of voting. I polled 545,000 – too little! – but had a good lead over Shin-

1 Home of Will Davis, q.v., Secretary of Bishop Auckland Constituency Labour Party.
2 George Thomas, later 1st Viscount Tonypandy (b. 1909). Labour M.P. for West Cardiff 1950–83; Cardiff Central 1945–50. Junior minister 1964–8. Secretary of State for Wales 1968–70. Speaker of the House of Commons 1976–83.

well, 410,000. Followed [by] Wilson with 397,000 and Phil Noel-Baker with 248,000. Then a scatter.

We shall be badly beaten at the election and then there'll be bad rows next year on N.E.C. and in Party. ...

Shall I retire at sixty-five from N.E.C.? Only if I could be pretty sure I'd be succeeded by an *effective younger* chap. And neither condition could be counted on.

October–November 1951[1]

THOUGHTS ON MY OWN FUTURE

Is this my last, or last-but-one, election campaign as a Parliamentary candidate?

When shall I retire from (1) N.E.C. and (2) Parliament? Make a good sunset. A 'planned sunset' is a bad phrase, but has the right idea.

> I'll lay me down beside my love
> With the sunset on my sword.
> (Herbert Trench, 'Apollo and the Seaman')[2]

My Love is the Labour Movement and the best of the young men in it. Or Henley[3]

> So be my passing
> My task accomplished and the long day done,
> My wages taken and in my heart
> Some late lark singing.
> Let me be gathered to the quiet west
> The sunset splendid and serene – Death

these words, often in my mind, may have given me that phrase about the 'song in my heart', which caught on so well with the critics.

Retire from N.E.C. in 1952 – don't stand again – and from Parliament at first election when I'm over seventy? Or is that too long?

But I don't want to dodder on, or even to start slipping. I'd like to die soon after retiring. No ignominious and useless dragged-out end;

---

1 Dalton labels the first two pages of this entry 12th October and the third page October–November, yet there is no break in the text.

2 Herbert Trench (1865–1923). Writer and poet. See *New Poems: Apollo and the Seaman*, Methuen, London, 1907:

> To lay you down beside your love
> With the sunset on your sword? ...

3 W. E. Henley (1849–1903). Poet and critic. The verse is from 'Margaritae Sororis' in *Echoes* (1886).

absorbing food and shelter and giving nothing in return (a nuisance, an uneconomic proposition). Or war may end it? ...

If I didn't run for National Executive it *might* just put back Shinwell – a bad political character and two years older than I am.

But I hope it would help – partly by setting an example and sowing a seed in people's minds – to bring on younger men, who had been *faithful* in their service to the Party (i.e. not Driberg) and who have it in them to serve still more responsibly – and to think things out and bring up new ideas, and exercise influence and join in taking big decisions. ...

I am now well past my best – physically, mentally and socially. But my best was pretty good – in all three – so there's no disaster yet.

I'll be a pretty good sixty-five, I hope, but best to go while going is good. And the decline may go rather fast in the next few years. I may be a bad seventy. I was at my high points politically in 1940–41 and in 1945–6, but that was largely determined by events outside me, though in these events I got and took my chance.

How about naming some on-comers in a resignation announcement speech – no need for tact any more. Hugh, Robens, Brown, Callaghan, Jay, Lindgren, Padley,[1] Freeman, Peart, Crosland, Darling,[2] Jenkins, Fienburgh. But not too many columnists this year.

Saturday 13th October
I think we're out – though Gallup Poll shows a narrowing margin and is subject to anti-Labour bias because interviewers are middle-class women.

And it is against all probability for us to be only just out. I think we shall lose not less than 50 seats net, i.e. a Tory majority of about 100. But that should mean we shouldn't lose many of our good young men. Tony hadn't come to Scarborough, and was glad he hadn't. It would have made him so angry. I might have been right to patch up peace, since election was coming so quick – he was still inclined to think we should have hung on – but *after* the election it would have to be fought out. And he, and a lot of other tough babies, would join us. ...

He had lunched with John Freeman the day after the Scarborough result, and John had been infinitely complacent. Everything had gone exactly as they had planned. John was counting on my becoming a

1 W. E. Padley (1916–84). Labour M.P. for Ogmore 1950–79. Junior minister 1964–7.
2 George Darling, later Baron (1905–85). Labour Co-op M.P. for Sheffield Hillsborough 1950–February 1974. Junior minister 1964–8.

Bevanite within a few months. I said I didn't think they could imagine they had won my goodwill by putting Driberg and Mikardo above me. They should, if they regarded me as a potential ally, not have discouraged C.L.P.s – as clearly they did – from voting for me. Tony said this would have been asking rather much. (And, after all, I *had* backed Gaitskell all through.) But he suggested that they *had* favoured me by recommending parties to vote only for *four* names – and not for *five* including Wilson. ...

Tony said he was out by 1000 in South Gloucester on latest Gallup Poll (the next Gallup Poll was better), but this ignores, I said, (a) his personality, (b) his record, (c) a woman against him, (d) more Liberals likely to vote Labour in South-West than nationally. All these factors favoured him.[1]

I said I thought I wouldn't stand for N.E. any more. ... Tony said he hoped I wouldn't decide this too quickly. I said I wouldn't. But I wanted to see younger people coming along. ...

Tony said Woodrow [Wyatt] wanted Parliamentary Labour Party to elect some members of N.E. But I brushed this aside as impracticable and not very desirable. We discussed future leadership. Clem should go on, partly because succession so difficult. I didn't like Herbert, and Nye was impossible. I said it was too soon for Hugh or Alf Robens, too late for me, probably – though not certainly – too late for Jim Griffiths. *He* should have been Foreign Secretary. Tony thought Stafford [Cripps] was the only possible *deus ex machina*. I said I didn't think his health could ever stand it and he had sometimes had very odd ideas. But let's wait, rather unhopefully, and see. I met Mervyn Stockwood for the first time, with Tony in the street, just outside the Grand Hotel. I rather liked him at first impact. Tony says he's a cynical Christian, but Clem should have made him a bishop.

Tony has finished his Fabian essay. He says it's very good indeed. I shall read it when the election's over.

Thursday 25th October
Polling Day. Weather very fine. Drive round all day, starting at 9 a.m. with an hour's break for lunch, and $\frac{1}{4}$ hour for tea, till 8.30 p.m. Visit every polling station except Hamsterley and Cockton Hill.

Then on wireless with Will [Davis] (Florrie[2] and dogs have gone to bed!) at 10 p.m. At 10.20 announced 'Recount at Watford'. That

---

1 Crosland held the South Gloucestershire constituency in the 1951 election. His majority fell only slightly – from 6,138 to 5,338.
2 Florence Davis. Married to Will Davis, q.v.

was John Freeman. I figured a tense scene. 'But', said I, 'that means
no Tory landslide.' That would easily have washed away Watford.

As night went on, rather reassuring picture begins to emerge. Our
vote well maintained, many seats held which I had feared might go –
and very few losses. Though Darlington is one!

15 'You Have Been Warned', 25th October 1951

9

Bevanism
1951–4

For most of the Attlee administration, the Labour Party had been a fragile coalition – a superficial unity concealing deep underlying divisions. With prominent pre-war left-wingers tied up in government jobs, the old battle line dividing libertarian, pacifist and fellow-travelling Left from the Party Establishment was temporarily submerged. Except over the nationalisation of iron and steel, and the issue of reducing the planned term of conscription, left-wing pressure counted for little between 1945 and 1951. Indeed, for most of this period there was no organised left-wing parliamentary group or faction.

The resignations over health charges, and Labour's defeat at the polls a few months later, ended the long truce. Now, at last, the pent-up emotions of a decade spilled over. After the 1951 election the supporters of Aneurin Bevan in the House of Commons organised themselves into a group with an elected chairman (Wilson was the first), holding weekly meetings. Reliable Bevanites consisted of the hard core of twenty-five M.P.s who had supported the pamphlet *One Way Only*. But on particular issues it was possible to rally a much larger number of sympathisers. Thus, fifty-seven M.P.s (the '57 varieties') voted against the Conservative Government's defence policy in 1952, in defiance of the Labour whip.

In some ways the battles of the 1950s were a return to the conflicts of the 1930s, when Bevan had sided with Cripps and the Socialist League, and had eventually been expelled from the Labour Party for giving public support to the Popular Front in defiance of N.E.C. edicts. But there were important differences. One was the increased size and importance of the P.L.P. In the 1930s, a Labour administration governing on its own was still an unfulfilled dream. In the 1950s, Labour front-benchers confidently expected to return to office. Before the war, the battle was about ideals; after the experience of the Attlee Government, it was a fight to decide how power should be exercised.

563

In this fight, differences of policy and of style were mixed up. Both sides faced a world of full employment, higher incomes and rising expectations, against a background of continued international tension and an increasing military dependence on the United States. Both Left and new Right were conscious of the need for Labour to adjust. The Bevanite Left wanted to breathe life into old principles, and to break the stultifying pattern of international alliances. The 'managerial' class of 1945, on the other hand, sought to harness new economic ideas to a broad progressive party that would abandon the class war. Meanwhile there was a personal jockeying for position among rival contenders for the leadership, as the date of Attlee's retirement was repeatedly postponed.

Dalton stayed in Parliament for eight years after the 1951 election, but he remained a serious politician for only four. Unlike most of his former Cabinet colleagues, he had no desire to return to ministerial office. The years in government, especially at the Treasury, had taken their toll, and he was aware of his own physical and mental decline. His interest now shifted from current issues to the careers of his 'young men' – M.P.s who enjoyed, tolerated or courted his company, and for whom he saw a bright future. Gaitskell, Jay, Callaghan, Jenkins, Brown, Robens, Healey and, above all, Crosland are among the names that occur most often in his diary in later years.

Yet Dalton did not always agree with his most prominent protégé, Hugh Gaitskell. His desire to advance the fortunes of Gaitskell was consistent and generous, later strengthened by an equally powerful desire to prevent Morrison from becoming Leader. But on one key issue, German rearmament, Dalton and Gaitskell were at odds. For a time, Dalton's prejudice against Germans, and his absolute opposition to German participation in any new scheme for European defence, brought him into alliance with the Bevanites, who opposed German rearmament for different reasons. Increasingly exasperated by Bevan, yet fiercely contemptuous of Morrison, Dalton continued to seek conciliation between Left and Right. Yet, as his fall from the N.E.C. showed, the middle ground was becoming untenable.

In the 1951 election, Dalton was returned for Bishop Auckland with a majority of 8,986 in a straight fight. Nationally, Labour again lost seats. The Conservatives increased their total to 321, compared with Labour's 295, with 6 Liberals and 3 Irish Nationalists. On the afternoon of 26th October, Attlee resigned and Churchill became Prime Minister for a second term.

Saturday 27th October
Have asked, beforehand, to see Attlee today – win or lose. Time fixed at 11 a.m. at Chequers. Drive down and stay to lunch – only Clem, Vi and a secretary. Go to see Cherry Cottage which they've bought and into which they'll soon move. Only seven miles from Chequers, rather like a pensioner's cottage just outside the front gates. An adapted cottage, with no approach and no view. A few not very good cherry trees block the light.

She is to live here. They'll have no pied-à-terre in London. He'll sleep, when he must, in a Club. (Hugh says to me three days later that she's a frightful woman, politically Tory, who wants him to give it all up.) Attlee and I speak of the future. We must have a new leadership, and give the younger people their chance. He and Stafford in 1931 in the House, but not on the N.E.C., and Herbert and I on the N.E.C. but not in the House, had a lot to do with policy making when old top end of party was blown off by MacDonald's treachery and Henderson's death. We've done all that now; written the first chapter of the Socialist story, in law and administration. What next? The younger people must write the second chapter.

He says Morrison was a terrible flop at the Foreign Office. We broach the possibility of having Jim Griffiths as a Second Deputy Chairman – Trade Unionist and non-Londoner. I suggest sending Milner to Lords. He spoke as though this hadn't occurred to him before. We think of Arthur Bottomley as Chief Whip. But Whip should be appointed, not elected.

Election results very good. Casualties minimised, especially among our young. How wise we Octobrists were!

Sunday 28th October
Stay in bed all day, and see and speak to no one. A heavy cold and a sore throat. But these wear off. I begin to write letters of condolence and congratulation.

Monday 29th October
Farewell to office – now Local Government and Planning, but to be renamed by Tories Housing and Local Government, in the charge of Macmillan. He won't be able to build any more, if as many as I. My last month (September) showed more than 17,000 completed – a good month. ...

Saw Jim Callaghan this afternoon. Not very keen on my idea of having Jim Griffiths as Second Deputy, along with Herbert. He is now working with Alf Robens and George Brown. I say they all ought to be on the Parliamentary Committee. He says Brown thinks it ought to be war to the knife with the Bevanites. Jim himself, of course, will calculate carefully!

Tuesday 30th October
Desmond Donnelly signs up. I congratulate him on a very fine result. He says the Bevanites are meeting tonight at 8.30 p.m. at Crossman's house[1] – very close to me! Donnelly will come and see me at 9.30 a.m. tomorrow to tell me their decision and drive me to the House. (Useful to be on good terms with young men with private cars, now that I no longer have a public one. And what a good listening post!)

Hugh at 11.30, and we talk for an hour. ... I made my proposal about Jim [Griffiths]. He was rather attracted by this. If Clem and Herbert fell out, Jim might be next Leader and P.M. This would help to keep out Nye. Hugh thinks Jim has a bit of a soft under-belly, but if *he* were his No. 2, [he] could control him. Naturally very anti-Bevanite. ...

He denied being completely in Morrison's pocket, as a result of Nye's attacks, but said he hoped I would resume relations with Morrison. I said I wouldn't run after him. I had reminded Clem at Chequers last Saturday that in 1935 I had backed Herbert against him, but much had changed since then. 'You've grown and he's shrunk.' Hugh will try to write some dollar articles though he has a little money of his own.[2] He thought it a mistake not to have had a row and a decisive vote at Scarborough!

John Freeman to see me in the afternoon. I say I hope Bevanites won't now form a continuing caucus within a caucus. He agrees and says he thinks they won't. I say I don't know what there really is to fight about, apart from personalities. Freeman wants the Hugh–Nye breach healed.

I spoke sharply of Mikardo and Driberg. I said I was angry to have been beaten by them at Scarborough. Of Barbara I felt quite different-ly. I said I *knew* that Mikardo and others had been intriguing with C.L.P.s to waste 3 votes and only to support 4 Bevanites. He said he didn't know this. They had been trying to get Barbara on and Shinwell off. His Watford people he had urged to work for the 4, plus Herbert,

---

1 Crossman lived at 9 Vincent Square. According to Crossman's diary (Janet Morgan, ed., *The Backbench Diaries of Richard Crossman*, Hamish Hamilton and Jonathan Cape, London, 1981, p. 27), 24 members of the 32-strong Keep Left Group attend-ed this meeting at which 'a long discussion took place on how to enlarge the Group and make it open to all who want to belong, without at the same time losing its cohesion.'
2 i.e. a private income.

Jim [Griffiths] and me. I denounced Mikardo's personal attack on T.U. leaders. ... I said it showed incredible levity for this large vote to be given to Driberg, less than a year after he had been publicly 'severely censured' for neglecting his Parliamentary duties. I said that counter organisation would be a frightful bore. The electorate had never been worked on like this before. This time some M.P.s had been refused information by their delegates as to how they were voting. He asked whether there was statistical evidence of wasted votes![1] I said Yes, very clear evidence. He said Driberg got his high vote because he was assiduous in addressing meetings all over the country and getting to know members of local parties. (I suppose he keeps an address book, and writes to them all just before Conference time!) This, he thinks, counts for more than the weekly article in *Reynolds*.

Freeman is still having great trouble with his ears (daily treatment at hospital) and with his sinus (very painful weekly wash out). He's below par. ... I like him a lot. ...

A most moving letter from Hugh, in reply to mine to him. This sort of incident makes my political life worth while. I re-read the preface and the first and last chapter of *Towards the Peace of Nations*.[2] The Germans killed the friends of my youth. Therefore, I have no friends, it is often remarked, of my own age. But I have sought and found them among those who are younger than myself.

Tony [Crosland] at lunch today, in front of Browaldh and others, said of Joad, with whom he dined last week, that Joad felt terribly the fact of growing old; he was fat and ugly now; no longer looked rakish and amusing, or played hockey at Hampstead; that he had been badly hurt by the railway ticket incident.[3] And Tony said this with such sympathy and understanding, though generally he seems so gay and out of sight of sorrow, that he moved me in a new way.

Tony often reminds me of Gladwyn [Jebb]. But Gladwyn is much colder and more cynical.

End of October
The election results are wonderful. We are out just at the right moment, and our casualties are wonderfully light.

---

1 'wasted votes': It was believed by the Right that Bevanite constituency delegates at Conference concentrated their voting power by voting only for leading left-wing candidates, and not for the maximum permissible number of seven, for seven places.
2 Published by Dalton in 1928. See above, p. 41n.
3 Early in 1948 Professor Cyril Joad, q.v., had been prosecuted for travelling on a train without a ticket, and convicted. The scandal permanently damaged his career as a popular pundit and broadcaster.

In my own constituency, the enemy didn't dig up past dirt – Stanley and the Lynskey Tribunal, or the Building Licences for the Grove[1] – though I took up all the papers, in case they should.

They tried to prove that I had caused local unemployment in the clothing industry, by my 'don't buy' speeches – but this, though the Lewins were very upset, didn't cut much ice. They made a fuss in the press because I had some shares in Courtauld's. And they alleged, particularly in Darlington, that I mimicked the Tory candidate's impediment of speech. And they put it about that I was now too old.

Pretty easy going compared with many other places! ...

If Clem dies soon, or if Vi persuades him to retire, there'll be a problem. Under Herbert it won't be a happy ship, nor a Socialist ship either. Nye can hardly hope to gather support in Parliamentary Party, for some time, sufficient to give him leadership. But he may appeal strongly to many in Opposition, and memories and moods are short. Hugh has a long way to go. Jim [Griffiths] looks the likeliest stop gap. But he's sixty-one already! and Nye is fifty-four. ...

Winston is feeling the burden ... His first speech in new Parliament on election of Speaker was very weak and confused. Maurice Webb said it reminded him so vividly of MacDonald in decline that he couldn't bear it, and went out. Winston is starting on the old game of getting people out of bed at 1 and 2 a.m. But he's seventy-seven now, and I don't believe he can stick it. The Government is largely 'government by cronies', as they say of Truman – Woolton, Leathers,[2] Cherwell,[3] Ismay,[4] Stuart,[5] etc. They have reconstituted the war-time Committee, except for Max [Beaverbrook] and Brendan [Bracken]. Max has left the country in a huff, and Brendan has refused office in the Cabinet on grounds of health (?). Alleged, they

1 'Building Licences for the Grove': see note 1 to entry for end of 1948 above, p. 446. Dalton was still worried by rumours of alleged irregularities in the granting of building licences to the Lewin family (proprietors of the West Auckland Clothing factory) in connection with their home, The Grove, Co. Durham.
2 F. L. Leathers, 1st Viscount (1883–1965). Secretary of State for Co-ordination of Transport, Fuel and Power 1951–3. Minister of War Transport 1941–5.
3 1st Viscount Cherwell, formerly Professor F. A. Lindemann (1886–1957). Pay-master-General (with a seat in the Cabinet) 1951–3. Personal Assistant to Churchill as Prime Minister 1940–42; Paymaster-General 1942–5.
4 General Sir Hastings Ismay, 1st Baron (1887–1965). Secretary of State for Com-monwealth Relations 1951–2. Chief of Staff to Minister of Defence (Churchill), and Deputy Secretary (Military) to the War Cabinet 1940–45. Secretary-General of N.A.T.O. 1952–7.
5 J. G. Stuart, later 1st Viscount (1897–1971). Secretary of State for Scotland 1951–7. Conservative M.P. for Moray and Nairn 1923–59. Government Chief Whip 1941–5. Opposition Chief Whip 1945–8.

thought, *inter alia*, that Winston shouldn't be Minister of Defence, and that Brendan refused the Admiralty, and Boothby has nothing, so far. Reported that Brendan and Boothby met Bevan and said, 'Tell us how to form a Bevan group!' Hudson and Elliott among others are also left out. Braithwaite[1] said, looking at tape, 'To be in this Government you must either be a member of the Churchill family, or the House of Lords.' Butler only 7th in hierarchy, below Woolton and Dai Fyfe.[2] Treasury officials working hard to get this altered!

Dispute on degree of success of Bevanites is being debated. Nye made a speech saying, 'I'm glad the candidates for whom I spoke all did so well', and when I said to him, jestingly, in the Smoke Room on the first day, 'You've lost some weight', he replied bumptiously and without a smile, 'I've been gaining some votes'. Philip Williams, egged on by Roy Jenkins and others, has written to *The Times*, confuting their statement (!) that Bevanites had done better than average. ...

Dick Crossman and I had a row in Smoke Room on first day. I attacked him for making a speech to Oxford University Labour Club saying that 'Bevanism' would, within twelve months, cease to be a heresy and become policy of Party. Only 'Bevanites' had been honest. I said what *is* 'Bevanism'? All this posturing and egoising! And this caucus of yours, why do you want to keep this up? He said, 'Caucus! You're the biggest caucus-sitter in the Party – Cabinet, National Executive, etc., but you object when anyone else sets up a caucus.' I said, 'These aren't exclusive groups.' He abused Hugh very bitterly.

Beginning of November

Attlee very strong in the Party; can do what he likes for the moment. His O.M. well deserved, and everyone praises him.

Tories very disappointed at small majority, very embarrassed by having to swallow their election promises, and many very bitter at being left out of the Government. Trying to create a 'panic' atmosphere, but I don't think it will go.

Our good young men very bright and eager – Jim Callaghan,

---

1 Probably Sir Albert Braithwaite (1893–1959). Conservative M.P. for Harrow West 1951–9; Buckrose 1926–45. But possibly J. G. Braithwaite, later 1st Bart (1895–1958). Parliamentary Secretary at the Ministry of Transport (later Transport and Aviation) 1951–3. Conservative M.P. for Bristol North-West 1950–55; Sheffield Hillsborough 1931–5; Holderness 1939–50.
2 Sir David Maxwell-Fyfe, later 1st Earl of Kilmuir (1900–67). Home Secretary 1951–4. Conservative M.P. for Liverpool West Derby 1935–54. Solicitor-General 1942–5; Attorney-General 1945. Lord Chancellor 1954–62.

Woodrow [Wyatt] and Roy [Jenkins]. Tony Crosland and Tony Benn less in a hurry. Benn may be half a Bevanite.

Thursday 1st November
First meeting of new, or rather old! Parliamentary Party. Many surprised and delighted to be back. No sense of defeat in recent election. Great ovation for Attlee, all rise and clap for several minutes.

Attlee, Morrison and Whiteley re-elected by acclamation. General atmosphere of 'Well done! No change.' It wouldn't have worked, or been wise, or been understood for me – or anyone else – to have proposed Griffiths as Second Deputy. Emrys Hughes proposed Nye, in opposition to Morrison, as Deputy. But Nye said simply, 'Thanks very much. But I'm not standing.' Greeted with moderate applause.

Saturday 10th November. Eve of Armistice Day
For thirty years I have been a continuously active party politician, in the Labour Party, having indeed first become a Socialist forty-four years ago. I have stuck to politics, because it has been fun, and because it is a drug, and because it has seemed to be a means of doing a lot of good.

But now, at the moment of ceasing to be a minister, I am come to the end of a long chapter. I am disoriented, and robbed of my slaves, and released, in an instant, from the pressure of responsibility. I am slowed down, physically and mentally, conscious of having a heart and flabby tummy muscles, and of being (sometimes) slow at the uptake, and of tending (sometimes) to repeat myself, and of being well past my best in every way. But I still have ideas about what should next be done.

I shan't be a minister again and, as I told Bob Fraser today, I don't want to live to be old – not beyond seventy, I think, six years hence. He said, 'Make it seventy-five!'

Tuesday 13th November
Voting for Parliamentary Committee announced. 259 voted, of whom 6 spoiled papers.

Griffiths	196
Hall	177
Gaitskell	175
Robens	136
Ede	132
Stokes	117
Callaghan	111
Dalton	110

Noel-Baker	110
Summerskill	107
Shinwell	102
Tony Greenwood[1]	91

Then followed 40 others with a wide scatter. Next in order.

Herbison	84
Strachey	74
Jay	61

McNeil had 50. Gordon Walker 48, Edwards 43.[2] George Brown under 40. Tail end Hector Hughes 26,[3] Bellenger 10.

Not at all a bsd Committee. Jim Griffiths, an alternative Leader, firmly on top. Hugh Gaitskell, Alf Robens and Jim Callaghan, good complementary elements in the Young Leadership, which must establish itself in this Parliament well up. No Bevanite ran, partly to preserve their future independence, partly because they feared they would be beaten.

I was irritated that *I* didn't poll more. I have neglected my Tea Room Flank in the last Parliament – and there's been no such vote open to the whole Parliamentary Party since 1939. And I daresay some of the Bevanites didn't vote for me, because I was a Gaitskellite, and some of the anti-Bevanites, because it will have [been] put round by Morrison and ? Tony Greenwood and his father and others that I was much too friendly with some of the Bevanites: in short was trimming. And had played for conciliation at Party Conferences. And no doubt I lost some votes through having been rude to some people, and rudely frank about others.

...

Politics is a highly competitive business and the number of people with sour faces is much bigger than usual today! I write to Hugh and Jim and speak to Alf, expressing pleasure.

Thursday 15th November
Desmond says that, among the Bevanites, Crossman, Foot and Mikardo are the factionists. Barbara [Castle], Freeman and he the anti-factionists.

1 Anthony Greenwood, later Baron (1911–82). Labour M.P. for Rossendale 1950–70; Heywood and Radcliffe 1946–50. Colonial Secretary 1964–5; Minister for Overseas Development 1965–6; Housing and Local Government 1966–70. Son of Arthur Greenwood, q.v.
2 Ness Edwards (1897–1968). Labour M.P. for Caerphilly 1939–68. Junior minister 1945–50. Postmaster-General 1950–51.
3 Hector Hughes, K.C. (1887–1970). Labour M.P. for Aberdeen North 1945–70.

Friday 16th November

Denis Healey thinks Churchill and Eden disagree on Europe. Churchill wants German Rearmament without conditions and a Franco-German alliance, even if Germany dominates. Eden is much more conscious of German danger.

Younger, Denis says, should be built up as a future Foreign Secretary. He is a bit of a 'Leftist', and has an inferiority complex towards, and a liking for, Nye. (Freeman, I recall, wanted him built up against Crossman.) ...

I spoke to Morrison about Crossman's idea of succeeding Younger.

16 'Search Parties', 15th November 1951

Morrison said he had never thought of it. I told him of Crossman in *Statesman*, and worse, in *Sunday Pictorial*, and of his statement to me, 'If there's a break, I shall go with Nye.' This bloody clever fool is always playing Dick Double Crossman.

I told Freeman I had scuppered Crossman, if, indeed, this was necessary. He was very pleased.

Sunday 18th November

Kenneth Younger to gossip in my flat. He has three children now, a girl aged 15½, and a girl and a boy born in the 1950 and 1951 elections. Between the first and the second there were several mishaps. ...

Younger had a very hard time at F.O., and at U.N., especially while Bevin was, in effect, out of action. The volume of work at the Foreign Office has increased enormously, especially through new Agencies – O.E.E.C., N.A.T.O., Council of Europe etc. – since 1945. When Eden had realised this, after two days at F.O., he went to Winston and told him he couldn't lead the House.

I told Younger that Crossman had wanted his job, when Morrison went to F.O. (I didn't tell him that Freeman had asked me to go into action on this.) Younger said he had always walked in Dick's shadow, two years his junior, at Winchester and at New College. So he couldn't ever resent Dick wanting, or taking, his job. Delicate soft masochism, I thought. I also quoted my conversation with Dick at end of last session, and Bellenger's remark that he would soon have been conditioned as a minister.[1] Younger said he would very soon be, and would make a first-class minister. ...

We praised Gladwyn. Younger said the other high ups at the Foreign Office were bitterly jealous of him, and would try to prevent his becoming Permanent Under-Secretary. Younger thought Strang and Makins were both straight, but not Bob Dixon, a courtier type and insecure. ...

Having been much in the Cabinet room, he had noticed, towards the end, when Bevin, Cripps and Bevan were all gone, a terrible lack of common purpose in the Cabinet. I said it had indeed got pretty bad!

It is a pity Younger hasn't more weight and voice, and presence. He has a good mind, experience already while still young, and a sound approach. I *think* he's our best bet for a future Foreign Secretary.

But next time may be too soon. So what do we do?

Monday 3rd December
I wrote to Olga [Davenport], in a roofer,[2] 'I'm glad I sound mellow' (Lionel Brett[3] had said this to her; he had been to lunch). 'Am falling deeply in love with my long lost Freedom after the Slave Years of Ministerial Self-Importance. I shall put this new Freedom to all sorts of uses, and perhaps write something about some of them.'

Monday 10th December
Returned from Newton Hall, after three nights with Walstons, wonderfully taken care of! Very good food and drink, put to bed in the afternoon – and, of course, breakfast in bed. Took a vow of obedience to Catherine. R.C. atmosphere very soothing ...

Max Habsburg,[4] Prince of Florence and final year undergraduate at Lincoln, Oxford to stay (very small and immature, except on titles

1 See entry for 2nd August 1951, p. 552.
2 'roofer': note of thanks for hospitality.
3 L. Brett, later 4th Viscount Esher (b. 1913). Architect Planner of Hatfield New Town 1949–59. Rector and Vice-Provost of the Royal College of Art 1971–8.
4 Prince Maximilian Habsburg-Lothringen. He entered Lincoln College, Oxford in 1951.

of Archdukes and Grand Dukes) and John Rothenstein and his wife,[1] and Christopher Sykes[2] among the weekend guests. I arrive on Friday night, staying in all Saturday (including sleeping in the afternoon) and on Sunday walk vigorously with Harry [Walston] in the morning, viewing cottages and drying machines.

Lunch party on Sunday includes Noel Annan and wife.[3] *He* says the Left has captured Economics at Cambridge – Joan Robinson,[4] Kahn,[5] Kaldor, etc. with Austin Robinson wearily in the chair. ...

To lunch on Sunday also (1) Henry Moore,[6] sculptor who praises Ruth for Battersea Exhibition – 'Why haven't I been allowed to talk to you?' I asked as he was going – Catherine says this'll be the joke in King's – (2) Young Runciman,[7] son of Sir Leslie,[8] to whom I gave a good Second – at Eton, up for Trinity Scholarship, but will try again next year. I urge him to finish at Eton. The great Last Year. He may be in Pop next year, but doubts whether all this adulation is good. I say, 'Yes. It gives you success and joy and confidence and Power of Leadership.'

Tuesday 11th December
Fabian Taxation Group. Second meeting. Tony [Crosland] now firmly in the chair. Nicky [Kaldor]'s paper on Expenditure tax, but Tony takes it slowly, as Hugh isn't here today. Balogh very polite to me, and after meeting, apologises if he has said a rude thing to me last time. I said I hadn't noticed it. Someone has spoken to him, perhaps Tony at Oxford last weekend. Tony had Harry Walston to lunch

1 J. K. Rothenstein, later Sir John (b. 1901). Art historian and critic. Director of the Tate Gallery 1936–64. Married to Elizabeth, née Whittington.
2 Christopher Sykes (b. 1907). Author and script-writer. B.B.C. Features Department producer 1949–68.
3 N. G. Annan, later Baron (b. 1916). Lecturer in Politics, Cambridge 1948–66. Fellow of King's College, Cambridge 1944–66; Provost 1956–66. Provost of University College, London 1966–78. Vice-Chancellor of London University 1978–81. Married to Gabriele, née Ullstein.
4 Joan Robinson, née Maurice (1903–83). Reader in Economics, Cambridge 1949–65; Professor of Economics 1965–71. Married to Austin Robinson, q.v.
5 R. F. Kahn, later Baron (b. 1905). Professor of Economics, Cambridge 1951–72. Fellow of King's College. Architect of the Keynesian 'multiplier', and formerly a close friend and colleague of Keynes. Temporary civil servant 1939–46.
6 Henry Moore (1898–1986). Sculptor. As Chairman of the L.C.C. Parks Committee, Ruth Dalton had introduced the practice of holding sculptural exhibitions in London parks.
7 W. G. Runciman (b. 1934). Later a writer on the philosophy of the social sciences. Fellow of Trinity College, Cambridge 1959–63, and since 1971. Chairman of Walter Runciman & Co. Ltd since 1976.
8 Sir Walter Leslie Runciman, 2nd Viscount, 1st Baron, 3rd Bart (b. 1900). Industrialist.

today, and says he heard say the weekend was a success. He and Roy [Jenkins] are off to Paris tonight to see Ike's H.Q.

Douglas Jay and I dine afterwards at the Crete.[1] We praise Attlee and I denounce Morrison. He praised Balogh as being often right and really on the Left. We discuss future leadership. He is for unity as am I. He thinks Hugh might have given in to Nye on teeth and glasses. I said this would only have postponed the clash. He thinks Nye may still be the Leader one day. He says Gordon Walker, Pakenham and McNeil want to drive him out of the Party. I say this is quite silly. He says Crossman is a German – his mother, he says, was. Hugh is in favour of making Nye and Wilson work their passage back. I say I feel very detached – interested only in Next Programme, Memoirs and Public Finance.[2]

Friday 14th December
Yesterday and today preparing Broadcast (Party Political) with help of Tony Benn (– very useful, moves through life like a cat, attractive, has reserves and sense of humour, but not quite to be trusted), Michael Young (better at this than at policy making) and Bill Pickles[3] (knows a good deal about it, but not quite on my line). They do most of the first part, on home affairs. I myself draft the second part, including German Rearmament.

Brian Abel-Smith to tea. I like him a lot, but he stayed $2\frac{1}{2}$ hours and then I had to push him out. Just missed office again at the Union by a narrow vote (against young Hurd[4] for Vice President). He won't stand again. He's doing economic research under Joan Robinson, who is more interested in politics than in economics now, and is a Bevanite. Abel-Smith is inclined to do something on inherited wealth, and propose something very drastic.

Meanwhile he's been invited to go with debating team to India and Pakistan, paid for by British Council. Should he go? I say Yes. His College approves of him, and he thinks he might stay up another two years. He might do some supervising in economics. I ask if he's badly

1 A Greek restaurant in Soho.
2 Dalton had started to write the first volume of his memoirs (*Call Back Yesterday*) and was revising his text-book *Principles of Public Finance*, with an additional section on his period as Chancellor.
3 William Pickles (d. 1979). Senior Lecturer, later Reader in political science, L.S.E. Former B.B.C. producer; specialist in French politics.
4 Douglas Hurd (b. 1930). Undergraduate at Trinity College, Cambridge. President of the Cambridge Union 1952. Political Secretary to Edward Heath as Opposition Leader and Prime Minister 1968–74. Conservative M.P. for Mid-Oxfordshire 1974–83; Witney since 1983. Minister of State, Foreign and Commonwealth Office 1979–83; Home Office 1983–4. Secretary of State for Northern Ireland 1984–5. Home Secretary since 1985.

bitten by the political bug. He says Yes. But should one go straight into Parliament from being a don? I said Tony Crosland (already mentioned by him in another connection) did.

He says Harry Walston ran into a lot of trouble at the election. They said he wasn't English, had stood as a Liberal and, worst of all, had his name on the *Conservative* Panel! A lot of this stuck. But Abel-Smith agrees with me that Catherine is very attractive – if only to hear her voice on the telephone. ...

Kaldor's lectures, he says, are a Box Office draw, and Annan has a most brilliant delivery.

The young men at Cambridge like Attlee very much indeed. Harold Wilson, he thought, was ageing and going grey early. Tony Crosland they had had again since the election; he was their favourite, he had such humour and personality and dealt so well with the Bevanites. (Tony told me they had never heard the anti-Bevanites' case before. He told them it wasn't a question of Left or Right, or of more Socialism or less Socialism, but simply of Optimism or Pessimism! ...)

Abel-Smith said Jack Ashley was marrying into a higher social stratum – a Girton girl who, till she met Jack, was the leading Tory.[1] They only met in his last term.

Abel-Smith is not so good looking, or so intellectually able, or so dashing, but he's the best young man for politics I've found at a university since Tony. Ruth, who stays part of the time, says he's very governing class. And why not? We want some more of that in a national party.

Tuesday 1st January 1952 West Leaze
... [R]uth and I have had three lots of inter-connected visitors for lunch. (1) Alan Taylor and his wife, Evelyn,[2] Tony's sister, on the 23rd (2) Tony himself on the 24th and (3) Dobs Little on the 27th. (1) and (3) fed on venison, (2) on chicken. All three successful, I think.

Thursday 3rd January
Today Hugh Gaitskell to lunch at flat. He thinks our economic position, both internally and externally, is much less serious [than] some suggest. ...

As to Bevan, Hugh thinks he just wants to lead the Party, and that is all the Bevanites want. But he may be cautious this year. I speak of Jim Griffiths. Hugh points out that he is getting on too (we look up ages, Jim is sixty-two this year). I say I am still for unity. He asks what

1 Jack Ashley, q.v., married Pauline Crispin in 1951.
2 A. J. P. Taylor married his second wife, Evelyn Crosland, sister of Anthony, in 1951.

do I want him to do. I say, 'Don't close your mind to the possibility of unity, and don't get manoeuvred into a too Right-wing position. Attack the Tories when they do wrong.' He says he'll do this last [thing], and has already told Treasury officials, whom he was invited by Butler to see, that there'll be a hell of a row if unemployment goes above 500,000. ...

Denis Healey to tea, is still in last three at Leeds, but unlikely to get it. My German broadcast[1] has done me nothing but good in the country, but there'll be a row no doubt, with Morrison in National Executive.

I think there is a slight restraint in my relations with Hugh. Quite friendly, but a little reserved and conscious of disagreement between us just below the surface. The relation is bound to be a bit tricky.

Hugh agrees with me that Tony would make the best Treasury minister among young M.P.s. Chris Mayhew, whom we both praise, for Service Department or Board of Trade.[2]

Monday 7th January

News today, Monday, that Denis got S.E. Leeds yesterday at selection conference. I had been afraid it would have gone to a useless local, Rafferty.[3]

I write to Denis. 'Wonderful. Foreign Secretary before 1972? It would be fun to know – or wouldn't it? You must have done better second go than first.' And now we must meet and discuss before International Sub – to take account of new situation. A good successor may not be easy to find.[4] And there will be jealousy and attempts to cut off his salary at a too early date. We have now to make our international policy.

Monday 14th January

Returned to London and see Denis. He is very delighted. Morgan

---

1 On 15th December, Dalton had delivered a broadcast in which he sharply attacked proposals for German rearmament, while keeping within the letter of the Labour Party official line. 'Dalton was obviously enormously titillated by the thought that Shinwell or Morrison would try to rebuke him and I suspect he was rather disappointed that they had not yet done so', Crossman noted after dinner together a few days later. 'This broadcast has its importance in the internal Party dissensions, since it very definitely swings the Party further towards the Left' (*Backbench Diaries*, entry for 19th December 1951, pp. 56–7).

2 The last two paragraphs appear in the text as separate notes added at the top of the two pages on which the entry for 3rd January 1952 was written.

3 John Rafferty. Leeds City councillor. Insurance agent. Labour candidate for Penrith and the Border 1951.

4 For Healey as Labour Party International Secretary.

Phillips has been very friendly, and paid his salary till the end of this month. This will mean only one week without salary, before his Parliamentary pay begins.

A surprising amount of irritation among E.C. members over Denis's selection, and I hear that Election Sub, including Clem, took a very narrow line on the general principle, and will recommend a very restrictive rule to N.E.C. next week. This will hinder recruitment of able young men to Transport House, or encourage them to leave and find another job, before trying for a constituency.

Nye says we are 'becoming as bad as the French Socialist Party' – all middle class intellectuals. He is in a bad mood, and I foresee trouble. We should have outgrown all this inverted snobbery. And where would Nye be without middle class?

Wednesday 23rd January

Row between Herbert and Nye. I have no use for either of them! ...

Today question was raised of what Churchill had said at Washington, especially on Korean War.[1] Nye said N.E.C. should issue a statement. Morrison said this would be for Parliamentary Party next week, after Churchill had made a statement in the House. Nye said, angrily, 'Don't play box and cox. N.E.C. issued statement on Budget.' (*What* a bore! Always going back to that!) Morrison said, rather irrelevantly, 'If anyone lost us votes in last two elections it was Nye. At least thirty seats.' Nye exploded and said, 'My advocacy in last two elections won more votes than Morrison in the whole of his life.' I said, 'Can't we have an end of this vainglorious rivalry!'

Much jealousy over Denis's candidature at Leeds. Nye in very bad mood. Grumbles at 'middle class people getting all good seats in Parliament. No working man stands a chance now. Middle class buy up seats. This should be investigated by Organisation Committee.' (Neither Denis nor Fienburgh *bought* seats against Trade Unionists!) ...

Nye is surrounded by middle class sycophants and hero-worshippers. N.E.C. made stupid decision that heads of departments at Transport House should resign on accepting *nomination* as Parliamentary candidate – as against selection. 16 to 6. Jim Griffiths, Sam Watson and I in minority.

---

1 The Prime Minister and Foreign Secretary (Eden) had sailed for New York on 31st December for an extended official visit to the United States and Canada. On 15th January, Churchill delivered an address to Congress in which he spoke of European defence, called for the presence of allied (not just British) troops at Suez, and promised full British support to the United States in policing any possible truce in Korea.

Friday 25th January
Lunching with Desmond Donnelly I referred to all this and said I was
equally fed up with Herbert and Nye. 'I love myself and hate my
colleagues' was no good. I thought of Jim Griffiths as successor to
Clem. Desmond said Nye did too. I said Nye was fifty-four, and
would never be Leader. ...

I said I couldn't tolerate middle-aged 'leaders' abusing the promising
younger people in the Party.

I said in reply to hints that I might take lead, that I was through with
ambition-ising. I had suffered fools gladly for decades, and wanted
now to be myself, and to say and write what *I* thought, without that
much muffling by collective responsibility.

Tuesday 29th January
Party Meeting. Bevanites pushing. Weak opposition. Gaitskell not
sufficiently combative against Tories.

Wednesday 30th January
German Rearmament. I raise this for the first time on Parliamentary
Committee. Morrison rather defensive. I say we must discuss it later.
Tony Greenwood says great majority of Party agree with what I said
in my broadcast. Good! I'm inclined to like this young man better!
He has poise, and a certain power of decision.

Thursday 31st January
Party Meeting. Foreign Affairs. Attlee from the Chair puts the point
about Winston's reference to 'a German Army' and repeats his own
points of last Friday, rather flatly.

Bing, following a hint from me in the passage just before the meeting, as first speaker in debate, says they all agree with what I said on
wireless on German Rearmament. And Shinwell, intervening later
and keeping Morrison out, says 'all agree with my broadcast'.

Tony Benn says – he has a very pleasant astringent humour – 'I
didn't know whether you looked more surprised, or Attlee and Morrison more angry', when this was said.

Sunday 3rd February
Trevor Evans,[1] *Daily Express*, rings up about all Nye's publicity last
week. Is it true he's planning to oust Attlee this week? I say, 'Don't
be silly! The Leader is chosen for a session at a time.' Also, 'The more
some people love Nye, the more others hate him.' Also, 'I'm bored
with green-eye.' This last remark, attributed to 'one of Socialist Big

1 T. M. Evans, later Sir Trevor (1902–81). Industrial correspondent of the *Daily
Express* 1930–67.

Five', goes into his Tuesday column.

Nye certainly gives the impression of intriguing all the time. I think he's in danger of speaking too much, in the House and at Party Meetings. But when he speaks in the House he exercises a hypnotic influence over many of our people. It's pathetic and dangerous to watch their eyes fixed on him.

Thursday 7th February

My mind has been moving for some time along the road of avoiding both Morrison and Bevan as future Party Leaders, or Prime Ministers. Each hates the other too much, and is altogether too personal in his approach to problems, as well as persons!

Today I say to Morgan Phillips that I think Jim Griffiths is the answer, if Clem gives up soon. (I hope he won't.) Morgan Phillips wonders whether Griffiths would run against Morrison, but says there is much to be said in his favour. (As a miner and a South Welshman he would steal a lot of Bevan's thunder.)

I also talk very straight to Griffiths about it. The other two are always at each other's throats. So it was in the Cabinet – so it is in the N.E. now. Either of them as Leader could seriously divide the Movement. Bevan keeps on living in the past (Hugh's Budget etc.) and forming a clique round him. Some say he doesn't want it, but I believe he does. It is very 'middle class', however you define it, and this makes his attacks on the 'middle class' (or National Executive elsewhere) sillier than ever. Morrison also has his clique, though not so obvious. He was, I say, a terrible failure at Foreign Office and still doesn't realise it. Griffiths agrees warmly. (He knows I wanted *him* to go there.) He says, in his emotional way, that our Movement must not be split. Our people count on it not being split. I say that if Attlee goes – I hope he won't for some years yet – Griffiths can hold it together better than any man. He is, I think, very pleased to hear me say this. He doesn't say he wouldn't run. I think he would, if he got enough backing. He says that we must keep in touch.

Morrison sitting next to me at a dinner to Nash[1] tonight, says half smiling, half resentful, that I ought to speak up when Nye talks nonsense at the N.E. He also says, 'I hear you've been talking.' But this conversation doesn't run on. He has some spy at some key hole, no doubt, on German Rearmament at least. The tide on this, I think, is turning my way. I'm pretty confident that I shall win in due course. But I am deliberately not rushing it for a week or two.

1 Sir Walter Nash, q.v. New Zealand Labour Party politician. Leader of the Opposition 1950–57.

I never forget Hugh in all this. But it would be soon to try to get the leadership for him in the near future. And I am a little chilled by his excess of 'responsibility'. I must try to stoke him up. Otherwise the chaps just won't follow him.

King George VI died in his sleep during the night of 5th to 6th February. The new Queen and the Duke of Edinburgh immediately returned by air from Kenya, where they were on an official visit.

Thursday 7th to Friday 8th February
Following the King's death, I attended two Accession Councils at St James's Palace. At the first, on Thursday afternoon, are Privy Councillors, Judges, and the Lord Mayor and Aldermen of the City of London. At the second, on Friday morning, only Privy Councillors including Judges.

Both are a Resurrection Parade, people one didn't remember were still alive, and some looking quite perky and self-important – Templewood, Belisha, Courthope,[1] Ammon, Hankey, Killearn,[2] Sir P. Loraine, etc.

At the first meeting we all sign the Proclamation (see *Times* of 8th February). I sign, by chance, between Harold Wilson and Nye Bevan!

At the second meeting, Queen Elizabeth the Second appears. She looks very small – high pitched, rather reedy voice. She does her part well, facing hundreds of old men in black clothes with long faces. She will take up this task 'which has come to me so early in life'. Killearn and Halifax get into the front row and block the view for many of us. Woolton's voice, as yesterday, is nauseating and oleaginous. He gets much worse as he grows older.

Duke of Edinburgh comes in from other door, in a slate coloured lounge suit – no black clothes handy, good sign. I think he'll be very good. I write to Tony, describing the scene, 'when you become a Minister of the Crown, you'll be seven years older than your sovereign.'

Monday 11th February
Shocking Party Meeting! Attlee proposes Parliamentary Committee Resolution, which, on last night's information, should have had a

---

1 Sir George Courthope, 1st Bart, 1st Baron (1877–1955). Conservative M.P. 1906–45.
2 Sir Miles Lampson, 1st Baron Killearn (1880–1964). Former diplomat. High Commissioner, then Ambassador, to Egypt and the Sudan 1934–46.

good majority, (1) censure on last week's events, (2) notice to reimpose standing orders, and (3) *all* Members to sign undertaking to abide by Party decisions in future.

Attlee moves quite well and firmly. But *no* follow up! We had agreed that, to exclude the haters, especially Morrison and Shinwell, only Attlee, whose stock was thought to be high, should speak. Alf Robens had collected names of stout trade unionists who would support – Mellish,[1] Jack Jones, Blyton, etc. Of these Mellish opened, with feeble compromising speech; Jones later bored meeting stiff and got the bird, for reading out boring quotes from an article he had written to his T.U. branch. Blyton, only arrived in early morning, didn't try to speak. Bevan made a violent speech, of nauseating egoism, and sweating with hatred. Strauss, Strachey, Marquand, McNeil and Younger had made a compromising resolution which they moved, and which was carried against Parliamentary Committee by 162 to 72!! I feel I would like to retire from Parliamentary politics altogether! No courage, no clarity! Strong hatreds and weak bladders!!

Thursday 21st February[2]
Bob Boothby says Macmillan didn't want his present job[3] (he was after the Foreign Office). So is always offering to resign, if he can't get his way, e.g. on housing subsidy. I get a good deal of gossip from Bob direct, and some indirectly from Dick Crossman and John Strachey.

Bob tells John that Eden's stock is falling very fast. If Winston went, Butler would be P.M. and Macmillan F.O. This is borne out by reception of Eden, on his return from Lisbon on 28th February 1952. He makes a very long and insubstantial statement, greeted by not one cheer, either at start or finish. They say he's nervy, and always losing his temper in Cabinet, Foreign Office and elsewhere.

Friday 22nd February
... [I] talk with Maurice Edelman and Tony Crosland in Smoke Room. Nye, they think, hasn't put a foot wrong since election. He'll go, they think, for Herbert for No. 2, not direct for No. 1. We couldn't, they think, win an election with him as Leader, but he might become Leader after ...

Maurice Edelman says that at a dinner, since the election, of the

---

1 R. J. Mellish, later Baron (b. 1913). Labour M.P. for Bermondsey 1950–82; Independent 1982–3. Junior minister 1964–9. Government Chief Whip 1969–70, 1974–6. Former Transport and General Workers' Union official.
2 Although dated 21st February, this entry was evidently written more than a week later.
3 Minister of Housing and Local Government 1951–4.

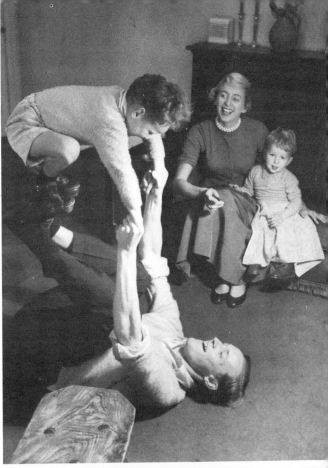

30 Sunday afternoon at the Benns',
1955

31 Douglas Jay on holiday with his
children, 1955

32 Ruth Dalton and Hugh Gaitskell, *c.* 1960

33 Dalton at West Leaze, 1961

1950 Club,[1] Attlee and Vi came, and he admitted that she wants him to give up, and then went on with some extraordinary Freudian dream story, clasping a furry hat in his hand and then waking up to find it was something else.

Defence estimates published at the end of February proposed an increase of £245 million in spending. An official Labour Amendment censured the Government for its administration of defence, but accepted the White Paper. A proposal by the Bevanites for a different Amendment declaring that the estimates were higher than the nation could afford, was rejected at a meeting of the P.L.P. on 4th March. Faced with a three-line whip instructing Labour M.P.s to abstain on the Government's motion and to support the Labour Amendment, the Bevanites decided to force a division on the first, and to abstain on the second. Fifty-seven Labour M.P.s voted against the White Paper, in defiance of the Whip, following the Commons debate on 5th March. This was the first major rebellion by back-benchers since November 1946. It hardened positions, and set a pattern for inter-party disputes which continued, intermittently, for most of the decade.

Friday 7th to Sunday 9th March
In Constituency. Annual meeting of C.L.P. goes well. ...

Later Michael Foot (long distance and awkward coincidence) speaks with me at good public meeting in Jubilee Hall. Back by train with him. Our conversation is friendly, but he now maintains that no M.P. can have his conduct decided for him by a majority vote of a private meeting. Not much sign of accommodation! Meanwhile all their weekend scribes in full cry.

This evening (9th) Tony Benn rings me up and we have a long talk on the telephone. He is all against a split. Thinks Parliamentary Committee may be beaten on proposal to withdraw whip unless undertaking given. Would Parliamentary Committee then resign! I said I thought not. Benn had spoken to many who were very doubtful of our wisdom. I spoke later to Chetwynd, who was doubtful, and Roy Jenkins, who was inclined to see it through.

Tuesday 8th April
Jim Callaghan thanked me for getting him in on the Finance Bill Second Reading Debate (I proposed him in Parliamentary Commit-

---

1 '1950 Club': Dalton had addressed them on 4th February.

tee). He had done very well. I said to him, 'My reward is your performance.'

Wednesday 9th April

Our crashing success in L.C.C. election and, to lesser extent, in other County Council elections, raises a danger that we may come back too soon. But I daresay Tories will hang on all the tighter. ...

Aneurin Bevan's book *In Place of Fear*[1] has had tremendous publicity. But it is *very* dull! Morrison is thought to be having a mild recovery. But he was very vexed at not being invited to speak at a dinner following the International Socialist Conference. He thinks Arthur Greenwood (in the chair) and I and Morgan Phillips prevented him – and we did. But he hadn't attended the conference. I'm afraid I'm hardly on speaking terms with him now. ...

Meeting of Parliamentary Committee, at which Jim Callaghan, Alf Robens and I, with some support from others, remould the Strasburg delegation. Alf Robens to lead it, Healey and Peart and Llywelyn Williams[2] to be included in reserves, Bottomley in first eight. Hynd to be out. Morrison sits silent through this, though it means displacing Gordon Walker from the leadership.

Grumping, particularly by Shinwell and Ede, about loss of control in the Chamber to the Bevanites. Jealous, frightened old men! Callaghan and I and others deny all this.

Some frank talk on Shawcross, led by Tony Greenwood. He is never here. Later at Committee's request, I ask him to speak on monopolies. But he will be in court and is getting rather dissatisfied about his position, and wondering whether he shouldn't resign his seat.

Of course he *should* have become either Lord Chief Justice or Master of the Rolls in the 1945–50 Parliament. He says to me that what he'd really [like] to speak on is *foreign affairs*. I daresay!

I refuse to speak on housing. Bring on younger people. 'We older men have had a very good innings ... ' Attlee watching to see which way cats jump these days. Very weak and inert in chair, meeting lasts much too long, nothing brought to a point.

Thursday 1st May

Hugh to lunch in my flat. He has decided, he says, not to run for N.E.C. this year. I said he was wise. He would get a bloody nose. I was inclined not to run – since I would have had twenty-five years, and

1 *In Place of Fear* (Heinemann, London, 1951) outlined Bevan's views on socialism and the direction of policy.
2 Llywelyn Williams (1911–65). Labour M.P. for Abertillery 1950–65.

will be sixty-five – but, because there was competition, and it would look cowardly, and I might have the wrong replacement, I would stand and fight. He says that he has spoken both to Attlee and Morrison about the latter leaving foreign affairs. He suggested to Attlee that Morrison should do more leading the House, as well as speaking on Home Front topics.

Hugh didn't think our recent row about German Rearmament very important.

Very pleased with way Finance Bill is going. No Bevanite trouble here. I still feel my relations with Hugh aren't as warm as I should like them, though there is no difficulty in discussing all these public affairs.

Friday 2nd May
A great personal victory!

This week I have done very well. On Sunday we were at Bonn – Wilfred Burke,[1] Mark Hewitson, Barbara Castle, Morgan Phillips and I – to confer with German and French Socialists. ...

Barbara and I flew back on Monday, above 10,000 feet so that we were rather sleepy and I could feel for two days that I had a heart – just that and no more. That afternoon I gave an oral account to Parliamentary Committee.

On Tuesday morning I dictated to Mavis Matthews[2] of Transport House a Report for N.E.C. This was round the table at N.E.C. meeting on the Wednesday morning (30th April 1952). I expounded it orally ending with my own personal conclusions. I said it was for consideration whether N.E.C. should, or should not, issue a public statement. I gave no lead on this. Hewitson said it was a fine report and he agreed with it all. Then someone (I forget who) moved that N.E.C. issue a statement. Barbara seconded. Morrison (with greatest ineptitude) opposed. Parliamentary Party was discussing and should be consulted. Summerskill supported him (she hates me!), but no one else till Jim Griffiths (weakly, wanting to be kind) moved an amendment that he should prepare a statement and communicate it to Parliamentary Committee and Parliamentary Party. I then said this wouldn't do. Not a dignified attitude for N.E.C. Only two alternatives, either for N.E.C. to make a statement and publish it straightaway or *not* to make a statement at all. I expressed no preference. Then they voted, and Jim's amendment was overwhelmingly defeated, only he, Morrison and Summerskill voting for it. I voted against, and so did Attlee and

1 W. A. Burke (1890–1968). Labour M.P. for Burnley 1935–59. Junior minister 1945–7.
2 Mavis Matthews. A Labour Party typist.

Peggy Herbison, and Eirene White, and Alice Horan.[1] Then on substantive motion that we issue a statement, Summerskill fell out. So there were only two against!

Then someone said, quite casually, that the statement should be on the lines of my conclusions (leaving out one on Constitution question in Germany), and this was accepted without a vote or further discussion.

Who to draft? Morgan Phillips and I and Attlee. Someone suggested Morrison, but he refused. So after the meeting I dictated, with help of Morgan and Mark Hewitson, in Morgan's office, a draft, and Morgan Phillips and I saw Attlee at 4, and he, after sitting silent for quite a long time, and then suggesting a small drafting improvement, agreed to it. And just before 5, Morgan Phillips and I gave it to Arthur Bax[2] to buzz into the press, and for the B.B.C.

Then Parliamentary Committee at 5.30. *Long* discussion on minor [?] things till nearly 7. Then we came to next week's Party Meeting – to discuss German Rearmament, etc. I tell them N.E.C. has issued statement and Attlee reads it out. Morrison, Shinwell, Stokes and Phil [Noel-Baker] furious – Shinwell most furious of all. He says we've sabotaged N.E.C. That 'some people', glaring at me, 'have been plugging this for a long time, and making speeches and writing about it outside, while others of us have kept quiet.' (!) What about his articles in *Daily Express* on Bevan's book and on Bevan and Morrison for leadership.

I take little part in discussion, being quite triumphant. Who will speak at Party Meeting? Attlee to open and gives a very good summary. Who to wind up? Jim [Callaghan] and Tony [Greenwood] suggest me. But Morrison suggests Phil and I didn't press my claim. I only say that, if N.E.C. statement attacked, I shall claim right to defend it. Shinwell says, 'Oh, well, if we're going to have a row, let's have a real row', etc.

Statement on tape at 6 p.m. Fred Peart took it to the Foreign Affairs Group while Phil Noel-Baker was reminiscing about 1920s and 1930s. Practically all in favour. I am tremendously complimented ... Most Labour M.P.s very satisfied. Morrison says this is 'caucus rule'. Gordon Walker echoes him. Few else!

---

1 Alice Horan (1895–1971). National Women's Officer of the General and Municipal Workers' Union, and a member of the Labour Party N.E.C. (Women's Section).
2 Arthur Bax. Transport House official. Secretary of the Labour Party Press and Publicity Department.

The N.E.C. statement on German rearmament, issued on 30th April, declared that fresh elections should be held in West Germany before any commitment could be made by the Adenauer Government for a German contribution to the European Defence Community; and it reaffirmed the need to rearm N.A.T.O. countries before rearming Germany. Crossman noted on 1st May: 'This was a really clever piece of Daltonian politics. Apparently he made his report on Bonn in such a persuasive form that the whole Executive almost automatically agreed, with the exception of Herbert Morrison, Jim Griffiths and Edith Summerskill.'[1]

Tuesday 6th May
Balogh to lunch at Josef's. He is all over me now. My *tour de force*, my personal triumph, etc. This reconciliation, for the time being, is complete.

Thursday 8th May
A. J. Irvine[2] tells a good story of Winston at some function with his fly-buttons undone. When his attention was tactfully drawn to this, he said, 'A dead bird won't fall out of the nest.'

Tuesday 13th May
George Brown and I talk. He thinks I'm in danger on N.E.C. I say, if it wasn't a lively year, I'd have stood down. Case for retiring age from N.E.C. at sixty-five. Anyhow I don't want to be a minister again. Let younger people come on. Brown argues against this. Wants me still to exercise influence. Crossman, he says, is no friend of mine. Only a week or two [ago] he was denouncing me in the Smoking Room as one of the more obstinate anti-Bevanites. 'They won't carry you', he says, of the Bevanites. I say I don't count on this. But the C.L.P. are a difficult electorate to organise beyond a certain point. Anyhow, I shan't break my neck if I'm beaten. He says this would be terribly sad. As to future leadership, I speak again of a third man. He says he thinks Jim Griffiths is weakening, and getting softer. I'm afraid he may be right.

Wednesday 14th May
Talk to Alf Robens. Very good. He'd make a third man, if he were a bit more established. We speak of draft resolution etc. He says,

1 *Backbench Diaries*, pp. 102–3.
2 A. J. Irvine, later Sir Arthur (1909–78). Labour M.P. for Liverpool Edge Hill 1947–78. Solicitor-General 1967–70.

'Don't piss into the wind.' Don't abandon leadership, but don't get needlessly across your troops.

Sunday 25th May
Much hatred is being worked up against me in Parliamentary Party as a 'near-Bevanite'. I can see this very clearly in many round faces which no longer smile at me! Anyhow I shan't stand for Parliamentary Committee again. I can't be bothered to be sucking up to all these dingy little people all the time, in Tea Room or elsewhere. I am too old for that, not wanting to be a minister again.

Tuesday 27th May
GERMAN REARMAMENT
We are being railroaded into this without any of the Attlee safe-guards.[1] A bunch of M.P.s – chiefly Bevanite – have put a motion on the paper in the terms of the N.E. declaration. They have thirty signatures, and hope to get more today. I hope they'll get a lot more who aren't Bevanite. ... This fight will have to be resumed.

Thursday 29th May
All night sitting on Finance Bill. I speak on Estate Duty. Tony [Crosland] and Roy [Jenkins] have been magnificent, and quite established themselves. Tony did a superb ragging speech against Woodrow [Wyatt]. 'Almost too flippant?' he asked after. No. No one else, on either side, could have done it. His Parliamentary Personality is achieved!

Hugh to dine at Josef's. I feel our relation much closer tonight than for a long time. We speak of the future. I say I'm disappointed in Jim Griffiths. I don't see who's to succeed Attlee now – until Hugh Gaits-kell, and that'll be some time yet. He hopes my relations less bad with Morrison now that latter is giving up Foreign Affairs. I say still pretty bad. He doesn't want to change things. He asks why I dislike

---

1 'the Attlee safeguards': in February 1951, Attlee had listed the conditions that the Labour Government would require to be fulfilled before consenting to a German contribution to the European Defence Community. These included the need for N.A.T.O. rearmament to precede German rearmament and the proper integration of German forces into a European force. In notes for a speech at a P.L.P. meeting on German rearmament on 13th May, Dalton wrote: 'February 1951 Attlee made conditions in speech in House of Commons. These followed long and animated discussions in Cabinet and were accepted with great satisfaction by his colleagues, the Parliamentary Party and Movement in the country. These still guide our policy including N.E.C. declaration. No-one ever authorised to set them aside.' (Included with Diary entry.)

Shawcross. I say he's insincere and vain. I tell Hugh that he nearly threw in his lot with the resigners. Hugh is impressed by this.

I say Tony is in a class by himself. He ought to be Hugh's Financial Secretary to Treasury, soon to be promoted to Minister of State for Economic Affairs. Roy to be Overseas Trade. Douglas Jay to be President Board of Trade.

We speak of ethics and [G. E.] Moore. Hugh says to love, and to be loved, is much the biggest thing in the world. I advise him to read Keynes on Moore.

Friday 30th May
London to Edale by train with Arthur Blenkinsop and Ted and Barbara Castle.

Whitsun Walk
Coming back in the train I had a row with Ted Castle – he wants to be candidate for Abingdon – over N.E.C. elections. He admitted that last year he'd advised Hornsey to 'plump for four Bevanites' including Driberg, but not to vote for me. I took strong objection to this. He said this year Harold Wilson would get on; the last place lay between me and Morrison. I could get it if I liked. I took all this ill!

Wednesday 11th June
I am playing with the idea of resigning from the Parliamentary Committee, and leaving Front Bench, on issue of ratification of agreements with Germany. The issue, in the Parliamentary Party, is largely bedevilled by Nye's attack on Clem in last Party Meeting before Whitsun, and in *Tribune* article. Shocking tactics! Rallying all moderates in loyalty behind Clem. They [should] have attacked Morrison.

I would sooner, if I have to choose, continue to have influence on N.E.C. than on Parliamentary Party.

If I resign on *this* from Parliamentary Committee, and Front Bench, and follow up with speeches, I should make myself safe on N.E.C. Feeling in the Movement is certainly against German Rearmament.

Before deciding, I must (1) watch events and sit put and (2) warn Attlee (3) consult a few – Hugh, Robens, Tony Greenwood – and ?Jim Callaghan on Parliamentary Committee – and Tony Crosland outside.

Speak later to Alf Robens, who has talked with Jim Callaghan, and thinks we can get agreement to vote against ratification, subject to our conditions. He hopes I won't think of resigning. And to George Brown, who takes the same view, I say it is 'demagogically very tempting'. He wonders.

Sunday 15th June. Weekend reflections
I am losing interest in current position, and especially in these personal
feuds. I shall not have much longer anyhow. At least I hope not. I
don't want senility.

Thursday 26th June
Tony [Crosland] came to lunch at my flat today.[1] ... He'd been lecturing in West Germany under Foreign Office auspices, and meeting lots
of people. West Germany was going ahead very fast.

Our future, as he sees it, is little better than a German satellite!
I said I was thinking of resigning from Parliamentary Committee on
German Rearmament, and speaking from below gangway. He was
horrified by this, and begged me, before deciding, to listen to some of
my younger friends; none of these except John Freeman, who wanted
Bevan to lead the Party, would take other view. I said I was being
resisted all the time on this [i.e. German Rearmament]. There was an
intolerable intrigue going on. He said there'd been intrigue on both
sides. ... He said of course I was bored. I said yes, and angry too.

He said I had a neurosis about German Rearmament; and my
hatred for Morrison was a matter for psychoanalysis. Something had
happened in this last year. I said there was no need for psychoanalysis. My feeling for Morrison wasn't hatred, but contempt. He
had let the side [down] completely as Foreign Secretary – and still
didn't realise it. He had wanted to delay the election – and this might
well have led to a massacre of our people – because he thought he
might soon get a truce in Korea. He was no longer a Socialist and
had no new ideas on the Home Front. And he was intriguing against
National Executive position, and Attlee conditions on German Rearmament. We spoke of Jim Griffiths – my Third Man, as against
Morrison and Bevan. I said he'd been of no use at all to me on this.
He'd taken a silly little point of dignity, put into his head by Morrison,
about some alleged meeting of back-bench N.E.C. members. I thought
we must look further down the line now for a Third Man; perhaps
Alf Robens. ...

Later [Tony] rang up, and we fixed that I would come to his flat on
Monday at 6 p.m. and have a drink with him and Roy Jenkins and

---

1 Dalton added here: '(Part of our talk in private diary, and some repetition here of
  that.)' Was there a second diary, running in tandem? Other references about the
  same time also suggest this possibility, at least for a short period. If so, none of it
  appears to have survived.

Jim Callaghan. He asked would I like Woodrow Wyatt too? I said No; he waffled. Or Douglas Jay and Denis Healey? I said I thought not. Not too big a meeting, and Healey didn't understand much about Parliamentary things yet.

That night, after our talk, I became very, very angry – not with Tony, but with some of my colleagues – and hardly slept at all.

When speaking to John Freeman about this a few days ago, he said he thought I had made my position on N.E.C., at one time in danger, safe now by my stand on German Rearmament, whether I resigned or not from Parliamentary Committee. If Morrison [was] pushed off N.E.C., it would be a pity and he would be very disruptive outside.

Saturday 28th June
At West Leaze, fuming over German Rearmament and failure of poor Tom Anderson[1] to keep Guthrie[2] and one or two troublemakers at Bishop Auckland in order.

I shall gradually disengage. ...

I don't think, if Parliaments last their normal length, I shall fight more than *one* more general election. If I'm beaten for N.E.C. this year, I shan't stand again. If I win, I shan't, I think (though this is a bit more open, involving future policy), stand next year.

Monday 30th June
To Tony's flat to meet Callaghan, Jenkins and Jay. Frank talk. I told them Germans were murderers, individuals excepted. They'd killed all my friends in First War, etc. *Deutschland über alles* was their song and they meant it. You couldn't tie them with snips of paper like E.D.C. [European Defence Community]. They said my resignation over German Rearmament would be a body blow at Clem, and a help to Bevan, and, said Roy, a body blow at Hugh. I said I couldn't help this. The fault would lie with them and Parliamentary Committee, who didn't support me. They said this was quite different from what I'd advised them when young – never resign, always accept majority view. I said this was good advice for young men, but I was already in the age of postscripts – and I wouldn't give way on principle. I re-capitulated my views on Germans and how the order to advance would be given in German, and we should be expected to obey.

---

1 Tom Anderson. Full-time Secretary-Agent for the Bishop Auckland Constituency Labour Party 1949–54.
2 Harold Guthrie. Bishop Auckland teacher and left-wing activist. Later constituency party secretary.

Roy, Tony and Jim all excused themselves from dining. Douglas accepted. ...

I sloshed Mallalieu at House of Commons for smearing Tony and Roy. He said I was drunk.

I told the young men I must go on the record and give a warning of what German Rearmament would mean. I wasn't going to be hushed up by the twopenny halfpenny little people on the Parliamentary Committee. That was why I spoke so often on this outside. Also I was personally committed by National Executive Declaration. They might run away. I couldn't. Tony said all this was so different from the realistic politician they had learned to know and respect.

I am very angry and worked up about it all. I see Europe going by default. Free economy Germany will be forging ahead; with all their gifts of efficiency displayed to the full. And we, in our mismanaged, mixed-economy, overpopulated little island, shall become a second-rate power, with no influence and continuing 'crises'.

I said I hoped I shouldn't be here to see too much of this, and I should advise all younger people to migrate to Canada or Australia.[1]

I find I have suddenly become totally bored by the House of Commons. It has become an unreal, far away nonsense. I looked in for a moment tonight, and saw them all sitting in rows – ugly idiots!

I said to the four young men, 'As soon as Germany is armed again, there'll be a bell tolling in the distance for someone. The Third World War will be on the way. They'll be getting the Death Ship into position for launching.'

Tuesday 1st July
Finally, after talk in Tony's flat *à quatre*, dining with Douglas Jay, and smashing into Mallalieu[2] (Freeman also being awkwardly present), I took Hugh back to my flat.

I stamped on the floor and was very indignant.

I said I loved him, but hated many of his lackeys; said I must resign from Parliamentary Committee if they went for ratification, in any form, of German Rearmament. But didn't want it rushed. If put off till autumn – after Party Conference, so that my resignation wouldn't

---

1 Marginal insertion: 'Polish airmen brought down 1 in 7 of German aircraft destroyed in Battle of Britain. When armed Germans with our support cross the Oder-Neisse line, we shall be practising old precept "forgive and forget"; forgive your enemies of yesterday, and forget your friends.'

2 Dalton wrote at the beginning of this entry: '... I am conscious of being very inclined to explode violently ... as I did to my four Young Men at Tony's flat yesterday, and later to Mallalieu in defence of two of my Young Men ...' Mallalieu was a Bevanite.

be said to strengthen Bevanites there – we should see where we stood then. I said he mustn't be too stiff.

Monday 7th July
Today I read of Zita Crossman's death,[1] and Tony Crosland tells me on the telephone that he and Hilary Sarson[2] are going to get married.

This is, as John Freeman, walking up and down the terrace, says to me, 'a very moving day'.

He has urged Tony to marry Hilary for some time. He keeps coming back to her. He has been a playboy long enough. More on this in private diary.[3]

Zita, whom we saw – Jim Callaghan and Douglas Jay and I, at XYZ – with Dick and their visitors only last Wednesday on the Terrace, and joked with – died of cerrebral (how spell the bloody word?) haemorrhage. She never recovered consciousness for the three days. If she had 'recovered', she would have been paralysed. They had no warning of this. And now *he* has a burst duodenal ulcer and a return of the phlebitis which nearly killed him in the war when he was working for me at M.E.W. I remember visiting him in hospital. Zita is to be buried on Thursday in the country. Dick, from Manor House Hospital, will go down. They were very devoted to each other.

Thursday 17th July
I've had two talks with Hugh, yesterday and today. He is very obstinate – and in danger of losing support of central mass of Party. He popped up at Party Meeting last week to interrupt me on gold payment to Germans for keeping our troops there. He said nothing was settled. I said that was what I complained of. He sits always beside Morrison on Platform at Party Meeting. I said to him last [night?] after XYZ, when he had been *very* talkative, and I think must have drunk a bit, 'Don't fight me too hard over German Rearmament. And don't just become Morrison's Jack in the Box.' He didn't take this well, and said, 'Well, if you're going to be offensive, I can be too. You sit on the fence. You used not to like people who sat on the fence.' I said that, as between Morrison and Bevan, it was very difficult to sit anywhere *but* on the fence. He said one must realise that there was a bitter struggle for leadership going on. It might last several years. The Bevanites might win. Then he'd have to consider whether he could

1 Inezita Crossman, formerly Baker, née Davis. She married Richard Crossman in 1939.
2 Hilary Sarson married Anthony Crosland in 1952. They divorced in 1957, and both remarried. She died in 1980.
3 See entry for 26th June 1952, p. 590, n. 1.

go on in public life. I said there were a lot of people in the middle who wanted their personal hatreds suppressed. He said this rested with the Bevanites. He was very tense and unsmiling.

Today he spoke again. I repeated, quoting George Chetwynd, that the middle mass – and I instanced the Party Meeting – was *very* tired of personal rivalries and bitterness. I said, picking up what he'd said about my sitting on the fence, that I thought I was right to try to keep the thing together, and not split from either end. He was glum and unresponsive. I said he was in danger of having an obsession about the Bevanites. He said I had an obsession about Morrison and was 'very unreasonable' about German Rearmament. This, anyhow, he said, would be settled soon.

He seemed to be looking forward to Morrison succeeding Attlee (who is, indeed, more and more frail and feeble, I fear). I said it would be a very unhappy ship. He said he had thought it all out.

Friday 18th to Sunday 20th July
Weekend at Walstons'. As always, very well cared for. Professor Richard Kahn to lunch on Saturday. I liked him, both as a chap and as a mind. Odd that we've never really met before. I'd known him, indirectly, as an obstructive civil servant at the Ministry of Production in the war, hindering my Development Area programme. I behaved very well, and modestly, as adjured by Tony beforehand.

Kahn talked good, but disturbing, sense on the Bank of England and the Treasury. No one outside the Bank knows what it's doing, or how, or whether it's right. He thinks it's worse since it was nationalised. (But this shouldn't be. I talk to Hugh some days later. We agree that Kahn would be the best economist to put on the Bank Court – and make an Executive Director. The Hungarians[1] wouldn't do. They'd bring down an Iron Curtain between themselves and the rest.) He thinks policy should begin to be discussed at 3rd Secretary level between Bank of England and Treasury.

Thursday 24th July
Today's Party Meeting approved, without comment, proposal of Parliamentary Committee that I, Shinwell and Chris Mayhew should speak for the Party on German Rearmament next week. (Afterwards Chris showed reluctance, not sure whether he could speak with conviction in light of last Party Meeting. He is, of course, in Herbert's pocket on this.) It was funny last night. When question of speakers arose, there was a silence. Then Jim Callaghan proposed me. More silence. Then I said that several Members *had* asked me why I never

1 Balogh and Kaldor.

spoke – in the House – on this, and I should be quite happy to speak in support of policy agreed at last Party Meeting. I was not in agreement, I knew, with a majority of members of the Parliamentary Committee on this. But I *was*, I thought, in agreement with majority of members of the Party. ... Party Meeting very ragged. Bevan raises again question of *British* Rearmament. Shrillness and altercation. George Brown makes a strong speech. Nye calls him, I'm told, a pimp and a bastard. Several people criticise each other. Crossman says he finds Gaitskell 'irritating'. Others ask for an end of these personalities. There is a good block of middle opinion forming in the Party – Chetwynd tells me a number of them met – to try to ride down all these personal hates and rivalries. ...

Later ... talk with George Brown. He is being very active in a number of groups in Parliamentary Party, (a) to try to strengthen leadership, buck up Attlee, get platform to lead, incidentally also to build up Morrison as Deputy, and to stop Jim Griffiths from being used as a Third Man, and (b) to fight the Bevanites. They're also trying to influence some votes for C.L.P. elections at Morecambe, against Bevanites. Some, he tells me, are doubtful whether, in addition to Morrison, Griffiths, Gaitskell and Alf Robens, to work for *me*, because they think I'm gunning for Morrison. George Brown hopes I won't give that impression. I speak, as before, very frankly about Morrison's terrible weaknesses. He has stopped growing, but not stopped intriguing. He *will* go on fighting me on German Rearmament, though I've got most of Party on my side, and am embarrassed by Bevanite support. I repeat that I have, more and more, an inclination to disengagement; wouldn't run for N.E. this year if I didn't think my seat was in danger, etc. It seems there are several groups in which George Brown is involved. Some of his colleagues are going to talk to Attlee. He himself to Morrison. The latter visited the Trade Union group last night. It was, says Brown, a pathetic flop. Not in touch with any sentiment in the Party; waiting, like a Buddha, for leadership to fall into his lap. We agreed that Attlee might outlast him, though Attlee had shown signs of ageing and weakening lately.

They had warned Griffiths not to let himself be made a catspaw. I said I'd seriously thought of him as an alternative, but lately had been disappointed in him. I said South Wales miners might support him, as against Bevan. Brown said they didn't think much of him in South Wales.

Brown also said that Gaitskell mustn't get too rigid and full of hatred. Some of his best friends must warn him. I said I'd tried, but without much result. Brown said that Stokes today had said to him that he was getting fed up with Gaitskell's attitude.

(I believe Dora's to blame; like Jennie and Bevan. Best a non-political wife, like Hilary for Tony, if you can't have, like me, a *wise* political wife!)

On 28th July, the Parliamentary Committee discussed its attitude to a Government motion to ratify the European Defence Community Treaty, and the Contract defining the future status of Germany. An Opposition Amendment was adopted (largely drafted by Dalton, but with an additional paragraph to reassure the Labour Right) attacking the Government's proposal and reaffirming the Attlee conditions of February 1951. This Amendment, strongly backed by the Bevanites, was put to a P.L.P. Meeting on 29th July.

Tuesday 29th July
GERMAN REARMAMENT
Tremendous personal triumph, my friends say. At Party Meeting in Westminster Hall our amendment is approved by 141 to 10; and the vote against the Government's substantive motion by 131 to 27. These are much larger majorities than I had expected. When Attlee announces Parliamentary Committee's recommendation, and reaches 2nd vote, there is loud applause from Bevanites and others, and loud and angry shouts of 'No' from the German Rearmers.

Later, in the Smoke Room, Nye asks how it went in the Parliamentary Committee yesterday. I say that, at the end, Morrison was practically isolated. He asks about Hugh. I say that he said that it was quite a reasonable amendment, and that he didn't resist the second vote. Nye is disappointed, I think, and slightly incredulous. He then says that Tony Crosland and Roy Jenkins voted with the 27 this morning. I say that neither of them was at the Party Meeting. He questions this. I say I am quite sure, and that one of them rang me up beforehand and that I told him he needn't come, because the majority was quite safe. This is a sidelight on the personal spites in Nye. It's all a crashing bore!

Last week I was at Durham for the Gala. Nye, Shawcross and Peggy Herbison the other visiting speakers. I spoke to Nye about tactics, following a talk with Dick Crossman. I said the important thing was to get the Parliamentary Party to vote against the Government motion on German Rearmament. To do this, I was prepared to concede something in the terms of our amendment. He agreed. I said that, if beaten in Parliamentary Committee, I wouldn't accept it, but would insist on its being brought to Party Meeting ... Gala as usual very moving. Travelled back with Shawcross and his wife. A careful conversation on both sides.

Monday 4th August
Now for the moment, *this* fight is over. It has taken me seven months to win this round – since my broadcast just before Christmas. The resistance, organised by Morrison, has been very persistent. Much ill has been spoken of me by the Morrisonites, and many faces, which used to smile at me always when we passed, do so no longer. (This may be partly, but not more than half, my fault too!) It is infuriating how this is all mixed up with Bevanism and anti-Bevanism – and the sickening Attlee–Bevan brawl, which broke out again on Friday morning, and half blanketed the reports of our debate, is the latest phase. And now Morrisonites are beginning to make anti-Bevanite speeches in the country – Gordon Walker, Stokes, etc. – attacking Bevanites for being 'a party within a party', etc. I don't see how this is going to heal up. It's getting worse, and more and more personal.

This is the first August since 1939 that I have not been a Minister of the Crown.

Wednesday 10th September
Lots of blokes electioneering for Morecambe. I made one speech, at Fabian Summer School at Frensham Heights, saying we must all be friends. I am repeating the substance of this at Evenwood this week. Tony says my young friends don't really like this bridge-building line. I said I thought it was sense and good Morecambe politics too. He thought it might be. I said I thought Herbert Morrison and I would be defeated by Crossman and Wilson.

Thursday 25th September
Hugh (whom I saw for ½ hour) thinks the last two places lie between himself, me, Wilson and Crossman. Mikardo, Shinwell and Phil [Noel-Baker] right out. And Alf Robens not registering. Hugh says his C.L.P. voted the same ticket as mine, likewise without prompting. He thinks Bevan is in a dilemma when Parliament meets again. If he runs for Parliamentary Committee, he'll get on, but no other Bevanites will, except, perhaps, Wilson. But then he can't go on attending and leaking to separate group. If he doesn't run, there'll be great annoyance with him among ordinary run of M.P.s.

The Labour Party Annual Conference opened at Morecambe on 29th September. Harry Earnshaw was in the chair.

September

MORECAMBE

This was the worst Labour Party Conference, for bad temper and general hatred, since 1926, the year of the General Strike when I was first elected to the National Executive, and the Chairman, Bob Williams,[1] so mishandled the Conference that he lost his seat.

And it was very cold and wet, and windy at Morecambe, and the accommodation was very dispersed and not very good.

Voting for National Executive as usual on Monday (29th September). I had made up my mind that I was off, but didn't discuss election much with anyone. I gave the Bishop Auckland vote to myself and six young non-Bevanites – Hugh, Jim Callaghan, Alf Robens, Tony Greenwood, Douglas Jay and George Lindgren. At 11 p.m., just as I was going to bed, Jim Callaghan rang up from a distant hotel, and we talked of National Executive election. I said I thought Mikardo and I were off, and Wilson and Hugh on. He said he thought this might well be.

He had not thought till twenty-four hours ago that I was in jeopardy, but he clearly thought so now. He'd got me the South-East Cardiff vote, but not, he regretted to say, Cardiff Borough. If I was to be succeeded by anyone, it couldn't be better than by Hugh Gaitskell from my point of view. I said I quite agreed, and that anyhow I shouldn't break my heart, as he knew, if I was off. He said he *did*, but he hoped I'd at least be irritated if beaten by Driberg, etc. He said it was because I was in danger that he'd rung me up. At such times, he thought, one's friends ought to ring one up and not keep away. I thanked him with a gay laugh. He'd said he was at the same hotel as Younger, Tony Greenwood and other friends of mine. They were all keeping their fingers crossed for me.

Tuesday 30th September

Second day of Conference. Morgan Phillips has postponed counting of votes for C.L.P. section till this morning, to avoid leaks. No interest in any of other sections. Announcement early in morning session.

Great Bevanite victory. Morrison and I both off, and Hugh Gaitskell next after me, not within striking distance.[2]

1 Robert Williams (1881–1936). Labour Party Chairman 1926. Secretary of the National Transport Workers' Federation 1912–25.
2 Voting for the seven successful candidates in the constituencies section of the N.E.C. was as follows (in thousands, with 1951 figures in brackets): Bevan 965 (858), Castle 868 (676), Driberg 744 (646), Griffiths 700 (597), Wilson 632 (396), Mikardo 630 (561), Crossman 620 (–). Runners up were Morrison 584 (595), Dalton 437 (545), Gaitskell 330 (–), Callaghan 196 (142), Shinwell 146 (410).

The figures show a tremendous concentration of the Bevanite vote; half vague emotion, half Mikardo's cunning organisation. The results were received with loud cheers from Bevanite elements, said to include quite a large number of Agents.

For me very irritating, as Jim said last night it *should* be, but much less with Morrison off too, than with me off alone. Jim is a great brick. He comes up at the lunch break, and again at the end of this afternoon, and companions [*sic*] me, ... and in the afternoon we go across for a drink at the Midland [Hotel]. Lots of people say they are so sorry. I evolve a standard reply. 'I think you're sorrier than I am.' To Dick Crossman, meeting him in the lounge at the Midland (with Massingham), I offer congratulations, and say, 'You'll find it awfully boring.' He says it wasn't *me* he wanted to put off!

This afternoon Morrison makes a speech, winding up on *Facing the Facts*,[1] which received a great ovation at the end. Rather nauseating, I think, after this morning's vote. But mostly, no doubt, from Trade Union delegates who didn't vote in C.L.P. section, and from those in that section who *did* vote for him. This speech is much written up in the press, and it is suggested that he should now become Leader in place of Attlee who played a very passive part throughout. (But what *could* he have done? Hardly declared, or implied, that vote for National Executive was wrong!)

Wednesday 1st October
Neither Morrison nor I condoled with one another. Nor did I congratulate any Bevanite except Dick.[2] I would have spoken a nice word to Barbara [Castle] if I'd run into her. But I didn't. Frightful row, with continuous booing from both sides, the following day. Deakin[3] and Lawther[4] very provocative.

I went off fairly early on the Friday, before the rush on the Special Train. I am very gloomy about the Party. We haven't had so strong hatreds since 1931 – and then one section left the Party, but now everyone is staying on. If we go on tearing each other to pieces in public and

---

1 '*Facing the Facts*': a Labour Party policy document published in the summer of 1952.
2 Dalton changed this in his memoirs to: 'I stayed all through the Conference ... And I congratulated Crossman and Wilson on their success' (HTA, p. 385).
3 Arthur Deakin (1890–1955). General Secretary of the Transport and General Workers' Union 1946–55.
4 Sir William Lawther (1889–1976). President of the Miners' Federation of Great Britain 1939–45; National Union of Mineworkers 1945–54. Labour M.P. 1929–31.

in private, the Tories may take a quick one, just after the Coronation, and win.[1]

The election for the Parliamentary Committee aroused special interest in 1952, partly because of changes in the voting rules, aimed at weakening the Left. The first ballot was held on 19th November, and the second on 27th November.

Tuesday 14th October

Interesting talk with George Brown. He thinks the Bevanites could get three or four candidates, if they run them, on the Parliamentary Committee. 'Keep Calm'[2] people – Strachey, Strauss, etc. – for unity at all costs. Brown thinks that now Griffiths is probable successor to Attlee. Morrison, he thinks, is out of it now and Bevan is impossible anyhow. I say I'm very glad to hear Brown say this. He says the trouble about Hugh is that he's too arrogant. No warmth to Trade Unionists. Seeking leadership too eagerly and too early.

Brown wants me to be a centre for younger people, who want an effective Party. He says Deakin, Evans,[3] etc. are inclined to think I'm not facing my responsibilities; they are now praising Morrison for whom they've cared little in the past. Brown wants me to commit myself more against Bevan. He thinks I contributed a bit to my defeat at Morecambe by my self-detachment. He says I'm not so old as I think. This next year I should make up my mind to play an important part.[4]

Friday 24th to Tuesday 28th October

Gloom and boredom over Party rows. Last week, 23rd, we carried by 188 to 51 at a Party Meeting a resolution, approving Clem's speech,

---

1 The Coronation was planned for June 1953.
2 John Strachey, G. R. Strauss and Kenneth Younger had formed a Keep Calm Group, aimed at non-aligned M.P.s. Though himself divided in his loyalties, Dalton dismissed the leaders of this new tendency as 'the sibilant sisters'.
3 L. Evans, later Sir Lincoln (1889–1970). General Secretary of the Iron and Steel Trades' Confederation 1946–53.
4 After the contest had taken place in November, Dalton inserted the following paragraph at the end of the entry for 14th October: '(… G.B. was busy over Parliamentary Committee elections. He said, after first declaration, that he'd got me some votes, but that it hadn't been altogether easy! I said, "Do get Shinwell off on second round." He said, rather angrily, "Don't try that one now. We must concentrate on one thing at a time." He meant keep A.B. off. He failed in that.)'

which was better and livelier than usual, calling on Bevanites to dis-band, and on all to cease attacking each other in press and speech.

But nothing is getting better. More hatred, and more love of hatred, in our Party than I ever remember. Nye's defects of character, and of entourage, are growing on him. Arrogance, conceit, personal ani-mosities – and the entourage egg him on. Now Mikardo and Co. are trying to undermine non-Bevanite M.P.s in their constituencies.

Monday 3rd November
Read in this morning's *Daily Herald* that Bevan will stand against Morrison for Deputy Leader this week. He will, of course, be easily beaten in a straight fight. But *what* a miserable choice! I ring up Jim Griffiths, remembering past talks, to sound him as to whether *he* would run. Not home. I'm afraid he won't. Since Morecambe there will be a concentration of right-wing effort behind Morrison. But I'll try to see Griffiths later today.

[Written later]

Saw Griffiths. I said it was, I dared say, rather late for him to intervene. But if anything happened to Attlee many would think *him*, rather than Morrison or Bevan, the best Leader. He said it *was* too late now – we should let things take their course. But he had pressed Attlee to go on, and had pressed Vi. *She* had been frightened by deaths of Ernie and Stafford and wanted Clem for a few years to herself.

Tuesday 11th November
Contest for deputy leadership. Morrison 194; Bevan 82. The latter's vote is large. I hadn't thought he'd get over 60. Much of it is a demon-strative vote, against leadership, Attlee as much as Morrison. Some just anti-Morrison. I myself abstained.

This, I think, is a clear pointer to Jim Griffiths, as Attlee's successor. He has just been elected Chairman of Policy Sub-Committee of N.E. (scoring 11 votes against 2 for Nye – Wilson and Mikardo).

Now there'll be a scramble for Parliamentary Committee. I suppose I must stand. I'm awfully allergic. I'm much more interested in writing my life and re-writing my *Public Finance*. The hatreds in this Labour Party are so hateful and so harmful that one would almost prefer not to be here.

Last weekend was much more agreeable. Friday night talking to Cambridge University Labour Club. They said it was very 'friendly'. Hugh had apparently lectured them, and said beforehand that he wouldn't answer questions on differences in Labour Party. Brian Abel-Smith, who remains rather shyly young and a little twisty-

faced and spotty complexioned, but whom I still definitely like, and
who liked having a day and a night, on my initiative, at Newton Hall,
and was treated nicely this time by Catherine [Walston], again on my
initiative – tells me that my only 'black' was when I praised Queens-
land over coffee, as a White Man's Country in the tropics. All these
young men are very much against racial and colour prejudice – all for
mixed marriages and miscegenation and a grey race emerging.

Thursday 13th November
Donnelly says that the Bevanite Group really *is* breaking up. The
Tribune corner is now on its own, uncontrolled by the rest. Nye is
anti-Barbara. Ted is terribly difficult about everything. Barbara is
taking too much benzedrine, or is very strained. Freeman has been
very intransigent against Nye and any of the Bevanites standing for
the Parliamentary Committee. The Keep Calmers tried to do a deal.
They sent Paget[1] to suggest to the Bevanites a common ticket, 8 or
9 Bevanites +3 or 4 Keep Calmers. This was contemptuously refused.

John Freeman would like to edit the *New Statesman*. Dick [Cross-
man] says that Kingsley Martin would like Freeman to succeed him,
but that the Board will appoint *him* (Dick) and not Freeman.

Thursday 27th November
Parliamentary Committee elections rather a triumph. I am elected
in top 6 in first round. Jim Griffiths, Chuter Ede, Hugh Gaitskell, Alf
Robens, Hugh Dalton and Jim Callaghan in that order. Nye on by
skin of his teeth. No change in first 12, even after eliminating top 6
and bottom 34. No other Bevanites. I'm sorry Tony Greenwood went
off, and that Shinwell didn't. Otherwise not too bad. I said I regarded
Wilson's defeat as reparation for Morecambe.

Long and affectionate talk with Nye. He drove me home after all
night sitting. I told him not to believe what some of his followers said
to him. He and I had been together on winning sides before – in
Cabinet and N.E. – and could be again. He said he and I had always
got on very well when I was Chancellor of the Exchequer. I said I had
backed him for *National* Health Service when Morrison wanted it
only Municipal. And we had fought on same side on iron and steel.
He spoke ill of Attlee and Morrison and said he despised Robens.
I praised Jim Callaghan. He said he knew how I felt about Hugh
Gaitskell; so wouldn't discuss.

For the moment there's a chance of mending the rents, I hope.

1 R. T. Paget, later Baron (b. 1908). Labour M.P. for Northampton 1945–February
1974.

Saturday 29th November
Tea with Tony and Hilary [Crosland] at their flat at 61 Queen's Gate.

Dine with Bob and Betty [Fraser] and Rosalind (now a big, healthy looking girl, though short sighted) at their flat in Hampstead.

Wednesday 3rd December
Nicholas Kaldor replying to Meade.[1] Against devaluation or 'floating rate' now; better have import cuts. We had decided on some new members – Roy already present, Robin Brook[2] to be approached by Hugh; Colin Clark to be invited by me to talk to XYZ, and we'll see whether he'll do; Richard Kahn to be approached by Kaldor.

Kaldor very long, and, when he replies, *so* long again that several people are looking at their watches and shuffling. I say suddenly, 'Everyone wants to go.' So Kaldor shuts up. It is 11.15.

Dalton spent three weeks over Christmas and the New Year in Israel and Cyprus, then a further week in his constituency.

Friday 27th February 1953
To West Leaze (Friday morning) by early train, to prepare for planting spinney. ...

Some political reflections.

The Labour Party is making no progress in the country. We don't look or sound like an effective alternative government. We are still squabbling. For the moment Bevan is out of the country, on a three weeks' trip to India. He has made a silly speech to the Indian Parliament, criticising U.S. and Soviet Union and saying that we need a Third Force of other nations, in which India would play a leading part. But this is so stale and stupid ('Force' in India!) that Nehru repudiates it, though politely, in a speech next day. There is, however, a great to-do on N.E.C. (how glad I am I'm not there! They sit from 10 to 12.30 without a break on 25th) about *Tribune* Brains Trusts[3]

---

1 J. E. Meade (b. 1907). Professor of Commerce, with special reference to International Trade, at the L.S.E. 1947–57. Economic Assistant, Economic Section of the Cabinet Office 1940–45; Director 1946–7. Professor of Political Economy and Fellow of Christ's College, Cambridge 1957–68.

2 R. E. Brook, later Sir Robin (b. 1908). Merchant banker. Chairman of the Colonial Development Corporation 1949–53. S.O.E. 1941–6, first as Personal Assistant to Jebb, and later in charge of the organisation of resistance in France. A Director of the Bank of England 1946–9.

3 '*Tribune* Brains Trusts': through *Tribune*, the Bevanites had organised roving panels of well-known left-wingers, who answered questions at public meetings.

and about rudeness of Lawther and *Daily Herald* to Bevanites.[1] Oh Hell! Just loving hating each other! 'Who', says some detached M.P. to me, 'thinks anything of a family, where husband and wife are always rowing in public?'

Nor is Tory rule so bad, or thought to be so, as we had prophesied. Unemployment, prices, wages, social services (especially housing), foreign affairs, all better than we expected. And no war! ...

Attlee's seventieth birthday celebration, with presentation of an illuminated Address, a Medallion and a silver dish for Vi was a *very* prosaic affair. M.P.s, General Council, N.E.C. and swarms of co-operators – all looking alike, small, stout, spectacled and insignificant! I am amazed at my tolerance, through so many decades, of so many dullards. Now, sitting above the clouds of political ambition, I can afford to be more choosy in my company, and less forthcoming to all and sundry.

Attlee makes a good, short speech. The rest were dull and too long – Greenwood, with inaccurate reminiscences of 1940, then O'Brien,[2] Fred Blower[3] and Herbert Morrison, who talks as though he and Attlee had always been bosom pals – first Labour mayors of Stepney and Hackney in successive years,[4] etc.

Vi, I hear, after wanting to pull Clem out of Parliament and have him all the time at Cherry Cottage, is now bored with C.C. and wants to pull out of it, and go back to No. 10 Downing Street. But I doubt if we can win next time and, if we lose by a majority large enough to make a further four or five years of Tory rule likely, I guess Clem *will* retire. And so should Herbert, and a few more of us. The succession is a frightful problem – worse than ever. Morrison is ageing and slow, and will never have a new idea, or a new phrase (unless someone supplies it) again. Jim Griffiths made *such* a nice Party Political Broadcast ... All about the Colonies, and their awakening,

---

1 *Tribune* had criticised Lincoln Evans, q.v., General Secretary of the Iron and Steel Trades' Confederation, for accepting a knighthood from the Conservative Government in the New Year Honours. The *Daily Herald* denounced this attack, and Sir William Lawther accused the Bevanites of attempting to undermine the leadership 'in the same way as Hitler and the Communists did'. The N.E.C. reprimanded the *Herald* and Lawther, while Deakin, of the T.G.W.U., defended them. (See M. Foot, *Aneurin Bevan: A Biography, Vol. I 1945–1960*, MacGibbon & Kee, London, 1973, pp. 393–4.)

2 T. O'Brien, later Sir Tom (1900–70). Labour M.P. for Nottingham North-West 1950–55; Nottingham West 1945–50, 1955–9. General Secretary of the National Association of Theatrical and Kine Employees 1932–70. Member of the T.U.C. General Council 1940–70.

3 J. W. Blower. Chairman of the Co-operative Union. Joint Chairman of the National Council of Labour.

4 1919 and 1920.

and our duty to them. But *totally* vague and lacking everything except patent sincerity, monotonous sing-song voice, and local preacher's moral tone. But maybe as Leader he'd be better than this. *Maybe*. But anyhow better than Herbert or Nye. Oh yes, still.

Tuesday 3rd March
Desmond Donnelly, rather depressed, has a long talk with me. Nye is away in India and Burma, and not back till nearly the end of this month. 'Policy making' on N.E. is going badly. Wilson on aircraft manufacture said many technicians were in favour of nationalising it; when asked to name some, he couldn't. (Wilson was over working. He came to speak for Donnelly in Pembrokeshire, and had had a blackout and had to stop and sit down in middle of speech. Had *I* ever had to do that, Donnelly asked, in any of the much greater periods of strain I had gone through? No I said.)

Thursday 5th March
Defence Debate. Goes pretty well. Half a dozen pacifists abstain ... Attlee opens all right, Phil [Noel-Baker] winds up, very nervously, very earnestly with that plaintive note in his voice which has become habitual, with *many* too many notes. He has long gone past his climax. Rather pathetic, remembering his form of decades back. Winston not at all provocative, but never mentions N.A.T.O. Good passage on jets, etc., to Middle East. Won't agree to anything which appreciably shifts balance against Israel in favour of Arab States. Hugh and I loudly applaud this, but no one else on either side makes much noise.
...

After the vote at 10 p.m. our people very well disciplined this time and no one challenges a second vote on main question. I am walking in the passage with Barbara Castle. Winston, pretty tight and physically supported by his son-in-law and P.P.S. Christopher Soames,[1] approaches from the other direction. He stops and says to me, 'Thank you very much for your support. I won't allow the balance to be tilted against Israel. I've always been a Zionist, and I've often had a very heavy time over it.' I say I've just seen them in Israel and they're doing jolly well. I mention General Yadin.[2] He isn't listening much, but,

1 Christopher Soames, later Baron (b. 1920). P.P.S. to Churchill as Prime Minister 1952–5. Conservative M.P. for Bedford 1950–66. Married to Churchill's daughter Mary. Junior minister 1955–8. Secretary of State for War 1958–60; Agriculture, Fisheries and Food 1960–64. Ambassador to France 1968–72. A Vice-President of the Commission of European Communities 1973–7. Governor of Southern Rhodesia 1979–80. Lord President of the Council and Leader of the House of Lords 1979–81.
2 General R. Y. Yadin (b. 1917). Israeli Chief of Staff 1949–52.

catching the words 'General' and 'Commander of their forces', says, 'You're coming to dine with Tito aren't you?' I said, 'Yes. Thank you very much for asking me.' (This was at No. 10 on the 18th; and I had already accepted the invitation.) 'Tito', Winston went on, 'likes uniforms, and medals and decorations. So we must all do our best, and each put on the best he has!' Then Soames guided him away. I think, though his speech was not quite clear, that he had used my Christian name, a thing which he had hardly ever done before, even when we were allies over British Rearmament before the war, or when I was one of his ministers during it.

Friday 6th March
Anyhow, next day, to please Winston and Tito (and perhaps myself), I walked about in Mayfair till I found a shop that supplied such things (Spinks in King Street, corner St James Street) and ordered ribbons and miniatures of the three medals I'm entitled to, to be set on a brooch for wear with evening dress. The young woman in charge rang up about the ribbon and miniature of my Italian Bronze medal,[1] and said they had it in stock. She hadn't recognised it at first, but, when I wrote it down in Italian, she said, 'Oh, of course, for military valour. A plain blue ribbon isn't it?' and I said, 'Yes.'

Thus I break a habit of $24\frac{1}{2}$ years of not wearing decorations at appropriate dinner parties and other social gatherings.

Winston at seventy-nine is still a very great personality. I have been reading, with much appreciation lately, his *Great Contemporaries*[2] borrowed from Bob Boothby.

Wednesday 18th March
Dine at No. 10 to meet Tito. Party of about thirty, our side represented by Attlee, Morrison and myself (wearing 'decorations' with evening dress for the first time in my life!). Trade Union leaders – Tom O'Brien, Vincent Tewson[3] and Tom Williamson[4] – very pleased with life. Winston plays up to them wonderfully. ...

Sit between a Yugoslav doctor, with very little English, and Lascelles.[5] Speak with latter of Nicolson's *George V*,[6] my forthcoming

1 Dalton had been awarded the *Medaglio di Bronzo al Valor Militare* by the Italian government, for bravery during the retreat from Caporetto in 1917.
2 W. S. Churchill, *Great Contemporaries*, Butterworth, London, 1937.
3 H. V. Tewson, later Sir Vincent (1898–1981). General Secretary of the T.U.C. 1946–60. Assistant-General Secretary 1931–46.
4 T. Williamson, later Baron (1897–1983). General Secretary of the General and Municipal Workers' Union 1946–61. Labour M.P. for Brigg 1945–8.
5 Sir Alan Lascelles, q.v., Private Secretary to George VI 1943–52; Elizabeth II 1952–3.
6 Harold Nicolson, *King George V: His Life and Reign*, Constable, London, 1952.

book, and Wheeler-Bennett[1] as biographer of George VI. Wheeler-Bennett was recommended by Nicolson. I say I think, from his previous writings, that he may be dull. Lascelles says that, compared with George V, it was a relatively straightforward reign. George V had to take a series of most difficult decisions, beginning at his accession. George VI had only one difficult problem, which only lasted half an hour, to choose between Halifax and Winston as Neville Chamberlain's successor in May 1940. Lascelles says George V had a most awkward and double-headed set up in his secretariat – Knollys[2] and Stamfordham, with dividing line never clear cut. I said it was lucky he had Knollys. Stamfordham, I thought, was sometimes a very rash counsellor (e.g. on the promise to Asquith to make peers, and on Baldwin's request for a dissolution in 1923).

I spoke of Wigram, Stamfordham's successor, but Lascelles dismissed him curtly. 'He was no good at all,' he said. I said I thought Nicolson had written an admirable book, but I disagreed with much of his emphasis and detail on 1931 and should say so in my book. Lascelles said, 'I think he got quite a lot from Herbert Morrison.' 'Yes', I said, 'and nothing to balance it from those who were on the other side in the Labour Cabinet.'

Crossman wrote in his diary on 30th March 1953: 'The big gossip today has been the Shawcross story ... I spent a great deal of time putting the story together from talks with Woodrow Wyatt, Harold Keeble, who is now Assistant Editor of the *Sunday Express*, and Hugh Dalton, whom Woodrow Wyatt, pledged to secrecy, had selected as his confidant.'[3] Shawcross was afraid that Wyatt's laudatory articles might be in breach of the convention banning 'advertising' by members of the Bar. Though still a Labour M.P., Shawcross acted as legal adviser in a private capacity to the Prime Minister.

Monday 23rd March
Dined at the House tonight at same time as Wyatt, Hugh, and Blenkinsop. Talk turned to Shawcross. Wyatt has undertaken to write four articles on him for *Sunday Express*. Hugh praises him highly, thinks

---

1 J. Wheeler-Bennett, later Sir John (1902–75). Historian. Fellow of New College, Oxford and Lecturer in International Politics 1950–57. Official biographer of George VI. Author of *King George VI: His Life and Reign*, Macmillan, London, 1958.
2 Sir Francis Knollys, 1st Viscount (1837–1924). Private Secretary to Edward VII 1901–10; George V 1910–13.
3 *Backbench Diaries*, pp. 213–14.

he has not only a very remarkable legal brain, easily best at the Bar, but that he is a national figure and, as such, of great value to the Party. I criticise him. His neglect of his Parliamentary duties has become an open scandal. He should not have rejected both Lord Chief Justice and Master of the Rolls when Attorney-General. A Socialist judge of high intelligence might have done things for the interpretation of our law. He and Frank Soskice sat tight for six years as Attorney-General and Solicitor-General and blocked all on legal side of Party. Shawcross admittedly wants Foreign Office – and no doubt to be P.M. after that. ... Bevan is against him, and thinks feeling in the Party, all over the country, has grown very much against him in the last month or two. Wyatt in *this* conversation is defending Shawcross, and I say that these articles are clearly designed as a build-up.

Afterwards I go to Smoke Room, by myself. Wyatt comes and sits near me, obviously wanting to continue conversation. So we do. He shows me a letter which Shawcross has sent him by hand today, but not marked personal or confidential. Shawcross writes that he has only heard in the last few days about these articles (Wyatt says he *saw* Shawcross and told him and talked to him about them on 4th March, nearly three weeks ago, and Shawcross made no objection and gave him much information about his life and career); that he would have to resign from the Bar if they were published, since this would be against 'etiquette of the Bar', and that he would indemnify Wyatt for his fees, if he didn't publish.

Wyatt says that *Sunday Express* published, yesterday, a notice of these forthcoming articles, headed 'Man or Superman?' with a very handsome photograph, the story of Hartley Shawcross's life, 'frank, intimate and authoritative'. (I said I thought these three epithets were unfortunate and clearly implied that Shawcross had been 'advertising' himself, in a broad sense, to Wyatt. Wyatt said that this blurb was composed not by him, but by the newspaper.) This morning, Wyatt hears, Shawcross talked with both Monckton[1] and Heald[2] (Attorney-General) who both said the articles should not be published, and Shawcross had also written today to Max Aitken,[3] the proprietor of the paper, a letter very similar to what he had written to Wyatt, also

1 Sir Walter Monckton, later 1st Viscount (1891–1965). Minister of Labour and National Service 1951–5. Conservative M.P. for Bristol West 1951–7. Solicitor-General 1945. Minister of Defence 1955–6; Paymaster-General 1956–7.
2 Sir Lionel Heald (1897–1981). Attorney-General 1951–4. Conservative M.P. for Chertsey 1950–70.
3 J. W. M. Aitken, later Sir Max, 2nd Bart (1910–85). Director and Chairman of the Board, Beaverbrook Newspapers Ltd 1964–77. Conservative M.P. 1945–50. Son of Lord Beaverbrook. Disclaimed peerage 1964.

containing the offer to 'indemnify' Wyatt. Monckton was approaching Winston, who was telephoning to Beaverbrook in the West Indies, to get the articles stopped. Wyatt said he felt he should go ahead. At this moment he received a telephone message to ring up Wintour,[1] Assistant Editor, *Sunday Express*. He went out, saying he would return. Soon after, Heald came in. So I went out, not wanting to compromise Wyatt or myself by talking in front of Heald. Later I met Wyatt in the corridor and we went to the Harcourt Room, at his suggestion, for a further talk. He was very full of it all. He had had a very long telephone conversation. Aitken had been under very heavy pressure. Winston had personally asked him not to publish. So had Attorney-General. So had Shawcross, who had called personally and said that at Aden he had been ill with bowel trouble and the doctor had said that, if he had any nervous strain, he might die. On this ground also he asked Aitken not to publish. Shawcross, Wyatt says, has 'pulled out every stop'. In Shawcross's letter to Wyatt he says he had understood that the articles wouldn't be published till after Easter. Wyatt thinks this means *after* Annual Meeting of Bar Council.

I advise Wyatt to sleep on it and not worry. He is concerned as to his own reputation as a journalist if his articles, so sensationally announced, don't now appear. I told him that I called Shawcross 'Sir Peacock'. This is self-esteem and hystèria.

Wyatt told me of the talk with Dick Crossman in the train. Wyatt had said Dick was 'irresponsible'. Dick replied, 'That is Attlee's fault. He made me irresponsible by denying me responsibility.' Dick said the fight in the Party would go on and on. They would never let it die. There would be new leaders of the Trade Unions who would be Bevanite, and new M.P.s the same, and many existing M.P.s talked Bevanism when they got to their constituencies, though at Westminster they talked and voted anti-Bevanite.

Meanwhile, with Bevan away in India, Pakistan and Burma, all has been quiet. None of the others really count in the House. They are only band-waggoners. There was no trouble this year on Defence.

Jim Callaghan, just back from U.S., liked Haverford College very much. He also had a few days in N.Y., Washington, where he saw McCarthy's[2] Committee of Enquiry in action, and Ann Arbor. A

---

1 Charles Wintour (b. 1917). Assistant Editor of the *Sunday Express* 1952–4. Managing Editor of the *Daily Express* 1957–9; Managing Director 1977–8. Director of the *Evening Standard* 1959–82.

2 Joseph McCarthy (1909–57). Republican Senator for Wisconsin 1946–57. Chairman of the Senate Committee on Government Operations and its permanent subcommittee on Investigations.

very good experience for him. I told him he was in last week's *Economist*. 'Mr Callaghan, the Chancellor of the Exchequer, yesterday rode in state to Grosvenor Square', to take over some symbol of American Aid in 1965.[1] Hugh was P.M. and Butler Leader of the Opposition. No one else mentioned.

Wednesday 25th March

Roy Jenkins to dine (Parliament adjourns, owing to Queen Mary's death,[2] and XYZ cancelled). He thinks the outlook is gloomy. Only the challenge of Bevan could make him vote for Morrison, if Attlee retired. Jim Griffiths, he thinks, is too weak, and not a sufficiently big public figure. He asks if I wouldn't like to be in the next Government, perhaps as Lord President. I say definitely no. No one over sixty-five, except P.M. whoever he is, should be in next Cabinet.

Saturday 28th March

Pleasant weekend at Newton Hall. Made much fuss of, as usual, breakfast in bed and good lunch party, including Myrdal (with sticks from a motor accident) and Nicky [Kaldor]. Catherine [Walston] gives me a canary yellow, high in the collar, pullover to compensate for the old blue one which one of her Jesuits ran off with. Brian Abel-Smith, on my suggestion, arrives for the night on Sunday, and drives me back to London on Monday afternoon (30th March). He has a job now with National Institute of Economic Research (in London) and is working on Redistribution of Social Services. He has been long enough in Cambridge and should do this work well, and make a reputation as an authority before coming into Parliament.

Tuesday 31st March

To Windsor in morning by special train for Queen Mary's funeral. Privy Councillors, diplomats, courtiers, military and old retainers. Morrison, alone of the eminent, in a soft black hat, not a top hat.

At St George's, I am conscious of being, in the nave, within a hundred yards of my parents' ashes in the south aisle. The building and the service are very beautiful.

Stokes sits beside me, and Shawcross beside him, talking audibly about his *Sunday Express* case. Eternal egoism!

---

1 Part of this prediction was accurate. Callaghan served as Chancellor of the Exchequer 1964–7.
2 Queen Mary, née Princess Mary of Teck (1868–1953). Widow of George V. She died on 24th March.

Across the way is Gromyko,[1] looking ill, in morning coat, etc., but elastic sided boots!

Back in the same carriage with Albert Alexander and his wife, Patrick Gordon Walker and his wife, and Herbert Morrison. We mention 1931. Morrison says the unemployed voted for their country and not for their sectional interest. They were patriots. I say they were frightened. I say I have written an account of this which will be out shortly. He warns me, rather heavily and sourly, not to violate my Privy Councillor's oath. I said I wasn't in the Cabinet or a P.C. then. I only went by what had been written, and what people had told me. (*He* blabbed a lot of inner Cabinet stuff to Harold Nicolson, but I didn't say this. I suppose he thinks my version may damage him.) ...

SHAWCROSS, WYATT AND SUNDAY EXPRESS
Sunday Express didn't publish. Winston intervened *twice* with Max Aitken. And Heald, Attorney-General, saw Wyatt and issued a statement on behalf of the Bar Council. Heald said, in Smoke Room to me and Hector McNeil, who is on terms of friendship with Shawcross, that Wyatt had said he didn't see why he shouldn't publish. I said I gather that Shawcross had *not* told Wyatt he objected, when the matter was first broached at beginning of March. Heald was inclined to disbelieve this. McNeil said Shawcross was [at risk] of a breakdown. He worked too hard, worried too much, and had too many doctors looking after him. I said he ought to go away, on medical advice, for several months, on a sea voyage. Heald said Shawcross was afraid that, if he did, he would lose his practice. Shawcross has also written, in *The Times* of yesterday, a long letter in favour of paying judges more. Why need *he* write this, just *now*?

Wednesday 15th April
Budget debate. First impression of Butler's Budget is that it will be popular, and hard to fight. But Hugh does very well on the second day, and raises great applause.

Tony [Crosland] winds up for us on second day. Not much of a house. But good, as usual, though not quite at his best. He says, rather rashly, 'We may have to put a tax on coal.'

Ellis Smith[2] says to me afterwards that, listening to Tony today, he felt he was listening to me thirty years ago. I say, 'Tell him that.'

1 A. A. Gromyko (b. 1909). Soviet Ambassador to Great Britain 1952–3. First Deputy Minister of Foreign Affairs 1949–52, 1953–7. Minister of Foreign Affairs since 1957.
2 Ellis Smith (1896–1969). Labour M.P. for Stoke-on-Trent South 1950–66; Stoke-on-Trent 1935–50. Junior minister 1945–6. General President of the United Patternmakers' Association.

Mark Hewitson says that, in the last fortnight, he's heard of petitions and counter-petitions for divorce that will blow up the Bevanite movement. And Nye working overtime to stop it.

Thursday 30th April
Callaghan said Morrison borrowed my book[1] from him while he was in the lavatory (obviously just time to look up references to himself), and said, handing it back, 'I didn't know the bugger kept a diary like that.'

Wednesday 17th June
Attlee said to me, referring to Soames's statement to press, 'I shouldn't think much of my P.P.S. if he said of me, "He's all right physically; it's only mental."'

Tuesday 23rd June
Meeting of Parliamentary Committee to decide on recommendation to Party Meeting on election of Parliamentary Committee at end of this Session. Basis of discussion last time's arrangement. Two ballots; at First must vote for 12 and all those with clear majority elected; rest to go to Second Ballot with twice number of candidates as there are still unfilled places; again all must vote for full number of vacant places. Nye in terrible state of indecision and excitement, especially towards Hugh. (I am more convinced every time I see him on such debating occasions that Nye is increasingly unfit to hold high office in Party; much too full of egoism and bile, and getting worse.) First vote on whether we insist at First Ballot that all must vote for 12. Finally carried with only 2 against – Nye and Shinwell. Nye says this deprives minorities of their results; consolidates Right Wing; gives 'you all' what you want. Will insist on speaking against this at Party Meeting. Taunts about National Executive elections (Morrison absent).

Then long confused wrangle about conditions of Second Ballot, and should anti-plumping rule[2] apply there too. I begin by being inclined to support existing arrangements, but Nye is getting some support for view that plumping *should* be allowed in Second Ballot, so, following Chuter Ede, I swing round against any Second Ballot. This is finally carried against a minority of 4 or 5 – Attlee, Hugh, Phil [Noel-Baker] and, I think, Willie Hall and Jim Callaghan. Atmosphere shocking! Jim Callaghan stands up to Nye boldly.

1 The first volume of Dalton's memoirs, *Call Back Yesterday: Memoirs 1887–1931* (Muller, London), was published at the beginning of May 1953.
2 'anti-plumping rule': the rule that M.P.s had to vote for as many candidates as there were places (twelve) on the Committee.

I dine with John Freeman, whom I still like a lot. Later we are joined by Dick Crossman, whom I like less. Both very excited, on Nye's side, about our decision tonight. Freeman says he'll tear up his voting paper; denied 'free elections'; I ask if he can't find 12 people out of 260 whom he can vote for. He says they want to be free to give weighted vote. Dick, as usual, more vehement. They will campaign against it. 'The weeklies and *Reynolds* have a very big influence', [he says] menacingly. But admits that Nye is always at his worst in Parliamentary Committee, or Party Meeting, or even on National Executive, because he feels inferiority complex, beaten before he starts. I say the Party is beaten before it starts at next general election and these rows are making it sure. Both seem to agree!

Thursday 25th June
Hugh to lunch alone in flat. Hadn't had a real talk with him for quite a while. Very easy and friendly today. I say I want to run him and Callaghan for N.E.C. I don't think there's much chance of putting any Bevanites off, but we must keep on trying. With Morrison and me, and Robens not standing, there'll be a good few votes at large. He doesn't think there'll be a change. He likes Jim Callaghan and he has a very good Parliamentary style, but his judgment is often weak, e.g. in discussion on methods of electing Parliamentary Committee. First he stood up to Nye very well, and then, without seeing the point, he almost gave away the anti-plumping rule at Second Ballot. I said Nye was getting more and more ego-soaked and impossible. He said Attlee was weaker and weaker. Clearly he wants Morrison to succeed him. ...

Hugh said Attlee was afraid of working men – Bevin most, but Bevan now too, and even Shinwell. I guess that what Hugh would like, would be for Attlee to retire and Morrison to become Leader and himself as No. 2. He said he'd have to make up his mind one day as to whether, if Morrison wasn't in for it, *he'd* run for No. 2, even against Jim Griffiths. I said I'd thought of Griffiths, as he knew, as a Third Man for Leader, but I'd been losing heart for this alternative. He was awfully weak. Hugh agreed, but thought on the whole he'd done well as Chairman of Policy Committee.

I sense that Hugh's stock stands very high in Parliamentary Party, which is what for him matters most.

Wednesday 8th July
Nye is getting worse and worse. Today at Party Meeting we had up recommendations for election of Parliamentary Committee. Two main proposals (1) single vote, with no Second Ballot, and (2) all must

vote for 12, i.e. no plumping. Chuter Ede proposed. No one advocated Second Ballot. But Lipton moved and Bing seconded that we allow plumping. Brief debate. Not much excitement. Morrison wound up. Then Nye broke in. He had been sitting in back row of platform, having arrived too late to get a seat in front. Most unsuccessful speech. Angry pouting face. He had been against this in Parliamentary Committee. It was a matter of procedure, so not governed by collective responsibility. Morrison, he said, hadn't been at meeting when this was discussed. Minorities as well as majorities should be represented on Parliamentary Committee. We had had very bad Parliamentary Committees in pre-war Parliaments, because minorities not represented. (I don't think there was an anti-plumping rule then.) ... Finally recommendation carried by 75 to 16. Minority all well-known Bevanites. But some of best known weren't there.

In the afternoon, at weekly meeting of Parliamentary Committee, another scene. First long grumble from Nye about our having let Tories get initiative in Foreign Affairs debate, and now waiting for Churchill to get better. Attlee irritated by this. Says we're all agreed about foreign affairs, but must be properly timed. After a bit more, I say rather impatiently to Nye, 'Can't we stop grizzling about the past and decide what to do next week?' ...

Then a letter from George Wigg is read, protesting that in vote against merger of War Pensions and National Health, a number including one member of Parliamentary Committee abstained. The one, it seems, is Nye. He is very rude and truculent. He had made a public declaration in favour of merger. Therefore he couldn't be expected to vote against it. (He had also made a speech at a thinly attended Party Meeting, arguing against vote, but had been outvoted.) Several then say that, if this is a precedent, there will just be anarchy. Also that this is only a matter of administrative detail, not a case of conscience. Nye then says, 'I refuse to discuss it.' Attlee rather nettled, 'But *we* are going to discuss it.' Nye then says, 'Then I shall leave the Committee', in high tantrum, picks up his papers and sweeps from the room. I say, 'He is getting sillier and sillier every day.' We decide that Attlee shall tell Party Meeting that we reject his action. He is in a state of increasingly irritated conceit. Losing ground fast in Parliamentary Party, and not, I think, making any advances in the country.

Thursday 9th July
Morrison, invited by N.U.M. and T.G.W.U., will be their nominee against Greenwood for Treasurer of Party. Way back to N.E.C. He will win, but there will be great bitterness. Not only among Bevanites, but among friends of Greenwood. Poor old veteran, aged seventy-

three, and ill, but *his* Conference.[1] Hunter[2] thinks this may help Nye in fight for deputy chairmanship next October. Memories of Conference, and Greenwood's overthrow, will still be strong. Hunter hears that Jimmy Glanville,[3] Billy Blyton and others are already saying they'll never vote for Morrison again.

I think, but don't say, that this strengthens very much the case for nominating Jim Griffiths, if he'll stand, so as to draw off from Nye the anti-Herbert vote (and from Herbert some of the anti-Nye vote).

There still remain two possibilities (1) Morrison not to consent to run *this* year, so as to let Greenwood have his Conference triumph and farewell, undefeated, and (2) Greenwood not to stand again. But I am inclined to rule out (2) certainly, and (1) probably. Morrison *can* get it, pretty surely, if he runs. And he seldom lets such chances slip.

On merits, of course Greenwood should have retired long ago. He is quite gaga.

Saturday 11th July
At West Leaze. I hear on the air that poor little Margaret Morrison[4] is dead. I remember her coming here with him in 1933 or thereabouts, when I told him I thought he ought to be Leader of the Party.[5] And Ruth and I wondered what sort of a show she'd make, poor little stammering creature, as P.M.'s wife. I gather she's been ill a long time. Probably cancer or some such beastliness.

Wednesday 15th July
Morrison's little wife Margaret was cremated this morning at Honor Oak. Attlee and wife, Hugh and wife, Soskice and wife, among others went. I had written him a letter.

This afternoon at usual meeting of Parliamentary Committee, discussed speakers for next week's Foreign Affairs debate, two days. ...

---

1 Arthur Greenwood was Chairman of the Labour Party 1952–3, and so was due to chair the 1953 Conference at Margate.
2 Leslie Hunter. Lobby Correspondent of the *Daily Herald*. Author of *The Road to Brighton Pier* (Barker, London, 1959), an account of the Labour Party's internal struggles in the mid-1950s.
3 James Glanville (1891–1958). Labour M.P. for Consett 1943–55.
4 Margaret Morrison, née Kent. Wife of Herbert Morrison. She died of stomach cancer on 11th July.
5 In fact it was 1935. The Morrisons stayed with the Daltons at West Leaze for the weekend of 5th–6th October 1935 (not 1933) just after George Lansbury's resignation as Leader. Dalton told Morrison during a walk on the Marlborough Downs that he would back him in the forthcoming leadership contest (see FY, p. 70).

Nye then says he thinks, since Morrison has been away for last two meetings of Parliamentary Committee and from last Party Meeting, that he is a most unsuitable speaker for next week. At that Hugh and Summerskill explode with indignation. Hugh says, 'He has been burying his wife this morning!' and moves we pass on to next business. We do.

Alice Bacon tells us that Arthur Greenwood – against whom, it will be remembered, Morrison is running for the treasurership, and is likely to beat him on 2nd day of Conference – can't make himself heard in the chair. He talks like a man with a cleft palate. He has been having further medical treatment. He just can't, physically, preside at the Conference.

Why the Hell can't he resign, and finish with it? This awful hanging on and on.

Tuesday 21st July
Bevan in Smoke Room, says, 'I don't believe in all this talk about apathy. I never address a meeting with less than a thousand people.' This man is so full of conceit that he'll burst soon!

Friday 23rd October
To Oxford. Lunch with Frank Pakenham. Meet his son Tom[1] and Trevor-Roper[2] and Blake[3] (Senior Censor of Christ Church) who works for Beaverbrook and edited Haig's Diaries. Oxford dons are much in the swim!

Thursday 29th October
Hugh to lunch. Conscious, as sometimes before, of a veil of reserve, though most who overheard would think our conversation very friendly. I tell him that, having gloomily abstained last year on Morrison v. Bevan for Deputy Leader, I have this time voted gloomily for Morrison, because Bevan has been so impossible in Parliamentary Committee and, in particular, so rude to Hugh. I say to Hugh half ragging, 'Don't get intriguing with Morrison for him to push out Attlee. Let things run on for a bit.' He says he will. It is planned, if Greenwood retires next year, for Hugh, with leading Trade Union backing, to become Treasurer of Party, with seat on N.E.C.

1 Thomas Pakenham (b. 1933). Oxford undergraduate. Later a professional historian.
2 Hugh Trevor-Roper, later Baron Dacre (b. 1914). Historian. Student of Christ Church, Oxford 1946–57. Regius Professor of Modern History, and Fellow of Oriel College 1957–80. Master of Peterhouse, Cambridge since 1980.
3 Robert Blake, later Baron (b. 1916). Historian. Student and Tutor in Politics, Christ Church, Oxford 1947–68. Censor 1950–55. Provost of Queen's College, Oxford since 1968.

Announced yesterday, Deputy Leader

| Herbert Morrison | 181 | (194 last year) |
| Aneurin Bevan | 76 | (82 last year) |

257 papers returned out of 292 issued.

So both lose votes, and relative position remains much the same. Bevan gets 29.6 per cent of votes this time, against 29.7 last time. Some voted for Bevan because they were anti-Morrison. And some were anti-both and abstained.

If either Jim Griffiths or Hugh Gaitskell had stood, Bevan would have polled less.

Thursday 5th November
Result of voting for Parliamentary Committee announced. No changes. We just fail by 3 votes to shift Shinwell, and by 1 vote keep off Harold Wilson. I would have preferred Wilson to Shinwell.[1]

Saturday 7th November
Gave Hilary [Crosland] two amethysts and Dobs [Little] a topaz.[2] Drinks before lunch at Tony and Hilary's flat, Ian and Dobs coming in. Then we all lunch at Imperial, near South Kensington station. Italian and rather poor. Gilbert Harding[3] at next table.

Tuesday 17th November
Talked with Desmond Donnelly, first time for some while. Still very free about Bevanite doings.

They've had several meetings lately, one week at Buscot,[4] and a meeting at Crossman's house, the first before, the second after, the elections to the Parliamentary Committee, which, of course, much disappointed them.

At the first meeting a few led by John Freeman, who is much the most intransigent of them all, and including Jennie [Lee], Barbara

1 Successful candidates in the election for the Parliamentary Committee were as follows (1952 figures in brackets): Griffiths 180 (194), Gaitskell 176 (179), Soskice 168 (111), Callaghan 160 (137), Dalton 159 (140), Ede 134 (189), Robens 133 (148), Summerskill 129 (130), Bevan 126 (108), Noel-Baker 118 (121), Shinwell 108 (124), Hall 106 (113). Runners-up were Wilson, Anthony Greenwood, Stewart and Strauss. Soskice, Callaghan, Dalton and Bevan were the only elected candidates who increased their votes.
2 Acquired by Dalton during his trip to Brazil in the summer.
3 Gilbert Harding (1907–60). Broadcaster.
4 Buscot Park: country house belonging to Gavin Faringdon (2nd Baron), a leading Fabian.

[Castle] and Mikardo, wanted to reconstitute the Group. Bevan was against, and it was agreed to wait till after Parliamentary Committee elections. At the second meeting Freeman and Barbara didn't turn up ... It was put off again. But Jennie said she didn't think Nye would be able to stay on the Parliamentary Committee for the whole year. Already hunting for some pretext to resign and make trouble!

Douglas Jay told me that Dick Crossman had been saying lately that they 'must find a new issue' between the Bevanites and the rest of the Party.

Wednesday 18th November
Parliamentary Committee. Clear that the whole bloody Bevanite trouble is being worked up again. Shinwell had a silly suggestion last session that the Committee should no longer choose Front Bench speakers, but that this should be left to the Chairman. Attlee having, as requested, thought it over, comes down in favour of present system. Generally accepted, so I have no need to speak. But Nye intervenes to say that present system is not satisfactory, since under it, 'some of us are permanently silenced on a wide range of subjects.' Asked if he means that, wanting to speak on a subject, he can't get chosen, he hints that he would sometimes want to speak, in addition to selected speakers, to put a slightly different point of view. After more grunts and grumbles, he says that it is a very doubtful advantage being a member of the Parliamentary Committee.

On 13th November *Tribune* published an article by J. P. W. Mallalieu complaining that Labour M.P.s advocated 'consolidation' among themselves, while demanding more socialism in public. 'Would it not be better if voting lists were published after Party Meetings,' wrote Mallalieu, 'as they are published after Divisions in the House of Commons?' On 18th November, with only Bevan dissenting, the Parliamentary Committee decided to reprimand Mallalieu. When the Parliamentary Committee met again on 25th November, the case provoked a bitter row between Bevan and Gaitskell. '[Bevan] says he has never been in favour of disciplinary measures, and has never invited them all the time he has been in the Party', Dalton recorded. 'Speaks of "danger of discipline". When Hugh Gaitskell says something of "dangers of *in*discipline", Nye fixes him straight across the table, with a glare of concentrated hatred, and says, "You're still too young in the Movement to know what you're talking about." Jim Callaghan says, "You're trying to find an excuse to resign from this Committee." He indignantly denies. Later, he leaves the room while we are still sitting, saying, "Whatever you agree to in your present mood, I am against it." [1]

Wednesday 2nd December
Party Meeting on Mallalieu case. I am in bed with enteritis – very boring, but not very painful. George Chetwynd, by pre-arrangement, rings up to report. And I hear also on phone later from Jim Callaghan and Douglas Jay.

Bevanites were present in force, spaced about the room. Mallalieu spoke very shortly, based his defence on freedom of press and no attack on named persons. Then debate got in a muddle. McLeavy,[2] always dull and heavy, moved that whip be taken away from Mallalieu at once. Attlee had to say this was out of order, because no notice. Woodburn in confused speech proposed next business. This was carried by 110 to 40 (approximately). Bevanites voted with majority. Minority was Trade Union diehards. But meeting accepted, or so it was recorded, Attlee's statement that Mallalieu had broken rule and that if anything like this happened again, Parliamentary Committee would have to take action about it!

I find myself with little enthusiasm for some of our anti-Bevanites, increasingly repelled by Bevan himself, and some of his supporters, and infuriated by their tactics and insinuations.

Saturday 20th February 1954
Bevanites fairly quiet. Nye making up to non-Bevanites, e.g. in Housing Bill Committee. Israeli Ambassador,[3] with whom I lunched on 4th February, wasn't very pleased with Nye's visit to Israel. He had upset everyone, trying to be bright and clever. ... All this made a bad impression and Jennie Lee ran round behind him, conscious of his bricks, and trying to undo the damage. Desmond [Donnelly] told me, on 11th February, that Wilson, whom he says the other Bevanites hate and despise, had been with Freeman and Baird to see Morrison and proposed that Morrison should be Leader and Nye Deputy Leader, getting rid of Attlee and blocking out Hugh. Nye was very angry when he heard about this, and said that this wasn't the way to set about things, and that you couldn't trust Morrison to play straight anyhow. Not clear what Morrison said! ...

George Brown new Chairman of Trade Union Group in House of

1 Diary, 25th November 1953, and see HTA, pp. 393–6.
2 Frank McLeavy, later Baron (1899–1976). Labour M.P. for Bradford East 1945–66.
3 Eliahu Elath. Israeli Ambassador to Britain 1952–60.

Commons, in place of Viant. He will buck the group up, and strength-en his own position. I congratulate him, but warn him not to upset people needlessly. On 29th January to Cardiff, speak with Jim Callaghan at Labour supper party at Penarth. Keen crowd. I do my best for him. On 30th January talk in my hotel bedroom before lunch. ... Jim's judgment on particular points in politics, not very sure. But he has a first class public face and 'platform personality', and is fun as a companion. Have been reading Roy [Jenkins]'s *Mr Balfour's Poodle*.[1] First class. His best so far.

On 17th February 1954, Dalton injured his back, virtually immobilising himself. His recovery was slow and painful – though providing an opportunity to bring his diary up to date and work on a new edition of *Public Finance*.

Wednesday 24th March

Slipped disc going very slow. Most irritating, when in all other respects I'm perfectly well. It is five weeks today that I first went out of action and a fortnight since I came out of the Nursing Home. I plan to go down, in the evening, tomorrow to the House to vote against Television Bill.[2] Then, I hope, a little more next week. Then, the week after that, it will be the Budget and a terrible bore if I can't be there and speak. We shall see! ...

I told Ruth that, with Parliaments of normal length, I didn't think I should stand more than *once* more. She said she had thought I should feel like that. In 1957 I shall be seventy. I certainly ought not to stand again after that. And I doubt whether I shall stand again for Parliamentary Committee. If there's a summer, or early autumn, election, there won't be another election in this Parliament. I want to be free to say openly that the Parliamentary leadership is much too old, and that more younger people should get their chances sooner.

Kenneth Younger came to see me in the flat. Very nice, quite intelligent, but still *so* mild mannered! No public face. We agreed that the Tories would win seats at a general election now. We had no attractive programme. People were content with the Tories. They

---

1 *Mr Balfour's Poodle: An account of the struggle between the House of Lords and the Government of Mr Asquith*, Heinemann, London, 1954.
2 The Second Reading of the Television Bill, ending the B.B.C. monopoly and setting up the Independent Television Authority, was moved by Sir David Maxwell-Fyfe, for the Government, on 25th March 1954. It was carried by 296 votes to 269.

had stolen the Socialists' clothes (full employment; welfare state, etc.). I said it must be disappointing to him, and others of his age, young ex-ministers, to have the prospect of waiting another six years for office. He said No. He didn't want it at present, or till the Party knew better what *it* wanted, and there was a better spirit.

I spoke of the much more intense interest taken by many young people in Africans, Indians, etc. He said, very truly, that, having done away with gross poverty, extremes of wealth here, this was where the emotions now went, and the moral indignation, that used to find a natural vent at home. I said that, when I first went to Bishop Auckland as prospective candidate in 1928, and met leading members of the Party, they were nearly all unemployed miners, shabby and hungry. Last month they were in evening dress (not optional), yes including some miners, at Civic Dinner of Labour controlled Council.

Sunday 11th April
Getting better in leg and back, but wearily slowly. Spoke in House (for first time this year! – I'd spoken last on Trieste before Christmas) in Budget debate on Thursday. I'd been apprehensive beforehand; feared I might be terribly immobile at Box, not easily able to 'give way' and get up again, might feel suddenly very tired and lose thread, and lose it suddenly through sudden pain.

None of this happened. I spoke for $\frac{1}{2}$ hour, and was rather clear and harmonious, and said some things the comrades liked. Felt much more confident of everything afterwards. ...

Fienburgh, who is writing [for the] *Statesman* weekly, says Freeman told him it was a terrible 'trauma' to cut loose from one's class. Fienburgh pooh-poohed this, and said, 'What about Attlee and Dalton: they don't show it.' Freeman admitted that I didn't, but said Attlee had never cut loose. ...

Attlee's *As It Happened*[1] is unbelievably laconic. No statesman who was not an Englishman could have written such a book. Understatement exaggerates its emphasis. But he fitted with the requirements of the time; lacks all positive political vices; is honest and infused by rather drab goodwill.

I am irritated at selection of Harold Guthrie, disloyal little Bevanite, much too clever for the rest of them, to be new part-time secretary at Bishop Auckland. I may have trouble with him.

In March 1954, Labour opinion was aroused by a much-publicised American H-Bomb test in the Pacific. A few weeks later, left-wing fears that Britain

1 C. R. Attlee, *As It Happened*, Heinemann, London, 1954.

might be about to support a new hard-line American foreign policy were
encouraged by a speech in which John Foster Dulles (the U.S. Secretary of
State) called for an Allied initiative against Chinese involvement in Indo-
China – where the French colonial war was approaching its climax at Dien
Bien Phu.

On 11th April, Dulles came to London to discuss joint action. Two days
later, Eden tried to calm both sides in the House of Commons by promising
support for collective defence in South-East Asia – but making this promise
in the most luke-warm and unspecific terms. Attlee and most of the Labour
front bench were willing to be reassured. Bevan, on the other hand, regarded
the statement as an outrage, and Attlee's passivity as a sell-out. The same
day, the British government signed an agreement with the European Defence
Community, subject to French ratification, committing Britain to participation in a European Army. On 14th April, Bevan resigned from the Parliamentary Committee, in opposition to the E.D.C. agreement (which the Committee
had accepted) and in protest at the failure of the leadership to repudiate
Eden's statement.

Tuesday 13th April
Back in the shit! Coming down after Questions, I am told, by all I
meet, of the scene at Question Time today. Eden made a statement,
quite satisfactory as far as it went, on his talk with Dulles. No ultimatum to China, as we feared Dulles might press for. Only an undertaking to 'examine the possibility' of collective defence in South-East
Asia, within terms of Charter of U.N.

Attlee, having only seen statement two or three minutes before,
raised two points (1) no good without Asians (2) not a buttress to
'French colonialism'. Then Bevan, said to be obviously 'out of control', rushed down bench and put several questions. 'Statement would
be resented by majority of people in country' ...... 'would be uni-
versally regarded as a surrender to American pressure.' Cheers from
the hystericals. But Stanley Evans rebuked Bevan by saying that
Attlee's 'restrained question and comment' would have support of
overwhelming majority of Parliamentary Party.

Meanwhile Tories in high delight, wonderful comeback after bad
time over Hydrogen Bomb and Budget.

At Parliamentary Committee Shinwell makes a long-winded
attack on Bevan's conduct in intervening, and seeming to challenge
Leader of Party on bench. Bevan speaks twice; second time, after

series of rebukes from other members, shouts, with eyes goggling –
and what an ugly, hating face, when he's crossed or angry – 'I address
meetings, very big meetings, and *I* know what people are thinking ......
I know the mind of the country.' I had said between his first and
second speech, 'I often listen with a heavy heart to the speeches of
some of my colleagues on the front bench. But I suffer in silence.
Sometimes I speak to them afterwards. Sometimes I don't trouble.'
And these hysterical anti-Americans in our Party make me awfully
pro-American. After reading Driberg's rubbish in *Reynolds*, I often
feel inclined to apply for a naturalisation certificate from American
Consul-General ...... Dulles a bogey man. But he wanted, they say,
collective ultimatum to China before Geneva. That's all out. Eden
has done something, though he's only a Tory. I remember how
Lawther once said, 'Don't tell workers to refuse a rise in wages just
because the employers offered it.' Attlee had the two main points
very well, I said.

Callaghan, a little inclined to lack judgment, wanted us to adopt
and issue a special resolution; others to summon a special Party
Meeting; to issue statements, etc. I, and others, cried this down, on
eve of Easter Recess.

Later, George Wigg said there was no discipline in the Party. 'Nye
sleeps with his politics.' She's always egging him on. Today she rushed
off to sign a resolution, immediately after Questions. If, said Wigg,
he'd married a woman who'd borne him children, he'd have had a
little love in his life. Anyhow he's further off than ever from leading
the Party.

I told Attlee I liked his book. He said, 'It's not nearly so interesting
as yours.' I said only an *English* statesman could have written such a
book, and not many of them. I said his understatements reminded
me of Dill,[1] to cynical Americans, on Battle of Britain, 'No, our air
force wasn't wholly inactive.'

Wednesday 14th April
Parliamentary Committee at 5.30. Nye scowling. Others solemnly
quiet. Attlee begins by sketching what he has in mind to say to Party
Meeting on Eden's statement. Quite sensible and unprovocative. Then
Nye says it wouldn't be fair, since he has stated his view, to take any
further part in discussion. He has decided that, to avoid any repetition

---

1 Field-Marshal Sir John Dill (1881–1944). Commander, First Army Corps in
France 1939–40; Chief of Imperial General Staff 1940–41; Head of British Joint
Staff Mission, U.S.A. 1941–4.

of yesterday's charge that on front bench he must never express disagreement with others, he will, after Easter Recess, withdraw to back
bench, where he can speak freely. So now he will withdraw from
Committee. Yesterday he had to listen to a lot of *impudent* speeches.
He won't continue this nervous strain. He gets up and walks out. As he
leaves, Attlee [says], 'Of course, if it's your nerves that are wrong, I
can't do anything about it.'

Clearly he slept with his politics last night. Some discussion of what
to do next. Had he resigned? Decided to wait and see. Attlee said he
would say at Party Meeting that it was unfortunate if one member of
front bench openly contradicted another. I said, 'Say "openly
contradicted the *Leader*".'

Later at Party Meeting Attlee stated case well and ended up with
rebuke, as agreed. And said he'd been asked by Parliamentary Committee to say this. Nye had been sitting on platform. Rose and
protested, and said he had no idea that this would be said on behalf
of Parliamentary Committee. Admitted he hadn't stayed till end of
meeting. Said he was going on to back bench. Rose and walked out
of door and reappeared to rear of meeting. Not very impressive.
Paget made sentimental appeal to him to reconsider. Very little support. Meeting broke up. I sense that Bevanites, many of them, are
upset by Nye's tactics. *Bad* pretext. It will have done him harm. 'What
a wonderful Easter egg!' said a Tory at the tape.

Friday 16th April
Good Friday. Televise 'In the News' with the inevitable Walter
Elliot, Van and David Ogmore. ...

I don't know how it went. I never do. But when, hearing part of it
played back afterwards at John Irwin's where we went for drinks, I
thought I sounded the most incisive of the four! Poor Van is crippled
with osteo-arthritis – far worse, and far more permanent I fear, than
my slipped disc. And his face is lined, with pain and sadness. And,
though his charm remains – though even this must weaken in a
chronically sick man – he is become old and rather feeble. He said
twice that he was over seventy. Ogmore is fat and pompous and slow.

Saturday 24th April
Bevanite weekend press a bit uncomfortable about his latest resignation, especially *New Statesman* which says he has probably put off
for ever his leadership of the Party, and speaks of his 'streak of
wilfulness'.

As runner-up in the Parliamentary Committee election, Harold Wilson was entitled to fill the vacancy created by Bevan's resignation. However, Wilson was a Bevanite and had resigned with Bevan in 1951. Hence his decision to step into Bevan's shoes was criticised by some left-wingers, including Bevan himself.

End April
Wilson has taken the vacant place, due to Bevan's resignation, on Parliamentary Committee. *New Statesman* thinks he must have had a 'fortnight of torment' making up his mind. A. J. Irvine announced publicly that he couldn't keep an engagement to speak in Wilson's constituency, because the latter's letter of acceptance referred to 'interest of party unity', and this implied that Bevan had been guilty of disturbing this unity.

'Wilsonism' we read of now in *The Economist*. But who is a Wilsonite? He's a clever little chap, with a sure political touch. But not magnetic. The original Bevanites are very split. Crossman and, I hear, Barbara Castle ... very sick with Bevan. Crossman said to him, 'How do you expect us to go on supporting you, when you make a bloody fool of yourself' (by resigning) 'without saying a word to us beforehand.' Crossman urged Wilson to take the vacancy. Wilson tried to get Bevan to let him say he took it with his agreement. Bevan furiously refused. Lower animals like Baird and Will Griffiths (who was so deeply moved by it all that he got so drunk in Smoke Room that he had to be taken home to [his] wife) follow Bevan to the end. Crossman says that Mikardo was also against Bevan's tactics (but I guess he'll stay Bevanite). Crossman says that Mikardo is 'an incorrigible intriguer and wrecker'.

Wednesday 5th May
And now *back in the shit* once more!
    Herbert Morrison has an article in *Socialist Commentary*[1] for May, out yesterday, the last three paragraphs of which are a strong attack by name on Bevan. '...... Electorally, Mr Bevan has I fear cost us much. That one word "vermin" so increased the intensity of Tory

1 '*Socialist Commentary*': a monthly periodical which supported the Morrisonian and Gaitskellite tendencies within the Labour Party. It started publication in 1954 as the journal of the Socialist Vanguard Group.

electoral effort and voting in 1950 that it may have cost us 30 to 50 seats. The resignations from the Labour Government near to the 1951 election hurt us badly ......' Everyone in P.L.P. is wildly excited. Parliamentary Committee meets tonight. Jim Callaghan says to me beforehand that we *must* condemn Morrison for a breach of the resolution of the P.L.P. of 23rd October 1952 [which] 'calls upon *all* Members to refrain from making attacks on one another either in the House, the press or on the platform'. I go to see Attlee before the meeting. He is disturbed and says this article is a clear breach of the resolution. He had no idea this was going to be published, though Morrison had shown it to him. (Later in Parliamentary Committee he says he didn't realise *Socialist Commentary* was published; he thought it was only circulated privately to M.P.s. Pretty feeble!) I suggest he should get Morrison to say he was sorry. Then it would all fall. ...

At Parliamentary Committee Shinwell, Summerskill and Hall are all rallying behind Morrison. Attlee had begun by saying that the article was a clear breach. Whiteley, though not saying much, hotly pro-Morrison, glaring, grimacing and interrupting. ... Morrison defended himself on the grounds of provocation in *Tribune*, *Statesman*, etc. Many of them were very angry about a cartoon showing some German Rearmers dancing round the May Pole with Nazi generals.

I left after an hour to lecture to the Fabians, Attlee having assured me that there would be no decision. ...

George Brown, later, told me that Morrison was now saying to him and others that they must all rally round him. And Brown was afraid that they must cover him. But clearly, he said, Morrison had now quite lost his judgment. He looked old and he was old. Brown blamed me, in a friendly half-banter, for having made it so clear that I was withdrawing from competitive leadership. There were no alternative leaders. I mentioned Alf Robens, but he dismissed him.

Jim Callaghan met Morrison in the Lobby and said that his policy was to take the whip away from both Morrison and Bevan for three months as a trial trip. Morrison, he said, didn't think this was funny.

Thursday 6th May
I dined late, with Paget and Roy Jenkins. I said that, if Morrison apologised, instead of arguing an impossible case, he would come back with a bang. But I doubted if he was big enough. Then, rather egotistically, I cited my own conduct in the Budget incident! They were both a bit more pro-Morrison than I (I had said he was obviously past it, and on the decline) but this too was their view.

Wednesday 12th May

Hugh lunched with me at the Akropolis.[1] Not too crowded. I want a substitute for Josef's, where one is welcomed, but not much seen or heard. Preferably, therefore, a restaurant slightly in decline. Hugh thinks the Akropolis is this, though the food and drink are quite good.

I warned him that Robens, Brown and Callaghan, three of his best political contemporaries, have separately told me lately that he's too rigid and doesn't pay attention to what they say. He thinks well of the first two, but distrusts Callaghan, and so, he says, do a lot of other people. He's a trimmer. I said I'd often been called that, and no doubt still was. He said that deliberately fence-sitting as a policy and in sight of all – my case – was one thing, but trying to persuade everyone that he was on your side of the fence – Callaghan's case – was another. I said Callaghan had a better Parliamentary style and poise than any of us. And I'd liked his asking Clem why he hadn't made him First Lord of the Admiralty instead of Pakenham. Gaitskell said Clem hadn't liked it at all, and reminded me of one of my old bits of advice to *him*, 'Never ask for anything, and never refuse anything.'

We spoke of Morrison and his gaffe in *Socialist Commentary*. What did I think he should do? I said begin by apologising, saying he oughtn't to have done it and he's sorry. Then he'd have the ball at his feet again, as Bevan would have done in like case recently. Hugh didn't think he would. I said there was a clear case, I thought, against any personal attacks in *Tribune*, by any one, since the three editors were all M.P.s. He thought it was very difficult to bring home. He asked what I thought of Frank Soskice. I said I liked him and admired his intelligence and his industry. But I didn't think he was a future Leader of the Party.

Donnelly, who has been at Geneva as *Daily Herald* correspondent at the Indo-China-Korea Conference, told me an odd yarn. He'd seen a lot of Chinese and Russians. When he came home, he wanted to tell Winston, who rather likes him, and rang up his office. Pitblado[2] (Private Secretary) said he must see Foreign Office first. So he did – Nutting[3] – and told him a long story. Then he went to Churchill, who received him very defensively, saying, 'I can't say anything. You must

1 A Greek restaurant in Charlotte Street, W.1.
2 D. B. Pitblado, later Sir David (b. 1912). Principal Private Secretary to three successive Prime Ministers (Attlee, Churchill, Eden) 1951–6. Permanent Secretary at the Ministry of Power 1966–9; Ministry of Technology 1969–70. Second Permanent Secretary in the Civil Service Department 1970–71.
3 H. A. Nutting, later Sir Anthony, 2nd Bart (b. 1920). Parliamentary Under-Secretary of State for Foreign Affairs 1951–4; Minister of State 1954–6. Conservative M.P. for Melton 1945–56. Resigned from the Government and the House of Commons over Suez in 1956. Later career as author and historian.

see the Foreign Office.' Desmond then went to his flat in Dolphin Square and noticed several times during the next twenty-four hours a man, whom he thought was a detective, sitting in the hall. Another man took turns with him. The porter didn't know who these men were. When he rang up Rosemary,[1] his wife, who was at Roch (their house in Pembrokeshire), he thought he heard a suspicious click, as though the phone was being tapped. When he arrived at Roch, his post next day wasn't delivered. He rang up Pitblado, from Roch, and said that he was being trailed by a detective, his telephone was being tapped and his mail tampered with. Was No. 10 responsible? Pitblado, obviously caught off guard, said, 'Oh I hope the Foreign Office haven't done anything silly!' Then went away and came back to say that he was sure Desmond was mistaken. Soon afterwards Desmond's mail arrived by a special dispatch rider. He didn't, rather foolishly, ask the dispatch rider any questions.

Friday 4th June

To West Leaze with Ruth for Whitsun. I can move more and more easily, but the slipped disc is a slow thing. Without me to lead them our Parliamentary Rambling Troupe rambles no more. ...

Bevan, following his resignation and in spite of Morrison's attack on him, has lost much ground in the House. In the country, or at least among the Bevanites in the C.L.P.s, it may be otherwise. There is a bad split in Bevanite leadership. Crossman and Wilson both against him. He said that he would regard Wilson taking his place on Parliamentary Committee as 'a gross act of personal disloyalty to myself'. Crossman said, 'Then you think Harold is expendable.' Bevan replied, 'Yes and so are you.' *New Statesman* next week declared that neither Morrison nor Bevan could now ever lead the Labour Party. I wonder if Freeman assented to this. No third man suggested!

I said to someone that I was charged with sitting on the fence, but 'I'd sooner sit on the fence than lie down in the shit on either side of it.' Tony, when I quoted this to him, replied, 'That is a civilian's answer. In war you have to lie in the shit.'

Saturday 19th June

Hugh has been nominated for Treasurer of the Party in succession to Greenwood, by Transport and General Workers. I hear that Bevan will oppose him – though this would mean that, if defeated, Bevan would be off the N.E. and his seniority claim to Vice-Chairman next year, and Chairman the year after, would lapse.[2] It looks likely, though

1 Rosemary Donnelly, née Taggart.
2 Because he could not simultaneously stand for the treasurership and for the constituencies section of the N.E.C., of which he was currently a member.

not certain, that Hugh will get enough big Union votes to win. If so, Bevan commits political suicide.

Freeman, to whom I say this, replies that it is all a consistent line, resigning from Cabinet in 1951 and from Parliamentary Committee this year, and now probably leaving N.E. in order to demonstrate to rank and file that 'leadership' is misleading them. Bing tells me that the mood of resigning is brought about by the poor vote he got for Parliamentary Committee last time, showing that his colleagues don't really want him. He has circulated to *all* M.P.s copies of articles in American journals by Wyatt and Healey attacking him. I tell Hugh that he should talk to Trade Union leaders in Marquess of Granby, opposite Transport House, and learn all their Christian names.

Friday 9th to Monday 12th July
... I have *two* books in hand, page proofs of *Public Finance* and typed fragments of Memoirs II. Brian Abel-Smith will join me in catching misprints in *Public Finance*. He lunched with me last week, after an interval, and I am commending him to Attlee, as an old Haileyburyer and on other grounds, and suggesting he be seen. ...

I spent last weekend in the constituency ... Saw Guthrie at his house and heard his tale of woe. Financial liabilities (Anderson didn't warn them of six months' rent owing, and made a mess up of a joint draw with Darlington C.L.P.). I said I didn't feel I could subscribe to current expenditure. This should be cleared with proceeds of sale of house, N.U.M. propaganda grant, N.U.R. affiliation if secured, and individual members' subscription. I pointed out that they had not yet begun to build a General Election Fund, and this might involve me in heavy expenditure. I also told him he couldn't be the Agent – being a teacher employed by Durham County Council he couldn't get leave. (I knew he was taking a correspondence course on Agency work, and I think he was thinking he *might* be the Agent.) He seemed to take all this well, but I don't trust him. I am having to take a bit more trouble to counter-organise – and am aiming at a Cell to include Will Davis, Will Longworth[1] (now President) and Jack Race (ex-President), all very loyal to me. ...

Hugh Gaitskell last week made sure of election as Labour Party Treasurer. What settled it was the decision of both the Miners and the Engineers to vote for him. ...

Will Bevan stand, or withdraw? Either way he'll lose prestige. If he stands, he'll be beaten and off the N.E. and his chairmanship postponed till limbo. People won't like these tactics, equivalent to resigning

---

1 Councillor W. Longworth. Secretary of Brusselton Miners' Lodge, in Dalton's constituency.

from the National Executive. If he withdraws, he can stay on the N.E. But then he'll be running away. I judge that the Bevan boom is well past its peak. And he is always so badly advised that he is likely to say something silly, which will antagonise the Unions. Tony [Crosland] said to me the other day that it's extraordinary how little harm his last resignation, from the Parliamentary Committee, and his conviction for dangerous driving and not stopping,[1] have done him in the C.L.P.s. I'm not sure. And one can't separate C.L.P.s from Trade Union delegates. I think it's soaking in that he isn't a team man, is unreliable and an egoist.

Bevanites have disappeared, as though by magic, from the House of Commons and their corner of the Smoking Room. They must be as mad as hell! But he's quarrelled with Crossman and Wilson. *New Statesman* announced the other day that neither Morrison nor Bevan can now ever lead the Party. And Wilson is trying to edge his way along on his own.

Meanwhile Hugh has had a great leap up. Permanently on N.E. with the Trade Unions behind him, and many C.L.P.s – 'broad based upon the workers' will'.[2]

I hope he'll rise to it, and not be too unaudacious at home, nor too clear cut abroad. Both are dangers.

Friday 16th July
To Constituency for the Gala.

Saturday 17th July
To Durham, arriving about 9.45. Big crowds, bigger than ever. Procession, which we join at the Hospital, moves very slowly. Pass the County Hotel – Sam Watson, Ernest Jones,[3] Archbishop of York,[4] Bessie Braddock, Nye Bevan, Shawcross and others on balcony – about 10.45. Much cheered, especially in last stages of the March; down the bank on to the Big Field. ...

Shawcross makes a Tory speech. 'Don't trust long-haired backroom boys who say you should nationalise this or that industry.' Don't change anything! Incredible what a smoothie can get away with here. The crowds are unresponsive, except to familiar fighting

---

1 On 3rd April Bevan was involved in a minor car crash. On 7th May he was fined £25 and disqualified for three months for dangerous driving and failing to report an accident.
2 See Diary, 6th March 1931 (p. 138 and n. 1).
3 W. E. Jones (1895–1973). President of the National Union of Mineworkers 1954–60. Member of T.U.C. General Council 1950–60.
4 The Most Revd C. F. Garbett (1875–1955). Archbishop of York 1942–55.

phrases. *Why* do the miners go on voting to hear this man? I told Sam afterwards that I thought they were bloody conservative – Attlee and Morrison one year, Bevan and Shawcross the next. Why not some of our younger people, especially Hugh Gaitskell? Bessie spoke a little too long, and the first band and banner marched off loudly before she'd finished. But the speeches here are nothing, the procession and the crowds are everything. Today 120 banners; 95 bands; more than 200,000 people. Bevan had been trying, at the other platform, to 'appeal to the miners over the heads of their leaders' as he had threatened Sam Watson. But they didn't, I think, realise what he was trying to do. He would always, he said, respect the decisions of the Trade Unions (very kind of him!) when they were reached democratically by the rank and file, but not when they were taken by bureaucrats.

After the official lunch, and when the great gathering had dispersed (I watched the band and banners going out from the County [Hotel] balcony), I went up to Sam Watson's where I am to spend the night. He and Jenny (wonderful good housekeeper) had a party of about fifty people, first on the lawn outside their house (old Peter Lee's house) across the drop to the cathedral; then in three sessions for a buffet supper. Nye and Shawcross came, but caught a night train. Nye was holding forth – 'He'd drunk a lot the night before, and was looking very tousled', Jenny Watson said – more and more egoistic and self-satisfied and boring. I asked him whether he was going on in his candidature. 'Yes, certainly,' he said. He complained that he was never allowed to appear on T.V. 'Who forbade him,' I asked. 'Herbert Morrison,' he said. I said Morrison had no such power. I appeared on T.V. from time to time and that couldn't please Morrison much. Oh, said Nye, he can't control everything, but he stops me. I was, Nye thought, very innocent, if I didn't know that. 'But', he said, 'none of this troubles me at all' (this went for leaving National Executive too), 'my sense of timing tells me that things will come out all right.'

After supper he started haranguing the Police Superintendent (who is a good political friend of ours). 'The police are an organised conspiracy for lying. It is a fable that they are incorruptible. They tell lies about the speed of motorists, and take bribes from prostitutes. Motoring cases should be heard by special courts. The police and the magistrates are most unfair to motorists.' I thought all this incredibly inept, after his recent experience – failing to stop after an accident, and a very mild fine. At last, bored and reclining in a chair, the rest standing, I said, 'I am a hiker. I regard motorists as a small privileged section of the capitalist class.'

Sunday 18th July

Breakfast in bed. Sam Watson comes in and talks. We had planned 'a serious talk' this morning. He relates a talk with Nye at the House of Commons, before the Miners' Blackpool Conference, when they decided to support Hugh Gaitskell for the treasurership. Nye said he supposed he would get the miners' vote. Sam said he didn't know, but Durham were voting for Hugh. Nye, very angry, said he would denounce Sam at the Gala. This was a conspiracy by bureaucrats, not a democratic decision. Sam: 'When you win a vote, you call it democracy; when you lose, you call it a conspiracy. What qualification have you for the treasurership anyhow?' ... Nye: 'Gaitskell is not symbolic of the Trade Union Movement.' Sam: 'Do you think you are?' Nye: 'Gaitskell's policy is very dangerous.' Sam: 'You could have fought it in the Cabinet. You could still fight it on the National Executive – if you were elected again in the C.L.P. Section. We think Gaitskell is a very brilliant and able man. We want both him and you on the E.C. If you say the present system of voting isn't democratic, would you like the whole Conference to vote for the whole E.C.?' Nye: '*I* should still get on.' Sam: 'Yes, but very few of your friends. Crossman, and Driberg, and Barbara Castle, and Mikardo, would all be off.' ...

I told Hugh of this talk afterwards. He is getting quite a good rally of C.L.P. nominations, some very unexpected. I said that Bevan's 'sense of timing' probably meant that he hoped to hold a pistol at the head of the next Labour Government, if it had only a small majority. Hugh said, 'Better not win than have that.'

Friday 30th July

Parliament into Recess today for just over $2\frac{1}{2}$ months, unless summoned back for some crisis. ...

One day this week I talked with – mainly listened to – Crossman. He criticised Nye a great deal, but at intervals interpolated that he was *so* brilliant – sometimes, he said, one had to wait a long time for it, but the idea or phrase was *so* original when at last it came. All this a bit overdone, I thought. Nye knew he would be beaten for the treasurership. But he had a death wish, like others of his followers. (Damned egocentric fools to cherish that, as practical politicians!) He and Jennie were retiring to their farm. Those two were getting on so well *now*. (Admitted that they weren't a little while back.) Nye was feeling his age (fifty-seven this year). He sometimes said now, 'Of course, you younger people will have to settle all these questions.'

And he was a frightfully bad politician. Now and then he said, 'We *must* get rid of Attlee', and couldn't see that, as things were, this would only bring in Morrison. His outbreak in the House, which led to his resignation from Parliamentary Committee, followed a lunch at which he had drunk a good deal, and had been urged to strike a clearer note on China than Attlee.[1]

Wednesday 8th to Sunday 26th September
While Ruth is in France ... I go to my constituency. In Bishop Auckland addressing women on International Affairs – including German

17 'September Morn at Scarborough', 28th September 1954

Rearmament – on the 9th, having dined well with Kendalls[2] the previous night on arrival. ...

On 26th back to London. Well, it's been a good trip. There's great political lethargy everywhere. Guthrie-ites not very strong. Don't trust him an inch, but he won't fight me in the open. Longworth first class. Now I needn't go again until January.

1 This fits Crossman's own diary account a week after the event: '... on Tuesday the 13th [April] at our Bevanite lunch, with Nye present, we spent most of the time discussing Indo-China and steaming Nye up to the need for a strong Party line' (*Backbench Diaries*, 21st April 1954, p. 310).
2 Frederick and Ann Kendall. Kendall was a German-born manufacturer who had established a button-making factory in Dalton's constituency before the war.

In 1954 Anthony Crosland and his first wife Hilary separated. Meanwhile, Crosland had begun work on *The Future of Socialism*, published in 1956. At the Scarborough Conference in October, Gaitskell was elected Party Treasurer by 4,338,000 votes to 2,032,000.

Mid-October

... [Crosland] has been supposed to be working on [his book on socialist policy] all this vacation. It's very sad, and I fear, quite expensive for him – this break with Hilary. I wanted him to go to the U.S. *before* he married her. ... Also his constituency is destroyed by Redistribution, if it comes as proposed. But he stands very well with Hugh, and Hugh is on the up grade. That will stand him well in the future.

I didn't go to the Annual Conference at Scarborough. I now enjoy *not* going, as much as I used to enjoy *going*.

I'm bored stiff as a board with Bevan. His hangers on have written him up to much more than Life Size, and he just can't live up to it. His egoism and arrogance grow worse and worse. His personal hatreds of 'comrades' stick out like ugly protruding teeth, as part of his normal aspect. He polled very badly for Treasurer and Hugh beat him by more than 2 to 1. Hugh will now dig in. If he can do something for the Agents, he will steal C.L.P. support away from Nye. *Tribune* was bitterly attacking him[1] last week for some speech, saying we don't disagree with Tories on foreign policy. He plays into the enemy's hands too often. He is being driven to the 'Right' by the shameless and personal attacks of the 'Left'. Does he really want to change British society? (Poor old Morrison doesn't.) I am very loyal to old friends and close co-operators in difficult past days. But Hugh makes me stir uneasily in my loyalty. I must talk to him.

'German Rearmament. Must we go on debating it?' Dalton wrote in the same entry. Following conferences in London and Paris in September and October, a nine-power agreement was signed ending the Allied occupation of West Germany, inviting Germany and Italy to join N.A.T.O., reaffirming American commitment to European defence, and promising a permanent British force on the Continent. The Foreign Secretary, personally responsible for this diplomatic coup, announced the main features of the London and

1 i.e. Gaitskell.

Paris Agreements in the House on 25th October. Attlee welcomed Eden's statement, but once again there was dissension in the ranks of the Opposition. An N.E.C. motion accepting German rearmament had been narrowly carried at Scarborough. Dalton, no longer on the N.E.C., remained bitterly hostile – as did the Bevanites, most constituency parties, and several other leaders not normally associated with the Labour Left.

Friday 5th to Monday 8th November
At West Leaze. Ruminate, half asleep, on tactics next week on German Rearmament. We are to have Party Meetings on this on Wednesday and Thursday morning and a Parliamentary Committee on Wednesday evening. On the Wednesday morning the platform is to listen to the floor, in the evening we are to decide on a recommendation to the Thursday morning meeting. I am away on Tuesday at Liverpool for West Derby by-election, which may be a convenient absence. I shall travel back by sleeper in time for the Wednesday morning meeting.

I have decided to write Attlee a short note on Monday saying that I am much troubled by the Paris Agreements and how they are to be handled by us (1) at the Party Meetings and (2) in the House.

I shall seek to see him on Monday. I shall say that I am against these Agreements and shall argue that we vote against them. If defeated in Parliamentary Committee, I shall ask, relying on precedents of 1936 and 1937, for members of minority [on] Parliamentary Committee to have the right to speak and vote according to their convictions in Party Meeting. If this is agreed, I shall try, from the platform, to persuade the Party Meeting. If I succeed, I shall be quite content; if I fail I'll accept majority decision and won't vote against. If, on the other hand, it is not conceded that I can speak from platform, I shall resign from Parliamentary Committee on Wednesday night and speak from floor on Thursday morning. I should then also speak from below gangway in House when Agreements come on.

I would rather remain on Committee, and speak from platform. But I shan't grieve if I *do* resign from Committee. It is lousy with old age pensioners. *And* I shall have great support in the country.

I won't speak of these tactics to anyone else till I have seen Attlee on Monday and got his reaction. Ruth, to whom I expound all this, is quite in favour.

Sunday 14th November
A bad week, in which the Parliamentary Committee and the Parliamentary Party decided to support the Paris Agreements of last month. These restore West German sovereignty, authorise West German

Rearmament, commit us to maintain four British divisions and a Tactical Air Force on the Continent and to pay for them ourselves, instead of charging the Germans with costs of Occupation.

The Parliamentary Committee was to meet on Tuesday afternoon (9th), the Party Meeting was to be on Wednesday (10th) and if necessary, Thursday (11th).

On Monday (8th) I sent a note to Attlee saying that I was troubled over the whole thing and that I would like to see him. I did so at 9 p.m. Our talk was quite friendly. He, having fought the Germans in W.W.I.,[1] is always more conscious than our conscientious objectors, Quakers, reserved occupations and youngsters, of the danger of rearming them. He asked, as usual, for my alternative, and I gave him my usual answer. I said I couldn't vote for the Paris Agreements. He said that perhaps we could all abstain. I recalled the precedents of 1936-7, when, on British Army vote, all members of the Parliamentary Committee spoke and voted as they thought at the Party Meeting.

He said he doubted whether this would be agreed to now. There were no Bevanites then. Now this would colour it. They would be using it as a precedent for everything.

I said I had it in mind to circulate to members of the Parliamentary Committee a short note, giving them notice of my intention to raise this point tomorrow. He agreed. I did so. He thought the Russians might be more reasonable after than before German Rearmament had been decided on. I said no word about resigning. But I then turned the talk to the great age of the Committee. Eight out of fifteen of us, I said, were over sixty-five. And we were called a 'Shadow Cabinet'. More shadows than future Cabinet Ministers, I said. He said with a smile, that he was the oldest of the lot. I said I didn't want *him* to retire, for several reasons. But I'd like to get rid of some of the others. I heard that old George Isaacs was a new candidate this time. He had no sense of shame or fitness. I should like to see some of our younger people on. Service on the Parliamentary Committee, though not comparable to service in the Cabinet, was still a very useful experience. I praised Kenneth Younger's speech on S.E.A.T.O. He had, I said, *almost* the gifts required for a Foreign Secretary and I could see few others. Attlee rose to Younger. He said, quite eagerly, 'He's very near it.' He said our younger people only seemed young to us. Between forty and fifty they were mature and experienced. Those who had come in 1945, had now been in Parliament for nine years, as long as he had been when he became Deputy Leader in 1931.

---

1 Attlee served in the South Lancashire Regiment and Tank Corps at Gallipoli, in Mesopotamia (where he was wounded) and in France.

I spoke afterwards with George Chetwynd. Very loyal and with his ear always to the ground. I said I was inclined to resign if refused freedom to vote and speak in the Party Meeting. He says that we shall be easily beaten this time. (He was right.) Many more opponents than supporters of German Rearmament are abroad, in Russia, China, etc. And many other opponents have grown weary. There's a general feeling that Scarborough settled it. If I speak, he says, it's important that I should get over that this *isn't* Scarborough, and the N.E. haven't yet carried out the Scarborough conditions, of consultation with other European Socialist Parties. Have I, he asks, faced the results of resigning? Do I really want to fall out of the Parliamentary Committee? I said, Yes; we're much too old. I want to see some younger people moving up. He said that, if I went, my place might not be taken by a younger person at all, or it might be the wrong sort of younger person.

On Tuesday morning (9th) I rang up Robens, Callaghan and Wilson. Robens said that we were bound by Scarborough; general arguments were no good any more. I must, if I was to succeed, prove that Scarborough didn't justify this vote. Scarborough was the test. Callaghan said he was with me, and would back me in Parliamentary Committee, including my argument for freedom to speak and vote. I said I was inclined to resign, if refused. He said resignations weren't popular. He thought the Party had lost interest in the whole question.

Wilson said that Scarborough hadn't been carried out. There had been no consultations as required by the resolution. He would say so at the Parliamentary Committee this afternoon. I went to the House of Commons at 3 p.m. Our Parliamentary Committee is at 5. We sat till 7.30, all on this one thing (we have another meeting tomorrow to discuss other business). The discussion was calm throughout. I said, when I began – and I spoke longer than usual – that I was going to be amiable. Shinwell was absent (his wife has just died), but the other 14 were there. In the end 4 were in favour of voting against the Paris Agreements (Chuter Ede, Callaghan, Wilson and I), the rest in favour. Robens crossed over, on Scarborough. I hadn't counted on any of the others. I had said that the vote for the Paris Agreements would be a Black Letter Day in the history of this country, Europe and the world. We had the usual exchange, quite stereotyped now, about the 'alternative'. I said, as often before, 'one more go' with the Russians, [for] free elections and unified government in Germany, but no West German Rearmament, plus East German Disarmament and occupying troops to remain, both in West and East Germany, for, say, ten years, during which renewed efforts to be made for real Disarmament, including nuclear weapons. There was no pretence by the majority that consultation had taken place since Scarborough. ... 'Events have moved quicker than we expected,' said Morrison. None really met my argument directly. Summerskill said that, if I'd been at Scarborough, I'd have recognised, as all did, that everyone there thought it was a straight vote, for or against German Rearmament. And everyone was relieved, when it was settled, one way or the other.

Then I raised the question of the 1936–7 precedents. Morrison said he'd tried to find the Minutes, but they had been destroyed, with many other papers, in the war. I said I had a typescript, recounting the whole thing, in my hand, a bit of my next volume of Memoirs. If there had been time, I could have read it aloud to them. 'And you', I said to Morrison, with a smile, 'are mentioned all right. How lucky that, if there is no official record, I have kept an unofficial one.' He said, still most agreeably, 'Others might challenge the accuracy of your record.' (Next day, meeting me in the passage, he said, 'You know you ought not to publish accounts of what happened in Party Meetings, and in private conversations. That would be very naughty.' I didn't pick this up, or begin to recall the precedents.)

I said it would be 'deceitful, cowardly and dishonourable' if I didn't, in the Party Meeting, stick to the line they all knew I took. These convictions went very deep down in me.

But several argued that, particularly in view of Bevanites, etc., they must go to the Party Meeting as a united committee. Hugh said I needn't come to the meeting. I said, 'That would be taking refuge in a coward's castle.'

Finally I said, 'I will tell you a way out of all your troubles. I will speak tomorrow at the Party Meeting from the floor, and vote as I feel, and as from first light tomorrow, or from some other convenient hour, there will be a vacancy on this Committee. I shall be much happier that way, and so will you.' But, of course, they weren't! And all began, in various tones, to try to persuade me to reconsider. I said very little. Only once, that, when people talked about conscience in politics in our Party, they generally thought about such things as Temperance and Birth Control. This went much deeper. 'Do you tell me', I said, 'that I may have a conscience about beer bottles and French letters, but not about the life and death of my generation?' Some were a bit shocked by this.

Then someone proposed that the four of us should be entitled to abstain at the Party Meeting when the vote was taken – though not to speak against the majority line. Robens, and Soskice, and I think, Jim Griffiths were for this line. I sat tight, and so did my three colleagues. Hugh was rather against the proposal. Morrison said he would like to know, before he voted, whether I accepted this or not.

I said I wasn't giving any snap answers. I should listen to what was said, and speak to the chairman later that night. Then Jim Callaghan said, 'Leave him to me. I'll work on him.' Then Soskice made a personal and sympathetic appeal. Then, by general acclamation, they agreed to the proposal, for silent abstention.

Then Jim and I went and drank and talked, and dined, and it was quite clear that *he* didn't want me to resign, or to resign himself. He said the steam was out of the debate. People wanted it finished. I shouldn't be able to swing the vote tomorrow.

And at the end I said, 'All right. You come with me to see the little man,[1] for you're implicated too, and we'll say we agree, provided he tells the Party Meeting that four of us are abstaining, by special agreement of Parliamentary Committee.' So we went and put it to him. Just as he was leaving for his train. And, without more ado, he said he agreed.

And I put it down on paper, and handed it to him next morning, Wednesday 10th, at the Party Meeting and, in a shambling sort of way, though not naming us, he said it.

The debate at the Party Meeting was scrappy ... Strachey, e.g., was very hesitating. This wouldn't mean war tomorrow, or next year, or the year after ...... But it was handing over the prominent position in Europe to Germany. Some wanted to close the debate, and take the vote, the first day. Charlie Pannell[2] and George Brown pressed for this. But Attlee said many more wanted to speak, and we must go on tomorrow.

Next day – Thursday 11th – I went in half an hour after the start. I sat, and so did Callaghan and Chuter [Ede] and Wilson, in the second row of the platform. Rather grimly. Michael Foot was shouting his head off when I arrived, not turning a vote, nor were any of the speakers on either side. Strauss moved an amendment and Tony Greenwood seconded (with a very unhappy opening, that 'debate this morning on a lower level than yesterday') that we should begin discussions with Russians at once, without waiting for ratification. No one who was against German Rearmament should have voted for this, but most did. Morrison wound up, not either effectively or aggressively. Amendment defeated by 115 to 82.

Main question (to support Paris Agreements) carried by 124 to 72. A very bad result! I could have done nothing with this. The whole

1 i.e. Attlee.
2 T. C. Pannell, later Baron (1902–80). Labour M.P. for Leeds West 1949–February 1974. Secretary of the Trade Union group of the P.L.P. Minister of Public Building and Works 1964–6.

resistance has crumbled. The Bevanites, and their discrediting, have contributed to this.

Rows in *Tribune* don't help.[1] Foot and [Morgan] Phillips panting about freedom. This is just not my idea of how to run a political party. I see no reason, except crass conservatism, for voting Labour now. The Tories are doing very well – Full Employment, Buy What You Like, More for all, Higher Pensions on the way, Growing Vision of Peace. And the Labour Party, like the Tories, wants to arm the Germans!

In the Parliamentary Committee election on 18th November, Dalton stood for the last time, polling 147 votes and moving up from fifth to fourth place, after Gaitskell, Griffiths and Soskice. Two days later he was taken ill with gastric flu followed by complications, and on 26th November he was admitted to hospital.

Christmas

After $2\frac{1}{2}$ weeks in the London Clinic, after a week in bed, in great discomfort, at West Leaze. I am pretty flabby and have to be cautious about food and drink. But I am promised that, when I have settled down again, I shall be fitter than for a long time.

I am visited in the flat by Tony [Crosland], just back from the U.S.A., and Roy Jenkins and Ian and Dobs [Little] and George Chetwynd, and have long telephone conversations with Jim Callaghan – and take two cautious lunches at the Akropolis with Tony, and Desmond Donnelly who looks rather ill (he is to have his tonsils out in January) and disoriented (following his row with the Bevanites) and I'm afraid rather hard up. He says all his trips – to Russia, China and East European satellites – only just covered expenses. ...

Feeling, however, in a gossipy mood, after Tom Jones,[2] I write Hugh a long gossipy letter about the political near future.

---

1 In October, *Tribune* had been in trouble with the N.E.C. for an article by Michael Foot attacking Arthur Deakin's behaviour during the London dock strike. This caused a row between Bevan (who wanted to attack Deakin even more strongly, in defiance of the N.E.C.) and Bevanite moderates such as Crossman and Wilson, who felt that to do so would merely lead to expulsion. 'All this had, of course, deflected a great deal of energy and attention from the German problem', Crossman noted on 11th November (*Backbench Diaries*, pp. 359–62).

2 While in the London Clinic, Dalton had been reading Thomas Jones's *Diary With Letters, 1931–50* (Oxford University Press, London, 1954). Jones, q.v., had been a Deputy Secretary to the Cabinet, and a personal friend of Lloyd George and Stanley Baldwin.

Bevan has been committing slow suicide – better so, I said, than that Bevanites should have some flaming dramatic battle. Other Bevanites are either losing ground, or losing him, or both. Many are now only tense, neurotic bores. Three M.P.s from quite different stables (in fact, Callaghan, Chetwynd and Donnelly) have recently said to me that they hope Attlee will hold the leadership long enough to pass it straight on to Hugh. With Bevan's suicide, and Griffiths's failure to stay the course (three years ago I thought he was a possible Third Man) and with the melancholy mediocrity of Morrison growing worse from month to month, the road is open for Hugh, especially if he makes more speeches like his last one attacking inequalities and profiteering. ...

I hope he won't feel too loyal to Morrison to push for the leadership himself. (Ruth doesn't think he will.)

10

The Hampstead Set
1955–60

Dalton's interest in defence concentrated narrowly on German rearmament. When this matter had been decided, he ceased to need Bevanite allies and moved closer to the Gaitskellite camp. On the issues that dominated Labour Party discussions over the next few years, he found little difficulty in agreeing with the Shadow Cabinet majority.

This was partly because of personal loyalty towards Hugh Gaitskell, whose political career he had carefully nurtured since before the war, and whose eventual succession to Attlee he helped to bring about. After the 1955 election, Dalton sought to improve Gaitskell's chances by announcing his own retirement from the Shadow Cabinet on grounds of age, in such a way as to embarrass senior colleagues who chose to remain. One of the veterans was Morrison, hitherto regarded as heir apparent. Morrison did not follow his example, but by the time of Attlee's retirement in December 1955, most Labour M.P.s were looking for a younger man. Apart from Morrison, the choice lay between Gaitskell and Bevan. Bevan had already been an M.P. for sixteen years when Gaitskell first entered Parliament. He was working-class, he was better known in the country, and he was popular in the constituency parties. But Gaitskell had support where it mattered most: among the leaders of the big unions and inside the P.L.P. These advantages were decisive.

After the leadership had been settled, relations between Bevan and Gaitskell improved. The Suez crisis, and then the prospect of forming another Labour government, brought a truce that was not seriously disrupted before Bevan's death. If the Labour Party had won the 1959 election, Gaitskell might have been able to govern at the head of a united Cabinet. Labour's third successive defeat, however, reopened the old battle between Left and Right. New controversies now arose, especially over unilateral nuclear disarmament, advocated by the Left (though not by Bevan), and over a proposed revision of the Party Constitution, advocated by the Right (though not by many trade union leaders).

642

By this time, Dalton was no longer at the centre of affairs, even within the Labour Party. The failure of his last intrigue – an attempt to fix a seat for Anthony Crosland in time for the 1955 election – left him lonely and disengaged, less concerned about the issues than the personalities. More and more, Dalton sought out the company of younger friends, mainly drawn from the so-called 'Hampstead Set' of Gaitskellite M.P.s. In the last years of his life, he lived his politics vicariously through the campaigns and careers of those he regarded as the coming generation of Labour leaders.

Saturday 8th January 1955

Tony [Crosland] is our first visitor, staying the night, at West Leaze since the completion of the cottage and the arrival of the Wilds.[1] He is most interesting and suggestive in his talk about the U.S. – whence he came back last month. ... If socialism = a classless society, isn't U.S. more socialist than U.K.? He will work these queries into his book. He took many notes in U.S., working very hard at this, even against the grain. ... He had been very happy there – happier than for a long time – and had got a tremendous lot out of it.

Ruth and he go [on] a walk together on Sunday (9th) and she comes back knowing and liking him, I think, much better than ever before. I am very glad of this.

His constituency problem is very tiresome. Ted Rees,[2] intelligent Regional Organiser, thinks the new South Gloucester will have a Tory majority of 2,000 to 3,000. I have a hunch that this is too optimistic anyhow. But Tony must decide within two months at outside whether to fight there or not, and meanwhile there is, apparently, nowhere else for him to go to. He has seen Len Williams,[3] who appeared friendly, and appreciated that Soskice, the *extrudé* from Leeds (probably Alice Bacon, but possibly Denis Healey) and Tony were the three highest priorities for any vacancies, but had nothing immediate to offer. ...

If he loses at the next election, he will be without an income – though, no doubt, he could soon pick something up again, but subsistence for Hilary will be a great nuisance here. And he will lose

---

1 Hugh's immobility following his slipped disc at the end of 1953, and problems with local domestic help, had persuaded the Daltons to build a staff cottage close to West Leaze for a housekeeper and gardener. A couple called Mr and Mrs Wild moved in after the cottage had been completed in November 1954.
2 Edward Rees, q.v. Labour Party South-West Regional Organiser.
3 Len Williams, later Sir Leonard (1904–72). Labour Party National Agent 1951–9; Deputy General Secretary 1959–62; General Secretary 1962–8. Governor-General of Mauritius 1968–72.

ground relatively being out of the House. I will push around and do what I can but it isn't easy.

Monday 28th February

Hugh to lunch, alone, at the flat. He was in a good mood, and I think that he and I are a bit closer again now than we were last year. I urge him to be active on Tony's behalf. He says that he has spoken to Attlee, Morrison and Whiteley about the possibility of ennobling Price (West Gloucester). The idea, he says, was well received by all, and Whiteley was to speak to Price. We mustn't let the idea hang fire.

We planned, half seriously half in jest, the next Labour Government. I asked if, pending the premiership, he was drawn towards the Foreign Office rather than the Treasury. He said no, but filling the Foreign Office was the most difficult of all the problems. I said that Wilson would be delighted to take the Treasury, if Hugh went elsewhere.

As to Foreign Office none of the possibles were really satisfactory. Younger, we agreed, should have another No. 1 job first, and see how he developed. A repetition of Morrison, we agreed, was quite out of the question. Hugh then asked what about Soskice or Robens? I was strongly against Soskice for this. The Home Office would be better if he wanted to be political. He was much too emotional (e.g. on capital punishment) and too anti-Russian for the Foreign Office. In the end, we thought Robens the most promising name. He had done well at Strasburg, had presence, and pretty good judgment, and, we thought, much power of growth. And he would be in the T.U.–F.O. tradition of our Party. ... For Shawcross, we supposed, the Wool-sack. Hugh wondered whether Tom Williams couldn't do Agriculture again. I said certainly not. He was too old, and constantly in pain. I didn't think he'd entertain the idea for a moment. George Brown was the obvious Minister of Agriculture. For Callaghan I suggested, and Hugh liked, Housing and Local Government. I said we must sweep out all the old people, and, if Attlee and Morrison were going on, the average age must be brought down drastically. I, for my part, didn't want to be in the next government – I had said this before – but would like to make my own attitude a lever to push out other old ones. Our Parliamentary Committee was stiff with old age pensioners. Some day I should make a strong speech or a striking declaration on this subject. Our new government should be almost wholly vintage of 1945 and after. He said, 'You are splendidly consistent.' What Bevanites? It depended, of course, on how Bevan and the rest behaved in the interval.

If their behaviour was tolerable, we considered for Bevan either Defence or Colonies. Hugh said we must remember that he was always in the hands of his officials. I said I had suggested Colonies in 1951, instead of Labour.

For Crossman we thought a No. 1 job outside the Cabinet, e.g. Transport, to renationalise lorries, etc. It must be an absorbing job to keep him out of other mischief.

Alternatively Wilson might take Colonies – he was keen on Under-developed Peoples, and always writing or talking about them. I encouraged Hugh to think of Douglas Jay for Board of Trade. At the Treasury he would have liked both Roy [Jenkins] and Tony, but I said I didn't think that would do. He wanted a Minister of State (Treasury) and for this thought of Chris Mayhew. Roy he thought would be an excellent F.S.T. [Financial Secretary at the Treasury]. We compared Roy and Tony. Roy much more assiduous, perhaps a better Parliamentarian, Tony with much better brain and wider sweep, and, I emphasised, with larger unused reserves of power, owing to his many preoccupations. Hugh thought Tony might go, at first, to Board of Trade to do all Overseas Trade, including nego-tiations. ... Later, if Mayhew went from the Treasury to a Service Department, Tony might succeed him. Hugh said the field of other possible Trade ministers was awfully bare. Perhaps Mulley?[1] (Later someone else suggested Fienburgh.)

Bottomley we thought was clearly Commonwealth Relations. Ungoed-Thomas[2] for Attorney-General and how about Mitchison[3] for Solicitor-General?

On 24th February, the P.L.P. discussed its attitude to the official announce-ment that Britain would make the hydrogen bomb. The Party approved the Shadow Cabinet's main proposal – for a motion which censured the Govern-ment for its defence strategy, but accepted the bomb as a necessary deterrent. Bevan, however, found this compromise unacceptable. During the debate in the House, he criticised his own leaders, challenged the deterrent strategy, and led some sixty Labour M.P.s to abstain on the censure motion. But the impact of this rebellion was reduced by the refusal of several Bevanites – including Wilson, Crossman and Freeman – to give support.

---

1 F. W. Mulley, later Baron (b. 1918). Labour M.P. for Sheffield Park 1950–83. Junior minister 1964–7. Joint Minister of State at the Foreign and Commonwealth Office, with responsibility for Disarmament 1967–9. Minister of Transport 1969–70, 1974–5. Secretary of State for Education and Science 1975–6; Defence 1976–9.
2 Sir Lynn Ungoed-Thomas (1904–72). Labour M.P. for Leicester North-East 1950–62; Llandaff and Barry 1945–50. Solicitor-General 1951.
3 G. R. Mitchison, later Lord (1890–1970). Labour M.P. for Kettering 1945–64. Junior minister 1964–6.

Monday 7th March

Back for a late lunch from West Leaze, where it was very cold and disagreeable (weather only). Find a summons to a special Parliamentary Committee at 4.30 this afternoon. This is to consider action following on Bevan's speech, and conduct in the House, last Wednesday, 2nd March. We must decide a line for Party Meeting on Wednesday, 9th March.

Final decision is to recommend to Party Meeting to withdraw the whip. If carried, this decision is communicated automatically to National Executive (as it was in recent case of Silverman,[1] Yates,[2] etc., who defied Party decision – due to my stand in Parliamentary Committee – to abstain on Paris Agreements. N.E. decided to take no action.)[3] Four of us voted, at the end, against this – Griffiths, Robens, Wilson and I – and Attlee, though he did not vote, being in the Chair, agreed with us. Our alternative was to recommend a severe vote of censure and to report this to the National Executive. I urged that the best next step would be to provoke Bevan to resign from the Party. He has less and less self-control and is in the habit of resigning. I said I thought that, if the terms of the censure motion were strong enough and if it was moved in a deliberately offensive speech, there was a good chance that he would resign. But they didn't like this. Jim Callaghan said it was too clever by half. (I replied that it was better to be too clever by half than too stupid by three-quarters.)

Those who were strong for withdrawing the whip were Callaghan, Ede and Summerskill – all of these came in early. They were supported by Morrison, Hall, Whiteley, Shinwell and Noel-Baker. Also by Soskice (after a slight wobble my way). Gaitskell did not come till

1 Sidney Silverman (1895–1968). Labour M.P. for Nelson and Colne 1935–68. Pacifist and campaigner against capital punishment. Later chairman of the left-wing 'Victory for Socialism' group, and a leading supporter of unilateral nuclear disarmament.
2 Victor Yates (1900–69). Labour M.P. for Birmingham Ladywood 1945–69.
3 The London and Paris Agreements on West German sovereignty and rearmament were debated in the House of Commons on 17th–18th November 1954. The Shadow Cabinet supported the Government. The Bevanites, however, threatened to defy the whip if ordered to vote in favour of ratification. Faced with the possibility of an embarrassing rebellion, the leadership decided to try to avoid a division by putting out a three-line whip in favour of abstention. Most Bevanites obeyed, but six pacifists, led by Silverman, forced a division and voted against ratification; one non-Bevanite Labour M.P., John McGovern, also defied the whip and voted with the Tories. On 22nd November the Shadow Cabinet asked that the whip should be withdrawn from all seven rebels, and the P.L.P. confirmed this sentence. Apart from Silverman, the other M.P.s who voted against ratification were Victor Yates, Emrys Hughes, George Craddock, S. O. Davies and Ernest Fernyhough. All were received back into the Parliamentary Party before the next election.

near the end, but was for withdrawing the whip. So the voting was 10 to 4 with the Chairman not voting.

It was recognised by all that proposing to withdraw the whip, and still more expulsion from the Party if decided by the N.E., would cause the hell of a stink in the constituencies, where little nests of Bevanites are active nearly everywhere. It gives the Tories a wonderful opportunity to cash in with an early election. But heavy trouble can't be avoided whatever we do. Hugh said that he believed, and thought that I agreed with him, that the Party would never do any good till Bevan was out. Several, Hugh and Morrison in particular, said that they thought he lost us votes on balance. Several said that you couldn't treat Silverman and Yates more severely than Bevan, whose offence was so much greater. This argument carried much weight, and it was thought that, unless we recommended the withdrawal of the whip, there would be an outbreak of anger from the loyalists. It was mentioned that some of these were now again raising an 'Attlee must go' movement, based on his alleged weakness and wobbling. 'A lot of Members are going about with their razors sharpened on both sides', someone said.

As to whether we could carry the recommendation to withdraw the whip through the Party Meeting, most seemed confident. But I am not at all sure. And, if the majority were small, it would look very weak. (George Chetwynd said to me afterwards that if Attlee told the meeting that they had to choose between him and Bevan, he would win. But I don't want it done that way. In the earlier part of our discussion in the Parliamentary Committee several suggested proposing a vote of confidence in the Leader, but this was not passed. Several, including myself, spoke strongly against it.)

It was insisted that secrecy was very essential – no mention to press or outside colleagues – particularly as a letter must be sent to Bevan tonight, giving him notice of our intentions. He is ill with flu, down at his farm,[1] and cancelled several meetings last week-end. No doubt, when he has the letter, all will leak from him and Jennie tomorrow.

Tuesday 8th March
And secrecy *was* wonderfully maintained. No morning paper carried anything. It broke in the *Evening Standard* in the afternoon. (George Hutchinson,[2] who spoke to me on Wednesday morning on the phone, was very proud of himself for this scoop.) Jennie, I heard, had been

1 Aneurin Bevan and Jennie Lee bought Asheridge Farm in the Chilterns in 1954.
2 George Hutchinson. Political correspondent of the *Evening Standard* 1953–60. Director of Publicity for the Conservative Party 1961–4.

telephoning from the farm to the House of Commons this morning.

I did not, till the middle of this afternoon, move about the House at all. ... Roy Jenkins then told me that he heard most of the names and how they had voted. He had just come back from some Fabian Committee. So I guess it was Harold Wilson who told him. Roy was very doubtful whether we should get withdrawal of the whip through the Party Meeting.

Meanwhile it must be postponed from tomorrow owing to Bevan's flu. This puts it off till next week. Meanwhile Bevanites everywhere will be busy. And other people's will to be strong will weaken. Time is on Bevan's side.

Thursday 10th March

Take Hutchinson (*Evening Standard*) to lunch ... and impress on him that we shall now all stand together on Parliamentary Committee, and shall all resign, and whips as well, if motion to withdraw the whip not carried; also that we shan't accept a separate motion of confidence. The only way to show confidence will be to vote for recommendation. (I hope Attlee will stand up to this next Wednesday.) I find that Hutchinson has the four names right, in his notebook.

See Hugh in my flat 5.45 to 6.15. We must stand firm or we are sunk. He will sketch a synopsis of a speech for Attlee and send me and Alf Robens copies. Alf might then give it to Attlee who is always most sensitive to working men. Talk with Robens, who is very firm and sensible: Jim Griffiths, much shocked by Morrison's attitude – agrees with me that he was thinking Attlee might crash, and he succeed – at last Parliamentary Committee. Jim Griffiths, still having kittens, tells me that George Chetwynd has asked him whether there is *any* way out, and they thought only if Bevan humbly apologised. But *that* isn't in character at all. Griffiths clearly still has a faint hope that it may happen, and I would like time to put the possibility around. But I don't feel inclined to. Hugh was very pleased with Jim Callaghan's firmness, and thinks I may have been responsible!

Friday 11th March

Morning papers full of it! And *Manchester Guardian*, first of them to print it, gets the *four* names right. Callaghan rings up and says that he's spoken to Attlee on the telephone and suggests that on Monday he should support U.N. inquiry into effects of nuclear tests and no more till we have reports. He thinks I might write to Attlee in that sense. I say I'll write something, and perhaps that, so that he gets it on Monday morning. Callaghan asks me not to suggest, even in joke, that one reason why he's so firm is because, if one Bevanite on N.E.C.

resigns, Callaghan will automatically succeed him. (If four went, Callaghan, Soskice, Harold Davies and Emrys Hughes would move in!) H. Massingham rings up, and I give him background. He asks why did Callaghan *move* withdrawal of whip? I say he didn't. He asks who was keenest on this line. I say you can guess, and indicate Deputy Leader,[1] Soskice and Shinwell. I play down Hugh's part. I say that, though I voted in minority, this is not a big question like German Rearmament, and I shall, therefore, without hesitation vote with the majority.

Saturday 12th March

Bevan issues statement from his farm that his differences with Attlee are not personal, but only on policy. Hugh, who is speaking tomorrow at Doncaster and had not intended to refer to this, rings up, and we discuss what he might *now* say. We both think something emphasising Bevan's conduct in the House on 2nd March. (As Ruth says, most people don't realise this at all.) I get a standard resolution from Bishop Auckland *Local* Labour Party.[2] The C.L.P. Executive meets tonight. I shall ring up Davis tomorrow and find out what they've done, if anything. Resolutions are beginning to come in, all, of course, pro-Bevan, from various C.L.P.s. Hugh and I are both a bit apprehensive that Attlee may weaken as this goes on. Today is only Saturday, and they have till Wednesday!

Sunday 13th March

Sunday press full of it, though Princess Margaret and Peter Townsend[3] divert some attention! New line put out by Bevanites is that Shadow Cabinet have broken Standing Orders, which provide that, before whip is withdrawn, a member shall have the right to be heard by Shadow Cabinet, as well as by Parliamentary Party. This point was raised at our meeting, but Standing Orders were read out, and appeared not to give this right when withdrawal of whip was at issue. (I hope we weren't misled on this!)

---

1 Herbert Morrison.
2 i.e. the local party for the town, as opposed to the Bishop Auckland constituency party made up of affiliated union branches, local parties and other bodies.
3 Group Captain Peter Townsend (b. 1914). Air Attaché in Brussels 1953–6. Equerry to George VI and Elizabeth II 1944–53. Townsend's relationship with Princess Margaret (b. 1930) caused controversy because he was divorced. In October 1955, Princess Margaret announced that, 'mindful of the Church's teaching that Christian marriage is indissoluble', she and Group Captain Townsend would not marry.

Will Davis on telephone tells me this afternoon that Bishop Auckland C.L.P. Executive last night was in good and quiet mood. ... They passed, he says, a harmless resolution of regret, which he did not feel he could oppose. But there was no strong feeling or virulent speeches, and they seemed to know that I had voted in the minority. Guthrie, he says, is in difficulty and there may be some change in arrangements for secretaryship. This sounds hopeful. I am to address G.M.C. [General Management Committee] on Saturday, 26th March, when I shall be in the constituency anyhow.

Sunday press makes hardly any reference to Bevan's growing defects of character and conduct, his inability to *discuss*, rather than *orate*, his intolerance of the great majority of his colleagues, his increasingly evil face, both when silent and when speechifying.

Monday 14th March

Hugh sends me, and Alf Robens, a note of the case against Bevan, to be put into Attlee's hands, by Robens as the only 'working man' of the three of us. This is fixed at Conference *à trois* at 7.30 p.m. in Room A, off Lower Passage; Robens to give it to Attlee after vote at 10 p.m.; to pick him up in Lobby and take him to his room.

Rumours today that Bevan may apologise on Wednesday, but this seems out of character, and Leslie Hunter tells me that Jennie, Foot and Mallalieu are pressing him *against* apology, others *towards* it.

Tuesday 15th March

Special meeting of Parliamentary Committee called at my suggestion 'to survey field before Wednesday's battle', at 11.30 a.m. Attlee starts with 'What do I do if he apologises?' Jim Griffiths the only really nervous man, though Attlee also a bit wobbly. Wilson says he's pretty sure there won't be an apology. Finally we conclude, with practical unanimity, that Attlee should say it's too late; he's had a week in which [to] write. We are firm for getting straight vote. Whiteley reports from his whips that 160 votes will be in our support and about 80 against. Total 293, but heavy sick list.

Finally agreed that Attlee won't take a vote of confidence in him or us; he'll say that opposition to our proposal is a vote of no confidence in us. But he wouldn't refuse an amendment of heavy censure, though this will be equivalent to no confidence in us. Quite strong today are Morrison, Gaitskell, Summerskill, Shinwell, Alf Robens and I. Jim Griffiths terrified. Wilson rather resigned. Jim Callaghan saying little, but not, I think, wobbling. Soskice strong, but absent in court. Whiteley very firm.

So it turns primarily on the Little Man tomorrow. If he's firm, he'll win, and by a firm majority.

I leave the House at 4.30; there are no votes and it's impossible now to pass anyone without being engaged in the eternal topic.

George Brown, to whom I speak by phone at Harry Walston's flat,[1] says *Evening Standard* gives 140 certain votes for platform tomorrow, and 80 against. He says Bevan was lunching with Crossman and other friends in the House today. Some, no doubt, were urging him to apologise tomorrow. I said that, if he showed signs of apologising, someone should interrupt, or better still, laugh mockingly. Then he would lose control. George said they had this laid down. Three sturdy chaps were prepared to do this. I explained my original tactical view, but said we were all solid now, except Griffiths and perhaps Wilson. He was sure we should win tomorrow, but by how much depended on how Attlee put it.

The Party Meeting to discuss the Parliamentary Committee's recommendation to withdraw the whip from Bevan took place on 16th March. According to Crossman: 'The meeting started with Attlee prosecuting quietly and I thought very effectively because he simply described a series of challenges to his leadership on the floor of the Chamber, which were terribly embarrassing, and then widened out to say that for three years the Party had been in a terrible mess and Nye had been chronically disloyal. Nye didn't want to speak then but was made to do so.'[2]

Wednesday 16th March
Bevan says he'll make a statement now, if he also has a right of reply later. But there are cries of 'only one speech' and so, with a defiant air, he starts. Clear at once that we shall not be embarrassed by an apology. Complains that he did not know, till Attlee spoke this morning, what charge against him was. Then replied to Attlee's speech, *or part of it*. Avoids most awkward points with skill. ... Attacks Brown ... by name, for recent speeches against him. Recalls that in 1947 Brown was working against Attlee's leadership.[3] Declares that it is false that he wants the leadership or is working for it. If so, he would be a fool, he says, to be taking the line he is. Then, his voice rising to the familiar scream, 'These are the men who are working against the leadership,

1 In The Albany, Piccadilly.
2 J. Morgan (ed.), *The Backbench Diaries of Richard Crossman*, Hamish Hamilton and Jonathan Cape, London, 1981, entry for 16th March 1955, p. 403.
3 See above, Diary entries for 25th and 30th July 1947, pp. 395–6 and 402–5.

those hatchet-faced men sitting on the platform.' 'It's a lie,' shouts one of them, I think Jim Callaghan. Then an attack on Douglas Jay, 'It's no use Jay sitting there smirking.' Then a declaration that he won't form a splinter party. And so to an end. Then Fred Lee moves, and Maurice Edelman seconds, an amendment that we deplore and censure Bevan's conduct, and urge Party to unite behind Attlee to turn the Tories out at the next election. Attlee had at first queried whether this would be in order, since it combines two elements – opposition to withdrawing the whip, and confidence in present leadership. But he doesn't insist, and Lee moves, pretty well, and Edelman seconds, less well. (He says you can't make a party virile by castrating it; howls of laughter.) As the debate goes on after this, a piece of paper is passed along the platform (I think in Hugh's writing) for signature, and then to be handed to Attlee, saying that he hasn't made it clear that we shall *all resign* unless whip withdrawn, and that unless he makes this clear, we are in danger of defeat. This is signed by all Parliamentary Committee (except Griffiths to whom I didn't show it, and Wilson who is diplomatically absent) and also by Whiteley. Attlee reads it and puts it on his desk. We hope he may be reserving a firm statement for the finish.

On 1947 – Brown, who makes an effective speech, says that in that year he thought Bevin would be the best P.M. and has never concealed this. Alice Bacon asks Bevan whether he remembers in that summer taking her by the arm and walking her down the corridor and saying that Attlee was hopelessly weak and that they must have Bevin as P.M. (Bevan screams, 'That's a lie.') Daines[1] asks Bevan whether he remembers at that same time taking him along to his Minister's room, and drawing the curtain, and saying that Attlee is much too weak and must be got rid of. Of other speakers, Tom Fraser[2] denounces Bevan very roundly, for persistent intrigue against leadership. Irvine, *for* Bevan, is, as usual, a gift to the other side, and gets into a slanging match with Bessie Braddock – 'an ex-Communist' versus 'an ex-Liberal'. T. Proctor[3] makes a malaprop anti-Bevan speech; Collick a rather effective speech, in favour of Lee's motion, but admitting Bevan's misdeeds. Attlee's reply is *not* strong. Referring to 1947, he says he knows that there were moves then to get rid of him, but they all came to nothing 'owing to Bevin's loyalty'. He adds neither new

1 Percy Daines (1902–57). Labour and Co-operative M.P. for East Ham North 1945–57.
2 Thomas Fraser (b. 1911). Labour M.P. for Hamilton 1943–67. Junior minister 1945–51. Minister of Transport 1964–5.
3 Tom Proctor (1896–1967). Labour M.P. for Eccles 1945–64.

points nor strength. When he sits down Elaine Burton,[1] very plucky woman, says she is in disagreement with her C.L.P. on this, but wants to know whether if motion defeated, Attlee and his colleagues would resign. Attlee says, in a weak voice, 'We should have to consider our position.'

Voted for Lee's amendment 124; against 138.
      for main question (withdrawal of whip) 141; against 112.

A very poor result, in a heavily attended meeting. It will now be more difficult for N.E.C. to expel Bevan.

Misfortunes (1) the week's delay, during which agitation in the country built itself up; (2) the refusal of Parliamentary Committee to accept my advice – to put down a heavy motion of censure and try to provoke a resignation; (3) the decision to withdraw the whip having been taken, Attlee's weakness this morning. Someone said, 'He was weak this morning because he wasn't sure which way the vote would go, and was determined, whichever way it went, to stay on as Leader.'

To one journalist I said, 'Well anyhow the Party was unanimous against Bevan. They all either voted to censure him severely or to withdraw the whip.' That was the best face I could put on it.

Friday 18th March
Took Tony to dine at a Drapers' Court Dinner. Rather soothing after all our row over Bevan, culminating in a Party Meeting which, the day before yesterday, by a small majority, withdrew the whip.

I think Tony likes the dinner which *is* good, as usual, and not spoilt by speeches. Afterwards he's picked up by Hugh Farmar,[2] who shows him round. He charms them all, including old Admiral Harris,[3] by whom he sat.

We then come back to my flat and talk. He is working very hard at the Book, and enjoys this Parliamentary lull. He is very pleased at how the Book is shaping.

He is very vexed with Hugh for taking, as he thinks, the wrong line over Bevan. He thinks my line – heavy censure motion and a good try to provoke Bevan into resignation – was the right line. He, with Roy Jenkins, Woodrow Wyatt, Mulley and Albu have been unconditional unquestioning Gaitskellites, but now they are going to tell him what they think of this last incident.

His constituency problem is sticky.

We must move quickly. Tony must see Len Williams this week.

1 E. F. Burton, later Baroness (b. 1904). Labour M.P. for Coventry South 1950–59.
2 H. W. Farmar (b. 1908). Clerk to the Drapers' Company 1952–73.
3 Rear-Admiral C. F. Harris (1887–1957). Master of the Drapers' Company 1953–4.

Wednesday 30th March
At Parliamentary Committee we discuss our reaction to proposal for early general election. In 1929 and 1945, the precedents now quoted for a spring election, there was co-operation by the Opposition in getting business through. But this would now mean facilitating Finance Bill and surrendering Supply Days. Most of us, including Attlee, Morrison and Gaitskell, in addition to myself, are against such co-operation. We want to see Eden Government[1] in office for summer months (six months till October). I argue that Eden will look very small after [the] big man – 'little diplomat in striped trousers' – first P.M. for a *very long time* who has never had either ministerial responsibility for a Home Front Department *or* any local government experience. Suggested we should convey to Churchill our view that a quick election wouldn't be playing the game. Steps taken to this end.

At the end of March, Dalton began to make inquiries about the possibility of gaining a peerage for Morgan Philips Price, elderly Labour M.P. for Gloucestershire West, in order to provide a constituency for Anthony Crosland, whose Gloucestershire South seat was adversely affected by boundary changes.

Thursday 31st March
Hugh tells me he has spoken to Attlee about Price (West Gloucester for Tony is the plot), but it didn't seem to be very urgently handled.

Yesterday the N.E.C. temporarily patched up the Bevan case. This has, no doubt, become necessary, owing to previous delays and hesitations. But, by a good majority, they carried a pretty stiff resolution; approving action of P.L.P. in withdrawing the whip, taking note of Bevan's apology, and warning that future breaches of discipline will be severely dealt with. Attlee and Jim Griffiths wanted to be less stiff and abstained.

Last weekend I was at Bishop Auckland and, at my own request, met G.M.C. About 70 attended.

I speak of need for unity, but insist that Bevan has done very badly. I detail his recent misdeeds. I cite Durham cases of Benfold and Mudd.[2] Each did much less than Bevan. Can't leave one law for big

1 The retirement of Churchill was now regarded as imminent, and Eden's succession as inevitable.
2 Benfold and Mudd: two councillors who had had the Labour whip withdrawn after a local dispute with the leader of Bishop Auckland council, Jim Middlewood, q.v.

fish and another for small. Harm done by Nydolaters. If he'd been big enough to say 'I'm sorry', it would have stopped things coming this far.

Then Nunn and Pickering and Guthrie (the 3 Bevanites) spoke. The other 67 sat silent. Nunn and Pickering were both pretty reasonable, and agreed with many of my points. But Nunn attacked Gaitskell and Morrison. Guthrie made a shocking speech jumping about and shouting, wildly excited. 'I am a Nydolater', he shouted. 'Bevan is at Darlington on 1st May. Come and hear him!' No attack on me, but a most infuriating performance.

Very little applause. Then Longworth says, in a few sentences, that we must respect majority decisions. Considerable applause. Then I reply, praise Nunn and Pickering and go for Guthrie, pretty vigorously. I say his is the one thoroughly unhelpful speech. 'To hear you speak', I say, 'one would think that Bevan was Lord God Almighty, and that all the rest of us were a lot of scallywags.' I also defended Hugh and said, quoting Bevan last year, that he had been chosen by rank and file of Miners to speak at Miners' Gala this year. Then, thinking I might seem to some to have hit Guthrie too hard, I said, 'Now I'll do what I've said Nye Bevan ought to do. If I've hurt your feelings, I'm sorry. Shake hands.' This rather took him aback, but he couldn't refuse.

Then, at the end of my speech, a pause. Then Jack Bell says he wants 'to move a vote of confidence in our Member'. This is seconded, and carried unanimously.

This evening's performance shows that I can beat Guthrie in G.M.C. if I put myself to do it. But *what* a bore! And on E.C. he can pull people his way. It is shocking how silent and inert all the decent people at the G.M.C. are.

I catch Attlee this evening to press point about Price. We have quite a long talk. I open with Price, casually mentioning Tony, but mainly praising Price. Attlee will see him. Can't, he says, get him into Dissolution Honours. This is always straight Party. But could get some new Peerages just after election, whichever way it went. (This is a bad blow!)

We then speak at length on next Labour Government, if we win next election. I say I don't believe we can, certainly not if it's a quick one. I say he *must* go on as Leader until Morrison is no longer an inevitable successor. I add, cryptically, that succession could then be settled in more than one way. He says he can't go on much longer, but is very critical of Morrison. He agrees with me that Morrison couldn't go back to the Foreign Office. He was pitiable there. And Attlee doesn't think Morrison could lead the House again. He's very unpopular,

Attlee hears. What, he asks, do I think of Morrison going back to the Home Office? He could do that. I say that if he'd take it, that would be admirable. We speak of others. (Not of Hugh, I not initiating, since he and Attlee have been so much at odds over Bevan. But I'm clear that Attlee would think of no one else as Chancellor of Exchequer.) Of Morrison he says one of his faults is that he doesn't know the difference between a big question and a small question.

He gives me an opening by saying that one must be drastic next time and make many changes. I then say that, if he and Morrison go on, no one else over sixty-five, except Jim Griffiths, who has a Trade Union value, should be in government. It seems that Attlee and I both watch ages. Of fifteen Shadow Cabinet, nine are now over sixty-five, and of these four are over seventy. I urge that Whiteley, Ede, Shinwell, Noel-Baker and Hall shouldn't be in next time. I don't want to be in, and if he keeps all these others out, I'll back him up publicly and privately, and write a suitable letter for publication at the right moment. (Likewise, if we don't win, we must get all this old lot off the Parliamentary Committee, and I'll not stand, and give a lead here too.)

Other possible Peers. John Dugdale (he agrees with me that he isn't a success in the House), John Strachey (he's inclined not to have him in next government), Phil Noel-Baker (but he's got a son active in politics) and Tom Williams (but he probably hasn't any money).

Foreign Office. He suggests Robens, and I back this up. He learns, he's been good at Strasburg, he has presence. Trade Unionist much better than a lawyer for this, he thinks. We recall our preference for Griffiths when Bevin went. But he's gone off since then. Shawcross. Woolsack, we both think. I say Party would be in an uproar if he was given anything else. Soskice. I say he'd never do for Foreign Office. Much too emotional. Remember that awful speech he made about capital punishment. How about Home Office? I ask. No, says Attlee, you don't want a lawyer at Home Office either. 'Let him stay where he is', i.e. go on as law officer. Bevan, if he's behaving? What about Defence? I suggest. But Attlee doesn't like this. Anyhow, I say, he wasn't a C.O. [Conscientious Objector] like Shinwell. Attlee says Shinwell won confidence of many generals. He asks about Colonies for Bevan? I remind him that I recommended this in 1950. He'd get very keen and he's full of colour prejudice (against whites). Wilson? Back to Board of Trade, he thinks. I said he wasn't too good there before. Jim Callaghan? I'm glad to find that Attlee is strongly in favour. I suggest Housing and Local Government. He thinks Transport and in the Cabinet. I suggest he should be moved to Home Front post, since not yet quite old enough to be Minister of Defence. George

Brown, we both agree, Agriculture, and Arthur Bottomley, we both agree, Commonwealth Relations. Anything left [for] Creech Jones? I wonder. Attlee thinks not. I suggest Education. He says, 'Michael Stewart is being groomed for that.' He wants Mayhew somewhere. Perhaps Admiralty? Attlee thinks Stokes at War Office – and I agree warmly – and de Freitas at Air. Crossman, I suggest, a heavy Home Front job outside the Cabinet. 'National Insurance and Pensions', says Attlee with a chuckle. Pakenham, Lord Privy Seal and Leader in Lords. 'Jowitt is no leader', he says, and Alexander is lame and doesn't fit. He still hankers after George Hall, but I urge very strongly that he's too old. Tom Fraser we both like very much. Obviously Secretary of State for Scotland next time. Hector McNeil never about. I say he always looks as though he drinks too much. [Ernest] Davies nothing next time. ... I suggest that Mitchison, though really too old, might be Solicitor-General. He has worked very hard and well. Attlee not unsympathetic. We both agree that Bob Mellish should be an Under-Secretary. We deplore lack of good younger miners. Attlee has noticed Roy Mason.[1] I think he might be tried somewhere. He asks me about Fred Lee. I say quite good up to a point, but comes to an end rather suddenly. I praised Lindgren, while not claiming too much for him.

This conversation took a long time. But it will be seen that we left many offices and persons undiscussed.

Friday 1st April

See Len Williams, primarily about a seat for Tony.

Televise tonight *In the News* with [Walter] Elliot, Boothby and Crossman. Less well run, by Miall,[2] a dull dog, and Michael Peacock,[3] a commonplace young man, than it used to be. ...

Most amusing part of the evening is at Boothby's house afterwards, where all gossip freely. Boothby is sure Winston is going on Tuesday (the 5th), but it's awful for him that London newspapers will still be out of action owing to strike!

---

1 Roy Mason (b. 1924). Labour M.P. for Barnsley 1953–83; Barnsley Central since 1983. Yorkshire Miners' Council 1949–53. Junior minister 1967–8. Postmaster-General 1968; Minister of Power 1968–9; President of the Board of Trade 1969–70. Secretary of State for Defence 1974–6; Northern Ireland 1976–9.
2 Leonard Miall (b. 1914). Head of B.B.C. Television Talks and Documentary Features 1954–61.
3 Michael Peacock (b. 1929). B.B.C. Television producer 1952–6. Producer of Panorama 1956–8; Editor 1959–66. Editor of B.B.C. TV News 1961–3. Controller of B.B.C. 1 Services 1965–7. Managing Director of London Weekend Television Ltd 1967–9. Governor of L.S.E. since 1982.

Eden, they say, is accepted, but without enthusiasm. Eden, Butler and Macmillan are 'not a triumvirate, but a trinity'. No friendship at the top here. But no present challenge from outside the three. Physically, Eden, though he was three times cut up, has made a wonderful recovery. He can still play tennis, and his movements at the box are much freer than either of the others. Butler is very tired (and what a job he has!) and felt the loss of his wife very much.[1] And Macmillan shuffles along like an old man. He had a gall bladder operation not long ago. Boothby thinks the others will be watching Eden and that he may well be pole-axed in eighteen months' time.

Crossman obviously hates Gaitskell more than he loves Bevan. Bevan, he says, has apologised, to keep himself in the Party, but he has no apology in his heart. The day after the N.E.C. reprieved him he had a Commonwealth Press Conference.[2] In first part, off the record, he attacked the Industrial Oligarchs and said he'd beat them yet. In the second part, he tried to veer against the H-bomb. The 'fall-out', he said, was a new factor. We must all think again.

Crossman praised his gifts. I said this was all fantastically exaggerated. And the main defects were visibly growing. He was no longer capable of discussion, but only of monologue. And he never went to the Tea Room. ... Crossman said, 'You don't go to the Tea Room either.' I said, 'Yes, I do, and I've never seen him there or you.' Crossman said Bevan would 'get the miners within two years'. I said he wouldn't. I knew a lot about miners. ... Crossman said Bevan was always thinking about his 'long term strategy', and had been very angry with [him], because, under the title 'Mr Attlee puts his foot down', the *New Statesman* had said that 'the great majority of Labour supporters loyally accept Mr Attlee as their Leader, Mr Gaitskell as their financial expert and Mr Bevan as the inspirer of their Socialist faith.' Bevan had told Crossman that this reference to Gaitskell was 'gross disloyalty'.

Boothby and I had remarked earlier to one another that these Wykehamists showed their hatred of one another too openly; we Etonians managed our relations, even when lethal, much more smoothly.

Crossman grumbled about Strasburg, and jeered at those we sent. They were quite undistinguished and knew no languages. Sneers at Robens and Chetwynd. And why was Edelman dropped? I said, 'When *you* were appointed, you wouldn't go.'

1 Sydney Butler, née Courtauld, died in December 1954. She had married R. A. Butler in 1926.
2 The Commonwealth Conference was meeting in London.

Saturday 2nd April

TONY CROSLAND AND I[1]

We dined tonight at the Akropolis, and he came back to my flat for a final drink.

His constituency problem is very difficult. Our hopes of getting Philips Price out of West Gloucester (a constituency which would suit Tony perfectly) in time for a change at the general election now seem almost gone.

On 5th April, Churchill resigned as Prime Minister. Next day, Sir Anthony Eden, the Foreign Secretary, succeeded him. An early election was now widely expected.

Monday 4th to Thursday 7th April
Intensive electioneering on behalf of my two young friends, Tony [Crosland] and Mike [Williams Thompson]. On the 5th, as expected, Winston *did* resign. The end, in the House, was flat. On Tuesday, his last day, he didn't come to answer his P.Q.s – as all had expected – and to bid his farewell. Nor did Eden show himself.

No newspapers in London![2] This meant a muffled going. Butler, to whom I said, 'I expect you had to push', replied, 'Yes, we had. You see at the end he couldn't do the business in Cabinet. He spent all his time composing his answers to P.Q.s.' Others related that he talked too much, and with no grasp of detail. Very conspicuously at the Commonwealth P.M.s' Conference.

Butler told me, on the 6th, that he himself would like a later election – this, if true, is contrary to all the popular guesses from outside the Cabinet.

On the 4th (or ? earlier), Monckton had hinted that the election might be delayed till October. Strong advice, I gathered, was being given to Eden to delay. 'The brave thing', said Monckton, 'would be for Eden to announce that there would be no election this year.' He himself, he said, didn't much mind which party was in, and didn't want to continue in office. But, on all the obvious party arguments, the case for going quick seems overwhelming.

1 Inserted at the top of the page: 'In the next few days I start forcing tactics of my own on Price, though Hugh Gaitskell and Tony were both a bit scared of this, and it seemed, on 7th April 1955, to be working very hopefully.'
2 A newspaper strike had begun a few days earlier, affecting all London daily and Sunday papers. It lasted until 21st April.

659

On the 6th tributes to the old boy in the House, and welcome to his successor. I shake Eden's hand as we go out behind the Chair. He is a bit emotional.

Monday 4th April

See Len Williams at 3. I explain that Tony wants to lie back and wait, and hates the idea of winning a marginal. He [would] sooner lose next time and take his chance of by-elections afterwards. And he feels he *might* pick up something at last moment. Of course I don't mention West Gloucester. I then suggest we should send Mike Williams Thompson's name to Grantham, and also to Frank Shepherd[1] for Eastleigh. Agreed. ...

I meet Price in the House. He is trying to get in debate on our adherence to Turkish–Iraqi Pact. I ask him to meet me afterwards, in dining room. He does. But people, including Crossman, are at next table. So I talk with Price about the Pamirs, etc. At last Crossman goes and I tackle Price on Peerage. He says he'd like it. He'd like 'a niche' for himself, here at Westminster, as he grows older. But adds that he spent his seventieth birthday hunting with I forget what hounds and has just told his constituency people that he'd like to fight again, and has been readopted.

He said 'No' to Whiteley the other day, because Whiteley put it 'very abruptly', and because Attlee had behaved so badly before about it. He then pours out a story. There have been two previous offers. First by Attlee in 1941, when Stansgate, Winster and Wedgwood and someone else went up. Price was offered it, and accepted after consulting his family. Then Attlee sent for him and said, 'I'm afraid it's off.' Price asked why, and Attlee said awkwardly and looking uncomfortable, 'I'm afraid I can't tell you.' Price was very indignant. I said that no doubt it was very difficult in the Coalition, and Winston and the Tories may have objected to so many Labour Peers.

Then, said Price, there was a second case in 1950, after the election. Attlee sent for him, and said he wanted his seat. Would he go to the Lords? He couldn't offer him any office, but he could, if he liked, be a Lord-in-Waiting. Price told me that at this, he had been angry, and said that neither he nor his seat was in the market, and that he had no wish to be a Lord-in-Waiting, and left Attlee's room. (In fact, the trouble in 1941 was that it was discovered that Price's wife[2] was a German – a valid objection – and also that, years before, he had been a suspected Communist – great nonsense in 1941!) But now, I told

1 Frank Shepherd. Secretary of the Southern Regional Council of the Labour Party 1947–59.
2 Elisa, née Balster. From Halberstadt, Germany. They married in 1919.

him, Attlee wanted him in the Lords, he needed greater strength there, and Price would bring it, especially in Agriculture and Forestry, and in Foreign Affairs. He seemed very pleased at this. I asked whether I could tell Attlee that he would like it, and he said yes. He began to speak about when it would come, and when he should tell constituents. I said Dissolution Honours were pure Party, but Attlee would fix it with Eden for an early date after. He said that Eden liked him, and had asked him to dinner recently to meet the Turkish Ambassador. He was becoming keener and keener as we talked. I advised him not to worry at present about telling his constituents, and thinking of dates of announcement. (Nor, most deliberately, did I touch on any question of successor, nor did he.) Crossman came back and rejoined us, and we had to change the conversation. Then, when we had got rid of Crossman, Price asked should he tell his family. I said it might be well to tell his wife, but not Peter nor Tanya yet. *Very good*!

I rang up Tony and said, 'Price wants a Peerage, and I hear from a high authority that there may be no election till next year.' (We had been assuming May.) He was dumbfounded at both these announcements!

Tuesday 5th April
I told Attlee that Price would like a Peerage. I suggested [he] should see him. He was glad of the news and said he would.

I had Frank Shepherd to the House of Commons at 5.30 and we drank beer. Then we took a taxi to Mike [Williams Thompson]'s flat, and propounded [*sic*] Eastleigh. Then Mike and I went off to dine at the Akropolis. Mike was clear he couldn't take it because chances not good enough. He could *become an M.P.*, and still run his business without loss of credit. But not if he ran and was beaten. This was a slightly new slant to me, but quite rational. So we agreed that both he and I would write to Shepherd next day, and tell the plain truth. (We did, and exchanged letters.) If a quick election comes, I don't see much chance of doing better for Mike. If it's delayed, something might turn up. But I'm disappointed not to have been able to do better for him.

Wednesday 6th April
I must get a move on over West Gloucester. I rang up Attlee and urged he should see Price *today*. (Tomorrow the House adjourns for Easter.) He says he will if he can be got hold of. I mention Tony as an argument for speed.

Then I try to track Price. I ring his London number. No reply. I get his Gloucestershire number from the whips' office and ring it. A servant says he is still in London today, but catching the 6.35 train home this evening. The servant thinks he will be at the House of Commons. I telephone twice to the House leaving a message for him to ring me up. No reply! I lunch in, and go early to the House. Price has not been seen there today! Just after 4, after the tributes to Winston, I go again to Clem's room, and urge him to see Price today. I tell him that Price thinks Eden will be agreeable. I again mention Tony. Clem says, 'He's a very promising young man, but there are other claimants without seats, e.g. Soskice and Summerskill.' I say with great assurance, 'Oh, *they* are all fixed. Soskice is going to Gorton and Summerskill to Warrington. I saw Len Williams yesterday. Crosland is the only one of any importance not yet placed.' He accepts this, not apparently being in touch with events. About 5 Price rushes up to me, very excited. He has only just got my telephone message. I say, 'My intelligence service is pretty good. You are proposing to catch the 6.35. You must cancel that. Attlee wants to see you today.' Price agrees. We go to Attlee's room. He isn't there. We fix 6.30 with Mrs Skelly[1] (Attlee's secretary) for the interview. I then tell Hugh, who is in the Library, how things stand. I am in the corridor just before 6.30. Attlee goes by. He says, 'I haven't seen him.' I said, 'I have. He's coming to see you at 6.30.' A few minutes later Price appears. I say, 'He's waiting for you. Good luck! Let's have a word afterwards.' Soon after 7, Attlee again appears, with a party who look like constituents. He breaks loose and says to me, 'It went very well. And he was very much pleased by the successor.' I asked, 'Do you mean the youngster?' He said, 'Yes.' (It was important that he, and not I, should first mention Tony to Price.)

I then found Price in the Library, and we went down to the Harcourt Room. He said, 'He was awfully nice. He told me that in 1941 it wasn't his fault. He said he *wanted* me to speak on Foreign Affairs in the Lords, as well as on Agriculture. He said he thought it could be arranged for Birthday Honours in June. I told him I knew Eden quite well, and he seemed very pleased.' And then, said Price, they had talked about a successor. 'You had advised me not to, but he introduced it.' 'Well,' I said, 'the important thing is your Peerage, and I didn't want to complicate a settlement of that.' He had mentioned Soskice to me as the sort of anti-Bevanite successor he would like. I had said that Soskice was going to Gorton, but had not mentioned Tony. 'Well,' said Price, 'he suggested to me Tony Crosland. And that would suit me very well indeed. We don't [want] any Bevanites. Down in the Forest we're united on that. In fact,' he said,

---

1 Mrs Beryl Skelly. Secretary to the Leader of the Opposition (Attlee, then Gaitskell) 1951–63.

eyeing me a little carefully, 'we passed a resolution and sent [it] to H.Q. in favour of the Paris Agreements.' 'Oh,' I said, 'that controversy is all over now. I held pro-Bevanite views on that. But that's finished. As a matter of fact, Crosland would agree with you on that. He's a strong anti-Bevanite. Do you know him at all?' 'Oh yes,' said Price, they had been County Members together, and he had a good opinion [of him]. I said, so had I. He was very useful in Budget debates, and had a good background, and good brains, and a good personality. (But I deliberately didn't lay it on at all thick.) 'How would it be to have him down for a night during the recess, and talk it all over with him?' Yes, he said, he'd like to do that. Would I be seeing him? I might be, I said, and I would give him Price's message, either orally or in writing.

That night I rang up Tony and said, 'Price invites you to spend a night with him during the Easter Recess, to arrange for your taking over the Forest.' He was amazed. When I told him what had happened he expressed much gratitude – I always discourage too much of that – and thought that my handling had been 'brilliant'. I only hope it comes off. There are still some difficulties about timing, e.g. [whether?] Birthday Honours are before dissolution.

Thursday 7th April
Lunch with Hugh at Hampstead, with Douglas Jay and 'the three wise young men' – Tony, Roy and Woodrow [Wyatt]. 'A booze up' as Hugh called it, finishing up a lot of Walston wine, with very agreeable cold pork, mayonnaise potato salad and cheese.

Fixed beforehand not to speak of West Gloucester in front of Woodrow, who I hope will get All Saints Birmingham, but don't want in the Forest. Tony and I – and Roy with car – stay behind afterwards, and Roy drives us back. Agreed that Tony shall write to Price and accept kind invitation to stay night. Later I ring up Price and ask how his wife likes the idea. He says very much. I then say I've seen Tony who will be most delighted to come, and is writing. I then ring Tony again and report. So far with *this* prolonged negotiation. It may still fail, but without my efforts of the last three days, it should never have begun to show any sign of succeeding.

The talk at and after lunch was very frank and interesting. The three young men, and Douglas Jay to some extent, were critical of Hugh over Bevan affair. They felt the Parliamentary Committee should not have gone for withdrawing the whip. (On this my position had been wiser.) They thought Hugh under-estimated difficulties in C.L.P.s. And that he was getting labelled Right Wing. And must devote more time and effort to attacking Tories. When they had

finished I agreed with most of what they'd said. Several of them also
said that Hugh mustn't quarrel with Attlee. I agreed with this. I said
I wanted Hugh to lead the Party and to succeed Attlee directly – and
not after a period of Morrison. Hugh, I was rather shocked to find,
is still playing with the idea of Morrison replacing Attlee, with himself
as Deputy: I said this wouldn't work. The M.P.s wouldn't prefer
Morrison to Attlee as Leader. Hugh said he had to do so much of the
anti-Bevan fighting because others did so little, and he said that some
of his Trade Union supporters sometimes asked him why his young
intellectual supporters didn't take a larger share. Hugh spoke, in his
reply, with earnestness, solemnity and, the young thought afterwards,
much cogency.

One trouble is that, as I said, having to defend yourself against
attacks from the so-called 'Left', you are driven into a perpetual
position of defence, and you haven't enough energy left for attacking
the Tories. But this must be fought down. BUTSKELL, a figure invented
by *The Economist*, though eagerly adopted by the Bevanites, must be
destroyed.

And I daresay Hugh thinks that *I* should have done more to fight
the Bevanites and support him. But (a) I have always been trying,
rather vainly, instead, to strengthen 'unity', and (b) I have been persistently involved, until a few months ago, with German Rearmament,
on which I was often embarrassed by Bevanite support.

Saturday 16th April
Tony rang up this morning from Bristol that his visit to Philips Price
had been very successful, though he didn't care for either his wife or
Peter. But Price was very keen to have him as successor, and drove
him round the constituency – though it seemed wise not to meet the
agent[1] or other leading local figures. Tony thinks it would be a dream
constituency. And he fancies himself as carrying on the Dilke tradition.[2] Price would vacate it for general election, if he could get something a little firmer from Attlee, whom he doesn't much trust in view
of past difficulties. Attlee is now lecturing for C.C.F. [Co-operative
Commonwealth Fellowship] in Canada, and it may be that *I* shall
have to speak to Eden about Price's Peerage. Look into this tomorrow.
Meanwhile no mention to Len Williams or Ted Rees (whose duty it
would be to report to Len Williams), in case either Summerskill or,
less probably, Soskice, is left displaced, and might be officially
[pushed ?] against Tony.

1 See below, p. 667 and n.
2 Sir Charles Dilke, 2nd Bart (1843–1911). Radical and republican. Liberal M.P.
  for the Forest of Dean 1892–1911.

On 15th April, four days before a tax-cutting Budget, Eden announced that there would be a general election on 26th May.

Thursday 21st April

Spoke on the Budget, opening from our side after Maudling,[1] who deputised for Thorneycroft,[2] [who was] ill. I had a good deal of fun, especially with the arithmetic of the income tax reductions, and of the greater relief given to non-earned than to earned incomes. 'Under the Tories,' I said, 'it pays to do no work.' Our people, those who were there, for this Parliament is dying fast, liked all this.

As to Tony and West Gloucester, I spoke to Hugh early on the phone. I have written Attlee a pressing letter about time getting short for Price's honour, and urging him to speak to Eden very soon. Attlee is due back at London Airport at 8 a.m. There is an N.E.C. this morning. He will get my letter early this afternoon. I asked Hugh to press him, this morning, to see Eden today.

He did so this afternoon. I saw him later and he said Eden was quite well disposed, but wanted to look up the precedents. I saw Price and told him this. He was flappier than usual. He said, 'Another complication has arisen.' His agent, whom he had taken into his confidence, said that it would cause great consternation if he didn't fight the general election at the last moment; it would be much resented if someone new was suddenly pushed in; and the Party would want someone, probably a Trade Union candidate with money.[3] I discouraged all this, and told Price that it was very common nowadays for C.L.P.s to choose people without money in preference to Trade Union nominees. He seemed very surprised, and asked if I could give an example. I said Tony in South Gloucester. I fear that he has

---

1 Reginald Maudling (1917–79). Minister of Supply from 7th April 1955 until 1957. Conservative M.P. for Barnet 1950–February 1974; Chipping Barnet February 1974–9. Economic Secretary at the Treasury 1952–5. Paymaster-General 1957–9; President of the Board of Trade 1959–61; Colonial Secretary 1961–2; Chancellor of the Exchequer 1962–4. Home Secretary 1970–72. Eden had moved Maudling from the Treasury to Supply as part of a government reshuffle immediately after becoming Prime Minister.

2 Peter Thorneycroft, later Baron (b. 1909). President of the Board of Trade 1951–7. Conservative M.P. for Monmouth 1945–66; Stafford 1938–45. Junior minister 1945. Chancellor of the Exchequer 1957–8. Minister of Aviation 1960–62; Defence 1962–4. Chairman of the Conservative Party Organisation 1975–81.

3 i.e. a 'sponsored' candidate – backed by a trade union willing to contribute towards election and other constituency expenses, which might include an agent's salary.

not only mentioned Tony to his agent, which we knew, but added, in reply no doubt to agent's questions, that he had no money.

That night, dining late in Members' Dining Room with T. O'Brien and others, I saw our new P.M. and his Chief Whip[1] at a table by themselves at the far end of the room. Nearly everyone else had gone. (Winston never lunched or dined here.) So I followed Eden and started on Bishop Auckland Festival, etc., and then went with him alone into his room. We talked, superficially, of the international scene, the coming election, etc. I said I found all this transition very moving. He and I had never seriously disagreed. At the end I spoke of Price. He said he's asked Patrick (Buchan-Hepburn) to look at the precedents; they had been talking of this immediately before at dinner. (I wasn't sure whether Attlee had distinguished between Dissolution and Birthday Honours. If we *could* get it in Dissolution Honours it would be much easier. But I didn't say this.) I praised Price, and said he was in a great stew, and couldn't say anything to anyone. Going out – all seeming in a very good mood – I said we also wanted his seat, and casually mentioned Tony. He laughed very much at this. But I think this mention was a good calculated risk. At least I hope so, and I had to decide quickly how far to go.

Friday 22nd April
Short sitting (11–4) on the Budget Resolutions.

I went down just before lunch, and to Attlee's room. Mrs Skelly says, 'Mr Philips Price has been in to see him.' I went in, and asked whether he had had a message yet from Eden. He said No. Price had come of his own accord to enquire. I saw Price who said he had put off going home till the 2.15 p.m. train, in case there was a message. He said, very miserably, 'I don't want to leave the Forest under a cloud.'

I urged him to bring no one else into confidence. He caught his 2.15 train. He said that Attlee had promised to ring him up if he had any news. But Attlee was away in the afternoon. At 4 p.m. as it finished, I had another quick word in the passage with Eden. He said Patrick hadn't sent him the note he had asked for. 'After all,' he said, 'I only heard about it yesterday.' This with a smile, but I felt I had gone to the utmost limit I could in pressing him. He said, 'We've had a Cabinet all this morning.'

I had arranged for Tony to go away with me when the House rose.

---

1 P. G. T. Buchan-Hepburn, later 1st Baron Hailes (1901–74). Government Chief Whip 1950–55. Conservative M.P. for Beckenham 1950–57; Liverpool East Toxteth 1931–50. Minister of Works 1955–7.

I told him all that had happened. I said I was discouraged, but there was still some hope.

It was clear to us both that the agent was the trouble ...

Saturday 23rd April

I spoke to Philips Price at his home at 11 a.m. I told him of my seeing Eden yesterday. I warned him again on discretion. He said he had decided to tell no one but Jenkins.[1] He said he wouldn't come up on Monday, but he had written me a letter. I said I would tell him of any events.

Monday 25th April

Ring Hugh. He thinks that if Eden agrees today on Price, Tony should not merely *ring up*, but go down to Bristol and see Ted Rees. We must, Hugh says, just bulldoze it through once the Price Peerage is secure. I say that probably Jenkins, Price's agent, is a weak man ... I would later, but now it's premature, suggest to Price that he should go on paying for a while, towards cost of organisation. Cost of election would be covered anyhow. Hugh asks if I mentioned Tony to Eden. I said yes, with a hunch that this was a worthwhile calculated risk. Hugh says he's glad I did. He thinks it was right. He thinks Tony should miss Dartford on Saturday if the Forest's on the cards.

Speaking to Tony, he reminded me that he belonged to Tom Williamson's Union,[2] and that they gave a little to his election expenses.

I rang back Hugh, and asked him to speak to Tom Williamson. If not Tony, they might pick a Bevanite. He said he would, as soon as Eden's answer, if good, comes in.

I receive a letter from Price. Compare this with his other letter a week ago! His agent has worked on him. We must bulldoze him.

Go down in the afternoon to the House. Meet Attlee in passage. No message from No. 10. He will ring him up. Hugh has prodded him. Hugh has flu and looks like death. Brief talk with him and Tony. We agree that Tony must take Ted Rees into his confidence, if he goes down and sees him, as we agree that he should as soon as a 'Yes' comes – if it *does* come – from No. 10.

See Attlee again – Hugh has gone home – at 6.30. No reply. He has asked Pitblado, P.S. at No. 10 who is dealing with it, to reply *tomorrow*! Either difficulties are being manufactured, or the P.M. is very busy.

---

1 G. T. D. Jenkins, of Lydney, Gloucestershire. West Gloucestershire C.L.P. agent.
2 The General and Municipal Workers' Union.

Don't miss the possibility of the latter! Tell Tony. I make no communication to Price today. I tell Attlee I'll see him again tomorrow afternoon. He says Railway Strike, threatened by A.S.L.E.F., will do us in.[1]

Passages full of wondering whispering waifs: Summerskill at one end. She goes to Warrington tomorrow to compete against Tommy Williams and three others. Woodrow Wyatt, twice rejected in Birmingham, asks me about Grantham. I mention Eastleigh too.

I feel very low, and am impatient with little group on Finance Bill Committee.

Tuesday 26th April
12.20. Rang Attlee. 'Any message from No. 10 yet?' 'No. I expect it this afternoon.'

Rang Tony and arranged to see him at the House at 4. Found Attlee on the Bench at 3.55. Sat beside him. He whispered, 'I've spoken to his secretary. He says they're working on it now.' Later, outside – he seems to have a weak bladder and to be always running to the rear – he says, 'They're working on it now. They say it's very complicated. It must be Honours List as a whole. I can't do any more.' I have about shot my bolt with Attlee today. Hugh must have a go tomorrow if no news. Today he's in Barnsley – I hope his flu won't snuff him out.

Walked with Tony on Terrace. He ran into Price but couldn't say much. Price didn't seem to understand how much more critical this *general* election was for Tony than Price. We agreed that Price should stay in London for some days, so that Ted Rees, if the right answer came, could see Jenkins, Price's agent, before Price returned. We agreed that it was very important what Attlee said to Price, if right answer came. He should be firm and clear on national importance of the vacancy. I said I wasn't confident about this. I couldn't play other people's games of chess for them, in these tricky conversations. Last night I said that I seemed to be trying to play chess on twelve boards simultaneously! We agreed that Hugh could weigh in here with Price, rather distantly, not knowing him well, but as Future P.M., etc. I said I doubted whether Price realised all this.

Later I took Price out on the Terrace, gave him the news, and urged him to stay in London, in case something came in. He said he'd planned to do this, till Friday. His wife, he said, had been very depressed over the weekend. *He* seemed a bit brighter, and chuckled

1 i.e. do Labour harm in the election. A strike over wages, originally called for 1st May, was cancelled at the last minute. This turned out to be only a postponement, and the engine drivers struck from the end of May until mid-June.

over 'it' being complicated. He was sure, from his experience of life, that 'it', an Honours List, always was. ... I told Price I had his letter, but didn't want to discuss that now. His Peerage, I said, was the thing.

Later I rang up Tony and told him all this. ... Tony thinks he *should* get Dartford, if he goes. He's on a short list of three, other two local. Pannell has been working for him. But Frank Shepherd told him that an attempt was made to keep him off the short list, by alleging that, at a private conference, he had said that he was against any more nationalisation.

At the end of our talk, I tried to persuade him that there wasn't all that difference between political life with a safe, and a not-so-safe, constituency. If he won Dartford this time, he'd hold it pretty easily next time. Things would be *against* us this time, *for* us next time. And that would be ten years.[1]

He was very grateful and appreciative of all I'd done, tried to make quite a long speech. I said, first, I hate to be beaten, and [had] for him a combination of affection and esteem. Without both I couldn't have gone even as far as this. (But I am very pessimistic now about getting him into the Forest, except by Dissolution Honours.)

House of Commons intolerable. 'What a shit hole this place is!' I wrote on a postcard and gave to Tony. Trying to talk in corridors, and even on Terrace, one is observed, if not overheard, everywhere – by undesirable people – and conclusions drawn.

Wednesday 27th April

10.45–1.15. Joint meeting at Transport House of Parliamentary Committee with N.E.C. on Election Manifesto. Improve it a good deal ...

See Tony, who earlier had said he thought he should be getting himself psychologically prepared for Dartford – he now says he hears from Dodds[2] that it's all tied up in favour of a local man, who will have half votes, at least, in his pocket at start.[3] I say I'll see Len Williams tomorrow morning. Tony says that Edna, Denis Healey's wife,[4] who knows the Forest, has heard a rumour that Price will withdraw at last moment, and people are guessing it's a Peerage. All very bloody! But Tony, as usual, with a gay smile. Sooner not stand,

1 In fact, Dartford was held by Labour without a break until 1970. The 1955 majority (4,198) was larger than in Gloucestershire West (4,020).
2 N. N. Dodds (1903–65). Labour and Co-operative M.P. for Dartford 1945–55; Erith and Crayford 1955–65.
3 Dartford selected the chairman of the constituency party, Sydney Irving, later Baron (b. 1918), as candidate. Labour M.P. for Dartford 1955–70, 1974–9. Junior whip 1964–6.
4 Edna Healey, née Edmunds.

and try for by-election afterwards. But I think he'd better stand *somewhere*, even if badly beaten.

Thursday 28th April

Back at House see Attlee. He has letter from Eden saying he'll put Price into Birthday Honours, though with warning about old objection (Communist Youth) and Winston having been impressed with it. Attlee says he'll ignore this. He asks me to collect Price. I say he must be firm with him, and insist on his resigning at general election. I find Price and congratulate him warmly; I see him again after he has seen Attlee. Very happy. I tell him to telephone, in guarded terms, to his wife. On not fighting general election still obstinately resistant, though he reports what Attlee said. I tell him this is now a matter for H.Q. I must tell Len Williams. He's a little awestruck, I think. ...

I then catch Tony and bring him back to my flat, and up to date. It is a wildly funny story anyhow!

Price still fretting about money. I tell him that Tony is member of M.G.W. [Municipal and General Workers'] and they might make him a grant towards organisation. This obviously interests Price more than anything else I've said (influence of Jenkins). I put it to him that he might contribute a bit himself. He agreed to this. But he isn't really interested now in Tony, or his merits as successor, only in his own position. What can he say, if he withdraws now? He'll be 'hated' in Forest for 'deserting' them. (Jenkins again – slick, eloquent Welshman.) I say, 'for private reasons'. They'll learn very soon, in a few weeks, what these are. He says what can I do during the campaign? Could I speak for him? No one would understand. And the procedure? His adoption meeting is on 7th May. There must be a week's notice. There must be time for new nominations. I say, 'Let's leave this to the experts. H.Q. will advise on all this. They're used to it. And now let's wait for Rees's report. And you see Len Williams next Wednesday.' And so I leave, not very hopefully, and only outwardly friendly to this silly selfish deaf old blockhead!

Sunday 1st May

I am very sad and depressed by all this. Tony has come worse out of all this than any of them. (But Soskice, I hear later, has lost Gorton today by three votes to Zilliacus, who offered £400 and Soskice only £100. Soskice leading in first three ballots!)

I write down a note of events – and post it to Tony. Causes (1) butchery of Redistribution (2) *quick* election (3) *slow* movement, in successive stages, of Price. Well, 'I done my damnedest; angels can do no more.'[1] Tony very appreciative. No one *really* helped much, not even Hugh.

Saturday 7th May
My hunch today is that Tories will have a majority of between 40 and 100. And then our internal row will start again! A gloomy near future for our Party. And in the further future, I shall be out of it.

I am *very* sad about Tony.

1955 General Election (26th May)
This was my 10th general election and, counting two byes, my twelfth Parliamentary. And it was the most tedious, apathetic, uninteresting and, I think, worst organised of them all. Partly, no doubt, this was subjective, owing to increasing age (I am now sixty-seven) and very limited future political ambitions.

There was great disinclination to attend meetings. (I held many fewer indoor meetings.) We all kidded ourselves that this was because the electors were viewing T.V. or listening in to sound radio. We were wrong. B.B.C. reported later that their political audiences were no larger, either on T.V. or sound, than on normal non-election days. And the audience for any politician depended on what other item went before or after. The plain truth was that people were not much interested in the election.

There were no burning issues, no unemployment, and much over-time. In my campaign I was reduced to saying that (1) prices – and here I read out and listed grocery prices at two dates – had risen dis-gracefully under the Tories who had promised to put value back into the £, and (2) Attlee rather than Eden should go to top-level talks!!

We lost surprisingly few seats. I grieve *very* much for Tony, and am mildly sorry about some of the others. There was no Peerage for Price![2] The Honours Advisory Committee dug up his anti-interven-tionist activities in Russia in 1920!

But I felt exceedingly unenthusiastic about Bishop Auckland. I felt I had had just about enough of *them*, and just couldn't bear to think of fighting another election there.

---

1 A line from a poem by R. W. Service, the Canadian poet and ballad writer, whom Dalton had admired as an undergraduate.
2 Philips Price remained as M.P. for Gloucestershire West until the 1959 election. He received no honour. While out of Parliament, Crosland completed *The Future of Socialism*, published in 1956.

In the general election, the Conservatives increased their 1951 majority of
17 to 59 – the first time in the twentieth century after a full Parliament that
a governing party had gained seats. In Bishop Auckland, Dalton's majority
fell to 5,845 in a straight fight with a Conservative. Faced with another four
or five years in Opposition, Dalton finally decided that this was to be his
last Parliament, and that he would stand down from the Shadow Cabinet.

He was not, however, a man to retire quietly. After careful planning, he
launched 'Operation Avalanche', a gesture of calculated contempt directed
at his most prominent contemporaries.[1] On 1st June he wrote to Attlee,
declaring that he would not himself stand again for the Parliamentary
Committee, and urging that all others over sixty-five should follow his
example – with the single exception of the Party Leader. Meanwhile, he took
care that the press should be informed. 'Seldom has it been such fun to do
one's duty', he wrote. For a time bitterness among his older colleagues
was intense. Three of them stood down – Ede, Hall and Shinwell – all
strenuously denying that they had been influenced by Dalton's campaign.
Griffiths, Gaitskell, Callaghan, Robens, Wilson, Summerskill, Bevan,
Brown, Noel-Baker, Greenwood, Stokes and Mitchison were elected to the
new Committee, in that order.

Wednesday 8th June

Swore in. Churchill, too, has suddenly gone very old. Like the fish
who live at a great depth, subject to tremendous pressure, and, when
they are brought up toward the surface, and the pressures relax, burst
and die. Attlee got a cheer, when, the Government Front Bench
having sworn, and the Opposition Front Bench being about to swear,
he shook the old boy's hand, sitting in his old corner seat below the
gangway, and led him to join the queue. The old boy signed his name
very slowly, and hesitated about putting in the name of his constituency. Later I saw him in the Smoking Room, and greeted him. But he
was unresponsive. He thought my latest action, he said glumly, would
not be popular on the back benches. I don't think we shall hear much
more from *him*.

Tony to dine at Akropolis. He says he's started again on the Book
and is pleased with it. He's had a number of invitations to lecture
and write. This is reassuring, and shows that he can earn fairly easily.
We agree that he should write nothing serious till he's finished the

1 See HTA, pp. 411–24.

Book. I give him an assessment of recent goings on. He thinks I adopted a very harsh line to the over sixty-fives at the Shadow Cabinet. He thinks now that he would be quite content to be out of the House for three years.

Friday 10th June
Letter from Ede to Attlee in the press. Very rude to me. Some papers, e.g. *Daily Herald*, play it down as 'ironical'. Clearly he was very much disconcerted by *my* letter. I think he's been in trouble in his own constituency on grounds of age. He told us in Parliamentary Committee that he would be in his constituency this weekend and would be asked whether he was following my example. I expect he read this letter to some of his constituents before sending it to the press.

Poor old boy! I think he must have been bottling up anti-Dalton emotions, and an inferiority complex, for years. Now it's all burst out! I can't think that this letter will do *him* much good, or *me* much harm. Too obviously bilious. And anyhow he's making another vacancy in the Shadow Cabinet, and that's what I wanted him to do.

Wednesday 6th July

BEVAN

His hair has suddenly gone quite white, and his bushy eyebrows too. And his face the colour of beetroot. This may be the fresh air of the farm, or it may be drink.

Today I was walking across the Park to lunch with Sadd[1] at the Athenaeum. I met Skinnard[2] ... (ex-M.P.). He spoke of this and then that. And then of Bevan. 'I hear he's been drinking too much,' he said. 'I saw him yesterday' – apparently at some Hospital Board do – 'and he looked awful.' ... Skinnard thought his wife was to blame for keeping him in a bad mood.

I then walked on to my date with Sadd. Hardly had we begun lunch when he said, unprompted by me, 'I hear Aneurin Bevan's drinking too much.' And this, from two different sources, within ten minutes.

That night I walked home with Crossman, and then to his house for a gossip. I related this. He said, as I knew, that he and Wilson and Barbara Castle had now practically pulled out. This left Bevan, he said, with a group who were all heavy drinkers – Bowles, Hale,[3] Baird,

---

1 Sir Clarence Sadd (1883–1962). Chief Executive and Vice-Chairman of Midland Bank 1944–8. Member of the National Investment Council 1945–8.
2 F. W. Skinnard (1902–84). Labour M.P. for Harrow East 1945–50.
3 Leslie Hale, q.v., Labour M.P. for West Oldham.

Delargy, etc. He added that Foot also drank too much. And that he (Crossman) had seen Bevan drinking at 3 p.m. – that early! And that his public row with Attlee, leading to his resignation over S.E.A.T.O., was immediately after a lot to drink, at lunch with him (Crossman).

Thursday 7th July
I told George Brown about the previous day. I said it would be the best solution if Bevan thus faded, rather discreditably, out of our front rank. I also told him that Crossman, before the Shadow Cabinet elections, had been going round saying that I was running Brown and Tony Greenwood. 'Variety with promise,' I said.

Monday 31st October
I wind up vote of censure on Government's Budget and Housing policy. A very great Parliamentary success, one of my best ever.

It went all the better because Morrison, moving the vote of censure, had been almost inconceivably bad. Took seventy minutes, made no points, delivered no punch, and got our people talking and going out. It was an utterly pathetic performance.

Attention now focused on the Party leadership. When would Attlee decide to retire? This question dominated Party Conference. For the third successive year, Dalton did not attend, using a recently fractured ankle as an excuse; but he listened eagerly to Conference gossip afterwards.

End of October
At the Margate Conference ... it was thought that Herbert Morrison had made something of a comeback. And that Hugh had also done well, declaring himself socialist in warmer fashion than the Bevanite propaganda had prepared delegates' minds for. Bevan, on the other hand, though he had afterwards made two good speeches, one mild and one clever, had begun with a wild outburst at the 'private' session, full of hate against 'Trade Union bosses', and had had a shatteringly adverse vote for Treasurer.

I said, hearing all this, the Leader isn't elected by the Conference, or even by the Trade Union bosses, but by the M.P.s, and I forecast that, when we got back to Westminster, especially with an autumn Budget coming, Hugh would go ahead and Morrison lose ground and that Bevan was now quite out of the hunt, though I heard that Bevanites might vote for Morrison to try to keep Hugh out ......

Meanwhile Attlee shows no clear sign of going. But it is becoming embarrassing that this uncertainty should continue. It is constantly discussed in the Press. (They even reported *me*, quite accurately, as saying to the Oxford University Labour Club in Margate week that, if Attlee went, we must have a younger man, not a caretaker Leader, approaching seventy years of age.) Now Shinwell writes to the *Star* attacking Chris Mayhew for writing that tide is now with Hugh, attacking 'old *school tie*', but praising old *men*. And he speaks in the same sense to his constituents. This won't help Morrison.

Thursday 3rd November[1]
I have a long talk on all this with George Brown. He is Chairman of Trade Union Group. Ness Edwards, he says, is for going to Clem, and he agrees. I warn Brown to be careful, and not upset the Group as a whole by precipitate action by a few members of the Group's Executive.

Brown says that he has now, since Margate, definitely become a Gaitskellite. He says that, especially after Morrison's shocking show on vote of censure last Monday, he doesn't think he'd get 10 votes – apart from possible tactical Bevanite support. He says that, since Monday, he had told Morrison this, and advised him not to contest the leadership now, but to stay on as Deputy, and be magnanimous to Hugh. This would be much easier, Brown says he told Morrison, than to be beaten for Leader and then consent to stay on as Deputy. And Brown says he pointed out, if Morrison ceased to be Deputy, he would be off the Parliamentary Committee *and* the National E.C. If, however, he stayed on as No. 2, he might take charge of organisation at Transport House – 'none of us want Wilson,' Brown added. I am much more doubtful of this, but don't comment.

Brown said Morrison had taken all this advice very ill, and had complained of being deserted by his friends. Gordon Walker, with whom Brown had once been very close, but less lately, and who had till now been an extreme Morrisonite, now, Brown says, shares his view that Morrison would be hopelessly beaten if he ran for the leadership. Brown hopes, following a recent talk with Gordon Walker, that the latter would also tell Morrison this. And Charlie Pannell, a very devoted Gaitskellite, who is Secretary of the Trade Union Group, said to me in the Tea Room, after last Monday's fiasco, that Morrison ought to be 'sealing up the No. 2 position', which means the same thing.

---

1 Much of this entry is labelled 'End of October 1955', while following in a continuous narrative from material headed '3rd November 1955'.

And now, says Brown tonight (3rd November), Morrison made an awful mess of Burgess and Maclean at tonight's Party Meeting,[1] and seems likely to make another Parliamentary fiasco next Monday ... when there is to be a House of Commons debate on all this on adjournment. He added that Morrison and Bevan were seen to be together in the Smoke Room tonight, having a drink (for which, he thinks, Bevan paid! Donnelly next morning on the phone confirmed this!).

My conclusion, so far, is that, barring something unforeseen, Hugh has the leadership in the bag, if it comes loose in the next few months.

Brown and I then spoke of deputy leadership, if Morrison didn't keep it. Brown hoped Hugh wasn't too set on Robens. Brown wasn't sure that Robens would grow. I said I thought Hugh would quite welcome Jim Griffiths, and so would I. No. 2 to Hugh must be a Trade Unionist, and to keep *this* a bit open would do no harm.

Attlee announced his retirement as Leader of the Labour Party on 7th December 1955. There were three candidates for the succession: Aneurin Bevan, Hugh Gaitskell and Herbert Morrison. In the previous contest in 1935, Dalton had led the campaign for Morrison; now he performed the same role for Morrison's younger rival, and his own personal friend, Gaitskell. When the votes were counted on 14th December, Gaitskell won on the first ballot by 157 to Bevan's 70, with a humiliating 40 for Morrison. Morrison rejected the consolation prize of Deputy, resigned his post, and effectively ended his career as a leading politician. Of the older generation of leaders, only Griffiths now remained.

Thursday 2nd February 1956
When the House resumed after the Christmas recess, there seemed to be a much more relaxed and friendly atmosphere in the Parliamentary Party. The position of the leadership had been settled. The Tories had been in trouble.

The deputy leadership vote was announced at a Party Meeting this evening. Griffiths 141, Bevan 111, majority 30. ... The result was received very quietly. Griffiths made a perfect little short speech. He

1 Herbert Morrison had been Foreign Secretary in May 1951 when the two Foreign Office spies, Guy Burgess and Donald Maclean, defected to the Soviet Union. The affair was topical again in the autumn of 1955 because of an official report (debated in the House on 25th September) and because of the revelations of Vladimir Petrov, which suggested the existence of a Third Man.

had lived all his life in the Movement. He would co-operate loyally with our new Leader, etc. Bevan, who was sitting on the platform with a most ugly, controlled, angry face, when asked by Hugh whether he would like to say anything, made a contemptuous, scowling gesture of refusal, seen by all, and remained seated. (There'll soon be more trouble, I thought, and so sure enough there was when he spoke two days later at Manchester.)[1] Lucky I stopped, or helped to stop, Robens from running for Deputy.[2]

I feel a little like a Creator who rested and beheld his handiwork after much hard labour and saw that it was good. Vacancies due to Attlee's and Morrison's departure from Shadow Cabinet filled by Tom Fraser and Kenneth Younger. Hugh Gaitskell Leader, Jim Griffiths, wonderfully loyal, Deputy and the other younger people on the Shadow Cabinet, of which the average age is now fifty-two – younger than that of Tory Cabinet.

Tonight at Party Meeting I saw in various parts of the floor Shinwell, Ede and Morrison – the latter making his first appearance since before Xmas. I am the only one of these veterans, I think, who [is] serene and happy.

The Bevan mystique is still a danger. Will Stones,[3] new M.P. for Consett, told me that he had voted for Hugh for Leader, because he thought he would appeal to the widest range of electors, but would vote for Bevan as Deputy. 'After all,' he said, 'his roots are in the working class.' (But Jim's, thought I, are much deeper and firmer. Bevan's have been shaken and loosened by the strong winds of social adulation, flattery of middle-class advisers, and by a disordered and malevolent egoism.)

End of February
Operation Avalanche (make this a chapter heading in Vol. III)[4] has gone damned well. Jolly good! I was the small stone which deliberately started it, and all the rest followed. Our younger people now must play themselves in, and get used to the light.

---

1 'two days later': although most of the entry is written as though on 2nd February, this sentence seems to refer to Bevan's speech at a *Tribune* meeting in Manchester on 4th February.
2 Lord Robens confirms that a letter from Dalton, advising him that Griffiths would probably win anyway, influenced him against standing for the deputy leadership (interview).
3 William Stones (1904–69). Labour M.P. for Consett 1955–66.
4 See *High Tide and After*, Chapter XLIV.

Thursday 1st March

I am very happy at the outstanding success of George Brown in Defence Debate. I've never heard him better. Grip and zip and self-confidence, though keyed up.

Friday 2nd March

I train for the North with Ernest Popplewell[1] and Dai Jones. I say how pleased I am.

They say how sad it is about Shinwell and Morrison. Shinwell now won't speak to any of them. He won't speak, says Popplewell, to any of the collier boys, and he hasn't spoken to Popplewell since they had that row in the Tea Room when Shinwell was proposing to carry on for one year with Morrison as Leader, in succession to Attlee. Jones confesses that he was approached to support idea that Hugh and Bevan should both stand aside to let Morrison have an unopposed return for Leader.[2] He agreed, but had no idea that anything would be published. Nor was it put to Hugh; Shinwell, they say, hates Hugh's guts, because once he was his Under-Secretary. I say it's very sad and very wrong, that these old men should be so selfish, so unaware of the ticking of the clock, and so unhappy. I'm very happy. I want to see young people coming on. This is an Eternal Movement. If *I* can do it, why can't *they*?

I know I can't make such a good speech now, as ten years ago. Why don't *they* know it? And Morrison's speeches were catastrophic lately. Why deny the obvious that, after about sixty or sixty-five, we're all 'over the hill, brother, over the hill'.

Though now Leader, Gaitskell did not retire as Party Treasurer until the autumn of 1956. In the contest to replace him, Bevan beat Brown by 3,029,000 votes to 2,755,000. This result temporarily mollified the Labour Left. Meanwhile, a new international crisis provided Gaitskell's first serious test. In

---

1 Ernest Popplewell, later Baron (1899–1977). Labour M.P. for Newcastle upon Tyne West 1945–66.
2 On 9th December, two days after Attlee had announced his retirement, Bevan received a letter from ten Labour M.P.s asking him to withdraw and to allow Morrison to be returned unopposed. Bevan (who had nothing to lose) issued a statement saying that he would stand down if Gaitskell did so as well. Gaitskell declined. D. T. Jones was one of the signatories of the letter, of which Shinwell was an instigator. (See B. Donoughue and G. W. Jones, *Herbert Morrison: Portrait of a Politician*, Weidenfeld & Nicolson, London, 1973, pp. 539–40.)

July, Colonel Nasser, the new Egyptian President, had announced the nationalisation of the Suez Canal Company. Gaitskell joined Eden in denouncing this as an act of aggression, and even compared Nasser to Hitler. Some Labour Party members, however, took a different view, and by the time of Party Conference in Blackpool, support for Nasser among the rank and file had become strong. Gaitskell managed to rally Conference without deserting his own position by arguing for economic, as opposed to military, action against Egypt. In the meantime, the Prime Minister had secretly agreed to a French proposal for a joint intervention in the event of an Israeli-Egyptian war.

Saturday 27th October

This first long session of the Parliament elected in 1955 ends next week. Hugh is very firmly established as Leader, most firmly of all with the Parliamentary Party, but more and more firmly in the Party in the country. He had, it seems, a great success at the recent Annual Conference at Blackpool. Bevan is terribly full of himself after beating George Brown for Treasurer. At first it was thought that he would challenge either Hugh for Leader or Griffiths for Deputy Leader at the end of this session. But this now seems unlikely. Griffiths is thought by some to be ageing quickly, and becoming rather ridiculous and ineffective. But I think this is exaggerated. He is *very* loyal and co-operative and we can't have two intellectuals, Hugh and Bevan, as Leader and Deputy.

Alternatively, Bevan may demand the Shadow Foreign Office, in place of Alf Robens. Hugh, with whom I talked some days ago, is inclined to keep Bevan on for at least another session. He *may* improve. The trouble, I'm afraid, is that he isn't really clever enough. Hugh is inclined to make as few changes as possible in the Shadow Government allocations.

There is no limit to Bevan's ambition, nor ever will be, nor, therefore, to his potential bad faith and jealousy. His megalomania is still almost unbelievable. The Chief Whip, Herbert Bowden,[1] told Hugh that, ten months ago, when Hugh had just beaten Bevan (and Morrison) for the leadership, Bevan said to him, 'There ought to be no *election* to the deputy leadership. Gaitskell should *appoint* me as Deputy Leader. I am the leader of the Party in the country.'

1 H. W. Bowden, later Baron Aylestone (b. 1905). Opposition Chief Whip 1955–64. Labour M.P. for Leicester South-West 1950–67; Leicester South 1945–50. Junior government whip 1949–51. Lord President and Leader of the House 1964–6. Secretary of State for Commonwealth Affairs 1966–7.

This year the National Executive must produce a Report on Ownership of Industry. It will be interesting to see what line, when forced down to detail, Bevan and the other Old Believers take.

Tony's *Future of Socialism* is selling well, and has had some good reviews. It may yet make trouble for him at a Selection Conference, but it is certainly building up his reputation in many different circles. He is very happy and cheerful – he dined with me last week – and is now pretty well off – Co-op, broadcasting and writing.

Friday 2nd November

A talk at dawn with Alf Robens in the Harcourt Room. He is a very nice man, an admirable colleague and very loyal to Hugh. He is very conscious that he has been a failure as Shadow Foreign Secretary and his poor press has got him down a bit. He has also, he says, had a lot of domestic troubles ... and this has got him down further.

He says he told Hugh two or three weeks ago that he knew he hadn't been a success, and was quite prepared, without any sense of grievance, to change to some other Shadow Department, if Hugh wished.

We spoke of Bevan. Robens thought that he would never be loyal to Hugh or content until *he* was No. 1. He recalled the famous story of Nye's question 'Where is the Power?' often told by himself and published in his *In Place of Fear*. He would play on Hugh's nerves, always overbid (e.g. on nationalisation programme). Hugh, Robens said, had such a heavy job anyhow that he should have peace and support in his inner circle. Bevan would never let him have this.

Robens was pessimistic about the possibilities of keeping Bevan out of second place in the Party. If he came out top of the poll for Shadow Cabinet, he would claim Shadow Foreign Office. He was already No. 2 in National Executive as Treasurer. I said I did not accept this, nor need others.

International events dominated British politics at the end of October and in early November 1956. In Hungary, opposition to the Communist regime had escalated into a popular rising. A succession of ministerial changes culminated in the coalition government of Imre Nagy, formed on 31st October. This announced Hungary's withdrawal from the Warsaw Pact. The Soviet Union responded by moving troops into Hungary and encircling strategic centres. Early on 4th November the Russians launched an attack which soon succeeded in crushing all opposition.

Meanwhile Western attention had been diverted by an escalation of the

Middle East crisis. On 29th October, Israeli troops invaded the Sinai in a 'pre-emptive' attack on the Egyptians. The following day, Eden told the House of Commons of an Anglo-French ultimatum: force would be used to restore peace to the Canal area unless an immediate cease-fire was followed by the withdrawal of troops on both sides to a distance of ten miles from the Canal. Nasser did not respond to this threat, and on 31st October French and British bombers began an assault on Egyptian military targets, despite American pressure against such action.

On 1st November, the Labour Opposition tabled a strongly worded motion of censure. On 2nd November, the United Nations Assembly called on Britain, France and Israel to halt their attack at once. At first, the British and French governments ignored their critics, and on 5th and 6th November an Anglo-French force invaded Egypt by air and sea at Port Said. By this time, however, the strength of international (and especially American) opposition had had its effect. On 5th November, the United Nations Secretary-General, Dag Hammarskjöld, persuaded the British and French to accept a cease-fire which would be policed by a United Nations Emergency Force. On the evening of 6th November, Eden announced an abrupt end to the allied operation.

Saturday 3rd November
House of Commons meets at noon, for three hours, and adjourns in uproar. Loud booing, and gestures at Eden, cries of 'Resign', 'Go' and 'Get out'.

Thus ends a tumultuous week. It began on Monday with Israeli crossing into Egypt and [was] followed by swift and complete Israeli victory in Sinai, rout of Egyptian Army and capture of large quantities of arms recently supplied by Russians and Czechs.

The myth of Egypt as a military power and a 'leader' of Arab world is smashed for ever. All this is wonderful! Israel will now be more secure than at any time since 1948. And of the other Arab states, none moved against Israel, in spite of all their Arab Leagues and Alliances. If they do now, Israel will be able to deal with them promptly and easily, with Egypt out already. Nor I think will either Suez or the Gulf of Akaba be blockaded against Israel any more.

But it is nauseating to find Tories *now* putting Israel's case against Egypt, when they ignored it before, when stated by many of us. So far, very good and I drink the health of the Israeli armed forces – very brave, dedicated and efficient.

But nothing else is good. Our Anglo-French armed attack on Egypt and declared intention to occupy Canal Zone 'temporarily', is followed

681

by our two countries being condemned by Security Council – whereat we both used the veto for the first time – and by General Assembly by 64 to 5 (our two selves, Israel and the Anzacs). And then we refuse even the recommendation, backed by this majority, for a Cease Fire. Eden and Selwyn Lloyd[1] (a miserable third rate, if ever there was one) both repeated today that our 'police operation' must be completed, in order to keep combatants (Israel and Egypt) apart, and 'to stop the war' between them. But they are apart already and the war has stopped, with an overwhelming Israeli victory.

Meanwhile the Canal is blocked by several blockships.

There is great feeling against H.M.G.'s policy, not only in the House of Commons, but in wide circles outside. I was away on Tuesday, Wednesday and most of Thursday in my constituency, where the Queen Mother[2] visited Bowes Museum to celebrate take-over by County Council. All a great success. While I'm away there are very angry scenes in the House; once the sitting was suspended for ½ hour owing to grave disorder. Our vote of censure on Thursday was defeated by 69. Only Stanley Evans deliberately abstained on our side, and none, I think, on theirs. But there are rumours of a number of ministers most unhappy and inclined to resign – Nutting, Boyle,[3] and in Cabinet, Macleod[4] and H. Amory.[5] Of private members on their side many are very ill at ease. David Price,[6] Desmond tells me, is practically decided to come out into the open. He has been very troubled for a week. At first he thought of asking for the whip to be withdrawn and perhaps of fighting a by-election as an Independent. If he did, he'd be beaten in a △ fight, and we'd win Eastleigh. ...

Hugh has done splendidly (and this is the general view of the Party) all this week. He feels clearly the moral and tactical danger to U.K. –

---

1 Selwyn Lloyd, q.v., Foreign Secretary 1955–60.

2 Queen Elizabeth, née Lady Elizabeth Bowes-Lyon (b. 1900).

3 Sir Edward Boyle, 3rd Bart, later Baron (1923–81). Economic Secretary to the Treasury 1955–6, when he resigned over Suez. Conservative M.P. for Handsworth November 1950–70. Junior minister 1954–5, 1957–9. Financial Secretary to the Treasury 1959–62. Minister of Education 1962–4. Vice-Chancellor of Leeds University 1970–81.

4 Iain Macleod (1913–70). Minister of Labour and National Service 1955–9. Conservative M.P. for Enfield West 1950–70. Minister of Health 1952–5; Colonial Secretary 1959–61; Chancellor of the Duchy of Lancaster and Leader of the House 1961–3. Chancellor of the Exchequer 1970.

5 Derick Heathcoat Amory, later 1st Viscount (1899–1981). Minister of Agriculture, Fisheries and Food 1954–8. Conservative M.P. for Tiverton 1945–60. Minister of Pensions 1951–3; Minister of State at the Board of Trade 1953–4. Chancellor of the Exchequer 1958–60.

6 D. E. C. Price, later Sir David (b. 1924). Conservative M.P. for Eastleigh since 1955. Junior minister 1962–4, 1970–72.

the split in the Commonwealth, the crack in the Anglo-American Alliance and the break in – and away from – the U.N. When again can it be strong and respected! Will not every potential aggressor feel able to repudiate its decisions with impunity?

And *today* the Security Council is considering a complaint on behalf of Hungary against a 'police operation' by Soviet Russia. *They* can cite our precedent!

The Party is organising a quick, widespread campaign of meetings. I have agreed to speak at Burton next Tuesday (a marginal constituency) and Wandsworth on the following Sunday. Meetings will be live again.

End 1956

It is a year now since Hugh became Leader. He is, I think, well dug in with our own Party. He has incurred a fierce hatred, so fierce as to surprise me, among the Tories, arising out of his attitude on Suez. 'Traitor Gaitskell', they call him. And the Tory build-up of Bevan, as a much more patriotic and national figure, has been most assiduously pursued. I can't find any evidence of a weakening of Hugh's support within the Party. Indeed Tory hatred is likely to strengthen it – and Bevan may suffer if he's too ardently portrayed by the enemy as a national saviour. ...

Meanwhile Hugh has made Bevan Shadow Foreign Secretary. This has, on the whole, been welcome, or at least recognised as inevitable, in view of Alf Robens's failure to shine in this role. He has been the persistent perfect gentleman, putting himself entirely in Hugh's hands and saying he won't resent it in any way if Hugh wants to shift him. Hugh has given him Labour plus all Fuel and Power – a pretty important assignment – and would like him built up in this new role.

After 1956, entries in Dalton's diary became less frequent, partly because his interest in current politics waned. Two things preoccupied him in 1957: his own impending retirement, and the publication in April of the second volume of his memoirs, *The Fateful Years*, which enraged Morrison and other senior colleagues, much to the author's delight.

In October 1957, Dalton told the General Management Committee of the Bishop Auckland Constituency Labour Party that he would not stand again as their candidate.

Sunday 17th February 1957

I am committed to writing an obit for Winston for the *New Statesman*, and for Attlee for the B.B.C. It looks as though the former, much the most difficult, will be needed very soon. It would be bad if both were needed on the same day, and neither written.

...

In our party politics we've won North Lewisham on a minority vote; our Party seems united still; Nye very indolent, sometimes sits in corner of Smoke Room drinking with third raters, and missing Party Meetings and even a Shadow Cabinet.

On 19th July, Dalton travelled by train to Durham with Hugh Gaitskell for the Miners' Gala.

Sunday 21st July

The Gala being over and the guests departed, I saw Sam Watson at his house and stayed for an excellent cold lunch, being the remains of the feast of the night before. ...

I told him that I should not stand again. I expected, from what Hugh told me, some resistance to this. But there was none, he having evidently thought the matter over in the interval, and nodding his head understandingly when I explained that on questions of youth and age I took a most obstinate and doctrinaire position. His chief reaction was that it was indispensable to find a suitable and able young man as my successor. 'With a bad candidate', he said, 'that seat might easily be lost.' I said I did not think it was quite as bad as that, but was most anxious that my successor should be young, able and acceptable; also that he should be loyal to Hugh, and not any sort of Bevanite. I said that I would have been very happy to be succeeded by a young miner, but that I was afraid that there was no one even remotely suitable. ... I said that I would also be quite happy if there was a young Trade Unionist from some other Union who could make the grade, but that here again, I did not think that any local personality would do. I said that, at this stage, I had no name to suggest, but that we should speak of this again later when we had both had time to look around. We joked about Shinwell. Watson said he hoped that he would follow my example but was not quite sure whether he would do so willingly. I said I had heard from his constituency and that I thought he might find it difficult to be re-adopted. I said that I should not think of making any public announcement until after the Labour Party Conference, or otherwise some poor Bishop Auckland delegate would be surrounded like a honeypot by bees. ...

When I related all this to Ruth, she said, quite truly, that one reason why there was such a lack of good young local possibles, was the heavy emigration of all the best talent in the area during the 1920s and 1930s. This is certainly true.

The Campaign for Nuclear Disarmament was founded in January 1958, with Canon John Collins as Chairman and Bertrand Russell as President. The first of a series of Aldermaston Marches, in protest at Britain's possession of nuclear weapons, took place the same year over the Easter weekend.

Gaitskell's attitude towards the new movement was cool. He called for a suspension of British nuclear tests and the removal of Thor missile bases, but defended the independent nuclear deterrent and British membership of N.A.T.O. Bevan was also opposed to unilateralism. At the 1957 Conference, he accused supporters of the campaign of suffering from an 'emotional spasm', and declared that he was not prepared to 'go naked into the conference chamber', without the nuclear deterrent. By backing official Party policy in this way, Bevan found himself at odds with many of his old friends and allies on the Labour Left.

Wednesday 2nd April 1958
Party Meeting in Westminster Hall to *discuss* joint declaration by the National Executive and the T.U.C. on 'Disarmament and Nuclear War'. The P.L.P. couldn't approve or disapprove this declaration, which, coming from the top level, bound them.

Bevan introduced it, quite well, without going into detail, but with a good background of tactics. And Brown wound up, when everyone was a bit satiated, with some remarks on different types of weapons. Most speakers gave the declaration general support, though there was a lot of argument to and fro, by 'experts', Wigg, Strachey, Paget, etc.

I spoke, having forewarned Hugh, towards the end. I had a great success, loudly cheered both in mid career and at the finish. He was very pleased and shook my hand afterwards. I said, 'Isn't it better to do it only occasionally, but then rather well?'

I complimented Bevan on his exposition, and said I was delighted with his statement that the leaders were now more united than they had ever been. I said that they were now giving a good lead to the rank and file. 'Let us now', I said, 'hold fast to the great simplicities, and not get bogged down in a mass of debatable detail, on which all the experts differed. ...'

Unilateral disarmament, in terms of whatever were the most formidable armaments of the day, had never been official Labour Party policy. It had never been approved at any Labour Party Annual Conference, or at any T.U.C. Not even at any meeting of the P.L.P. But, as Bevan had said, the Tory press gives much more publicity to our disagreements than to our agreements. And there was a danger that our Unilateral Nuclear Disarmers, with their march to Aldermaston, etc., would get much publicity and create the impression that they spoke for the Labour Party. This policy would make no mass appeal to the electors. It might appeal to small groups of excited people, mostly middle class. But, speaking of those I know best, you would never get it accepted by the Durham Miners (cheers) nor by any Workmen's Club that I had ever been in, and I had been in a good many (laughter and cheers). Lansbury did a lot of harm to the Labour Party in the thirties, for all his fine qualities. He helped to create the impression that the Labour Party was not to be trusted with responsibility for Defence. That impression was very widespread. It prevented us from winning power in the thirties. Had we done so, we might have stopped the Second World War (cheers). That might happen again. Finally, don't think a world of 'conventional weapons' would be a peaceful paradise. We must have General Disarmament to cover them all.

Thursday 3rd to Monday 14th April

EASTER RECESS

I am at West Leaze, and Ruth from 31st March to 11th April in Paris and in Belgium.

At West Leaze it is tiresomely cold. I write a little of Vol. III ... Tony [Crosland] stays one night here, and Mike [Williams Thompson] two nights; my two most regular visitors in the last few years. Both very satisfactory, in their different ways.

I am troubled about George Brown. Historically, he has been very much one of my protégés, and I have tried to help him as recently as the last Shadow Cabinet election, when I canvassed for him because I thought he would have a small and discrediting vote, even though he retained his seat.

But I am not at all sure whether he is loyal to our present Leader, or whether he is not plotting for some new combination. One must never forget that most of the stories of dissensions and personal rivalries in the Labour Party in the enemy press are primarily designed to make trouble, and to shake morale in our own ranks. But sometimes these stories have grains of truth.

One story, in a Sunday paper this recess, says that Brown is planning with Bevan, that the latter should become Deputy Leader, in place of Jim Griffiths, and thus not be confined to Foreign Affairs, but have 'a roving commission'. But this would be intolerable for Hugh – two Kings in Babylon. Nor do I think it would have much support, *unless Griffiths voluntarily retired.* This must be prevented and I'll do my share.

Next autumn we shall be entering, probably, the last session of this Parliament. It would be a very great mistake to change the leadership pattern so late in the Parliament. The story went on to suggest that Brown thought that *he* should succeed Bevan as Shadow Foreign Secretary, when Bevan became Deputy Leader. But this I find most unlikely.

The root of this particular malaise is that Brown is still most sensitively class conscious. He finds it difficult to be a really good comrade with an 'intellectual', defined as a person who has been at a Public School and University. (I hope I may exempt myself from this disqualification in view of our past relationship. But he said some very silly things to me after reading my *Fateful Years*, in which I gave him, I thought, a pretty good lift, particularly for his speech in favour of expelling Cripps in 1939. He said that he and Sophie[1] both agreed, reading my book, that all my real intimacies and friendships were with 'intellectuals', who knew how to play up to me, and not with Trade Unionists. I was only interested in University types, e.g. Jay and Mayhew. I nearly made a list of references to disprove this, but couldn't be bothered.) Brown also told me, in the last few months, that he now finds it much easier to discuss things with Bevan than with Hugh, and that he finds himself much more often in agreement with Bevan than he used to do.

Frank Cousins[2] is also a relevant figure. Brown says that Cousins doesn't like Hugh, though the latter had taken a lot of trouble socially with Cousins. ...

George Brown is obviously liable to be influenced by Cousins, as General Secretary of Transport and General Workers' Union, though on question of Defence, and some other political issues, Brown wouldn't accept Cousins's views, e.g. on H-bombs.

Brown is also disappointed that, though he's Chairman of Parlia-

---

1 Sophie Brown, née Levene. The Browns married in 1937.
2 Frank Cousins (1904–86). General Secretary of the Transport and General Workers' Union 1956–69, apart from a period (1964–6) when he was Minister of Technology. Labour M.P. 1965–6. Married to Annie, née Judd.

mentary Trade Union Group, as well as Shadow Defence Minister, Cousins won't give him any official position in his Union's political policy-making set up. Before Cousins became General Secretary, he used to tell Brown that he *ought* to have such a position. Now that Cousins has become General Secretary, he's changed his mind. He doesn't want a rival.

Just before Christmas, 1957, I had a very unsatisfactory experience with Brown. He and I (and Sophie) spent a week-end at the Walstons. The party should have included Fred Peart, on my suggestion, and Will Carron[1] and other T.U. leaders, on Brown's suggestion. But none of these came.

Brown finally brought Sophie, but he told me that *she* had made a scene the day before. She didn't want to come, the Walstons were not the sort of people she wanted to be with, not what she meant by socialism, etc. But Brown was terribly class conscious and touchy. I noted that he was not getting better in these respects, though perhaps still least bad with me. But he was very tiresome in conversation. (To Catherine [Walston] alone he said, 'I'm only a lorry driver's son; not rich like you.' Later I heard that he had been having difficulties about money – in spite of increase in M.P.s' salaries. Neither of his two daughters are earning.)

He has an obsession with XYZ. He once came as a guest to talk about agriculture, and Richard Kahn, then still a member, had attacked him very rudely and, I daresay, destructively. I wasn't there that night.

'Not a single Trade Unionist belongs to it,' he said. I said that not many took much interest in the sort of subjects we discussed, e.g. liquidity ratios, exchange control within the sterling area, etc. To which he replied, 'You ask Charlie Pannell and Bob Mellish to join and you'll see.' I said that neither of these, though both were good friends of mine, had shown the faintest sign of interest in such matters, either by speaking of them in the House, or ever attending meetings of the Economic and Financial Group of Labour M.P.s when such questions were discussed.

Finally, after I had again tediously explained, in outline, about XYZ he [said], 'I don't mind your dining together, if you don't talk too much about it.' I asked who talked. He said Jay and Diamond, and added that this was a new development. I spoke to both Jay and Diamond, who denied the accusation!

Further complaint about Hugh not seeing enough of the Party. I said he and the Chief Whip visited all (geographical) Whips' groups

---

1 William Carron, later Baron (1902–69). President of the Amalgamated Engineering Union 1956–67.

in turn, and there could be discussions and questions. He thought these visits were 'too formal'. I disagreed. He said Hugh should sometimes go to the Tea Room. I said this would mean that he would be monopolised by one or two. I preferred visits to the groups. Then he and Sophie said Hugh and Dora should give a series of tea parties, for Labour M.P.s *and wives*! 'And wives! Good God!' I cried, in a real angry outburst. What else do they [think] a Party Leader has to do.

All this was tiresome enough, and this weekend left a bad taste in my mouth. Much of the above was in the presence of strangers to the Labour Party.

There was also before Xmas a burst of anti-Gaitskell stuff in the Sunday press (both the cheap and dear varieties). *Observer*, *Sunday Times* and *Sunday Express* (Crossbencher in on this).

'Among Trade Unionists a vast distaste for intellectuals.' A middle-class woman supporter of the Party asked me, 'Is it true?' I said, 'The enemy press prints stuff like this, in order that people like you shall ask that question of people like me.'

Malicious trivialities. 'Who has Leader's private telephone number?' (wisely not in book, as mine ever since 1924!) 'Who calls in regularly on a Sunday morning, on the heights of Hampstead, for a very dry sherry?' 'The wealthy and personable Jack Diamond', greeted much more warmly by the Leader than recent Trade Union victors at by-elections. The Leader, entering the dining room, sits by Dingle Foot and Megan [Lloyd George], and 'spurns' the tables where Trade Unionists sit.

I half suspect George Brown of giving some of this 'background gossip' to the press. Hugh's 'Iago'? But Jim Callaghan says it's Wigg, most disloyal in talks to the press and to Tory M.P.s about us.

Wednesday 18th June
Good gossip with Hugh whom I had not seen since before Whitsun. An extra week's Parliamentary recess at Whitsun, making just over a fortnight, is very agreeable.

Hugh seems happy and fit and full of common sense and good judgment; particularly happy at the rapid flowering of Julia,[1] now nineteen, living in Rome with a family.

Hence to education. I praise the Party's latest Policy Pamphlet on this subject. Best of the series so far. Well written – exceptionally well for such a document. Emphasises the important obvious, with clarity and an occasional real ray of fresh sunlight. Tawney was on the

1 Julia Gaitskell, later Mrs McNeal (b. 1939). The Gaitskells' elder daughter.

working party, chaired by Michael Stewart. He can still help others to write.

I am particularly glad that they propose to do nothing about Public Schools in the next five years. This avoids a political blunder of the first magnitude, the rousing of a most violent opposition among Old Boys, worse than 'lower than vermin'. This would have been the fiercest resistance to any Labour proposal since 1945, would have been very skilfully conducted, and would have distracted attention from many other much more important educational (and other) problems, which we must solve first. And, in the last resort, there would have been a new Eton in Canada or Northern France, and a new Winchester in Eire! Flemingism[1] maybe would cost too much.

Hugh isn't sure yet who should be Minister of Education. Not very keen on Stewart, who has no children. I am for Jay – a more plausible figure among teachers, children and local authorities than among businessmen (as President of the Board of Trade). I've said this to Hugh before, but don't repeat it today. But I shall return to it, particularly as I like the Education Report very much, and should like to see a big push in Education as our biggest home front effort next time.

Bevan was with Hugh at the International, and at the British Embassy in Brussels. This relationship is fascinating. Hugh is the stronger character, as well as much the best brain. When the two are together, he can prevent Bevan from running wild, though he makes concessions, not of great importance, to his excitable moods. When Bevan is on his own, he is inclined to run out of control, e.g. in his first article in *Tribune* attacking de Gaulle.[2] This habit of writing regular articles, said Hugh, is a great nuisance, and very undesirable in a future Foreign Secretary.

Bevan enjoyed himself in our Brussels Embassy, where George Labouchere,[3] our Ambassador, is very keen on modern art. Bevan when relaxed, and off political shop, and without Jennie, can be very charming and amusing. To avoid what happened in our Washington Embassy, where Bevan gave no tips and didn't write a roofer, Hugh

---

1 In 1944 the Fleming Report (commissioned by the then President of the Board of Education, R. A. Butler) recommended that public schools should allocate a quarter of their places to scholarship pupils from the state sector. The proposal was never implemented.
2 General Charles de Gaulle (1890–1970). French Prime Minister 1944–6, 1958–9. President 1959–69. He took office as premier on 2nd June.
3 Sir George Labouchere (b. 1905). Ambassador to Belgium 1955–60. Married to Rachel, née Hamilton-Russell.

asked, at Brussels Embassy, what tipping scale was, and paid for Bevan as well, informing him. And he hinted at the roofer, Lady Labouchere having pleased Bevan.

He also discussed with Bevan the question of evening dress. They had quite a talk about this. It would be natural to wear a dinner jacket to dine at the Embassy, and Hugh did. Bevan didn't. Hugh said to Bevan that he would really have to face appearing in evening dress soon. Bevan said that he liked to be well dressed. He was not one of those who deliberately put on old clothes in order to meet his constituents, or to address a meeting of unemployed men. (This, I said to Hugh, is a repetition of what Jennie Lee wrote in last week's *Tribune*.) But, said Bevan, he objected to being told by other people what to wear, and he objected to 'uniform'. Hugh suggested that he might like to wear a purple velvet smoking jacket with a black tie in the evening. Bevan seemed rather taken with this idea, but finally said that he realised that, if he was Foreign Secretary, he would have to conform to wearing evening dress.

Hugh said that Bevan's relations with Michael Foot were now very bad, and that Foot was trying to stir up Beaverbrook to attack Bevan. He also said that Foot still had a cottage on Beaverbrook's Cherkeley estate, and saw a good deal of the old man. He had heard from an American journalist that Foot was down there last weekend. I said that I noticed references to Bevan in the *Express* (both *Sunday* and *Daily*) which suggested that Bevan was no longer on the White List.

Crossbencher recently had a paragraph, estimating the Bevan family income at £11,600 p.a. And the *Daily Express* reported that he and Jennie were godparents to children of '44-year-old' Howard Samuel 'wealthy property-owner ... and director of the Socialist magazine *Tribune*', now being sued for divorce by 'his 34-year-old artist wife, Miss Jane Lane'.[1]

Finally Hugh and I spoke of Cousins, who, in effect, is surrendering after seven week London bus strike.[2] Hugh says that all General

---

1 Howard Samuel (1914–61). Property magnate. With Jack Hylton, Samuel was mainly responsible for financing *Tribune* in the 1950s, and was one of the three directors of the paper (with Michael Foot and Jennie Lee). Samuel and his wife divorced, but remarried each other in 1959.
2 'seven week London bus strike': in May and June a strike of busmen paralysed passenger transport in London. Forty-nine thousand workers were involved. The issues were a wage claim, the resistance of the Government to a fare increase, and the refusal of the workers to accept a reduction in services. The strike ended on 20th June.

Council of T.U.C. now either hate or despise Cousins so much that the danger is that they will move too much to the right. Ted Hill,[1] good old boilermakers' leader, very rough and crude, spoke contemptuously to Hugh of Cousins's failure to lead, trailing his London bus negotiating committee of thirteen men round with him everywhere.

Hugh and I agreed that there is nothing seriously wrong with the internal state of the Party. Politics aren't exciting, to most people, now, and you can't change that at present. After seven years in Opposition it's not surprising that many M.P.s are bored and don't attend debates. All this would change if we won the election and, hard though the Tory press tries to prove the contrary, all the indications are that, unless we make bloody fools of ourselves, we shall win it easily.

On 25th March 1959, Dalton suffered a mild stroke. By the end of May his speech was normal, but he remained physically weak.

On 7th September Harold Macmillan, who had succeeded Eden as Prime Minister in January 1957, announced that the general election would be held on 8th October. The 1959 contest was the second election at which the Tories were able to campaign on a record of rising living standards and continued full employment. 'Life is better with the Conservatives', they claimed. 'Don't let Labour ruin it.' The Labour Party could offer no convincing answer. The Conservatives obtained their best result since the war: 365 seats and an overall majority in the House of Commons of 100.

Thursday 8th October
This morning Ruth and I voted at Aldbourne for Cave,[2] and then went by mid-morning train to London.

I had spoken for Cave at Ludgershall (3rd October), Pewsey (5th October), Swindon Town Hall (for Francis Noel-Baker)[3] and Marl-

---

1 E. J. Hill, later Baron (d. 1969). General Secretary of the United Society of Boilermakers 1948–63.
2 Wilfrid Cave (b. 1907). Labour candidate for Devizes (the constituency which contained the Daltons' house at Aldbourne) in 1945, 1950, 1955 and 1959.
3 F. E. Noel-Baker (b. 1920). Labour M.P. for Swindon 1955–68; Brentford and Chiswick 1945–50. Son of Philip Noel-Baker, q.v.

borough Town Hall (cheerful questioning and Hall half full of boys from Marlborough)[1] on 6th October and Wroughton (eve of poll) on 7th October. Meetings better attended than at last election. But *'non sum qualis eram'*. I tire much too easily and my points go over less well. At Pewsey I addressed them sitting, quite audibly, but became too tired to stand.

I had had a firm hunch for the last three days of the campaign that we were going to win – and so had Hugh himself and many of our leaders and good candidates. I just noted that the Tory–Lab gap in the *News Chronicle* Poll had not merely narrowed, but actually vanished last week, and in the last four days the *Daily Mirror*, largest circulation in the country, especially among the young, had come thundering into action, admirably set out, to move the Don't Knows our way. On polling day *News Chronicle* published a last poll, saying that the Don't Knows (so high a percentage) were coming off the fence with a majority in favour of the Tories. Nonetheless I felt reasonably hopeful, as Ruth and I settled down in the flat to hear the results. ...

From the start the results went wrong. No. 1 Billericay, containing the New Town of Basildon, recruited by good Labour votes from West and East Ham. Surely a Labour gain. But no, held by Tories with 4,000 majority. True we held the two Salford seats but then came a stream of disappointments. Battersea South, and Watford both held by Tories, and a Tory gain from Labour at Acton. And so, on and on.

Hugh conceded the election about 1 a.m. We sat up till 2.30 a.m. waiting for some of my closest friends, especially Denis Howell[2] and Jim Callaghan. Earlier Tony had only held Grimsby by *101*! After 1½ recounts. And he had expected, he had written me half way through the fight, to win by 4,500 (Younger had had 3,500 last time). Denis Howell was out by 20, after 2 recounts. This loss grieved me more than any other result. He was very much one of my Poodles, *very* shrewd (rarest of qualities in Labour Party nowadays). Very loyal, forward looking, with wide interests. ...

And Jim Callaghan was in, but by less than 1,000.

---

1 i.e. the public school.
2 D. H. Howell (b. 1923). Labour M.P. for Birmingham All Saints 1955–9; Birmingham Small Heath since 1961. Junior minister 1964–9. Minister of State at the Ministry of Housing and Local Government 1969–70; Department of the Environment 1974–9.

Friday 9th October

That night I slept little and woke with difficulty next day (Friday). ...

I got on to Dora Gaitskell. How did I feel. 'Very angry with the electors and very proud of Hugh.' I spoke to him and he said, 'Come round (to 18 Frognal Gardens)[1] on Sunday morning and I'll try to get some of the intelligent young men along.'[2] I rang Tony and told him I was sure Hugh would like *him* there.

Saturday 10th October

Roy Jenkins and Jennifer came round for a drink on Saturday. Very crushed, especially she. It is very difficult to explain. Our leadership and organisation were so much better than ever before. Hugh was expert on T.V. But Birmingham is in the depths. Apart from Roy, now that Denis Howell is out, the Labour M.P.s are sheer trash. Denis now has no job and no money, wife and two young children and buying his house. Roy had spoken to Hugh who hoped he might get Denis job as National Youth Officer at Transport House, or even successor to Carol Johnson.[3]

Sunday 11th October

Tony drove me up to 18 Frognal Gardens. At Grimsby they were astounded by the result. All had seemed going well. The canvassers were revived a bit by a 'Victory Social' on Friday night. His Tory opponent, whom he had thought unimportant, was passed off at the end as a key man in Fishing Industry.[4] This was rather obscure to me but may have been very damaging.

At 11 a.m. at 18 Frognal Gardens there were Hugh, myself, Douglas Jay, Gordon Walker, Herbert Bowden (Chief Whip), Tony, Roy and Jennifer, John Harris[5] (nice looking young man, who came late and took no part in talk; Hugh had told me that he was wonderful as an A.D.C., and he would like to get him into the House later. I must meet

1 The Gaitskells' home in Hampstead.
2 Insertion: 'built round John Harris'. J. H. Harris, later Baron (b. 1930), helped Gaitskell with his campaign in 1959, and stayed with the Party Leader as Personal Assistant and Public Relations Officer. He was Minister of State at the Home Office 1974–9.
3 C. A. Johnson (b. 1903). Secretary of the P.L.P. 1943–59. Labour M.P. for Lewisham South 1959–February 1974.
4 Crosland's Conservative opponent in Grimsby was Wilfred Pearson (b. 1908), a wholesale fish merchant and a local man.
5 See above, n. 2.

him again). They want me to contribute to *Forward* series,[1] but 'not yet' I said. Tony also said practically nothing. He was going on, he told me, to lunch with his mother, and Roy and Jennifer drove me home, and I lunched with Roy at Speranza. (One of my economies now is not to pay for other people's meals, but I broke this rule for Roy today.)

Douglas Jay started off with a great oration on the moral of the election defeat. He wanted (1) to drop 'nationalisation', (2) drop the Trade Unions, (3) drop the name 'Labour Party', and become 'Labour and Radical' or 'Labour and Progressive', or 'the People's Party' (suggested by Cole long ago), (4) drop the principle of political independence, and make agreements, even up to merger, with the Liberals. Otherwise, he said, we should never win. And he'd sacrifice a lot in order to win. I said I thought this was rather wild, pouring out the baby with the bathwater and throwing the bath after them. But we should coldly and carefully study all the evidence. Most of this went into Jay's opening article in *Forward*'s new Open Forum.[2] If it goes on like this, it will catch up and pass the circulation of *Tribune*. Others too were more cautious than Jay. Gordon Walker wanted a scientific enquiry, 'market research' by N.E.C. to find out what attracted and repelled people in certain age and occupation groups. It would be worth while paying a good price for that. He too thought the Trade Union connection might be loosened. The association, plus unofficial strikes, etc., he was sure did us much harm. Bowden was very practical, and Hugh said little in front of so many. He is, I said to Brian Abel-Smith (on 19th October), 'resolutely, but cautiously revisionist', and 'that phrase means a lot'.

Party Constitution might be revised, some new formula on public or common ownership substituted for 1918 text (Webb & Henderson before end of W.W.1). 'Common ownership of all means of production, distribution and exchange.' Party Constitution might also be changed by having National Executive elected by Unions, local parties regrouped regionally (here I said that Jim Middleton had once suggested this, and Hugh said, 'How surprisingly sensible!') and Parliamentary Party with shift of authority towards Parliamentary leadership. But any such changes will take time, and need most care-

---

1 '*Forward*': a Gaitskellite publication.
2 The 16th October issue of *Forward* contained an article by Douglas Jay arguing that Labour should drop steel nationalisation and shed its working-class image in order to win a future election. This annoyed the Labour Left, which believed that Jay's words had been inspired by Gaitskell. Although this entry is dated 11th October, it was evidently written several days later.

ful handling. Hugh, very wisely, listens more than talks to groups like
this.

Jim and Audrey Callaghan[1] to dine (at flat). Better placed than
most. He still has his Parliamentary salary, his seat on both executives,
and his police job.[2] Good! He says children of Socialists in Housing
Estates often voted Tory. One old boy in Cardiff told him that his
son had said, 'All right, Dad, Labour may suit you, but I'm voting
Conservative this time.'

Friday 16th October
I saw Hugh alone at House of Commons.

I said I thought Jay's article in *Forward*, on lines of his talk on
Sunday (11th), was rather badly timed. He replied that we couldn't
accept that Left (*Tribune*) could continually attack, and Right never
reply.

I spoke of Life Peerage for myself and said I would still like it (as
when we had spoken of it in July). But chiefly in order more easily to
keep in touch with my young friends in the Commons, i.e. to retain
membership of Westminster Club. Following our agreement in July,
I hadn't made any communication to P.M., nor had I run into him
casually. But I bet Morrison had approached him! Hugh says he
didn't know this, only that in 1955 Morrison had refused offer of a
Peerage then. I said that P.M. might approach Hugh and suggest, in
well worn formula, that he would like 'to strengthen the Labour Party
in the Lords'. Hugh said he didn't think it likely that P.M. would
approach him in near future on this. But he would get Chief Whip
(Bowden) to 'take some soundings'. There I left it.

And in the next few weeks, as I gradually begin to work out the new
rhythm of my life, and become more and more intent on finishing my
Vol. III, the attraction of a Life Peerage weakens a bit. If we'd won
the Election, and I had been a Life Peer and Minister without Portfolio, or even a Life Peer with some official standing, to help with
Government business, it would have been interesting. But now, indefinitely in Opposition, it was much less interesting, and attendance
to duties might even be something of an unwelcome tie.

But I said that, now that I *was* retired from the House of Commons,
I should no longer pretend, to myself or anyone else, that I was still a
Member. I shouldn't hang about the place, or listen through keyholes,
or run about picking up gossip, or trying to influence details. I was
retired, and now the younger ones must run the show. I said this with

1 Audrey Callaghan, née Moulton.
2 From 1955 to 1964, Callaghan was retained as a consultant by the Police Federation.

a certain air of finality, and he said ... that he knew I should always be available for consultation and advice.

He also said that his next visitor was Shinwell, who wanted to suggest that the Shadow Cabinet should not be elected, but should be chosen by the Leader. Does he think he'll be chosen at *his* age?

Friday 1st January 1960
My Life Peerage is announced, on the air at 8 a.m. and in the newspapers. I had been uncertain till today whether it was really true, though I had a letter from Macmillan in the first days of December, asking whether I would like it, and had heard from Hugh soon after the election, that it was being handled on Chief Whip level, and from Bowden at Lobby level at end of November that all was clear and it would be in New Year's Honours list.

At West Leaze in the warm comfort of the study, it is easy to deal with telephone calls, receive visits from press and photographers, and telegrams and letters. Many, and a very varied body, of my friends, are very pleased.

Most, by a large majority, when I was still uncertain, urged me to take it. 'Still a platform', if I wanted to speak. But this didn't appeal to me much. What appealed to me most was that I should thus retain my membership of the Westminster Club, though 'at the other end of the Passage'. After thirty-one years as M.P. (with thirteen years, nearly half, as a minister) I shall like to keep in touch with events in House of Commons and with my many friends there, including particularly young men on Labour side; and to make occasional use – though I must not overdo it – of right of entry to Commoners' Dining Room and Smoking Room. And sit in Peers' Gallery watching the beasts fighting in the old Arena.

At the Blackpool Party Conference in November, Gaitskell made a speech attacking nationalisation as an aim in itself and criticising Clause IV of the Labour Party Constitution, which called for 'the common ownership of the means of production, distribution and exchange'. Hostilities in the Labour Party were resumed. On this issue, however, the big unions opposed the Party leadership.

In another controversy, forces were more evenly balanced. The Campaign for Nuclear Disarmament had continued to gather strength. At the Scarborough Party Conference in 1960, unilateralism was narrowly adopted as Party policy – backed by the Transport Workers, Engineers, Railwaymen and Shop Workers. This was 1935 in reverse: a pacifistic conference voting down a defence-minded Leader. Unlike Lansbury, however, Gaitskell announced his intention to 'fight, fight and fight again'. The Scarborough decision was reversed at Brighton in 1961.

Wednesday 4th May
Roy Jenkins to see me. Just after A.E.U. against advice of E.C. had voted for Unilateral Nuclear Disarmament, against *any* change in Clause 4, and in favour of a shopping list of new nationalisation. We both felt that the position had become impossible for Hugh. What [line] should he take and when? I said he should soon publicly declare that if Party went for unilateral disarmament he could not continue to lead it. Roy said this was a conservative view; we stuck to what we had said since 1934; we were for *multilateral* disarmament. But, he thought, Hugh should also say something positive and forward looking to attract support from non-members, e.g. an anti Trade Union declaration. We couldn't go on being pushed about, on matters of policy, by snap divisions at Trade Union Conference by narrow margins, while delegates were waiting for tea. I was doubtful about this, too like Jay's nonsense, which put us wrong on both feet when this fuss started. Perhaps Hugh had been wrong on Clause 4, too compliant. Perhaps, I added, wrong at Blackpool, to raise Clause 4.

Roy told me this: Crossman, when Clause 4 was on, said that, of course, he didn't care a damn about more nationalisation and was quite prepared to support Hugh's line. 'But when he made it an issue of personal loyalty, I had to vote against him'!!

Thursday 12th May
Hugh, whom I hadn't seen for some time, dined with me alone (Ruth had provided some good cold food and drink) at the flat.

A.E.U. had just voted for nuclear unilateral disarmament. I said the slide to N.U.D. [Nuclear Unilateral Disarmament] had now gone so far that I doubted if we could now stop it. I thought it likely that both Miners and N.U.R. would go same way. Large prefabricated majority for this at T.U.C. and on Annual Conference, was being rapidly built up, and perhaps in favour of Clause 4 as well. If these were carried, then could Hugh go on as Leader?

Hugh didn't take quite such a dark picture as I did. But he said that, if he resigned the leadership, it wouldn't mean that he would retire from politics. He would sit below the gangway, and many in P.L.P. would follow him. He would tell P.L.P. that he couldn't go on as Leader. He didn't know whom they'd choose. The new official leadership and front bench wouldn't be impressive. I asked him if his constituents in Leeds were firm. He said Yes. He said George Brown was often difficult. His final words were a request to me to see Brown, and persuade him not to concoct some humbugging with Cousins. We wanted the issue clear cut.[1] This was a very sad talk. I told Hugh that Brown had said that ambitious young Parliamentarians were saying, 'How long will Hugh Gaitskell last? I don't want to be dragged down with him, if he goes.'

A special meeting of the N.E.C. on 13th July decided to abandon the attempt to revise the Constitution. Attention now focused on the defence issue.

Aneurin Bevan underwent an operation for cancer at the end of December 1959. He died on 6th July 1960.

Wednesday 13th July
Today Hugh and the N.E.C. gave up the ghost on Clause 4. It will remain unchanged in the Party Constitution. The substitute statement on Aims, agreed some months ago, will be printed in the N.E.'s report for the Year. ...

Of course, the press will naturally, and logically, describe this as a great defeat and rebuff for Hugh. But both I in my two last letters to him, and Tony, with whom I talked last night, were very eager to see Clause 4 buried. When Hugh made his Blackpool speech, I agreed with it. But neither he nor I realised the massive boneheadedness in all sections of the Party, D.L.P.s, T.U.s and P.L.P. It has been a most staggering, and almost unbelievable, experience. ...

Memorial Service for Nye in Westminster Abbey on 26th July. Of course, I shan't go. Utterly unreal and inappropriate! He was an 'unbeliever' and never pretended, as so many do, to be anything [else]. (In this, if in nothing else, he and Ernie Bevin were alike.) When Nye was cremated – in a crematorium near Tredegar – there was no religious service at all. No Minister of Religion was present; no prayers, no hymns, no spoken word. The silence was broken only by part of Beethoven's Sixth Symphony – one of Nye's favourites – played on a gramophone.

I remember when Nye was Minister of Health, and fighting fierce opposition to his National Health Service, that in a speech he said,

---

1 Later insertion: 'Efforts to have a talk with George Brown failed. He was first in hospital, then cried off a Drapers' Dinner; then in U.S.'

'I say, Let the little children come unto me.' How angry the Christians were. I think I remember the present Archbishop of Canterbury[1] publicly rebuking him.

Other item: [today is] the A.E.U. Having voted for Unilateralism at their Conference, their Executive announced that they would only decide how to vote at Labour Party Conference – for or against Unilateralism, and for or against Party's new Defence Plan when their delegates assemble at Scarborough. This Party can't be run like this, and long survive. What do these half-wits think people outside think of them, and their wriggles?

Talking with Tony yesterday, we thought George Brown, though very awkward, vain, sensitive and fundamentally self-seeking and unfaithful, 'It's almost a full time job handling him' said Tony, would be the best Deputy Leader. The Gaitskellite vote, dispersed but not negligible in the P.L.P., should be pushed towards him, so that he would win by T.U. plus Gaitskellites. Wilson would get 'the Left', ex-Bevanites, etc. But no warmth, only a carbon copy of Hugh. Two Economic Dons from Oxford. Jim Callaghan isn't really in the running yet, but [has] ability in some directions, promise and poise. But too obviously a trimmer, and doesn't seem to have any deep convictions. I quote David Butler's[2] question to me, 'Has he got a resignation inside him?' and Desmond Donnelly's, 'Oh, if I did that, I might lose my seat on the National Executive.' Donnelly: 'But this[3] is much more important than a seat on the National Executive.' Callaghan: 'But I don't want to lose my seat on the N.E. just at this moment.' And some say Callaghan's intellectual grip isn't tightening, as it should be.

Talk with Tony on consequences of a Conference vote for Unilateralism. I said my hunch was that Unilateralism would win. Tony said many pundits thought otherwise; hoped A.E.U. would strike back, etc. I doubted all this. If Unilateralism won, Hugh couldn't accept this. Tony wondered whether a majority of P.L.P. would vote to disregard Conference vote. I doubted this. Boneheadedness would work against this. I doubted whether many would follow Hugh on to back-benches. This move, even if inevitable, since he was so deeply committed on Defence, and was individually entitled to his conscientious objection, might turn [out], like Clause 4, to be a tactical miscalculation. Gives a lead, but no one following. But Brown was

---

1 Geoffrey Fisher, later Lord (1887–1972). Archbishop of Canterbury 1945–61.
2 D. E. Butler (b. 1924). Political scientist. Official Fellow of Nuffield College, Oxford since 1954.
3 Insertion: '(I forget what)'.

also pretty deeply committed on Defence against unilateralists. Not much joy ahead here. Only certain that Tories will win next election, probably with further increased majority, and probably the next but one likewise.

I told Tony that Desmond had told me that Crossman had told him that Nye was going to stab Hugh in the back after Hugh's Blackpool speech, but then unfortunately fell ill. Crossman is one of the most unfaithful deceivers, with a coating of intellectual cheap glitter.

The diary breaks off here. Over the next year, Dalton struggled to complete the final volume of his memoirs, *High Tide and After*, published on 5th February 1962. He died in St Pancras Hospital on 12th February 1962.

Appendix:
Main Characters

Alexander: Albert Victor Alexander, later 1st Earl (1885–1965). Labour and Co-operative M.P. for Hillsborough 1922–31, 1935–50. Parliamentary Secretary at the Board of Trade 1924. First Lord of the Admiralty 1929–31, 1940–45, 1945–6. Minister of Defence 1947–50; Chancellor of the Duchy of Lancaster 1950–51.

Attlee: Clement Richard Attlee, later 1st Earl (1883–1967). Labour M.P. for Limehouse 1922–50; West Walthamstow 1950–55. Under-Secretary of State for War 1924; Chancellor of the Duchy of Lancaster 1930–31; Postmaster-General 1931. Lord Privy Seal 1940–42; Deputy Prime Minister 1942–5; Secretary of State for Dominion Affairs 1942–5. Prime Minister 1945–51. Minister of Defence 1945–6. Leader of the Labour Party 1935–55.

Bevan: Aneurin Bevan (1897–1960). Labour M.P. for Ebbw Vale 1929–60. Minister of Health 1945–51; Minister of Labour and National Service 1951. Treasurer of the Labour Party 1956–60; Deputy Leader 1959–60.

Bevin: Ernest Bevin (1881–1951). Labour M.P. for Central Wandsworth 1940–50; East Woolwich 1950–51. Minister of Labour and National Service 1940–45. Foreign Secretary 1945–51; Lord Privy Seal 1951. Member of the General Council of the T.U.C. 1925–40. National Organiser of the Dockers' Union 1910–21; General Secretary of the Transport and General Workers' Union 1921–40.

Brown: George Alfred Brown, later Baron George-Brown (1914–85). Labour M.P. for Belper 1945–70. Joint Parliamentary Secretary at the Ministry of Agriculture and Fisheries

703

1947–51; Minister of Works 1951. First Secretary of State and Secretary of State for Economic Affairs 1964–6; Foreign Secretary 1966–8. Deputy Leader of the Labour Party 1960–70.

Callaghan: Leonard James Callaghan (b. 1912). Labour M.P. for South Cardiff 1945–50; South-East Cardiff 1950–83; Cardiff South and Penarth since 1983. Parliamentary Secretary at the Ministry of Transport 1947–50; Parliamentary and Financial Secretary at the Admiralty 1950–51. Chancellor of the Exchequer 1964–7; Home Secretary 1967–70. Foreign Secretary 1974–6. Prime Minister 1976–9. Treasurer of the Labour Party 1967–76; Leader of the Labour Party 1976–80. Delegate to the Council of Europe, Strasburg 1948–50, 1954. Assistant Secretary to the Inland Revenue Staff Federation 1936–47.

Chamberlain: Arthur Neville Chamberlain (1869–1940). Conservative M.P. for Birmingham Ladywood 1918–29; Edgbaston 1929–40. Postmaster-General 1922–3; Paymaster-General 1923; Minister of Health 1923, 1924–9, 1931. Chancellor of the Exchequer 1923–4, 1931–7. Prime Minister 1937–40; Lord President of the Council 1940. Chairman of the Conservative Party 1930–31.

Churchill: Winston Leonard Spencer Churchill, later Sir Winston (1874–1965). Conservative M.P. for Oldham 1900–4; Liberal M.P. for Oldham 1904–6; North-West Manchester 1906–8; Dundee 1908–22. Conservative M.P. for Epping 1924–45; Woodford 1945–64. Parliamentary Under-Secretary at the Colonial Office 1905–8; President of the Board of Trade 1908–10. Home Secretary 1910–11; First Lord of the Admiralty 1911–15, 1939–40. Chancellor of the Duchy of Lancaster 1915. Minister of Munitions 1917–19; Secretary of State for War and Air 1919–21; Secretary of State for the Colonies 1921–2. Chancellor of the Exchequer 1924–9. Prime Minister 1940–45, 1951–5. Minister of Defence 1940–45.

Cripps: Sir Richard Stafford Cripps (1889–1952). Labour M.P. for East Bristol 1931–50; South-East Bristol February–October 1950. Solicitor-General 1930–31. Ambassador to the Soviet Union 1940–42. Lord Privy Seal and Leader of the House of Commons 1942; Minister of Aircraft Production 1942–5. President of the Board of Trade 1945–7; Minister of Economic Affairs 1947; Chancellor of the Exchequer 1947–50.

Crosland: Charles Anthony Raven Crosland (1918–77). Labour

M.P. for South Gloucestershire 1950–55; Grimsby 1959–77. Minister of State for Economic Affairs 1964–5; Secretary of State for Education and Science 1965–7; President of the Board of Trade 1967–9. Secretary of State for Local Government and Regional Planning 1969–70; the Environment 1974–6; Foreign and Commonwealth Affairs 1976–7.

Crossman: Richard Howard Stafford Crossman (1907–74). Labour M.P. for East Coventry 1945–74. Minister of Housing and Local Government 1964–6; Lord President of the Council and Leader of the House of Commons 1966–8; Secretary of State for Social Services 1968–70. Assistant Editor of the *New Statesman and Nation* 1938–55; Editor of the *New Statesman* 1970–72. Deputy Director of Psychological Warfare, Allied Forces' Headquarters, Algiers 1943. Assistant Chief of the Psychological Warfare Division, S.H.A.E.F. 1944–5. Member of the Anglo-American Palestine Commission 1946.

Dalton, Hugh: Edward Hugh John Neale Dalton, later Baron (1887–1962). Labour M.P. for Peckham 1924–9; Bishop Auckland 1929–31, 1935–59. Parliamentary Under-Secretary of State for Foreign Affairs 1929–31. Minister of Economic Warfare 1940–42; President of the Board of Trade 1942–5; Chancellor of the Exchequer 1945–7. Chancellor of the Duchy of Lancaster 1948–50; Minister of Town and Country Planning 1950–51; Minister of Local Government and Planning 1951.

Dalton, Ruth: Florence Ruth Dalton, née Hamilton Fox (1890–1966). Labour M.P. for Bishop Auckland February–May 1929. Member of London County Council 1925–31; Alderman 1936–42, 1946–52. Married Hugh Dalton 1914. Assistant Secretary of the Workers' Educational Association 1918–19. Worked in the Ministry of Supply, based in Manchester, as liaison officer with hostels for women workers in the North of England 1941–4. United Nations Relief and Rehabilitation Administration 1944–5. Member of the Arts Council 1957–62.

Eden: Robert Anthony Eden, later Sir Anthony, 1st Earl of Avon (1897–1977). Conservative M.P. for Warwick and Leamington 1923–57. Parliamentary Private Secretary to the Foreign Secretary 1926–9. Parliamentary Under-Secretary for Foreign Affairs 1931–3; Lord Privy Seal 1933–5; Minister without Portfolio, League of Nations Affairs 1935. Secretary of State for Foreign Affairs 1935–8, 1940–45, 1951–5;

Dominion Affairs 1939–40; War May–December 1940.
Leader of the House of Commons 1942–5. Deputy Leader
of the Opposition 1945–51. Prime Minister and Leader of
the Conservative Party 1955–7.

Gaitskell: Hugh Todd Naylor Gaitskell (1906–63). Labour M.P. for
South Leeds 1945–63. Principal Private Secretary to Dalton
as Minister of Economic Warfare 1940–42. Principal
Assistant Secretary, Board of Trade 1942–5. Parliamentary
Secretary, Minister of Fuel and Power 1946–7. Minister of
Fuel and Power 1947–50. Minister of State for Economic
Affairs 1950. Chancellor of the Exchequer 1950–51. Leader
of the Labour Party 1955–63.

Greenwood: Arthur Greenwood (1880–1954). Labour M.P. for Nelson
and Colne 1922–31; Wakefield 1932–54. Parliamentary
Secretary at the Ministry of Health 1924. Minister of
Health 1929–31. Minister without Portfolio and Member
of the War Cabinet 1940–42. Lord Privy Seal 1945–7.
Paymaster-General 1946–7; Minister without Portfolio
1947. Deputy Leader of the Labour Party 1935–54.

Griffiths: James Griffiths (1890–1975). Labour M.P. for Llanelli
1936–70. Minister of National Insurance 1945–50; Secretary of State for the Colonies 1950–51. Secretary of State
for Wales 1964–6.

Halifax: Edward Frederick Lindley Wood, 1st Baron Irwin, 3rd
Viscount Halifax, later 1st Earl (1881–1959). Conservative
M.P. for Ripon 1910–25. Under-Secretary of State for the
Colonies 1921–2. President of the Board of Education
1922–4, 1932–5. Minister of Agriculture and Fisheries
1924–5. Viceroy of India 1926–31. Secretary of State for
War 1935; Lord Privy Seal 1935–7; Leader of the House
of Lords 1935–8, 1940; Lord President of the Council 1937–
8; Foreign Secretary 1938–40. Ambassador to the U.S.A.
1941–6.

Henderson: Arthur Henderson (1863–1935). Labour M.P. for Barnard
Castle 1903–18; Widnes 1919–22; East Newcastle 1923;
Burnley 1924–31; Clay Cross 1933–5. President of the
Board of Education 1915–16; Paymaster-General 1916;
Minister without Portfolio 1916–17. Home Secretary 1924.
Foreign Secretary 1929–31. Chairman of the Disarmament
Conference, Geneva 1931–5. Chairman of the Parlia-
mentary Labour Party 1908–10, 1914–17. Secretary of the
Labour Party 1912–35. Leader of the Labour Party 1931–2.

Jay: Douglas Patrick Thomas Jay (b. 1907). Labour M.P. for

North Battersea 1946–83. Journalist at *The Times* 1929–33; *The Economist* 1933–7; City Editor of the *Daily Herald* 1937–41. Assistant Secretary at the Ministry of Supply 1941–3; Principal Assistant Secretary at the Board of Trade 1943–5. Personal Assistant to the Prime Minister 1945–6. Parliamentary Private Secretary to Dalton as Chancellor of the Exchequer 1947. Economic Secretary to the Treasury 1947–50; Financial Secretary to the Treasury 1950–51. President of the Board of Trade 1964–7.

Jebb: Hubert Miles Gladwyn Jebb, later Sir Gladwyn, 1st Baron Gladwyn (b. 1900). Private Secretary to Dalton as Parliamentary Under-Secretary of State for Foreign Affairs 1929–31. Private Secretary to the Permanent Under-Secretary of State 1937–40; Chief Executive Officer, Special Operations Executive 1940–42; Head of Reconstruction Department 1942. Counsellor at the Foreign Office 1943–6. Acting Secretary-General of the United Nations 1946. Assistant Under-Secretary and United Nations Adviser 1946–7. U.K. Representative at the United Nations 1950–54. Ambassador to France 1954–60.

Keynes: John Maynard Keynes, later 1st Baron (1883–1946). Fellow of King's College, Cambridge 1909–46. Civil servant at the India Office 1906–8; Treasury 1915–19. Principal Representative of the Treasury at the Paris Peace Conference and Deputy for the Chancellor of Exchequer on the Supreme Economic Council January–June 1919. Member of the Committee on Finance and Industry 1929–31. Leader of the British delegation negotiating the American Loan in Washington September–December 1945. Governor of the International Bank for Reconstruction and Development 1946. Editor of *Economic Journal* 1911–44.

MacDonald: James Ramsay MacDonald (1866–1937). Labour M.P. for Leicester 1906–18; Aberavon 1922–9; Seaham 1929–31. National Labour M.P. for Seaham 1931–5; Scottish Universities 1936–7. Prime Minister and Foreign Secretary 1924. Prime Minister 1929–35; Lord President of the Council 1935–7. Chairman of the I.L.P. 1906–9; Leader of the Labour Party 1911–14, 1922–31.

Morrison: Herbert Stanley Morrison, later Baron (1888–1965). Labour M.P. for South Hackney 1923–4, 1929–31, 1935–45; East Lewisham 1945–50; South Lewisham 1950–59. Minister of Transport 1929–31. Minister of Supply 1940; Home Secretary and Minister of Home Security 1940–45. Member of the War Cabinet 1942–5. Deputy Prime Minister 1945–51. Lord President of the Council and Leader of the House of Commons 1945–51; Foreign Secretary March–October 1951. Deputy Leader of the Opposition 1951–5. Member of London County Council 1922–45; Leader 1934–40.

Mosley: Oswald Ernald Mosley, later Sir Oswald, 6th Bart (1896–1981). Conservative M.P. for Harrow 1918–22; Independent M.P. for Harrow 1922–4. Labour M.P. for Smethwick 1926–31. Chancellor of the Duchy of Lancaster 1929–30. Founded New Party 1931; British Union of Fascists 1932; Union Movement 1948. Imprisoned under Defence Regulation 18B 1940–45.

Noel-Baker: Philip John Noel-Baker, later Baron (1889–1982). Labour M.P. for Coventry 1929–31; Derby 1936–50; Derby South 1950–70. Parliamentary Private Secretary to the Foreign Secretary 1929–31. Parliamentary Secretary at the Ministry of War Transport 1942–5. Minister of State at the Foreign Office 1945–6. Secretary of State for Air 1946–7; Commonwealth Relations 1947–50. Minister of Fuel and Power 1950–51. League of Nations Section of British Delegation to the Paris Peace Conference 1919; League of Nations Secretariat 1919–22. Principal Assistant to the President of the Disarmament Conference at Geneva 1932–3.

Shinwell: Emanuel Shinwell, later Baron (1884–1986). Labour M.P. for Linlithgow 1922–4, 1928–31; Seaham 1935–50; Easington 1950–70. Financial Secretary at the War Office 1929–30. Parliamentary Secretary at the Department of Mines at the Board of Trade 1924, 1930–31. Minister of Fuel and Power 1945–7; Secretary of State for War 1947–50; Minister of Defence 1950–51. Chairman of the Parliamentary Labour Party 1964–7.

Vansittart: Sir Robert Gilbert Vansittart, later 1st Baron (1881–1957). Assistant Under-Secretary of State for Foreign Affairs and Principal Private Secretary to the Prime Minister 1928–30; Permanent Under-Secretary of State for Foreign Affairs 1930–38; Chief Diplomatic Adviser to the Foreign Secretary 1938–41.

Index

The index includes a glossary of nicknames

709

712

717

731

733